second edition

INTERNATIONAL BUSINESS

Environment and Management

Christopher M. Korth

University of South Carolina

PRENTICE-HALL, INC., Englewood Cliffs, New Jersey 07632

Library of Congress Cataloging in Publication Data

Korth, Christopher M.
   International business, environment and management.

   Rev. ed. of: International business, an introduction to
the world of the multinational firm/Richard D. Hays,
Christopher M. Korth, Manucher Roudiani. 1971, c1972.
   Includes bibliographies and index.
   1. International business enterprises.   I. Hays,
Richard D.   International business, an introduction to
the world of the multinational firm.   II. Title.
HD62.4.K67   1985   658'.049   84-8196
ISBN 0-13-472457-7

Editorial/production supervision
and interior design by Margaret Rizzi
Cover design by Wanda Lubelska Design
Manufacturing buyer: Ed O'Dougherty

Printed in the United States of America

10 9 8 7 6 5 4 3 2 1

ISBN 0-13-472457-7   01

Prentice-Hall International, Inc., *London*
Prentice-Hall of Australia Pty. Limited, *Sydney*
Editora Prentice-Hall do Brasil, Ltda., *Rio de Janeiro*
Prentice-Hall Canada Inc., *Toronto*
Prentice-Hall of India Private Limited, *New Delhi*
Prentice-Hall of Japan, Inc., *Tokyo*
Prentice-Hall of Southeast Asia Pte. Ltd., *Singapore*
Whitehall Books Limited, *Wellington, New Zealand*

Dedicated to all the wonderful ladies,
both young and not so young, in my life:

Shirley,
Katie, Jennie, Elizabeth, Sarah,
Kae, and Sonja

Contents

PART
II   **INTERNATIONAL BUSINESS:
OPPORTUNITIES AND BARRIERS**

PART

V INTERNATIONAL BUSINESS OPERATIONS

Preface

In the past twenty years the economies of the world have become more tightly intertwined than ever before. The devaluation of the U.S. dollar, soaring oil prices, severe trade imbalances, the impact of multinational corporations, the international debt crisis, and the widespread call for expanded controls on international trade are only a few of the major international economic developments that affect our everyday life.

For business firms, the world economy has similarly become much more important. International trade has grown very rapidly. Many more firms are involved in international trade than in the past, and such trade has often become a very significant part of the firm's operations. Commercial banks have become involved in international lending and foreign-exchange trading on an unprecedented scale. Foreign banks have become important financial institutions in most countries. More and more companies are investing abroad. Conversely, foreign companies, either via new investments or via acquisitions of existing local firms, have become major competitors to local producers in most countries.

As a direct result of these and other related changes that so greatly expand the significance of world business, in the business sector as well as among the awareness of the general public, international business has grown rapidly. Furthermore, the greatly enhanced role of international business and the unique problems and opportunities that it brings have stretched the horizons of economics and the various management functions, such as finance, marketing, personnel, organization, control, and public relations. Unfortunately, the traditional business school courses generally offered in colleges and universities in these fields do not adequately prepare students for international business activities.

International business as a clearly defined field of *study*, one which long lagged behind the very rapid postwar growth of international business, has expanded in recent years at an even faster rate than has the international business phenomenon itself. It is still a very young field with many growing pains. An additional difficulty in the development of the study of international business arises from its scope, since, quite obviously, it is a wide-ranging field comprising elements of all the various business operations. However, since international business studies take prospective business managers beyond the borders of their native countries, whole new dimensions must be added to that already long list of variable factors concerning the familiar domestic environment. Aspects of the domestic environment that have always been constants are now becoming variables, for example, the political, business, and monetary systems; social customs; language. Thus a whole new sphere of study is required.

The study of business in most business schools is basically a study of domestic business. However, for a growing number of companies, large and small, such training is inadequate, since their managers and prospective managers also need to know the basics of managing international business operations—exporting; importing; licensing; foreign exchange; Euromarkets; foreign investments; and the special features of the world economic, social, and political environment in which the companies function. Indeed, even domestic companies with no international business operations are affected by many developments in the world environment and should understand them.

This book is designed to introduce business students to this expanded world; it is a survey of both levels of the international manager's world: the environment (economic, political, and social) within which he or she will be operating and the new international dimensions of traditional business operations. A survey of a very complex field cannot possibly concentrate on any particular segment of international business in any exhaustive detail. What is presented here, therefore, is a broad but concrete introduction for the general reader.

The reader with previous exposure to international business will find in this book a convenient integration of the diverse elements of the field. However, no attempt has been made to produce "the" definitive work in this field; indeed it is questionable if such an effort would even be possible for such a complex field. Rather, in this survey the reader is introduced to the entire scope of international business, both its environment and managerial functions, so that he or she may decide what field to study in greater detail. The list of suggested readings at the end of each chapter offers a selection of worthwhile literature available in each specific subject area.

International business is very different from domestic business in many respects. Nevertheless, the study of international environments and international operations of business have been badly neglected in business schools. This is especially true in the United States. In order to overcome this tendency, the American Assembly of Collegiate Schools of Business (AACSB), the major accrediting agency for American business schools, has adopted a requirement that graduate and undergraduate curricula be internationalized. However, this has proven to be an elusive goal and business courses nonetheless tend to put overwhelming emphasis on the domestic, when they should be internationalized. This book is designed for a course that will at least begin the process of overcoming this deficiency.

THE STRUCTURE OF THE BOOK

International Business: Environment and Management is divided into the following five sections:

Part I. International Business—an overview of the scope of international business with a framework that identifies the role of the multinational corporation and provides an orientation for the entire book.

Part II. International Business: Opportunities and Barriers—the theoretical basis for and obstacles to international trade and investment.

Part III. International Economic Environment—a look at some of the most unique aspects of the economic environment of the multinational corporation—the world monetary system, foreign exchange markets, international money and capital markets, multinational organizations, and balance of payments.

Part IV. The Multinational Corporation and the Nation State— the special nature of the multinational corporation and the problems that arise from its relations with both its home and host governments.

Part V. International Business Operations—individual examinations of the international aspects of the major functional areas of business—organization, marketing, personnel, finance, and accounting, plus special discussions of exporting and importing, the management of foreign exchange, and taxation.

Every chapter concludes with a summary, a list of key words, questions relating to the chapter, and a list of additional suggested readings. Before reading each chapter, the reader is advised to read the summary, the vocabulary list, and the questions. This introduces the reader to both the general subject of the chapter and to the important, specific concepts that are introduced in the chapter.

At the end of the book is an extensive glossary of the most important terms introduced in the book.

The first edition of this text was entitled *International Business: An Introduction to the World of the Multinational Firm*. It was a combination of both text and readings and comprised eleven chapters. I had the benefit of two coauthors when writing that edition: Richard D. Hays and Manucher Roudiani. Unfortunately, neither of them was available to assist in the writing of this second edition.

This second edition is a complete rewriting: It has no readings and comprises twenty-two chapters. It is much more extensive than was the first edition.

I would like to thank those who contributed to the writing of this book. Special thanks are due to three colleagues of mine at the College of Business of the University of South Carolina each of whom contributed a chapter, which I revised as necessary to fit the needs, style, and content of the rest of the book: Brian Toyne (Chapter 17, "Marketing Management in International Operations"), Thomas Evans (Chapter 19, "Accounting for International Operations"), and Ronald Taylor (Chapter 22, "International Taxation"). In addition, among those many who contributed useful suggestions were Douglas Nigh, Jean Boddewyn, John Fayerweather, David Ricks, and John Daniels and William Hauworth, who offered detailed comments. I am also very grateful to a number of other academic and business colleagues who reviewed various chapters of the book and made valuable suggestions: Raj Aggarwal, Jeffrey Arpan, Richard Collister, Michael Dundorf, Richard Farmer, James Korth, Joseph Kvasnicka, John Mathis, Joseph Monahan, Lee Nehrt, Robert Shulman, William Sihler, Arnold Stebinger, Lee Travis, and Vern Terpstra. Last, but not least, I would like to thank my secretary, Dee Williams, and my wife, Shirley, for typing the numerous drafts.

1

The Nature of International Business

WHAT IS INTERNATIONAL BUSINESS?

The international sphere of the business world has crept only gradually into the consciousness of most businesses. This is especially true in the United States, where the huge domestic market is sufficient to satisfy most companies. However, the scale of business activities stretching beyond a nation's borders is so vast and the impact of such activities in even the largest countries is so significant upon businesses, governments, and entire economies, that this unique sector of business activities warrants the study of all business students.

Many corporations in Europe and elsewhere have generally been less isolated from international aspects of business than those in the United States. Because of the proximity of foreign borders and the limitations of their own natural resources and market size, much of the trade and investments of these businesses could indeed be called *international business*. Now more than ever before, every economy, regardless of its size or the political orientation of its government, must recognize its great interdependence with the economies of the rest of the world. This has major implications for corporate managers.

INTERNATIONAL BUSINESS

International business includes any type of business activity that crosses national borders. It includes the international transmission of almost any type of economic resource—merchandise, services (such as technology, skilled labor, transportation), and capital.

Study and research about international business encompass all the *uniquely international managerial processes* in which the international business is involved. They also cover the impact of the *environment* upon the companies involved in the international field, along with the impact of the companies upon the environment. This book surveys both the environment and the managerial operations that are unique to international business.

Although more restricted definitions of international business are used by some authors, the fairly broad approach to the subject described above best fits the objectives and scope of this book.

The study of international business focuses on the particular problems and opportunities that emerge because a firm is operating in more than one country. In a very real sense, international business involves the broadest and most generalized study of the field of business. As previously mentioned, traditional study of management examines business in a basically domestic environment as adapted to a fairly unique environment, for example, that of the United States. Many of the parameters and environmental variables that are very important in international business (such as foreign legal systems, foreign exchange markets, cultural differences, and different rates of inflation) are either largely irrelevant to domestic business or are so reduced in range and complexity as to be of greatly diminished significance. *Thus, it might be said that domestic business is a special limited case of international business.*

MULTINATIONAL CORPORATIONS

The concept of international business is relatively straightforward and noncontroversial. The same cannot be said, however, for the terms applied to the companies that engage in international business. Also, the definitions of these terms are subject to wide variations.

If a company has a very specific and narrow international business activity, then a specific term may well be available to clearly label the nature and range of the activity. For example, a company may be simply an *importing company* or a *foreign freight forwarder.*[1] Little confusion or conflict exists over such terms.

---

[1]The term *foreign freight forwarder* is defined in the glossary at the end of the book.

Unfortunately, the same cannot be said for the terms to apply to companies engaged in a variety of international business activities: trade, licensing, foreign production, and so forth. A bewildering variety of terms assaults the reader—global, transnational, supernational (or supranational), world, multinational, international, and so forth. Such adjectives are further coupled with several different types of business entities, for example, corporation, company, enterprise, firm. Thus, writings in the field are spiced with titles such as *multinational enterprise* and *transnational corporation,* the latter term being favored by the United Nations. Tides of preferences ebb and flow; for example, when the first edition of this book was written, the term *multinational firm* was prominent and was employed in the title of the first edition of this book.

The search for an appropriate term is more than merely an exercise in semantics. It can indeed serve a very useful purpose. However, until more standardization of terminology and definition occurs, the reader is advised to remain flexible. Someday several of the terms cited above (or some yet to be devised) may be used to identify different groups of companies engaged in extensive and/or varied types of international activities. Until this occurs, it is best to minimize the confusion by utilizing a single term to encompass a wide range of such activities.

The term that is used in this textbook is *multinational corporation,* which is probably the most prevalent term currently in use.

Perspective of observer: One final observation needs to be made: The perspective of the viewer is critical in understanding the full meaning of a term. In this text we use the term *multinational corporation* from the perspective of the corporate manager. However, when other observers, such as government officials of the host government, labor union leaders, or social workers, use this term or any of those mentioned above, they often mean something much broader: For example, from their perspectives *any* foreign direct investor may be seen as a multinational (or transnational or global) corporation. This perspective is much too broad for the purposes of our discussion.

For our purposes, the *multinational corporation (MNC)* is a company whose managers view its domestic, home-country activities as merely a part of its worldwide activities. When resources are allocated within the MNC, domestic proposals are not given preference but are evaluated on a comparable basis with various international proposals. This definition focuses on the managerial perspective, the managerial decision process, and the corporate organizational structure. It does *not* address such issues as the scale of foreign sales, assets and profits, the nationality of owners and managers, or the location of headquarters and research and development facilities. These issues are sometimes used by writers as criteria for defining MNCs. This is part of the confusion of terminology in the field. Some of these issues will be addressed in subsequent chapters.

DOMESTIC VERSUS INTERNATIONAL BUSINESS

As noted above, managerial training generally has a very strong domestic bias. Thus, courses on business management in the United States tend to be a study of American management. Similarly, in Germany they tend to be a study of German management. Such ethnocentric bias is understandable and exists in most major industrial countries. However, it leaves a significant gap in the training of the manager whose company's activities might stretch across national boundaries. The purpose of this textbook is to expand this limited perspective to a view of business as a worldwide phenomenon; to introduce the reader to basic elements of the international environment and to a much wider variety of business conditions; and, hopefully, to enhance the reader's interest in and sensitivity to the basic differences between different countries in culture, economy, politics, and so forth.

International business includes all elements of the domestic environment that local managers must confront—governmental, legal, cultural, and economic factors. However, within the domestic environment, many of the ingredients with which the domestic managers need have little concern (even if they operate nationwide) are constants: a single language, a common currency, reasonably homogeneous culture, and well-developed infrastructure. Such factors, as a result, are often constraints that can be expected, accepted, and ignored.

In international business, however, there are few fixed constraints. This book is designed to prepare and forewarn the reader about the many potential opportunities and difficulties that may be encountered in the field of international business. Of course, the differences vary considerably depending upon the location of the international business operations. For example, *cultural differences* are much greater for American executives in most of Asia or Africa than in Europe. Similarly, *legal differences* are likely to be far greater in countries whose legal system is based primarily on some foundation other than common law; for example, the Napoleonic Code in France, the Koranic law in Saudi Arabia, or the Communist systems of law are much more foreign to Americans than the systems in Canada or Australia.

Also, for managers accustomed to dealing with private-sector customers and competitors, where economic factors play the principal (although not the only) role, *political differences* between the home and host country can pose major hurdles. For example, the role of politics and noneconomic factors in marketing to or competing with Communist and other governments can be a shock. Consider the following managerial scenarios: negotiating for years with a succession of different levels of bureaucrats in East Germany; having the U.S. government unexpectedly refuse to grant an export license for technical equipment to the USSR; or being refused contracts with Arab countries, because the company has economic ties with Israel.

This book alone cannot prepare the reader to confront *all* the potential differences; rather, its purpose is only to provide a broad survey of the subject. However, by introducing the reader to the background of and theoretical basis for international business, the differences in the international environment, and the resulting applications for business operations, the business manager will be forewarned and will also be better able to utilize more specialized training in exporting, importing, international finance, international marketing, international personnel, and so forth.

PATTERNS OF INTERNATIONAL BUSINESS

The difficulties and risks of engaging in a major change in the nature of a business are great. This is true domestically as well as internationally. Before the Ford Motor Company built factories throughout the United States, it first shipped cars from Michigan (in effect, they "exported" to the rest of the country; conversely, the rest of the country "imported" from Detroit). Also, in many industries, companies with inadequate production capacity commonly license their technology to other *domestic* companies.

To assemble or manufacture on a significant scale in different parts of the United States is expensive, complex, and risky; "exporting" to other parts of the country or licensing is generally simpler, cheaper, and less risky than actually marketing, assembling, or manufacturing in these areas. Eventually, however, the expanding company is likely to grow beyond its local origins, as Detroit's auto industry did by setting up assembly and manufacturing operations in many parts of the United States.

When the external trappings of international business are stripped away, there is a great similarity to such domestic American business. After all, the United States is a very large, very diverse economy. If it had not been for an historical process that produced a single, united, coast-to-coast nation (instead of English, Spanish, French, Mexican, Dutch, and Russian colonies or a northern federation and a southern confederation), the Ford Motor Company would need to worry about confronting Napoleonic law in Missouri as well as in Louisiana; speaking

Dutch in New York; receiving pounds sterling in Massachusetts, Mexican pesos in Texas, and confederate dollars in South Carolina.

As a result, most of the forms of business organization that are employed in international business are basically the same as their domestic counterparts: trading, licensing, direct marketing, assembling, manufacturing, and so forth. However, their relative significance will differ and often very greatly.

FOUR DEGREES OF CORPORATE INTERNATIONALIZATION

Companies differ markedly in the extent and patterns of international business. They vary from the strictly domestic company with no awareness of any international business activity on its part (even though, as with the corner variety store, many of the goods on its shelves may actually have been imported by the store's suppliers) to the theoretical notion of a company with no obvious national identity and with a completely international outlook.

In between these two extremes are four degrees of internationalization. These different phases of international orientation correspond to the previously mentioned evolution of the Ford Motor Company from a "domestic" Detroit company to one whose vision and activities extended outward to markets beyond that of the local area.

Following our definition of the multinational corporation, this division of companies into the various classifications is a function of the perspective of corporate management and the importance of the role played by the firm's international activities in managerial decision making.

Table 1.1 illustrates how these different phases of internationalization relate to one another.

The typical evolutionary transformation carries a company through a series of growth processes by which it is able to mature as an international company. The process is very different for different companies. However, a generalized pattern is possible to observe. In Table 1.1 this pattern is shown as four degrees or phases of internationalization.

First-degree internationalization: The first phase of internationalization for a company is when its international activities are limited to exporting and/or importing of an indirect or even a passive nature. Included in this category are companies that utilize the services of other companies to act as their interface with foreign customers or suppliers. As will be seen in Chapter 16, there is an extensive series of specialized companies, ranging from buying and selling agents, freight forwarders and customhouse brokers, to sophisticated international

TABLE 1.1 Four Degrees of Internationalization

	First-Degree Internationalization	Second-Degree Internationalization	Third-Degree Internationalization	Fourth-Degree Internationalization
Nature of contact with foreign markets	Indirect, passive	Direct, active	Direct, active	Direct, active
Locus of international operations	Domestic	Domestic	Domestic and international	Domestic and international
Orientation of company	Domestic	Domestic	Primarily domestic	Multinational[a]
Type of international activity	Foreign trade of goods and services	Foreign trade of goods and services	Foreign trade, foreign assistance contracts, foreign direct investment	Foreign trade, foreign assistance contracts, foreign direct investment
Organizational structure	Traditional domestic	International department	International division	Global structure[b]

[a]Domestic operations are viewed as only part of whole.
[b]Corporate structure will be examined in Chapter 15.

trading companies (the most highly developed of which are the Japanese trading companies such as Mitsui, Marubeni, and Mitsubishi).

The company engaged in this first degree of internationalization may be involved with either merchandise or services. The company may order imported *merchandise* that is for sale through a sales agent. Alternatively, the company may offer a useful *service* that is marketed for it abroad through another company. For example, a regional bank may be invited into an international loan syndication by a larger, money-center bank or a foreign bank. Likewise, an insurance company may be offered a chance to reinsure some international risks upon which another company has offered the basic insurance. Each of these is an example of indirect exporting or importing of either goods or services.

At this stage of internationalization the company will likely be handling its importing and/or exporting as a mere adjunct to one of its existing departments. The international portion of its activities is not significant enough to warrant a special international department. It might very well be handled on a part-time basis by those involved.

Second-degree internationalization: The second phase of internationalization occurs when a company takes its international destiny into its own hands. Again, the activity can be exporting or importing of either a good or a service. However, in this phase of internationalization the company *actively and directly solicits* such international business. It still undoubtedly uses some of the international trade specialists mentioned in the previous section. However, the company is much more directly involved in finding suppliers or customers, communicating with them, and trying to expand the trade. Nevertheless, the trade is still conducted from the company's domestic base.

The company in this stage of internationalization does not have staff who are permanently stationed abroad. It probably will, indeed should, have "traveling officers," who periodically travel abroad to "get to know the territory." There are too many unique characteristics, including opportunities and pitfalls, in international business for the company to be engaged in much foreign trade without its senior officers being familiar with the field in which their company is involved. For example, the importer may well find it useful to visit its major foreign suppliers in order to develop a closer relationship, improve the flow of communication, maintain quality standards, and so forth. Similarly, the billion-dollar bank (which is small by international standards) should have calling officers who personally know the foreign countries to which the bank lends money, even though the loans may primarily be relatively short-term trade credits to high-quality borrowers. Any company should know its customers well.

At this stage of internationalization the company has typically created a special export or import department or even division. Nevertheless, the company is still essentially a domestic company, although with a growing international interest.

Third-degree internationalization: The third phase of internationalization involves the use of permanent management abroad. This could occur with the import company that has its own purchasing managers abroad. It could also involve the exporter who has permanent sales staff abroad. These two types of importers or exporters of either goods or services are similar to the company in the second degree of internationalization, except that these companies now have a permanent foreign representation.

This third degree of internationalization can also involve companies that actually produce their merchandise or services abroad—companies that offer technical or managerial assistance to companies or governments abroad, banks and insurance companies that sell their services from a foreign base, and also companies that manufacture their goods abroad.

The distinguishing characteristics of the third degree of internationalization are that, although the company is *still essentially domestically oriented,* it is involved directly in the purchase, sale, and/or manufacture of its goods or services abroad and *permanently utilizes its own personnel abroad.* The company is likely to be organized with an international division rather than merely a department. The international side of its operations has reached a much higher level of significance for the company.

Fourth-degree internationalization: The fourth and final degree of internationalization exists when a company's orientation has shifted from the domestic to the international. At this phase, a company's domestic operations are no longer considered to be of a higher priority than are the international. The corporate management is now looking dispassionately at the purchase, sale, and/or production options between domestic or international locations; *the domestic part of the company no longer dominates.* The company is no longer a domestic company with some degree of international interest. Instead it is a *multinational company* that may have a very strong domestic interest. Its foreign activities can include any type of international business activity.

The concept of the multinational corporation has different connotations for different groups—the government of the investing company, the government of the host country, labor unions, the United Nations, and so forth. In many instances such outside observers perceive *any* type of foreign direct investment to be multinational.

Here our perspective of the multinational company is strictly from the point of view of the *management* of the firm: Thus, in this fourth degree of internationalization, *the management perceives itself to be multinational* in orientation.

CORPORATE ATTITUDE

A key to understanding the degree of international involvement of a corporation is the attitude of its management. As was suggested above, the dividing lines between the various degrees of internationalization of a business corporation are qualitative, not quantitative. The divisions do not depend on some arbitrary percentage of sales or profits that accrue from international operations. For example, if a company makes no effort to promote its goods abroad but is perfectly willing to satisfy any orders from another country, then its internationalization is only first degree, even if such sales represent 15 or 20 percent of its sales. On the other hand, if a company is actively promoting its products overseas and views such sales as a continuing part of its operations, then such a corporation is involved in international business to at least a second-degree extent. Indeed, if a company views its international operations as a vital part of its operations and organizes itself accordingly—with an international division or department—then it has indeed reached the third degree of internationalization, even if international sales or profits represent only 5 or 10 percent of the corporate totals.

Managerial attitude continues to be a vital consideration, even when a firm becomes *multinational*. Howard Perlmutter developed a widely used scenario that distinguishes between three management perspectives of the world.[2] The first perspective perceives all countries as basically the same as the manager's own country and views the company's international operations as mere extensions of its domestic operations; this view is *ethnocentric*. It tends to naively ignore differences between countries.

The second view tends to perceive each country and the firm's operations in that country as rather unique, dissimilar entities; this view is called *polycentric*. It tends to exaggerate the differences between countries.

The third view is the most truly international. Its perspective recognizes similarities and dissimilarities between countries. Accordingly, the manager and company with this perspective try to be realistic,

---

[2]Howard Perlmutter, "The Tortuous Evolution of the Multinational Corporation," *Columbia Journal of World Business,* January–February 1969, pp. 9-18.

neither underestimating nor overestimating differences between countries. Perlmutter termed this view *geocentric.*

Companies with first and second degrees of internationalization tend to be strongly ethnocentric, although some might be somewhat polycentric. Corporations with multinational operations should generally qualify as geocentric. Unfortunately, some are polycentric or even ethnocentric.

Neither managers nor firms are always consistent in their views of the world. Sometimes the same manager or firm may think and act geocentrically, whereas in other instances they may think and act polycentrically or even ethnocentrically. An interesting book, *Big Business Blunders*, illustrates errors in managerial judgment.[3] Many of these errors are often very costly, and they illustrate the failure of companies, often very large and profitable ones, to think and act geocentrically.

TYPES OF INTERNATIONAL BUSINESS OPERATIONS

Related to the phases of internationalization of corporations mentioned above are a variety of different types of international business operations.

EXPORTS AND IMPORTS OF GOODS AND SERVICES

The simplest form of international business is normally the first international step of almost any company—*foreign trade.* This includes the two-way flow of both merchandise and services. The reader is likely to be most familiar with international merchandise trade—the *import* of goods such as oil, textiles, cars, televisions, and coffee, and the *export* of products such as grains, airplanes, machine tools, and chemicals.

Also of great importance can be international trade in *services.* This includes *personal services* such as tourism, transportation, banking, insurance, brokerage, retailing, wholesaling, telecommunications, consulting, and management or technical contracts (for example, drilling and construction). It also includes *impersonal services* such as the rental of patents, processes, trademarks, and copyrights as well as movies, TV shows, and magazines. Examples of service transactions include the

---

[3]David Ricks, *Big Business Blunders.* Homewood, Ill.: Dow Jones Irwin, 1983.

expenditures of Japanese who fly on Pan American Airlines and who vacation in the United States, the sale of foreign currencies by banks, the offering by Merrill Lynch (the world's largest stockbroker) of brokerage services internationally, and the foreign offices of Sears, McDonald's, and Hilton Hotels.

EXPORTS AND IMPORTS OF PORTFOLIO CAPITAL

Closely related to other types of exports and imports are flows of capital resulting from the purchase or sale of marketable securities (bonds and commercial paper), nonsecurity-type financial investments (bank accounts), and noncontrolling amounts of common stock. This is known as *portfolio investment*. It does not usually involve direct overseas management. For example, an American may be able to deposit money in a London bank at a higher interest rate or borrow it at a lower rate than could be obtained in the United States. (If the account is denominated in U.S. dollars, this transaction is part of the so-called Eurodollar market.) Likewise, an investor from Holland might buy stock in Polaroid on the New York Stock Exchange.

DIRECT INVESTMENT

Finally, the most complicated form of international business involves the actual ownership and control of foreign operations. This *direct investment* must, as its name implies, involve direct participation in the management of foreign enterprises. Multinational firms are the epitome of direct investors, but many direct investments are also made by companies whose international orientation may only be third degree.

Because of the greater uncertainties and risks and the vast sizes of many international ventures, cooperative arrangements in the area of direct investment tend to be more common abroad than domestically. Examples include joint ventures, banking consortiums, and mixed ventures in which the foreign government is a partner. Government participation in such endeavors is sometimes the preference of the private-sector investor, but much more frequently it is forced upon the investor by the government—either before or after the investment has been made.

FRAMEWORK FOR STUDY

The study of such an important force as international business, operating in a very complex environment, ideally requires a systematic framework by which its details and structures can be presented to the reader.

The outline of this framework is the topic of the remainder of this chapter.

STUDY OF INTERNATIONAL BUSINESS ADMINISTRATION

International business is concerned with business between different national environments. Unlike ethnocentric attitudes—those whose horizons are limited to or centered upon a single country—people with interest in international business must be prepared to look well beyond the prevailing conditions in one country to seek a much more geocentric (or world-centered) knowledge and attitude.

International business differs from general business administration in that its operations straddle national boundaries. Thus, in its simplest form, international business involves one firm, two nations, and the flows of goods, services, funds, people, and information between these two nations, either to or from the firm.

FRAMEWORK OF THE BOOK

Part I, "Introduction to International Business," is comprised solely of this introductory chapter.

Part II, "International Business: Opportunities and Barriers" (Chapters 2 through 4), deals with the theory of international trade and finance and explains why flows of goods, services, and factors of production occur from one country to another. Figures 1.1 and 1.2 illustrate the basic models discussed in Part II.

Figure 1.1 suggests the complicated relationship that exists even for a firm that operates simply within its own *domestic environment* and that has no international opportunities or problems as yet. All firms send flows of goods, services, salaries and wages, taxes, payments, information, pollution, and so forth into the environment within which they operates. At the same time, all firms are affected by the socio-cultural, politico-legal, and economic influences of the environment. For domestic firms, many of these environmental factors serve as constants that require little, if any, management time (for example, language and currency). For foreign firms, however, even these factors are often variables that warrant special concern.

Figure 1.2 illustrates the basic model of international business activity as discussed in Chapters 2 and 3. Two firms located in two different countries engage in some form of economic interchange. Since national borders are crossed, the business functions become more complicated, but at this phase there are no obstacles to such economic activity.

The major assumption underlying the whole theory of internation-

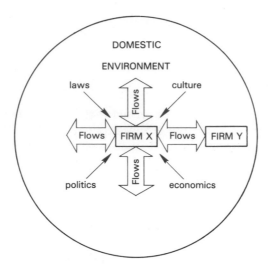

Flows: goods, services, funds, people, information, taxes

Domestic Constraints:

   Socio-cultural: work ethic, education, attitudes, and so forth

   Economic: inflation, interest rates, competition, labor unions, money and capital markets

   Politico-legal: monetary and fiscal policies, antitrust, employ- ment and labor policies, pollution and safety policies, and so forth

FIGURE 1.1   The Firm and Its *Domestic* Environment

al trade and finance is that economic rationality is the only motivation to action. However, even each local environment becomes more compli- cated as uniquely international elements of the environment now con- front the firm, elements that were not part of the relevant environment of the wholly domestic firm—foreign currencies, special laws, special institutions (either to aid or hinder international activities), and so forth. (Note that Firm X and Firm Y in Figure 1.2 may be independent companies, or they could be parts of the same company that are located in different countries.) This model in Figure 1.2 thus becomes the skele- ton of a framework with which to study international business.

As indicated in Figure 1.2, Chapter 2 examines the theory of trade flows (of goods and services), whereas Chapter 3 looks at the theory of the flows of capital and other factors of production—capital, people, and technology.

As indicated in Figure 1.3, Chapter 4 examines the interference to trade flows caused by (1) *tariffs* and other *trade controls*, which interfere with free movement of goods and services; (2) *exchange controls*, which

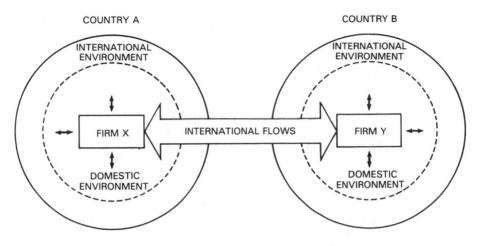

International flows: goods and services (Chapter 2); capital, people,
technology (Chapter 3)

FIGURE 1.2   The Firm and Its *International* Environments

interfere with free access to foreign exchange markets at a single exchange rate; and (3) *capital controls,* which are designed to interfere
with money and capital movements. Such obstacles occur in either the
originating or receiving country and can obstruct either outflows or
inflows and are part of the international environments of each country.

Part III, "International Economic Environment" (Chapters 5
through 10), discusses analyses of international concepts; once the basic

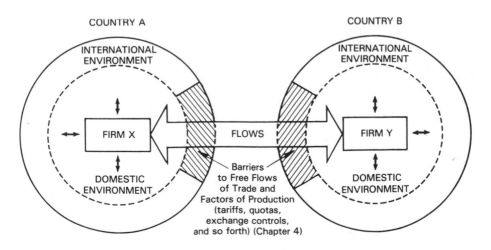

FIGURE 1.3   Barriers to Free International Movements of Trade and Factor Flows

differences that can occur in different national economies and the means by which these differences can affect international business have been examined, our focus will shift to an analysis of truly international concepts. This analysis has two aspects: the international constraints and opportunities arising from the individual countries and those that arise from sources outside of those countries. As was seen in Figure 1.2, the constraints of the simple domestic environment are augmented by corresponding international constraints of at least two countries when economic flows cross national borders. The most unique elements, but certainly not all, of the international environment are in the economic sphere.

In addition to the trade and capital flow barriers, which are covered in Chapter 4, five other major elements of the international economic environment are studied in Chapters 5 through 9. These elements are illustrated in Figure 1.4 as international institutions that overlap both countries. In Chapter 5 the international monetary system is examined. Chapter 6 analyzes foreign currencies and foreign-exchange markets. In Chapter 7 the focus shifts to the private money and capital markets of the world, for example, the major domestic markets and international banking. Chapter 8 focuses on the international financial markets known as *Euromarkets*. Chapter 9 is a survey of major international

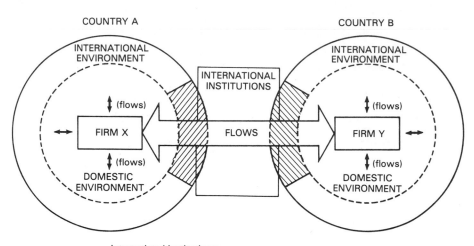

International institutions:

   World monetary system (Chapter 5)

   Foreign exchange markets (Chapter 6)

   International financial markets (Chapter 7)

   Euromarkets (Chapter 8)

   Multinational organizations (Chapter 9)

FIGURE 1.4   The Total Environment of International Business

economic organizations other than the International Monetary Fund (IMF): the World Bank Group, the General Agreement on Tariffs and Trade (GATT), major development banks, and economic integration organizations, such as the European Economic Community (EEC) and European Monetary System (EMS) in Western Europe and Council of Mutual Economic Assistance (CMEA or COMECON) in Eastern Europe. After these five basic elements of the international environment are examined, Chapter 10 looks at the basic nature and purposes of the balance of payments—the financial statement that measures the totals of one country's international transactions with those of the other nations of the world.

Part IV, "The Multinational Corporation and the Nation State" (Chapters 11 through 14), begins the study of international management per se. Chapter 11 is a study of companies' first ventures abroad: exporting-importing, licensing (patents and copyrights), management contracts, and portfolio investments. Also included is foreign market analysis.

When a firm's involvement abroad advances far enough that it becomes multinational, it may well find itself not only strongly affected by the host countries within which it operates but also strongly impacting upon them. Chapters 12 and 13 look at the MNC's impact, favorable and unfavorable, upon both its home and host countries. Finally, Chapter 14 studies the mutual dependency that exists between the multinational firm and host country; it is generally a positive-sum relationship, which requires carefully and clearly defined compromises between the two parties.

Part V, "International Business Operations" (Chapters 15 through 22), is divided into individual categories of international managerial functions: organization (Chapter 15), export and import procedures and financing (Chapter 16), marketing (Chapter 17), personnel (Chapter 18), accounting (Chapter 19), finance (Chapter 20), managment of foreign exchange exposure (Chapter 21), and international taxation (Chapter 22).

SUMMARY

International business is any form of business activity that crosses a national border: exports and imports of goods or services, licensing, management contracts, and portfolio and direct investments. Firms can engage in international business either directly or through intermediaries.

Multinational corporations are a special breed among companies actively engaged in international business, whose international activities are perceived to be as important as their domestic operations and whose domestic operations are viewed as being only a portion of their worldwide operations.

From the perspective of others, such as officials of a host government or leaders of the local labor unions in the host country or even those back in the home country of the investing company, the term *multinational corporation* is applied to a much vaster array of international companies. Indeed, it might refer to any company making a direct foreign investment. However, we are examining the environment and operations of the MNC from the perspective of the firm itself. Therefore, for our purposes the multinational corporation is one in which the domestic operations do not play a disproportionately large role but are instead weighed along with the various international alternatives.

Most companies actively engaged in international business do not qualify as MNCs. Many of them may evolve to such a status. However, in the meantime they are basically domestic companies with some degree of international activity. Such involvement may be casual, and have no long-term significance to the company, or it may have some marginal significance but still be only of subsidiary interest to corporate management. The international activities of many other firms are integral to corporate success and profitability, but they are still viewed as only an adjunct to the domestic operations, which remain the company's principal focus.

This book surveys the entire field of international business—its environment and its operations. The examination of both aspects is useful for an understanding of any of these phases of international business activity.

KEY TERMS*

DIRECT INVESTMENT	INTERNATIONAL	POLYCENTRIC
ETHNOCENTRIC	BUSINESS	PORTFOLIO INVESTMENT
GEOCENTRIC	MULTINATIONAL	
	CORPORATION (MNC)	

REVIEW QUESTIONS

1. What is international business?
2. What is the difference between a multinational corporation and a company engaged in international business?

---

*Definitions for the Key Terms appearing in this book can be found in the Glossary at the end of the text.

3. Discuss the four degrees of internationalization of a company from being domestic to becoming multinational.
4. What are some of the major economic and legal ways in which international business differs from domestic business?
5. Distinguish between portfolio and direct investment.
6. Exporting is better than importing! Discuss this statement.
7. What are the three basic managerial perspectives of the world? How do they compare with the perspectives of workers and the general public?
8. The company that is engaged in international business must confront four different levels of environmental constraints (see Figure 1.3). Discuss each.

SUGGESTED REFERENCES

AHARONI, YAIR "On the Definition of the Multinational Firm," *Quarterly Review of Economics and Business,* Autumn 1971, pp. 27–37.

BALL, DONALD A., AND WENDELL H. MCCULLOCH, JR. *International Business.* Plano, Tex.: Business Publications, 1982.

BERKMAN, HAROLD W., AND IVAN R. VERNON *Contemporary Perspectives in International Business.* Chicago, Ill.: Rand McNally College Publishing Co., 1979.

BROOKE, MICHAEL Z., AND H. LEE REMMERS *International Management and Business Policy.* Boston: Houghton Mifflin Co., 1978.

FARMER, RICHARD N., AND BARRY RICHMAN *International Business: An Operational Theory* (3rd ed.). Bloomington, Indiana: Cedarwood Press, 1980.

HANER, F. T. *Multinational Management.* Columbus, Ohio: Charles E. Merrill Publishing Company, 1973.

KOLDE, ENDEL-JAKOB *International Business Enterprise* (2nd ed.). Englewood Cliffs, N.J.: Prentice-Hall, Inc., 1973.

—— *Environment of International Business.* Boston: Kent, 1982.

MASON, H. HAL, ROBERT R. MILLER, AND DALE R. WEIGEL *International Business* (2nd ed.). New York: John Wiley & Sons, Inc., 1981.

NORDYKE, JAMES *Comparative Business Environment.* Cincinnati, Ohio: Southwestern Publishing Company, 1977.

PERLMUTTER, HOWARD V. "Social Architectural Problems of the Multinational Firm," *Quarterly Journal of AIESEC International,* August 1967.

PHATAK, ARVIND V. *Managing Multinational Corporations.* New York: Praeger Publishers, 1974.

RICKS, DAVID   *Big Business Blunders.* Homewood, Ill.: Dow Jones Irwin, 1983.

ROBINSON, RICHARD D.   *International Business Management* (2nd ed.). Hinsdale, Ill.: Dryden Press, 1978.

ROBOCK, STEFAN H., AND KENNETH SIMMONDS   *International Business and Multinational Enterprises* (3d ed.). Homewood, Ill.: Richard D. Irwin, Inc., 1980.

ROOT, FRANKLIN R.   *International Trade and Investment* (4th ed.). Cincinnati, Ohio: Southwestern Publishing Company, 1978.

RUTENBERG, DAVID   *Multinational Management.* Boston: Little, Brown & Company, 1982.

VERNON, RAYMOND, AND LOUIS T. WELLS, JR.   *Manager in the International Economy* (4th ed.). Englewood Cliffs, N.J.: Prentice-Hall, Inc., 1981.

WILKINS, MYRA   *The Emergence of Multinational Enterprise.* Cambridge, Mass.: Harvard University Press, 1970.

———   *The Maturing of Multinational Enterprise.* Cambridge, Mass.: Harvard University Press, 1974.

2

The Basis
for International
Trade

International business is a far more complicated and sophisticated field than domestic business. An understanding of the basic causes for the various forms of international business has fascinated economists for centuries. The greatest amount of effort by far has been expended on developing an understanding of the international trade of merchandise. International trade theory is examined in this chapter. In the next chapter we consider the basis for other forms of international business, especially capital flows.

THE BASIS FOR TRADE

Why does a nation, especially one as large and economically powerful as the United States, become deeply involved in foreign trade and international investment? Wouldn't it be better if the United States "went it alone," relying only on itself? The answer to this question basically lies in the differences existing among countries.

The ability of a country to export successfully depends on four basic considerations:

1. availability of the necessary productive resources
2. environmental conditions

3. opportunity, ability, and effort of the producer to trade
4. competitiveness of the local producers abroad

Availability of Productive Resources

From an economic perspective, the basic ingredients of an economy are its *factors of production:* land (including raw materials), labor, capital, technology, and entrepreneurship. It is the differences in (1) the distribution of these resources and (2) the extent of their development that basically accounts for much of the international interchange of economic factors and/or the products and services that the basic factors can be used to produce.

Distribution of natural resources: Nature has not endowed all regions of the world equally in the distribution of natural resources. For example, the oil resources of Saudi Arabia, the extensive arable land of Argentina, and the mild climates and abundant rainfall of many tropical and subtropical areas of the world contrast sharply with the apparent dearth of rich natural resources of Saharan countries such as Chad and Mali, the shortage of arable land and fresh water in much of the Middle East (at least until more economical means of water desalinization are devised), and the harsh climates of northern Siberia and Canada. People too are a natural resource. Compare the relatively thinly populated countries such as Australia and Canada with densely populated areas such as El Salvador, the Netherlands, and India. These differences affect the types of products and services a country or region can produce, the quantity it can produce, the manner in which it can produce, and how economically it can produce.

Historical development: The productive ability of a region depends not only on its raw resources (including its people), but also on how these basic natural resources have been treated and developed over time. Different histories of social, political, economic, and technological development tend to increase or to decrease the differences among countries. For instance, there are significant variations among countries in educational levels, technological levels, industrial capacities, transportation systems, the availability of investment capital, and the social mobility of workers. As a result, some countries can produce certain products better or less expensively than other countries, even than those whose resource base is similar, but less highly developed. On the other hand, social, economic, and especially political and military developments can turn back the clock of progress: The destruction of the sophisticated economies of the Incas and Mayas by the conquistadors and the modern destruction of Cambodia by its own leaders and by Vietnam are examples.

Indeed, this imbalance in *resource endowments* (natural and developed) of different regions is not restricted to international environments alone; imbalances in productive advantages occur within a nation as well as among nations. For instance, the climatic advantages of Florida over Montana in the production of oranges are analogous to Spain's advantages over Sweden in the same respect.

Few nations are as richly endowed as the United States in resources, in the historical development of such resources, in the general ability to produce the goods and services demanded by its economy, and in the size of its domestic market. Thus, international trade is *relatively* less important to the United States than to most countries. However, the United States is virtually devoid of certain resources, such as tin, chromium, nickel, and platinum, and relatively short in numerous other resources, such as copper, gold, and, of course, oil. Furthermore, although many other products could be produced here, the cost of doing so would be far greater than the cost of importing the products, for example, tea, coffee, bananas, and natural rubber. Finally, there is also a strong demand for the importation of large quantities of such products as foreign cameras, textiles, steel, and automobiles, despite large American industries in these fields. Indeed, the extent of foreign trade by the United States in absolute terms is very great, and the impact of the U.S. exports and imports on the rest of the world is enormous. (As either an importer or exporter, the United States is involved in 25 to 30 percent of total world trade.)

CONDITIONS OF THE ECONOMIC ENVIRONMENT

A country with the necessary natural resources and the historical development of productive capacity and infrastructure has a critical edge over countries that lack such assets. However, such assets are not sufficient in themselves to guarantee success in international trade; for example, American producers as a whole have tended to be less successful as exporters than their European or Japanese counterparts.

Many environmental conditions can interfere with the opportunities for utilizing favorable natural resources, industry, and infrastructure. Prominent among these are inflation, exchange rates, labor conditions, the attitude of government, and laws.

Inflation: Cost increases are a critical problem in a company's ability to compete either domestically or internationally. In the late 1960s, a period of relatively stable world prices began to come to an end, and it totally disappeared in the 1970s. Massive governmental budgetary deficits, "printing-press" monetary policies, chronic increases in oil prices, currency instability, and "stickiness" in the downward movement of prices combined to cause chronic upward movement of prices on a worldwide basis—in both oil-importing and oil-exporting countries, in both developed and less-developed countries, and in both free market and Communist economies. In the 1980s, countries such as Germany and Switzerland were praised for keeping inflation in the 4 to 6 percent range, a range that would have been viewed as high in the 1950s and 1960s!

Obviously, a producer whose prices increase more rapidly than those of competitors will, with all else being equal, find it difficult to compete.

Exchange rates: Differences in rates of inflation can be offset by changes in exchange rates (the prices of currencies in foreign exchange markets). Thus, if French prices rise (inflate) more rapidly than in the Netherlands, then a decline in the value of the French franc relative to the Dutch guilder will help to adjust for the domestic inflationary differences. Therefore, French producers will be able to continue to compete with Dutch producers in third countries, in the Netherlands, and in France.

However, if a currency's international value does not decline as price differences would suggest, then local producers will not be able to export as successfully nor compete as successfully with imports as formerly. This was a serious problem for many U.S. exporters when the U.S. dollar was highly overvalued in the late 1960s and early 1970s and again in the early 1980s.

Conversely, a currency that doesn't rise in value when its domestic inflation is relatively low provides an artificial advantage to both its exporters and import competitors.

Labor conditions: Adequately developed productive capacity and infrastructure provide the necessary base for export success. However, disruption of production or distribution can eliminate those advantages. Recurring major labor disruptions in the United States and United Kingdom in such areas as steel, trucking, and the ports are serious hurdles for American and British exporters.

Governmental attitudes: As will be seen in subsequent chapters, some governments strongly encourage and abet the export sector of their economies. Other governments are essentially neutral or even obstructive to exporting.

Also, governmental expenditures can be a critical factor in supporting critical industries. For example, military purchases of aircraft are an important factor in the international commercial success of the American, French, and Israeli aircraft industries. Similarly, the U.S. space program has provided a strong impetus to domestic electronic companies.

Laws: Laws generally reflect governmental attitudes. Labor laws, tax laws, and patent laws are just three of the critical legal areas that can affect the competitiveness of exporters. For example, the value-added tax system, which is widely used in Europe, provides for the rebate to producers of domestic taxes paid on exported goods.

THE OPPORTUNITY, THE ABILITY, AND THE EFFORT OF THE PRODUCER TO TRADE

If a country or region has been fortunate in the availability of natural resources and has developed these and other factors of production (for example, capital, technology, and entrepreneurship), this is still no guarantee of success in international trade. There also needs to be the necessary demand, an awareness of this demand by the supplier, the availability of appropriate distribution channels, freedom from governmental barriers, and, very importantly, the necessary desire and effort on the part of the exporter.

Demand: Quite obviously there must be foreign demand for the good or service produced. When UNIVAC developed the original computer, little foreign demand for computers was expected, since the first models were quite expensive. However, foreign demand can often be developed where none existed before, as Pepsi is in the process of attempting in the Soviet Union. Or there might simply be much more potential demand abroad than had ever been realized, as was the case with hand-held calculators.

Knowledge of market opportunities: Even if potential foreign demand exists for a product, the producer must be aware of the demand; this knowledge can be attained either directly or via an intermediary. Many producers are very ignorant of their foreign opportunities. For example, most American companies are notoriously lacking in this respect. Producers in most other developed countries, such as Germany, The Netherlands, and Japan, are much more attuned to world markets. Companies in most developing countries are also commonly quite weak in seeking out foreign markets, although there are notable exceptions, such as South Korea, Taiwan, and Brazil.

Foreign distribution channels: Even in the 1980s there are many areas of the world, especially in less-developed countries, that lack reasonable transportation and storage facilities. Due to this lack, a market may simply not be prepared to buy many types of products. For example, frozen foods would be impossible to sell to regions where frozen-storage facilities do not exist.

Minimum of governmental controls: Within a single nation today, the flow of trade may still be quite free: Money is normally used in order to facilitate trade, and a minimum of barriers typically exist for trade in most products. For instance, in the United Kingdom as well as in the United States, Coca-Cola is traded (for money) throughout the country. In such free markets, as noted previously, various geographical areas have different climatic, raw material, or labor advantages and have developed their industrial capacities to different extents and, as a consequence, tend to produce and trade products which their advantages make possible (Pennsylvania's coal, Texas' oil, Vermont's maple sugar, Idaho's potatoes, Minnesota's iron ore, Michigan's automobiles, South Carolina's textiles, and so forth).

However, trade between nations is subject to numerous restrictions. As will be thoroughly discussed in Chapter 4, *all* national governments impose import restraints on foreign-made goods and services. Most governments also impose some form of export, exchange, or capital controls. Such controls either restrict or totally ban some types of trade. Examples of export controls are controls on exports of military equipment, banning of trade with certain countries, and so forth.

Desire and effort: Even when all of the conditions noted above offer satisfactory opportunities for international trade, many companies fail to respond. Some companies simply lack the desire to try. Other companies have the desire but never make an adequate effort.

The importance of desire and effort in determining success in international trade cannot be overemphasized. Management is a critical factor. Countries such as Japan and South Korea are very poor in raw materials; however, they have been very successful in importing materials and components for use in local manufacturing of goods both for local use and exporting.

COMPETITIVENESS OF LOCAL PRODUCERS ABROAD

The fourth of the four basic elements that determine the ability of a country to export successfully is the capacity of local producers abroad to compete.

Production costs: Clearly a vital element in the ability of local producers to compete is the relative cost of production. High labor, capital, and energy costs, to name a few, can open the road for very strong competition from abroad. Note, for example, the success of Japanese electronics products in the United States.

Competition: The existence of strong, aggressive competitors in a foreign market can be a strong disincentive to successful and profitable exporting. Companies that have learned to innovate, produce, and market effectively against strong competition at home are often able to successfully resist competition from abroad. Also, local tradition or governmental action can strengthen local companies vis à vis imports.

TRADE BY BARTER

Trade was once very simple: The number of goods available were few; there were no currencies and no national boundaries. Eventually, however, the number of products increased, and political boundaries developed. Money was developed to facilitate trade. Also, governments began acting to either facilitate or impede trade.

Although the existence of money usually facilitates trade relative to barter, with the primary exception of periods of hyperinflation, the existence of many different currencies complicates and reduces many of the advantages of money. Therefore, before examining trade involving the use of money, we first explore trade via barter, so that the reader will be better prepared to understand the theory under conditions of monetary exchange, which is examined later in this chapter.

Barter is, of course, very common in many native markets in poor countries of the world. It is also increasing in importance among wealthy countries. Communist countries have long relied heavily upon barter for trade among themselves and with developing countries. Also companies in non-Communist, developed countries have bartered such products as pipeline with Eastern Europe in exchange for some of the natural gas to be transported by the pipeline and with factories in exchange for a share of their output. (General Motors once even bartered cars for strawberries!) In addition, a number of the major oil exporters, such as Iran and Nigeria, have bartered oil and natural gas in exchange for manufactured goods (including weapons). Thus, an examination of barter is of more than simply theoretical interest.[1]

ABSOLUTE AND COMPARATIVE ADVANTAGE
AS THE BASES FOR INTERNATIONAL TRADE

Absolute advantage: The flow of trade and investments arises from an economic advantage that one region has over another in the output or the marketing of a particular good or service. In the examples given thus far in this chapter, trade occurs because of the *absolute advantage* of one of the regions in the production of a product. This

---

[1]For a more extended discussion of barter in the 1980s, see Christopher M. Korth, "Barter—An Old Practice Yields New Profits," *Business,* September–October 1981.

TABLE 2.1   Units of Output (Per Unit of Input)

	Oranges	Lumber
Country A	6	4
Country B	3	6
Comparative efficiency	2 : 1	2 : 3 or $\frac{2}{3}$: 1

means that it costs less (in terms of labor, land, capital, and so forth) for that region to produce copper or oranges or Coca-Cola than it does for the other region; the less efficient region will therefore desire to trade for some of its needs.

If the second region in turn has absolute advantages in other products, a basis exists for trade. As can be seen in Table 2.1, country A can produce oranges twice as efficiently as can country B, whereas the latter is 50 percent more productive than A in the output of lumber; thus, there is a natural tendency for country A to exchange oranges for country B's lumber.

Unfortunately, this procedure has obvious limitations. As the observer may quickly point out, the quantity of a product that a country would be willing to accept in exchange for its exports is not unlimited; the ability and desire of country B to consume oranges from country A may be inadequate relative to the latter's desire for lumber. Perhaps in addition to oranges, country A also has an absolute advantage in wheat; it could then offer both products for country B's lumber. Nevertheless, it is very unlikely that their absolute advantages and demand conditions would be perfectly complementary. As a result, trade opportunities would be severely limited. Thus, successful barter relies upon what economists call a "double coincidence of wants," which imposes a severe limitation on the development of trade. Some of these bilateral limitations can be overcome by multilateral barter. However, even this type of system has severe limitations.

Comparative advantage: Fortunately, however, economists noted long ago that this imbalance of absolute advantages need not prevent further trade from occurring. Rather, they were able to show that it can be quite rational and economically profitable for a nation to import goods that it could itself produce at a lower resource cost than could other countries, that is, import goods in which it has absolute production cost advantages. Conversely, countries can successfuly export goods in which they have absolute production cost *dis*advantages. This phenomenon is called the *theory of comparative advantage* or the *theory of comparative cost*.

TABLE 2.2 Units of Output (Per Unit of Input)

	Clothing	Food	Domestic Exchange Ratio
Country A	10	6	5 : 3
Country B	5	4	5 : 4
Comparative efficiency	2 : 1	1.5 : 1	

Comparative advantage refers to the significance of *relative* cost differences between countries that are more important (for trading purposes) than the absolute cost differences mentioned above. Relative cost difference refers to one country's need to sacrifice less of product X in order to produce an additional unit of product Y than the other country; therefore, a comparative advantage exists. Either the country with the absolute cost advantage or that with the absolute cost disadvantage may have the comparative cost advantage in a given product! For example, although in country A it may be possible to produce 10 units of clothing or 6 units of food with 1 unit of labor input, land, or capital,[2] in country B the outputs are only 5 units of clothing and 4 units of food for the same unit of input. These conditions are listed in Table 2.2. In the absence of international trade, trade occurs domestically in the same exchange ratios as production. In our example above, the ratios would be 10 : 6 (or 5 : 3) in country A and 5 : 4 in country B; these are the *domestic exchange ratios*.

As can be seen in Table 2.2, country A has an absolute advantage in the production of both commodities; that is, for the same amount of effort, A can produce twice as much clothing as and 50 percent more food than B. Obviously, country B would feel that it could gain from trade. Less obviously, however, country A can find trade to its advantage also. An understanding of this principle is vital in order to understand much of the trade that actually occurs. The reader must learn to think of the relative (comparative) rather than the absolute relationship.

Before assuming that A is not interested in trade, the reader ought to ask *what* and *how much* producers in country A must be offered in order to be interested in trade. Obviously, if country B offers country A more than 5 units of clothing in exchange for 3 units of food, which is the domestic exchange ratio observed in Table 2.2, then A would benefit by concentrating more of its resources in the production of food and by trading for some or all of its clothing needs. Conversely, if A were to be offered more than 3 units of food in international trade in exchange for 5

---

[2]It makes no difference what units are chosen, as long as the amounts of effort are equal. The units could be grams, individual units, multiunit boxes, full railroad cars, or even shiploads.

units of clothing, it would again gain by trade if it concentrated on the production of clothing.

But will producers in country B be willing to offer producers in country A more than 5 units of clothing in exchange for 3 units of food or more than 3 units of food in exchange for 5 units of clothing? Country B can, by sacrificing 4 units of food, produce for itself 5 units of clothing. Therefore, B will offer *up to but not more than* 4 units of food to A in exchange for 5 units of clothing.

If, therefore, A can gain by receiving more than 3 units of food in exchange for 5 units of clothing, and if B were willing to offer up to 4 units of food for that much clothing, then a basis for trade between the two countries exists (that is, between the exchange ratios of 5 : 3 and 5 : 4), *even for products in which all the absolute cost advantages of production belong to one country* (A in our example). Country B therefore has a comparative advantage (its lower absolute *dis*advantage) in food, whereas A has its comparative advantage (its greater absolute advantage) in clothing.

Comparative advantages thus identify the products in which each country can specialize in international trade if it is offered a sufficient amount of another product—as much as or more than would be offered in domestic trade. The country that must sacrifice the least amount of output of one product or service in order to release the labor or other factor of production needed to produce another product (its more relatively efficient product) has a comparative advantage in the latter good or service. Clothing is the more relatively efficient product for country A, since it need sacrifice less food production than country B to produce more clothing; food is the more relatively efficient product for country B, since it would need to sacrifice less clothing than would country A to produce more food.

TERMS OF TRADE

The *exchange ratio between exports and imports* is called the *terms of trade.* This ratio settles somewhere between or at the two extremes of 5 : 4 and 5 : 3. At any other exchange ratio, either A or B would be made worse off and would refuse to trade. For instance, at an international exchange ratio of 5 units of clothing to 2 units of food, both countries would want to produce only food—a highly unsatisfactory situation. Similarly, at a ratio of 5 : 5, only clothing would be produced. Only within the range between 5 : 3 and 5 :4 could a satisfactory balance occur.

Exactly where the terms of trade settle between these two extremes depends upon the relative demand and supply conditions in each country for the other country's exports. Both countries benefit by trade at terms within these limits, but the distribution of *gains from trade* varies. The gains from trade are the *increases in total production that occur as the result of trade* (that is, the increased benefits resulting from *specialization* in each country in the product in which it has a comparative advantage).

Country A can indeed gain from trade, even though it has absolute advantages in the production of both goods (that is, it can produce more of either with a particular amount of input effort). Once again the point ought to be emphasized that it is the *ratios* of productive efficiency between the goods that are important. These ratios measure the comparative rather than the absolute sacrifice that production of the goods involves. *There will always be a comparative advantage for every country in something,* unless the ratios of the domestic opportunity costs are equal in both countries.[3] This provides a basic rationale for trade.

SPECIALIZATION

The shift of resources away from less efficient employment into the production of goods in which countries have relatively greater efficiency is the process of *specialization.* Specialization leads not only to the acquisition of what otherwise might be unattainable, but to an overall increase in the total production of the products traded (that is, gains from trade). Clearly, this increased output must occur if *both* parties are to benefit from trade. Also, as noted above, this basic feature of specialization leads to the result that either or both regions might cease to produce items that they are currently producing and might even give up production of what they can produce more cheaply (in terms of resource employment) than can competitive regions.

PRODUCTION AND CONSUMPTION POSSIBILITIES

Figure 2.1 illustrates the various output combinations for country A from the data in Table 2.2. If all labor (let us assume 100 units) is devoted to production of clothing, the total output in country A would be 1000 units (point *W*); on the other hand, if all labor is employed in food production, A's total output is 600 units (point *X*).[4] Line *WX* is called a *production-possibilities line.* It shows the various *maximum* combina-

---

[3]The reader may wish to analyze this special situation for the following case:

	Clothing	Food
Country A	10	8
Country B	5	4

[4]*Constant costs* are assumed in this example, that is, efficiency is not affected as more and more labor is concentrated in the production of one good. To assume *increasing or decreasing costs* would be more realistic; however, it would not greatly affect our conclusions and would only complicate the discussion.

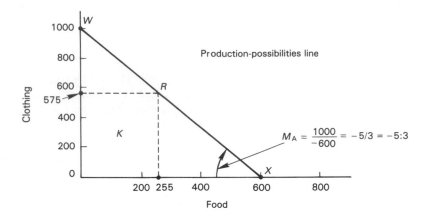

FIGURE 2.1   Production Possibilities for Country A (100 Units of Labor)

tions of *output* that country A can produce with its labor supply. In the absence of foreign trade, *WX* also becomes A's *consumption-possibilities line*. This line is an illustration of all the *maximum* combinations that are available to a country for *consumption*. Obviously, *in the absence of trade,* a country can consume no more than it produces. The domestic exchange ratio in A of 5 : 3 is measured by the slope $(-\frac{5}{3})$ of WX.[5] Any combination of production and consumption of food and clothing below this line is also possible, for example, point *K*, but such a combination would correspond to a lower standard of living than is attainable, would be less efficient, and would cause unemployment. At any given time, a country will be producing and consuming at only one point on its production-consumption diagram; just what combination of goods is produced and consumed depends largely upon demand and supply conditions; one possible combination is shown at point *R* in Figure 2.1, where 575 units of clothing are produced by $57\frac{1}{2}$ units of labor and 255 units of food are produced by $42\frac{1}{2}$ units of labor.[6]

GAINS FROM TRADE

As has been seen, the introduction of *trade permits a country to consume more than it could produce by itself.* Trade also permits the world to consume more than if each country consumed only its own

---

[5]*M* Refers to the slope of the line.

[6]$\dfrac{575 \text{ units of clothing}}{1000 \text{ units of clothing}} = \dfrac{x \text{ units of labor}}{100 \text{ units of labor}}$

$x = 57\frac{1}{2}$ units of labor to use in the manufacture of clothing, which leaves $42\frac{1}{2}$ units available for food production.

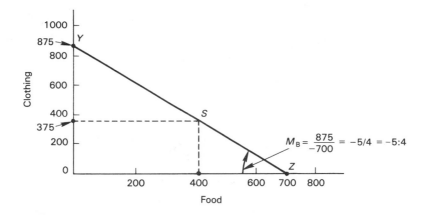

FIGURE 2.2 Production Possibilities for Country B (175 Units of Labor)

production. No country will be economically worse off. *Standards of living can rise in every country.* These are the *gains from specialization.* A graphical presentation of this may be helpful to the reader.

Figure 2.2 shows the production-possibilitites line, *YZ*, for country B for 175 units of labor; also, as was seen above, in the absence of international trade it is B's consumption-possibilities line as well. The domestic exchange ratio of 5 : 4 (the productive efficiency in B) is measured by $-\frac{5}{4}$, the slope of *YZ*. If B's full productive capacity is applied to the output of clothing, total output will be 875 units of clothing (point *Y*). Likewise, the maximum output of food (when there is no output of clothing) is 700 units—point *Z*. A possible production-consumption combination in the absence of trade is shown at point *S*: 375 units of clothing (produced by 75 units of labor) and 400 units of food (produced by 100 units of labor).

If trade now occurs, the consumption-possibilities lines of both countries shift (but, of course, not the production-possibilities lines, which are not affected by trade) in order to indicate increased consumption possibilities. These can be seen in Figures 2.3 and 2.4. The new lines, *WX'* and *Y'Z*, are called *trade-possibilities lines.* They indicate the *maximum quantities* of the commodities that each country can obtain at a particular exchange ratio via specializing in the production of one good and trading for the other. As can be seen, the totals available with free trade are greater than those available without trade. When country A is free to specialize by concentrating greater and greater amounts of its resources in the production of clothing while relying on country B for food, and vice versa, the total productive output of the world will rise.

The slopes of the trade-possibilities line of each country are now equal—$M_A = M_B = -5 : 3.4$ (see Figures 2.3 and 2.4). They represent

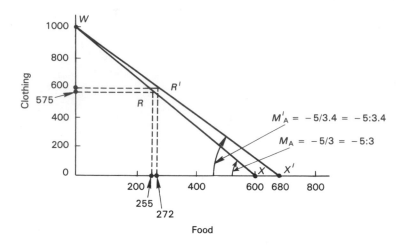

FIGURE 2.3 Trade Possibilities for Country A

the *international terms of trade,* which are different from and fall in between the domestic terms of trade of both countries (5 : 3 in country A and 5 : 4 in country B).[7]

For each exchange ratio (that is, a particular terms-of-trade figure), there is a distinct trade-possibilities line. In this example the terms of trade are assumed to be 5 : 3.4. If it is assumed that at this ratio country B desires to export the exact amount of food that A wishes and that A is willing to export the amount of food that B demands (that is, if this is an *equilibrium exchange ratio,* namely that at this exchange ratio the demand and supply conditions in each country are satisfied and therefore that the market is cleared, with all production being consumed), then R' (in Figure 2.3) and S' (in Figure 2.4) might represent the new consumption combinations in the two countries. Remember that only one exchange ratio clears the market under the supply and demand conditions that apply at a given point in time. Similarly, only one R' and S' exist at that exchange ratio. Different demand and supply conditions produce either a shift in the existing trade possibilities line (with the same exchange ratio) or a move to a new trade-possibilities line (with a different exchange ratio). In either event the consumption patterns and the sharing of the gains from trade would change.

Note that clothing consumption in A (600 units) plus clothing

---

[7]Except in the special case where the international terms of trade are exactly the same as the domestic terms of trade of either country (that is, at either 5 : 3 or 5 : 4). This might occur, for example, in trade between a very large and a very small country; the latter may be unable to affect domestic prices of the former. Trade would still occur, but the small country would get all the gains from trade, although the large country would be no worse off. This special case is a basic argument on behalf of preferential trading arrangements between poor, small countries and wealthy, large countries.

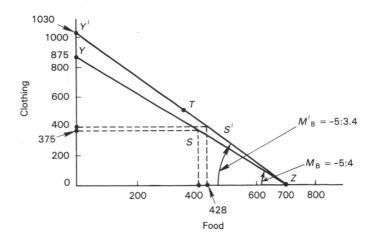

FIGURE 2.4   Trade Possibilities for Country B

consumption in B (400 units imported from A) exactly equals country A's maximum productive capability (1000 units). Similarly, food consumption in A (272 units imported from B) plus food consumption in B (428 units) exactly equals country B's maximum productive capacity (700 units).

Note also that both countries would then be consuming more of each product than they had been able to do in the absence of trade *despite the fact that there has been no change in the production capabilities of each country!* Each country, by specializing in the product in which it has the comparative advantage, increases total world production of that product and gains from specialization. By trading, the countries share those gains (i.e., the gains from trade).

Table 2.3 summarizes the output and consumption conditions before and after trade and illustrates the gains from trade. At this particular exchange ratio and with an equilibrium position on the consumption-possibilities line of each country, B would gain the most from trade (line 8), but the distribution of the gains from trade would be different with any other exchange rate and country A could gain the most under other supply and demand conditions.

Both countries are now able to consume more of each product. However, if the logic of the trade-possibilities line is pursued, note that it is very possible for a nation to choose less of one product *with* trade than in the absence of trade (point T in Figure 2.4) in order to receive a correspondingly greater amount of the other good. This situation is rare, but consumer tastes often surprise the "experts."

If, as a result of demand conditions, an exchange ratio of 5 units of clothing for 3.4 units of food does not result in equilibrium, the terms of

TABLE 2.3

	Exchange Ratio	Clothing: Production (a) – Exports (b) + Imports (c) = Consumption (d)								Food: Production (a) – Exports (b) + Imports (c) = Consumption (d)							
		a		b		c		d		a		b		c		d
Situation *before trade*																	
1. Country A	5 : 3	575	–	0	+	0	=	575		255	–	0	+	0	=	255
2. Country B	5 : 4	375	–	0	+	0	=	375		400	–	0	+	0	=	400
3. World	none	950						950		655						655
Situation *after trade*																	
4. Country A	5 : 3.4	1000	–	400	+	0	=	600		0	–	0	+	272	=	272
5. Country B	5 : 3.4	0	–	0	+	400	=	400		700	–	272	+	0	=	428
6. World	5 : 3.4	1000						1000		700						700
Gain from trade																	
7. Country A								+ 25*								+ 17*
8. Country B								+ 25**								+ 28**
9. World								+ 50								+ 45

*line 4 minus line 1.

**line 5 minus line 2.

36

trade (and therefore the trade-possibilities lines) must change. The gains from trade will likewise shift somewhat from one country to the other; but as long as the exchange ratio remains between 5 : 3 and 5 : 4, both countries benefit. Outside this range, no trade would occur, since both countries would try to specialize in the production of the same product.

REFINEMENT OF TRADE THEORY UNDER BARTER

Incomplete specialization: Frequently each country would continue to produce both products. This results from economic factors and a reluctance to rely upon a single supplier as well as political and sociological factors, such as when the government decides to maintain at least some domestic production in order to avoid the danger of foreign supplies being cut off by war.

Furthermore, countries A and B have been assumed to be of similar size in terms of productive output. As a result, each country is able to specialize completely and to supply the total demand for its comparatively more efficient output. If one of the countries is significantly smaller than the other, it might specialize completely in the production of one product and still be unable to satisfy total demand. The other country would therefore have to continue to produce both goods. In this event, the larger country's economy would be less affected by international trade pressures than the smaller country's economy. As a result, the smaller country's price structure would be affected more, and therefore more of the gains from trade would accrue to the smaller country. Thus, if Japan liberalizes trade with the Philippines, both countries will benefit, but the Philippines will receive more benefit. This is a major argument for liberalizing international trade as a means of assisting poor countries by means other than foreign aid, which is never in sufficient supply. Also, if increasing costs instead of constant or decreasing costs are assumed, each country might continue to produce some of both products even with trade.

The analysis above involves the simplest of conceivable trade situations: one input, two countries, two products, no trade barriers, no currencies (that is, barter is necessary), and no movement of the factors of production.

Multicommodity trade: The real situation is much more complicated. At the very minimum, the respective demands for the other country's export will not ordinarily balance. As a result, single-commodity trade normally expands to multicommodity trade. This is possible because *comparative advantages ordinarily exist for both countries in a number of products*. The more that trade expands in order to reap the benefits of specialization, the greater the rewards for the world.

Multicountry trade: Even multicommodity trade between only two countries has limitations. However, the diversity of productive resources is too great for two countries (even if they were of the size of the U.S. and the USSR, let alone if they were El Salvador and Upper Volta) to be able to completely satisfy the trading needs of each other. For instance, the production capabilities of both the U.S. and the USSR in such products as natural rubber, tea, coffee, and bananas are very limited. In order for specialization to provide the maximum world benefits from trade, it must become multilateral or many-sided. *Multicountry trade* means that the trade between A and B does not have to exactly balance (as was necessary in the model above), but that A can buy from B, which buys from C, which buys from A, and so on. Such an arrangement permits even greater reliance upon specialization and makes it possible for nations to surmount shortcomings in their natural resource endowments in the most effective way.

However, even these multicommodity and multilateral adjustments to the original barter model depart significantly from most actual conditions. They are obviously gross oversimplifications, and in certain respects the development of international economic theory lags far behind the development of international business. Nevertheless, this analysis does provide a basic framework for examining many important aspects of the complex world of international business.

With this examination of basic trade theory behind us, we can now turn to some major adjustments and adaptations to the basic theory. The balance of this chapter involves consideration of (1) international trade under conditions other than barter, (2) inadequacies of such basic trade theories, and (3) a modern trade theory. Chapter 3 examines capital flows and the mobility of other factors of production. Chapter 4 examines barriers to free trade and factor mobility.

MONETARY EXCHANGE

Most world trade does not occur on a barter basis. Even within a given country, consumers would find it very difficult to take the goods or services that their families produce, such as beef, tools, or haircuts, and barter for their daily needs. Likewise, a gas station owner is not equipped to accept eggs and potatoes in exchange for gasoline. Instead, societies long ago recognized the convenience of using money. The same is true, of course, for trade between countries.

Money has many advantages, and the elimination of the need for barter is only one of them. In addition to these *standard of value* and *unit of exchange* functions, money serves invaluably as a *store of value*. Many products, such as eggs, butter, and milk, cannot be stored for long, and most services, such as haircuts, taxi rides, and so forth, cannot be

TABLE 2.4   Units of Output (Per Day of Worker Input)

	Clothing	Food	Domestic Exchange Ratio (Barter)
Country A	10	6	5 : 3
Country B	5	4	5 : 4

stored at all. In addition, many "storable" goods can only be stored with great difficulty and expense. Money is also a *standard of deferred payment,* whereby financial obligations can be satisfied at some future date. The ability to receive and store money is, therefore, obviously a great advantage to all sectors of an economy.

Although the use of money simplifies the exchange procedure, it also adds some problems. Some of these problems will become apparent in the following discussion. Nevertheless, *the introduction of money will not alter the fundamental principles observed in previous sections.*

In order to examine how money fits into our example, consider two currencies—pesos in country A and francs in country B—and refer to Table 2.4, which is the same as Table 2.2. Table 2.4 illustrates *output efficiencies* (units of output per unit of labor input). Next assume that wages are 90 pesos in country A and 40 francs in country B. Based on these wages, Table 2.5 shows the per-unit price of these goods in domestic currency units. Obviously, the price of each good is still determined by the efficiency of production; the prices in Table 2.5 are, therefore, a function of the efficiency of outputs in Table 2.4 and the wages paid. For instance, at the wage level in country A (90 pesos), clothing costs 9 pesos and food 15 pesos per unit of output, that is, 90 ÷ 10 for clothing and 90 ÷ 6 for food. In country B clothing costs 8 francs and food 10 francs.

Note that the exchange ratios when expressed in terms of currency in Table 2.5 are the inverse of those expressed in terms of barter ratios in Table 2.4. Thus a ratio of 5 : 3 for country A becomes 3 : 5. The results of our analysis of trade theory are unchanged, but the reasoning process must be adjusted. Indeed, comparative advantages can be as readily identified as in the earlier discussion.

In country A only three-fifths as much of its currency (that is, 9 pesos) must be paid for clothing as for food (15 pesos). In country B, 8 units of its currency must be paid for clothing versus 10 units for food (a 4 : 5 ratio). Therefore, it is still *relatively* cheaper for country A to produce clothing, regardless of the difference in currencies and whether the currencies can be exchanged, that is, whether they are *convertible* into each other. The comparative advantage in clothing therefore belongs to country A, whether productive efficiency is expressed in units of output or in local currency prices. This is true at all times: *The use of currencies has no effect on comparative advantages.*

However, the determination of absolute advantage is impossible

TABLE 2.5   Price in Domestic Currency (Per Unit of Output)

	Clothing	Food	Domestic Exchange Ratio (Money)
Country A (pesos)	9	15	3 : 5
Country B (francs)	8	10	4 : 5

unless pesos can somehow be equated with francs (either in pesos, francs, or a third currency such as dollars or deutschemarks). Who is to say whether 9 pesos of clothing represents more or less efficient production than 8 francs of clothing? What is lacking is a means of transforming prices in francs into prices in pesos and vice versa.

CURRENCY EXCHANGE RATES

Currencies have prices just as do food and clothing. The price of one currency in terms of another is called the *exchange rate*. It helps to determine whether country A's or country B's clothing or food is less expensive. The consideration of exchange rates is, ironically, a return to a consideration of barter. Since there are limits to the willingness of people to hold the currency of another country, they "barter" their foreign currency holdings to find a price satisfactory to everyone for country A's pesos in terms of country B's francs. Of course the procedure is not quite that simple; decisions are not usually made by individuals but by many individuals acting in the currency market. However, this is the basic mechanism for arriving at rates of exchange.[8]

In the example above, if the exchange ratio is 1 peso = 10 francs (or 1 franc = 0.1 peso), country B has *absolute monetary cost advantages* in both commodities (see Table 2.6). In this situation, A would like to import both food and clothing (paying 0.8 pesos instead of 9 pesos for clothing and 1 peso instead of 15 pesos for food), and B would desire to

TABLE 2.6   Country B's Monetary Cost Advantages

	Prices in Pesos (P)	
	Clothing	Food
Country A	9 P	15P
Country B	0.8P	1P

Exchange rate: 1 franc equals 0.1 peso.

---

[8]The question of foreign exchange is explored more fully in Chapter 6, "Foreign Exchange Markets."

buy nothing from A. The result would be a strong demand for francs and no demand for pesos. Trade would not result unless one of two things occurred: (1) a better balance in prices resulting from a major increase in B's prices, a major decline in A's prices, or both, or (2) a change in the exchange rate.

ADJUSTMENT VIA PRICE CHANGES

Without changing the exchange rate, the prices could be brought into relative alignment by rising wages in B and falling wages in A. Such shifts might be occasioned by the availability of a large initial stock of monetary gold in the hands of country A. If gold could be used—either directly for purchasing B's goods or indirectly in exchange for francs—there would be a shift of gold to country B. Also, there would be very strong demand for B's products and labor. As a result, very strong inflationary pressures would occur, driving up B's prices. At the same time, demand for A's products and labor would collapse, which would drive down the wages and prices in that country. Eventually, even without any change in the exchange ratio, the prices (if unobstructed) would realign themselves until a point was reached at which B would gain by buying from A.

As the previous analysis showed, A has a comparative advantage in the production of clothing; this would again be the product in which A would specialize. With prices falling in A and rising in B, it is impossible to tell just where realignment would occur. Obviously, however, given an initial situation in which prices prevent trade, prices must shift until the price of one of the goods is at least equal in both countries before trade can occur. Since the existence of an exchange rate makes it possible to conveniently express the prices of both countries in one currency, even though we are now assuming that none of the adjustment occurs because of a change in the exchange rate, the necessity of this shift needs no further emphasis. Also, the range of possible trading prices is determined when the wage rates have been so adjusted that each country asks a lower price for only one of the commodities. If the prices diverge again so that either country charges less for both goods, only a flow of reserve assets such as gold will bring about trade, or it will be necessary either to barter as described above or to adjust the exchange rate.

Unfortunately, this analysis has several flaws when applied to most trading nations today. First, although wage rates are able to rise in most countries (for example, country B), they are quite "sticky" in a downward direction, since wage earners in country A are quite reluctant to accept sharp cuts in wages. Second, the time lag required to attain trade conditions that are attractive to both countries can be lengthy, and the social cost to country A in terms of unemployment and falling standards of living can be considerable. Third, a high rate of inflation in B usually meets resistance. As a result, the governments are under strong pressure to alleviate such trends as recession, inflation, or stagflation.

Traditional reactions have been the imposition of tariffs, quotas, and exchange restrictions, which are discussed in Chapter 4. Such steps obviously interfere with trade and the attainment of the benefits from specialization. Positive provisions, such as those in the U.S. Trade Expansion Act of 1962 for government assistance for workers and companies that are adversely affected by liberalization of trade, also exist and need not interfere with the attainment of gains from trade. Nevertheless, domestic pressure can be very strong on both governments to prevent the "natural" adjustments via either recession and slumping prices (in A) or rapid inflation (in B). Fortunately wage adjustments do not have to bear the full brunt of the adjustment.

ADJUSTMENT VIA EXCHANGE RATE CHANGES

It is also possible to alter the trade relationships by changing the exchange rate. In fact, if exchange rates in the example above are free to fluctuate with demand changes, the price of francs in terms of pesos would fall rapidly to a level at which a demand for pesos would develop in country B, even with no change in the wage or price level in either country. Consider Table 2.7. At an exchange rate of 1 peso = 1 franc, no trade would occur, since B still has no incentive to import. Likewise, at an exchange rate of 1 peso = 0.5 franc, country A would have no incentive to import. The exact range of relevant exchange rates can be found by taking the ratio of each price in country A (in pesos) divided by the corresponding price in country B (in francs), that is, between 9 : 8 and 12 : 8. At any exchange rate between these two extremes, *both* nations would gain from trade.[9]

Thus, either the adjustment of domestic prices at a constant exchange ratio or a change in the exchange ratio with relatively constant prices can maintain equilibrium. Naturally, a combination of the two could also be highly effective. In actual practice each of these three alternatives has been employed.

Until 1971 it was very unusual for exchange rates to fluctuate freely.[10] The norm had been for each currency to be "pegged" at a specific value and allowed to fluctuate only within a very narrow range around this *par value*.[11] As a result, exchange rate changes were normally the results of government decisions, and governments were usually

---

[9]The reader should work out an example in order to prove to his or her own satisfaction that the use of prices between these ratios, for example, 10 : 8, yields conditions that are conducive to trade.

[10]Canada had been the major nation to most recently utilize a "floating price" for its currency for any extended period—1960–1962.

[11]See Chapter 5, "World Monetary System."

TABLE 2.7 Prices and Ratios[a]

	Price per Unit of Output	
	Clothing	Food
Country A (pesos)	9	15
Country B (francs)	8	10
Ratio: $P_A : P_B$	9 : 8	$15 : 10 = 3 : 2 = 12 : 8$

[a]This table is identical to Table 2.5.

reluctant to institute such changes frequently.[12] Instead, great reliance was often placed upon restraining a economy that was experiencing a new outflow of money. Such flows of money involve nontrade factors, such as investments, foreign aid, loans, as well as trade factors, and governments commonly restrain various combinations of these flows.[13] Controls thus prevent free movements in these flows.

Here are a few examples of how governments utilized the alternatives listed above prior to 1971. In the mid-1960s Italy instituted a series of recessionary steps that were successful in bringing balance to its international monetary flows without requiring a change in the exchange rate of the lira. Nevertheless, the cost to the domestic economy in terms of unemployment and reduced economic output was high. However, in the late 1960s, the United Kingdom and France failed in similar efforts; when they eventually *devalued* their currencies (that is, changed the value downward), they also designed recessionary steps to help relieve the pressure that led to the devaluation.

The first half of the 1970s witnessed a highly disruptive monetary revolution in the international monetary system that had existed since the end of World War II to a very different type that persists today. Beginning with the *floating* of the dollar in August 1971 (efforts were no longer being made by the U.S. government to support the value of the dollar in terms of gold or other currencies), the international monetary system moved rapidly away from the fixed exchange rate system. In December 1971 fixed rates were reimposed, but by early 1973 the patch job tore apart; the world's first widespread, long-term use of nonfixed exchange rates in modern times has followed.

Thus, under conditions of monetary exchange the use of diverse currencies greatly complicates our examination of trade. Although the availability of money itself facilitates trade, the existence of national boundaries and governmental interference in economic transactions greatly complicate it. If the prevailing exchange rate is unrealistic or if government barriers to trade and factor flows are obstructive, interna-

---

[12]Exceptions were such countries as Brazil, Colombia, and Chile, which had been "devaluing" their currencies at least once per year. (There are exceptions to every generalization.)

[13]To be discussed in Chapter 3, "The Basis for International Factor Movements."

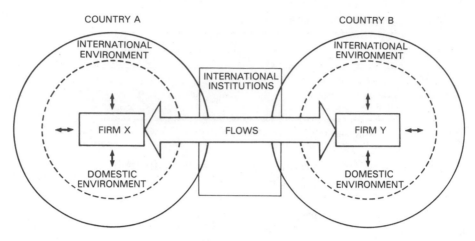

FIGURE 2.5   The Environment of International Business

tional transactions decline, and illegal flows such as smuggling and black markets develop.

As has been seen, the redressing of an imbalance in international economics can be adjusted by a variety of actions. In terms of the international environmental model (Chapter 1) these adjustments can occur in either the domestic constraints or the international constraints (Figure 2.5). Even intergovernmental institutions can be involved, although generally their function is to try to reduce such constraints. These different sectors of the international business environment are examined in subsequent chapters.

INADEQUACIES OF TRADITIONAL TRADE THEORIES

Basic trade theory, like most theory, is based on some convenient, simplified assumptions. Unfortunately, the nature of some of these assumptions greatly limits the applicability and efficiency of the theory.

First, there are a series of what might be called *natural barriers to trade*. Trade theory generally ignores considerations such as transportation and insurance expenditures plus the lack of knowledge of opportunities, which could greatly affect the "tradeability" of a product. Brick, which has a high transportation cost relative to value and therefore is not traded extensively internationally, would be a classic example.

Also, traditional theory assumes perfect knowledge of international trading opportunities, an active interest in trading, and rapid response by managers to the trading incentives. However, in practice executives are often unaware of their trade opportunities. Those who are aware often either are hampered by fears of the complexities of international trade or simply suffer from inertia, which prevents them from seizing an opportunity.

We have already noted that the assumption of rapid adjustments in costs and prices is highly unrealistic. In the absence of such rapid adjustments, few governments are prepared to pay the price of high inflation, recession, and unemployment in order to raise or lower prices to a level necessary for international equilibrium. Even exchange rate alterations have significant time lags before the expected trade-flow adjustments occur. This is another area where governments, for a wide variety of reasons—some of which have economic substance, but some of which are as economically irrational as a government's fear of loss of prestige—interfere with alterations in the value of currency.

Other "natural barriers" to trade involve the assumptions in trade theory of homogeneous products, of free and perfect competition, and of the immobility of factors of production. However, it is simple to demonstrate that many, if not most, products are not homogeneous (for instance, wine, TVs), that oligopolies or quasi-monopolies exist in many fields (computers, automobiles), and that such factors of production as capital, technology, management, and even unskilled labor are mobile.

In addition to the natural barriers to trade which trade theory generally does a poor job of considering, there are other factors with which trade theorists have not really been able to cope. One factor involves taste differences; for example, a dress or perfume might be saleable at a much higher price if labelled "made in France."

Perhaps the most serious shortcoming of traditional trade theory has been the failure to incorporate the role of business corporations, especially multinational companies, into the theories. Since the actual trading decisions are basically made on the microeconomic level by business managers (not by the government of country A or B), this inadequacy of traditional theory greatly limits applicability.

Multinational corporations operate from a multinational, not a national, perspective, which makes them a very unique type of entity. International trade and other flows involving such corporations are often between different affiliates of the company rather than with different companies. As a result, special considerations, such as minimizing tax liability or not competing with other affiliates of the same company, can often be dominant factors in the company's international decisions.

Traditional trade theory is a necessary base to our understanding of international business. In addition, it still underlies the thinking of many academicians, managers, labor leaders, and government officials. Therefore, an understanding of traditional theory is vital in order to understand much of the commentary in such areas as balance-of-payments adjustments, exchange rate adjustments of foreign currencies, and protectionism by use of tariffs and quotas. Also, such theory does satisfactorily explain much international commodity trade, such as the international trade of wheat.

However, international business theory, even trade theory, needs much more development and refinement. In the next section a more modern theory, which has relevance to both international trade and capital flows, is introduced.

PRODUCT LIFE CYCLE

A theory that has gained substantial attention in the past fifteen years focuses on an easily recognized pattern in the life of many products. This pattern is analogous to the childhood, adolescent, maturity, and old-age phases of human life. The model is known as the *product life-cycle (PLC) theory.*[14] Note that PLC is not a general theory, but it offers a valid explanation for certain trade and investment patterns.

Essentially, the PLC theory states that many new products (as opposed to commodities) pass through four basic phases: the new-product phase, the growth phase, the maturity phase, and the standardized-product phase. (See Figure 2.6.)

In the first phase, the *introduction* or the *new-product phase,* a producer introduces a new product; it is effectively in a monopolistic position during much of this phase. Costs (both production and marketing) are high; the price is correspondingly high. Most initial consumption is domestic, although foreign consumption is commonly of increasing importance.

In the second phase, or *growth phase,* production becomes increasingly routinized, so that costs and prices are likely to decline significantly. Competition grows and cost effectiveness becomes of increasing importance. Foreign markets also rise greatly in significance as prices and domestic marketing opportunity decline and as output and international awareness of the product grow. Exports from the country of initial production grow, but foreign production also grows rapidly; the speed of development of the latter is partially a function of the importance of such factors as labor costs, tariff barriers, and transportation costs.

In the third phase, the *maturity phase,* production spreads throughout many parts of the world. Domestic production begins declining as imports grow and exports decline.

In the fourth phase, the *standardized-product* or *decline phase,* production becomes highly routinized and therefore susceptible to the employment of relatively simple equipment and/or relatively unskilled labor. Costs and prices fall even further; they become vital factors in

---

[14]Raymond Vernon, "International Investment and International Trade in the Product Cycle," *Quarterly Journal of Economics,* May 1966, pp. 190–207.

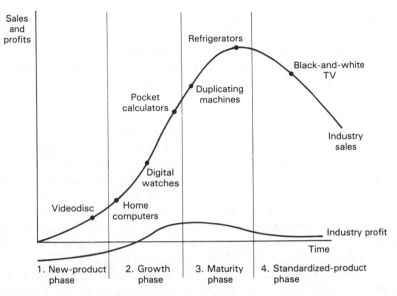

SOURCE: Adapted from Louis E. Boone and David L. Kurtz, *Foundations of Marketing* (Hinsdale, Ill.: Dryden Press, 1977), p. 167.

FIGURE 2.6 Product Life Cycle

both sales and location of production. Production becomes very wide-spread. The country of initial production may well experience declining production and find a shift from a status as net exporter to one of net importer. Also, at this phase many products that were once innovations virtually become commodities, for example, aluminum foil.

The product life-cycle approach thus offers an insight into some trade patterns that traditional theory fails to explain. PLC also has important bearing upon international capital flows, as will be seen in the next chapter. In the new-product phase, little foreign investment occurs. In the maturing-product phase, as foreign demand grows, the initial company might be producing some of the foreign output from its own facilities abroad. In the standardized-product phase, the initial company might even phase out domestic production in deference to its own foreign production and import back into its own country.

Both traditional trade theory (essentially a macroview) and the product life-cycle model (a microview) help provide important insights into the basic explanations to international trade. However, neither approach provides a complete theoretical basis for trade, nor do they do so together. Indeed, no general theory of international trade exists. Perhaps no meaningful general theory is feasible. Nevertheless, these two approaches are valuable tools in developing an understanding of the basic rationale of international business.

SUMMARY

Before advancing to detailed examinations of many different aspects of international business, it is useful to consider the theoretical base of the field. Most of the existing theory focuses upon international trade, which was the subject of this chapter.

Traditional trade theory was employed to examine the nature of trade (1) with barter and (2) with money. Comparative, rather than absolute, advantage was seen to be the underlying explanation for much of the trade that occurs. Trade by encouraging specialization leads to gains from specialization, which are shared between the trading countries in the form of gains from trade. The basic supply and demand conditions also lead to international terms of trade, which further affect the distribution of such gains. When currencies are employed, changes in exchange rates are also important factors in determining international prices and therefore patterns of international trade.

The product life cycle helps to explain some trade patterns that traditional theory has proven inadequate to explain. Its emphasis is upon the business firm.

In Chapter 3 this reflection upon the theoretical basis for international business is extended to a consideration of the basis for capital and other factor flows.

KEY TERMS

ABSOLUTE ADVANTAGE
BARTER
COMPARATIVE ADVANTAGE
FACTORS OF PRODUCTION

FUNCTIONS OF MONEY
STANDARD OF
DEFERRED PAYMENT
STANDARD OF VALUE
STORE OF VALUE
UNIT OF EXCHANGE

GAINS FROM
SPECIALIZATION
GAINS FROM TRADE
HYPERINFLATION
PRODUCT LIFE CYCLE
SPECIALIZATION
TERMS OF TRADE

REVIEW QUESTIONS

1. What two factors affect the availability of productive resources?
2. What impact does that availability (in question 1) have upon a country's ability and willingness to trade?
3. Explain how a country's ability to trade is affected by
   - **a.** labor conditions
   - **b.** laws
   - **c.** government
   - **d.** inflation
   - **e.** exchange rates
4. What impact do market conditions abroad have upon a country's ability to trade?
5. Distinguish between absolute advantage and comparative advan-

tage. Which is more significant for an understanding of international trade? Why?

6. What are world gains from trade? What produces them?
7. What is barter? What are its shortcomings? advantages? When might you expect barter to increase in the modern world?
8. If there is trade imbalance for a country in the modern world, what two basic economic adjustments can reverse that trend?
9. Explain the product life cycle. To what kind of products does it most readily apply?

Suggested references

Balassa, Bela *Changing Patterns in Foreign Trade and Payments.* New York: Norton, 1978.

Caves, Richard E., and Harry G. Johnson, eds., *Readings in International Economics.* Homewood, Ill.: Richard D. Irwin, Inc., 1968.

Heller, Robert *International Trade: Theory and Empirical Evidence* (2nd ed.). Englewood Cliffs, N.J.: Prentice-Hall, Inc., 1973.

Hogendorn, Jan S., and Wilson B. Brown *New International Economics.* Reading, Mass.: Addison-Wesley Publishing Co., Inc., 1979.

International Monetary Fund. *Direction of Trade Annual.*

Kenen, Peter, and Raymond Lubitz *International Economics* (3rd ed.). Englewood Cliffs, N.J.: Prentice-Hall, Inc., 1971.

Kindleberger, Charles, and Peter H. Lindert *International Economics* (6th ed.). Homewood, Ill.: Richard D. Irwin, Inc., 1978.

Korth, Christopher M. "Barter—An Old Practice Yields New Profits," *Business,* September–October 1981.

Rink, David R., and John E. Swan "Product Life Cycle Research: A Literature Review," *Journal of Business Research,* 1979.

Snider, Delbert *International Economics.* Homewood, Ill.: Richard D. Irwin, Inc., 1979.

United Nations *Yearbook for Trade Statistics* (annual).

Vernon, Raymond "International Investment and International Trade in the Product Cycle," *Quarterly Journal of Economics,* May 1966.

———ed., *Technology Factor in International Trade.* New York: Columbia University Press, 1970.

Walter, Ingo *International Economics: Theory and Policy.* Willowdale, Ontario: Ronald, 1976.

Wells, Louis T. "A Product Life Cycle for International Trade?" *Journal of Marketing,* July 1968.

3

The Basis for International Factor Movements

INTERNATIONAL FACTOR FLOWS

INTERNATIONAL FACTOR FLOWS VERSUS INTERNATIONAL TRADE FLOWS

The last chapter examined the means by which international trade can help to offset differences between countries in the availability of productive resources. Such conclusions, it was noted, are valid whether reference is made to differences in the natural distribution of factor endowments (raw material, population, and climate) or differences resulting from historical developments (monetary capital, plant and equipment, technology, infrastructure, trained human resources, political climate, and cultural attitudes).

It was seen that, as a result of comparative advantage, both a very poor country, such as Mali, with few natural resources, poor infrastructure, and little capital equipment, as well as a wealthy, highly developed country, such as Canada, can benefit from free trade. This traditional, simplistic view of the basis for trade has been modified in recent years with intensive examinations of the impact of managerial decisions upon the extent of and patterns of trade, as was examined under the product life cycle. Nevertheless, international trade is a vital ingredient in help-

TABLE 3.1 Degree of Mobility of Factors

Nature of Factors	Relatively Mobile	Relatively Immobile
Depletable		
Nonreplenishable and nonrenewable		
Raw materials	X	
Replenishable or renewable		
Land (agricultural)		X
Water		X
Climate		X
Capital[1]	X	
Labor	X	
Entrepreneurship	X	
Nondepletable		
Technology	X	

[1]Economists use the term *capital* to refer to plant and equipment (*real capital*) as well as to *monetary capital;* we will always use the term to mean "monetary capital."

ing to bridge the gaps that exist between countries in their productive resources.

However, trade is not the only means by which the unequal distribution of resources can be overcome and by which the severe imbalances between standards of living in different parts of the world can be reduced. Some factors of production can also move or be moved. Table 3.1 indicates the relative mobility of factors. It also categorizes the factors according to their susceptibility to depletion and their capacity for replenishment or renewal. For example, raw materials are depletable and nonrenewable but mobile. Capital is also depletable and mobile but in addition it is renewable.

As illustrations of factor mobility, millions of workers have migrated (either temporarily or permanently) from Southern Europe, Northern Africa, and Asia Minor to Northern Europe in order to bridge the "labor gap." Similarly, managers have worked abroad to help overcome "managerial and entrepreneurial gaps." Also, countries such as Japan, Taiwan, and Brazil have aggressively rented foreign technology in order to bridge the "technology gap." In addition, massive flows of capital in the form of bank loans, trade credit, portfolio investments, and direct investments have served to bridge the "capital gap."

International trade essentially *offsets* differences in endowments of the factors of production, whereas *factor movements* actually *reduce such differences*. Both trade and factor movements help to equalize the availability of output throughout the world and to reduce differences in the prices paid to factors of production, thereby raising living standards in all the countries affected by the flows.

This chapter examines the basic cause of and results from such factor flows. The emphasis is on capital flows. However, much of what is said regarding such flows will also be applicable to movements of other types of productive factors; the final section of the chapter discusses the flows of labor and technology.

WHY FACTOR FLOWS OCCUR

Most international economic transactions, whether of trade or factor flows, occur for similar reasons. As seen in the last chapter, trade can be initiated either as a result of demand for foreign goods and services or as a result of a desire to expand sales markets (for both demand and supply reasons). Profit and economic efficiency motives are the basic forces underlying both the demand and supply incentives for international trade. These forces also explain most factor movements.

From the supply side, the search for more profitable employment of factors of production is the primary underlying motive for most international factor flows. Similarly, from the demand side, the basic motive is for gaining access to a component or consumable good, service, or capital that helps the company's profitability by, for example, lowering costs or increasing marketability.

Much of the supply incentive in international technology transfer results from a desire to tap additional markets, such as through the rental or sale of pharmaceutical or chemical patents. Rentals of trademarks and copyrights are similar flows of intangible assets. Labor, whether unskilled, technical, or managerial, often flows to places where opportunity and potential return are greater. Capital commonly flows to where interest, profits, and capital gains promise to be greater. From the demand side, international flows can be initiated in similar fashion: The company that needs capital, managers, technology, and so forth initiates the search in response to its need to lower costs, improve its productive efficiency, or to introduce new products to its customers.

Both supply and demand motivations are frequently much more complicated than a mere search for greater profitability. Many other motivations exist; some are also economically quite rational, but some can be quite irrational economically, even when they are rational from a political or sociological perspective.

For example, a California winery that acquires a distribution office for its wines in France might be seeking the prestige of claiming that even European connoisseurs enjoy its wines. The technician who accepts an overseas assignment might be primarily seeking adventure, training, or the opportunity to flee from political or social constraints at home. The Arab millionnaire who invests in U.S. real estate may be primarily interested in having another place to live in the future in the event of political shifts at home. The purchaser of goods or services from a particular company might be influenced by an improper personal payment.

There are, of course, numerous other examples of factor flows that have economic rationale other than international profit or other noneconomic rationale. Nevertheless, most international factor flows do reflect a search for higher returns, either directly or indirectly. This chapter focuses on the complex rationales for such flows; the primary emphasis is upon money and capital flows.

As will be seen, the market for international capital is large and efficient. On the other hand, markets for labor and technology tend to be fragmented and much less efficient. Lacking the homogeneity of money and capital instruments, the labor and technology markets suffer from poor information flows. Also, the international labor markets are the most politically and socially sensitive of all international markets; as a result, they are the most heavily regulated.

FORMS OF CAPITAL MOVEMENT

There are essentially two major forms of capital movement. One type involves the lending and borrowing of money, a rental process similar to the rental of a building or of technology. Lending and borrowing involve investments both in marketable (negotiable) forms of debt, such as bonds, notes, certificates of deposit, and commercial paper, and in nonmarketable forms, such as, bank deposits, bank loans, and private placements.[2]

An important distinction is made between short-term forms (less than twelve months) and long-term forms. Another important distinction is made between the public and private sectors as both lenders and borrowers.[3]

The second type of capital movement involves investments in the equity of a company. This can be in either marketable stock or private investments. Table 3.2 outlines the major types of debt and equity.

If a long-term investment does *not* involve managerial control of a foreign company (for example, the purchase of long-term debt issues or of a noncontrolling share of equity), it is known as a *portfolio investment*. If the equity investment is sufficient to acquire managerial control, this special form of investment is known as a *direct investment*. Such direct

---

[2]See the Glossary at the end of the book for a definition of the term *private placements*.

[3]The public sector includes not only the central government of a country but also provincial (or state) and city governments, governmental agencies, and international agencies (the World Bank).

TABLE 3.2   Forms of Capital Instruments

Type of Funds Obtained	Private Sector Users of Funds	Public Sector Users of Funds
equity	common stock[a] preferred stock[a]	—
long- and medium-term debt	private placements[b] term loans from banks[b] bonds[c]	private placements[b] term loans from banks[b] bonds[c]
short-term debt	trade credit[b] private placements[b] bank loans[b] commercial paper[c] bankers acceptances[c]	trade credit[b] private placements[b] bank loans[b] bills (Treasury bills)[c]

[a]May or may not be marketable.
[b]Not readily marketable.
[c]Readily marketable.

investment can involve either the construction of new facilities abroad or the acquisition of existing foreign facilities. It can also involve either sole ownership or partial ownership, such as a joint venture.

SOURCES OF CAPITAL

In the scenario presented in the last chapter, a country's productive resources were seen to be either the result of natural resource endowment or the historical development of such resources. Monetary capital is also the result of such historical development; it is not a "natural" resource but instead must be accumulated over time as a result of the willingness of a society to defer consumption.

If a nation consumes all that it produces, it has no output available for commitment to expanding its productive capacity; part of production must be in the form of productive equipment in order for future productive capacity to be increased. If a nation spends all that it earns, it has no savings available for investment. Present consumption must be deferred in order to accumulate savings for the future.

Savings can originate in either the household sector, the corporate sector, or the government sector. The ability of a society to save and the locus of most saving depend upon a variety of factors—per capita income, the rate of economic growth, the nature of the economic system (private enterprise or government enterprise), the financial infrastructure (insurance companies, pension funds), the tax system, the rate of inflation, the political outlook, and the culture are only some of the relevant factors.

Countries differ significantly in their ability to defer consumption. Less-developed countries generally have a low capacity to generate investment capital; all of the capital that they do generate can usually be productively employed domestically. Developed countries undoubtedly have a much greater capacity for generating investment capital. Indeed, most of the private-sector investment capital in the world is generated in the industrial countries. Table 3.3 illustrates savings ratios for a variety of countries.

Thus, a high-income country with a high rate of economic growth where the government does not have an extensive social security program and where the culture encourages thrift, such as Japan, can have a very high rate of saving. However, due to the extremely high rate of economic growth in Japan in the 1950s, 1960s, and early 1970s, the Japanese economy absorbed most of the capital that was generated; this, coupled with capital controls, has meant that Japan has not been a major capital exporter.

On the other hand, high-income countries with extensive social security programs such as the United States and the United Kingdom have relatively low saving rates (see Table 3.3). Nevertheless, if the gross size of an economy is large and the investment ratio is low, a country with a low saving rate can sometimes generate a relatively high level of gross savings and be a large net contributor of capital internationally. The United States falls into this category.

In some countries, especially Communist countries, the government is the primary source of savings and investments.

In highly inflationary economies there is a strong tendency to buy rather than save, because financial investments in those countries do not

TABLE 3.3   Savings Ratios in Selected Countries[a]

	1960	1965	1970	1975	1979
United States	10	12	8	6	8
United Kingdom	11	12	14	6	10
Germany	23	20	21	12	14
France	16	18	18	14	13
Sweden	16	17	17	15	8
Canada	8	13	11	12	13
Japan	28	22	31	22	21
South Africa	14	15	13	16	22
India	9	11	12	15	19[b]
Zambia	NA	30	31	−5	6
Panama	0	6	13	15	7

[a]Savings as a percent of disposable income.
[b]1978.

SOURCE: United Nations, *Yearbook of National Accounts Statistics,* vol. 2 (1980), pp. 662–80.

usually offset the ravages of inflation, such as in Argentina. Also, if the political outlook is clouded, there is a strong temptation, for those who are able, to move funds abroad rather than to employ the funds locally.

A country's capacity to generate excess financial capital is indicative of its capacity to become a net exporter of capital. Such savings can be channeled through various intermediaries. Many capital-exporting countries of the world, such as the OPEC nations of Saudi Arabia and Kuwait, do not have very highly developed capital markets themselves. They must utilize major foreign and international financial markets.

Optimally, the financial markets would produce a completely efficient distribution of money and capital throughout the world. They are relatively efficient in comparison to most nonfinancial markets, but many barriers to the optimal distribution of financial resources still exist. For example, the observation has been made that shortcomings in the financial markets themselves produces a less-than-socially-optimal distribution of the capital that is available.

> .... Capital flows internationally in deep channels dictated by institutional considerations as well as by differences in the managerial productivity of capital.... Well-established attitudes of investors, practices of investment banking houses, governmental intervention and controls have all contributed to confining capital movements to well-worn paths.... The flow of capital is *not* like that of broad rivers which equalize levels over a vast area, but like that of irrigation canals and ditches which bring moisture to some areas and not to others, even though the latter areas may be on a lower level and need it more.[4]

Chapter 7 discusses the major financial markets of the world. As will be seen then, there are only a few major domestic money and capital markets in the world and even fewer major international money and capital markets, that is, the *Euromarkets*. In most instances, the major domestic money and capital markets and the major Euromarkets are not in the same countries.

THE BASIS FOR INTERNATIONAL CAPITAL FLOWS

As has already been noted, the explanation for the causes of international money and capital flows is not simple. No one has been able to develop a general theory of international capital movements. Instead, what exists are several different approaches, each of which is only a partial

---

[4]Charles P. Kindleberger and Peter H. Lindert, *International Economics,* 6th ed. Homewood, Ill.: Richard D. Irwin, Inc., 1978.

explanation. As with the natural sciences, where many individual researchers made separate contributions to the field of knowledge before a major synthesis could be made, many individual economists and business analysts have made and are continuing to make separate contributions to our understanding of the rationale of capital flows. It may be many years before a general synthesis of these diverse ideas can be made.

This book examines some of the major approaches and ties them together into a cohesive pattern, rather like a jigsaw puzzle where the general picture has been assembled enough to be recognized, but where some critical parts are still missing.

CLASSICAL THEORY OF INTERNATIONAL CAPITAL FLOWS

Although the bulk of international economic theory has concentrated on issues of international trade, a solid body of thought also developed on the theory of international capital flows. Such writings concentrated upon the foreign portfolio investment (FPI), since FPIs, especially long-term debt investment, dominated the foreign investment flows of the last century.

Foreign portfolio investment: The FPI process is generally simpler than that of the foreign direct investment. The former usually involves shorter time horizons, simpler investment goals, more complete market information, and more competitive and efficient markets. As a result, classical theories of international capital flows, which make assumptions about such conditions, are much more helpful in understanding FPIs than foreign direct investment. However, market conditions even for FPIs are far more complicated than in the simplified markets envisioned by the classical analysts. So also are the decision processes of the investors more complicated in the real world. Among the investment motives that complicate the theoretical examination of the FPI flows are such factors as *portfolio diversification,* which might lead to an investment with a lower rate of return than alternative investments but which might provide better portfolio balance via a reduction of systematic risk.[5]

Other reasons for the choice of an investment include diversification to avoid political risk (much of the Arab and Latin American investment in the United States is believed to be for this purpose) or speculation to obtain profits not through the direct return on the invest-

---

[5]See *portfolio effect* in the Glossary at the end of the book.

ment via interest, dividends, or capital gains but from foreign exchange rate fluctuations.

The nineteenth-century portfolio investments were most commonly in the form of pound sterling or French franc–denominated bonds. A very major share of the financing needs—especially for infrastructural projects such as railroads—of such countries as the United States, Germany, and the republics of Latin America were financed by London and Paris.[6]

The traditional theory falls well short of adequately explaining the very sophisticated and complicated developments in the foreign portfolio investment field during the last generation. These changes have followed from the modern developments in such corporate financial functions as asset and liability management, cash budgeting, and capital budgeting.[7] These developments in turn reflect changes in the environment (for example, high inflation and floating currencies), tools available (for example, modern communication techniques, computers, and portfolio and investment theories), and growth in the scale of international capital flows and of the infrastructural vehicles (for example, the Euromarkets) through which they will flow. (See Chapter 8 for a more detailed discussion of the Euromarkets.)

Foreign direct investment (FDI): In the 1800s FDI was vastly overshadowed by portfolio investments, except for such strong FDI patterns as investments by the British and French into their colonies and some investments by investors of the same two countries or by other investors into noncolonial countries. These investments were primarily for raw material extraction, agricultural plantations, and trade facilities.

As a result, the theory of foreign direct investment remained rather underdeveloped and in the shadow of the theory of FPI. Considering the relative scale of FDI at the time, this pattern is understandable. However, given the massive scale of FDI today, an understanding of the rationale for foreign direct investments is one of the most critical, and certainly one of the most politically sensitive, issues in the field of international economics.

The bulk of the discussion in the rest of this chapter focuses on studies during the past two decades that have concentrated upon FDI. Nevertheless, many of the elements of foreign investment that complicate the FDI decision also affect the portfolio investment decision, for

---

[6]Several interesting views of nineteenth-century international finance can be found in *Bankers and Pashas* by David S. Landes, *The Merchant Bankers* by Joseph Wechsberg, and *The Impact of Western Man* by W. Woodruff.

[7]These subjects are discussed in Chapter 20.

example, noneconomic investment criteria and imperfections in the markets, such as inadequate information and barriers, whether they are
governmentally or managerially imposed. They are also examined here.

The modern applicability of classical capital theory: Traditional theories of capital flows can still be of use in understanding some
of the basis for modern international capital flows. Although, for improved understanding, substantial modifications in many of the assumptions of the classical theorists need to be made. One condition in the
market is actually even truer today than in the 1800s: the extent of
quality of the knowledge of international market conditions and the
efficiency of those markets. However, despite this improved correlation
between the assumptions of classical theory and the actual market
conditions, classical theory still fails to explain much of the international money and capital flows today.

Too many of the other simplifying assumptions of the classical
theorists, coupled with their restricted horizons, limit the applicability
and value of their theories in the international money and capital
markets of the 1980s. Foreign direct investment, as it has already been
seen, was not adequately examined. Also capital flow theorists generally
assumed a high degree of competition, no significant interference by
governments, nonaffiliated participants, and few barriers (either natural, such as transaction costs; or artificial, such as taxes or capital
controls). The conclusion of such studies was that capital will flow from
where capital is abundant to where it is scarce or, to put it another way,
from where the rates of return are low to where they are high.

Without any doubt, a significant amount of foreign investment does
indeed search out its highest return. Such pressures help to enhance the
efficiency of the international financial markets. We will be returning in
later chapters to some of the ways in which such tendencies affect
international financial markets and the multinational companies that
utilize them. For example, dynamic cash management by corporate
treasurers helps to keep the Euromarkets closely aligned with the corresponding domestic markets. Also, as interest rates change in the security
markets of different currencies, actions by corporate treasurers to earn
high interest cause predictable and logical changes in the forward exchange rates of currencies. (See Chapter 6 for a more detailed discussion
of foreign exchange markets.)

As with international trade theory, classical international money-
and-capital-flow theory is essentially macroeconomic in its perspective.
However, in reality international money and capital flows are very
much related to managerial decisions. Also, flows are often between
affiliated entities. Therefore, we need to examine such flows from a
microeconomic perspective. In addition, in order to obtain a better theory

of international capital movements, the role of government must be analyzed in a different light than that of the classical theorists.

HISTORICAL DEVELOPMENTS FAVORING FOREIGN INVESTMENT

Foreign investment, especially portfolio investment, has been practiced for centuries, indeed, for thousands of years. However, there has been a revolutionary change in the arena of foreign investment since the 1950s.

Economic and business developments: One obvious cause for the great increase in international capital flows is the substantial growth in real income and real standards of living in many countries throughout the world. Even in many chronically poor countries, such as India, and Indonesia, the total income has increased sufficiently to generate substantial amounts of capital for investing domestically and creating markets for goods and services that can attract investments from abroad.

Corresponding to the tremendous increase in world living standards during the past century, corporations have grown to be large enough so that they are more inclined to look beyond their domestic borders, are large enough to be able to afford foreign investments, and have the capacity to bear the risks involved.

At the same time the technological revolution has produced a great increase in the sophistication of not only products but also productive techniques. As a result, industrial and service production has become much more complicated than in previous generations. Companies are needed that are large enough to be able to bear greater costs and larger risks and to attain higher levels of productive and managerial sophistication. This makes it impossible for most countries throughout the world to have the capability, via either the private or the public sector, to produce all the goods and services demanded by their people. This provides an opportunity for foreign companies to tread where local companies fear or are unable to tread. Foreign direct investment can be invaluable to infusing not only capital but other, and often more important, factors such as management and technology.

Parallel to these revolutionary changes in national incomes, products, productive techniques, and corporate sophistication have been the revolutionary improvements in the international infrastructure in such areas as communication, transportation, banking, insurance, and brokerage. Such developments have greatly facilitated both the opportunities for learning about investment alternatives available and the means of acting upon those options.

Governmental developments: Finally a factor that assumes greater and greater significance as the years pass is that governments are playing an ever-increasing role in both domestic and international markets. (The next chapter details how governmental action can interfere with international trade and financial and other flows.) Governments are viewed in traditional theory as essentially passive observers of the international money and capital markets. Even the domestic money supply and international exchange rates were once largely subject to the impersonal supply and demand forces of the market; both money supplies and exchange rates were subject to the yoke of the *gold standard*.[8] Governments were much less likely to intervene in the 1880s than in the 1980s. Taxes and controls were sometimes imposed, but the governments were not normally active participants in the markets.

In the last two generations, governments have become very interventionist. They are much more willing to impose taxes, exchange controls, and capital controls than in the past. (See Chapter 4 for a discussion of international trade and capital-flow barriers.) Also control of the domestic money supply is now an active goal of monetary policy. Furthermore, exchange rates are manipulated for domestic motives—and not just economic motives but often political as well. Floating exchange rates have probably reduced the extent of such manipulation, but they certainly have not eliminated it. (Recall, for instance the Japanese policy of the mid-1970s, the British policy under Prime Minister Margaret Thatcher in the late 1970s and early 1980s, and the policy of the U.S. central bank, the Federal Reserve Bank, under Paul Volcker after September 1979).

However, governmental action is not all one-sided; it sometimes also aids and abets such flows in many ways, sometimes in a "push-and-pull" fashion. For example, governments of industrial countries often provide a "push" to foreign investment by offering insurance and guarantee programs for new investments by their domestic companies in *less-developed countries* (LDCs); this is part of the governments' foreign assistance programs. An example is the Overseas Private Investment Corporation of the U.S. government, which provides investment insurance and investment loan guarantees for FDI by U.S. companies in LDCs. Also, the governments of countries (industrial as well as LDC) attempt to "pull" foreign investment by actively encouraging the inflows of direct investment from abroad as part of their programs to encourage rapid and diversified economic growth. For example, the government of Ontario, Canada, offered such an attractive package of incentives to

---

[8]The gold standard never worked as efficiently nor was it ever as pervasive as its defenders in the 1970s and 1980s would like us to believe. However, the gold standard was nevertheless an important element in the international economy in the two generations prior to World War I. See the Glossary at the end of the book.

Ford Motor Company that the company made a major investment there instead of in the United States.[9]

Governments have also extended their efforts to encourage a greater internationalization of their economies through participation in such developments as the General Agreement on Tariff and Trade (GATT) and economic integration programs, such as the European Economic Community (discussed in Chapter 9).

MOTIVATION FOR FOREIGN DIRECT INVESTMENT

In theory (at least classical theory) foreign investment is a conceptually simple process. However, in practice it is seldom very simple. A complex of motivations is typically involved. That is why it has proven so difficult for traditional theory to adequately explain such flows or for new theories to satisfactorily fill the gap. Fortunately, significant progress has occurred in the last two decades, although much more needs to be done.

There are several underlying forces or patterns that clearly underlie most investments. The first such force is, of course, the profit motive. However, as will be seen, there are investments that definitely do not qualify as profit-oriented investments. Also, there are many other investments that may not appear at first to be profit-oriented but which, when seen in the proper perspective, are indeed made for the purpose of maximum profitability. The profitability, however, may be long-term in nature, may need to be seen on a corporatewide basis, or may increase profits elsewhere in the company, such as in the aftermarket.

Virtually all FDIs, whether the pursuit of profits is the primary criterion or not, are made for one of two basic, *strategic motives* (or a combination of the two). Investments seek either markets or increased operating efficiency. These are, of course, domestic motivations as well; international investment operates in a broader area than domestic investment but is not very different basically.

Market seekers: One of the most obvious goals for many direct investments involves the desire to tap another market. As was seen in the previous chapter, such markets are commonly served via exports.

However, many foreign markets cannot be served via exports, and some which have been served by exports in the past can no longer be served through that channel in the future.

For example, the advent of the European Economic Community threatened many American exports because trade barriers such as tar-

---

[9]As is seen in the next chapter, such excessive incentives can be just as disruptive to the efficiency of international capital flows as are controls to limit such investment.

iffs between member countries were going to be dismantled; as a result, U.S. exports would continue to bear the brunt of the tariffs, whereas exports from one member country to another would eventually be free of tariffs. American companies, seeing the handwriting on the wall (and also becoming more aware of the size of the European market), made many investments behind the EEC tariff wall. Without such investments, traditional markets were likely to be lost to the U.S. companies for the same reason Volkswagen began assembling VWs in the United States when the soaring value of the deutschemark made exports infeasible—the excessive cost of imported goods.

In other instances direct investments are made, because that may be the only way a foreign market can be tapped. In order to sell its petroleum products in the United States, British Petroleum bought a distribution network from existing companies. Coca-Cola cannot economically be shipped long distances and so is bottled in numerous foreign locations. In order to be able to sell in Paris and Tokyo and elsewhere overseas, fast-food outlets such as McDonald's or Kentucky Fried Chicken must serve foreign customers in their local market. Except for financial services, most services must be sold on the spot in the foreign market.

Exporting inevitably involves certain inherent diseconomies relative to local foreign production: greater costs of communication and transportation, slower reaction time to changing consumer demands, and greater difficulties of providing after-the-sale servicing of products. In addition to these "natural" barriers to effective competition through exports, governments chronically provide a wide variety of artificial barriers that help to tip the scale toward the need for foreign production in lieu of exports for serving foreign markets. Such investments may be directed either toward serving the market in which the investment occurs or serving associated countries; for example, General Motors' investment in Belgium may well have France and other EEC partners of Belgium as its major market.

In addition to such barriers, changing cost differentials can also shift the balance toward foreign production. These cost changes can result from either domestic inflation, changes in the exchange rate (or failure to change), or a combination of the two. For example, a high exchange rate in the United Kingdom in the late 1970s and early 1980s made British exports less competitive overseas. The pound sterling should have been weakened, so that British goods could maintain their competitiveness. Instead, rising revenues from oil exports coupled with high interest rates actually caused the pound to rise, thereby compounding the burden on the exporters of British merchandise.

It is sometimes asserted that FDIs reduce exports. Such charges frequently tend to be nothing more than naive, chauvinistic claims. For example, as noted above, many foreign investments are made because the export market is likely to be lost in any event. Also, a number of studies have shown that companies that invest abroad often tend to increase their exports as a result of foreign investment. This can result from exports of subassemblies and other components or from the subsequent sale of replacement parts and accessary equipment. Also, other companies often enjoy increased export demand as well, for example, exporters of productive equipment.

Not all charges that FDIs reduce exports are unfounded. Companies sometimes diversify productive capacity in order to reduce their exposure to productive disruption, such as can result from labor disputes. Companies also sometimes invest abroad in order to avoid governmental controls. These motives as well as others can promote foreign investments, even if they are not necessarily more economical than production at home. However, the reader will hopefully realize the complexity of the motivations that can lead to foreign investment and not be deluded by naive charges or sensational claims, either pro or con. FDI may lead to either lower exports or increased exports for a company and a country; each case must be analyzed on its own merit.

Seekers of increased operating efficiency: The second basic strategic motive for foreign direct investment involves the search for ways of increasing the efficiency of production and marketing; this can be accomplished by investing where resources are either of better quality or of lower price. Gaining access to lower-cost or higher-quality *factors of production* is one variety. For example, oil companies often build oil refineries near oil fields, and companies that plan to assemble abroad choose countries or even regions within countries where the work force is noted for its quality and adaptability. Growers obviously must locate where the soil, climate, altitude, and topography of the land are appropriate.

The product life cycle, which was discussed in the last chapter, illustrates how new products, especially those of a technical nature, tend to be produced in the more industrial countries when the products are first introduced. However, as the market and the productive technology mature, there is often a tendency for production to shift overseas to locations where production costs, especially labor costs, are less expensive.

A second path to greater productive efficiency can be via a search for a lower-cost or higher-quality *infrastructure*. For example, foreign banks are drawn to London, where the financial and legal infrastructure facilitates their operations. Also aluminum and copper companies need to find relatively low-cost energy for their smelters; thus they frequently build their smelters near hydroelectric projects.

Productive and marketing efficiency can also be increased internationally in other ways. *Economies of scale,* for example, can often be obtained through *vertical* or *horizontal integration,*[10] from buying, selling, or shipping in larger quantities, or from more efficient purchasing, research and development, transportation, or financing. The spreading of fixed costs such as administrative overhead can be an important appeal of expanded facilities, including those located overseas.

Many companies invest abroad in order to utilize idle or underutilized resources. Automobile companies sometimes introduce a model overseas after it is no longer produced at home. The design costs have already been amortized. Some of the used equipment can be reused. The company is thereby able to reduce the costs of its foreign operations, and the host country is able to obtain locally produced merchandise at a lower price than if the design is "up to date" and the equipment brand new. Ford utilized this approach in Argentina, and Volkswagen in Brazil.

Similar use is made of patents, productive processes, trademarks, and copyrights. If the foreign market cannot be adequately served by exports, a foreign direct investment that can utilize these resources can be very attractive. In some instances, such as foreign pharmaceutical patents in Italy, patent protection can be lost unless it is utilized locally: "Use it or lose it." Thus, a firm can feel strong pressure to use the patent in the face of such an implied threat. As will be seen later, there are alternatives to FDI for countering such a threat (for example, by licensing the patents to another company), but this is not always an attractive solution.

Even the emphasis in classical theory on interest sensitivity of money and capital meets this criterion. If higher return can be realized elsewhere, a shift of portfolio funds can eliminate underutilization of the funds.

Quite clearly, the seeking of markets and the seeking of operating efficiency can coincide; they are not mutually exclusive. For example, the decision to build a manufacturing plant inside a protected market such as Brazil may not only provide new markets but can also result in some of the productive and marketing efficiencies just mentioned.

THE NEW "ECONOMIC MAN"

Management theory often uses an analog to the classical economic man model. In management theory, the managerial decision maker should be objective, systematic, thorough, and unbiased, although with a more complicated set of decision criteria than that of the classical

---

[10]See Glossary at the end of the book for a definition of these terms.

economic man. When applied to the international investor, this would imply a truly world view with no biases and with a systematic effort to consider investment alternatives throughout the world on a consistent basis.

Managerial shortcomings in FDI decision making: The FDI decison process does indeed exhibit many of the rational elements that, from a managerial perspective, we would ideally like to see and would expect to see. However, we are not dealing with the ideal "economic man." We are observing managers and investors who exhibit biases, ignorance, fears, and, perhaps most unfortunately, plain managerial inertia.

External influences: Internally generated programs of investment analysis are often not sufficient to lead to systematic analysis of foreign investment opportunities. Aharoni noted in his study that *external motivation* can be critical in a company's FDI decision.[11] This can, of course, occur for a multinational firm as well as for a neophyte foreign investor. However, it is probably more critical for the firm with little or no foreign experience.

Such outside incentive might result from strong *competitive pressure*. For example, U.S. television producers faced very strong competiton from Japanese producers. RCA moved much of its production to the Orient and was eventually joined by Zenith. Ironically, several of the major Japanese companies are now producing a significant share of their U.S. television sales in U.S. factories as a result of the rapid rise in the value of the yen and the threat of import controls!

Another source of outside incentive for a company to involve itself in foreign direct investment is an invitation from another company. Such invitations often come from customers or suppliers, but they can even come from competitors who wish to share in the development of a major or politically risky foreign venture. For example, banks are often involved in a type of joint venture with other banks overseas known as a *consortium*. Also, mining companies often join with other companies in the same industry in developing very expensive extractive projects. Note, however, that cooperation between companies in the same industry, especially those from within the same country, can be obstructed by governmental opposition to collaborative action between major competitors. This is especially a problem for American companies, whereas in many other countries, such as France and Japan, the government often encourages cooperation between its domestic companies, especially in international ventures.

---

[11]Yair Aharoni, *The Foreign Direct Investment Decision Process* (Boston: Graduate School of Business, Harvard University, 1966).

Governments sometimes also encourage foreign investment by their domestic companies as extensions of governmental policy. Such encouragement may be noncooperative or it may be cooperative, the government helping via loans, guarantees, insurance grants, or simply influence abroad.

Patterns of bias in foreign direct investment: The evidence is overwhelming that the average international investor, while exhibiting some "economic man" characteristics, is very much distracted by non-economic influences and analytical shortcuts that can result in a less than theoretically ideal allocation of the world's investment capital and often of the investors' own capital. This allocation results from both limitations in the market and limitations of the decision makers.

Direct investment of American companies overseas is shown in Table 3.4. As can be seen, 21 percent of FDI by U.S. companies is in Canada; almost 40 percent is in English-speaking countries. Another 18 percent is in the Western Hemisphere, outside of Canada. The percentage of U.S. FDI in the Western Hemisphere was actually higher in earlier decades (for example, 28 percent in 1970) before political conditions in Latin America very sharply reduced the attractiveness of many of the Latin countries for foreign investors.

The patterns that are evident in Table 3.4 indicate what might be called *geographical bias* (investing close to home), *cultural bias* (investing in countries with similar cultures, especially with the same language [*linguistic bias*]), and *historical bias* (investing in countries with which the investor's country has had historical ties). In many instances the pattern of historical bias in investment preferences is fostered by the government of the investor. Investment is seen as a channel for main-

TABLE 3.4 Geographical Distribution of U.S. Foreign Direct Investment

	1950	1960	1970	1980
Foreign Direct Investment	11,788a	31,865	75,480	213,468
Western Hemisphere (not Canada)	4,576	8,365	12,462	38,275
Canada	3,579	11,179	21,015	44,640
Europe	1,733	6,691	25,255	95,686
United Kingdom	847	3,234	8,016	28,099
Japan		254	1,482	6,274
Australia, New Zealand, South Africa	705	1,195	4,067	10,484
Other Asian and Pacific		984	2,260	8,397
Other African	147	639	2,427	3,730
Middle East	692	1,139	1,545	2,281

aAll figures are in millions of U.S. dollars.

SOURCE: *Statistical Abstract of the U.S.,* 1961, p. 867; *Statistical Abstract of the U.S.,* 1971, p. 755; *Statistical Abstract of the U.S.,* 1981, p. 836.

taining a strong national influence in those countries. For example, the government of France strongly encourages French investment in former colonies, such as the Ivory Coast, and attempts to facilitate investment via its own political influence in those countries.

MONOPOLISTIC COMPETITION IN FDI

Corporate decision makers are often able to overcome the shackles of bias, ignorance, fear, and inertia. Much foreign investment is indeed actually made on the basis of rational analysis.

One of the most useful theories for the managerial process of foreign investment decision making was formulated by Stephen Hymer.[12] He felt that because of the inherent advantages that the local competitor has relative to the foreign investor, the latter must have its own unique offsetting oligopolistic or even monopolistic advantages in order to be able to compete successfully in the foreign market. These advantages can be of many different types: patents, research and development programs, productive techniques, managerial sophistication, economies of scale, captive export markets or inputs, access to large sums of capital, ability to absorb risk, trademarks, and so forth.

This theory assumes that the firm's managers have the initiative and capability to implement the investment scenario noted above. Yair Aharoni, in his pioneering study, identified the following international motivations as a critical element in the foreign investment decision process of many firms: the recognition of the available resources (management, capital, technology, equipment, and so forth) or of the advantages from international rationalization and the gaining of greater economies of scale.

In markets where the necessary factors are readily available to all participants, there will be less opportunity for successful investment from abroad. As has been seen, certain factors (for example, capital, technology, and management) can often be imported by the local company. If this is possible, it will lessen whatever oligopolistic advantages the foreign investor may have. However, it may be more difficult for the local company to overcome the nonfactor monopolies of the foreign company, for example, brand names such as Coca-Cola.

Foreign investors sometimes have lower profit expectations than do local companies. In other instances the foreign investor may foresee greater profit potential than the local competitor. In either case, the foreign investor may be willing to pay more for locally available, but

---

[12]Stephen H. Hymer, *International Operations of National Firms: A Study of Direct Foreign Investment* (Cambridge, Mass.: MIT Press, 1976).

limited, resources (for instance, top management, plant sites, or minerals). This can occur even when both parties are funding at the same cost of capital.

Hymer's view of competing companies with different strengths via their access to monopolistic assets helps explain the somewhat puzzling situation of cross investments in the same industry. The companies do not need comparable profit outlooks in order for each to find investment in the other's market to be attractive. This is especially true in oligopolistic industries.

Even if market knowledge and trading are perfect, investors themselves are differentiated. They prefer to invest in what they know best and in what they feel most comfortable. What exists in reality is *differentiated capital*—the same capital (even direct-investment capital) in different hands may well be limited to different channels of investment; for example, capital in the hands of General Motors may be biased toward automotive investments.

OTHER MOTIVATIONS FOR FDI

Thus far, this examination of the anatomy of foreign direct investment has focused on what are basically very profit-oriented bases for foreign investment (even where biased patterns of FDI are apparent). However, there are other motives for FDI. Some of them are quite rational; others are very irrational (from the perspective of corporate profitability).

Defensive investment: Alexander Lamfalussy pointed out years ago that many investments are made for essentially defensive reasons, the focus being more on the intent of avoiding either losses or a reduction of competitive position rather than making a profit.[13] For example, if Procter and Gamble should enter a country in which none of its major competitors is producing, there is an excellent chance that companies like Colgate and Unilever will soon follow. This defensive investment by the latter two companies is not done for the profit potential, especially in the short term (indeed there will normally be losses from such investments that may well extend to the long term). Rather, it is done in order to prevent Procter and Gamble from monopolizing a market that could be profitable for a single company and from developing greater worldwide economies of scale. Defensive investment also suggests why Procter and Gamble and Colgate invest in the United Kingdom and the Netherlands (the countries of Unilever's joint headquarters) and why Unilever

---

[13]Alexander Lamfalussy, *Investment and Growth in Mature Economies* (Oxford, England: Basil Blackwell and Mott, Ltd., 1961).

invests in the United States (the home country of Procter and Gamble and Colgate). Such cross-investments can increase the competitive pressure even in the competitor's home market. This is often done to reduce the likelihood of that company earning excessive profits at home, which could subsidize its ventures elsewhere. Such competition obviously works very much to the consumers' advantage in the form of lower prices and greater variety of choice.

Defensive investment can also be an effort to preempt a competitor's access to a valuable and limited factor of production. Thus, a coal company might buy more mining properties than it really needs in order to keep such resources out of the "avaricious grasp" of its competitors. Such investments are, of course, examples of types of investments that are not not conducive to greater economic efficiency in the markets. Governments, especially of countries with relatively limited natural resources, are understandably wary of nonproductive ownership of their critical resources.

Defensive investments have been suggested by some writers as types of investments that are not profit-oriented. While this may indeed be true in the short term, the firm may very well feel that it is indeed a profit-oriented decision in the long run: its long-term interests are buttressed by preventing the strengthening of a competitor.

Self-insurance: Another special type of FDI motivation centers around the desire for self-insurance. Such observations are consistent with theoretical studies of the *portfolio effect:* In diversifying its markets and its productive bases, the company in effect develops a portfolio of markets or factories, which together can reduce the overall risk to the company of (1) slumping or lost markets by recession in the home country or by exclusion from a profitable foreign market, (2) disrupted production from labor strikes or civil unrest, or (3) expropriated production facilities. By diversifying in a carefully planned pattern to systematically reduce risk, the company has provided a certain degree of insurance for itself.

Corporate image: Many companies seem almost obsessed with the desire to enhance their "international image" by opening operations in as many countries as possible, whether the basic economic conditions warrant it or not. Not too surprisingly, companies subsequently sometimes find it desirable to divest some of their ventures: "Invest in haste and repent at leisure."

On the other hand, companies sometimes feel that they enhance their image and competitive position by investing in a foreign market so as to be seen as a local company in that market. For example, if the investor's home country does not enjoy an image as a quality producer, it may invest in a major foreign market or even a third country in order to enjoy the aura of quality of its work force. For example, a "made in Ruritania" label might not help sales and might, in fact, hinder them. The same Ruritanian company might be able to initiate production in another country whose reputation for quality production is good. As a result, it might be able to sell quite successfully in that country and elsewhere.

Follow-the-leader: Follow-the-leader may be a popular children's game, but it can be a disastrous investment policy. Sometimes it is done for defensive investment purposes. In other instances it is done with very inadequate planning. Many American banks rushed to open up offices in London after most of the major banks had done so. As a result, there were far too many American banks in the market, and many of them had very unhappy experiences. Unfortunately, because of corporate image it is not always as easy to withdraw from a market as it is to enter it—for public relations and prestige reasons if not for legal reasons. (It was a cliché for several years in London that there were many banks who were ready to withdraw. However, while there were many who were willing to be the second bank to withdraw, no one wanted to bear the onus and bad publicity of being the first bank to leave.)

Some of the banks that opened offices in London have remained there profitably. However, that is not necessarily to say that they have succeeded because of good judgment. Success may have been in spite of a lack of appropriate motivation and investment analysis. Nevertheless, even follow-the-leader has some economic rationale. There are some other investment motivations that cannot be so charitably described.

Personal motivations for FDI: Some investments are made or avoided on the basis of essentially emotional or personal motives. If the company is fortunate, the true motivation may coincide with economic conditions that allow the company to stumble into a favorable investment and avoid a poor one. But in many cases the results are unsatisfactory. The company that invests in Costa Rica because the chairman wants to retire there—although it is unlikely that this is the reason given for his or her strong predilection for the country—is one example. (Many domestic corporate investments in such projects as yachts, airplanes, and mountain retreats reflect a similar noneconomic rationale.) An example of negative motivation involves the company president who refused to invest in one Middle Eastern country because the inefficiency of the transportation and communication infrastructure disrupted his vacation plans. These motivations are generally the least defensible rationales for promoting or avoiding a particular project.

Governmental incentives: The vast array of governmental incentives and disincentives can either be a siren's song or a repulsive obstacle to FDI. Governments that wish to encourage investment in certain countries (for example, less-developed countries) or to attract investment from abroad often offer subsidies, tax credits, and guarantees, as a means of encouraging the desired investment. Unfortunately, such appeals sometimes entice companies to make investments that are not really warranted, at least not without, and often even with, such "sweeteners."

In the same vein, governments sometimes use threats to encourage investment. In 1976 the government of Argentina was able to obtain $1 billion from a syndicate of large international banks by threatening that only the banks that participated in that loan were going to be able to do business in Argentina in the future when, hopefully, the chaotic situation, which still prevailed in the country, would improve. The long-term appeal of the country succeeded, and the desired funds were obtained, although not without a lot of misgivings on the part of many of the banks.

Foreign direct investment can thus be seen to be a very complex decision process. The failure for theorists to devise an all-encompassing theory results basically from this high degree of complexity and not from a lack of will or of effort. It may indeed prove impossible to ever develop a comprehensive theory. Nevertheless, the progress already made and developments to come will expand our understanding of the FDI phenomenon.

The existing body of knowledge is already extensive enough to provide us with the necessary overview to continue our exploration of international business. In Part IV of this book attention is focused on the managerial process of the analysis of international business opportunities, with special concentration on foreign direct investment.

LABOR FLOWS

International labor flows are of interest in three different categories: unskilled (and semiskilled), technological, and managerial (including entrepreneurial).

Unskilled and semiskilled labor flows occur on very large scales in various parts of the world. Northern European countries have been the hosts for millions of workers from Italy, Spain, Portugal, northern Africa, Yugoslavia, Greece, Turkey, and other Mediterranean countries. Similarly, millions of workers moved to the United States from Mexico, Cuba, and other Latin American countries. Some labor flows can be very long distance. For example, tens of thousands of Chinese were employed on the Tan-Zam railroad in Tanzania and Zambia, and more than 50,000 South Koreans worked on various construction contracts in Saudi Arabia at one time.

In some instances the workers come on a contract and leave when the contract is finished, such as was the case with Chinese workers in Africa and Korean workers in Saudi Arabia. Many of the millions of "guest workers" in Europe are also on contract, but hundreds of thousands of them have remained after the termination of their contracts. A large number of the foreign workers in the United States have come illegally and also intend to remain permanently.

The rationale for these flows of relatively unskilled and semiskilled labor is a very complex problem. A significant part of it is certainly the basic economic motive of seeking higher return for one's labor: They are "pulled" abroad by the job potential. As a result, the balance of payments of each of the countries that supplies laborers is strongly aided by large inflows of remittance from workers overseas to their families still at home (even when the worker is not planning to return).

However, the scenario is complicated by those who flee for political or religious reasons (the "push" motive). Hundreds of thousands of Palestinians, Cubans, Ugandans, Vietnamese, and so forth are a grim testimony to such migratory pressures.

After stripping away the political and religious motivations, we can identify worker flows primarily for income purposes but also for learning purposes, such as to obtain training in useful skills. Also a small proportion may be motivated by other personal motives such as a desire to travel or simply to get away from family or locale.

There is also a distinct dichotomy that explains the rationale for *technological and managerial flows*. First is the so-called brain drain involving the permanent emigration of highly skilled professionals, managers, technicians, and so forth. In a limited number of instances, the flow of the highly skilled is encouraged by governments seeking to export dissidents, for example, from Cuba. However, in the vast majority of cases the "brain drain" is viewed as an undesirable loss for the "exporting" country. Such flows represent a complex of sociological motives with very strong economic undertones: job opportunity, social opportunity, income, job conditions, political freedom, and so forth.

The other stream of technological and managerial flow is of a distinctly temporary nature involving the assignment of managers and technicians abroad. The individual mobility and visibility of the highly skilled are generally much greater than those of the unskilled and semiskilled. Many of the skilled are able to obtain individual contracts abroad. However, a much larger number are sent abroad by their companies.

Increasing immigration (and even guest worker) controls are being imposed by various countries to limit the impact of foreigners. Such controls are generally more generous to the highly skilled, but some countries, such as Switzerland, tightly control the influx even of professionals, even if they have a job waiting for them, and even if the job is a nonpermanent assignment!

Just as capital investment can be either long or short term, so also personnel flows can involve either short-term or long-term appointments but seldom a permanent assignment. (However, in past generations it was not at all unusual for British and French companies to send personnel abroad virtually for life; transportation was simply too slow to permit the rotating types of assignments so common today.) This temporary exporting of skills can range from the short-term assignments of Oklahoma oilfield workers in the jungles of Ecuador to the long-term assignment of the Japanese manager who runs the company's distribution network in Brazil.

The international market for unskilled and semiskilled labor tends to be very disjointed and inefficient. Occasionally, a government or major corporation undertakes the responsibility for gathering, sending, and supervising large groups of laborers abroad. For example, the Korean workers mentioned above went to Saudi Arabia under a contract between private companies and the Saudi government, and the Chinese workers mentioned above worked on the Tan-Zam railroad under the auspices of the Chinese government. More commonly, such flows are erratic and irregular; the workers either move individually or in small groups. The flows tend to develop slowly, but once the number of workers from a particular foreign country begins to build up in a host country, it becomes easier for subsequent workers from that country to follow (not unlike the follow-the-leader mentality of companies described above). For example, there are disproportionately large numbers of Turks in Germany, Algerians in France, and Mexicans in the United States. Obviously, geographical proximity can play a large role in determining such ties. But there are many other examples that do not follow the geographical pattern. However, it can be noted as a general fact that these markets are inefficient economically: A laborer's chance of gaining admittance to a foreign country, even on a temporary work basis, is often subject to historical accident, whether or not any others from his or her country have been able to pave the way.

FLOWS OF TECHNOLOGY

Technology is another factor of production that is internationally mobile but that has very imperfect markets. There is such a bewildering complexity of technology that the dissemination of knowledge about what is available is very inefficient. An entire industry is developing for the primary purpose of trying to help companies learn about the technology that is available in their fields. Even with such developments, the markets remain very fragmented and inefficient.

Technology can either be licensed (rented), sold, or invested. It is almost inevitably made available for profit-related purposes—either for the direct income from rental or sale or in lieu of capital as one company's investment in a joint venture.

The licensing or sale of technology can be a very attractive extension of the economic utilization of an asset. If the technology is no longer in use by the company that controls it, licensing gives new life to a sterile asset. If the technology can be made available abroad, it can help to introduce a company's products into a new market. It may be the only way of entering some highly restricted markets. The technology may need to be licensed in some countries if its protection is not to be lost in those markets.

However, licensing is not an unmitigated blessing. The strongest argument against licensing is that it may provide the basis for strengthening and even training a future competitor. More will be said of this in later chapters.

WHY MORE INTERNATIONAL FACTOR FLOWS
DO NOT OCCUR

The "economic man" would not be distracted by noneconomic elements of his environment but would systematically search out and exploit investment opportunities wherever they might exist. He would not be deterred by his own personal shortcomings. However, he would be constrained by governmental rules and policies. Within this scenario it might be reasonably expected that factors of production, together with flows of goods and services, would flow in the optimal fashion throughout the world. The net result would be an increase in living standards throughout the world.

Since the economic man must give way to the managers with a free will, with personal and managerial flaws, with governmental irrationality, and with continued infrastructural inefficiencies, it is no surprise that international flows, despite their tremendous growth in the past two decades, are far less than they would be under optimal conditions. Nevertheless, they have played a very major role in raising living standards throughout the world.

SUMMARY

International flows of the factors of production can help to relieve imbalances in the distribution of natural resources, just as international trade can. The factors that are most readily movable are capital, labor, and technology. The markets for the latter two are very fragmented and inefficient. Nevertheless, a very significant flow of both labor and technology occurs annually.

The international market for money and capital is much larger, more integrated, and more efficient than the markets for labor and technology. A very significant degree of integration has occurred between the major markets of the world.

The process of foreign investment decision making is very complicated. Classical theory is very useful in aiding our understanding of foreign portfolio investment. However, classical theory is only of very limited use in aiding our understanding of foreign direct investment. FDI must basically be analyzed from a microeconomic, or managerial, perspective in order to gain much understanding. Unfortunately, its complexity thus far prevents a grand unifying theory. Yet much can be learned by studying partial theories.

The next chapter examines in detail the problem of barriers, environmental as well as managerial.

KEY TERMS

DEFENSIVE INVESTMENT	FACTOR OF	LESS-DEVELOPED
ECONOMIC MAN	PRODUCTION	COUNTRY (LDC)
ECONOMY OF SCALE	HORIZONTAL	STRATEGIC MOTIVE
EUROMARKET	INTEGRATION	VERTICAL INTEGRATION
	INFRASTRUCTURE	

REVIEW QUESTIONS

1. Compare the roles of international trade and factor movements in raising worldwide standards of living.

2. Other than the profit or income motive, what are some reasons why capital, technology, and labor move from country to country?

3. What is the difference between direct and portfolio investment?

4. Discuss the major economic and business developments that have prompted the rapid growth of foreign investment in the past few decades.

5. Discuss the major political developments that have prompted the rapid growth of foreign investment in the past few decades.

6. Identify and discuss the two basic strategic motives that underlie most direct investments.

7. What patterns of investment bias tend to influence many FDI decisions?

8. Summarize the basis for the arguments that monopolistic competition explains many FDI decisions.

9. Are defensive investments reasonable? Explain.

10. There is no one explanation for all, or even most, FDI. Of the various theories discussed, which do *you* think is the most important? Why?

11. Discuss some of the major reasons for international labor flows.

References

ADAMS, WALTER, ed. *Brain Drain.* New York: Macmillan, Inc., 1979.

AHARONI, YAIR *The Foreign Direct Investment Decision Process,* Boston: Graduate School of Business Administration, Harvard University, 1966.

ALIBER, ROBERT "A Theory of Direct Foreign Investment," in Charles P. Kindleberger, ed., *International Corporation.* Cambridge, Mass.: MIT Press, 1970.

BANK FOR INTERNATIONAL SETTLEMENTS *Annual Report* (annually). Basel, Switzerland

BLAKE, DAVID "International Labor and the Regulation of Multinational Corporations: Proposals and Prospects," *San Diego Law Review,* November 1973.

GERAKIS, ANDREAS S., AND S. THAVANITHY "Wave of Middle East Migration Raises Questions of Policy in Many Countries," *IMF Survey,* September 4, 1978.

HEENAN, DAVID A., AND WARREN J. KEEGAN "The Rise of Third World Multinationals," *Harvard Business Review,* January–February 1979.

HYMER, STEPHEN H. *International Operations of National Firms: A Study of Direct Foreign Investment.* Cambridge, Mass.: MIT Press, 1976.

KEESING, DONALD B. "Labor Skills and Comparative Advantage," *American Economic Review,* May 1966.

KINDLEBERGER, CHARLES P. *American Business Abroad: 6 Lectures on Direct Investment.* New Haven, Conn.: Yale University Press, 1969.

LAMFALUSSY, ALEXANDER *Investment and Growth in Mature Economies.* Oxford, England: Basil Blackwell and Mott, Ltd., 1961.

LOVELL, ENID *Appraising Foreign Licensing Performance.* New York: National Industrial Conference Board, 1969.

MASON, R. HAL "Some Observations on the Choice of Technology by Multinational Firms in Developing Countries," *Review of Economics and Statistics,* March 1973.

RAGAZZI, GIORGIO "Theories of the Determinants of Direct Foreign Investment," *Staff Papers* (International Monetary Fund), July 1973.

ROBOCK, STEFAN H.   *The International Technology Process.* Washington, D.C.:
National Academy of Sciences, 1980.

VERNON, RAYMOND   "International Investment and International Trade in the
Product Cycle," *Quarterly Journal of Economics,* May 1966, pp. 190–207.

———— *Sovereignty at Bay.* New York: Basic Books, Inc., Publishers, 1971.

———— ed., *The Technology Factor in International Trade.* New York: Columbia
University Press, 1970.

4

Barriers to International Business

Chapters 2 and 3 carefully examined why trade and factor flows occur. However, the totals of such flows could be much greater. In this chapter we will examine why the logic of Chapters 2 and 3 has *not* led to even greater growth in international trade and factor flows due to managerial and governmental trade barriers.

Thus far we have seen that there are many comparative advantages a company can have that permit a company to compete abroad effectively. These comparative advantages can occur in such areas as design, production, promotion, delivery, financing, servicing, and so forth. Also, services, financial capital, or goods could be the area of the company's specialization and trade.

Finally, it should be remembered that comparative advantages can exist on the purchasing or consumption side as well as on the selling or production side. For example, an importing company such as Pier I Imports has strong advantages in finding suppliers, helping suppliers develop special products, enforcing quality control, and so forth. Likewise, a mass purchaser such as Sears or General Electric can bring many purchasing economies of scale, much knowledge of markets, and much technical expertise to its relations with suppliers.

The failure of businesses to recognize and take greater advantage of international markets and their failure to become providers and acquirers of goods, services, and factors of production in this market are the result of two conditions.

1. managerial barriers (lack of effort)
2. artificial barriers (mostly government-imposed)

Both these major groupings—managerial and governmental barriers—are examined in this chapter.

MANAGERIAL BARRIERS

Relatively few companies ever grow as rapidly as they are capable or ever reach their full potential. Numerous comparative advantages exist, or could be readily developed, to expand a company's markets. These advantages are either not employed at all or are employed inadequately. Many explanations exist for such failure to act. Most fall under one or more of the following reasons:

1. limited ambition
2. unrecognized opportunity
3. lack of skills
4. fear
5. inertia

LIMITED AMBITION

For many companies the major cause of failure to grow is simply satisfaction with the status quo or with local growth potential. They have the potential to expand but not the desire. This is an example of what the behaviorist Herbert Simon has referred to as *satisficing*—settling for less than the optimal. For example, a company might be quite satisfied with its rate of return, total profitability, rate of growth, extent of market penetration, economies of scale, and so forth. It might not feel a need to try harder. Such satisficing is quite common and understandable; consider, for instance, the highly successful restaurateur who is satisfied with a single location and the local dairy that has no desire to expand beyond the growth necessary to serve the local market. Such limited-growth companies are legion and play a valuable role in the modern economy.

Given their goals, limited-growth companies are often very successful. However, many of them could become far more succesful if they were to try. This is true internationally as well as domestically. Many domestic companies simply give little thought to foreign markets.

This limited horizon is especially true of companies in the United States, where a massive domestic market and geographical isolation from most other major economies tend to cause most companies to look no further than the U.S. borders. This is unfortunate, because many companies could find very profitable opportunities abroad, often more profitable than their home markets.

UNRECOGNIZED OPPORTUNITY

Numerous companies exist that have both the potential for growth and the willingness to grow, but yet they still fail to do so.

The most obvious reason companies do not seek to develop new markets under these circumstances is simply their failure to recognize that new markets exist. This can be due to either *lack of opportunity* to explore new markets or *lack of effort* to find out what opportunities exist. For example, the native weaver in Ecuador or woodcarver in Ghana may have little opportunity to learn about and develop export markets. A large company, however, has no such excuse; if McDonald's had not made the effort to find out, it might never have known that a market existed for its hamburgers in Tokyo that would pay more than $2.00 for one hamburger!

The full burden of recognizing export opportunities need not fall solely on the individual company. Most national governments and many state governments are actively involved not only in enhancing international awareness, but also in actively promoting the exports of companies. Such governments try to inform companies of the opportunities that are available and often try to actively aid their exporting efforts.

Such support efforts by governments are most commonly limited to encouraging exports and attracting foreign investment. However, as was seen in Chapters 2 and 3, most increases in international transactions *of any type* reflect comparative advantages, encourage specialization and diffusion of technology, and thereby enhance the standard of living of the world.

Governments are generally much less helpful in identifying sources of imports or markets and sources for factor flows. The overwhelming international economic interest of governments tends to focus on exports. For example, the Export-Import Bank of the U.S. was created to help facilitate two-way trade but has never financed any import: It should more rightfully be called the U.S. Export Bank!

Other organizations such as commercial banks and export management companies (discussed in Chapter 16) are also commonly in a position to help a company identify foreign market opportunities.

LACK OF SKILLS

However, even if a company has potential, has the will to "go international," and is aware of the opportunities, it may well be thwarted by the complexities and unfamiliar mechanisms of international transactions. Again, governmental agencies as well as commercial companies and universities are commonly available to help the novice company. Such assistance can take the form of educational efforts (seminars or consulting) or the provision of specialist services (export freight forwarders or customs house brokers).

International business is indeed a very unique part of the business world. However, there is a very substantial support structure to aid businesses until they themselves are able to perform such services. This support structure is examined in Chapter 16.

FEAR

Even if the opportunity for the exporting or importing of merchandise, the licensing of patents, or a foreign portfolio or direct investment is recognized, and if the necessary skills and desires exist, companies commonly fail to take advantage of them.

Many of these companies simply suffer from fear and excessive caution. Prudent caution is desirable, indeed necessary, for wise business decisions. However, many companies refrain from internationalization because of excessive and unrealistic fears. Any business growth entails risk, adjustments, and new problems. One of the principal goals of this book is to illustrate how the numerous new variables involved in international business can be understood and how adjustment to them can be made.

Some of the psychological barriers that hamstring many businesses when they confront international opportunity include the fear of the unknown or of what is foreign—different currencies, laws, documentation requirements, taxation, political systems, languages, and customs. Psychological barriers can also involve fear of being foreign oneself (in having alien status), fear of managerial difficulties, or fear of governmental action (either domestic or foreign).

Indeed, it *does* need to be recognized that there are inherent diseconomies, as well as economies, in foreign operations—communication and transportation difficulties, legal complications, and so forth. Internationalization will likely add new strain upon the management of a company. However, the benefits of exporting, importing, and investing frequently far outweigh the costs. Excessive fears obstruct many potentially profitable opportunities. In this book many of the variables that give rise to such fears are put into perspective.

INERTIA

Finally, and perhaps most unfortunately, business opportunities are not seized because of managerial inertia (simple failure to act). Many companies with the resources, opportunities, knowledge, and realistic perspectives still fail to exercise the initiative necessary to explore new ventures. Also, unfortunately, this obstacle to trade is one that study cannot overcome. All that can be done here is to introduce the reader to the environment and managerial techniques of international business. The initiative for internationalization must come from the individual and his or her company.

GOVERNMENTAL BARRIERS TO FREE TRADE

If markets were free of artificial barriers, comparative advantages and managerial barriers would dictate how trade and factor flow patterns are likely to develop. Unfortunately, however, governments have invented a myriad of special obstacles to restrict the free flow of goods, services, and factors of production. These artificial obstacles fall into several categories as follows:

1. trade controls
2. capital controls
3. exchange controls
4. controls on other factors of production

TRADE CONTROLS

Governments have instituted a bewildering variety of trade controls. GATT (to be discussed later in this chapter) has identified more than 800 variations. The major classes of these are discussed in this section.

Reasons for trade barriers: The arguments in support of free trade and capital flows generally rest upon economic rationale—namely, that unobstructed flows permit greater economic efficiency and higher productivity via international specialization. The entire world, and indeed every country, would generally be better off if flows are unobstructed.

However, while the world, nations, and even most regions would enjoy higher living standards as a result of the freedom of trade and factor flows, some individuals and groups would be worse off. Thus these groups are often protected, for example, much of the U.S. textile industry or the auto industry in most developing countries. In addition, the losses suffered by such groups tend to be quite concentrated and noticeable. On the other hand, the gains from free trade and factor flows for the entire country, although much greater in total than the losses of those who are adversely affected, are spread over much or all the economy and are less readily quantifiable. As a result, those who would be hurt by freedom of trade and factor flows tend to frequently speak much louder than those who benefit. Therefore, the will of the minority often overrides the welfare of the majority.

The economy will likely suffer if the government of a country accedes to protective pressures, regardless of the specific nature of the argument and regardless of whether the interested group represents the private or governmental sector. *Protectionism* means that a higher price must be paid by the majority in order to benefit the few.

The list of arguments on behalf of controls is long. The list of "reasonable" arguments from the viewpoint of the public good (as opposed to that of special interest groups) is very short. Even in these cases, however, both national and world efficiency, income, and living standards will decline. The following paragraphs weigh some of these potentially reasonable arguments.

1. *Revenue*—In the absence of an effective system of domestic taxes, a tariff can be important in financing government expenditures. This was a major reason for American tariffs for more than 100 years after the founding of the nation, although tariff revenues now contribute much less than 1 percent of U.S. government revenues. This is now a relatively minor factor for most developed nations, but it is still very important for many developing economies and for other countries with poor internal tax collection systems.

2. *Stimulation of economic development*—This argument requests only a "transitional" tariff until an *infant industry* can develop managers and trained workers and reach scales of output efficient enough to attain its comparative advantage and to enable it to face fair competition without tariffs. However, even if such industries can be identified (not an easy task), "transitional" tariffs usually create vested interests that are very reluctant to see the tariff eliminated; "transitional" tariffs usually become permanent. Thus most "infant" industries never mature. Even if such

industries could be indentified, a government production subsidy would usually be preferable to a tariff, since the true cost to the economy can readily be identified. However, politicians prefer to hide these costs.

3. *Protection of domestic industry and workers*—Free trade hurts some industries and workers whose efficiency or quality are too low and price too high. (The common battle cry in the latter case is "cheap foreign labor" or "unfair peasant wages abroad.") Unlike infant industries, these industries do not usually offer the pretext of becoming competitive in the future. Trade controls, by limiting the extent of foreign competition, can permit lower-quality local products to be sold, (for instance, the numerous low-quality consumer and industrial goods in Eastern Europe) or can increase the domestic price high enough for the high-cost local companies to be profitable (note, for example, the many types of U.S. shoes and textiles). Thus the companies and workers in the particular protected industry benefit, but the consumers must pay more for what they buy, often accept lower-quality goods, and perhaps accept less variety.

4. *Shift in the distribution of the gains from trade*—It is sometimes possible for a nation to increase its share of the international gains from trade or to redistribute the gains from trade between different groups within that country, or both, by the judicious use of obstacles to free trade. If economic welfare can successfully be transferred in a socially desirable way between sectors of a country to an extent that is very difficult by alternative means, the social results may justify the economic cost. For example, an entrenched aristocracy may be quite successful in avoiding a direct assault on its wealth in the form of income, capital gains, or property taxes, but may be unable to avoid high tariffs on luxury goods. Such revenues can be used to finance programs for either the general good or the good of specific groups, such as the poor.

5. *National defense*—It is sometimes argued that industries that would be vital in time of war should be protected if they are relatively inefficient, that the exploration for vital resources should be encouraged by tariffs or quotas, that export barriers should be imposed to protect the available supply of such materials, or that strategic materials should not be shipped to potential enemies. National security requirements place political or military considerations above economic rationality. Yet it may be completely justifiable from a government's perspective, at least in terms of past wars or even future, limited, nonnuclear wars. However, subsidies are less disruptive and costly, for example, the subsidization of a merchant marine for national security reasons.

6. *Retention of scarce materials*—Limitations on exports can also be used to (a) conserve nonrenewable or otherwise scarce resources; (b) encourage the development of local processing industries; for example, various OPEC countries are limiting the availability of oil for export in order to increase the domestic processing of oil into refined products that are even more profitable than crude exports; (c) help restrain domestic price rises by increasing the local supply of a good; for example, in the mid-1970s the U.S. government placed limits on the exports of soybeans in order to increase domestic supply and depress the domestic price, because the domestic as well as the international price was rising too high; or (d) attempt to increase the world price of the product by limiting its supply; for example,

the international coffee and copper producers' cartels[1] have attempted this, although with only very limited success. Also, as was noted in item 5 above, export of scarce materials may be limited or prevented for military reasons.

7. *Protection of the international value of a currency and the maintenance of international reserves*—By reducing imports or by artificially stimulating export trade, controls can be used to attempt to reduce the balance of trade deficit. This can help to strengthen the international value of a currency and to build up or avoid the depletion of a country's international reserves. (See also Chapter 5)

8. *Punishment of objectionable behavior of foreign countries or companies*— Trade barriers are sometimes imposed for either political reasons (discrimination against Communist countries) or for economic reasons; for example, corrective duties in response to such actions as dumping, subsidies, or smuggling.

   Corrective duties are applied as punishments for traders who fail to play by the "rules of the game." If a foreign exporter sells a product more cheaply in the import market (net of duties, transportation, and insurance costs) than the company sells in its home market, it is said to be *dumping* its goods in that foreign market. Dumping most usually occurs because of excess supply. For example, Japanese television manufacturers were dumping their television sets in the United States during the recession of the mid-1970s. However, it may occur in order to enlarge one's share in a foreign market or even to cripple foreign competition, called *predatory dumping*. In order to offset the advantages of the dumper, antidumping duties are often applied in addition to the normal duties.

   Another form of corrective duty is a *countervailing duty,* which is designed to offset subsidies paid to foreign producers by their governments. *Penalty duties* are applied against infractions of trade regulations. For example, a tourist who is caught smuggling goods through customs may need to pay not only the normal duty on the smuggled items but also an additional penalty duty.

9. *Support of domestic controls*—Legal domestic controls on easily importable items such as alcoholic beverages, weapons, or toys with lead-based paints need to be supplemented with import controls if legal imports are not to simply supplant local production. (Smuggling, of course, is outside of legal channels. Indeed, it is often done in order to escape strong trade controls.)

Falseness of protectionism arguments: Most arguments for protectionism are *economically* fallacious and generally result from naivete or self-interest. The reader should view protectionistic rhetoric with great skepticism.

Even when the arguments have some merit, the reader should remember that protectionism involves a high price for the country. One need ask whether or not a less costly and less distorting alternative is

---

[1]See Chapter 9 for a more detailed discussion of cartels.

available. Some aruments, such as national defense and protection of health, are clear exceptions: There is an economic cost for such military or social benefits. Also, sometimes other social goals, such as employment or income redistribution, are overriding considerations. Once again, however, such efforts are distorting, inefficient, and expensive; the price may be acceptable in certain circumstances, but it is important for the proponents of protectionistic actions to be aware of the costs as well as the benefits!

TARIFFS

The most universally employed of all trade barriers is the *tariff*—a schedule of taxes or duties levied on products as they cross national borders. The terms *tariff* and *duty* are often used interchangeably, although the former refers to a schedule or table of duties.

Where is a tariff levied? Tariffs may be levied on a product when it is exported, imported, or in transit through a third country. *Transit duties* have virtually disappeared, but in the past they were sometimes levied by Arab tribes against desert caravans, by American Indians against wagon trains on cattle drives, and by feudal European barons against travelers on their roads. Transit duties were a very early form of taxation.

Export duties are utilized primarily by certain developing countries as a source of governmental revenues. For example, oil-exporting countries heavily tax oil that is exported by private-sector producers; also, many banana-exporting countries tax the export of bananas. Such duties are not common, however, because obviously they shift comparative advantages against the exporting nations themselves. *Export duties are specifically forbidden by the Constitution of the United States.*

Import duties are by far the most significant type of tariff. They are in virtually universal use today.

Methods of applying tariffs: *Regular tariff duties* can be levied in several basic fashions. An *ad valorem duty* is levied as a percentage of the value of the product (for example, 15 percent of the cost). A *specific duty,* on the other hand, is expressed as a fixed amount of money per some quantitative unit (for example, $1.25 per pound, ton, gallon, barrel, bushel, meter, or piece). Finally, a *compound duty* is a combination of specific and ad valorem duties (for example, 15 percent of total value plus 70 cents per piece).

The penalties mentioned above and countervailing and other corrective duties are applied in addition to these regular tariff duties.

U.S. TARIFF HISTORY

The history of tariffs in the United States has experienced extreme volatility. Figure 4.1 illustrates the tariff history of the United States. The U.S. government relied heavily on tariff revenues to finance its budget in the eighteenth, nineteenth, and early twentieth centuries. Also, the "infant industry" argument was very popular; indeed Alexander Hamilton, the first U.S. Secretary of the Treasury, gave a classic exposition of this argument for tariffs. His exposition is still frequently quoted.

As the new country attempted to stand on its own two feet economically following independence, stimulation of domestic U.S. production was a prime consideration. The Napoleonic wars significantly reduced the importation of manufactured goods from Europe; this was a strong stimulant for domestic industry. In order to prevent being overwhelmed with European imports following the Napoleonic wars, average U.S. duties climbed to very high levels. This rising tide of protectionism, which basically reflected the will of the industrial Northern states, reached its crest with the Tariff Act of 1828 (dubbed the "Tariff of Abominations" by the basically agricultural Southern states, which preferred access to the inexpensive imports from Europe). Threats of secession occurred as early as this—thirty-three years before the Civil War.

Average tariff levels fell very substantially thereafter until the outbreak of the Civil War in 1861. In order to raise funds for the war, duties were more than doubled—bringing them back to the levels that had followed the Napoleonic wars. In Europe, meanwhile, many countries were reducing tariffs. These new, high U.S. tariff levels prevailed for more than fifty years, until the *Underwood Tariff of 1913* briefly lowered average duties down to the levels of the 1850s. However, the advent of World War I made this reduction more form than substance, since normal commerical trade was seriously disrupted.

Following World War I, as a serious recession developed, the *Fordney-McCumber Act of 1922* again pushed tariff levels up sharply. The onset of the Great Depression led to the infamous *Hawley-Smoot Tariff Act of 1930,* which pushed U.S. tariffs up to all-time highs—as an effort to stimulate domestic industry and agriculture. It also invited prompt and serious retaliation from other major industrial countries. As a result, international trade plummetted, the Depression was aggravated, and the spirit of international cooperation and goodwill substantially deteriorated, probably hastening and then aggravating World War II.

The Roosevelt administration rejected the high-tariff approach to economic stimulation. The U.S. Congress passed the *Reciprocal Trade Agreements Act of 1934,* which, after seventy-five years, finally put the U.S. back on the road toward lower tariffs. U.S. tariffs have been reduced almost steadily over the past fifty years to some of the lowest levels in history. The *Trade Expansion Act of 1962* and the *Trade Reform Act of 1974* have been recent major efforts to maintain the momentum. However, since tariffs on even dutiable imports have fallen to less than 10 percent (see Figure 4.1), the thrust of recent efforts toward relaxing trade barriers has focused on the very thorny issues of nontariff barriers. These barriers and international negotiations to reduce all trade barriers are discussed later in this chapter.

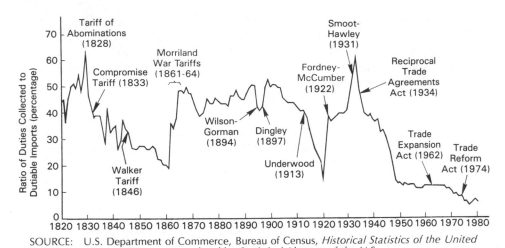

SOURCE: U.S. Department of Commerce, Bureau of Census, *Historical Statistics of the United States,* 1978, p. 888; updated by *Statistical Abstract of the U.S.*

FIGURE 4.1   Average U.S. Duties on Dutiable Imports

It is not only major tariff legislation that affects average tariff levels. Inflation, as well as the rates of duties themselves, affect the average duty on imported goods. Ad valorem duties, which are a function of prices, rise and fall proportionately with changes in import prices. However, specific duties, which are tied to some quantitative measure other than costs, do not change along with prices. Therefore, during periods of falling prices, average duty levels increase because of the inflexible impact of specific duties; whereas in periods of rising prices, average duty levels decline.

The greater the significance of *specific* duties relative to ad valorem duties, the greater the impact on average duties from price changes. For example, if the duties on a particular product are 40 percent of value (an ad valorem duty) plus $1.00 per pound (specific duty), the total duties and average of duties relative to cost would be as follows for an initial period (t_1), during a period of falling prices (t_2), and during a period of rising prices (t_3), as follows:

	t_1	t_2	t_3
1. Price per pound	$10.00	$6.00	$20.00
2. 40 percent duty	4.00	2.40	8.00
3. $1 per pound duty	1.00	1.00	1.00
4. Total duties	5.00	3.40	9.00
5. Average duty	50%	56⅔%	45%

If only ad valorem duties (line 2 above) are applied, the average duty remains unchanged at 40 percent, but the duty paid changes from $4.00 to $2.40 to $8.00. If only specific duties (line 3) are charged, the total duty remains unchanged at $1.00, but the average rate changes as the price changes (rising when prices decline and vice versa). Similarly, but to a lesser extreme, a compound duty (line 4) of both ad valorem and specific duties would tend to change as shown: rising during a period of falling prices (t_2: from 50 to $56\frac{2}{3}$ percent) and falling during a period of rising prices (t_3: from 50 to 45 percent). The larger the specific duty is, then, the greater the fluctuations in line 5.

NONTARIFF BARRIERS (NTBs)

In addition to tariffs, the inventive minds of government officials have devised a myriad of other barriers to trade. The major varieties of these are discussed in this section.

Quotas: Perhaps the simplest form of trade control is the *quota*— a quantitative limit on the volume or value of trade permitted. For example, the importation of a particular product may be limited to a particular tonnage or dollar value per year or, more flexibly, to a fixed percentage of domestic production. Despite international efforts to eliminate them, quotas are very common today.

The advantages of quotas is the speed and ease with which they can be imposed and their strength as weapons of discrimination.[2] Also, quotas are sometimes adopted multinationally as a means of stabilizing markets. For example, *commodity agreements* for products such as copper and coffee involve the allocation of quotas. These commodity agreements sometimes include the governments of the consuming country as well as of the producing country, and the agreement might therefore involve both *import quotas* and *export quotas*.[3] Because of their specific limit on quantity, quotas can be much more disruptive to trade than can other barriers such as tariffs. Retaliation is common in regard to tariffs as well as quotas, but because tariffs modify trade patterns instead of quantitatively limiting the volume of trade, because the effects are therefore harder to measure, and because tariffs provide some tax revenue, tariffs are commonly viewed with more favor than quotas.

One final difficulty with quotas is that the quotas must often be allocated among importers. It is very difficult for a government to be entirely fair about such allocations, especially since conditions in the market change. As a result, the possessors of import licenses for quota-controlled goods can often buy the goods at lower prices than their

---

[2]For instance, the United States discriminates in its trade regulations against most Communist countries, and its practices include many *embargoes* (quotas of zero).

[3]See Chapter 9 for a more detailed discussion of commodity agreements.

competitors in the domestic market. If the allocation of quotas is controlled by the government, favoritism and bribery are constant problems. Even when free from such trends, quotas tend to be based on previous imports, which penalizes newer but often more rapidly expanding and often more efficient companies. These companies must then rely on alternate, more expensive supplies. The auctioning of quotas would be a more efficient system of allocation than governmental allocation.

Quotas can be applied globally or on the basis of origin, for example, bilaterally or with reference to specific exporters. The following report from the International Monetary Fund indicates how some recent bilateral quotas have been applied.

> France took steps to limit the volume of textile imports from India and Korea; and the Benelux countries [Belgium, Netherlands, and Luxembourg] introduced quotas on cotton fabrics and dresses from Egypt, India, Macao, Morocco, Singapore and Tunisia. In addition to placing quantitative limits on imports of television sets from Korea, the United Kingdom introduced quotas on imports of various clothing items from Pakistan and the Philippines. . . . Italy introduced a quota on imports of certain makes of motorcycles from (Japan). . . . Malta introduced quotas on . . . telegraphic equipment, adding machines, and timber; temporary prohibitions were also imposed on . . . luxury automobiles, cigarettes, fresh meat and pesticides. In Portugal, quotas were introduced on [such products as] foodstuffs, domestic appliances and automobiles.[4]

Quotas tend to be even more pervasive in many developing countries. Furthermore, their use is growing rapidly. This reflects such factors as inflation, recession, high unemployment, and balance-of-payments imbalances of much of the 1970s and early 1980s. However, quotas are also replacing tariffs, which have been declining for three decades as a result of international cooperation. International negotiations (which will be discussed below) have tried to discourage and reduce quotas, but have not been highly successful so far.

Export restraint agreements: Governments are increasingly coercing other governments to accept "voluntary" export restraint agreements, through which the government of an exporting country is induced to limit the volume or value of exports to the importing country. This is, in effect, a special type of quota—an export quota. The United States has been a major employer of this technique. It has concluded "bilateral export restraint agreements with . . .

> . . . the Republic of China with respect to footwear and color television sets, Hong Kong with respect to textiles, Korea with respect to footwear, textiles and color television sets and with Japan as regards color television sets.[5]"

---

[4]International Monetary Fund, *29th Annual Report on Exchange Restrictions*, 1978, pp. 6–7. (Now called the *Annual Report on Exchange Arrangements and Exchange Restrictions*.)

[5]Ibid., p. 7.

Licenses: Permission to trade can take many different forms. For example, the government may simply exercise its will by dictate—specifically telling traders what is or is not to be traded and by whom. Such limitations are commonly in the form of import or export *licenses,* or permits to trade. Governments also sometimes set up *trading monopolies;* for instance, Italian purchases of foreign tobacco are conducted by a governmental import company, and most foreign trade by Communist countries is handled by international trade organizations (ITOs).

"Buy-national" laws: Policies that give legal preference to locally manufactured goods strongly discriminate against foreign producers. These policies generally apply to governmental purchases, but laws have been passed that cover private-sector purchases as well. As with all other trade barriers, "buy national" regulations increase the cost to consumers and the government and also limit their choice. For example, U.S. government procurement of military clothing must be from U.S. sources, unless the supply is inadequate or the price "unreasonable." As a result, the Defense Department pays much more for its uniforms than it would if foreign manufacturers could bid on such contracts. This example involves a policy primarily directed toward promoting domestic employment and industry. "Buy-national" laws often have a national security rationale—so that the domestic productive capacity is available in case of war.

A related practice that discriminates against foreign producers is the procedure for bidding. The United States uses a system involving a well-publicized call for bids (public tender), so that any firm, domestic or foreign, has a chance. Most countries, however, only invite a limited number of potential bidders (selective bidding): nontraditional bidders (including most foreign bidders) are excluded.

Customs-valuation methods: Since ad valorem duties are applied against the price of imported goods, the method of valuation of goods that is used for application of duties by the customs office is very important. Generally the applicable price is the cost of purchase abroad, the so-called *free-on-board (FOB) basis,* as is used in the U.S., or cost plus insurance and freight, *CIF*—as is prevalent in Europe. However, for many years the reference price for the application of duties on imports of benzenoid chemicals, wool-knit gloves, rubber-soled footwear, and canned clams into the United States was the "American selling price" (ASP) instead of the foreign purchase price. Since the ASP was always higher, this method led to higher duties.

Advance deposits: Another popular barrier to trade in many countries is the requirement that deposits of some portion of the purchase price (up to 100 percent or more) be made with a government agency for as long as six, twelve, or even eighteen months in advance of the intended importation. Generally, advance deposits earn no interest. The cost to a company of funding such a deposit can add greatly to the cost of importation, especially in countries where the cost of borrowing may be 20 percent, 40 percent or even higher. Advance deposits can be a very effective barrier in reducing imports.

Health and safety standards: Regulations designed to protect the health and safety of citizens are patently reasonable. However, it is easy to promulgate what are, in effect even if not in intent, antitrade regulations under the guise of safety requirements. For example, the U.S. safety requirements for auto bumpers that were originally issued would have eliminated most imports of European cars; since this was not the intent of the standard, it was modified to prevent this effect.

Arbitrary product standards: One of the clumsiest, but not necessarily ineffective, obstacles to trade is the promulgation of product standards with biased technical specifications. For example, American tomato producers were able to get a regulation passed controlling the import of small tomatoes. This regulation greatly reduced the inflow of Mexican tomatoes. U.S. wine companies were thwarted in their efforts to follow this example when they lobbied for a law to standardize the size of wine bottles. Such a law would have effectively barred the importation of many foreign wines, which come in a wide variety of bottle sizes.

These represent only a handful of the hundreds of nontariff barriers developed by various countries. Many more will undoubtedly be invented in the future. However, even this brief list suggests the complexities of some trade controls and the difficulties that must be faced when governments try to eliminate or regulate the use of trade barriers.

ARTIFICIAL STIMULATION OF TRADE

The controls previously discussed are oriented toward the limiting of trade by artificial means. However, governments also often attempt to *encourage trade* (usually *exportation* of goods or services) by artificial means. This is also a type of obstacle to free and economically efficient trade. Gains from trade should result from economic efficiencies, not from government support, which essentially involves the government absorbing some of the costs of production or distribution. These costs are not passed on to the consumer.

Some forms of governmental stimulation of exports are generally acceptable internationally.[6] Others are generally condemned.

---

[6]The General Agreement on Tariff and Trade (GATT) is discussed later in this chapter.

Acceptable stimulants: Some forms of governmental assistance that are generally acceptable under international agreement are as follows:

1. *The rebate of indirect taxes:* Indirect taxes are basically charged to domestic, but not foreign, buyers; any indirect taxes that have already been paid can be rebated to the seller, for example, the *value-added tax* (*VAT*), which is prevalent in much of Europe.[7] In contrast, *the rebate of direct taxes* (for example, taxes on profit or property) on exported items is not acceptable. This can work to the disadvantage of producers in countries where direct taxes represent the major share of tax burdens.

2. *Market research:* As noted above, many governments provide information regarding export opportunities to exporters.

3. *International trade shows:* Many national or regional governments help to finance trade shows abroad that help promote products of the companies in that country or region.

4. *Trade-promotion offices:* Permanent product-information offices in foreign countries can stimulate demand for exports of a country or region.

5. *Government-sponsored research:* Government studies can lead to the development of exportable products, for example, the U.S. space program.

6. *Free-trade zones:* These zones are areas where *imported* goods can be processed for re-export without paying duties, since they will not be used locally.

7. *Trade-financing programs:* A government agency can finance or guarantee exports, for instance, the export-import banks of Japan and the United States and the Export Credits Guarantee Department in the United Kingdom.

8. *Insurance programs:* Insurance is necessary to protect receivables from international trade; government agencies sometimes provide such protection.

Unacceptable stimulants: The most glaring example of generally *unacceptable governmental assistance* in promoting exports involves *direct subsidies*—direct financial support by the government for exports. These subsidies may involve special tax cuts (such as are given to the domestic international sales corporation [DISC] in the United States[8]); direct financial payment by the government per unit of exports; production assistance in the form of low-interest loans or wage assistance for factories that principally produce for export, such as the British shipbuilding industry; or subsidization of export credit, insurance, or transportation.

PERMANENCY OF TRADE BARRIERS

Unfortunately, protectionism is such an insidious temptation that protectionistic demands tend to crop up in most industries. Even many

---

[7]See Chapter 22 for a detailed discussion of the value-added tax.
[8]See Chapter 22 for a more detailed discussion of the domestic international sales corporation.

self-proclaimed "free-traders" advance claims for assistance of their own industry, while simultaneously, and perhaps hypocritically, resisting similar protection for others. U.S. farmers, allegedly among the strongest and most independent advocates of the free enterprise system, demand and benefit handsomely from such assistance as tight controls on imports of beef and price supports that subsidize exports as well as domestic sales. The arguments for protectionism are often very shallow. For example, "in the U.S., [producers] of peanuts, candles, thumbtacks, umbrella frames [and] gloves . . . have all asked for protection on grounds of national security"![9]

Another major difficulty with the imposition of trade obstacles is that, once they are introduced, a strong interest group is created that has a very important stake in preserving the protection. Protected companies either could not survive without the "fence" protecting them or, though capable of competing, are enjoying domestic monopoly profits which they are loathe to lose. An example of the former are certain sectors of the U.S. textile industry, which have been protected ever since their "infant industries" argument was accepted almost 200 years ago.

Unfortunately, governmental discussions of trade barriers within a country seldom include balanced representation of all interested groups. The largest group that is affected—the consumers—is generally poorly represented. As a result, very persuasive industry groups can be very successful in promoting their parochial interests to the disadvantage of the majority of consumers in that country.

THE REDUCTION OF TRADE BARRIERS

Trade obstacles would be much less of a problem if they were indeed "transitory." However, history has shown that it is much easier to erect controls than to dismantle them.

Governments would generally like to be free to impose trade controls without other governments doing the same. Although government officials are often unable to see how their own country's controls are bad for *their own* country, they almost universally recognize that the trade controls of another country are bad for their own country.

There have been isolated incidents of *unilateral* efforts to substantially reduce trade controls; the British aggressively pursued free trade during much of the nineteenth century. Recall, for instance, the repeal of the so-called Corn Laws, which restricted grain imports.

GATT: Probably the most notable endeavor in history to combat trade barriers has been a multilateral effort known as the *General Agreement on Tariffs and Trade.* GATT was put into operation in the

---

[9]Franklin Root, *International Trade and Investment,* 4th ed. (Cincinnati: Southwestern Publishing Company, 1978), p. 156.

late 1940s in order to facilitate the growth of post–World War II international trade. This was an effort to undo the foolish trade controls of the 1930s, which had helped to cripple international trade, deepen the Depression, and aggravate international relations.

The General Agreement on Tariffs and Trade is, as its name suggests, an agreement rather than a formal international regulation or organization. Originally, a formal organization (the International Trade Organization) had been planned by the allies toward the end of World War II.[10] While waiting for the ITO to be approved, the governments decided to implement an informal, interim agreement (GATT), which would terminate when the ITO became operational. However, when the U.S. Senate refused to approve the ITO treaty, GATT became permanent.

The General Agreement on Tariffs and Trade has not only survived, but has thrived for more than thirty-five years. That is a record that even many formal organizations and treaties could envy. GATT persists because it continues to perform a widely desirable and mutually beneficial service.

The goals of GATT are basically (1) to reduce tariffs, (2) to reduce nontariff barriers (NTBs), (3) to eliminate discrimination in trade practices, and (4) to provide a forum for negotiation of trade disputes.

During the 1930s a wall of massive trade barriers was erected by most countries. During the past three decades a series of seven GATT negotiations (the so-called Kennedy Round of the 1960s and the Tokyo Round of the 1970s) led to a substantial reduction of tariffs. However, the negotiations have generally been noticeably less successful in combating most nontariff barriers.

The Tokyo Round: The latest round of multilateral trade negotiations was launched under the auspices of GATT in Tokyo in September 1973 by the major industrial nations and many developing countries, but with little participation of the Communist countries.

What followed was "5½ years of tedious negotiations and often acrimonious debate among the 99 participating nations."[11] However, when the new agreement was finally signed by the negotiators, solid progress had again been made—not only in the form of tariff reductions, but also with some limited progress in combating nontariff barriers.

Significant reductions were agreed to by the major industrial nations. Beginning January 1, 1980, and continuing over an eight-year period, the average duties on thousands of industrial goods is to be reduced by an average of 33 percent. However, the overall impact of this development may be somewhat misleading: The actual 33 percent de-

---

[10]See the discussion of the Bretton Woods Conference in the next chapter.
[11]"GATT's Roundup," *Wall Street Journal,* April 12, 1979, p. 1.

cline is from an average of only 8.3 to 5.7 percent.[12] In earlier years when tariffs were much higher, a 33 percent cut could produce major results, but a 33 percent cut from a low level is of limited value. In some product categories the declines are very significant (for example, chemicals, nonelectrical machinery, and wood products); whereas in many others the impacts of inflation and fluctuations in the exchange rates are much more important.

Of potentially greater significance is the limited success achieved in nontariff barriers, which includes:

1. *a customs valuation code,* which it is hoped will reduce the use of arbitrary methods of determining the value of imported goods—the basis for application of ad valorem duties.
2. *an arrangement covering import licensing procedures,* which is intended to make them less discriminatory, simpler, and more open to critical review.
3. *a code on government procurements,* which greatly increases the range of government purchases that will be open to bidding from foreign companies, although most communications equipment, some power-generating equipment, and, of course, defense products, are excluded.
4. *a code on subsidies and countervailing duties,* which forbids subsidies on exports of industrial and primary minerals and places limits on agricultural subsidies. It also limits the imposition of countervailing duties to whenever "material injury" to domestic industry can actually be demonstrated; the use of countervailing duties to offset dumping has been significantly limited.

In general, tariff levels are, by historical standards, at very low levels (see Figure 4.1 earlier in the chapter). Nevertheless, since the mid-1970s, a worldwide tide of rising protectionism has appeared. This trend reflected widespread economic weakness, high unemployment, and balance-of-payments difficulties. As a result, the Tokyo Round of GATT negotiations was very difficult. Also, there will be continuing pressure on governments to impose trade barriers, especially NTBs, in the coming years in order to "protect" domestic jobs. Indeed, fears of trade wars stemming from competitive imposition of trade barriers are widespread.

GOVERNMENTAL BARRIERS
TO FREE FACTOR MOVEMENT

In addition to the extensive array of trade controls, governments have also devised an extensive array of other controls over the free movement of the factors of production: capital, people, and technology.

---

[12]Hang-Sheng Cheng, "The Tokyo Round," *Weekly Letter,* Federal Reserve Bank of San Francisco, July 13, 1979, p. 1.

EXCHANGE CONTROLS

Exchange controls interfere with the ability to freely exchange one currency for another at a realistic exchange rate and within a reasonable period of time. When a currency can be freely exchanged, it is said to be *convertible.* Currencies that cannot be easily and promptly exchanged at a fair price are *incovertible.*

In the interwar period, free convertibility of currencies was one of the many victims of the economic myopia of most of the world's leading powers. Yet, even after World War II and despite the prodding of the International Monetary Fund, most leading currencies did not regain full convertibility until 1958, and most less-developed countries still have imperfect convertibility. (The U.S. and Canadian dollars were, however, freely convertible throughout the postwar period.)

In an unregulated market, inconvertibility can be caused by a sharp imbalance in supply and demand conditions in the foreign exchange markets. Or a government can deliberately make its currency inconvertible by controlling supply or demand or by tightly regulating the exchange process.

Unfortunately, some form of exchange control is very common. Communist countries tend to utilize controls as a general policy in order to isolate their economies from outside influences or to regulate or modify the use of their foreign exchange markets. Controlling foreign exchange markets is especially common in less-developed countries, but not even the most industrialized countries refrain from this interference.[13]

The most common types of exchange controls utilized by various governments include *multiple exchange rates* and *rationing.* Multiple exchange rate systems involve the use of different rates for different types of transactions. For instance, importers may have to pay one of a variety of rates when they buy foreign currencies, depending on how the government sets the priority of the good to be imported. For example, pharmaceuticals may be granted a very favorable exchange rate, and jewelry may receive a very unfavorable rate. A limited supply of foreign exchange may be rationed on a similar priority basis or on a first-come, first-served basis. Also, foreign tourists may be encouraged and local tourists who wish to go abroad discouraged by the exchange rates. Belgium has used both a "commerical" and "financial" exchange rate for many years. Other countries, such as Argentina, have used as many as five to ten different exchange rates at the same time.

In the process of exercising such controls, the official exchange

---

[13]International Monetary Fund, *Annual Report on Exchange Arrangements and Exchange Restrictions,* any issue.

rates are often just shams; they are political tools often having very little relation to economic reality. Not too surprisingly, currency *black markets* frequently develop as a result of the artificiality of these rates or the control over who may use the market, for what purposes, and to what extent. Sometimes governments tacitly accept the domestic existence of such illegal markets; they are then known as *gray markets*. If the controls are oppressive enough, then an active *parallel market* will often arise outside the country—even for minor currencies.

CAPITAL CONTROLS

Closely related to exchange controls are another set of regulations also designed to interfere with the movement of money and capital across national borders. They are often used along with exchange controls. Money and capital controls determine *who* can move funds and under *what conditions,* and exchange controls dictate the *price* at which those who are allowed to use foreign exchange markets can exchange those funds for foreign currencies.

There are many different types of capital controls. For example, there may be limits (or *quotas*) on the amount of foreign exchange that may be purchased by a particular party; this involves limiting the amount of capital that can be moved abroad for such purposes as the payment of debts, the purchase of assets, or the payment of dividends to foreign parties.

Capital controls can also take the form of *taxes* on the outflow of capital. For instance, in Brazil, the higher a dividend payment is (relative to a company's equity), the more tax levied on that payment. This tax is in addition to any domestic profit and other taxes that have already been paid in Brazil.

Other capital controls can involve the imposition of a *waiting period* or the need for a *deposit* with a governmental agency of the funds to be remitted for some period prior to the time of the payment. These deposits, of course, as in the case of merchandise import deposits, earn no interest.

Money and capital controls are almost universal. The American markets have traditionally been the least obstructed. However, even there, when the U.S. balance of payments slipped into what appeared to be a serious deficit in the mid-1960s, capital controls were imposed between 1963 and 1973 to discourage the outflow of money and capital from the United States. There were three controls: the *Interest Equalization Tax* (introduced in 1963), which was directed at discouraging foreigners from raising funds in the U.S. capital markets; the *Foreign Credit Restraint Program* (1965), which was designed to discourage foreigners from borrowing from U.S. banks and other financial institutions; and the *Foreign Direct Investment Regulations* (1968), which attempted to discourage U.S. companies from investing abroad with U.S. funds, especially in the industrialized countries of Western Europe.[14]

Money and capital controls also often extend to the individual. Tourists from many countries, including major industrial countries, such as the United Kingdom and France, have often been restricted regarding how much money they can take out of their own countries. On the other hand, some East European countries have imposed controls on *incoming* tourists, which mandate a minimum purchase of the local (usually inconvertible) currency. Many countries also restrict the amount of *their own currency* that can be brought into their country (to discourage participation in parallel foreign exchange markets abroad).

Capital controls are generally intended to discourage the outflow of funds. There have, however, been several instances when controls have been directed toward discouraging the *inflow* of funds. This strange situation develops when currencies get too strong. Switzerland and Germany have used such controls. Perhaps the most extreme situation involved Switzerland, which for a number of years in the 1970s actually imposed a *negative* interest rate upon foreigners depositing large amounts of funds. Thus, instead of receiving *more* Swiss francs back after an investment period, the investor received back *fewer* francs!

Financial controls versus a change in currency value: Money, capital, and exchange controls are often used by a government in order to avoid lowering or increasing its currency's value. This was the basic motivation for the aforementioned U.S. and Swiss capital controls and the Argentine exchange controls. However, the two types of controls are often used together, such as was done by Mexico in 1982.

CONTROLS OVER THE MOVEMENT OF PEOPLE

There is widespread movement of people between countries throughout the world, both permanent (that is, migration) or temporary for such purposes as business or education.

All countries regulate *immigration*, usually by controlling the total number of immigrants. There have been a few countries, primarily Argentina and Brazil, which (even in recent years) have actively encouraged immigration. On the other hand, some countries, primarily Communist countries, have laws discouraging *emigration*.

---

[14]Christopher M. Korth and James C. Wood, "Business' Latest Albatross: The Foreign Direct Investment Regulations," *MSU Business Topics,* Winter 1971, pp. 55–60.

Despite the existence of stringent controls, there have been loop-holes that have permitted some large migrations. For example, Puerto Ricans can migrate readily to the United States, and, until a tightening of immigration laws, there was a large-scale movement of Indians, Paki-stanis, and others from British colonies and former colonies into the United Kingdom. Similarly, in response to political upheaval in foreign countries, the immigration gates are sometimes temporarily opened—the large-scale movements of Cubans and Vietnamese to the United States, and of former residents of Algeria to France and from Angola to Portugal following independence of those former colonies.

Migration within the European Economic Community is technical-ly free, and indeed much migration does occur. However, obstacles continue to obstruct many who would like to migrate (for example, from Southern Italy to France).

Illegal migration is universal and is sometimes on a massive scale. (For example, millions of Mexicans have illegally entered the United States.) Such flows generally represent the poor, the illiterate, and the untrained; educated, trained, and wealthy individuals are much more readily accepted into most countries, since they are less likely to impose an economic burden on their host country.

"People controls" also extensively regulate temporary movement of people across national borders. Communist and some developing coun-tries are very restrictive of their own citizens traveling abroad or of foreigners entering their country (Burma and Nepal are examples of the latter case).

There is a large-scale movement of students into the major industri-alized countries for educational purposes. Because of a tendency for many of these students to attempt to remain abroad after graduation, *student visas* from the host countries generally limit the period of the stay to discourage excessively extended schooling abroad. Student visas often need to be periodically renewed.

From the perspective of the multinational corporation, the most difficult control on the movement of people involves the ability to bring expatriates in for temporary (but often long-term) job assignments. Some countries do this as an incentive for foreign countries to hire and train local nationals. Such controls are very common, especially in developing countries, but even industrialized countries are sometimes very obstruc-tive, incuding the United States. A few countries, primarily Switzerland, impose very onerous controls, principally to restrain the number of foreigners in the country regardless of the extent of their skills. These controls on the inflow, either temporary or permanent, of foreigners are also sometimes imposed to discourage the "brain drain" of their best educated people. Countries such as India, Pakistan, Egypt, and Taiwan are examples of countries that have had a serious "brain drain" problem for many years. The problem mainly involves people who have been educated abroad, usually in one of the major industrialized countries, where they have acquired valuable skills but have also acquired an appreciation for the standard of living, personal freedom, and working conditions. These people are reluctant to return home.

Some countries allow large numbers of foreign workers to enter for temporary assignments. This pattern is especially prevalent in Western Europe, where millions of legal international migrant workers are employed in Germany, France, and other primarily Northern European countries where there are labor shortages or where local residents are reluctant to do the dirty jobs. These guest workers come primarily from Southern Europe (Portugal, Spain, Italy, and Greece), Eastern Europe (primarily Yugoslavia), North Africa (Algeria and Tunisia), and Turkey.

As the reader might well imagine, once large numbers of these workers have been admitted to a country, it is often very difficult to expel them. Many simply disappear illegally into the large colonies of foreign workers and their families. Also, many local laws and court decisions have strengthened the legal basis upon which these workers can demand legal residence.

A different type of large-scale, temporary movement of workers involves bringing large numbers of workers under contract to a foreign country for a major construction project. For example, South Korean construction companies have tens of thousands of workers in the Middle East, especially in Saudi Arabia.

CONTROLS OVER THE MOVEMENT OF TECHNOLOGY

Technology can be transferred in many ways: export of sophisticated equipment, provision of technical and managerial training, journals and books, personal visits, and the licensing of patents. In general, there has been relatively extensive freedom in the movement of technology. The more technologically advanced nations earn substantial amounts from licensing fees and export receipts annually from their technologically sophisticated exports.

For many years there have been some controls over the export of technology: controls over sales to certain countries, of certain equipment, and for certain purposes. For example, the industrialized nations of the Western World have the Coordinating Group Consultative Committee (COCOM), a coordinated effort that is directed at restricting the sale to Communist countries of technology that can readily be used for military purposes.[15] Similarly, the export of nuclear fuel and equipment

---

[15]Christopher M. Korth and Sharon Selander, "The China Market: Boom or Bust?" *Michigan Business Review*, July 1972, pp. 20–29.

has been controlled in an effort to stem the proliferation of nuclear weapons.

Sometimes these controls are imposed for political rather than for strictly military reasons. For example, the United States in 1982, because of the Soviet Union's invasion of Afghanistan and its suppression of political dissent in Poland, for many months embargoed the sale of sophisticated equipment for the construction of a natural gas pipeline from the Soviet Union into Western Europe. (U.S. allies did not participate in the embargo.) Since the embargo was opposed by the European countries and since some of the equipment was being produced by American companies in Europe or by European companies under license to American firms, who were forbidden to sell the equipment, the effort caused a serious rift between the United States and its European allies.

Demand for controls over the outflows of technology is growing. Another strong source of demands for controls comes from labor unions that claim that the export of high technology leads to the export of jobs when foreign countries obtain the capability to produce using the technology.

Controls over technology export are not yet onerous. However, the trend is not encouraging.

SUMMARY

The economic and social benefits of free trade were discussed in Chapters 2 and 3. Unfortunately, a variety of managerial and governmental obstacles exist that significantly impede trade expansion. The managerial obstacles are constantly present. However, significant progress in reducing governmental barriers was made in the decades prior to the 1970s.

The wave of protectionism through the use of nontariff barriers in the 1970s was a disquieting development following a generation of trade liberalization. The era of high inflation, economic weakness, and volatility of currency exchange rates are the roots of protectionism. The overvaluation of the U.S. dollar in the mid-1980s greatly hurt the U.S. trade balance—and provoked strong protectionist sentiment from many U.S. companies and labor unions. Unfortunately, such economic trends are likely to affect governments' actions regarding trade for many years to come.

The completion of the Tokyo Round of GATT negotiations promises continued declines in tariffs—but tariffs are no longer the principal obstacle to trade. Progress toward limiting nontariff barriers offers hope, but the codes can be circumvented and may well prove difficult to enforce. Nevertheless, they are a necessary step in the right direction. We can only wait patiently to observe the implementation of the new rules, which may well represent a significant reversal of protectionistic trends or they might simply be nuisances that governmental ingenuity can circumvent. In the former case, international trade will grow rapidly. In the latter case, the growth of trade could be substantially retarded. Living standards and the cost of living would suffer as a result.

Barriers to the unimpeded flow of capital, people, and technology are also significant hurdles for multinational companies. Although not as complicated as trade barriers, these obstacles nevertheless impose serious constraints on international managerial freedom. Exchange and capital controls are discussed further as part of the next two chapters.

KEY TERMS

BLACK MARKET
BRAIN DRAIN
"BUY NATIONAL" LAWS
CAPITAL CONTROL
COCOM
CONVERTIBLE CURRENCY
COST, INSURANCE, AND
  FREIGHT (CIF)
COUNTERVAILING
  DUTIES
DUMPING
DUTY
  AD VALOREM
  COMPOUND
  PENALTY
  SPECIFIC

EMBARGO
EXCHANGE CONTROL
EXPORT RESTRAINT
  AGREEMENT
FREE ON BOARD (FOB)
GENERAL AGREEMENT
  ON TARIFFS AND
  TRADE (GATT)
INCONVERTIBLE
  CURRENCY
INFANT INDUSTRY
INTERNATIONAL TRADE
  ORGANIZATION
LICENSING

MOST-FAVORED NATION
MULTIPLE EXCHANGE
  RATES
NONTARIFF BARRIER
PREDATORY DUMPING
QUOTA
SUBSIDY
TARIFF
TRADE CONTROL
TRADING MONOPOLY
VISA

REVIEW QUESTIONS

1. Discuss five ways in which management can be responsible for failing to take advantage of export (or import) opportunities.

2. If you worked for a company guilty of failing to take advantage of export or import opportunitites, how would you educate the company's management about the opportunities that were being missed? How would you overcome those managerial barriers?

3. Discuss the pros and cons of the following arguments against free trade:
   a. "infant industry"
   b. protection of domestic industry and workers
   c. national defense

4. If an import trade control was imposed, which would you prefer—a tariff or a quota? Why?
5. How can subsidies be considered a barrier to trade?
6. Why are NTBs becoming a more serious problem than tariffs?
7. Many trade barriers are introduced as temporary controls. Why do they tend to be so difficult to remove?
8. Who gains and who loses from import tariffs?
9. There is widespread lobbying for the increase of barriers to imports. Such requests are coming from both management and labor in an increasing number of industries in many countries. Why do you think that the pressure has been increasing so much? What is your position regarding these requests; that is, do you support the "free traders" or the "trade restricters"?

SUGGESTED REFERENCES

BALASSA, BELA *Trade Liberalization Among Industrial Countries: Objectives and Alternatives.* New York: McGraw-Hill Book Company, 1967.

BALDWIN, ROBERT E. "Nontariff Distortions of International Trade," *International Trade and Finance,* 1971.

——— "Trade and Employment Effects in the United States of Multilateral Tariff Reductions," *American Economic Review,* May 1976.

COMMITTEE FOR ECONOMIC DEVELOPMENT *Nontariff Distortions of Trade,* 1969.

GENERAL AGREEMENT ON TARIFFS AND TRADE *Annual Report.*

GRAY, H. PETER *International Trade, Investments and Payments.* Boston: Houghton Mifflin Co., 1979.

INTERNATIONAL MONETARY FUND *Annual Report on Exchange Arrangements and Exchange Restrictions.* (Any annual issue)

ROOT, FRANKLIN *International Trade and Investment* (4th ed.). Cincinnati: Southwestern Publishing Company, 1978.

UNITED NATIONS *Restrictive Business Practices,* 1971.

U.S. DEPARTMENT OF COMMERCE *Need for Better Identification and Analysis of Nontariff Barriers to Trade,* 1974.

YEAGER, LELAND B., AND DAVID G. TUERCK *Trade Policy and the Price System.* Scranton, Pa.: International Textbook, 1966.

5

The World Monetary System

As has been seen, the international economic arena does not always operate smoothly. The decade of the 1930s was an especially difficult economic period worldwide. The 1970s proved to be another period of great strain on the international economy. Some of the gravest strains during these periods occurred in the international monetary system. An understanding of the international monetary system and its major institutions is vital for the student of international business. This chapter examines the modern international financial system with special emphasis upon the *International Monetary Fund* (IMF), the international organization whose prime focus is maintaining stability and freedom in the foreign exchange markets. The examination begins with a consideration of the basic roles of money—domestic and international.

MONEY

THE DEVELOPMENT OF MONEY

As was discussed in Chapter 2, the inefficiencies of barter eventually led to the use of some commodity to serve as money. Many of the items that have been used as money at some time or other down through the years were functional commodities with intrinsic value, such as cattle, grain, salt, rice, furs, beer, slaves, iron, nylons, candy, cigarettes, diamonds, and even women, as well as precious metals such as gold and silver. Also, items with little alternative value have been employed as money: seashells, beads, woodpecker scalps, large rocks, and even cigarette butts. Indeed, *anything can serve as money that is readily accepted by others,* who in turn have the intention of spending that item rather than consuming it. Of course, some goods are more satisfactory for this purpose than others.

Each type of commodity money has obvious shortcomings. Cattle, slaves, and diamonds are not readily divisible. Cattle and slaves can die (although they can also reproduce). Some monetary commodities deteriorate easily, (for instance, beer and iron).[1] Many are difficult to transport and store (e.g. furs and stones). Candy is generally less desirable in summer than in winter. Supplies of some commodities, such as woodpecker scalps, are too limited; some are too common, such as iron; and some too seasonal, for instance, grain.

For these and other reasons commodity moneys have been replaced by paper moneys. Such paper has little intrinsic value but instead is valued for what it will buy. *The intrinsic usefulness of money is now a minor factor in its value.*

Paper money was first used by the Chinese. It first appeared in the Western world as receipts for goods held in a vault (e.g. the promissory notes of goldsmiths), in a warehouse (e.g. tobacco or cotton receipts) or even claims on future inventories (e.g. claims on crops in a field or on the merchandise in a ship which had not yet arrived at port).

Eventually merchandise receipts gave way to paper currency. Originally currency represented claims on some commodity owned by the issuer of the currency (usually a government or its agent). For example, gold certificates and silver certificates, which the U.S. Government would exchange for gold and silver, were basic components of the U.S. money supply for many years. (Gold certificates became invalid in 1934 and silver certificates in 1964.)

People clung stubbornly to the idea that paper money had to represent a claim for some commodity. Centuries ago when it was found that some goldsmiths had more gold receipts outstanding than gold in the vaults it was a cause for scandal. Decisions by the U.S. Government to progressively reduce and finally eliminate the gold and silver backing

---

[1]Paul Samuelson in his basic textbook, *Economics,* 11th edition, New York: McGraw Hill Book Co., 1980, p. 260, quotes from a book of W. Stanley Jevons in the mid-1800s: "Mademoiselle Zelie . . . gave a concert in the Society Islands. In exchange . . . she was to receive a third part of the receipts. . . . Her share was . . . 3 pigs, 23 turkeys, 44 chickens, 5000 cocoa-nuts, besides considerable quantities of bananas, lemons, and oranges . . . (which) in Paris . . . would have been good remuneration for 5 songs. In the Society Islands, however, pieces of money were scarce; and as Mademoiselle could not consume any considerable portion of the receipts herself, it became necessary . . . to feed the pigs and poultry with the fruit."

for the dollar were always met by strong opposition. Part of this opposition, of course, came from gold and silver mining interests, but most of it came from the general population, which feared that if the money could not be exchanged for a precious metal, it would be worthless.

Similarly, when silver was removed from U.S. coins in the 1960s, many people feared that coins would lose their value. However, people found that vending machines still took their coins and that stores still took their dollars, even without any precious metal content or backing. This reflects the true basis for money's value—what it will buy—which results from its *public acceptability*. To serve as money neither paper currency nor coin need any intrinsic value or even any government backing! For a government to declare that money is *legal tender* may help its acceptablity, but money does not need to be legal tender to be acceptable and useful. Money, even paper currency and coins, does not even need to be issued by a country's government. Commercial banks and even stores are sometimes the source of money in some countries.

MULTIPLE CURRENCIES

The optimal monetary situation in the world would be a single worldwide currency of stable value to serve all four basic monetary functions anywhere in the world.

Unfortunately, there are more than 150 currencies in the world. Almost every government wants its own currency plus its own independent monetary policies as part of its sovereign rights. The existence of multiple currencies is one of the many penalties that the modern international economy must face because of the failure of world governments to cooperate more effectively.

If a single world currency existed and if trade and capital controls were avoided, then international trade could occur as easily as domestic trade. Trade patterns might be very different and much more efficient than they are today. Many of the world's population, consumption, and production centers are closer to major centers in other countries than to those of their own countries (for example, Windsor in Canada and Detroit in the United States; Innsbruck in Austria and Munich in Germany; Buenos Aires in Argentina and Montevideo in Uruguay).

However, since most sovereign states have their own individual currencies, international trade must rely on some other mechanism, such as

1. barter
2. acceptance by the seller of the buyer's currency (for example, the widespread use of the U.S. dollar and formerly of the British pound sterling as proxies for true world currencies)
3. exchange of currencies

A very major share of world trade today does require the exchange-ability of currencies. Even if a French exporter is willing to sell his or her goods for U.S. dollars, he or she will usually need to *convert* those dollars into French francs in order to pay production expenses.

The next chapter examines the mechanism for exchanging currencies. Buying and selling of currencies by companies, banks, and governments (the role of individuals is very minor) operate within a highly developed system of governmentally created international mechanisms. The majority of these mechanisms involve the *International Monetary Fund.* However, the IMF is a post–World War II phenomenon. Prior to 1946, other means had evolved to facilitate and stabilize international monetary flows.

PRE-1930

The history of international monetary systems has been very chaotic in general. Prior to the late 1800s there was not really a system at all. However, by the late 1870s the evolution to the gold standard was becoming quite prominent. That system undoubtedly provided a valuable element of stability at a time when most countries, even most of the major industrial powers (including the United States), were erratically developing their *domestic* monetary systems.

However, the gold standard proved to be very inflexible, and its participants often failed to play by the "rules of the game." As a result, many studies have indicated that the gold standard was never really as successful as its modern adherents would like to believe.[2] Whatever the system's merits, the gold standard unraveled with the advent of World War I and never really recovered. Stumbling efforts to reconstruct the system were still being made up to the Great Depression, but that economic trauma followed by World War II ended all pretenses of maintaining a true gold standard.

THE 1930s

The economic trauma of the 1930s was a massive blow to both domestic and international economic conditions. The spreading depression brought efforts by most major countries to try to export their domestic problems in a vain hope of strengthening their domestic economies. This "beggar-my-neighbor" policy led to soaring trade barriers, and exchange and capital controls. This was the zenith of American trade protectionism, when the Hawley-Smoot Tariff Act of 1930 was

---

[2]See Arthur I. Bloomfield, *Monetary Policy Under the International Gold Standard: 1800–1914* (Federal Reserve Bank of New York); also Robert Triffin, *Our International Monetary System: Yesterday, Today and Tomorrow* (New York: Random House, Inc., 1966).

enacted (see Chapter 4). Not too surprisingly, such actions led to retaliation from other nations.

Countries failed miserably in their efforts to export their economic difficulties. They succeeded only in expanding and aggravating the Great Depression. As we have seen in Chapters 2–4, such results should not have been too surprising: Increased interference with the movement of goods and the factors of production generally leads to reduced economic efficiency and reduced world income. This indeed occurred.

This unilateralism, protectionism, and general isolationism, which resulted from the misguided and shortsighted nationalism of the period, not only disrupted international trade and factor-flow patterns, but it also produced a deterioration in political as well as economic ties between countries. Many analysts feel that this condition contributed significantly to the pressures that led to World War II. It also made it more difficult for some of the Allies (for instance, France and the United Kingdom) to cooperate in resisting Hitler's aggression.

THE INTERNATIONAL MONETARY FUND: PHASE 1

BRETTON WOODS

With the memory of this breakdown of world trade and monetary flows fresh in their minds and with the awareness of the contribution that this situation had made toward the horrible war that was then being waged, representatives of many of the Allied nations met in 1944 at Bretton Woods, New Hampshire, in order to plan and control the international financial and trading relations of the postwar world.

The planning at Bretton Woods was broken into three major areas: monetary problems, financing problems, and trade problems. Correspondingly, three international bodies were designed to deal respectively with these problems: the International Monetary Fund, International Bank for Reconstruction and Development, and the International Trade Organization, which was replaced by the GATT.[3]

GOALS OF THE IMF

The International Monetary Fund was designed to

1. promote international monetary cooperation
2. facilitate international trade as a means of raising employment and incomes

---

[3]The International Bank for Reconstruction and Development is examined in Chapter 9.

3. promote exchange stability, maintain orderly exchange arrangements, and avoid competitive exchange depreciation
4. assist in the establishment of a multilateral system of payments without restrictions on foreign currency exchange
5. make the general resources of the Fund available as loans to help countries adjust to temporary international payment problems and
6. shorten the duration and severity of international payments disequilibrium.[4]

MEMBERSHIP IN THE IMF

In order to oversee the efforts to pursue these goals, the IMF was designed as a formal and permanent organization with its headquarters in Washington, D.C. Membership in the Fund is open to any country willing to abide by its regulations. Only national governments and not corporations or other private-sector entities can be members or take advantage of the Fund's resources. More than 140 countries are members. Most non-Communist countries belong as well as some Communist countries such as Yugoslavia, Romania, Vietnam, the People's Republic of China, and Hungary.

All member countries must buy into the International Monetary Fund. They do this by paying their *subscription quota* to the Fund. Prior to the 1970s this meant that their membership subscription quota was to be paid 25 percent in gold and 75 percent in the country's own currency. The quota is determined by the relative economic strength and importance in world trade and finance of each country; the United States by far has the largest quota. These subscriptions quotas

1. provide the resources for IMF loans to member countries;
2. are the major factor in determining how much a member can borrow from the Fund;
3. determine the member's voting strength; and
4. serve as the basis for the allocation of special drawing rights, which are discussed later in this chapter.

STABILITY OF CURRENCY EXCHANGE RATES

Par value: Stability of exchange rates was one of the cornerstones of the IMF during its first quarter of a century. A member country was required

1. to reach an agreement with the Fund for a specifically stated value of its currency (its *par value*)

---

[4]Article 1, Articles of Agreement of the International Monetary Fund.

2. to prevent the market value of its currency from rising or falling by more than 1 percent from par value (its *intervention points*) and
3. not to change the par value without consulting the IMF.

There was no magic formula for the determination of an exchange rate. Governments usually made educated guesses regarding what exchange rate might prove acceptable not only to themselves but also to the markets. If the IMF approved, that rate would go into effect. (Even if the IMF failed to approve the proposed rate, the government could still put the rate into effect and either seek subsequent approval or simply do without such approval. However, the latter could affect the currency's international acceptability and would affect the country's access to financial assistance from the IMF.)

This par value was usually expressed in terms of U.S. dollars, although direct valuation in terms of gold was equally acceptable. However, since the dollar had an arbitrary value in terms of gold (the U.S. dollar equaled 1/35 ounce of gold, or gold was officially valued at $35.00 an ounce—in 1971 this was changed to $38.00 an ounce and in 1973 to $42.22 an ounce), and since the U.S. Treasury maintained this price for gold, all currencies were either directly or indirectly valued in terms of the dollar (or, alternately, in terms of gold). This relationship, therefore, determined the exchange rate between any other two currencies. (If the British pound sterling [£] was valued at $2.40 and the French franc [FF] at $0.20, then £1 = FF 12, since £1 = $2.40 = FF 12.)

Intervention points: A currency was not normally valued in foreign exchange markets at exactly its par value, because under the IMF system it was allowed to "float" according to market demand between 1 percent above and 1 percent below its par value. Thus, the British pound might fluctuate in value between $2.376 and $2.424. These limits were called the *intervention points* for a currency, because IMF regulations required that the nation's government prevent the value of its currency from exceeding these limits by intervening as necessary.

If more local currency was being demanded from abroad than being supplied, the price would naturally rise; the nation's government would enter the exchange market either when or before the upper intervention point (the ceiling) was reached and buy the excess foreign currencies *by supplying its own currency.* On the other hand, if more of the local currency was being sold than people were buying, its price would fall. Once again, the government had to intervene, but under those conditions the price (exchange rate) could be held within the intervention points (that is, lower intervention point [the floor] only if the government *bought its own currency* using international reserves or international borrowings). These reserves are a supply of liquid assets available to monetary authorities for the purpose of supporting the value of the national currency. These assets can be sold in foreign exchange markets or directly to foreign governments when the demand for the local currency is insufficient to cover the demand for foreign currencies.[5]

Convertibility: Closely related to the functions of the IMF described above are the encouragement and maintenance of convertibility, the easy exchange of one currency into other currencies. As was seen in the previous chapter, currencies that cannot readily be exchanged have varying degrees of inconvertibility. As with all its other major functions, the Fund seeks in this respect to foster an orderly and effective international financial system.

Loans from the IMF: A government's monetary reserves often prove inadequate to accomplish stabilization. When this happens, the nation may borrow from the IMF. The IMF does not itself intervene in the foreign exchange markets, but it extends loans so that members have greater capacity to intervene. The function of this loan facility is to "buy time," so that the government can take the necessary steps to end the "temporary" currency imbalance. The resources that the Fund has available to lend to its members come primarily from the subscription quotas the members themselves contribute. These quotas are periodically increased; as a result, the IMF's resources have grown substantially since its inception and exceed $70 billion at this writing. (See Figure 5.1.)

When a member country borrows from the Fund, it must offer in exchange an equivalent amount of its own currency as collateral. Thus, the IMF's holdings of that currency increase. The Fund automatically lends to a member until the Fund's holdings of that country's currency equal 100 percent of the nation's subscription quota. When the country first joined the IMF, this automatic line of credit was equal to 25 percent of its quota, since originally the quota was paid 75 percent in its own currency and 25 percent in gold. As a result, that 25 percent of automatic credit line was formerly referred to as the *gold tranche* but is now called its *reserve tranche*. (*Tranche* means "a portion or share.")

Even if a country's reserve tranche should become exhausted, the International Monetary Fund can provide further assistance. The next category of loans is called the *credit tranche*. This occurs when the Fund's holdings of the country's currency exceed 100 percent of the member's quota but are less than 200 percent; it is divided into four credit tranches of 25 percent each. This portion of credit is not automat-

---

[5]The portion of international reserves that is in the form of foreign exchange (FX) can be used *directly* in the FX markets. Other liquid assets in this fund (for example, gold and special drawing rights) first need to be sold for a foreign currency before they could be used in the FX markets, although such assets could also be transferred directly to a foreign government without being sold for currency. International monetary reserves are discussed later in this chapter.

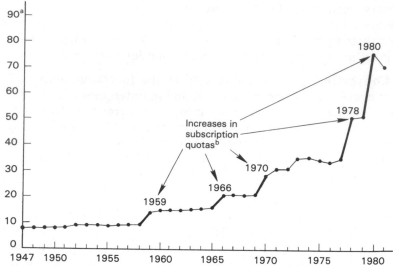

aAll figures are in billions of dollars.
bSubscription quotas are denominated in special drawing rights or SDRs, which will be discussed later in this chapter. The volatility of quotas in the years since 1970 (including the decline in 1981) is the result of fluctuations in the value of the SDR.The SDR totals have been translated into U.S. dollars in the figure.

SOURCE: *International Financial Statistics.* Various issues.

FIGURE 5.1   Contributions Paid in to the IMF (Subscription Quotas)

ic. Generally, the more credit tranches borrowed, the more stringent are the demands placed by the IMF upon the borrower in terms of monetary and fiscal action expected. Remember that these loans are made to help *temporarily* shore up a nation's currency—until corrective action can be taken. If the country will not or cannot take the necessary steps, the Fund may be unwilling to provide help for the purpose of maintaining the present value of its currency.

Provisions also exist for additional borrowings under other IMF lending facilities.[6]

Par-value changes: It sometimes happens that even IMF support is not sufficient to maintain the prevailing par value of a currency. Under these conditions, the IMF works in cooperation with the country in order to choose a "reasonable" new par value and to bring about an orderly and effective transition to a new exchange rate. As noted above, the choice of a new rate of exchange is at best a "guesstimate." No one, not even a government or the IMF, can know the "real" value of currency.

---

[6]See Table 5.1 later in the chapter.

Sickness of the IMF: The International Monetary Fund succeeded remarkably well for the first quarter century of its existence. It benefited from and contributed to an extensive period of international economic growth, relatively low inflation, and an increasing internationalization of the world economy.

During this period international trade and capital flows expanded rapidly, world income grew at an unprecedented pace, the ravaged countries of Europe and Asia made total economic recoveries from the destruction of World War II, and the development of many less-developed countries advanced at the most rapid rate in history.

However, the IMF system, as originally designed, was to prove to be unable to survive when this period of economic stability was succeeded by the economic strains of the 1970s. The principal flaw in the system was the mechanism for changing exchange rates.

Actually, as originally designed, the IMF provided for small and systematic changes in the values of currencies—small, periodic mini-revaluations of strong currencies and mini-devaluations of weak currencies. If this mechanism had actually been implemented as it had been intended, it would have prevented the buildup of excessive pressure in foreign exchange markets. The breakup of the fixed–exchange rate system could have been delayed, perhaps long enough to have permitted orderly reform of the IMF system.

Unfortunately, instead of a stable system of flexible exchange rates, what developed was a stable system of inflexible exchange rates. Since currencies had fixed par values that were maintained by governments, market forces were not permitted to determine the value of a currency, except within the narrow confines of the intervention points. It was up to the governmental forces to make the decision regarding a change in currency value. This could have worked effectively if governments were willing to revalue or devalue when market pressures indicated, but governments became wedded to a notion of the sanctity of the fixed value of their currencies relative to other currencies.[7] Thus, it became almost a matter of honor to resist a change. A devaluation came to be seen as an admission to failure in economic policy—which it indeed generally is— since it most commonly reflects a rate of domestic inflation that is more rapid than foreign inflation. A revaluation was seen by the "strong-currency" countries as being a punishment for success, reflecting their ability to control domestic prices.

As countries, weak and strong, ignored economic realities, the pressures of the unrealistic exchange rates grew. The inflationary countries became less able to compete in international trade since their

---

[7]A similar flaw had weakened the gold standard—a reluctance to change the gold value of currencies. See Kurt Dew, "Gold Policy: the Thirties and the Seventies," *Business Review* (Federal Reserve Bank of San Francisco), Winter 1974–1975, p. 17.

comparative advantages were artificially eroded by the failure of adjustments in the exchange rates to maintain pace with inflation. Also, such unrealistically high exchange rates generally tended to even discourage some of the capital flows that could have offset the declining trade performance. Similarly, the low-inflation countries experienced an artificial stimulus to their exports and capital inflows.

Such distortions obviously have some finite limits. However, when such limits were reached, it was too late for small adjustments. In the mid-1960s the United States introduced capital controls: the Interest Equalization Tax, the Foreign Direct Investment Regulations, and the Foreign Credit Restraint Program. The British pound sterling, then the second most important currency in the world, was belatedly devalued—by more than 15 percent in November 1967. It pulled with it a number of currencies that were closely tied to sterling, such as the Israeli pound, Spanish peseta, and many British Commonwealth currencies.

In 1968 the drain on the U.S. gold supply became so great that support of private gold markets at $35 per ounce by the United States and some of its major allies (via the so-called London gold pool) was suspended. A "two-tiered" system of gold prices emerged—the official or intergovernment market at $35 per ounce (a price maintained by the willingness of the U.S. Treasury to buy or sell gold at that price) and the private market at whatever price market forces (industry, jewelers, dentists, hoarders, and so forth) dictated.

In 1969 the French franc was devalued by almost 10 percent. In 1970 the IMF attempted to shore up confidence in the international monetary system and reduce reliance upon the increasingly shaky U.S. dollar by creating "paper gold," a new asset called the special drawing right (SDR).[8] However, the amount of SDRs issued has been relatively small compared to the availability of the U.S. dollar and the value (especially the *market* value) of gold.

Each year the international financial pressures mounted. Finally, in August 1971 the U.S. government thought "the unthinkable" and refused to support the dollar any longer with gold sales. That move was accompanied by a package of temporary moves, such as an import surcharge and price controls, but the end of gold convertibility for the dollar was permanent, although the dollar remained convertible into other currencies. This move, in effect, allowed the value of the dollar to float downward in comparison to other currencies. It threw the markets into great confusion.

Most observers, including almost all governments, were anxious to see a return to fixed exchange rates. As a result, only four months later on December 18, 1971, the major industrial countries signed the *Smith-*

---

[8]SDRs are discussed later in the chapter.

sonian Agreement, which provided for (1) an average devaluation of the dollar of approximately 10 percent against the major European currencies, (2) an increase in the price of gold to $38 per ounce, and (3) an increase of the intervention bands to ± 2¼ percent above and below a currency's par value.

However, the dollar continued to weaken; the 10 percent devaluation proved to be quite inadequate. As a result, a second devaluation of approximately 10 percent occurred in February 1973 with monetary gold rising to $42.22 an ounce. Within one month it was apparent that the adjustment effort was a dismal failure: Soon most major currencies were floating with little effort to maintain any pretext of par values.

The IMF was not prepared for crisis when it came. Despite ample forewarning of impending troubles, it floundered when the old system collapsed. It lacked contingency plans and was slow to respond.

"The IMF is dead! Long live the IMF!" These were stunning blows to the Fund. It was widely believed that this was the beginning of a sharp decline in the role played by the IMF. However, the organization has demonstrated its resiliency: It is now stronger and plays a bigger role than ever, even without fixed par values.

THE INTERNATIONAL MONETARY FUND: PHASE II

Mark Twain once wrote to a newspaper editor, "The rumors of my death are a little premature." So also were the pronouncements of the demise of the IMF in the early 1970s. The IMF bounced back with increased vigor and responsibility. Nevertheless, many difficulties still beset the Fund and the world monetary system.

The basic problems for the IMF involved the inflexibility of exchange rates and the inability of the Fund to provide financial assistance to countries with foreign exchange problems. The problem grew to one of declining confidence in the international financial system itself.

FLOATING EXCHANGE RATES

The problem of exchange rates stemmed from the refusal of countries to make small, periodic changes in the values of their currencies as was prescribed in the Articles of Agreement of the International Monetary Fund. Countries were satisfying their obligation to maintain the value of their currencies to an excessive extent: Once a par value was in effect, the governments clung to it desperately. When the Bretton Woods Agreements came unhinged, the need for an end to this inflexibility was most glaring. With the collapse of the efforts of the Smithsonian Agreements to reestablish stability, the system of par value dissolved. Since March 1973, *floating currencies* have been the order of the day between most of the major currencies. When a currency floats, its government has no specific responsibility to intervene, nor is there a par value. (See the boxed-in text.)

Floating exchange rates introduced a much greater element of uncertainty into international transactions. In contrast to the long periods of stability in the exchange rates that had prevailed under the Bretton Woods format, the post-1972 era witnessed high volatility in exchange rates.

CHANGE IN EXCHANGE RATES

Under the old Bretton Woods system of the IMF, countries had an obligation to maintain the value of their currencies by fiscal and monetary actions (including intervention in the foreign exchange markets). When a government finally chose to change the value of its currency (a decision that was typically made under heavy economic and/or diplomatic pressure), a formal declaration was made by the government of a new fixed rate; that is, the new par value. If the change was to a lower value, the action was referred to as a *devaluation*. If the government declared a new higher rate for the currency (a less-common occurrence than devaluation), it was called a *revaluation* or an *up-valuation*. Therefore, the terms *devaluation* and *revaluation* refer to specific governmental action that leads to a new *fixed value* for a currency. This procedure is still followed by most smaller economies of the world which tie their currencies to the dollar or—as in the case of a number of former French colonies—to the French franc, and by the members of the European Monetary System (EMS) relative to one another. (See Table 5.1 later in the chapter.)

Under a system of floating exchange rates, governments do not make such formal declarations of a new currency value, but rather allow the market forces (with smaller or larger amounts of governmental intervention) to drive the exchange rate to different and variable values, rather than fixed values. If the movement is downward, it is referred to as a *depreciation,* and if the movement of the currency is upward, it is called an *appreciation*.

	Upward Movement	Downward Movement
Formal Governmental Action	revaluation (up-valuation)	devaluation
Market Forces	appreciation	depreciation

Note that within a fixed-rate system such as the EMS formal changes (devaluations or revaluations) are periodically made, but that these currencies are allowed to appreciate or depreciate within a range around the par or central value ($\pm 2\frac{1}{4}$ percent in the case of most EMS currencies).

Figure 5.2 illustrates the movement of the trade-weighted value of the U.S. dollar, German deutsche mark, British sterling, and Japanese yen since 1970. Note the relative stability prior to 1972. The changes in the U.S. dollar's value against the composite picture of currencies in the figure have generally been much more moderate than those of the other currencies primarily because of the U.S dollar's strength against the Canadian dollar and because of the importance of trade with Canada as a part of total U.S. trade. Nevertheless, all the currencies have been quite volatile.

The problem of financial inflexibility was solved for, but not by, the International Monetary Fund. Indeed, the solution was forced upon it by events. When the effort at resolving the rapidly mounting crisis via the Smithsonion Agreement failed in early 1973, the old system (of par values and intervention points) dissolved. Five years later in 1978, the Second Amendment to the Articles of Agreement of the IMF accepted the new situation.

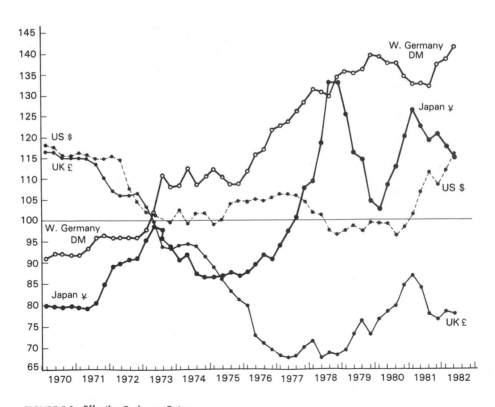

FIGURE 5.2   Effective Exchange Rates

Types of float: Under the system of floating rates, governments ideally should abstain from interference in the foreign exchange markets. Indeed, in 1973 there was extensive discussion of whether international reserves were even going to be of significant value anymore!

However, governments soon demonstrated their inability to resist the temptation to intervene lustily in the markets. New terminology evolved to describe the extent of governmental interference in the foreign exchange markets.

a. *Clean float:* no governmental intervention (this is a hypothetical state, since all governments intervene to some extent). (See Figure 5.3a.)

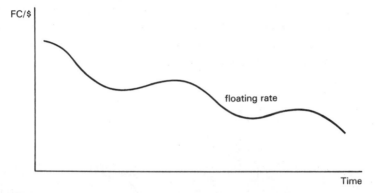

FIGURE 5.3a   A Clean Float

b. *Managed float:* governmental intervention directed at smoothing out some of the extreme volatility of its currency in the financial markets. The government permits the market to appreciate or depreciate the currency but attempts to see that it occurs in a more "orderly" fashion. The German government's intervention has generally been of the managed float variety. (See Figure 5.3b.)

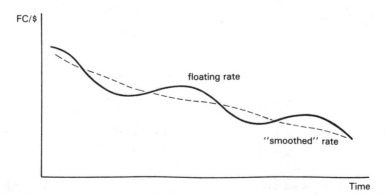

FIGURE 5.3b   The Managed Float

c. *Dirty float:* governmental intervention directed at obstructing the effect of normal market forces. Figure 5.3c illustrates the exchange rate that normal free-market forces would produce and the actual rate. The Japanese government was a prominent employer of the dirty float during much of the mid-1970s, as it attempted to prevent the yen from rising in value. However, its massive purchase of foreign currencies eventually caused an unsatisfactorily high rate of growth in the yen money supply. As a result, the bank of Japan later reverted to a managed float.

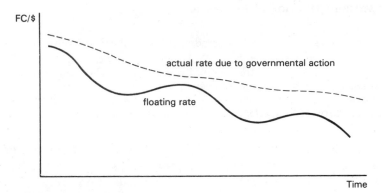

FIGURE 5.3c   Dirty Float

In addition to these three forms of floating, of course, there are many governments that still maintain fixed exchange rates for their currencies. (See Figure 5.3d). As can be seen from a comparison of Figures 5.3c and 5.3d, the fixed exchange rate is basically a modified form of dirty float. Most Latin American currencies maintain fixed exchange rates relative to the U.S. dollar.

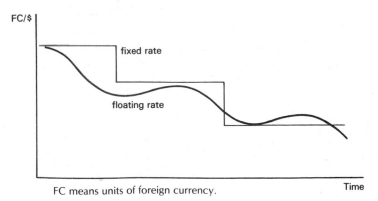

FIGURE 5.3d   Fixed Rate

Return to fixed rates? Floating rates have been mandated by the developments of the 1970s. Even most observers who would like to see a return to fixed exchange rates realize that the high rates of inflation and the massive balance of payments imbalances, which have prevailed worldwide since the early 1970s, make a return to fixed exchange rates an impossibility in the near future. When, and if, these problems are resolved, there will undoubtedly be many who will push for a return to something more akin to the old system of fixed exchange rates. The European Monetary System (see boxed-in text) suggests some of the variants that might be possible:

1. wider bands (as was indeed introduced under the Smithsonian Agreement)
2. provisions for periodic but small changes in the exchange rates. This was, of course, intended in the original design of the IMF, but new provisions would need to be designed to ensure that members actually live up to this obligation; it would involve a system of *crawling pegs* (that is, par values) or sliding parities (*mini-devaluations* or *mini-revaluations*).

In addition to the European Monetary System, a number of Latin American countries have been utilizing a system of periodic, small changes (mini-devaluations) in their currencies for many years. The procedure was pioneered by Chile but was brought to greatest prominence by Brazil. Colombia, Argentina, and Uruguay have also employed it at various times. Their systems of mini-devaluations are designed to remove much of the excessive pressures and distortions that can be caused by excessive delay of devaluations and to thereby reduce much of the uncertainty and speculation.

THE EUROPEAN MONETARY SYSTEM

Ten European countries are members of the European Economic Community (EEC). This endeavor has resulted in substantially integrating many facets of the economies of the United Kingdom, France, Germany, Italy, the Netherlands, Belgium, Luxembourg, Denmark, Ireland, and Greece. The old system of fixed exchange rates was a stable aid to this system. Floating exchange rates between members (at least at a time of extreme financial volatility) introduced serious strains into the organization. Accordingly, most of the members of the EEC, with the primary exception of the United Kingdom, instituted a regional adjunct to the EEC in early 1979. This effort at monetary integration is called the European Monetary System (EMS).

The European Monetary System is the ambitious child of the so-called snake, a less formal effort by several of the European currencies to stabilize their exchange rates relative to one another. Membership in the snake had been very erratic, however, and it was really nothing more than a deutschemark bloc. The EMS, on the other hand, while still primarily a DM-dominated bloc of currencies, has proved to be more durable than the snake.

The EMS in many ways is a throwback to the old IMF.

1. There are established exchange rates, which are called *central rates* rather than par values, but the intention is basically the same.
2. There are intervention limits. The limits are $\pm$ 2¼ percent (the same as had been introduced temporarily under the Smithsonian Agreement) except for Italy, which has a very liberal $\pm$ 6 percent.
3. Countries have an obligation to intervene as necessary in order to prevent their currencies from violating those limits.

In addition, the EMS has financial resources which its members have contributed. However, unlike the IMF, the EMS can use its resources to intervene itself in the financial markets.

Although the European Monetary System is dedicated to maintaining the relative stability of exchange rates between its members, there is no comparable commitment vis à vis nonmembers. As a result, the EMS currencies float as a unit against nonmember currencies, for example, the U.S. dollar, the Japanese yen, and even the pound sterling. Individual members can act in unison with nonmembers, such as action between Germany and the United States, but the EMS as a whole does not. Of course, if Germany and the United States are successful in moderating the movements between those two currencies, then their actions will, of necessity, also affect the exchange rates between each of the other members of the EMS and the dollar.

The goals of the EMS are much more ambitious than were those of the IMF. Stability between exchange rates is seen as only an initial step toward the *ultimate goal of full monetary integration.* This would entail eventually the creation of a new European currency, the *ECU (European currency unit),* which would supplant the deutsche mark, French franc, guilder, and so forth. It already exists as a unit of account within the group—but not as a currency.

In order for a joint currency to be feasible, the various member countries will need to institute a common monetary agency with a single monetary program for the entire group. This is highly ambitious and fraught with many difficulties, but the members are to be commended for their daring vision. Nevertheless, it is very easy for the observer to be quite skeptical of the prospects for success of joint efforts to arrive at common monetary policies between such inflation-prone members of the EMS as France and Italy and such monetarily cautious countries as Germany and the Netherlands.

If the European Monetary System succeeds as envisioned, then Europe may indeed become a massive common market. However, although Europe continues to migrate toward this ideal, it is doubtful that this effort will be able to match the success of the European Economic Community itself. Therefore, the EEC will likely remain more of a customs union than a true common market.[9]

---

[9]Customs union and common market will be discussed in Chapter 9.

TABLE 5.1 Exchange-Rate Systems Used by Members of the IMF (as of December 31, 1983)[1]

Currency Pegged to					Flexibility Limited in Terms of a Single Currency or Group of Currencies		More Flexible		
US Dollar	French Franc	Other Currency	SDR	Other Composite[2]	Single Currency[3]	Cooperative Arrangements[4]	Adjusted According to a Set of Indicators[5]	Other Managed Floating	Independently Floating
Antigua & Barbuda	Benin	Bhutan (Indian Rupee)	Burma	Algeria	Afghanistan	Belgium	Brazil	Argentina	Australia
Bahamas	Cameroon	Equatorial Guinea (Spanish Peseta)	Burundi	Austria	Bahrain	Denmark	Chile	Costa Rica	Canada
Barbados	C. African Republic	Gambia, The (Pound Sterling)	Guinea	Bangladesh	Ghana	France	Colombia	Ecuador	Israel
Belize	Chad	Lesotho (South African Rand)	Guinea-Bissau	Botswana	Guyana	Germany	Portugal	Greece	Japan
Bolivia	Comoros	Swaziland (South African Rand)	Iran, I.R. of	Cape Verde	Maldives	Ireland	Somalia	Iceland	Lebanon
Djibouti	Congo		Jordan	China, P.R.	Qatar	Italy		India	South Africa
Dominica	Gabon		Kenya	Cyprus	Saudi Arabia	Luxembourg		Indonesia	United Kingdom
Dominican Republic	Ivory Coast		Malawi	Fiji	Thailand	Netherlands		Jamaica	United States
Egypt	Mali		Rwanda	Finland	United Arab Emirates			Korea	Uruguay
El Salvador	Niger		São Tomé & Principe	Hungary				Mexico	
Ethiopia	Senegal		Seychelles	Kuwait				Morocco	
Grenada	Togo		Vanuatu	Madagascar				New Zealand	
Guatemala	Upper Volta		Viet Nam	Malaysia				Nigeria	
Haiti				Malta				Pakistan	
Honduras				Mauritania				Peru	
Iraq				Mauritius				Philippines	
Lao P.D. Republic				Nepal				Spain	
Liberia				Norway				Sri Lanka	
Libya				Papua New Guinea				Turkey	
Nicaragua				Romania				Uganda	
Oman				Singapore				Western Samoa	
Panama				Solomon Islands				Yugoslavia	
				Sweden				Zaire	

124

Paraguay
St. Lucia
St. Vincent
Sierre Leone

Sudan
Suriname
Syrian Arab
    Republic
Trinidad and
    Tobago
Venezuela

Yemen Arab
    Republic
Yemen, P.D.
    Republic

Tanzania
Tunisia
Zambia
Zimbabwe

[1]Excluding the currency of Democratic Kampuchea, for which no current information is available. For members with dual or multiple exchange markets, the arrangement shown is that in the major market.

[2]Comprises currencies which are pegged to various "baskets" of currencies of the members' own choice, as distinct from the SDR basket.

[3]Exchange rates of all currencies have shown limited flexibility in terms of the U.S. dollar.

[4]Refers to the cooperative arrangement maintained under the European Monetary System.

[5]Includes exchange arrangements under which the exchange rate is adjusted at relatively frequent intervals, on the basis of indicators determined by the respective member countries.

SOURCE: *International Financial Statistics* (International Monetary Fund), February 1984, p. 15.

Table 5.1 outlines the type of financial regime that each member of the IMF employs. Note that most Latin American and many Middle Eastern, African, and Asian currencies continue to have a fixed rate of exchange in terms of the U.S. dollar. Also note that a number of former French colonies still maintain a tie between their currencies and the French franc. Many other, mostly smaller, countries tie the value of their currencies to a basket or composite of major currencies; the most common composite is the SDR, which is discussed later in the chapter.

FINANCIAL ASSISTANCE

In another vein, the IMF has continued to innovate in order to improve its ability to provide assistance for countries experiencing difficulties in maintaining the stability of their currencies' exchange rates. This has been accomplished, first, by significant enlargement of the Fund's resources via major increases in the subscription quotas of its members.

In addition to this increase in resources for the Fund, there has also been a proliferation of special lending facilities. These are outlined in Table 5.2.

The increased resources and the greater flexibility, permitted by the wider variety of lending facilities plus some new policies as to how the facilities are to be employed, have greatly increased the influence of the Fund. Thus, instead of losing its clout when the old "Bretton Woods system" died, the IMF has more clout in international affairs than ever before. It has acquired much more self-confidence in its relations with members.

ADVISORY ASSISTANCE

Countries, no less than individuals, sometimes need financial advice. Ever since its inception, the IMF has provided a valuable and wide-ranging service of providing financial advice to its members. Much of this assistance comes as a result of specific requests from countries, such as help in setting up a central bank or in setting up a balance of payments accounting system). In addition, as noted earlier, the so-called credit tranches and special credit facilities generally involve the requirement that the borrowing country take certain recommended fiscal and/or monetary actions in order to remedy some of its difficulties. Even countries as large as Italy and even the United Kingdom have at times been required to implement actions required by the Fund in order to qualify for financial assistance from the Fund. In addition, commercial banks have sometimes made their loans to governments conditional upon the government implementing the suggestions of the IMF. This is

TABLE 5.2   Financial Facilities of the IMF and the Conditions of Their Use

TRANCHE POLICIES

Reserve Tranche

Condition—balance of payments need.

First Credit Tranche

Program representing reasonable efforts to overcome balance of payments difficulties; performance criteria and installments not used.

Higher Credit Tranches

Program giving substantial justification of member's efforts to overcome balance of payments difficulties; resources normally provided in the form of stand-by arrangements which include performance criteria and drawings in installments.

COMPENSATORY FINANCING FACILITY (1963)

Existence of temporary export shortfall for reasons beyond the member's control: member cooperates with Fund in an effort to find appropriate solutions for any balance of payments difficulties.

BUFFER STOCK FINANCING FACILITY (1969)

Existence of an international buffer stock accepted as suitable by Fund; member expected to cooperate with Fund as in the case of compensatory financing.

EXTENDED FACILITY (1974)

Medium-term program for up to three years to overcome structural balance of payments maladjustments; detailed statement of policies and measures for first and subsequent 12-month periods; resources provided in the form of extended arrangements which include performance criteria and drawings in installments.

TRUST FUND (1976)

Provides balance-of-payments loans on very concessionary terms to member developing countries that qualify for assistance.

SUPPLEMENTARY FINANCING FACILITY (1979)

For use in support of programs under stand-by arrangments reaching into the upper credit tranche or beyond, or under extended arrangements, subject to relevant policies on conditionality, phasing, and performance criteria.

SOURCE: adapted from *IMF Survey: Supplement,* September 1979, p. 7.

very important, since banks themselves are not the appropriate institution to be directly advising governments on monetary and fiscal policy.
Also, this parallelism of lending policies between the IMF and banks
makes it more difficult for the borrowers to avoid the strictures of the
Fund by utilizing commerical credit in lieu of IMF credit.

Nobody likes to receive painful advice. Governments are certainly
no exception. However, for domestic political reasons, governments also
are notorious for not taking sound, but difficult, economic actions until
strong pressure is applied or until economic conditions deteriorate to
critical levels. This function of the Fund therefore is a very important
instrument in encouraging governments to take appropriate economic
action sooner, perhaps, than they would if they were acting on their own
volition. Nevertheless, the IMF has been strongly criticized because the
"medicine" it prescribes can have high social costs, such as rising unemployment.

INTERNATIONAL LIQUIDITY

Official governmental liquidity is the total supply of all monetary assets—gold, convertible currencies, and special drawing rights—plus the
borrowing facilities for these assets that are held by central governmental authorities (treasuries or central banks). Figure 5.4 summarizes the
major sources of liquidity.

The prime significance of official liquidity is to serve as a pool of
resources for use when the stability of the national currency is threatened. Such supporting action can occur either via the use of the resources of the stabilization fund in the financial markets or via direct
actions with other governments.

PRIMARY LIQUIDITY

Monetary reserves or international reserves (see item 1 in Figure
5.4) are assets that are *unconditionally* available for whatever use the
government chooses. They are most commonly used for financing intervention in the foreign exchange markets. They are a country's "primary" reserves, since they are automatically and immediately available.
Monetary reserves are sometimes referred to as *owned assets,* but this is
a misnomer since many countries borrow money to enlarge their reserves.

Monetary gold (item 1a in Figure 5.4) is gold that a government is
free to sell or pledge as collateral. As seen above, until the demise of the
old IMF in early 1973, there was an official price for monetary gold.
When countries bought or sold gold among themselves, the price was
fixed. At that time, the governments were forbidden by international

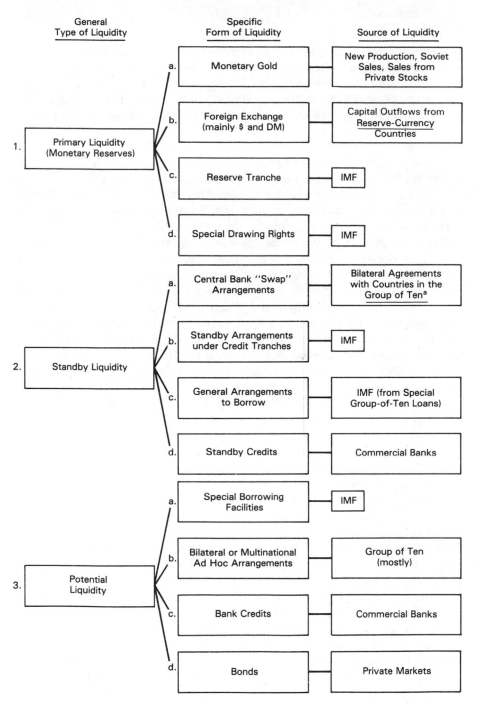

General Type of Liquidity	Specific Form of Liquidity	Source of Liquidity
1. Primary Liquidity (Monetary Reserves)	a. Monetary Gold	New Production, Soviet Sales, Sales from Private Stocks
	b. Foreign Exchange (mainly $ and DM)	Capital Outflows from Reserve-Currency Countries
	c. Reserve Tranche	IMF
	d. Special Drawing Rights	IMF
2. Standby Liquidity	a. Central Bank "Swap" Arrangements	Bilateral Agreements with Countries in the Group of Ten[a]
	b. Standby Arrangements under Credit Tranches	IMF
	c. General Arrangements to Borrow	IMF (from Special Group-of-Ten Loans)
	d. Standby Credits	Commercial Banks
3. Potential Liquidity	a. Special Borrowing Facilities	IMF
	b. Bilateral or Multinational Ad Hoc Arrangements	Group of Ten (mostly)
	c. Bank Credits	Commercial Banks
	d. Bonds	Private Markets

[a]Group of ten: United States, United Kingdom, Germany, France, Netherlands, Belgium, Italy, Sweden, Canada, and Japan, plus Switzerland as an associate member.

FIGURE 5.4   International Liquidity at a Glance

agreement from selling gold in the private markets where the price was much higher. Since the late 1970s there has been no official price for gold; governments have been free to trade gold between themselves at open-market prices. Nevertheless, there has been very little intergovernmental selling, although there has been a limited amount of pledging of gold for intergovernmental loans, for example, from the German to the Italian government in the mid-1970s. Gold has become a very sterile element of international reserves. This condition may very well change in the future, but for now gold is for holding, not for using.

The members of the International Monetary Fund decided in 1975 to discourage the future use of gold as a monetary asset. This was done because of the limited availability of the metal: Production had been falling and private-sector demands were absorbing all annual production. This decision has since been vindicated, in the eyes of many "experts," by the extremely high volatility of the market price of the metal. Such an unstable commodity makes a poor monetary asset. However, other "experts" are so appalled by the very rapid rates of growth of money supply and the ensuing high rates of inflation that they would like to see a return to the discipline of the old ways of using gold at a fixed price as a key element in the international financial system.

The IMF put its beliefs into action by selling 50 percent of all of its gold holdings, half back to its member at the old official price and half in a series of public auctions. The United States supported this action by holding a series of gold auctions of its own. However, as noted, most other governments have chosen to hold on to or to even increase their gold stocks. If gold is ever "reinstated," those governments want to be prepared. Despite its sales of gold, the United States continues to hold by far the largest share of the world's monetary gold.

The *foreign exchange portion* (item 1b in Figure 5.4) of the monetary reserve assets includes all holdings of *reserve currencies,* a small group of major foreign currencies which central banks are willing to hold as part of their monetary reserves. The U.S. dollar is by far the most significant of these currencies, with the German mark also very important. To a lesser extent the British pound, the Swiss franc, the Japanese yen, the French franc, and a few others are also part of this group. These currency holdings result from capital outflows coupled with the willingness of the other countries to hold the currencies.

Reserve tranche (item 1c) is an unconditional interest-free line of credit available from the IMF. Its size is originally determined by the portion of the IMF member's quota which was paid in gold, SDRs, or foreign currency.

Special drawing rights (SDRs) (item 1d) sometimes referred to as *paper gold,* which became operational on January 1, 1970, are the most recent addition to reserve assets. SDRs represent the first effort on the part of the IMF or any international organization in world history to actually create credit *by fiat,* without the backing of equivalent monetary assets. Unlike the traditional credit provisions of the Fund, SDRs are based simply upon the agreement of its member participants to accept them, although members are not required to participate in the SDR program.

The monetary value of the special drawing rights is equal to the weighted average of the value of the world's five major currencies. It is recalculated daily. Figure 5.5 shows how the SDR's value has fluctuated since its inception in 1970.

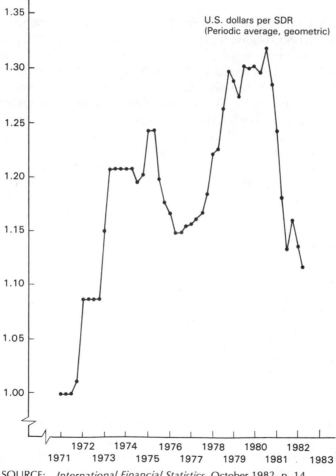

SOURCE: *International Financial Statistics,* October 1982, p. 14.

FIGURE 5.5   Change in the Value of SDR

The SDR is *not a currency*. It is an accounting creation that *exists only in financial records*. Furthermore, only governments and international agencies can own and use SDRs. For example, loans from the IMF are denominated in SDRs. Also, SDRs can be loaned, used for payment, or pledged as loan security by central governments.

The SDR is not an instrument that can be used by the private sector. Nevertheless, the SDR may be used by anyone as a unit of account. Thus, international private-sector loans are sometimes denominated in SDRs. However, the actual transactions involve currencies (usually U.S. dollars). Thus, if 1 SDR = \$1.10, then a 1 million SDR loan would involve the lending of \$1.1 million (1,000,000 SDR × \$1.10). Also, interest and principal would, although denominated in SDRs, be paid in dollars.

SDRs got off to a slow start. They were issued annually in 1970, 1971, and 1972 and totaled less than \$10 billion. However, no additional allotments were made until 1979. In the intervening years, monetary reserves had risen very rapidly (Figure 5.6), so that the relative significance of SDRs shrank rapidly. Nevertheless, the IMF is envisioning a strong role for the SDR. The major idea involves the creation of a substitution account. Under this proposal the IMF would use SDRs to buy excess holdings of dollars and other reserve currencies offered by countries from their monetary reserves.

Figures 5.6 and 5.7 illustrate the growth and changing composition of monetary reserves. Obviously, reserve currencies are the major component. The size of the gold portion is misleading. If the monetary gold stock is valued at the old official price (see *b* in Figure 5.6), its value is understated. If it is valued at market prices (see *a* in Figure 5.6), its value is overstated because, if large quantities of gold were sold on the market, the market price would be depressed and the higher price could not actually be realized. Nevertheless, it is clear that gold is an important element of international monetary reserves.

The monetary reserves category corresponds to the narrow concept of liquidity; it excludes the near-liquid assets described below. However, the following types of assets play a very important role and are, therefore, broadly speaking, part of international liquidity.

STANDBY LIQUIDITY

Standby liquidity— the second group of assets based on the degree of liquidity and the ease of acquisition for a government—involves lines of credit that have been negotiated in advance. (See item 2 in Figure 5.4.) *Swap arrangements* (item 2a) are bilateral agreements between governments that provide for an exchange of currencies for relatively short periods. Both countries can thereby increase their reserves by equal amounts. The initiating country needs the other country's currency for

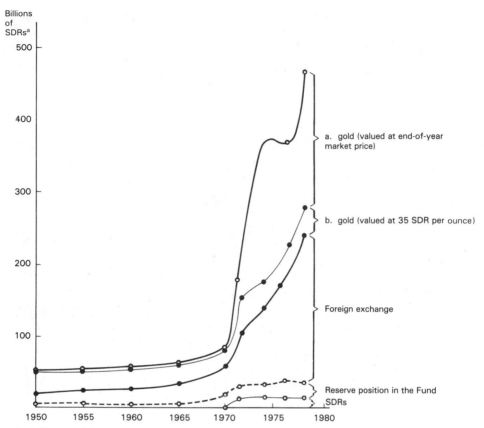

Billions
of
SDRs[a]

a. gold (valued at end-of-year market price)

b. gold (valued at 35 SDR per ounce)

Foreign exchange

Reserve position in the Fund

SDRs

[a]In billions of dollars.
[b]Gold valued at official IMF price of SDR 35/oz.
*No reserve position in IMF years indicated.

FIGURE 5.6   The Composition of International Monetary Reserves

foreign exchange market intervention. The other country takes the funds received and invests them in U.S. Treasury bills, for instance.

   IMF standing arrangements under credit tranche (item 2b) was discussed above and refers to the amount of borrowing that is permitted from the Fund in excess of a country's quota—up to 100 percent above the quota.

   The *general arrangements to borrow (GAB)* (item 2c) is the instrument with which eleven major financial countries have agreed to funnel additional funds through the IMF in order to buttress its credit facilities for aiding threatened reserve currencies.

   Swap arrangements and GAB are essentially tools for the major currencies, but credit tranche is available to all Fund members. *Standby credits* are prearranged lines of credit with commercial banks.

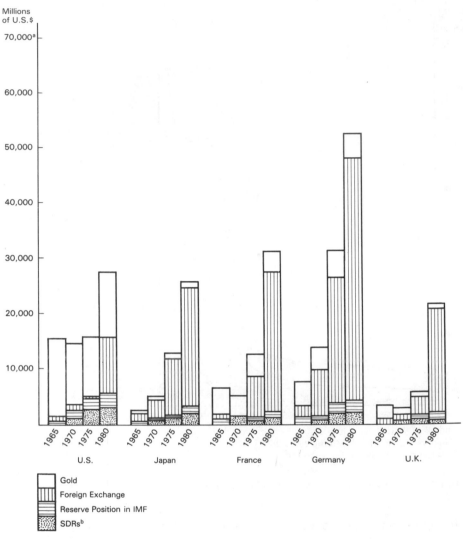

Gold
Foreign Exchange
Reserve Position in IMF
SDRs[b]

[a]In millions of U.S. dollars.
[b]There were no SDRs in 1965.

FIGURE 5.7   Composition of International Reserves for Selected Industrial Countries

POTENTIAL LIQUIDITY

The final category in Figure 5.4, *potential liquidity*, consists of extraordinary lines of credit. These must be negotiated on an ad hoc basis. In the case of bonds, the sale typically takes extensive planning; it cannot be done quickly.

There is thus available to national monetary authorities a wide array of financial resources for the purpose of shoring up unsteady currencies.

EFFECTS OF CURRENCY-VALUE CHANGES

When a currency rises or falls in value, that development has many wide-ranging and sometimes conflicting consequences. Table 5.3 outlines many of the most common effects. The table takes the perspective of a change in the value of the local currency. However, if the reader remembers that a devaluation (or depreciation) of a foreign currency is the same as a revaluation (or appreciation) of the local currency and that a revaluation (or appreciation) of a foreign currency is equivalent to a devaluation (or depreciation) of the local currency, then this table can be used to analyze the most likely impact of currency-value changes either locally or abroad.

Also, it should be borne in mind that these are generalized results. In order to determine the results in a particular country at a particular point in time, it would be necessary to know many other variables, for example, the elasticities of supply and demand, the degree of prosperity or slack in the economy and abroad, political and social conditions both at home and abroad, and so forth.

The table is divided into the following three sections:

A. Ordinary effects of currency-value changes
B. Local groups ordinarily affected *favorably* by the currency-value change
C. Local groups ordinarily affected *unfavorably* by the currency-value change

The left side of the table lists results of downward movements in the local currency, and the right side lists results from upward currency movements.

As can be seen in Table 5.3, a downward movement in a currency's value is inflationary: It will increase almost all prices of imported goods and even prices of many exported goods, which rise to the levels of the world markets. As a result of the devaluation, these levels are higher in terms of local currency. In contrast, an upward movement in a currency's value is anti-inflationary: The prices of imports decrease as do those of some exported goods, which may decline domestically as well as internationally in order to meet world market prices.

An important implication of the declining prices resulting from increases in a currency's value was seen with the rather mild impact upon many of the European economies for several years in the late 1970s due to OPEC's increases in oil prices. Since the oil was priced in dollars, the European currency price of oil rose only moderately as those currencies increased in value against the dollar. However, when those curren-

TABLE 5.3 Impacts of a Change in the Value of a Local Currency

	Devaluation	Revaluation
Definition	*Formal* change downward in a currency's value (*Depreciation* is an informal change downward [float]).	*Formal* change upward in a currency's value (*Appreciation* is an informal upward change [float]).
A. Effects	1. Imports increase in price	1. Imports decrease in price
	2. Exported goods may also increase in price locally but decrease in price as viewed from abroad	2. Exports increase in price (as viewed from abroad) but may fall locally
	3. Local investment becomes less expensive for foreign investors[a]	3. Local investment becomes more expensive for foreign investors[a]
	4. Foreign investment becomes more expensive for local investors[a]	4. Foreign investment becomes less expensive for local investors[a]
	5. Local economic statistics are adversely affected relative to rest of world, especially *inflation* and *GNP*	5. Local economic statistics are favorably affected relative to rest of world, especially *inflation* and *GNP*
	6. Delayed inflows (lags) and accelerated outflows (leads) return to normal	6. Accelerated inflows (leads) and delayed outflows (lags) return to normal
B. Ordinarily, effects are relatively *favorable* upon	1. Local import-competing industries	1. Local consumers
	2. Local exporting industries	2. Local importing industries
	3. Local export-competing industries	3. Local debtors with foreign currency payables
	4. Local money and capital markets and borrowers	4. Local tourists who wish to travel abroad
	5. Local creditors with foreign currency receivables	
	6. Local tourist industries	
C. Ordinarily, effects are relatively *unfavorable* upon	1. Local consumers	1. Local import-competing industries
	2. Local importing industries	2. Local exporting industries
	3. Local debtors with foreign currency payables	3. Local export-competing industries
	4. Local tourists who wish to travel abroad	4. Local money and capital markets and borrowers
		5. Local creditors with foreign currency receivables
		6. Local tourist industries

[a]The rate of return won't necessarily be significantly altered for either debt securities or stock investments.

cies later declined relative to the dollar, the delayed impact of the oil price hikes was felt.

Downward movements in the value of a currency make foreign direct investment more expensive and make local investment more attractive to foreigners. For example, a sharp increase in European investment in the United States in the late 1970s and early 1980s occurred when the weakened value of the dollar was coupled with relatively low prices in the U.S. stock markets. Upward movements in the value of a currency, of course, have the opposite effect.

In anticipation of the change in the value of a currency, there is commonly a disruption of normal money and capital flows, such as the speeding up of payment on a debt in a currency that is expected to strengthen, while slowing down payment in currencies that are expected to weaken. These effects are examples of what are called *leads and lags*. After the currency change occurs, these effects will unwind themselves; this result is somewhat favorable for a weakened currency and somewhat adverse for the strengthened currency.

The second section of the table shows that downward movements of a local currency are favorable to such industries as import competitors, exporters, creditors with foreign currency receivables, and the local tourist industry, since more foreigners may visit the country and fewer local residents are able to afford to travel abroad. Upward movements of a currency favor such groups as consumers (who are able to buy imported goods less expensively), importing industries, debtors with foreign currency payables, and local tourists who wish to travel abroad.

The groups that are hurt by a downward currency movement are those who are helped by an upward movement. Likewise, those who are helped by a downward movement are those who are hurt in the event of an upward movement. (See sections B and C of Table 5.3.)

SUMMARY

The international monetary system has changed greatly since the early 1970s, For governments, the new system poses numerous difficulties. Coming, as it did, at the same time as the soaring oil prices and massive balance-of-payments imbalances, governments have found their economies being buffeted by international economic tides to a much greater extent than previously.

The IMF has become a much more important source of assistance for even major industrial countries. The Fund has changed greatly in function in the face of the new realities of the international financial system. It is both more mature and more flexible. However, the system is still very much in a condition of flux. As a result, both the IMF and the world's governments continue to find the 1990s to be a challenging period.

For the international manager also, such developments as floating exchange rates and the much greater degree of volatility of exchange rates accompanying floating have brought about a much greater degree of uncertainty in the foreign exchange markets. The next chapter examines the nature of those markets.

KEY TERMS

APPRECIATION
BRETTON WOODS
CONVERTIBILITY
DEPRECIATION
DEVALUATION
EUROPEAN MONETARY
  SYSTEM
FLOAT
  CLEAN
  DIRTY
  MANAGED
GENERAL
  ARRANGEMENTS TO
  BORROW

IMF
INCONVERTIBILITY
INTERNATIONAL
  RESERVES
INTERVENTION POINT
LIQUIDITY
MONETARY RESERVES
PAR VALUE
RESERVE CURRENCY
REVALUATION
SPECIAL DRAWING
  RIGHT (SDR)
STABILIZATION FUND

STANDARD OF
  DEFERRED PAYMENT
  OR RECEIPT
STANDARD OF VALUE
STORE OF VALUE
SUBSCRIPTION QUOTA
SWAP ARRANGEMENT
TRANCHE
  CREDIT
  GOLD
  RESERVE
UNIT OF ACCOUNT
UNIT OF EXCHANGE

REVIEW QUESTIONS

1. What is necessary in order for something to be used as money?
2. What problems was the conference at Bretton Woods trying to resolve? What organizations were created to resolve the different problems?
3. What are the basic goals of the IMF.
4. Who are the members of the IMF? How do they qualify for membership?
5. What brought about the collapse of the old IMF system?
6. What are a government's goals under the three different types of float?
7. How does a government intervene to strengthen its currency? to weaken its currency?
8. What happens to stop a government from continuing to strengthen its currency? weaken its currency? (that is, how long can the government continue to intervene?)

9. What are the results to the domestic economy of an overvalued currency? of an undervalued currency?
10. What groups are hurt or helped by currency-value changes?

SUGGESTED REFERENCES

ABRAMS, RICHARD K. "Federal Reserve Intervention Policy," *Economic Review* (Federal Reserve Bank of Kansas City), March 1979; pp. 15–23.

ALIBER, ROBERT *International Money Game* (2nd ed.). New York: Basic Books, Inc., Publishers, 1976.

BLOOMFIELD, ARTHUR I. *Monetary Policy Under the International Gold Standard: 1880–1914.* New York: Federal Reserve Bank of New York (monograph).

COHEN, BENJAMIN J. *Organizing the World's Money.* New York: Basic Books, Inc., Publishers, 1977.

EVANS, THOMAS G. *Currency Carousel.* New York: Dow Jones, 1977.

FEDERAL RESERVE BANK OF SAN FRANCISCO *Search for Uncertainty in Uncertain World,* (pamphlet).

ROLFE, SIDNEY, AND JAMES L. BURTLE *Great Wheel.* New York: McGraw-Hill Book Company, 1973.

SOLOMON, ROBERT *International Monetary System, 1945–1976.* New York: Harper & Row Publishers, Inc., 1977.

TRIFFIN, ROBERT *Our International Monetary System: Yesterday, Today and Tomorrow.* New York: Random House, Inc., 1966.

6

Foreign
Exchange

In the last chapter we examined the nature of money and of the world monetary system as it exists today under the benevolent guidance of the IMF. Now we turn to the "micro" side of this system—the foreign exchange markets—where various currencies are actually traded.

An understanding of the foreign exchange markets, both their pitfalls and the mechanisms for avoiding the risks, is critical to anyone attempting to understand international business. Even if a company is able to export or import and borrow or invest abroad in its own currency, managers must understand the impact of foreign exchange markets upon their customers or suppliers.

Foreign exchange markets are not easy to understand for most people. Therefore, more review questions have been included at the end of this chapter than in other chapters. The reader is strongly recommended to work all exercises.

The previous chapter offered an overview of the foreign exchange markets. This chapter examines them in detail. Chapter 21 discusses how corporate managers respond to the risks and uncertainty of being exposed to fluctuations of exchange rates.

FOREIGN EXCHANGE MARKETS

The term *foreign exchange (FX)* is used loosely to mean a foreign currency. More precisely, it refers to an interchange of foreign currencies such as the exchange of American dollars in the *foreign exchange market* for British pounds.

A foreign exchange market is not so much a place as a process. It is the financial system for the exchange of currencies. In most countries there is no one, specific, physical marketplace for the exchange of currencies. Instead, the foreign exchange market is comprised of the system of corporations, banks, and brokers who buy and sell currencies. Virtually all this buying and selling is done via telephone or telex, very seldom is it done in person.

"RULES OF THE GAME"

Foreign exchange markets are generally rather informal arrangements. There is relatively little governmental regulation. There are no schools for training or standardized competency tests to be passed.

It is basically a market in which a participant's word is his or her bond: Verbal agreements are binding contracts. In order to be accepted as a participant an individual must not only know how to participate (skills must mostly be learned on the job), but others must believe that he or she will actually live up to his or her word. Someone who violates the rules simply won't be able to operate in the market.

THE PARTICIPANTS

The customers: Most supply and demand forces within the foreign exchange markets generally come from *institutional investors* (such as investment bankers) and *corporations,* whose involvement basically results from their ordinary operations arising from international trade and factor flows. Companies also become involved in the foreign exchange markets through extraordinary operations designed either to defend a company against fluctuations in the value of currencies in which they have claims and liabilities, or sometimes to speculate outright on changes in currency values.

Banks which do not have their own foreign exchange trading operations are also important sources of supply and demand.

Governments are a special breed in the foreign exchange markets. When they buy or sell foreign currencies as commercial transactions (for example, to pay for foreign purchases), their role is little different from that of corporations. However, governments often buy or sell currencies for the deliberate purpose of affecting the market. This is done in order to either strengthen or weaken its currency in the FX market. This "intervention" in the market is discussed in detail later in this chapter.

Individuals who buy foreign currencies to travel or to pay a bill from a foreign country or to transfer funds to someone overseas are very insignificant factors in the market. They are served by an office at the bank other than the foreign exchange desk.

International agencies (for instance, the International Monetary Fund or the International Bank for Reconstruction and Development) are another distinct group of less-important customers.

The FX trading desks of commercial banks: When corporations, governments, or international agencies desire to trade, they do not usually deal directly with one another. Instead, they generally utilize the *foreign exchange departments* of banks—*the FX traders.* The banks themselves are the basic "makers of the market": They generally buy and sell from their own portfolios of foreign currencies. Thus, if the treasurer of IBM Corporation phones the foreign exchange trading desk at Manufacturers Hanover Trust Company to buy DM 10 million or to sell £1 million, then the bank will sell from or buy those currencies for its own account.

The FX trading desks of commercial banks are not essentially in the business of pursuing profits via investments in various currencies. Rather, the traders (who are also called *FX dealers*) can operate quite successfully simply as a result of the small difference between the price at which they buy currencies and the price at which they sell them; this difference is called the *spread.*

Since the FX dealers are constantly buying or selling currencies for their own account, they do have inventories, or *positions,* in the various currencies which they trade. Although all the banks with FX trading operations are "makers of markets" for the major currencies (for instance, the U.S. dollar, German deutsche mark, British pound sterling, French franc, and Japanese yen), they do not all actively participate in markets for less significant currencies. If the bank has contracted to buy more of a particular currency than it has contracted to sell, it is said to have a *long position* in that currency. If it has contracted to sell more than to buy, its position is *short.* If purchases equal sales, then it has a *square position.*

FX brokers: Just as corporations, business organizations, and so forth do not normally seek to make FX deals themselves but instead utilize banks, the banks themselves generally do not deal directly with one another. Instead, they contact *FX brokers,* specialists who bring orders to buy and sell together. There is no law requiring the use of brokers, but banks commonly find this arrangement more convenient than dealing directly with one another. The brokers for their part generally deal only with banks, not corporations, and so forth.

The brokers usually do *not* buy or sell for their own accounts. A broker will bring two banks together. For example, a broker will direct a bank wishing to sell FF 15 million to a bank that has them to sell. The broker will charge a small *commission* to both the buyer and seller.

EXCHANGE RATES

Since there is no universal world currency, a currency is valued in the foreign exchange markets in terms of other currencies in the market. The price of one currency in terms of another is called the *exchange rate*. For a single currency there can be more than 150 different exchange rates. For example 1 U.S. dollar might be worth 2.5 deutschemarks, 25 pesos, 220 yen, or 1600 lire—all at the same time.

SOURCES OF FX INFORMATION

There are a variety of sources of information on the values of the major currencies. Newspapers such as the *New York Times,* the *Wall Street Journal,* and the *Financial Times* (London) publish the *previous day's* exchange rates on a daily basis (see Figure 6.1) along with the stock and bond prices. More complete information together with commentary upon market trends is published in weekly newsletters published by some of the major banks.

For more up-to-date data on prevailing quotations, corporate treasurers, bank traders, and brokers can subscribe to the Reuters Market Report. These quotes, which can be read directly off a television-like screen, indicate very recent quotes of dozens of banks.

It is important to bear in mind that none of the FX rates listed in the newletters, newspapers, or even in any of the electronic information services (e.g., Reuters Market Report or Telerate) are offers to trade. They are merely indicative rates. The bank's FX traders need to be contacted directly in order to obtain a firm quote.

It is also important for the reader to understand that these are wholesale quotes. For example, typical minimum amounts that would be traded in the United States would be:

pound sterling:	£	500,000
deutschemark:	DM	2,000,000
French franc:	FF	6,000,000
Japanese yen:	¥	200,000,000
Italian lira:	Lit	1,500,000,000

Such quotes are very different from quotes which individuals, who are buying or selling small amounts, would receive at the customer desk. The retail customer FX desk typically will not even be in the same department of the bank as the wholesale FX dealer. Since the amounts traded in the former are so small, the spreads on quotes to individuals need to be large to make the service profitable to the bank. Therefore,

Foreign Exchange

Friday, February 3, 1984

The New York foreign exchange selling rates below apply to trading among banks in amounts of $1 million and more, as quoted at 3 p.m. Eastern time by Bankers Trust Co. Retail transactions provide fewer units of foreign currency per dollar.

Country	U.S. $ equiv. Friday	Thurs.	Currency per U.S. $ Friday	Thurs.
Argentina (Peso)	.03921	.03921	25.502	25.502
Australia (Dollar)	.9230	.9237	1.0834	1.0826
Austria (Schilling)	.05115	.05141	19.55	19.45
Belgium (Franc)				
Commercial rate	.01782	.01758	56.105	56.885
Financial rate	.01739	.01724	57.500	58.000
Brazil (Cruzeiro)	.0009722	.0009722	1028.50	1028.50
Britain (Pound)	1.4330	1.4227	.6978	.7028
30-Day Forward	1.4335	1.4233	.6976	.7026
90-Day Forward	1.4347	1.4245	.6970	.7020
180-Day Forward	1.4362	1.4259	.6963	.7013
Canada (Dollar)	.8029	.8027	1.2455	1.2458
30-Day Forward	.8028	.8027	1.2456	1.2458
90-Day Forward	.8028	.8027	1.2456	1.2458
180-Day Forward	.8028	.8026	1.2456	1.2459
Chile (Official rate)	.01135	.01135	88.04	88.04
China (Yuan)	.4834	.4834	2.0686	2.0686
Colombia (Peso)	.01108	.01108	90.19	90.19
Denmark (Krone)	.1008	.0999	9.9200	10.0100
Ecuador (Sucre)				
Official rate	.01791	.01791	55.81	55.81
Floating rate	.01129	.01129	88.55	88.55
Finland (Markka)	.1708	.1706	5.8550	5.8600
France (Franc)	.1189	.1179	8.4050	8.4750
30-Day Forward	.1185	.1177	8.4350	8.4960
90-Day Forward	.1173	.1166	8.5200	8.5760
180-Day Forward	.1160	.1152	8.6200	8.6750
Greece (Drachma)	.009813	.009775	101.90	102.30
Hong Kong (Dollar)	.1283	.1282	7.7935	7.7965
India (Rupee)	.0931	.0931	10.7411	10.7411
Indonesia (Rupiah)	.001004	.001004	996.00	996.00
Ireland (Punt)	1.1235	1.1200	.8900	.8928
Israel (Shekel)	.008053	.008053	124.17	124.17
Italy (Lira)	.0005955	.0005896	1679.20	1696.00
Japan (Yen)	.004298	.004280	232.65	233.60
30-Day Forward	.004310	.004292	232.02	232.96
90-Day Forward	.004333	.004317	230.74	231.64
180-Day Forward	.004372	.004355	228.70	229.61
Lebanon (Pound)	.1706	.1706	5.86	5.86
Malaysia (Ringgit)	.4285	.4280	2.3335	2.3360
Mexico (Peso)				
Floating rate	.006024	.006024	166.00	166.00
Netherlands (Guilder)	.3242	.3211	3.0840	3.1135
New Zealand (Dollar)	.6560	.6535	1.5244	1.5302
Norway (Krone)	.1288	.1277	7.7600	7.8275
Pakistan (Rupee)	.07490	.07407	13.35	13.50
Peru (Sol)	.0004262	.0004262	2346.15	2346.15
Philippines (Peso)	.01742	.01742	14.00	14.00
Portugal (Escudo)	.007352	.007352	136.00	136.00
Saudi Arabia (Riyal)	.2849	.2848	3.5100	3.5105
Singapore (Dollar)	.4703	.4703	2.1260	2.1260
South Africa (Rand)	.8100	.7940	1.2345	1.2594
South Korea (Won)	.001250	.001250	799.60	799.60
Spain (Peseta)	.006443	.006391	155.20	156.45
Sweden (Krona)	.1238	.1232	8.0750	8.1160
Switzerland (Franc)	.4552	.4510	2.1965	2.2170
30-Day Forward	.4577	.4534	2.1848	2.2052
90-Day Forward	.4625	.4582	2.1621	2.1823
180-Day Forward	.4694	.4649	2.1300	2.1506
Taiwan (Dollar)	.02488	.02488	40.19	40.19
Thailand (Baht)	.04387	.04387	22.79	22.79
Uruguay (New Peso)				
Financial	.02144	.02144	46.63	46.63
Venezuela (Bolivar)				
Official rate	.1941	.1941	5.15	5.15
Floating rate	.07698	.07698	12.99	12.99
W. Germany (Mark)	.3659	.3621	2.7325	2.7610
30-Day Forward	.3671	.3633	2.7237	2.7523
90-Day Forward	.3695	.3657	2.7059	2.7342
180-Day Forward	.3729	.3690	2.6814	2.7098
SDR	1.04185	1.03981	.959836	.961719

Special Drawing Rights are based on exchange rates for the U.S., West German, British, French and Japanese currencies. Source: International Monetary Fund.
z-Not quoted.

FIGURE 6.1　Foreign Exchange Quotations

individuals would not receive quotes that are nearly as attractive as those in Figure 6.1.

In addition to the retail FX desks of a commercial bank, in major cities of some countries there are specialized retail FX companies that buy and sell relatively small amounts of foreign currencies. A major example in the United States is Deak-Perera in large cities like New York and Chicago.

CROSS RATES

Note that if $1 = 25 pesos and $1 = 250 yen, then 25 pesos = 250 yen, or 1 peso = 10 yen. This exchange rate between these two currencies, which we determined because we knew the exchange rates of both currencies in terms of the dollar, is known as the *cross rate* between those two currencies. The cross rate is calculated indirectly because of the direct relationships of both currencies in terms of a third (the U.S. dollar in this case, although any third currency in which both currencies are quoted could be used). The cross rate is an important relationship for many pairs of currencies since market equilibrium would require that when any of these three exchange rates change, then at least one of the other two must change as well. For example, if the dollar-yen exchange rate changes to $1 = 200 yen, then 25 pesos = 200 yen (or 1 peso = 8 yen) if the peso has not changed relative to the dollar. If 1 peso still equals 10 yen, then $1 now equals only 20 pesos.

For many pairs of currencies there are few or no direct markets. They must be traded through a third currency. For example, a purchase of Peruvian soles with Dutch guilders will typically first involve the purchase of dollars with guilders and then soles with dollars. Thus, the exchange rate between the guilder and the sol would have been determined by the cross rate between the two currencies, and the cross rate would result from the exchange rate of both currencies in terms of the dollar.

Banks in the United States do not offer much cross-rate trading on a broad scale. Therefore, a customer who wants to sell deutschemarks and buy lire would first have to sell the deutschemarks for dollar and then buy lire with the dollar. However, overseas it is quite common for banks to do cross-rate trading and charge only a single spread, such as is done in Paris, where one can buy deutschemarks for pounds sterling.

QUOTATIONS OF EXCHANGE RATE

Quotations of FX rates can be very confusing. The quotations are, of course, prices for currencies. However, the pricing system for currencies is very different from the pricing system in a grocery store or department store.

First, as seen above, each currency has many different prices—the number of deutschemarks per dollar, yen per dollar, and so forth. (Nothing simple like apples at 49¢ per pound or gasoline at $1.50 per gallon!)

Second, exchange rates may be quoted as DM/$ (for example, DM 1.7500 = $1) or $/DM. ($0.5714 = DM 1). For the currency in the numerator, this is said to be a *direct quote*. Thus, DM 1.7500/$1 is German direct, whereas $0.5714/DM is U.S. direct. Conversely, for the currency in the denominator, it is said to be an *indirect quote*. Thus, DM

1.7500/$ is U.S. indirect whereas \$0.5714/DM is German indirect. Note that the indirect is simply the reciprocal or inverse of the direct quote.

$$\text{indirect quote} = \frac{1}{\text{direct quote}}$$

$$\text{DM2.0000/\$} = \frac{1}{\text{\$0.5000/DM}}$$

Similarly,

$$\text{direct quote} = \frac{1}{\text{indirect quote}}$$

$$\text{\$0.5000/DM} = \frac{1}{\text{DM2.0000/\$}}$$

Figure 6.1 lists FX quotes in both dollar direct (columns 1 and 2) and dollar indirect terms (columns 3 and 4).

It has become the custom in recent years for FX dealers to quote the more valuable currency in the denominator (e.g., DM/$, FF/$ and $/£).

Third, price quotes usually involve both *buy and sell quotes* (also called *bid and ask* or *bid and offer quotes,* that is, bid to buy and offer to sell). *The buy quote is always given first.* For example, when a corporation calls its bank's FX trading desk for the deutschemark quote for dollars, it might be told DM 1.7500–1.7520. This means the bank would buy $1 for DM 1.7500 or sell $1 for DM 1.7520. Since the bank must earn its profit from the "spread" between the two quotes, obviously the first quote (that is, the buy quote) must be less than the second, the sell quote. This is certainly more complex than a woman's clothing store, which lists a selling price, but never a buying price!

Actually, participants in the FX markets use their own special brand of shorthand to minimize the awkwardness of FX quotations. Thus, the quotation noted above would actually appear as DM 1.7500–20. The "20" for the sell quote must be understood to be only the last two decimals (that is, DM 0.0020) of the actual quote; all preceding numbers (DM 1.75) are understood to be the same as for the buy quote.

Fourth, price quotations for major currencies can be obtained for today but also for next month or even six months or more from today. The market for buying or selling today is called the *spot market.* (Actually, it usually provides for closing a contract in one business day.) The market for closing contracts on all subsequent days, such as for three months, is called the *forward market.* Thus, the dollar might be quoted as follows:

SPOT	ONE-MONTH	THREE-MONTH	SIX-MONTH
DM 1.7500–20	DM 1.7200–30	DM 1.6600–50	DM 1.5700–75

Quotes could be obtained for any intervening period as well (e.g., two weeks).

If the forward quote is less than spot, the currency (dollar in this case) is selling at a *discount*. If the forward is more than the spot, the reference currency is trading at a *premium*. If the dollar is at a discount, then the deutsche mark is trading at a premium and vice versa.

Note that the spread between the buy and sell quotes increases as the maturity of the contract increases, because the bank, which is buying or selling out of its own portfolio, needs more protection (reward) for the greater uncertainty of longer contracts. When forward contracts are signed, no money is paid or received: Money will change hands only at a future data—the *settlement date*.

The method of explicitly stating forward quotes as noted above involves what is called *outright quotations*. Another form of shorthand is generally used by sophisticated participants in the market called *swap quotations*, which involve stating forward quotes as the *difference* between the forward and spot quotes. Thus, the quotes mentioned above could also be written as follows:

SPOT	ONE-MONTH	THREE-MONTH	SIX-MONTH
DM 1.7500–20	300–290	900–870	1800–1745

Decimals are not used with swap quotes, but it is understood that there are as many decimals in the swap quote as in the outright spot quote (for example, .0300–.0290 and so forth).

In order to convert swap quotations into outright quotations, they must be either *added to* or *subtracted from* spot quotes. If the swap buy quote is larger than the swap sell quote (such as in 300–290), then both are subtracted from the spot quotes. This occurs because the currency being quoted (the dollar in this case) is trading at a forward discount. For example, the outright quotes for the swap quotes given above on the dollar can be calculated as follows:

SPOT	ONE-MONTH		THREE-MONTH		SIX-MONTH	
DM 1.7500–20	1.7500	1.7520	1.7500	1.7520	1.7500	1.7520
	−.0300	−.0290	−.0900	−.0870	−.1800	−.1745
	1.7200	1.7230	1.6600	1.6650	1.5700	1.5775

This is exactly as was seen in the outright quotes above.

If, on the other hand, the forward buy quote is less than the forward sell quote, then the currency being quoted is selling at a forward premium. In this event, the swap quotes must be *added* to the spot quotes.

Whether to add or subtract swap quotes to the spot quotes is always confusing at first. However, a simple rule of thumb is that if, when you add or subtract the swap quotes to the spot quotes, the *spreads* between the buy and sell quotes *increase* (as they should when the maturities get longer), then the correct method was used. If the spread *decreases,* something is wrong!

DETERMINATION OF EXCHANGE RATES: THE SPOT MARKET

The rate of exchange between two currencies is basically the result of two forces: the market forces of supply and demand plus governmental interference.

Supply and demand: Forces in the FX markets result from a diverse and complicated set of pressures. Some of these are "ordinary" market forces, while others are extraordinary.

Ordinary market forces are those that occur under normal market conditions. Included are both the effects of trade and of capital flows. Thus, the purchase and sales of currencies, which accompany such transactions as grain exports; machine tool imports; tourist expenditures; the payment of dividends, foreign aid, and workers' remittances; short-term investments; and direct investments could all affect the value of a currency in FX markets.

Such "ordinary" market forces are not usually balanced. As a result, countries run balance of payments surpluses or deficits (see Chapter 10).

In addition, fluctuations in such "ordinary" market forces can occur. For example, as economies move through economic boom and recession cycles, import demand varies. Also, interest-rate movements, which tend to accompany such economic swings, affect capital flows: When an economy is strong, interest rates rise. This condition tends to attract funds from abroad and to decrease the outflow of funds from the domestic economy.

Even within these normal business cycles there are seasonal patterns that can affect currencies. For example, large net inflows resulting from tourist expenditures tend to strengthen the Spanish peseta and, to a lesser extent, the lira each summer. On the other hand, heavy capital expatriation tends to weaken the Canadian dollar each December.

However, the pressures that can affect a country's balance of payments may or may not affect its currency's value and vice versa. For example, imports into the United States for which a U.S. company pays dollars would not necessarily affect the value of the U.S. dollar if the exporter does not sell those dollars but instead invests the receipts in the U.S. dollar or Eurodollar markets. On the other hand, if a company were to borrow Eurodollars and use them to buy British pounds, this action would affect the dollar's value without necessarily affecting the U.S. balance of payments.

All the situations above are examples of ordinary market forces. They are normal pressures that occur as a result of basic market conditions. In addition, extraordinary pressure can develop that can temporarily, but often severely, distort the FX markets. Political and social turmoils or anticipation of them are prominent examples. Apprehension of the possibility of Communist Party victories in French and Italian elections periodically weakens those currencies. Likewise, rioting in South Korea in 1980 produced downward pressure on its currency.

Major developments or anticipation of them can also produce *upward* pressures on a currency. For example, if an anticipated change of government is viewed as favorable by the market, the impact would be to strengthen a currency.

The extraordinary development can also be economic. For example, an announcement of a major oil find would be very bullish (creating an extreme upward movement) for a currency.

Another prominent extraordinary economic development results from anticipated major changes of exchange rates. As is discussed below, governments often resist the tendency of ordinary market pressures to increase or decrease the value of the government's currency. When the distortion becomes too great, companies acting defensively and speculators are tempted to take extraordinary actions in anticipation of the delayed change—a change which will likely be much greater because it was delayed. This type of situation is discussed in detail below.

Normal market forces: Currencies are basically commodities. In the absence of governmental interference, basic market supply and demand forces determine a currency's value, just as they do in commodity markets for wheat, copper, or frozen pork bellies.

Figure 6.2 illustrates market equilibrium for the British pound sterling at one point in time. Under the supply and demand conditions that have been assumed in the diagram, equilibrium of the exchange rate for the pound sterling is realized at a quantity q_1 and a price of $1.50/£.

As with many other supply and demand situations, shifts in either the supply or demand pressures change the price (that is, the exchange rate) for the pound. In Figure 6.3 an increase in demand conditions (from $D_£$ to $D'_£$) with no change in supply conditions leads to an increase in the exchange rate ($D'_£$) for sterling (to $1.60 in this example), even though the supply of pounds offered has also increased to q_2. This could result from an increase in British exports or an increase in British interest rates, either change would increase demand for the pound sterling.

Governmental interference: Some governments arbitrarily choose an exchange rate (or rates) for their currency and impose it by governmental fiat. This is often abetted by extensive trade, exchange,

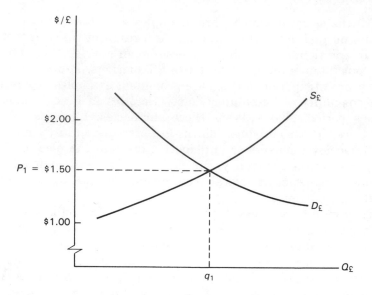

FIGURE 6.2   Free-Market Supply and Demand for the Pound Sterling (£)

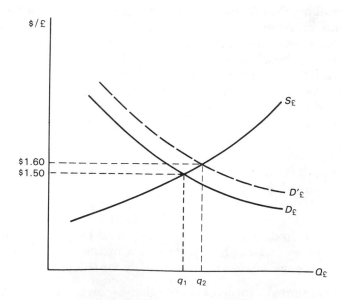

FIGURE 6.3   An Increase in Demand for the Pound Sterling Without Any Increase in Supply

and capital controls, as discussed in Chapter 4. However, the basic
method for governmental determination of an exchange rate requires
that the government be prepared to adjust demand and supply conditions for its currency in response to changes in private foreign exchange
markets. This can be done in many instances without extraordinary
controls. For example, Figure 6.4 illustrates how the British government
could respond to increased demand for the pound sterling in the FX
markets (that is, from $D_£$ to $D'_£$) by increasing the supply of the currency
(from $S_£$ to $S'_£$) via the government's own intervention in the FX markets. In the absence of governmental response to the increased demand,
the price increases to \$1.60 (as seen in Figure 6.3). By actually shifting
the supply curve and by increasing the supply of sterling to q_3, the
British government could keep the price from rising above \$1.50. In this
process the government buys foreign currencies with the sterling; the
government's holdings of foreign currencies in its international reserves
would therefore increase.

In Figure 6.5 a related but different change has occurred in the
market. The *market supply curve* for the pound sterling has shifted from
point a to $S''_£$, as opposed to the shift in the *market demand curve* in
Figure 6.4. Without a governmental response, the quantity of sterling
traded in the FX markets would decline to q_4, with a corresponding
increase in the exchange rate to \$1.55. In this situation the British
government could again respond by buying foreign currencies with ster-

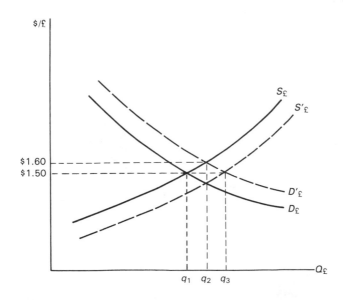

FIGURE 6.4   Governmental Increase of the Supply of £ ($S'_£$) in Response
to an Increase in Private-Sector Demand for £ ($D'_£$)

ling and thereby increasing the supply of sterling so that $S''_£$ shifts back to $S_£$ (movement to point b). The exchange rate would again return to $1.50.

In both of the two examples above, there would have been an insufficient supply of sterling relative to demand in the market. This could result from either a private-sector *increase in the demand* for the pound sterling (Figure 6.3) or a private-sector *decrease in the supply* of pound sterling (Figure 6.5) The government's response in either case was to buy foreign currencies by selling sterling. This selling of sterling is, of course, an increase in the British money supply. The purchase of foreign currencies increases the British government's international reserves.

In Figure 6.6 a different type of problem confronts the British government—a *decrease in demand* for sterling (movement c), which causes an excess supply of the pound and leads to a decline in its value to $1.40. In this situation, the government cannot respond as it did in Figures 6.4 and 6.5, since by selling additional sterling it would simply aggravate the excess supply conditions even more. In order to rectify conditions of inadequate demand for its currency, the British government could respond in the FX markets by buying sterling, that is, by increasing the demand for the pound (movement d). This is accomplished by using the government's holdings of foreign currencies (in its international reserves) to absorb sterling from the market. Once again the FX rate for the pound sterling would return to the government-imposed equilibrium of $1.50.

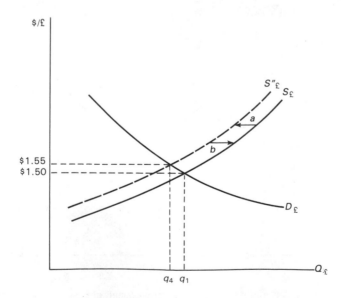

FIGURE 6.5   Governmental Increase in the Supply of £ (back to $S_£$) in Response to a Decline to $S''_£$ in the Private-Sector Supply of £

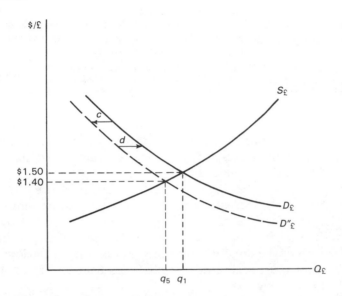

FIGURE 6.6 Governmental Increase in the Demand for £ (Back to $D_\pounds$) in Response to a Decrease in Private-Sector Demand ($D''_\pounds$)

Note that in the exhibits above it was assumed that the British government intervened in the FX markets to maintain the old equilibrium price for sterling. As is seen in Chapter 5, such governmental intervention was required under the Bretton Woods agreement. By using its international reserves (see Figure 6.6), a government can buy its own currency in the FX markets and thereby increase the demand for its own currency (and also decrease the currency's supply and the level of the government's international reserves). On the other hand, in Figures 6.4 and 6.5 it was seen that by buying foreign currency with its own currency—and thereby increasing the supply of its own currency in the FX markets as well as the money supply and its holdings of international reserves—a government can also maintain equilibrium in the foreign exchange market when there is insufficient supply of its currency in the private markets.

These examples illustrate several important points that were introduced in the previous chapter:

1. A country's own currency cannot be part of that country's international reserves, but can be used to acquire such reserves.
2. A government's ability to strengthen its own currency in the FX markets is limited by its capacity for buying its currency with FX. Such foreign currencies come from its primary and secondary international reserves.
3. This process of purchasing its own currency reduces the money supply.

4. There is no *absolute* limit to a government's ability to buy FX with its own currency, since a government controls the supply of its own currency and can increase that supply as much as it desires.

5. The acquisition of foreign currency increases the domestic money supply, which may cause inflation. This situation imposes a *relative* limit (but not absolute) upon a government's ability to buy FX with its own currency.

Thus, a government can continue to maintain the demand for its own currency as long as its international reserves are sufficient or until this process of buying up its own currency contracts the domestic money supply to an undesirable extent.

Similarly, a government can resist upward pressure on its currency's value by simply increasing its money supply to accommodate the growing demand for it in the foreign exchange markets. However, increases in the money supply that exceed the basic increases dictated by the real growth of the domestic economy can be very inflationary. Thus, the government must seek a delicate balance between its FX goals and its domestic monetary goals.

As long as a government is willing and able to buy and sell its currency in almost limitless quantities, it has the capacity to name the value of its currency. This same process applies to other commodities as well. For example, the U.S. government almost single-handedly maintained the value of gold at $35 per ounce from 1934 to 1971 by the simple measure of being prepared to either buy or sell it at that price (adjusted for small transactions costs). Similarly, the European Economic Community maintains the market price of such basic commodities as butter by either supplying or demanding butter in sufficient quantities to clear the market. Mostly it demands butter, since at the artificially high price that is maintained the supply is usually excessive. Also, domestic monetary policy can accomplish a similar result with interest rates by varying the money supply. For example, the U.S. central bank—the Federal Reserve—kept interest rates unrealistically low in the late 1970s by increasing the money supply at an excessive rate.

The effects of changing interest rates: The illustrations in Figures 6.4, 6.5, and 6.6 are examples of efforts by a government to modify movements in the FX value of its own currency. In those examples the procedure involved changes in the government's supply of or demand for its own currency. The reader should be aware, however, that a government can also induce changes in the private sector by changing the domestic interest rate. By allowing (or causing) the domestic interest rate to rise relative to foreign rates, a government can keep interest-rate–sensitive domestic funds from being so anxious to move abroad and can encourage funds from abroad to move into the country. Conversely, declines in domestic interest rates have the opposite effect by encouraging outflows and discouraging inflows. Thus, interest-rate policy can be used in conjunction with or in lieu of FX market intervention to affect a currency's value.

FX actions by foreign governments: It should also be noted that if there is insufficient demand for the pound sterling relative to the U.S. dollar, then there must be excessive demand for the dollar. Any imbalance in the FX markets is therefore bilateral. It affects a minimum of two currencies (and usually other currencies as well). The imbalance can be attacked from either or both countries. For example, instead of the United Kingdom acting to combat the excessive demand of sterling (as illustrated in Figure 6.4), the U.S. government or even a third party such as the European Economic community could have been the source of the governmental intervention in the FX markets. Coordinated international efforts are common. The British government might even lend pounds sterling to other governments to facilitate such intervention, for example, the swap lines discussed in Chapter 5.

Purchasing-power parity: Many forces have been identified as sources of pressure that lead to changes in the values of spot market exchange rates. Extraordinary forces can temporarily distort the markets. Governmental intervention can also cause temporary distortion and often for extensive periods. However, over the long run, which may vary from less than a year to many years, the principal explanatory variable to relative movements in exchange rates is the *difference in inflation rates*. This notion is expressed in the *purchasing-power parity (PPP) theory*.

The essential idea of PPP is that the normal FX market forces will sooner or later be affected by differences in inflation rates. The theory suggests that the exchange rate between two currencies will move to maintain equality in the buying power (that is, *parity* in purchasing power) of the two currencies. For example, if, at an initial rate of exchange of £1 = $2, £100 will buy the same assortment of goods and services in the United Kingdom as $200 will in the United States, then PPP exists between the two countries. If inflation rates are the same in both countries, then the purchasing power of £100 remains approximately equal to $200, although, as a result of inflation, the real value of both currencies will have declined.

If, however, the rates of inflation between two countries vary, then the buying power of £100 will not remain equal to $200. For example, if inflation is 10 percent in the United States and only 5 percent in the United Kingdom, then £100 would be able to buy more than $200. (Again, bear in mind that because of inflation neither amount of money would buy as much as it did before prices rose. Thus, neither £100 nor $200 will buy as much as formerly, but £100 will now buy more than $200 does now.) Under these conditions, holders of dollars could buy more goods by buying pounds with dollars and importing from the United Kingdom. So long as the exchange rate remains unchanged, this trend would continue. As a result, there would be an upward pressure upon sterling and a corresponding downward pressure upon the dollar.[1]

If the two currencies are free to move, movement in the exchange rate continues until £1 will exchange for an amount of dollars that will buy as much in the United States as the pound will buy in the United Kingdom. Table 6.1 shows what would happen over a three-year period of 10 percent inflation in the United States and 5 percent inflation in the United Kingdom.

As can be seen in the exhibit, since prices in the United States are shown to be rising faster than in the United Kingdom, then the value of sterling should be rising relative to the dollar—if extraordinary market forces and/or governmental intervention do not distort the basic market pressures. If the value of sterling rises sufficiently to maintain purchasing-power parity, then what the basket of goods now costs in the United Kingdom should be equal to what the same amount of money will buy when translated into U.S. dollars and spent in the United States. Since British prices have risen 15.76 percent in the three years (as shown by the price index of 115.76 in column 3 of Table 6.1), what formerly cost £100 now costs £115.76. What formerly cost $200 in the United States now costs $266.20, since there has been a 33.10 percent increase in prices (as indicated by the price index of 133.10). The purchasing-power parity exchange rate (X) is calculated by dividing the cost of the basket of goods in the United States by the cost of the same collection of goods in the United Kingdom:

$$X = \frac{\$266.19}{115.76} = \$2.2995$$

The PPPs are shown in columns 4 and 5 of Table 6.1. In the third year that value is $2.2995/£.

The reader should note, however, that the theory of purchasing-power parity, while supported by many empirical studies, is not easy to apply to daily situations. First, as noted above, PPP helps us to gauge medium to long-term FX trends, not short-term trends. Other dynamic forces in the market (for example, interest rates, political developments,

---

[1]Review Chapter 2 if you are unclear about the economic impact of these diverging pressures upon the two economies.

TABLE 6.1   Purchasing-Power Parity Betweeen the United States and the United
Kingdom

(1)	(2)	(3)	PPP Exchange Rates	
Year	U.S. Price Index[a]	U.K. Price Index[b]	$/£[c]	£/$[d]
0	100.00	100.00	$2.0000	£0.5000
1	110.00	105.00	$2.0952	£0.4773
2	121.00	110.25	$2.1950	£0.4556
3	133.10	115.76	$2.2995	£0.4349

[a]Based upon inflation of 10 percent per year.

[b]Based upon inflation of 5 percent per year.

[c]Found by multiplying $2.0000 times the U.S. Price Index divided by the U.K. Price Index.

[d]The reciprocal of the $/£ exchange rate. It can also be calculated by multiplying £0.5000 times the U.K. Price Index divided by the U.S. Price Index.

and so forth) can cause extensive variation from PPP projections. Also, access to the appropriate price indexes is not always available: The appropriate indexes are those of internationally traded goods and services, indexes that may well be inadequate or even nonexistent or defined differently by different countries.

Thus, it can be seen that, while purchasing-power parity is a useful tool for understanding movements over time of spot rates, it has definite limitations over the short to medium term.

Summary of spot market forces: In the preceding discussion we have seen that spot market exchange rates reflect

1. international trade flows,
2. international capital flows,
3. extraordinary trade and capital flows, and
4. governmental intervention.

International trade flows are heavily affected by inflation. It is this force that most directly is reflected by purchasing-power parity. However, capital flows also are affected by inflation via interest rates and thereby can help to contribute to the exchange market pressures which result in PPP.

Interest rates basically reflect several ingredients, as follows:

1. *real rate of return:* A basic reward for the investor, even if there are no risks involved.

2. *inflation premium:* Interest rates reflect inflation rates since investors demand protection from the loss of value of the investment caused by inflation; the real rate of return plus the inflation premium are the essential components of the so-called default-free rate of return (for example, the interest rate on U.S. Treasury bills).

3. *risk premium:* An extra "cushion" to protect investors from risks other than inflation. Thus, local corporations, municipal governments, and often foreign governments typically pay higher interest rates than do national governments. However, in some circumstances foreign borrowers may pay interest rates that are even lower than those paid by the national government (for example, when the U.S. government sold DM-denominated obligations in Germany in 1978 and 1979, it paid even lower interest than the German government).

If interest rates are allowed to fully reflect inflation in both countries, then interest rates would have a neutral influence upon exchange rates. However, governments have a long record of preventing interest rates from reaching their natural level during inflationary periods. A classic example was the refusal of the Federal Reserve Bank to permit the prime interest rate in the late 1970s to rise above 12 percent, even when the annual rate of inflation was 3 to 5 percent higher. Not only were investors not gaining adequate protection from inflation, but they were not realizing a real rate of return or even an adequate return for other types of risk. In effect, the "real" rate of interest was negative. This is a delightful condition for borrowers but quite unsatisfactory for investors.

Under such circumstances, highly liquid capital (often called *hot money*) has a strong tendency to avoid that country from abroad and to flee the country from within. This adds to the devaluation pressure on the currency, as indeed happened to the dollar, which was under significant downward pressure during most of the 1970s. Unfortunately, this distortion to ordinary FX pressures cannot only supplement the trade pressures but, like any distortion, can overdo it. On several occasions, the value of the dollar fell unrealistically low.

FORWARD EXCHANGE RATES

The spot market is an absolute necessity for international transactions. Without it, trade between countries with different currencies would be extremely difficult. The forward market does not bear the same degree of necessity as does the spot market. However, it has a degree of sophistication that greatly increases the efficiency of the international markets. It provides a very valuable tool for protecting corporations against the vagaries of movement in FX rates.

Forward markets only exist for a relatively small group of major, and relatively uncontrolled, currencies. Nevertheless, those are the currencies in which the vast majority of international transactions are denominated.

When a forward exchange contract is signed, the forward buy and sell quotes in effect at that point in time are the exchange rates that apply, although *no payment is generally made until the settlement date of the contract*. Notice that once again one of the parties is typically going to be a bank. Once again, the bank's profit comes from its spread between the buy and sell quotes. Also, if a broker is involved in the transactions, his or her revenue is in the form of a commission.

Forward contracts are *legally binding commitments* for all parties concerned. Despite the informal nature of the market, participants can operate with a high degree of certainty that their contracts will be fulfilled by the other party, even if the currency value has moved to the severe disadvantage of that party. For example, regardless of how uncomfortable it may be for a treasurer to pay 1500 lire per dollar as specified in a forward contract when the actual future spot rate turns out to be only 1400, the contract must be honored.

Students often ask, "Who loses on a forward contract if my company is gaining?" Nobody actually loses from an *a priori* perspective. We would not enter into the contract unless we preferred the greater certainty of the contract. The same is true of the other party. When the actual date of the contract arrives, we may decide in retrospect that we were either extremely wise for having protected ourselves or that we had protected ourselves unnecessarily and had missed the chance to have profited from a more favorable exchange rate. However tempting this 20/20 hindsight might be, it is a fool's endeavor. The manager must make the decisions and then learn to live with them. Some of the decisions will be favorable, and others will be unfavorable. Unfortunately, the unfavorable outcomes could not be identified at the time the decisions were made. If the favorable outcomes outweigh the unfavorable, the manager will have done well.

The forward exchange markets involve a positive-sum relationship. Some parties will be willing to absorb small net losses as insurance against the possibility of large losses. Also, a German treasurer might gladly lock in a forward market loss if the forward discount on dollars is less than the interest premium on dollars. Thus, there are fewer *perceived* losses in the market than gains!

Users of forward contracts: Forward markets play a variety of roles for corporations. They are seldom used by governments for intervention in the markets but can be of use to governments for the same transaction motives as for corporations. As with the spot market, the forward market is important for both trade and capital flows. A participant in an international transaction whose domestic currency is being used in the transaction does not need to be worried about exchange risks such as is the case for the U.S. exporter who denominates its foreign sales in U.S. dollars. Likewise, if the other participant either has the foreign currency in his or her control (for instance, a Eurodollar account) or is willing to accumulate the foreign currency, he or she might not be greatly concerned about exchange risks. However, if a participant whose currency is not being used either does not have the currency in which he or she must pay or is not willing to hold the currency he or she will receive, then exchange risks become real problems.

Exchange risks result from any kind of development in the foreign exchange markets that could be damaging. They include not only the risk of an unfavorable movement in the exchange rate but also the risk of exchange or capital controls. Forward contracts provide a form of insurance against such risks. Controls could be made retroactive to include outstanding forward contracts; this would reduce or totally eliminate the advantage of a forward contract as protection. Generally, however, controls are applied only to subsequent contracts: thus a forward contract that is arranged before new controls go into effect is usually exempt from the controls.

Importers use forward markets to buy the needed foreign exchange for settlement of future contracts. By purchasing the foreign currency forward, importers are guaranteeing the exact cost of the contracts in their own currency. If the foreign currency should *increase* in value in the interim (and an increase is the basic fear of importers and other debtors), the importer bears none of the added cost. However, note that they also would have foregone the potential savings if that foreign currency declines in value!

Exporters use forward markets to sell their anticipated receipts. They are thereby guaranteed an exact receipt in their own currency. They have been protected against the possible decline in the value of the foreign currency (and a decline is the basic fear of exporters and other creditors), but they have also given up the potential gain if the currency were to have gone up in value. *Utilization of the forward markets is essentially a type of insurance.* The user pays the price of foregoing possible gains in order to gain protection against possible losses.

Another major user of forwards are investors in money-market instruments such as government bills, negotiable certificates of deposits (CDs), commercial paper, bankers' acceptances, and so forth. Sophisticated corporate treasurers have come to treat the entire money and capital markets of the world as a single entity. They can invest as easily in Eurodollar CDs as in domestic U.S. CDs. They could also as easily invest in Eurodeutsche mark CDs or domestic sterling CDs in London. As long as no currencies are exchanged, there is no currency risk. However, when the corporation invests in a foreign currency, it must either accept the FX risks or seek to protect itself.

A common form of protection against FX risk is to sell forward the anticipated foreign currency receipts (that is, both the investment and the interest earned). Since corporate treasurers are basically conservative individuals who move money around the world in pursuit of interest-rate advantages but are not comfortable with exchange risks, they generally cover their exposed contracts in this manner. For example, if interest rates are 8 percent in Germany and 12 percent in the United States, then the German treasurer might be inclined to buy dollars with excess DMs and invest the dollar proceeds in the United States. At the same time, in order to ensure that his or her future receipts in DM are protected, the anticipated receipts of the dollar-denominated principal and interest are sold forward. Like the exporter in the paragraph above, this procedure will guarantee the local currency value of the future receipts.

The reader must remember in all these discussions that interest rates and FX premiums and discounts are *always* stated on an *annual basis,* so that they are indeed in comparable terms. $100 invested at 12 percent for three months does not yield $112 [$100 + $100 (12 percent)] but only $103.

$$\$103 = \$100 + \$100\left(12\% \times \frac{3 \text{ months}}{12 \text{ months}}\right)$$

This is the principal plus the interest for three months (one-fourth of a year). Similarly, if the pound sterling is trading at $2, an 8 percent premium on six-month forwards equals $2.08, not $2.16!

$$\$2.00 + \$2.00\left(8\% \times \frac{6 \text{ months}}{12 \text{ months}} = \$2.08\right)$$

Exporters and importers have no formula to tell them when to stop buying or selling forward contracts. They will continue to do so as long as they prefer its costs to the risk of being uncovered. Unlike the exporter and importer however, the short-term investor has an absolute limit to guide his or her investment decisions. For reasons to be seen shortly, a currency is trading at a forward *discount* when interest rates in that currency are *higher* than those overseas. If the German treasurer can earn 12 percent in the United States and only 8 percent in Germany, U.S. investments will remain attractive until the forward discount on the dollar equals or exceeds the 4 percent advantage of U.S. interest rates.

Treasurers acting either defensively or speculatively can also find the forward market useful. If, for example, the currency is expected to decline in value by more than the amount of the forward discount, then the currency could be *sold forward* at the discounted rate with the intention of buying it in the future spot market when the contract matures at a lower price in order to settle the contract. Similarly, if it is thought that the currency will rise more in the future spot market than the current premium in the forward market, then the currency can be *bought forward* with the intention of selling in the future spot market at a higher price. In either case the anticipated discrepancy between the current forward rate and the forecasted future spot rate provide the corporate treasurer with a profit. If, however, the forecast was wrong, the company would lose!

Note that with both the transactions above the company does not have an offsetting contract to the forward purchase or sale of a currency, unlike the exporter, importer, or money-market investor who is merely seeking to protect his or her investment. Instead, the company is seeking to earn a profit in an exchange market when it exercises the necessary offsetting contract in the future.[2]

Determination of forward rates: The principal element in the determination of the forward rate is the spot rate. When the spot rate moves, so does the forward rate, and in the same direction and generally in a similar magnitude. Thus, if a government intervenes in the spot market and causes a currency to rise, then the forward rates are likely to move simultaneously and without governmental assistance. Similarly, large balance-of-payments deficits will likely drag a currency's spot rate down, and the forward rates with it.

As noted above, corporate treasurers often buy and sell foreign exchange forward in order to cover anticipated import payments or export receipts. All else being equal, such actions would by themselves tend to move a currency into either a premium or discount according to the psychology of the market at that particular point in time for that particular forward date.

However, there is another force at work in the forward markets that generally overwhelms such actions by corporate treasurers to cover their commercial transactions. It was pointed out above that treasurers also utilize forward markets aggressively as an adjunct to their investments of short-term funds in foreign currencies. For example, if the

---

[2]Covering and other hedging operations of FX exposure management are examined in detail in Chapter 21.

American treasurer invests in Eurosterling for thirty days, he or she is likely at the same time to sell the anticipated sterling receipts in the forward market. Investments in Eurosterling remain attractive until the forward discount on sterling approximately equals the interest-rate advantage of sterling-denominated investments over dollar-denominated investments. Indeed, the amounts of short-term funds available to be moved from dollars into sterling are of such great magnitude that they will *force* the forward discount to increase until it equals the interest-rate differential. At that point there will be parity in the *effective interest rates* between sterling investments and dollar investments. This *interest-rate parity* is what *generally causes the degree of forward premium or discount.*

For example, if country A is a high-interest country while country B is a low-interest country, then at interest-rate parity:

$$\begin{array}{ccc} \text{annualized} & \text{annualized} & \text{annualized} \\ \text{percentage interest} - & \text{percentage} & = \text{percentage interest} \\ \text{in A} & \text{forward discount} & \text{in B} \\ & \text{on A's currency} & \end{array}$$

Similarly,

$$\begin{array}{ccc} \text{annualized} & \text{annualized} & \text{annualized} \\ \text{percentage interest} + & \text{percentage} & = \text{percentage interest} \\ \text{in B} & \text{forward premium} & \text{in A} \\ & \text{on B's currency} & \end{array}$$

This relationship holds whether a treasurer is investing or funding (borrowing). Foreign currency funds can be *borrowed* and converted to the local currency if a forward purchase of the borrowed currency is available to protect the borrower. Thus, when the markets are fully efficient and interest-rate parity is operating fully, corporate treasurers are basically indifferent between investing or funding in high-interest, medium-interest, or low-interest countries. In actuality, small discrepancies do occur, and corporate treasurers are often able to find differential advantages in different markets at different times.

Before understanding the concept of interest-rate parity, it is a normal assumption to believe that forward rates are the market's estimates of what the future spot rates will be. Many economists and other observers of the market think that even with the interest-rate parity the forward markets are still a reasonable predictor of future spot rates. For treasurers who believe this, it should make no difference whether or not they cover their transactions in the forward market, since they expect that the exchange rate will be the same in either case. However, there are many other observers who believe that the forward rate is a poor predictor of the future spot rate. For them, it pays to attempt to forecast the future spot rate and decide whether or not to cover their transactions or to hedge their other exposure depending upon how their forecast compares with the forward rates.

There are times when interest-rate parity is clearly violated in the forward markets. When this occurs, it is the result of extraordinary forces that have overwhelmed the ordinary market forces: expectations of political or social instability, major currency-value changes, and so forth. Under such circumstances, corporations in acting defensively or speculatively are estimating that the forward discount or premium is inadequate. The sum of their actions is to drive the discount or premium beyond the point of interest-rate parity. Indeed, if forward rates are not in conformity with interest-rate parity, then *speculation* is likely to be the cause.

Summary of forward-rate forces: In the discussion above we have seen that the forward-market exchange rates reflect

1. the spot rate
2. interest-rate parity
3. ordinary protective actions of importers and exporters
4. extraordinary market pressures (defensive and speculative) arising from expectations of disruptive events
5. governmental intervention (only rarely)

The forward rate generally moves proportionately with the spot rate unless shifting interest rates at the same time cause a shift in interest-rate parity. Since one of the principal ingredients of the interest rate is the rate of inflation, when prices are rising, interest rates generally rise. This rise, as has just been seen, tends to attract money from abroad and leads to an increase in the forward discount on that country's currency. Thus, through this mechanism of interest-rate parity, inflation is reflected in the forward rates for a currency, unless the government's actions affecting interest rates thwart the workings of the market.

Ordinary actions by exporters and importers to protect themselves from possible adverse consequences in the movement in the value of a currency usually must operate within the parameters set by the interest-rate pressures as they pushed the forward markets to interest-rate parity. The forward rate directly reflects the market's expectations of future spot rates only if the mood of the market is expecting a significant adverse or unusually favorable development and if it is strong enough to cause the joint action of all market participants to push the forward rates beyond what interest-rate parity would dictate. Only rarely do governments actively get involved in that part of the FX markets, except in the United Kingdom, where the Bank of England has sometimes shown a strong propensity to intervene even in the forward market.

ARBITRAGE

Interest-rate parity results from the simultaneous actions of many corporate treasurers trying to make the most profitable investment without bearing any FX risk. If their investments lead them into other currencies, they protect themselves by selling the currency forward at the same time that they buy it spot. This procedure is known as *covered-interest arbitrage*. *Arbitrage* is the procedure of *simultaneously* buying and selling a financial or commercial contract. Similarly, a foreign exchange trader may be able to make a profit by buying deutsche marks in New York with dollars while simultaneously selling the DM in Frankfort, Germany, for dollars (exchange-rate arbitrage).

The essence of arbitrage is that simultaneous contracts to buy and sell the same, or a closely related, contract are made, so that the *arbitrageur* never takes a net position and therefore is never exposed to adverse movements in the value of the contract. The price discrepancies for which the arbitrageur is watching are generally very small, and they disappear very quickly. Seldom can anyone who is not an active participant in the market recognize and take advantage of arbitrage opportunities. The arbitrage differentials are generally very small, but since the size of the contracts is large, attractive profits can sometimes be made. One of the most attractive features about arbitrage is that, since the contracts are simultaneous and exactly offsetting, the arbitrageur does not need to put up any money!

The arbitrage function is quite valuable for the markets since it keeps prices in various markets from getting out of balance.

CURRENCY FUTURES AND CURRENCY OPTIONS

Two additional developments of recent vintage in the FX market are the future and the option. A *currency future* is analogous to the forward market but exists outside of the traditional FX channels. Currency futures were developed by the International Money Market in Chicago in the mid-1970s. A future contract, like other financial or commodity futures contracts, permits the buyer or seller to obtain a guaranteed future price—very similar to the forward market. Currency futures have become an important part of FX trading. As a result, major FX trading banks, both U.S. and European, have become members and active participants of the IMM.

The *currency option* which was developed by the IMM in the early 1980s is a contract which permits the buyer or the seller to buy or sell within a specified period of time *if he or she chooses*. It is not a contract which mandates buying or selling but rather offers the opportunity—if the buyer or seller chooses—to texercise the contract. If market conditions are not attractive, the contractee can allow the contract to die unused.

SUMMARY

Foreign exchange markets are a vital element of international business. They are widely used by corporations, governments, international organizations, and smaller banks. Such retail customers can buy and sell foreign currencies via the FX trading desks of major banks. The banks, which buy and sell for their own accounts in serving their customers, utilize FX brokers if their portfolios get out of balance. All these transactions are typically handled by phone or cable and are settled by cable or mail. Seldom are transactions done in person.

There are really two FX markets: The *spot market,* which reflects current ordinary and extraordinary private-sector pressures plus governmental intervention, and the *forward market,* which reflects the spot market, and *interest-rate parity* plus extraordinary pressures.

With access to the spot and forward markets, a corporate treasurer is no longer constrained to the exclusive use of that company's home currency. He or she can quickly, easily, and safely buy or sell in other currencies, even with future settlement. Furthermore, the spot and forward markets are the keys that permit integration of all of the world's money and capital markets. As a result, the corporate treasurer can invest or fund in foreign currencies almost as easily as in his or her home currency.

In the next chapter, the nature of the major money and capital markets of the world (domestic, foreign, and international) are explored.

KEY TERMS

ARBITRAGE	HARD CURRENCY	PURSCHASING-POWER
BID (OR BUY) QUOTE	INDIRECT QUOTATION	PARITY
BROKER	INTEREST-RATE PARITY	SETTLEMENT DATE
CROSS RATE	NOMINAL INTEREST RATE	SOFT CURRENCY
DEALER (OR TRADER)	OFFER (OR ASK OR SELL)	SPECULATION
DIRECT QUOTATION	QUOTE	SPOT MARKET
DISCOUNT	OUTRIGHT QUOTATION	SPREAD
EFFECTIVE INTEREST RATE	PREMIUM	SWAP QUOTE
FORWARD MARKET		

REVIEW QUESTIONS

1. Who are the primary "makers" in the FX markets?
2. If you personally wanted to buy a foreign currency for a vacation abroad, how would the quote you receive from the bank differ from

the quote received by a corporation? Why would your quote be better or worse than that of the corporation?

3. What *two* pieces of information do you need to convert swap quotes to outright quotes?

4. How does purchasing-power parity affect exchange rates?

5. How does interest rate parity affect exchange rates?

6. How does arbitrage work?

7. Given a spot quotation of Ps 2.2250–70/$.
   a. The bank will buy $ at _____ .
   b. The bank will sell $ at _____ .
   c. You can buy Ps at _____ .
   d. You can sell Ps at _____ .

8. Given a spot quotation of Ps 2.2250–70/$ (without inverting the exchange rate).
   a. The bank will buy Ps at _____ .
   b. The bank will sell Ps at _____ .
   c. You can buy $ at _____ .
   d. You can sell $ at _____ .

9. a. With a spot quotation of Ps 2.2250–70/$, which currency is being quoted directly? indirectly?
   b. With a quotation of $1.6525–40/£, which currency is being quoted directly? indirectly?

10. Calculate the forward swap quotes for the following outright quotations:

	SPOT	1-MONTH	3-MONTHS	6-MONTHS
a.	Ps 1.2250-70	1.2300-1.2325	1.2400-1.2475	1.2550-1.2690
b.	$1.6525-40	1.6620-1.6640	1.6800-1.6855	1.7045-1.7150

11. a. In question 10(a), are interest rates higher in $ or Ps? How do you know?
    b. In question 10(b), are interest rates higher in $ or £? How do you know?

12. Interest rates for ninety-day treasury bills (T-bills) are 16 percent in the United States and 8 percent in Ruritania. The exchange rates are $1.5780/RP spot and $1.6100/RP forward three months.[3]
    a. If you have $1 million available to invest for ninety days, how much would you earn in the United States? (Assume no transactions costs.)

[3] RP is the abbreviation for the Ruritanian peso, the currency of Ruritania.

b. If the $1 million was invested for ninety days in Ruritania and covered in the forward market, how much would you earn (translated into $)? (Assume no transactions costs. Think carefully in choosing the appropriate exchange rate at which you buy RP and sell RP.)

13. Given the following quotations, calculate the various cross rates:

		DM	FF	Lit	£
DM 2/$1	DM				
FF 6/$1	FF				
Lit 1500/$1	Lit				
$1.75/£1	£				

SUGGESTED REFERENCES

ALIBER, ROBERT Z. *International Money Game.* New York: Basic Books, Inc., 1976.

CONINX, RAYMOND G. F. *Foreign Exchange Today.* New York: Halstead Press, 1978.

COOMBS, CHARLES A. *Arena of International Finance.* New York: John Wiley & Sons, Inc., 1976.

EINZIG, PAUL *Textbook on Foreign Exchange.* New York: St. Martin's Press, Inc., 1969.

FEDERAL RESERVE BANK OF NEW YORK "Treasury and Federal Reserve Foreign Exchange Operations," *Quarterly Review*, any issue.

FRENKEL, JACOB A., AND HARRY G. JOHNSON, eds. *Economics of Exchange Rates.* Reading, Mass: Addison-Wesley Publishing Co., Inc., 1978.

KOHLHAGEN, STEVEN "Performance of Foreign Exchange Markets: 1971–74," *Journal of International Business Studies,* Fall 1975.

KUBARYCH, ROGER M. *Foreign Exchange Markets in the United States.* New York: Federal Reserve Bank of New York, 1978.

MANDICH, DONALD R., ed., *Foreign Exchange Trading Techniques and Controls.* Washington, D.C.: American Bankers Association, 1976.

RIEHL, HEINZ, AND RITA M. RODRIQUEZ *Foreign Exchange Markets.* New York: McGraw-Hill Book Company, 1977.

7

Major Financial Centers and International Banking

A thorough understanding of the basic nature of money and capital markets is critical for the corporate decision maker. Just as has been seen with regard to other aspects of international business, the opportunities that present themselves to the corporate treasurer who has an international perspective are far greater than those that are available to the treasurer who has a strictly domestic orientation. A company does not even have to be an international company in order to be able to benefit from access to the international money and capital markets.

The major international money and capital markets of the world are widely dispersed. The first section of this chapter discusses the location of the major markets, including the so-called offshore markets. The second section examines the nature of the international money and capital markets. International banking is discussed in the last section. The special category of Euromarkets is examined in the next chapter.

MAJOR MONEY AND CAPITAL MARKETS

THE UNITED STATES

The United States is by far the largest economy in the world. As befits the largest economy, it also has the largest and, in many ways, the most sophisticated, money and capital market in the world. Both the *depth* of the market (the vast amount of funds available) and the *breadth* of the market (the wide variety of different financial instruments and services) make the American market very attractive to both domestic and foreign participants. For example, $500 million or even $1,000 million loan syndications and bond issues are not uncommon. Often reference is made to the "New York markets." This is a proxy for the U.S. markets as a whole, and a very misleading proxy at that. Because of the size and pattern of development of the United States, a very diverse financial system has developed. Not only New York, but Chicago and San Francisco are major banking centers. Chicago and Kansas city are major centers for commodity trading. Hartford, Connecticut, is the major insurance center.

The U.S. market has several other very attractive features for foreign investors and seekers of fund. The country's political stability makes it a chronic haven even for European investors. Also, the general absence of money and capital controls is another advantage. The U.S. dollar is virtually the only currency in the world that has been convertible throughout the postwar period; the major European currencies only regained full convertibility in 1958. Even under the capital control program between 1963 and 1973, foreigners were always able to borrow in the United States—although it became financially unattractive to do so because of the interest equalization tax—and to repatriate their U.S. investments.

The United States–Iranian conflict from 1979 to 1981, when the U.S. Government ordered American banks to freeze Iranian assets, cast a shadow over this record of freedom, which will probably never be totally erased. However, the unique nature of that impasse reduced the negative impact on the American markets even during the crisis, and the negative impact will likely fade further with the passage of time.

Another big advantage for the U.S. markets is the major role played by American companies in international trade and capital flows and the unique role of the dollar. Although challenged for primacy in recent years by Germany and Japan, the United States has played the dominant role in international trade in the postwar era. Also, the large-scale capital outflows by the U.S. companies for foreign investments carried significant American weight. Virtually all these flows were dollar-denominated. In addition, *much of the trade and capital flows between most other countries is denominated and paid for in U.S. dollars.* As noted in previous chapters, despite all the recent change and upheaval in the international financial markets, the world is still basically on a dollar standard. For example, most international commodities are priced in dollars; this includes the massive value of international oil trade. Also, since the currencies of Eastern Europe and of most developing countries are subject to extensive amounts of capital controls, the dollar is the currency in which much or most Latin American, Asian, Middle Eastern, and Eastern European trade is denominated.[1]

Despite their international role, the U.S. markets are actually some of the most tightly regulated financial markets in the world. This is an advantage in many circumstances for investors, but it is generally a disadvantage for seekers of funds who must generally bear most of the onus and expense of complying with such regulations. Some of the tightest controls involve the banking system, which is one of the most complex and tightly controlled banking systems in the world. For example, the United States is the only country in the world that does not permit nationwide banking. (The term *national banking* is very much a misnomer when applied to the American banking system. It simply means that a bank has a national charter from the Comptroller of the Currency in Washington, D.C. A "national" bank could be a small one-office bank with $10 million or even less in assets). Few banks have been able to branch across state lines, and in some states no branching at all is permitted. These restrictions obviously severely limit the efficiency of the majority of banks, which could never compete very effectively with larger banks.

THE UNITED KINGDOM

The other great financial market in the world is in the United Kingdom. The term *London markets* is often used as a proxy for the British markets as a whole. To a much greater extent than with the "New York markets," this is a reasonable proxy. London is indeed the center of British banking, insurance, commodity trading, and the shipping industry as well. The financial district of London is centered in the old, medieval city of London—a one–square-mile area commonly known in financial circles as "the City."

British preeminence derives from causes similar to those of the U.S. position. Political stability is a factor as it is in the United States. However, much of the basis is historical, based on what Britain and the pound sterling *used* to be. At one time Britain played much of the economic role in the world which is now played by the United States. Once sterling played a role very similar to that of the dollar today. However, today the British economy is smaller than the German, Japanese, and French economies, let alone that of the United States. Furthermore, sterling now has a less significant international role than do the deutschemark, Swiss franc, and Japanese yen.

---

[1]The picture is not as clear for most of sub-Saharan Africa where colonial trade patterns still play a very large role in those economies. For example, a very significant amount of the trade between many of the former French and British colonies is still with France and the United Kingdom, respectively, and is commonly denominated in francs and sterling.

However, during the days of British and sterling preeminence, the London financial markets developed a degree of sophistication, which in some ways still leaves London at an advantage over the U.S. markets. Also, since the United Kingdom is in the same time zone as Continental Europe and is close to Middle Eastern time zones, the London market has another not so inconsequential advantage over the U.S. markets.

Other factors have also played a role in London's success, especially relative to other major economic powers. The most crucial of these is the general regulatory environment—banks and financial markets in Britain simply have far more freedom than do the comparable institutions on the continent and in Japan.

OTHER MAJOR MONEY AND CAPITAL MARKETS

Germany, Japan, and France: There are no other major domestic financial markets that match the significance of the United States and the United Kingdom in the world economy. Even Germany, Japan, and France, while enjoying strong banking systems, are not nearly as strong, diversified, or as sophisticated as the former two markets.[2] The economies of these three nations are at least as large as that of the United Kingdom and, in the case of Japan and Germany, much larger. However, in these nations, the secondary[3] money and capital markets have never developed to the extent that they have in the United States and the United Kingdom. The markets are indeed growing, and some of the governmental obstacles are being dismantled; but there is no doubt that none of these markets can match those of the United States and the United Kingdom.

However, the increasing role of the deutschemark and the yen as transaction and reserve currencies will continue to increase the international role of even the domestic markets of those countries. Their governments have resisted this trend for a long time, but the tides of international finance are hard to resist: Their currencies and their financial markets will assume an increasing role in the future, not just in Germany and Japan but in France, Italy, and a few other countries as well.

Switzerland: For many years Switzerland has been a very special case. Despite the small size of the Swiss economy, the money and capital markets have developed a high degree of sophistication. Most of the Swiss role is the result of the pass-through of investments by foreigners, but there is also a large amount of Swiss franc-denominated domestic credit that is extended annually to foreigners.

---

[2]Of the top twenty-five banks in the world, fifteen are Japanese, German, or French.

[3]*Secondary markets* refer to the *resale* of negotiable (i.e., marketable) securities such as Treasury bills, certificates of deposit, common stock, and corporate bonds. The initial sale of a newly issued negotiable debt and equity is known as the *primary market.*

Switzerland is a traditional haven for international flows of capital. Most funds that pass through the country do so without affecting the domestic markets. This appeal of the Swiss markets is strongly aided by the famous (or infamous) secrecy laws, the political stability, the neutrality of the country, and the almost chronic fiscal and monetary conservatism, which have fostered low inflation, low interest rates, and a strong currency. Switzerland recognized the economic advantages of becoming a major financial center long before any of the other current "offshore" leaders did (see the next section). As a result, the Swiss have established a very strong reputation in commercial and merchant banking as very sophisticated and respected specialists who are known colloquially as the "gnomes of Zurich," despite the fact that the Swiss "gnomes" are the same general size as other Europeans and do not all work in Zurich!

OFFSHORE MONEY AND CAPITAL MARKETS

In addition to these large domestic financial markets, there are certain financial market centers that have developed in spite of the lack of any significant domestic base. These developed solely as international financial centers (as opposed to domestic centers). They are essentially financial *entrepots,* that is, collection and processing centers that help facilitate the financial intermediation between providers of funds from outside that country to users of funds in other countries. The local markets are generally insignificant and typically are deliberately isolated from the international financial market in that same center.

Many offshore financial centers have risen to prominence in the past two decades. Most of these are on islands and therefore accurately qualify as being "offshore." The major centers in the Western Hemisphere are in the Bahamas (that is, Nassau), the Cayman Islands, and Panama. In Asia the principal centers are in Singapore and Hong Kong. In the Middle East, Bahrain has supplanted the war-torn country of Lebanon as the major financial center. In Europe, Luxembourg is the only major offshore center, although some writers would include Switzerland as an offshore center as well.

International banking facilities: A new and unique offshore center came into existence in 1981 when the United States began permitting *international banking facilities* (IBFs). Like banks in other offshore centers, IBFs are able to accept foreign currency deposits and invest those same currencies. However, unlike other offshore markets, IBFs can also take deposits in and invest the local onshore currency—the U.S. dollar. In order to keep the IBFs "offshore," their transactions must be with customers abroad (including the foreign offices of U.S. companies). As long as they do that, they are free from most U.S. banking laws. This reduces their cost of funds so that they can compete successfully with banks in other offshore centers. IBFs can exist in any state in the United States that permits them, and many states—including all of the major states with active international banks—do permit them.

THE NATURE OF MONEY AND CAPITAL MARKETS

The treasurer who is willing to look at financial markets both at home and abroad—for either financing or investing needs—will find three arenas for consideration.

1. domestic markets at home
2. domestic markets abroad
3. Euromarkets

DOMESTIC MONEY AND CAPITAL MARKETS AT HOME AND ABROAD

A company's local home market is, of course, the traditional market with which the financial decision maker is already well aware. The home market is the system of financial instruments and institutions that university classes thoroughly discuss and where the company has done all of its traditional financing and investing. The two core elements are the equity (stock) market and the debt market (bonds, notes, commercial paper, certificates of deposit, bank loans, private placements, and so forth). The debt markets encompass both short and long-term components and involve both negotiable (marketable) debt, such as bonds and commercial paper, and nonnegotiable debt, such as bank loans and private placements. These local markets are subject to the control of local laws. They only involve the local currency. For instance, the local money and capital markets in the United Kingdom involve all pound sterling–denominated financing and investment but none of the foreign currency–denominated activity in the country.

The local domestic market may be a very insular market that is rather effectively isolated from foreign financial markets, or it can be a very "open" market that invites foreign participants as either providers or takers of funds or both. The difference between the two varieties is largely a function of two elements: (1) the size and sophistication of the local market and (2) the attitude, policies, and laws of the local government.

Obviously, very small and unsophisticated markets have little appeal to international financiers. Also, governments in those countries tend to have a very natural protective instinct to prevent the international financial community from dominating such an immature market. (This is a variety of the infant industry argument.)

In addition, however, many governments of modern, sophisticated economies are also perennially protective of their domestic financial markets. Even countries such as Japan, Germany, and France are guilty of such policies. Also, the U.S. goverment, while generally permitting relatively open money and capital markets, was guilty of very restrictive capital controls in the 1964–1974 period (see Chapter 4). Indeed, it is the exception rather than the rule for domestic financial markets to be generally open to foreign participation. Such controls typically involve limitations on foreign takers of funds (borrowers) that would lead to capital outflows. However, in two instances (Germany and Switzerland) the controls have often been to restrain the *inflow* of foreign capital; such inflows can expand the domestic money supply to an undesirable extent.

When domestic financial markets are open to foreign participation, the participants are not only foreign corporations but also governments and international institutions as both users and suppliers of funds. Such activity can often be very vigorous.

Foreign participation in the bond market and the banking market is generally the most active. However, there are also many foreign companies whose shares of stock are listed on such exchanges as New York, London, Amsterdam, and Tokyo.[4]

Only a few countries permit listings of equity issues by foreign companies. Such stock issues are different from those listed in the home market of the companies: They are special issues registered with and approved by the local authorities. This stock can only be traded in that particular country, since there is no truly international market for equity stocks; they can be bought or sold by foreigners, but trading generally takes place only in the country where the stock was *issued*.

Bond markets are commonly more accessible to foreigners than equity markets. However, it is generally only the industrial countries and larger developing countries that have very viable and active bond markets. Some of these exclude foreign participation, especially foreign borrowing, or limit any local funding for use in local investments of the foreign companies. Such issues of bonds by foreigners in the domestic capital market are known as *foreign bonds*.

Several of the more prominent markets for foreign bonds have acquired market nicknames. For example, when foreign companies, governments, or international institutions float foreign bonds in the United States, the issues are commonly known as *Yankee bonds*. Similarly, yen-denominated issues that have been floated in Tokyo have been nick-

---

[4]For example, see the *Wall Street Journal* or *Financial Times,* any issue.

TABLE 7.1 New International Bond Issues[a]

	1970	1971	1972	1973	1974	1975	1976	1977	1978	1979	1980	1981	1982	1983
Eurobonds[b]	3.0	3.6	6.3	4.2	2.1	8.6	14.5	17.8	14.1	18.7	24.0	31.6	51.6	48.5
Foreign bonds	1.6	2.6[c]	3.4	3.6	4.7[c]	11.3	18.2	16.2	20.2	22.3	18.0[c]	21.6	26.4	27.2
in the United States ("Yankee bonds")	1.2	1.1	1.4	1.0	3.3	6.5	10.6	7.4	5.8	4.5	3.4	7.6	5.9	4.4
in Germany	0.1	0.3	0.5	0.4	0.3	1.1	1.3	2.2	3.8	5.4	4.8	1.3	3.0	2.6
in Switzerland	0.2	0.7	0.8	1.5	0.9	3.3	5.4	5.0	5.7	9.8	7.6	8.3	11.4	14.1
elsewhere	0.1	0.6	0.7	0.7	0.3	0.5	0.9	1.6	4.9	2.6	2.1	4.4	6.1	6.1
Total	4.6	6.3[c]	9.7	7.8	6.9[c]	19.9	32.7	34.0	34.3	41.0	42.0	53.0	78.0	75.7

[a]All figures in $billions ($1,000,000,000).
[b]See Chapter 8 for a discussion of Eurobonds.
[c]Errors are due to rounding.

SOURCE: *World Financial Markets* (Morgan Guaranty Trust Co.), various issues.

named *samurai bonds*. A rebirth of foreign issues in the domestic sterling bond market bears the title *bulldog bonds*.

Table 7.1 shows the pattern of growth of the international bond markets. Note that the international bond market is comprised of the Eurobond market plus that portion of the domestic markets that was issued by foreigners. As Figure 7.1 shows, the total of new international bond issues has grown dramatically. The total remained modest until 1975 when new issues soared. Since then both Eurobonds and foreign bonds have shown rapid growth—although the Eurobond market became dominant in the early 1980s.

There are three major foreign-bond markets: in the United States, Switzerland, and Germany. The pattern of growth in these three markets has been very erratic (see Figure 7.2). The "Yankee bond" portion soared in the 1974–1976 period after the interest equalization tax was removed; however, after that the market slumped. (In the next chapter, on the other hand, it will be seen that in the Eurobond market the U.S. dollar is still the overwhelming choice.) The Swiss franc market began growing rapidly in 1975 and became the largest portion in 1978. The DM market reached significant proportions in 1978 when it also surpassed

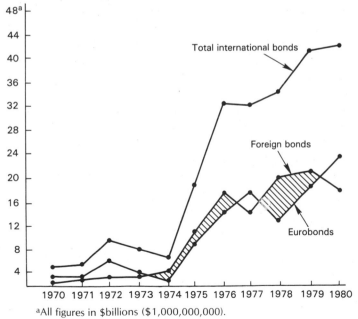

[a]All figures in $billions ($1,000,000,000).

SOURCE: *World Financial Markets* (Morgan Guaranty Trust Co.), various issues.

FIGURE 7.1 New International Bond Issues

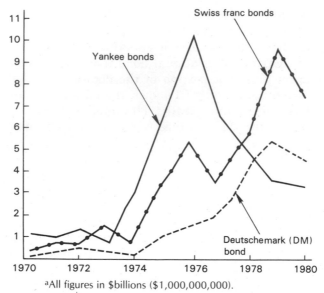

^aAll figures in $billions ($1,000,000,000).

SOURCE: *World Financial Markets* (Morgan Guaranty Trust Co.),
          various issues.

FIGURE 7.2   Foreign Bonds by Currency

the Yankee-bond total—although it also faded in the early 1980s. (In the next chapter it will be seen that DM-denominated Eurobonds are second only to dollars in the Eurobond market.)

These markets will likely continue to grow in coming years, and the Yankee bond will undoubtedly rebound. Also, the Japanese market will continue to increase: in 1984 Japan agreed to relax its controls against foreign access to its capital markets.

Domestic banking is more highly developed in most countries than are the equity and bond markets. This development has been aided in most countries by the active participation of local offices of foreign banks. International banking is examined in the last section of this chapter.

It is imperative that the reader understand that, regardless of the nationality of the issuer of these debt and equity issues in a domestic market, the markets are totally under the authority of the local government authorities. The local government can grant participation or remove permission. Foreign governments and international agencies have little influence in the regulation. The foreign participant must register with the local regulatory authority, must utilize local investment banks or commercial banks, and must obey all applicable laws. Also such issues will always be denominated and paid for in the local domestic currency.

INTERNATIONAL MONEY AND CAPITAL MARKETS

The domestic money and capital markets mentioned above, whether in the home country of a company or in foreign countries, are just as the name implies—domestic—and are subject to any applicable local laws, such as reserve requirements, deposit insurance, registration requirements, use of the local currency, use of local investment bankers, and so forth. However, very dynamic international or "stateless" international money and capital markets have sprung up in the past generation. These have helped to reshape the financial markets of the world, have tied the disparate domestic markets much more closely together, and have been very instrumental in promoting the growth of international trade and investment. Indeed they have become so prevalent that they are very controversial, are the object of a great amount of scrutiny, and have faced repeated calls for international controls. These international money and capital markets are commonly known as the *Euromarkets*. They are examined in the next chapter.

INTERNATIONAL BANKING

There have been international banks of major significance for many centuries. Of course, the early financial institutions bore little resemblance to their present-day counterparts. Nevertheless, their role in international affairs—political as well as economic—was considerable. Banking houses such as the Fuggers, the Medici, and the Rothschilds helped to finance companies, governments, voyages of discovery, colonial operations, and much more.

The banks of the two major modern colonial powers, Great Britain and France, have long been established overseas. American, German, and Japanese banks "went international" much later. Domestic opportunity often plays a major role in the timing of the international investment decisions of not only banks but also any other type of corporation. Strong domestic economies with ample banking potential delayed the international thrust of banks in those countries. So also did banking regulations, which in some countries have prevented and distorted the international role of a nation's banks. For example, American national banks were forbidden to branch overseas until 1914. Also, Japanese banks on occasion have been largely driven out of the international loan syndication market when the Bank of Japan objected to the growth and terms of their international lending (for example, as in the mid-1970s). Likewise, the Swiss banks were also very constrained by governmental regulation of their international merchant banking until the late 1970s.

Except for the colonial experience and the long-existing international financial expertise of bankers in such special financial centers as Switzerland, banks developed their international prominence much later than did their industrial and commercial counterparts. However, the thrust finally came in the past two decades. The major American banks found their international wings in the late 1960s. Their major Japanese and European counterparts followed aggressively in the 1970s.

To a large extent, banks were dragged into international banking by the rapid pace of events. The explosion of foreign investment by industrial and commercial corporations in the 1950s and 1960s was a prime influence as the banks of different countries "followed the flag" of their domestic customers abroad. Also, the capital controls imposed by the U.S. government in the 1960s fostered the expansion of the Eurodollar market. This served to attract American banks, which soon dominated the markets and also appealed to the banks as a means of financing their domestic operations via their foreign branches and subsidiaries.

Once they got overseas, many of the banks found international banking to be a very profitable business. Also, it opened new banking dimensions. From an original emphasis upon servicing their domestic customers' international activities, banks have commonly evolved to service foreign customers as well, including foreign governments, for example, via recycling deposits from surplus countries back to deficit countries. They even provide consumer banking services to individuals. Once the initial barriers to internationalization have been overcome, banks have found it to be much easier to advance to new horizons.

RANGE OF INTERNATIONAL ACTIVITIES

Short-term loans: International banks provide a bewildering variety of services. The basic service for most banks involves *trade financing*—the financial services that aid importers and exporters. Much of this is handled by banks from their home offices. Domestically, the bulk of trade is financed on an open account basis with the credit being provided to the buyer by the seller. Internationally—where buyers and sellers are commonly separated by not only long distances but national borders, languages, and currencies—open-account selling is fraught with far more risk. As a result, specialized tools such as *letters of credit* and *bankers' acceptances* were developed in order to lubricate the wheels of international trade; these tools are generally not utilized in domestic trade. They will be discussed in Chapter 16.

In addition to trade financing, banks provide a substantial amount of short-term financing for other purposes, such as for working capital needs. Also, Eurobanks often lend to their parent or other affiliate in order to help fund their needs, usually on a short-term basis.

Term financing: In addition to short-term financing, international banks have also become deeply involved in international medium- and long-term credits (jointly called *term loans*). This has been a relatively recent development away from the traditional division between the short-term nature of the commercial bank market and the long-term nature of the public debt market. However, in the last two decades there has been a strong movement toward the blurring of traditional roles in the financial markets. This is abundantly apparent in many domestic markets as well, where such developments as the *commercial paper market* have been infringing upon the traditional functions of banks.[5]

Such term loans have become the core of the overseas international activities of banks, as opposed to the domestic international activities such as trade financing, which even banks without international offices can provide to their customers. For example, the Eurocurrency markets are of this nature: The Eurobanks play the crucial role in the world economy of taking numerous, relatively small and ordinarily short-term deposits and reinvesting them long-term in much larger quantities. In the *petrodollar* crisis, the major international banks played *the key role* by taking huge deposits from the oil-exporting countries (primarily OPEC) and transforming them into credits for the importing countries.

Ancillary services: In addition to the basic functions of trade and term financing, international commercial banks also provide an extremely diverse variety of ancillary services. Many of these are adjuncts to the two basic functions, such as foreign exchange trading, credit checks, documentary collections, money transfers, courier services, and so forth. However, other services are quite distinct. In Chapter 20 (Financial Management in International Operations) some of these other services are examined.

OVERSEAS BANKING FACILITIES

Correspondent banking: The simplest type of foreign office for a bank is simply to make arrangements with independent foreign banks to act on the bank's behalf in foreign countries. This is analogous to domestic banking, whereby a bank in Dallas or Munich or Osaka arranges with banks in other areas of the country to act on its behalf in their regions. These helpful banks are called *correspondent banks*. They

---

[5]Commercial paper is a negotiable short-term promissory note of corporations. These notes have been strong competition to traditional short-term financing from commercial banks.

are very critical in the United States where nationwide banking does not exist. Correspondent banking is also of critical importance internationally where even the very largest banks often need some help in servicing their customers' needs worldwide. It is not unusual for a bank to have hundreds of international correspondents.

Representative office: The simplest type of foreign office a bank would own directly (remember that a correspondent bank is a totally independent bank, not part of the bank's own divisions) is a *representative office*. A "rep office," as its name suggests, represents its bank in a country, but it cannot legally offer banking services in that country. For example, from a bank's rep office in Mexico its personnel can visit customers, arrange deposits or loans, handle complaints, and so forth, but it can neither accept deposits nor make loans. Any financial services must be handled by offices of that bank in another country where the foreign bank has an office that is able to provide such services. For example, the representative office might arrange for a deposit to be made in the bank's branch in Nassau or for a loan to be made out of its Panamanian branch or subsidiary.

The reason that a bank might have only a rep office rather than a branch, for instance, is that in many countries (for example, Mexico, Brazil, and Saudi Arabia) the local government permits foreign banks to set up rep offices only, rather than more sophisticated offices. Any foreign banks that do have branches in those countries had the offices before the law was passed.[6]

Agency: An *agency* is a type of banking office that can make loans directly to customers but cannot accept deposits. It is therefore more flexible than a representative office. Some countries permit agencies but not anything more sophisticated. Obviously, the basic intent of these governments is to encourage an inflow of funds from abroad by forcing the foreign banks to fund their loans from overseas rather than by tapping the domestic deposit market. This incentive for capital inflows tends to strengthen a country's balance of payments, at least in the short term.

Branch: A bank office that can perform most or all of a bank's traditional banking services is a *branch*. It is permitted not only to extend loans but also to fund such loans from domestic sources via the taking of deposits. Only a country that has a strong domestic banking

---

[6]The willingness to accept the existing status of banks that were already in a country before a law banning any new banks (except as representatives) was passed, is known as *grandfathering*.

system or that is trying to greatly strengthen a weak banking system by the infusion of foreign banks will ordinarily accept foreign branches.

These foreign offices of banks (whether they are rep offices, agencies, or branches) are not separate corporations but are actually mere extensions of the parent bank, which bears full legal responsibility for them. They are generally tightly regulated and can only do what the local banking authorities permit. These characteristics describe the general nature of such offices; in actual practice, for instance, there can be significant differences between what a branch might be able to do in one country and what it might be able to do in another.

Sometimes offices of foreign banks are able to do what similar offices of domestic banks can do—that is, they are treated according to the same rules as are local banks. In other cases, the foreign banks' offices are at somewhat of a disadvantage relative to local banks because of the local banking laws. In a few isolated cases, foreign banks are actually at an advantage relative to the local banks. Somewhat surprisingly, the United States was for many years in that category. The reason was that the rather archaic and sometimes conflicting banking laws in the United States were designed to prevent American banks from branching across state lines or taking over a bank in another state. However, prior to 1978 foreign banks were not subject to many of these limitations. As a result, it was possible for a bank such as Barclays (a British bank) to buy banks in both New York and California, something that American banks could not do.

Much of the international banking activity in such offshore money centers as Nassau and Singapore is handled by branches. These branches book both foreign deposits and loans and lend to the parent bank.

Subsidiary: The most flexible type of foreign office is a *subsidiary*. Unlike representative offices, agencies, and branches, subsidiaries are *separate legal entities* from their parents. They are locally incorporated companies that are legally independent from the parent; as a result, the parent in general does not have the legal obligation to support the subsidiary. This is a very important distinction in terms both of a bank's contingent liabilities and in terms of the types of activities in which it is free to engage. A banking subsidiary often can do things that a parent bank cannot. One of the most important functions for a bank's foreign subsidiary is *investment* or *merchant banking*.[7]

Investment banking involves activities such as underwriting and selling new equity and debt issues and the organization of financial

---

[7]The terms *investment* and *merchant banking* are not exactly identical; however, they are commonly used interchangeably.

packages for major investment projects. The nature of investment banking is very different from commercial banking. Typically the merchant banks do not provide their own funds to the seeker of funds. (The term *investment banking* is somewhat of a misnomer, since they neither do banking, in the commercial banking sense, nor do they make investments!) Investment banking subsidiaries are attractive to the parent because of the fees they bring in. It is a nonasset-type of financial activity for banks. The subsidiaries earn attractive income in the form of fees without having to put new assets on their books in the form of loans. However, it is quite common for a bank's investment banking subsidiary to obtain part of the funds for a project it is financing from the bank's commercial banking operations.

THE SPREADING INTEGRATION OF BANKING PRACTICES

An interesting byproduct of the internationalization of banks from different countries is the introduction of new banking techniques from abroad. For example, the issuance of *certificates of deposit* (short-term, negotiable promissory notes of banks) (CDs) by U.S. banks and the traditional American practice of loan *syndications* have become integral parts of the Eurocurrency markets. Similarly, the decline in the use of *compensating balances*[8] and the use of loans priced according to an objective index (for example, the prevailing interest rate on commercial paper or CDs) instead of the prime rate have been substantially accelerated by the influx of foreign banks into the United States.

SUMMARY

The international money and capital markets are very valuable tools for the corporate treasurer, even for corporations that are not multinational. The availability of local domestic markets, foreign domestic markets, and the Euromarkets greatly expands the company's flexibility. These markets are available not only for funding needs but also for investing needs.

International banking is basically an extension of domestic banking. However, it includes so many unique features that the corporate decision maker also needs to be fully familiar with the services of international banks. The next chapter extends this discussion to the topic of the Euromarkets, the major part of which (the Eurocurrency market) is an international banking market.

---

[8]See the Glossary at the end of the book for a definition of *compensating balances.*

KEY TERMS

AGENCY
BRANCH
CAPITAL MARKETS
CERTIFICATE OF DEPOSIT
(CD)
COMMERCIAL PAPER
CORRESPONDENT BANK
FOREIGN BOND

INTERNATIONAL
BANKING FACILITY (IBF)
INVESTMENT BANK
MERCHANT BANK
MONEY MARKETS
NEGOTIABLE
OFFSHORE MARKET
PRIMARY MARKET

REPRESENTATIVE OFFICE
SECONDARY MARKET
SUBSIDIARY
SYNDICATION
TERM LOAN
TRADE FINANCING

REVIEW QUESTIONS

1. Which are the world's major financial markets? What makes them unique?
2. What is meant by offshore markets? What are the major offshore markets?
3. How do IBFs differ from other offshore markets? Where are IBFs located?
4. What can a bank do through its offshore activities that it cannot do onshore?
5. What are foreign bonds? What are Yankee bonds?
6. What are the various types of foreign offices that a bank can have? What are their characteristics?
7. What is a correspondent bank? How does a commercial bank use one?
8. How do investment banks differ from commercial banks?

SUGGESTED REFERENCES

ANGELINI, ANTHONY, MAXIMO ENG, AND FRANCIS A. LEES *International Lending, Risk and the Euromarkets.* New York: Macmillan, Inc., 1979.

BAUGHN, WILLIAM H., AND DONALD R. MANDICH, eds. *International Banking Handbook.* Homewood, Ill.: Dow Jones-Irwin, 1983.

KORTH, CHRISTOPHER M. "Evolving Role of U.S. Banks in International Finance," *Bankers Magazine,* July–August 1980.

KORTH, CHRISTOPHER M. "Risk Minimization for International Lending in Regional Banks," *Columbia Journal of World Business,* Winter 1981.

LEES, FRANCIS A. *International Banking and Finance.* New York: Halstead Press, 1974.

LEES, FRANCIS, AND MAXIMO ENG   *International Financial Markets.* New York: Praeger Publishers, 1975.

MATHIS, F. JOHN, ed.   *Offshore Lending by U.S. Commercial Banks* (2d ed.) Washington, D.C.: Bankers Association for Foreign Trade, 1981.

OPPENHEIMER, PETER K.   *International Banking* (4th ed.) Washington, D.C.: American Bankers Association, 1982.

ROBBINS, SIDNEY, ROBERT STOBAUGH, ET AL.   *How to Use International Capital Markets.* Financial Executives Research Foundation, 1976.

ROUSSAKIS, EMMANUEL N., ed.   *International Banking: Principles and Practices.* New York: Praeger Publishers, 1983.

SIHLER, WILLIAM, ed.   *Classics in Commercial Bank Lending.* Philadelphia, PA.: Robert Morris Associates, 1981.

8

Euromarkets

The company that becomes involved in international business encounters, as we have seen, numerous environmental conditions that are very different from those that exist in domestic markets. Some of these new situations can open up important new vistas for the alert and imaginative company. One of the most important of these is the *Euromarket*.

Not only do Euromarkets offer new funding options but also new investing alternatives. As a result, both cash budgeting and capital budgeting have taken on entirely new dimensions for hundreds of companies worldwide. This is obviously of inestimable value for companies in countries with weak domestic money and capital markets. However, it is also of great importance to companies in all of the major industrialized countries.

THE NATURE OF EUROMARKETS

The crux of the concept of Euromarkets is that they are *free from governmental controls*—controls involving registration of new issues, deposit reserves, and deposit insurance are all absent. Another major feature is that *the local currency is seldom part of the local Euromarket.* (IBFs in the U.S. are the one major exception.) For example, any transaction currency can be a Eurocurrency in London except the pound sterling. Any financial transaction in London involving the pound will fall under the legal authority of the British regulatory agencies and will not therefore qualify as part of a Euromarket. Of course, in any other Euromarket sterling could indeed be a Eurocurrency, for instance, in Singapore.

There are two major portions of the Euromarkets: the *Eurocurrency* and the *Eurobond* markets. In addition, there is a small *Euro–commercial-paper* market, but it is not very significant; in many ways it can be viewed as a short-term adjunct to the Eurobond market, that is, the short- and long-term international debt markets for negotiable instruments. Reference is also sometimes made to the "Euro-equity market." This is very misleading, however, since it actually refers to stocks of foreign companies listed on a local stock exchange, denominated in the local currency, and registered with the local authorities. Therefore this is quite clearly not a Euro-equity market at all.

EUROBOND MARKET

The *Eurobond market* is an international market for bonds that are not registered in any country. A normal domestic bond (whether issued by a domestic or foreign entity) must be registered with the appropriate local authorities (for instance, the Securities and Exchange Commission in the United States) and must be underwritten by a group of locally licensed investment bankers. A Eurobond *requires no registration*—indeed, there is no international authority with whom to register—and can be underwritten by underwriters from any country or countries. Also, a Eurobond would be in a different currency than the domestic currency.

The Eurobond market provides an alternative for the borrower who wishes to reach new sources of funds and who wishes to avoid the regulation and expense of floating the bond in a domestic market. Eurobonds are negotiable, long-term debt instruments issued by borrowers with high credit ratings. There is a secondary market for them in the international markets—although, of course, a deutschemark–denominated Eurobond, for example, could not be sold in Germany. Because the borrower is able to raise the funds so quickly, flexibly, and with a minimum of noninterest expenses, the borrower generally pays a higher interest rate than in the comparable domestic market. The investor demands, of course, the higher return since there are fewer safeguards in the unregulated Euromarket. The investor also has the advantage of generally being able to avoid withholding taxes and the reporting of income to the tax authorities of the investor's home country.

Eurobonds also have some other general characteristics: They are usually *bearer bonds* (that is, ownership is not registered and interest is paid when detachable coupons are submitted by the bearer), and they are usually unsecured (that is, they are "full faith and credit obligations" of the borrower). Some of them are *fixed-rate obligations;* others are *floating-rate bonds* with an interest rate that is changed periodically—usually every six months—depending upon market conditions.

The Eurobond market has adopted several special formats from the domestic U.S. markets that have helped to broaden the appeal of the market. Important among these "sweeteners" are convertibility and the issuance of stock warrants attached to the bond.

Growth of the Eurobond market: The vast majority of Eurobonds are either dollar-denominated or deutschemark–denominated; the dollar portion alone generally exceeds 60 percent (see Table 8.1). The market remained relatively small until 1976; since then it has grown to be a very significant financial market. Figure 8.1 charts the growth of the market as well as the relative dollar and deutschemark portions.

EUROCURRENCY MARKET

The *Eurocurrency market* is the core of the Euromarkets. The Eurocurrency market is an *international bank market.* It is thus very different from the Eurobond market. *There is no such thing as a "Eurodollar bond."* There are dollar-denominated Eurobonds and there are Eurodollar deposits and loans in banks, but there are no Eurodollar bonds.

Eurocurrencies are usually deposits of a currency in a bank outside of the country which issued the currency, for example, a DM, but not a DM that is deposited anywhere in Germany and not a pound sterling deposited in London. Since the bank has accepted a deposit denominated in that currency, interest is paid and the loan is repaid in the same currency.

This same pattern would apply for deposits made in any currency: the U.S. dollar, pound sterling, Japanese yen, and deutschemark, for example (that is, the *Eurodollar, Eurosterling, Euroyen,* and *Euro–deutschemark*). Any currency that banks will accept on deposit outside of the country that issued that currency is a Eurocurrency. However, in practice there is only a very limited number of currencies that are accepted.

There is nothing unique about Eurocurrencies other than that they have been deposited outside of the country of issue and are *largely beyond the monetary control of the monetary authorities* in that country. For example, *Eurodollars are no different than domestic dollars,* except that they are overseas. They have the same value. They can be used in

TABLE 8.1 Eurobonds: New Issues

	1972	1973	1974	1975	1976	1977	1978	1979	1980	1981	1982	1983
U.S. $-denominated	3.9	2.4	1.0	3.7	9.3	11.6	7.3	12.6	16.4	26.8	44.0	38.4
DM-denominated	1.1	1.0	0.3	2.3	2.7	4.1	5.3	3.6	3.6	1.3	2.6	3.8
Other	1.3	0.8	0.8	2.6	2.5	2.1	1.5	2.5	4.0	3.5	5.0	6.3
Total	6.3	4.2	2.1	8.6	14.5	17.8	14.1	18.7	24.0	31.6	51.6	48.5
U.S. $-denominated as percent of total	62%	57%	48%	43%	64%	65%	52%	67%	68%	85%	85%	79%

aAll figures are in billions of U.S. dollars ($1,000,000,000).

SOURCE: *World Financial Markets* (Morgan Guaranty Trust Co.), various issues.

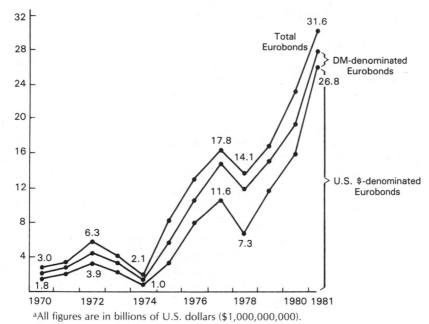

aAll figures are in billions of U.S. dollars ($1,000,000,000).

SOURCE: *World Financial Markets* (Morgan Guaranty Trust Co.), various issues.

FIGURE 8.1   New Eurobond Issues

the same way. They suffer from the same inflation. They can be traded on the same foreign exchange markets.

Actual cash is seldom used in international corporate transactions. Funds are indeed moved around the world in vast quantities, but they are moved in the form of checks or cable transfers. It would be very unusual indeed for someone to walk into a Eurobank in London with $100,000 in cash in order to create a Eurodollar deposit; it could be done but would be most unusual. Similarly, the borrower of $2 million would not be interested in receiving cash. Cash is simply too bulky, inconvenient, and risky.

The banks that are involved in the Eurocurrency markets, called *Eurobanks,* can be banks of any nationality. Thus, the bank in London in which dollars are deposited to create Eurodollars could be a branch or subsidiary of an American bank, of a British bank, or of any other country. For example, American banks can accept Eurodollar deposits outside of the United States. Of course, they can also accept Eurosterling or Euro-DM deposits abroad. However, if the sterling is deposited in the U.S. bank's British office, it is not Eurosterling but simply domestic sterling.

ORIGIN OF THE EUROMARKETS

The terms *Eurodollar, Eurobank,* and so forth are of recent vintage. However, the basic process of deposits of foreign currencies goes back hundreds of years. The modern Euromarket (and really the first *international* money and capital market of major proportions in all history) only developed in the late 1950s. Like many other major developments, the birth of the Euromarkets is clouded with uncertainty. One plausible explanation ironically credits the Soviet Union and its Eastern European partners with being the impetus that propelled the creation of this classic capitalist institution. In the mid-1950s at the height of the cold war and at a time when the U.S. dollar was absolutely preeminent as a transaction and vehicle currency (the other major industrialized countries still had inconvertible currencies), the Soviet Union wanted to keep its international reserves in dollars but not in the United States. Thus, they wished to hold U.S. dollar-denominated assets outside the United States. Banks in London and on the continent accepted these deposits. Many other depositors soon took advantage of the new option that was available to them: *Eurodeposits.*

The U.S. capital controls of 1963–1973 later served to increase the appeal of the Euromarkets. Since funds were difficult to raise in the United States, a strong increase in demand arose for *Euroloans.* At the same time, since American corporations found it difficult to bring funds out of the United States again if they had repatriated them from overseas, U.S. companies sharply reduced their repatriation of foreign earnings and investments. Much of these funds went into the Euromarket.

A third major impetus to the Euromarkets came with the oil crisis of the 1970s. The *petrodollars* (OPEC oil surpluses) poured into the major Eurobanks, which acted as a major conduit for recycling such funds back to governmental borrowers who badly needed funds to pay for their oil-induced balance-of-payments deficits.

MORE THAN EURODOLLARS

OTHER EUROCURRENCIES

When the market first evolved, it involved dollars deposited in Europe. This remained the basic nature of the market for more than a decade. Thus, it was called the *Eurodollar* market; indeed, the dollar still represents 75 percent of all Eurocurrencies (see Table 8.2).

However, in the 1970s several other currencies, especially the deutschemark, began to grow to maturity as vehicles for international transactions and reserves. Therefore, very appropriately, the term *Euro-*

TABLE 8.2 Size of the Eurocurrency Markets[a]
(rounded to nearest $5 billion; end of year)

	1970	1971	1972	1973	1974	1975	1976	1977	1978	1979	1980	1981
Estimated Size												
1. Gross liabilities	105	145	200	305	375	460	565	695	895	1185	1515	1800
2. Net claims	65	85	110	160	215	250	310	380	485	600	760	890
a. Claims on nonbanks	25	35	45	65	100	115	150	195	245	295	400	485
b. Claims on central banks and commercial banks outside of Euromarket area	30	35	45	75	95	115	135	155	195	245	285	325
c. Conversion of Eurofunds into domestic funds by Eurobanks	10	15	20	20	20	20	25	30	45	60	75	80
3. Eurodollars as percentage of gross liabilities in all Eurocurrencies (line 1)	81%	76%	78%	73%	77%	78%	79%	76%	74%	72%	74%	75%

[a]Based upon foreign currency liabilities and claims of banks in major European countries, the Bahamas, Bahrain, Cayman Islands, Netherlands Antilles, Panama, Canada, Japan, Hong Kong, and Singapore.

SOURCE: *World Financial Markets* (Morgan Guaranty Trust Co.), various issues.

currency supplanted the less-accurate term *Eurodollar* as the title for the entire market, although Eurodollar is still the term for the dollar portion of the market.

LOCATION OF EUROMARKETS

The term *Eurocurrency,* however, is also a misnomer. Just as the market evolved away from almost total reliance upon dollars, so also did it migrate away from Europe primarily to the offshore money centers. A market of which only 50 percent is located in Europe cannot accurately be termed a *Euro*market. Accordingly, reference is often made to the *Asia-currency* and *Latin-currency* markets. Actually they are only subsectors of the Eurocurrency market, which continues to be the term for not only the European portion of the markets but also the entire worldwide market as well.[1] However, because of the location, safety, and size of the smaller regional markets, deposit and lending terms do vary slightly from those in London.

London was the natural choice as the major *Eurocenter.* As was seen in the previous chapter, London has a long history as a financial center. As a result, it has developed an excellent financial infrastructure and a large cadre of financial professionals. Anxious to maintain the city's preeminence, Parliament passed the legislation that was needed.

The development of other major Eurocenters was not usually as obvious. In most cases, countries (or cities) with some advantages of location and infrastructure made a conscious effort to create major financial centers where none had existed before—locations without a substantial domestic market to support it.

In order to attract the jobs, income, travelers, and prestige of an international financial center, such unlikely places as the Bahamas, the Cayman Islands, Panama, Singapore, Hong Kong, and Bahrain have passed tax and regulatory legislation designed to attract foreign banks. The laws allow banks a high degree of flexibility and a minimum of costs in order to woo them away from the more traditional financial centers such as the United States, France, Germany, and Japan—all of which have regulatory and tax laws that prevent or discourage international banking from developing on as large a scale as would otherwise have occurred. For example, until 1981 (with the creation of IBFs), the U.S. government prevented U.S. banks from accepting foreign currency–denominated deposits in the United States.

In contrast, the government of Singapore has allowed the formation of offshore banks that are free of reserve requirements, exempt from

---

[1]The term *xenocurrency* (foreign currency) has been suggested. It is a more appropriate term but has not gained wide acceptance. Also, *world-currency market* would be a possibility.

withholding and other taxes on nonresidents' income on foreign-currency deposits, and exempt from capital controls. These banks are tightly restricted in their ability to service the local Singaporean economy. (Thus, a clear distinction is maintained between the domestic market and Asia-currency markets.) The offices must also be branches rather than subsidiaries, so that the banks' home offices must bear a much greater degree of responsibility for any possible insolvency.

The Latin-currency market (primarily located in the Bahamas, the Cayman Islands, and Panama) and the Asia currency market (primarily Singapore and Hong Kong) also have an advantage over Europe since they are in significantly different time zones.

London definitely dominates the worldwide Euromarkets. It is the largest, most sophisticated, and perhaps the safest of the Euromarkets. However, from the corporate point of view, any of these markets can satisfy the company's financial needs. As a result, corporate treasurers around the world can obtain banking services twenty-four hours a day in some major Euromarket somewhere in the world.

EURODEPOSITS

Deposits in the Euromarkets can only be *time deposits*. They can be either standard, nonnegotiable time deposits or certificates of deposit, which are negotiable. There are no demand deposits (checking accounts) in the Euromarkets. Thus, Eurodeposits are not, as such, part of any country's basic money supply.

EFFECTS OF EURODEPOSITS

However, Eurodeposits do have a very close tie with the monetary system of the country whose currency is used. When a Eurodeposit is created, the investor deposits a check or arranges for a cable transfer. Either of these methods involves the transfer of funds from the depositor's checking account. For example, if 400 units of a currency are deposited in a *Euroaccount,* the investor has exchanged a domestic demand deposit for a Eurocurrency time deposit. This can be shown with the use of T-accounts:

EUROCURRENCY DEPOSITOR

Assets		Liabilities
Demand deposit (in domestic bank)	−400	
Eurodeposit (time deposit)	+400	

The Eurobank has now assumed a Eurocurrency liability, but what asset has it acquired in exchange? It now has an interbank demand deposit in the bank in the country whose currency was deposited:

EUROBANK 1			
Demand deposit (in the country whose currency was deposited)	+400	Eurodeposit	+400

The impact upon the bank on whom the check or cable transfer was drawn should be clear: It has simply exchanged demand deposit liabilities.

DOMESTIC BANK	
Assets	Liabilities
	Demand deposit (customer) −400
	Interbank demand deposit (Eurobank 1) +400

Since demand deposits are commonly considered part of the money supply of a country, does that mean that part of the domestic money supply has now moved abroad? Actually, it has not moved at all: It is still in the original domestic bank, only the ownership of the funds has changed. Whether or not part of the domestic money supply is now in the account of a Eurobank is a matter of the government's definition of M-1 money supply (i.e., demand deposits plus currency in circulation). In 1980 the U.S. definition of the basic money supply was redefined to exclude all interbank demand deposits; formerly, only domestic interbank deposits had been excluded. Thus, in some countries the interbank demand deposits are included as part of the basic money supply, whereas in other countries they are not.

SOURCES OF EURODEPOSITS

Eurodeposits can come from many sources. Corporations (whether multinational or not), governments, international agencies, and even individuals can open *Euro-accounts*. the size of the minimum deposit is usually large—typically in excess of $100,000 or its equivalent—but some banks accept deposits of as little as $10,000.

The OPEC governments have been very large depositors in the Euromarkets. By depositing their dollar receipts in the Eurodollar market they avoided moving that portion of their funds into the direct jurisdiction of the U.S. government (especially if the deposits were in non-American banks), yet kept the funds in a very liquid form.

The OPEC countries realized the importance of an efficient recycling of their petrodollar surpluses in order to help finance some of the deficit countries. However, the OPEC countries lack the banking system to accomplish such recycling themselves. Furthermore, they are unwilling to make the loans directly on any major scale. Thus, they welcome both the efficiency and insurance provided by the Eurobanks, who acted as intermediaries. Thereby, if a borrower should default on a loan, it would be the bank and not the OPEC country that would have to absorb the loss.

EURO-INVESTMENTS

Since the Eurobank has assumed a foreign currency obligation (that is, foreign to the local market in which the bank is accepting Eurodeposits, although it either may or may not be the bank's own home currency), it would be bearing the risk of loss from currency depreciation or devaluation if the bank made a *cross-currency* loan. Eurobanks sometimes make these loans if an increase in the value of the other currency is anticipated or if the cross-currency risk can be covered by selling the other currency in the forward market. However, the vast majority of all Euro-investments are in the same currency as the deposit.

There are a variety of investment opportunities available to the Eurobank:

1. interbank *Euroloans*
2. loans to its own affiliate in the country whose currency was deposited
3. loans to corporations and governments
4. investment in negotiable securities

INTERBANK EUROLOANS

A very major portion of the funds deposited in the major Eurobanks is reloaned to other, typically smaller banks in the *interbank market*. This is especially true of Eurodollars deposited in American banks and Euro–deutschemarks deposited in German banks, and so forth.

LIBOR: As was seen in Table 8.2 there is a very active interbank Euromarket. Active banks have specific rates at which they are prepared to either buy or sell *Eurofunds* within the interbank market, rates of which are analogous to the buy and sell quotes in the foreign exchange markets. In the Euromarkets in London these are known as the *London interbank bid and offer rates*. Banks know that they can borrow at another bank's offer rate. This cost plus a small markup becomes the borrowing bank's own *London interbank offer rate* (*LIBOR*).

It should be clear that the bank that receives the original primary deposit has a lower funding cost than the banks that need to borrow in the interbank market. There are even several tiers of rates that different primary depositories must pay. The higher a bank's credit rating, the lower the rate of interest that it must pay to depositors. (This is analogous to the domestic markets where the most credit-worthy banks pay less when they sell large certificates of deposit than do banks with a lower credit rating.)

In a similar vein, the more credit-worthy the bank is that is borrowing in the interbank market, the lower the rate offered to it. Each bank thus offers different rates, depending on the quality of the bank to which it is lending. For example, a prime quality bank might be quoted LIBOR whereas a less credit-worthy bank would be offered LIBOR plus an increment of perhaps $\frac{1}{16}$ or $\frac{1}{8}$. Banks also have different LIBORs for different currencies. For example, at the same time that the bank is offering a Eurodollar LIBOR of 14 percent, it may be offering 10 percent on the Euro–deutschemark).

LIBOR plus: LIBOR is, as the name suggests, the rate offered in the interbank market. Nonbank borrowers are generally quoted a higher rate. Since the lending bank knows that it could lend the funds at its own LIBOR in the interbank market, it may charge a higher rate to corporate or governmental borrowers, who are not viewed quite as favorably as are prime banks. Thus, in order to make a satisfactory return, the Euro-banks typically price their loans at LIBOR plus some prevailing "spread." The *spread* is the differential between the LIBOR and the lending rate. Thus, if a loan is made at LIBOR plus 1 percent, then when LIBOR is 12 percent the loan is at 13 percent. The size of the spread depends upon the quality of the borrower and upon credit conditions in the market.

Euroloans can be for any maturity from overnight to fifteen or more years. If the loan is for longer than six months, the loan is generally made at a *floating rate,* that is, every six months the LIBOR base is changed to reflect credit conditions at that time. This is to protect the lender; but if interest rates decline, it can also benefit the borrower. (Of course, if rates rise, the lender is protected, but the borrower pays more.)

Banks can normally fund their Euroloans in the interbank market for six-month periods; longer funding is much more difficult and expensive. Therefore, by simply *rolling over* the loans each six months the banks are lending at rates that reasonably approximate their funding costs. For example, the LIBOR + 1 percent loan mentioned above was initiated at 13 percent, that is, when LIBOR was 12 percent. Six months later, if LIBOR had risen to 15 percent, then the rollover would be at 16 percent. However, the pricing system can also work to the borrower's advantage. If LIBOR falls to 8 percent, then the roll-over is 9 percent, substantially less than when the loan was first drawn down (i.e., when the funds were received by the borrower). Thus, in the spring of 1980, many borrowers took loans at a time when LIBOR was 18 percent and even higher. By the time of the roll-over six months later, the LIBOR rate had plunged to under 12 percent.

When banks fund their Euroloans, they generally prefer to borrow for the same maturity period as the loan they intend to make; this balance is called *matched funding*. For example, a six-month loan would be funded with a six-month deposit or interbank loan. However, banks often engage in an aggressive funding practice of borrowing short term and lending long term (for example, borrowing thirty-day funds and lending for six months). This is known as *short funding* and is done when the bank is anticipating a drop in interest rates. It is a regular part of the *interest-rate cycle*—match funding (or even *longfunding*) when interest rates are rising and short funding when rates are falling.

If the bank's forecast is correct when it shortfunded, then it would profit handsomely, as its true funding cost will drop below the LIBOR reference price on the loan. However, if the bank is wrong in its forecast and funding rates rise, then the bank may well lose money on the loan. Banks must watch their interest rates very closely when they are short funding; if rates begin to move against them, they must act quickly to tie down their funding needs before rates go even higher.

A Eurobank might use its own quoted LIBOR rate as the basis for pricing its loan. Also, Eurobanks often use the daily published LIBOR quote of the *Financial Times*. This quote is based upon the average of quotes of a representative Eurobank from each of five countries: Morgan Guaranty Trust Company (United States), Deutsche Bank (Germany), Barclays (United Kingdom), Banque Nationale de Paris (France), and Bank of Tokyo (Japan). Alternatively, if the loan is from a syndicate of banks, then an average of the LIBOR quotes of some or all of the banks in the syndicate might be used.

Continuing with our example from the T-accounts above, when the interbank deposit is made, the effects on the three banks involved are as follows. Note that for the domestic bank the impact is again merely a transfer of a liquid liability, similar to when the original deposit was made.

EUROBANK 1

Assets		Liabilities
Interbank demand deposit	−400	
Interbank Euroloan (time deposit)	+400	

EUROBANK 2

Interbank demand deposit (in the country whose currency was deposited)	+400	Interbank Euroloan (time deposit)	+400

DOMESTIC BANK

		Interbank demand deposit (Eurobank 1)	−400
		Interbank demand deposit (Eurobank 2)	+400

LOANS TO AFFILIATES

Another major use of Eurofunds is for loans to be extended within the same banking organization. This could be either to the parent company or to some other affiliate. The most common target would be to the affiliate in the country whose currency has been deposited or borrowed. For example, the London office of an American bank could be used to funnel funds back to its home office in the United States, either because the Eurofunds were cheaper or because of the domestic credit stringency in the United States. Non-American banks can finance some of their U.S. operations in the same fashion, but the flows are larger for American banks.

The net flows can move either way: In some years there has been a net inflow to the United States and in other years a net outflow to the Eurobank branches abroad. For example, the inflows have periodically been used to avoid tight money conditions in the United States. This is because Eurodollar borrowings were not originally subject to reserve requirements for banks in the States. This obviously gave these funds an added cost advantage. In order to discourage the use of these intrabank borrowings, the Federal Reserve in 1969 imposed a reserve requirement on borrowings from foreign affiliates or even from unaffiliated banks. The reserve requirement has fluctuated over the years as the Federal Reserve relaxes or tightens its attitude toward such drawings. For example, in the spring of 1980, when the dollar was under downward pressure in the foreign exchange markets, the Federal Reserve reduced the reserve requirement to zero percent. This was a technical difference from eliminating the requirement altogether, since everyone was reminded that the rule was still on the books and could be raised above zero

percent at any time in the future. Indeed, later that year the requirements were again changed.

T-accounts for loans to affiliates are essentially the same as with
interbank loans, and again the effect upon the domestic bank is merely a
transfer of liquid liabilities. If the domestic bank and parent bank are
the same, the transfer would involve only accounts of the affiliated
offices.

LOANS TO CORPORATIONS AND GOVERNMENTS

A significant share of Eurodeposits must eventually leave the banking system. The largest share goes into loans to corporations and governments or international institutions (for example, the World Bank). The
channeling of loans to those ultimate borrowers can occur directly from
the Eurobank or via the interbank or intrabank flows mentioned above.

As seen in Table 8.2 above, the size of the Euromarkets is awesome.
They have developed the capacity to finance very large credits via
multibank syndications. Billion and even multibillion dollar credits are
not unusual, although they are appropriately recognized even in sophisticated banking circles as "jumbos."

The existence of the Euromarket provides corporate treasurers
with a major adjunct to their domestic markets. Just as with commercial
banks, the international markets can be a very appealing alternative
when domestic credit conditions get very tight. Indeed, as has been
noted, the U.S. credit controls between 1963 and 1973 gave the Euromarkets a strong impetus. Foreign borrowers were effectively frozen out of
borrowing in the domestic U.S. markets for overseas purposes, and
American borrowers were largely prevented from taking funds out of the
United States, even their own retained earnings. As a result, a very
strong demand arose for access to dollars overseas. The Euromarkets
have never lost their allure since then. Also, it has been seen that the
massive increases in oil prices in 1973 and 1979–1980 contributed to the
growth of these markets. The OPEC countries, which receive mostly
dollars for their oil, have deposited heavily in the Eurodollar market,
and the deficit countries have borrowed heavily to finance their import
needs.

INVESTMENT IN NEGOTIABLE SECURITIES

Loans are not the only channel for the investment of Eurofunds.
Eurobanks can also employ their funds in investments in marketable
securities. Such investments, which are typically short term in order to
maintain liquidity, have the advantage (unlike loans) of being readily
marketable before maturity. Of course, banks also attempt to balance

the maturity structure of their *loan* portfolio carefully as well—so that there is a steady inflow of funds from maturing credits. However, the secondary markets provide an alternative for not only attractive investments but also as insurance against a possible shortfall in funds.

Some of the principal alternatives to which a bank has recourse are U.S. Treasury bills, commercial paper (either in the Euro or domestic markets), negotiable certificates of deposit (also either in the Euro or domestic markets), and bankers' acceptances. These are all high-quality, short-term instruments for which there is a well-developed secondary market. Thus the two critical conditions of liquidity are met: easy disposability and low risk of significant loss on the value of the principal and interest.

Finally, it should be noted that not all of a bank's Eurodeposits are actually loaned out. Although there are no reserve requirements (as indeed there are not in most countries' domestic markets), banks prudently maintain some minimum level of *precautionary reserves* as working capital to meet any unforeseen demands.

INTEREST RATES IN THE EUROMARKETS

Eurofunds are essentially indistinguishable from domestic funds of the same currency. They can move freely across national borders. They can be freely exchanged for other currencies at the same exchange rates as funds of domestic origin. There is virtually nothing that domestic-originated funds can do that Eurofunds cannot, and there are a number of advantages, as has been seen, that the latter has over domestic-sourced funds, such as avoiding capital export controls that existed in the United States in the late 1960s and early 1970s.

There is thus a very close tie between the two markets. A constant choice by both depositors and borrowers and the action of interest-rate *arbitrageurs* serves to keep the Eurorates, both deposit and lending, very close to the corresponding domestic rates.[2]

The basic relationship between the Euromarkets and domestic markets is that, in general, *deposit rates on Eurodeposits are slightly higher* and *lending rates are slightly lower* than those of their domestic counterparts. Since the costs of deposit taking are lower for Eurobanks, they can afford to pay more on deposits. They have no reserve requirements or deposit insurance, only accept large deposits, and do not have the high expense of an extensive branch network. The depositors generally expect a higher return, since there is less protection than for domestic deposits.

Likewise, the lower costs for the bank make it possible for it to lend

---

[2]See the Glossary for a definition of the term *arbitrageur*.

at a slightly lower interest rate than a domestic bank. Domestic market conditions act as an anchor for credit conditions in the Euromarket. Since most depositors and borrowers always have the option of switching to the domestic market, the Euromarket has to buy business by offering more attractive rates.

There have been periods when Eurorates have penetrated the constraints imposed by domestic conditions. This is caused by legal or psychological obstacles. The U.S. capital controls imposed such a legal constraint prior to 1974. The OPEC nations' fears about the possible seizure of their funds in the United States may also have prompted them to put a disproportionate amount of their funds in the Euromarkets. However, arbitraging from other depositors and between banks tends to eliminate most of that distortion. Only when controls are in effect is the efficiency of the market significantly obstructed.

DESTRUCTION OF EUROCURRENCIES

As was seen above, the creation of Eurocurrencies occurs only when a foreign currency is deposited in a bank. The subsequent lending or investing of these deposits does not increase the actual, net size of the Euromarkets (see Table 8.2). Similarly, the repayment of loans or the sale of negotiable securities by a Eurobank does not reduce the size of the market. *Only the withdrawal of the original deposit can cause a reduction or destruction of Eurocurrencies*. Thus, if a depositor withdraws DM 1 million from a Euro-DM account with a bank in London and repatriates them to Germany, then the size of the Euro–deutschemark market has declined. However, if the deposit is not removed, but instead a DM 1 million loan is repaid to the Eurobank, the size of the Euro-DM market would be unchanged. The basic reason is, of course, that the underlying demand deposit in a domestic German bank is still there.

SUMMARY

The unique features of the Euromarkets can be summarized in a few basic points:

1. A Eurocurrency is really no different from the corresponding domestic currency, except that it is deposited abroad.
2. The Eurocurrency market is a *banking market*.
3. Eurobonds are a very different type of Euromarket from Eurocurrencies, as different as domestic bond markets are from domestic banking markets.

4. The essence of Euromarkets is that they are largely beyond the control of domestic banking authorities, either of the country of the currency or of the country in which the market operates.

5. In general, investors can earn slightly more and borrowers pay slightly less in the Euromarkets than in comparable domestic markets.

KEY TERMS

ARBITRAGE	EUROMARKET	PETRODOLLAR
ASIA CURRENCY	FLOATING RATE	RECYCLING
CROSS CURRENCY	INTERBANK	ROLLOVER
EUROBANK	LATIN CURRENCY	SHORT FUNDING
EUROBOND	LIBOR	SPREAD
EUROCURRENCY	MATCHED FUNDING	XENOCURRENCY
EURODOLLAR		

REVIEW QUESTIONS

1. What are the Euromarkets? What is their greatest attraction?
2. What is a Eurobond?
3. What is a Eurocurrency? What is a Eurodollar?
4. What is an Asia-currency or Latin-currency market?
5. How is a Eurocurrency created? How is it destroyed?
6. Why is the term *Eurodollar bond* incorrect?
7. Where is the principal Euromarket located? Why?
8. Can U.S. banks trade Eurodollars? Explain.
9. Can British banks do Eurobanking in London? Explain.
10. Can Eurosterling be traded in London?
11. Why is the term *Euro-equity* wrong?
12. What three developments were major factors in the growth of the Euromarkets?
13. What is the general relationship between deposit and lending interest rates in the Euromarkets and in the corresponding domestic market of the same currency?

SUGGESTED REFERENCES

DAVIS, STEVEN I.　*Euro-bank,* New York: Halsted Press, 1976.

DUFEY, GUNTER, AND IAN H. GIDDY　*The International Money Market.* Englewood Cliffs, N.J.: Prentice-Hall, Inc., 1978.

EINZIG, PAUL *Eurodollar System.* New York: Macmillan, Inc., 1967.

FIRST NATIONAL BANK OF CHICAGO, *Eurobond Market,* 1978.

KORTH, CHRISTOPHER M. "The Eurocurrency Market" in William H. Baughn and Donald R. Mandich, eds., *The International Banking Handbook.* Homewood, Ill.: Dow Jones-Irwin, 1983.

KORTH, CHRISTOPHER M. "International Financial Markets" in William H. Baughn and Donald R. Mandich, eds., *The International Banking Handbook.* Homewood Ill.: Dow Jones-Irwin, 1983.

MCKENZIE, GEORGE W. *Economics of the Eurocurrency System.* New York: Halsted Press, 1976.

MENDELSOHN, M.S. *Money on the Move.* New York: McGraw-Hill Book Company, 1980.

QUINN, BRIAN S. *New Euromarkets.* New York: Halsted Press, 1975.

9

Multinational Economic Organizations

INTRODUCTION

There are more than 170 countries in the world today. Such fragmentation tends to produce economic, political, and military weakness for the individual countries and magnifies the potential for international conflicts. Each country is a sovereign entity with sovereign control over the people and institutions within its borders and over the activities of groups that cross its borders.

History has amply demonstrated the difficulties and dangers of political and economic fragmentation. As a result, governments have created a myriad of multinational institutions in order to overcome the shortcomings of such separation. These organizations are of several types. Table 9.1 summarizes the major organizations that illustrate each of the following categories:

1. The first group of international organizations comprises those that are basically forums for discussion of mutual problems and opportunities (for example, the Organization of Petroleum Exporting Countries). These institutions generally have little authority to operate either independently or on behalf of member states. Nevertheless, they serve a very valuable function for their members by bringing them together to discuss, and often to resolve, major issues.

TABLE 9.1 Major International Organizations

---

1. DISCUSSION FORUMS

> United Nations: General Assembly and Security Council
> General Agreement on Tariffs and Trade (GATT)
> Organization of Petroleum Exporting Countries (OPEC)
> Bank for International Settlements (BIS)
> Organization of Economic Cooperation and Development (OECD)

2. INDEPENDENT AUTHORITIES

> International Monetary Fund (IMF)
> International Bank for Reconstruction and Development (IBRD or World
>   Bank)
> Inter-American Development Bank
> Asian Development Bank
> African Development Bank
> Functional organs of the United Nations such as the World Health Organi-
>   zation

3. MULTINATIONAL INTEGRATION

> European Economic Community (EEC)
> European Monetary System (EMS)
> Council of Mutual Economic Assistance (CMEA or COMECON)
> North Atlantic Treaty Organization (NATO)
> Warsaw Pact

---

2. The second group is comprised of institutions that have been set up with independent, multinational authority and powers (for example, the IMF). They are designed to perform functions that the individual states cannot or will not perform on their own.

3. The third group includes only those institutions that actually integrate some portion of the economic or political activities of member countries (for example, the European Economic Community). Such efforts are the most ambitious of all.

GATT was discussed in Chapter 4 and the IMF in Chapter 5. Military organizations such as NATO and the Warsaw Pact are not relevant to our discussion. And the UN is a very diverse organization which addresses a wide range of issues with interest to multinational companies, for example, via the International Labor Organization, the Center for the Study of the Transnational (or multinational) Corporation, and suggested codes of conduct for multinationals. However, we are primarily interested in the international organizations that have the major impact upon corporations or the environment within which firms operate, for example, the World Bank, major regional development banks (such as the Inter-American Development Bank), the European Economic Community, and international cartels such as OPEC. These and other major international institutions provide the focus for the rest of the chapter.

DEVELOPMENT BANKS

The problem of economic and social development is immense and growing. In the last generation a handful of countries have made the jump from being less developed to rapidly developing. However, these have mostly had the advantage of an abundance of raw materials, such as is the case with Saudi Arabia and Brazil, or a strong work ethic, such as in South Korea and Singapore. Other relevant factors include proximity to major foreign markets, such as have Mexico and Spain, and the incentive of an external military threat, such as is experienced by Taiwan.

However, for most countries the conditions have not been as conducive to rapid development. Numerous programs such as foreign aid have been created to alleviate the problem. Nevertheless, the problem of underdevelopment is severe: Many different types of assistance must be mobilized to overcome the hurdles confronting development. One of the most significant of these efforts involves *development banks.*

Development banks are investment funds. They do not accept deposits and are very unlike commercial banks. They extend loans and sometimes make equity investments. Development banks exist at three levels: worldwide, regional, and national. The following discussion focuses on the worldwide and regional development banks.

INTERNATIONAL BANK FOR RECONSTRUCTION AND DEVELOPMENT (IBRD)

As was mentioned in the discussion of the International Monetary Fund, Bretton Woods was the site of a major international economic conference during World War II. The aim of the conference was, first, to ensure that the international economic breakdown of the 1930s, which resulted from artificial barriers to trade and capital flows and arbitrary manipulations of the exchange rates, would be undone and not permitted to recur. The second aim was to provide international aid for the war-ravaged countries to foster reconstruction and, for the less-developed countries, to foster development.

Bretton Woods led directly or indirectly to the establishment of three organizations: the IMF, the International Bank for Reconstruction and Development (IBRD), and the General Agreement on Tariffs and Trade (GATT). The IBRD is examined in this section; the other two organizations were discussed in earlier chapters.

One of the major concerns of the Bretton Woods conferees was the very serious problem of the reconstruction of war-ravaged Europe and Asia. Coupled with this was the compelling need to help aid the economic and social development of less-developed countries (LDCs). The IBRD was designed to fill these needs. It is a worldwide development bank.

Any member of the IMF may elect to join the IBRD; there are more than 130 members. The basic function of the IBRD (or *World Bank,* as it is misleadingly called) is to make loans to its needy members. The financial resources come partially from members' contributions (quotas) but primarily from borrowing in private capital markets.

The resources of the World Bank have grown significantly since its foundation in 1946. Table 9.2 illustrates how much its resources have grown. They doubled between 1970 and 1975 and doubled again by 1980 to a total of more than $50 billion.

Since the majority of the World Bank's resources depend upon its borrowing capacity, it is critical that the organization maintains a prime credit rating. It does this by the following:

1. extending *loans only,* it makes no equity investments
2. charging rates of interest that fully cover both its borrowing and administrative costs
3. lending only to countries with reasonable credit ratings, although it does not lend to developed countries
4. extending loans only for economically attractive and self-financing projects
5. requiring guarantees from the government to whose country the loan is being extended
6. financing only part of any project
7. insisting upon repayment only in hard currencies
8. having limited recourse to its members for additional contributions as part of their membership quota

The Bank has been very successful in maintaining its prime credit rating. Furthermore, it has been able to do this without ever having to have recourse to calling for the supplemental contributions of its members, as per item 8 above.

Although the IBRD had as its primary initial objective the reconstruction of the war-ravaged countries, its resources proved very inadequate for the task. Accordingly, when the U.S. government introduced the Marshall Plan with its significantly greater resources, the IBRD shifted its activities almost totally to the task of economic and social development of the LDCs. Now its loans go only to developing countries,

TABLE 9.2 The World Bank

	Assets		Loans				Borrowings		Capital
	Total Assets	Total Assets minus Undisbursed Loans	Total Disbursed	Total Disbursed and Undisbursed	New Disbursement	New Commitments	Total Outstanding	New Net	Capital Stock (Paid-in)
1950	2,102[a]	1,976	614	740	166	316	290[b]	36[b]	1,670
1955	3,312	2,869	1,680	2,136	274	350	852	75	1,806
1960	5,550	4,673	2,807	3,683	544	659	2,073	168	2,025
1965	7,721	6,059	3,829	5,492	606	1,023	2,724	232	2,168
1970	11,628	8,702	5,963	8,889	754	1,580	4,568	487	2,316
1975	26,026	18,351	12,188	19,863	1,995	4,320	12,275	2,639	3,082
1980	57,183	39,071	26,703	44,804	4,363	7,644	29,635	3,382	3,996

[a]All figures are in millions of U.S. dollars.
[b]Estimate.

SOURCE: *World Bank Annual Report*, Washington, D.C.: International Bank for Reconstruction and Development, various issues.

not to industrialized countries, which have the capacity to finance their needs by the alternative means, or not to the poorest countries, which generally do not qualify because of their poor credit ratings.

The International Bank for Reconstruction and Development is careful to avoid competing with private-sector lenders. Not only might competition lead to antagonism, but it might discourage direct flows of private-sector financial flows to developing countries—something the Bank is anxious to promote. Moreover, in order to encourage loans from commercial banks, the IBRD often offers a guarantee to banks on part of some bank loans.

Unfortunately, because of the need to maintain its credit rating, the World Bank is very restricted in the type of projects it can finance. There are many worthwhile projects that its charter or prudence do not allow it to finance. In order to surmount these limitations and to increase its contribution to economic and social development, two subsidiary organizations have been created.

International Finance Corporation (IFC):   Early experience at the World Bank indicated that, because of the stringency of the conditions under which loans could be made, the IBRD was not able to offer financial help for many worthy investments. Therefore, in 1956 a sister organization, the International Finance Corporation, was created. The IFC is designed to make loans *without government guarantees* (and therefore for investments *only in the private sector*) and even equity investments (that is, to have partial ownership rather than simply make loans). In fact, even its loans may have provisions for profit sharing.

As in the case of the IBRD, the fostering of private money and capital markets is of paramount importance. Toward this end the International Finance Corporation is anxious to sell its investments when a venture becomes successful enough to attract private investors.

However, since the IFC makes nonguaranteed loans and equity investments, its risks are greater than are those of the IBRD. As a result, the *IFC's credit rating does not permit it to borrow in the private capital markets.* Accordingly, all the institution's resources must come from member government contributions. This, of course, makes the IFC much more dependent upon the generosity of member governments than is its parent organization. However, it also allows the IFC to be more flexible in credit terms, currency of repayment, and so forth.

International Development Association (IDA):   Even the IFC had certain limitations regarding the variety and stipulations of its loans. Therefore, in 1960 the third organization of the *World Bank Group* was created. The International Development Association (sometimes called the *soft-loan window* of the World Bank) provides money for so-called nonproductive loans—housing, sanitation projects, and so on.

Also, the stipulations can be very generous—no interest charges, ten-year "periods of grace" (no repayment of principal for the first ten years), and up to fifty years for repayment. The IDA is even less credit-worthy than the IFC. Therefore all of its resources must also come directly from member-government contributions.

REGIONAL DEVELOPMENT BANKS

The job of financing international economic and social development is so immense that even the extensive resources of the World Bank Group are inadequate. To help meet the tremendous demands for assistance, a number of other international financing organizations, mostly public but some private, have been created. Although they are not part of the World Bank Group, many of these are somewhat similar, and they, at least indirectly, owe their existence to the example set by the IBRD. Like the IBRD, they receive their funds primarily from member contributions but also from debt financing—not from deposits.

The goals and method of operations of the development banks are generally comparable to those of the World Bank, but they each have a much more limited geographical focus. The major development banks are as follows:

Inter-American Development Bank
Asian Development Bank
African Development Bank
European Investment Bank
International Bank for Economic Cooperation ⎫
                                            ⎬ in Eastern Europe
International Investment Bank   ⎭

THE INTER-AMERICAN DEVELOPMENT BANK (IDB)

The largest and most prominent of the international development banks is the Inter-American Development Bank. The IDB is a regional bank that seeks to accelerate economic and social development in the developing countries of the Western Hemisphere. In addition to the potential borrowing countries, many non-borrowing countries (the U.S., Canada, and many developed countries outside of the Western Hemisphere) are capital-contributing (but not capital-borrowing) members.

The bank makes two different types of loans, each of which comes from a different "fund": the ordinary capital resources fund and the fund for special operations.

The *ordinary capital resources fund* is used to make productive loans at conventional terms to governments or private organizations capable of bearing the debt. Such loans must be repaid in the currency in which the loans were made and guaranteed by the government of the recipient nation. These loans are similar in many respects to IBRD loans. The funds for the ordinary capital resources fund are provided by member-country quotas and borrowing in world capital markets. Also, the ordinary capital resources are buttressed by an additional, and much larger, amount of "callable" capital, which is used as security for borrowing in world capital markets.

The *Fund for Special Operations (FSO)* provides funds on a less stringent basis than that associated with ordinary capital funds. Loans are not restricted to directly productive employment; for instance, housing and improvement of water and sewage facilities are legitimate purposes. Also, these long-term, relatively low-interest loans are often repayable in the currency of the borrower. The FSO's resources are contributions from member countries. This fund is similar in activity to the IDA, which it actually antedates.

The other regional development banks operate in similar fashion. In addition, there are *national* development banks that operate in a parallel fashion within countries; a country may have several of those development banks, each focusing upon a different sector of the economy, for instance, mining and agriculture.

ASIAN DEVELOPMENT BANK (AsDB)

The Far Eastern counterpart of the Inter-American Development Bank is the Asian Development Bank, which was opened in 1966. Its members include not only Asian countries, which can be both contributing and borrowing members, but also non-Asian countries, which can be contributing members only. The United States, Canada, the United Kingdom, and many Western European countries are among the nonregional members. Its headquarters is in Manila in the Philippines.

The AsDB's financial resources come primarily from member-country contributions plus borrowings from money and capital markets. Although its loans can extend for as long as thirty years and grace periods can be as long as seven years on the repayment of principal, the interest rates and credit record of the organization, as well as the backing of its member governments, have maintained a strong credit rating. Most of the loans are extended to governments or governmental agencies. Much of the AsDB's lending involves cofinancing with commercial banks. Technical assistance is also an important service of the organization.

The Asian Development Bank has a "soft-loan window"—the *Asian Development Fund*—which is analogous to the Fund for Special Operations of the Inter-American Development Bank. The Asian Development Fund extends loans for as long as forty years with a ten-year grace period and a very nominal 1 percent interest rate. Obviously, the credit rating of the Bank would be impaired with such loans in its portfolio. However, the AsDF's funds come from special contributions of its members; it cannot borrow from private markets.

AFRICAN DEVELOPMENT BANK (AfDB)

In the same year as the initiation of the Asian Development Bank, a similar organization was begun in Africa. In that year the Organization of African Unity created the African Development Bank, which is headquartered in Abidjan, Ivory Coast. The AfDB, like the IDB and the AsDB, was designed to provide financial and technical assistance to member countries. The AfDB was, until the early 1980s, more restrictive than either of the other two groups: Only African countries (and only independent African countries at that) could be members. The organization is now willing to accept non-African countries as contributing, but not borrowing, members.

The African Development Bank receives its funds from both its members' subscribed capital contributions and also from private-sector borrowings. It has a good credit rating, which qualifies it for commercial credits. In order to qualify for commercial bank funds and public offerings, the AfDB maintains conservative lending policies and interest rates. Loans are made only to governments or their agencies. Interest rates are close to commercial rates. Loans can be for as long as twenty years with three- to five-year grace periods. In addition to the loans, the Bank also provides guarantees and technical assistance.

The African Development Bank also has its own "soft-loan window" analogous to the Fund for Special Operations of the IDB and the Asian Development Fund of the AsDB. The *African Development Fund* was founded in 1972. Unlike the parent organization, the AfDF has included as members from its very beginning not only African countries but also many other countries such as the United States, the United Kingdom, Germany, Brazil, Japan, and South Korea. These soft loans can be for as long as fifty years, include ten years of grace, and be repaid at interest rates of 1 percent in the ten years after the grace period and 3 percent after that.

DEVELOPMENT BANKS AND INTERNATIONAL BUSINESSES

As the discussion above indicates, development banks exist primarily in developing countries. Although national development banks can exist in any country, the IBRD and the regional development banks lend only to the less economically advanced countries.

The resources of development banks are directed toward projects within these countries. Often foreign companies can be participants in the projects, occasionally as part owner or, more likely, as contractors or suppliers. This is the principal impact of these organizations upon international business.

The development banks help to facilitate and partially fund billions of dollars of international trade annually. The portion they finance is generally only the foreign currency share, which is, of course, the most critical part as far as foreign suppliers or contractors are concerned. Also, since these international institutions generally have prime credit ratings, their participation, approval, and guarantees help to promote these types of projects, even to the extent of facilitating additional financing from commercial banks, which is indeed a major priority of all development banks.

ECONOMIC INTEGRATION

International development banks are not the only regional cooperative efforts in existence. Another very potent movement of the post–World War II era has been the trend toward regional integration. The best known of such efforts is the *European Economic Community (EEC)*. However, integrative efforts have sprouted up in many parts of the globe.

BASIC FORMS OF ECONOMIC INTEGRATION

Economic integration schemes can basically be broken down into the following four types:

1. free trade area
2. customs union
3. common market
4. full economic and political union

Free trade area: A *free trade area* is a collection of countries which have agreed to remove trade barriers between themselves, while each member retains its individual trade barriers vis-à-vis nonmember countries. The most prominent example of this type of union is the *European Free Trade Association.* However, EFTA has declined greatly in significance since three of its members (the United Kingdom, Ireland, and Denmark) opted in the mid-1970s to join the EEC. Other free trade areas include the Latin American Free Trade Association (LAFTA), the Caribbean Free Trade Area (CARIFTA), and the Association of Southeast Asian Nations (ASEAN).

Customs union: A *customs union* goes one step beyond a free trade area. Not only do the members agree to dismantle all trade barriers between themselves but also to utilize a common set of trade barriers with nonmembers. The best-known customs union is the European Economic Community. Unlike EFTA, the EEC is continuing to be very strong—indeed, the defection of the United Kingdom, Ireland, and Denmark from EFTA to the EEC was a very favorable trend for the latter group. The other members are Germany, France, Netherlands, Belgium, Luxembourg, Italy, and Greece.

The *Central American Common Market (CACM)* was at one time a fairly successful imitator of the EEC experiment. However, war and continuing domestic and international unrest have torn CACM apart and prevented its rebuilding.

Common market: A *common market* not only eliminates internal trade barriers (à la a free trade area) and institutes common external trade barriers for nonmembers (à la a customs union), but in addition it opens up the internal markets to free factor flows. Thus, capital, technology, and labor would be free to migrate anywhere within the common market area without encountering any obstacles not encountered by similar domestic factors of production. This has proven to be an elusive goal.

The EEC and the CACM were originally planned as common markets; indeed, the EEC is often, but erroneously, called the European Common Market. However, such free factor mobility has encountered such strong opposition, that neither group ever attained common market status. Nevertheless, as was discussed in Chapter 5, in early 1979 the European Economic Community created the *European Monetary System (EMS)*, which is a further step in pursuit of that goal.

Full economic and political union: The integration groups that were described above are integrating their markets to various extents. However, in each instance the member countries intend to retain the vast majority of their *individual sovereignty*.

The ultimate move toward full integration would require the sacrifice of most international sovereignty in the creation of total integration. Several major countries have been created in the past from just such integration. The United States, Canada, and Australia are three examples of successful integrative efforts, although the French Canadian separatist movement is causing great strain in the Canadian confederation. Also, the amalgamation of Zanzibar with Tanganyika yielded Tanzania. Other more recent efforts at full integration have largely been unsuccessful. Examples have been abortive efforts to merge Egypt with Syria (to form the United Arab Republic) and Malaysia with Singapore.

Nevertheless, the world is fragmented into many small and very poor countries. Partial integration can help many of them to realize the economies of large markets. Therefore, further attempts by the groups mentioned above and others to integrate into regional blocs are likely to be seen in the future. In addition, recurring efforts at full integration are also likely to occur. The difficulties of successful integration are immense. A very strong will to succeed and a willingness to compromise and make sacrifices of sovereignty are necessary.

However, without cooperative regional efforts, the smaller countries are always going to remain in the shadow of the larger countries, and their potential for growth will be reduced. Even the wealthy countries of Europe continue to recognize the benefits of integration. Poor countries in Latin American, Asia, Africa, and the Middle East have much to gain from integration.

ADVANTAGES OF INTEGRATION

There are many ways in which economic cooperation can benefit its participants; the greater the willingness to make sacrifices and to cooperate, the greater are the potential gains.

One of the most attractive prospects from integration is that import costs such as tariffs and other trade barriers are reduced and finally eliminated. Companies that import thus have a strong interest in integration.

The prospect of much larger export markets is a strong inducement because of the efficiencies of large-scale production that may not be possible in smaller national markets—more efficient sizes of factories; greater specialization of the work force and machines; longer production runs; and internal economies of scale in purchasing, marketing, and financing. These are just some of the many developments that can lead to lower costs and higher living standards.

In addition, many so-called external economies of scale often result from the integration of national transportation, power, communication, financing, and labor markets. These also lead to greater efficiency and lower costs.

DIFFICULTIES OF INTEGRATION

Obviously the higher the degree of integration, the more concessions each member must make and the more sovereignty it must sacrifice. Similarly, the barriers to success grow with the extent of the desired integration. Nevertheless, these examples of ongoing integration and other efforts still in the planning stage attest to the recognition by a very fragmented world that working together can benefit all participants.

Unfortunately, most integration efforts between less-developed countries (LDCs) have progressed far more slowly than in Europe. The most significant barriers have probably been political—an unwillingness to compromise and make significant concessions and a tendency for regional wars to erupt, such as occurred between Tanzania and Uganda as well as in Central America.

However, most groups of LDCs also have major economic disadvantages that limit the near-term potential of such integration. For instance, they have not historically traded extensively among themselves —most rely heavily on the export of primary products (minerals, petroleum, foodstuffs) and import manufactured goods. As a result they have much more potential as competitors than as trading partners.

Another obstacle to economic integration in developing countries is the great difficulty of integrating transportation and power networks and so forth, which is a much larger problem in LDCs than in Europe. Also, literacy levels are low, and the industrial base or infrastructure must be constructed, not simply rebuilt as was true in Europe after World War II.

Integration requires adjustments in the economic practices of various countries, since success in some areas can lead to decline in others. Each country can expect to experience declines in some of its industries; some geographic regions may suffer, whereas others may gain. A major responsibility of the governments is to encourage new industry to locate in adversely affected areas and to invest heavily in the infrastructure of the major industrial areas. Integrational efforts are, therefore, phased in over a period of years in order to cushion the effects, and readjustment funds are often provided for the declining areas.

Nevertheless, the potential from integration is very great in developing countries, perhaps greater than in Europe. The LDCs are just too small and too economically underdeveloped in most cases to grow rapidly as individual units.

Significance of Economic Integration for International Business

Like any change, economic integration affects different companies in vastly different ways. For example, the company that has enjoyed a privileged and highly profitable position behind high tariff walls is not likely to favor removal of those tariffs. In general, import-competing companies do not encourage integration.

On the other hand, the company that sees the removal of trade barriers as an opportunity to greatly expand its markets by being able to ship to neighboring countries free of barriers, sees integration as a fortunate development.

The traditional exporters to the markets that are absorbed into the economic union also have a very strong interest. They tend to view these markets as more attractive than in the past, since they are now so much larger. However, at the same time, as an outsider, that company's shipments are still subject to trade controls, whereas competitors within the new economic group face decreasing barriers. Thus, companies abroad may face the prospect of losing traditional markets, because they are outside the integrated group of countries. As a result, there is a strong incentive to invest inside the new grouping. Thus, *economic integration tends to serve as an incentive to attract foreign investment.* This was the strongest impetus to the rapid increase of U.S. investments in the EEC countries in the late 1950s and early 1960s.

TRADE RESTRICTION AGREEMENTS

The market system does not always work to the total satisfaction of any one individual; each of us can identify flaws. At such moments many or most of us might at least monetarily wish for an alternative system that would satisfy our needs more readily. However, on balance and with careful reflection, most observers (at least in the non-Communist world) recognize that the existing market system, for all its possible limitations, does the most economically efficient job of supplying the vast array of merchandise and services that a modern economy demands.

However, there are many individuals and groups who are strongly attracted to some type of controls, which, by definition, obstruct the free operation of the market system. In the United States, collusive efforts by buyers or sellers are generally banned, unless they are specifically introduced by the federal or state governments; for example, the wage and price controls of the early 1970s and the chronic program of agricultural price supports.

It should not be surprising, therefore, that in foreign countries, which in general are less free-market oriented than in the United States, there can often be very strong interest in collusive producing, selling, or buying efforts. This is especially true in developing countries, which frequently rely very heavily on foreign exchange receipts from a very limited range of product exports. The fascination for these countries is seldom focused upon keeping prices down or even very often upon increasing supply or access to products and services. Overwhelmingly the interest of developing countries is for increasing the price of those raw materials upon which those countries rely for much of their export earnings.

The perceived need of these developing countries for some form of controls would likely be much less if alternative satisfactory arrangements were available to help foster their economic and social growth. For example, if the level of foreign aid dispensed by the developed countries was more satisfactory (instead of declining in real terms), or if the developing countries could obtain more generous preferential access to the markets of developed countries for a more diversified basket of the poorer-countries' exports, there might be much less interest in international controls.

However, there is substantial dissatisfaction among the poorer countries (and some of the not-so-poor) and a very strong interest in some form of cartel or international commodity agreement. This interest was heightened by the sharp rise of the prices of most imported goods since the early 1970s and the high volatility of earnings of most commodities.

No one can dispute the existence of sharp rises in the prices of most goods and services, which have been felt by rich and poor alike. However, a United Nations study demonstrated that between 1950 and 1974 the price increases of a wide list of internationally traded commodities actually exceeded the average increase in the prices of manufactured goods.[1] But averages conceal many variations. For some commodities the price increases exceeded that of manufactured goods, whereas for many other commodities the price increases failed to match the increases of general prices.

However, the true problem does not so much involve the overall movements in prices but rather the *volatility* in prices of commodities relative to manufactured goods. Such price volatility disrupts developmental programs and causes severe hardship on many poorer countries with little export diversification. This variability has many causes. *Demand pressures* can vary substantially at different phases of the economic cycle and in response to technological innovation or consumer taste changes.

Supply pressures can likewise significantly alter the availability of commodities. Supplies can decline due to weather (for example, a drought in Chile sharply reduced Chilean copper output and frost in Brazil sharply reduced Brazilian coffee production), other natural calam-

---

[1] United Nations, "Evolution of Basic Commodity Prices Since 1950," Document A/9544, 1974.

ities (such as typhoons, earthquakes or floods), domestic insurrection or other domestic turmoil (for instance, the Iranian crisis that followed the overthrow of the Shah in 1979 and also the Nigerian civil war), and international conflict (such as the Angolan invasion into Zaire, which severely disrupted the latter's copper output).

Commodity supplies can also increase sharply—for example, new sources of production, such as the opening of new mines or the sharp increase of agricultural production such as Brazil's major venture into soybean production and Malaysia's into palm oil or the advent of new technology, such as the sharp increases in harvests in some countries following the introduction of new seeds of grains in the 1970s.

As a result of these experiences, producing countries (especially developing countries) have suggested many international cooperative efforts to increase and stabilize their incomes.

CARTEL

A *cartel* is an agreement among producers that seeks to artificially increase prices by *arbitrary price raises,* by *reducing supplies,* or by *allocating markets.* Such cartels can be either private-sector (in the past there have been cartels in matches, wood pulp, oil, cement, and lead) or public-sector, such as OPEC, rubber, and potash.

An example of the imposition of a government-sponsored cartel was that of the British government in restricting rubber output on rubber plantations in Malaya in the 1920s. The program was temporarily successful but led to unintended results, such as a sharp increase in the production and world market share of Indonesia, a sharp increase in the use of reclaimed rubber, and the development of synthetic rubber!

INTERNATIONAL COMMODITY
PRICE AGREEMENT (ICA)

An ICA is similar in many ways to a cartel but *includes customers as well as suppliers in the agreement.* Example of past efforts toward international commodity agreements have occurred with coffee, sugar, and tin.

In general, the record of success of ICAs has been unsatisfactory; as a result, they have vitually all collapsed. Like most types of artificial controls, they contain the seeds of their own destruction. If the stresses and distortions that ICAs create are very significant (and there would be no reason to set them up in the first place unless they would be capable of significantly altering the basic market pressures), market responses often overwhelm the controls. Some of the negative effects of ICAs that can lead to their demise are as follows:

1. If demand is highly elastic, then demand can decline sufficiently to offset the intended gains from rising prices. Also, if demand falls, then prices will begin to slip unless the producers can cooperate to restrict output.
2. If the price is too high, then strong opposition may develop in the consuming countries.
3. High prices may also induce increases in supply from nonmembers or even from members who might be willing to risk collapse of the agreement for the sake of taking extra advantage of the restraint of its partners.
4. These production increases may have resulted from a poor and wasteful allocation of resources.
5. High prices may well encourage the development of substitutes. Substitutes can come either from other natural products (for example, aluminum for copper, tea for coffee, cotton for wool) or through the development of synthetics (for example, synthetic rubber, synthetic fibers, margarine, plastics).

The search for restrictive agreements to bolster the income of producers of primary goods is always with us. However, their distortion of the market generally bears the seeds of their collapse. The record of such efforts, except for OPEC, is generally bad.

SUMMARY

The international organizations examined in this chapter fall into three broad categories: (1) development banks, (2) groups that promote economic integration, and (3) groups that try to profit from cooperative manipulation of the world market for a particular commodity and thereby obstruct market forces.

Development banks can be very important for international businesses. Institutions such as the World Bank and Inter-American Development Bank finance billions of dollars annually of the import portion of development projects. This can be valuable business to exporters in other countries.

There have been many schemes for regional economic integration. By far the most successful has been the European Economic Community. However, even the less ambitious schemes offer the promise of larger integrated markets to international businesses, but also the prospect of more competition.

Development banks and economic integration are elements of the international environment that tend to improve the climate for international trade. However, cartels and commodity price agreements are groups that deliberately manipulate international commodity markets; they interfere with international trade. As we all know from OPEC, it is possible for these groups to have a very strong impact.

KEY TERMS

ASSOCIATION OF
   SOUTHEAST ASIAN
   NATIONS (ASEAN)
CARTEL
CENTRAL AMERICAN
   COMMON MARKET
   (CACM)
COMMON MARKET
COUNCIL OF MUTUAL
   ECONOMIC
   ASSISTANCE
   (CMEA OR COMECON)
CUSTOMS UNION
DEVELOPMENT BANK
EUROPEAN ECONOMIC
   COMMUNITY (EEC)

EUROPEAN FREE TRADE
   ASSOCIATION (EFTA)
FREE TRADE AREA
INTERAMERICAN
   DEVELOPMENT BANK
   (IDB)
INTERNATIONAL BANK
   FOR
   RECONSTRUCTION
   AND DEVELOPMENT
   (IBRD)
INTERNATIONAL
   COMMODITY PRICE
   AGREEMENT (ICA)

INTERNATIONAL
   DEVELOPMENT
   ASSOCIATION (IDA)
INTERNATIONAL
   FINANCE
   CORPORATION (IFC)
ORGANIZATION OF
   PETROLEUM
   EXPORTING
   COUNTRIES (OPEC)
SOVEREIGNTY
WORLD BANK
WORLD BANK GROUP

REVIEW QUESTIONS

1. What were the three basic problems with which the Bretton Woods Conference was concerned?
2. What organizations were eventually created to address the three problems in question 1?
3. Can any country belong the World Bank? Can all members borrow from it?
4. How does the IBRD maintain a prime credit rating?
5. How do the lending policies of the IBRD differ from those of the IFC and IDA? Explain each.
6. Distinguish between the four basic types of economic integration.
7. How would you view integration if you are a local producer? An importer? An exporter? A foreign investor?
8. How would a cartel affect your company if you are a producer of the commodity? If you are a buyer?

SUGGESTED REFERENCES

AMERICAN ACADEMY OF POLITICAL AND SOCIAL SCIENCES *Annals* (special issue: *European Community After 20 Years*). November 1978.

BAKER, JAMES *International Finance Corporation*. New York: Praeger Publishers, 1978.

BALASSA, BELA *Theory of Economic Integration*. Homewood, Ill.: Richard D. Irwin, Inc., 1961.

DE VRIES, MARGARET G. *International Monetary Fund, 1966–1971*. International Monetary Fund, Washington, D.C., 1977.

EUROPEAN COMMUNITY INFORMATION SERVICE *General Report on Activities of the Community* (annual).

INTER-AMERICAN DEVELOPMENT BANK *Annual Report.*

INTERNATIONAL BANK FOR RECONSTRUCTION AND DEVELOPMENT *Annual Report.*

INTERNATIONAL MONETARY FUND *Annual Report.*

VAN MEERHAEGHE, M.A.G. *International Economic Institutions*. London: Longmans, Green & Co., Ltd., 1966.

WORLD BANK *Annual Report.*

10

Balance
of
Payments

In Chapters 2 and 3 the bases for and the barriers to international transactions were discussed. The combination of these and other forces lead to extensive economic interaction between any country and other countries in the world. In order to gauge the nature of the economic interaction between one country and the rest of the world, economists have developed an accounting system to measure the extent and pattern of international transactions for a country. That macroeconomic accounting system is known as the *balance of payments* (*BOP*).

Any reader of the business press or even any regular observer of the evening news has often heard of the balance of payments and its subsection, the *balance of trade*. Judging by the solemnity of the announcements or accompanying commentary (for example, "the U.S. dollar strengthened in the foreign-exchange markets when today's announcement of the U.S. trade deficit was less than the market had anticipated"), the average person senses that whatever this balance of payments and balance of trade are they must be important.

However, these concepts are not really understood by most people. It is commonly agreed that the concepts are very important, but few people can explain exactly why. A feeling that "something should be done" about "the problems of the balance of payments" is widespread. However, neither the actual nature of the balance itself nor the problems that may arise from a lack of balance are well understood. Therefore, it is not surprising that precisely *what* should be done is not clear to most people.

THE NATURE OF THE BALANCE OF PAYMENTS

The balance of payments has traditionally been useful as a gauge of the pressure upon a country's exchange rate. This view of the BOP has always been of limited validity and has very little value under our existing system of floating exchange rates. However, the BOP remains a very popular record of the scale and pattern of a country's international transactions. Also, rightly or wrongly, it continues to guide (or misguide) governmental policy makers. Accordingly, the international business manager needs to be familiar with the BOP.

DEFINITION

The *balance of payments* is a summary of the flows during a certain period of time of all economic transactions between the residents of a given country (or group of countries) and the residents of the rest of the world.

Flows: The BOP measures flows of economic transactions. It is *not a measure of the level* of foreign assets and liabilities. As such, the BOP tables are analogous to a corporation's source-and-application-of-funds statement or to a family's record of its income and expenditures.

Time period: The balance of payments records economic flows during a specified period of time. This is usually one calendar year, although some countries such as Japan use different fiscal years. However, the BOP is also generally reported on a quarterly basis.

Residents of a country: The economic transactions can involve corporations, governments, individuals, or any other "residents" of a country; tourists, itinerent corporate executives, or employees of foreign governments are not classified as residents. Virtually all other persons and institutions are legal residents.

Occasionally, balance-of-payments tables are set up for regions or multicountry groups of countries rather than for an individual country. For example, the balance of payments of the European Economic Community with the rest of the world.

Economic transactions: The balance of payments attempts to measure all international economic transactions, even if no money actually changes hands and even if the transactions are not legal. This ambitious goal leads to a number of difficulties for the statisticians. For some countries, smuggling (or "unrecorded border transactions" as they are sometimes euphemistically called) is a significant form of international transaction; BOP accountants attempt to estimate the total of smuggling. For many other countries, *remittances* from immigrants or temporary foreign workers or gifts from individuals and charitable institutions are a significant item in the international transactions of a country, even though there is no *quid pro quo* exchange. These also are recorded in the BOP tables. In a similar vein, foreign aid of one government to another is recorded. Also recorded is international barter (such as petroleum for industrial equipment) in which no money exchanges hands. Thus, some observers have suggested that this system of accounts should be called the *balance of transactions* rather than the balance of payments.

Cross-border transactions: The critical determinant of whether or not a particular transaction should be included in a country's BOP is whether or not it crossed the nation's border. If a transaction does not cross a nation's border, the country's BOP is not affected. Thus, an automobile that is manufactured in Detroit and shipped to Florida is not part of the U.S. balance of payments. Nor is French wine that is produced in the Loire Valley and sold in Paris part of the French BOP.

Currency of transactions: The currency of a transaction that does cross a nation's border is irrelevant for balance-of-payment purposes. The transaction may be denominated in the local currency, a foreign currency, a basket of currencies (such as SDRs), or perhaps not any currency at all as in the case of barter. Thus, it makes no difference for BOP purposes whether an Italian importer pays for the goods or services in lire, in U.S. dollars (as is normal for international trade in most commodities such as petroleum, copper, and wheat), or some other currency such as pounds sterling, Japanese yen, or Guatemalan quetzales.

On the other hand, an economic transaction *does not affect* a nation's balance of payments unless it crosses that country's border, even though that country's currency is involved. For example, a Saudi Arabian shipment of petroleum to Japan that is priced and paid for in U.S. dollars *does not affect* the U.S. balance of payments, since it does not cross the U.S. border. However, it will affect the payments balances of both Saudi Arabia and Japan.

DOUBLE-ENTRY ACCOUNTING

The balance of payments is based on a double-entry accounting system analogous to corporate financial statements. Theoretically each transaction must be reflected with both a debit and a credit entry. Thus, when all debits are totaled, the sum equals the total of all of the credit entries. That is why the system is called a *balance* of payments.

Debits are transactions that give rise to payments from the country to somewhere else in the world, either from expending money or using credit. Debits involve the *use of funds,* the application of external purchasing power. They represent *either increases in assets or reductions in liabilities.* Examples include imports, the purchase of financial assets from foreigners, paying off of foreign liabilities, and an increase in official reserve assets.

Credits are transactions that give rise to increases in financial

TABLE 10.1 Examples of BOP Double-Entry Accounting

CURRENT ACCOUNT	
Merchandise Account	
Dr[a]	*Cr*[b]
Import of goods (increase of asset)	Export of goods (decrease of asset)
Unilateral Transfers Account	
Dr	*Cr*
Gifts or aid sent abroad—an accounting offset to the export of such goods or aid (increase of "asset")	Gifts or aid from abroad—an accounting offset to the import of such goods or aid (decrease of "asset")

CAPITAL ACCOUNT	
Direct-Investment Account	
Dr	*Cr*
Purchase or construction of factory abroad (increase of asset)	Purchase or construction of domestic factory by foreigners (decrease of asset)
Debt-Financing Account	
Dr	*Cr*
Domestic bank loan to a company abroad (increase of asset)	Payment of loan funds to foreign company (decrease of asset)
Receipt of loan funds from abroad (increase of asset)	Note payable to bank abroad increased (increase of liability)
Repayment by domestic company of loan from foreign bank (decrease of liability)	Domestic bank's loan is repaid by foreign borrower (decrease of asset)

RESERVE ACCOUNT	
Reserve Account	
Dr	*Cr*
Acquisition of foreign exchange reserves (increase of asset)	Sale of monetary gold (decrease of asset)

[a]Debit (Dr) means an increase in assets or decrease in liabilities.

[b]Credit (Cr) means a decrease in assets or increase in liabilities.

receipts—the means of international payment—either by getting money or receiving credit. They are sources of funds or external purchasing power. Credits represent either reductions in assets or increases in liabilities. Examples include exports, the sale of financial assets to foreigners, borrowing from foreigners, and a reduction of official reserve assets.

Table 10.1 illustrates how various international debits and credits affect balance-of-payments accounts.

Every transaction has a pair of offsetting debit and credit entries. If all these entries could be accurately measured, then the BOP tables would balance, with total assets equaling total liabilities. However, unlike corporate financial accounts, the diversity, complexity, sheer magnitude, and the method of calculating the totals of various categories of international transactions make it impossible for governmental statisticians to accumulate a total record of all individual international transactions of all residents of that country. Thus, while total debits must *conceptually* equal all credits, in practice the data are collected in such a fashion that, even in the countries with the most sophisticated BOP accounting systems, the totals of the balance-of-payments table are only reasonable approximations. Very few totals in BOP tables are based on totals that are known with certainty (as is also true of national income accounts such as the GNP tables).

Since the balance of payments measures all economic transactions of a country with the rest of the world, then the summary of the BOP deficits and surpluses of all of the countries in the world should equal zero. Conceptually it does, since one country's credit should match another country's debit. Also, the total of individual accounts should equal the total of their counterparts on a worldwide basis. For example, the total of all worldwide exports should equal the total for all imports, since one country's exports are another country's imports. Again, conceptually they do balance. However, for the same statistical reasons noted above, in actual practice some discrepancies do exist when comparing the worldwide totals.

THE BALANCE-OF-PAYMENTS FORMAT

Table 10.2 is an outline of the general BOP format used by the International Monetary Fund. Unfortunately, IMF balance-of-payments statistics are stated in SDRs, a unit of account that is not familiar to most analysts. The process of conversion from SDRs to a local currency is cumbersome.

Governments generally use a BOP format similar to that of the IMF but with rearrangement of some of the data, especially in the capital or financial accounts. Table 10.3 shows the U.S. BOP format with data for sample years.

TABLE 10.2 Balance of Payments: IMF Format

CURRENT ACCOUNT

merchandise (= goods = visibles)
services (= invisibles)
unrequited (= unilateral) transfers

CAPITAL ACCOUNT

direct investment and other long-term capital
short-term capital

ERRORS AND OMISSIONS (= STATISTICAL DISCREPANCY)

TOTAL CHANGE IN RESERVES

SOURCE: *International Monetary Fund, Balance of Payments Yearbook* (any issue).

TABLE 10.3 The U.S. Balance of Payments

	1960	1965	1970	1975	1980
Current account	+ 2.8[a]	+ 5.4	+ 2.3	+ 18.3	+ 3.7
Exports of goods and services[b]	+28.9	+41.1	+65.7	+155.7	+344.7
Merchandise (= goods = visibles)					
excluding military	+19.7	+26.5	+42.5	+107.1	+224.0
Services (= invisibles)	+ 9.2	+14.6	+23.2	+ 48.6	+120.7
Imports of goods and services[b]	− 23.7	− 32.8	− 60.1	− 132.8	− 333.9
Merchandise, excluding military	− 14.8	− 21.5	− 39.9	− 98.0	− 249.3
Services	− 8.9	− 11.3	− 20.2	− 34.8	− 84.6
Unilateral Transfers	− 2.3	− 2.8	− 3.3	− 4.6	− 7.1
Capital and reserve accounts[c]	− 1.8	− 5.0	− 2.0	− 24.0	− 33.3
U.S. assets abroad, net					
(increase = capital outflow, (−) entry)	− 4.1	− 5.7	− 9.3	− 39.7	− 84.8
U.S. official reserve assets, net	+ 2.1	+ 1.2	+ 2.5	− 0.8	− 8.2
Other U.S. government assets, net	− 1.1	− 1.6	− 1.6	− 3.5	− 5.2
U.S. private assets, net	− 5.1	− 5.3	− 10.2	− 35.4	− 71.5
Foreign assets in the U.S., net					
(increase = capital inflow, (+) entry)	+ 2.3	+ 0.7	+ 6.4	+ 15.7	+ 50.3
Foreign official assets in U.S., net	+ 1.5	+ 0.1	+ 6.9	+ 7.0	+ 15.5
Other foreign assets in U.S., net	+ 0.8	+ 0.6	− 0.6	+ 8.6	+ 34.8
Allocation of SDRs	0	0	+ 0.9	0	+ 1.2
Statistical discrepancy (= errors and omissions)	− 1.0	− 0.5	− 0.2	+ 5.8	+ 29.6

[a]All figures are in billions of U.S. dollars ($1,000,000,000).

[b]Exports of goods and services are always (+) entries. Imports of goods and services are always (−) entries. Other accounts can be either *net* (+) or (−) entries.

[c]These are traditional terms that help to distinguish financial accounts from the current accounts. However, they are no longer used by the U.S. government. Note that these accounts are given on a *net* basis—that is, the difference between inflows and outflows.

SOURCES: *Survey of Current Business,* June 1980, pp. 32–33, and June 1981, p. 39.

The rest of this section examines the major subsections of balance-of-payments tables in greater detail.

CURRENT ACCOUNT

The first major section of the typical balance-of-payments table is the record of the transactions that involve goods, services, and unrequited (or unilateral) transfers, commonly called the *current account*. It records a country's trade in goods and services and the flow of gifts, pensions, and workers' remittances between that country and the rest of the world. Table 10.4 lists the major items in the current account.

BALANCE OF TRADE (BOT)

Merchandise trade: The first part of the current account is the one with which the public is typically most familiar— the *merchandise-trade account,* also called *trade in goods* or *trade in "visibles".* Merchan-

TABLE 10.4   Current Account

Merchandise (= goods = visibles)
    exports
    Imports
               Balance of trade (BOT)

Services (= invisibles)
    exports
        transportion and travel
        income on overseas investments
            distributed (that is, paid to parent)
            undistributed (that is, reinvested abroad, not paid to
               parent)
        fees and royalties
        other private-sector services
        government services
    imports
        (same subcategories as for service exports above)
               Balance of services (BOS)
                    Balance of goods and services (BOGS)

Unilateral (= unrequited) transfers
    private (for example, gifts; charity; and workers' remittances and
        pensions)
    government (for example, foreign aid and pensions)
              Balance on current account (BOCA)

---

dise trade includes trade in all commodities (for example, minerals, agricultural products, and other unprocessed goods) and all processed and manufactured goods. Most references to exports and imports refer to this account.

The difference between exports and imports is known as the *balance of trade*. It is a measure of whether a country is a net international supplier or recipient of merchandise.

Surplus versus deficit: The balance-of-trade total is a very misunderstood and widely abused number. There is a strong tendency to assume that a BOT surplus is preferable to a BOT deficit. This is not necessarily true. The optimal BOT for a country must reflect the country's specific stage of economic development and the strength of the country's industrial, service, and capital markets. Developing countries such as Brazil, Egypt, and India, as well as industrialized countries with chronic balance-of-service surpluses, such as Switzerland and the United Kingdom, tend to run chronic BOT deficits. This is a normal, acceptable, and nonthreatening condition as long as the service, transfer, and capital accounts can finance the BOT deficit. Surplus in the service and transfer account, and/or deficit in the capital account (that is, net capital imports) provide the financial resources needed to finance the trade deficit.

In a similar vein, a balance-of-trade surplus provides the financial resources to a country to be a net importer of international services, a net provider of unilateral transfers, and/or a net exporter of capital. For three generations prior to the 1970s, the United States had a trade surplus. Since 1973, many of the OPEC countries have fallen into this category.

Figure 10.1 illustrates the totals of exports, imports, and balance of trade for several major exporting countries. Table 10.5 shows the breakdown of the U.S. trade account into its major components.

BALANCE OF SERVICES (BOS)

The second portion of the current account involves trade in services or "invisibles." Included under this heading are a wide diversity of types of transactions of both the private and government sectors:

1. trade in services
    a. transportation
    b. travel (hotels and restaurants)
    c. banking
    d. insurance
    e. brokerage

2. return on assets abroad (income)
   a. fees (consulting, management, technical services, and so forth)
   b. royalties
   c. dividends
   d. interest
   e. earnings reinvested abroad

It is relatively easy for most observers to understand the inclusion of most of these items as services. However, the inclusion of interest and dividend payments and earnings reinvested abroad is not quite so obvious as is the inclusion of the others. Some analysts would argue that these items could just as readily be included under short-term capital flows, which will be discussed in a moment. However, the somewhat arbitrary decision has generally been accepted to include these as services, since they represent payment for the provision of financial ser-

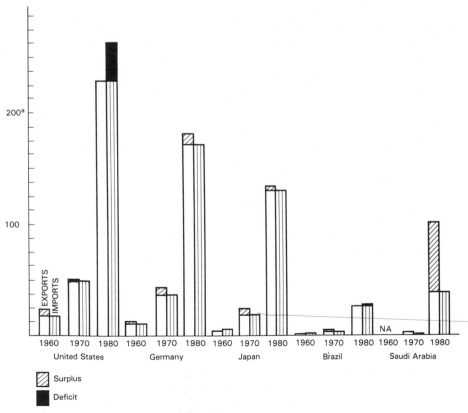

ᵃAll figures are in billions of U.S. dollars ($1,000,000,000).

FIGURE 10.1   International Merchandise Trade of Selected Countries

TABLE 10.5 Major Categories of U.S. Merchandise Trade

	Exports			Imports			Net		
	1970	1975	1980	1970	1975	1980	1970	1975	1980
Agricultural products, total	7,174[a]	21,889	41,256	5,665	9,490	17,425	1,509	12,399	23,831
Nonagricultural products, total	35,420	84,268	175,336	34,298	86,651	223,409	1,121	− 2,383	−48,073
Total merchandise trade	42,593	106,102	216,592	39,963	96,116	240,834	2,630	9,986	−24,242
Major categories									
Food and live animals	4,349	15,484	27,744	5,379	8,503	15,763	−1,030	6,981	11,981
Crude materials, inedible, except fuels	4,609	9,784	23,791	3,312	5,564	10,496	1,296	4,219	13,295
Mineral fuels, lubricants, and so forth	1,594	4,470	7,982	3,081	26,476	79,058	−1,487	−22,006	−71,075
Chemicals	3,826	8,691	20,740	1,450	3,696	8,583	2,376	4,995	12,158
Manufactured goods	5,067	10,919	22,255	8,437	14,703	32,190	−3,370	− 3,783	− 9,936
Machinery, total	11,372	28,476	55,790	5,289	11,727	31,904	6,082	16,749	23,886
Transport equipment, total	6,504	17,191	28,839	5,882	11,737	28,642	622	5,453	197
Motor vehicles and parts	3,549	10,036	14,590	5,067	9,921	24,134	−1,517	116	− 9,544
Other	5,273	11,088	29,452	7,132	13,710	34,199	−1,859	− 2,622	− 4,747

[a]All figures are in millions of U.S. dollars.

SOURCES: *Survey of Current Business*, July 1971, pp. S21–23; December 1976, pp. S22–24; December 1981, pp. S19–20.

vices in the form of debt and equity funds. Table 10.6 illustrates the scale of exports of services for selected major countries.

The difference between the exports of services and imports of services is the *balance of services*. The sum of the balance of trade and the balance of services is the *balance of goods and services* [*BOGS*].

Just as with the balance of trade, a balance-of-services deficit or surplus, and indeed even a balance-of-goods-and-services deficit or surplus, is neither good nor bad. Deficits and surpluses must be evaluated as part of the entire balance-of-payments position of a country. This is examined more fully in the following sections.

UNILATERAL TRANSFERS

The third component of the current account involves *unilateral* (or *unrequited*) *transfers*. (See Table 10.3.) This includes both private-sector personal gifts, charitable assistance, *remittances* of workers to their families, pensions, and governmental foreign-aid programs. Note, however, that the actual transfer of goods, services, or money appears elsewhere in the tables of the balance of payments. The shipment of actual merchandise is recorded as an export. The transfer of financial resources is recorded as a capital flow. What, then, is the unilateral-transfer account? It is a contra-account or counterpart entry (a "plug" entry), which is the necessary offsetting debit or credit in order to maintain conceptual balance in this double-entry accounting system. It is analogous to "good will" on a corporate balance sheet.

For most countries, the unilateral-transfer account is not a major account when compared with the goods, services, and capital accounts. However, for many developing countries flows such as foreign aid (for example, for Egypt, Senegal, and Thailand) and workers' remittances (for example, for Portugal, Turkey, Algeria, and Mexico) are very significant as marginal sources of financing for trade and/or service deficits.

BALANCE ON CURRENT ACCOUNT (BOCA)

The balance of goods and services plus the balance on unilateral transfers is the *balance on current account*. A BOCA deficit indicates the amount that must be financed by the reserve and capital accounts (that is, from depletion of reserves or from capital inflows). A BOCA surplus is the contribution to the reserve and capital accounts, that is, for increase in that country's international reserves or available for investing abroad. The BOCA is the most important of the various subcategories of the BOP and is commonly referred to as *the* balance of payments. Table 10.7 illustrates current account trends for selected countries.

TABLE 10.6 International Service Trade of Selected Countries

	1970			1975			1980		
	Export	Import	Net	Export	Import	Net	Export	Import	Net
US	+23.19[a]	−19.79	+3.40	+48.70	−34.55	+14.15	+117.86	−83.74	+34.12
UK	+11.43	− 9.23	+2.20	+23.69	−18.63	+ 5.06	+ 55.97	−47.13	+ 8.84
Germany	+ 8.67	−10.84	−2.17	+22.96	−28.47	− 5.51	+ 51.32	−63.41	−12.09
Japan	+ 4.01	− 5.79	−1.78	+13.58	−18.84	− 5.26	+ 31.49	−42.84	−11.35
France	+ 6.06	− 5.63	+0.43	+19.13	−17.54	+ 1.59	+ 53.48	−44.79	+ 8.69
Italy	+ 5.84	− 4.79	+1.05	+10.99	−10.69	+ 0.30	+ 28.18	−22.77	+ 5.41
Saudi Arabia	+ 0.28	− 1.21	−0.93	+ 3.20	− 6.50	− 3.30	+ 11.27	−34.28	−23.01
Brazil	+ 0.38	− 1.19	−0.81	+ 1.45	− 4.91	− 3.46	+ 3.14	−13.30	−10.16
Mexico	+ 1.51	− 1.79	−0.28	+ 3.35	− 4.26	− 0.91	+ 8.47	−13.98	− 5.51

[a]All figures are in billions of U.S. dollars ($1,000,000,000).

SOURCE: *IFS*, December 1977, pp. 74, 142, 150, 196, 206, 250, 366, 370, 377; January 1983, pp. 98, 168, 176, 232, 242, 273, 288, 424, 428.

TABLE 10.7   Balance on Current Account for Selected Countries

	1960	1965	1970	1975	1980
United States	2.82a	5.44	2.36	17.68	1.48
Germany	1.11	−1.69	0.67	3.89	−16.45
Japan	0.14	0.93	1.97	−0.68	−10.75
Brazil	−0.52	0.28	−0.84	−7.05	−12.82
Saudi Arabia	0.22	0.13	0.07	13.88	45.41

aAll figures are in billions of U.S. dollars.

SOURCE: *International Financial Statistics: 1978 Supplement,* pp. 92–93, 168–69, 228–29, 368–69, 398–99; and *International Financial Statistics,* January 1983, pp. 98, 197, 242, 273, 428.

CAPITAL ACCOUNT

The capital account includes such international flows as direct investments, portfolio investments, bank loans, trade credits, private placements, and government loans.[1]

Two common arrangements of the capital account were shown for the IMF (Table 10.2) and the United States (Table 10.3). The IMF organizes all capital flows according to maturity: long-term capital versus short-term capital. The U.S. government categorizes capital flows according to the locus (and ownership) of the asset: U.S. assets abroad versus foreign assets in the United States. The capital account could also have as its major divisions the distinction between the government and the private sectors. Any of these formats can provide comparable information; indeed, if the capital-account tables are detailed enough, the three formats can be interchanged. Table 10.8 illustrates these three basic approaches to organizing the capital account.

As indicated above in the discussion of the current account, there is nothing necessarily good or bad about capital-account deficits or surpluses. A country that runs a current-account surplus has funds available to be a capital exporter (or to increase its reserves). Likewise, a country with a BOCA deficit needs to be a net importer of capital (or to draw down its reserves) in order to finance the deficit. Either condition could be a normal, satisfactory, equilibrium condition for a country.

Some major aspects of the capital account are discussed below.

FOREIGN DIRECT INVESTMENT

When companies build factories, stores, mines, and so forth abroad or buy existing facilities, the companies have managerial control over

---

[1]*Private placements* are private loan (or equity) arrangements that involve only nonmarketable securities; such arrangements do not generally require approval from the regulatory authorities.

TABLE 10.8   Capital Account: Alternative Formats

    A. Organization based upon maturity of assets
        (for example, the IMF)
       Long-term capital flows
          versus
       Short-term capital flows
    B. Organization based upon location and
        ownership of assets (for instance, the United
        States)
       Foreign assets owned by local residents
          versus
       Domestic assets owned by foreign residents
    C. Organization based upon the nature of the
        owner of assets
       Government sector
          versus
       Private sector

---

the assets. *When an investment gives a country managerial control,* it is called a *foreign direct investment (FDI).*

Direct investments are not limited to 100 percent ownership of foreign facilities. *Joint ventures,* for instance, are generally considered FDIs. As long as the company is able to exercise effective managerial control, the conditions for a direct investment are met. Two or three or even more companies in a joint venture could qualify on this basis.

In a managerial sense, there is no absolute formula that distinguishes a direct from an indirect investment. In some cases a 40 percent or even larger investment (though less than 50 percent) might not bring managerial control, if the balance of the capital is owned by one entity or cohesive group. In other instances 5 percent or even less of the capital of a company might bring effective control, if the rest of the capital is widely distributed.

For BOP reporting purposes, governments or the IMF must choose a mechanical definition for foreign direct investment. The IMF uses whatever definition the reporting government uses. The U.S. government arbitrarily identifies any purchase of 10 percent or more of equity as an FDI; prior to 1974 the percentage was 25 percent.

Remember, however, that these measures are from a *statistical* perspective. From a *managerial* perspective, FDI is a measure of *control,* not percentage of ownership.

Foreign Portfolio Investment

If equity investment in another country does not bring managerial control, the investment is called a *foreign portfolio investment* (sometimes also called an *indirect investment*). Long-term *debt* investments are also portfolio investments: corporate bonds, government treasury notes and bonds, and private placements.

Portfolio investments are generally made for the investment income that they provide, primarily from interest and dividends. However, sometimes there may be additional motives, for example, in order to gain favorable supply or pricing considerations from a supplier or sometimes because government debt has been given in compensation for expropriation.[2]

In addition to portfolio investment, there are a few other, mostly nonmarketable types of long-term capital, such as drawings on bank loans, long-term lines of credit, and loans from governments. Also included are repayments on some long-term government loans and contributions to international organizations (including subscription quotas).

Short-term capital: The distinction between long- and short-term capital is arbitrary. Equity investments are always considered long term, since they have no maturity. Debt investments are generally considered long term if at the time of the investment there is more than one year before the maturity of the instrument.

Therefore, short-term investments are those whose original maturity was one year or less. These include assets such as demand deposits, short-term time deposits (including most certificates of deposit), government treasury bills, commercial paper of corporations, letters of credit, and so forth.[3]

RESERVE ACCOUNT

Most BOP formats have a clearly identifiable section that corresponds to changes in a government's international reserves. The IMF clearly identifies it as such in its detailed BOP presentation (see Table 10.2). The U.S. government titles it "U.S. official reserve assets, net." As noted in Chapter 5, the primary reserve assets are only those highly liquid assets

---

[2]*Expropriation* is the seizure by a government of private property with compensation paid. For a more complete discussion, see Chapter 14.

[3]A *certificate of deposit* is a special type of time deposit. In large denominations (usually in excess of $100,000), they are negotiable, or marketable. *Commercial paper* is a short-term marketable promissory note of a corporation with a prime credit rating. A *letter of credit* is a bank's or corporation's promise to pay on behalf of another at some time in the future. See Chapter 16.

that can quickly and unconditionally be converted into desired foreign currencies, as follows:

1. monetary gold
2. special drawing rights
3. reserve position in the IMF
4. foreign currencies[4]

ERRORS AND OMISSIONS

Companies export and import hundreds of billions of dollars or pounds sterling or hundreds of trillions of yen worth of goods each year. Similarly, tourists spend tens of billions of dollars abroad annually. Banks and other financial institutions lend and invest tens of billions of dollars across borders. Yet the governments whose countries are affected by these transactions can only *estimate* the flow of these transactions across their borders from incomplete reports and statistical samples. Governments, of course, usually have a much more accurate idea of the totals from *their own* international activities. Nevertheless, when the totals of all of these different debits and credits are summed, it should come as no surprise that the balance of payments never actually balances: There are errors of estimation, omissions of relevant data, and differences in timing.

Unlike corporate accounting, the statistical gaps do not pose an embarrassing dilemma for BOP statisticians. Since the totals must balance, a "plug" figure called "errors and omissions" is inserted to bring the totals into balance. It must be added either to total recorded payments or to total receipts, so that the two totals balance. This is analogous to the "statistical discrepancy" account in national income accounting (GNP). (How many students of corporate financial accounting wish that they could have it so good on homework problems and exams!)

This "plug" does not mean that the BOP tables are therefore of little value. Indeed, they provide very valuable information in countries that have measured the BOP with care. However, the reader must bear in mind the limitations imposed by this lack of total accuracy; the tables must be interpreted accordingly. This fact also leads to a situation that would be totally unacceptable from corporate financial records but that is a fact of life in both BOP and GNP tabulations—namely, that periodic revisions are frequently forthcoming. The reasons for this should be apparent from the comments above.

---

[4]The asset "foreign currencies," it should be recalled, is not actually in the form of currency. Instead it is invested in such highly liquid assets as demand deposits, treasury bills, Eurodeposits, and special deposits with foreign central banks.

SUMMARY

The *balance of payments* is a measure of the international economic flows that occur between the residents of a country and the rest of the world during a specific period of time (e.g., one year or one-quarter of a year). The BOP indicates such things as whether the country is a net importer or net exporter of goods and services and capital. It also shows whether a country's international reserves are increasing or decreasing.

The principal BOP subtotals are the *balance of trade* and the *balance on current account.* Despite its notoriety, the BOT is only one small portion of the overall BOP; it involves only the net balance on merchandise trade. Therefore, its significance is not nearly as great as is normally assumed.

The BOCA is a much more extensive concept and of much greater value than the BOT. The BOCA measures the net export or import of not only merchandise trade but also trade in services and flows of *unilateral transfers.* It indicates whether the country is a net exporter or importer of capital and/or whether the country needs to augment or reduce its international reserves.

Balance-of-payments statistics must be used with great care. There is a strong tendency for many observers, such as corporate managers, journalists, government officials, and the public, to misinterpret the numbers. Some countries are chronic net importers of goods, services, and transfers (that is, the BOCA) and also chronic importers of capital to pay for the current account deficit. Other countries have just the opposite pattern. Yet neither pattern is necessarily any worse than the other

The evaluation of BOP tables is not something to be done casually. The reader should become thoroughly familiar with the BOP concepts but should at the same time realize that an accurate evaluation of the full implications of the balance of payments is complicated.

KEY TERMS

BALANCE ON CURRENT ACCOUNT	BALANCE OF TRADE	ERRORS AND OMISSIONS
BALANCE OF PAYMENTS	CAPITAL ACCOUNT	JOINT VENTURE
BALANCE OF SERVICES	CURRENT ACCOUNT	PORTFOLIO INVESTMENT
	DIRECT INVESTMENT	UNILATERAL TRANSFER

REVIEW QUESTIONS

1. What is the balance of payments?
2. What is the balance of trade?

3. What is the balance on current account?

4. Are transactions abroad between two foreign countries that are denominated in £ part of the British balance of payments?

5. If a French franc–denominated transaction crosses the British border (an import), is that part of the balance of payments in the United Kingdom? in France?

6. How can there be BOP deficits or surpluses if it is a *balance* of payments?

7. What are unilateral transfers? Give several examples from both the governmental and private sectors.

8. Discuss the statement: "A BOT deficit may be good for a country."

9. What types of factors account for large errors and omissions in the balance of payments, either surplus or deficit? (See Table 10.3.) Where do the discrepancies occur?

10. Define direct and portfolio foreign investments.

SUGGESTED REFERENCES

COHEN, BENJAMIN J. *Balance of Payments Policy.* New York: Penguin Books, 1970.

FEDERAL RESERVE BOARD *Federal Reserve Bulletin* (various monthly issues).

INTERNATIONAL MONETARY FUND *Balance of Payments Concepts and Definitions,* 1968.

INTERNATIONAL MONETARY FUND *Balance of Payments Yearbook* (annual plus updates).

JANSSEN, RICHARD F. "U.S. Companies Profit from Investments They Made Years Ago in Plants Overseas," *Wall Street Journal,* March 11, 1981.

KEMP, DONALD "Balance of Payment Concepts—What Do They Really Mean?" *Review* (Federal Reserve Bank of St. Louis), July 1975.

KUWAYAMA, PATRICIA H. "Measuring the U.S. Balance of Payments," *Monthly Review* (Federal Reserve Bank of New York), August 1975.

STERN, ROBERT *Balance of Payments.* Chicago: Aldine Publishing Company, 1973.

STEVENS, ROBERT WARREN *Primer on the Dollar in the World Economy.* New York: Random House, Inc., 1972.

U.S. DEPARTMENT OF COMMERCE *Survey of Current Business* (various monthly issues).

11

The Domestic Company Looks Abroad

When a company considers becoming involved in international operations—either to acquire resources abroad or to sell abroad—there are several alternatives that can be followed. We have already examined the basic nature of exporting, importing, licensing, portfolio investment, direct investment, and so forth. In this chapter we examine the managerial task of determining which form of organization and international activity is most appropriate for a particular company, at a particular point in time, and for a particular product, whether merchandise or a service.

A systematic and objective analysis of involvement in international operations of whatever variety should ideally involve the following steps:

1. a careful analysis of the company itself—its resources, its goals, its strengths, and its weaknesses
2. a careful consideration of the likely impact of the proposed international activity upon the overall firm
3. selection of the optimal type of international activity
4. a systematic market analysis—including a careful examination of possible governmental policies and actions in both the home and host countries
5. selection of the specific foreign market or markets in which the company will become involved as buyer or seller

As the five steps listed above suggest, the company must first have a very clear understanding of not only what it would like to do but also what it is capable of doing. This understanding should be coupled with the likely impact of the alternative types of international activities upon the overall welfare of the entire corporation. Then it must analyze the various risks before choosing the appropriate country or countries for the firm.

The problem of risk analysis in international activities is very complicated. Following is a list of some of the most important (these risks are examined in detail in this and later chapters):

1.   Customer or supplier risk: This risk involves the likelihood that the buyer or the seller company will fail through its own fault to live up to its contract with the company, that is, by the failure of a supplier to provide what has been promised or the failure of a customer to pay its debts.

2.   Managerial risk: This risk involves the company itself (not its customer or supplier) failing through its own fault, whether from poor planning or market studies, poor management, inadequate financial commitment, or whatever other managerial reason.

3.   Economic risk: This risk concerns the economy (whether in the home country, the host country, or a third-country market), which can adversely affect the operations of the company via such adverse trends as inflation, recession, tight credit conditions, foreign exchange volatility, or even natural catastrophe.

4.   Political or sovereign risk: There is always the threat that governmental action (whether of first- second-, or third-country origin) will negatively affect the company via actions such as international controls (for example, on trade, exchange, or monetary controls), expropriation or confiscation, war or insurrection, or simply refusing to repay its own international debts.

5.   Socio-cultural risk: There is also the risk that cultural or other sociological developments such as religious attitudes or unrest, tribal conflicts, and so forth could seriously interfere with the efficient and profitable international operations of the firm.

Thus the dimensions that must be considered in this process of analysis for international operations include the firm itself, other firms with which it must deal, and the various environments within which it must operate. All these basic international managerial tasks are integrated in this chapter via the examination of these major processes:

1.   research and planning for international operations
2.   assessing foreign market and source potential
3.   analysis of country risk

RESEARCH AND PLANNING
FOR INTERNATIONAL OPERATIONS

In many instances the evolutionary movement overseas of some of a firm's activities is not properly planned and integrated by the company. Nevertheless, few investments occur without some degree of planning and analysis. Unfortunately, the process of international research is a complicated and imprecise process. There are many different possible approaches to every variety of international research, whether the research is directed at the opportunities or the risks of international business operations. As will be shown, there are an immense variety of variables that might be considered for any and all of the various types of international research, whether it is market research, foreign exchange risk analysis, funding alternatives, country-risk analysis, or any of the other variables that are examined in the chapter.

There are many different ways in which a company can become involved in international operations. Most of our discussion thus far has focused upon international trade and international direct investments. However, these are only a few of the major options available. Correspondingly, there is no general approach to international business research. The analytical approach is a function of the *type* of international activity which the company is contemplating.

EXPORT AND IMPORT OF MERCHANDISE

International trade, whether exporting or importing, is the most common way for companies to begin their international business operations. Sometimes this business is unexpected, for example, a company receives unsolicited export orders from a foreign company or a domestic company starts receiving foreign supplies from its wholesalers.

Many other companies deliberately initiate the purchase or selling activity as a result of their own perceived opportunities or problems. For example, competitive pressure can induce domestic companies to investigate the opportunities of imports or exports, such as Chrysler's distribution of cars manufactured by Mitsubishi. Similarly, cyclicality in the domestic demand for its sales, the threat to a company's supplies resulting from a domestic strike in the supplier's industry (as has happened in the U.S. steel industry), or the inability of domestic suppliers to provide all a company's needs in a strong economy are all reasons that can induce domestic companies to evaluate either imports or exports.

Exporters: The domestic company that is approached by a foreign buyer is naturally concerned about the ability of the customer to pay for the goods or services to be purchased. However, either payment in advance or utilization of standard financial tools of international trade such as letters of credit and bankers' acceptances provide the exporter with not only assurance of payment but also an opportunity to accelerate payment on the receivables (at a discount) by the sale of the bankers' acceptance.[1]

Other political concerns of the exporter could include such factors as the currency of the sale and the legal jurisdiction for the settlement of any disputes between the buyer and the seller. As will be seen in the discussion of foreign exchange risk management in Chapter 21, the forward-exchange markets and the *money markets* (foreign as well as domestic) provide protection against foreign exchange risks.

The question of legal jurisdiction can be quite complicated. Very commonly the legal system of the exporter is accepted by the importer as one of the terms of the contract. However, if the efficiency and/or the impartiality of the exporter's legal system are questioned by the buyer, the importer may request an alternative legal jurisdiction—either that of the buyer or that of a third country. American and British courts are often chosen for such purposes.

Importers: The neophyte importer is in an analogous position to the exporter. However, many of the special risks and problems fall more heavily upon the buyer than the seller, for example, fluctuating foreign exchange rates, finding a satisfactory means of payment, and accepting the legal jurisdiction chosen by the seller. However, the alternatives mentioned above for the protection of the seller can also be invaluable to the buyer: the forward-exchange and money markets and the use of letters of credit and banker's acceptances.

Importers in some "hard-currency" countries are often able to arrange billing and payment in their own currency. This arrangement, of course, shifts the currency risk to the exporter. However, in most countries exporters actually prefer (or may be required by government decree) to receive payment in a major currency, especially the U.S. dollar. As noted above, it is very common for the currency used to be foreign to both the exporter and the importer.

The question of legal jurisdiction for the importer is analogous to that of the exporter. The agreed jurisdiction can be that of the exporter, the importer, or a third country.

If the importer requires a sophisticated purchasing program, then a significant amount of import research may be necessary; the wide range of frequently changing imports by Pier 1 Imports is an example. The other extreme involves a company that imports commodities, such as wheat or iron ore, that are highly competitive, and for which quality standards are well developed and widely used.

---

[1]These and other instruments of international trade are discussed in Chapter 16.

EXPORTS AND IMPORT OF SERVICES

As the examination of the balance of payments showed, the second major category of the current account is the balance of trade in services. Services (or "invisibles") are a very major part of the balance of payments of most countries today: bank earnings, insurance premiums, international transportation, licensing and franchising fees, management contracts, and so forth. For many companies such activities become a very major part of their international operations.

The provision of financial services can be performed quite satisfactorily in many cases without the creation of foreign offices or with the establishment of only a "shell" office at most in a place such as Nassau or the Cayman Islands. For example, insurance, especially corporate or shipping insurance, can be provided abroad from domestic offices. Similarly, commercial banks can provide a wide range of foreign financial and nonfinancial services from their domestic offices—lending, foreign exchange, cash management, and so forth.

In a similar vein, many companies that are reluctant to make direct investments abroad but that are unable to service foreign markets via exports or are unable to service their domestic needs via imports, find an attractive alternative in the use of *licenses.* Many things can be licensed: patents, productive or marketing techniques, trademarks, copyrights, and so forth. (For example, the first edition of this book was licensed for translation into Spanish.) In some countries, such as Italy, local patent protection can be lost under some circumstances, unless it is employed locally, either *directly* via investment and production there or *indirectly* via licensing.

Companies that license their own intangible assets must be careful to protect the quality of the foreign use of that asset. Sometimes the foreign use of the license may result in something very different from the original, sometimes with the permission of the licensor. For example, the popular German beer, Lowenbrau, has been licensed for sale in the United States by the Miller Brewing Company. However, the product that is manufactured and sold in the United States under that name bears little resemblance to the original.

Franchising is another form of the licensing of trademarks and processes. As with other forms of licensing, domestic companies can use franchising to expand abroad at minimum expenditure and financial risk to themselves. They cannot only gain significant economies of scale, but franchising agreements often involve export contracts as well. Pepsi-Cola, for example, licenses the use of its name and the right to manufacture and sell its drink abroad. Part of the contract, however, involves the requirement that the foreign licensee buy the syrup from Pepsi—therefore, the company enjoys both royalty and export advantages.

The other side of the equation, of course, is that licenses can also be imported. This allows local companies to benefit from the foreign asset at a lower cost than would be true from a direct investment by foreigners.

Another type of international service that has been growing very rapidly is *advisory and management contracts*. For example, the Pohang Steel Company of South Korea, in a major expansion program, bought some sophisticated production equipment from American producers and hired Allegheny Ludlum to provide managerial assistance for several years to help run the equipment and to train Koreans to run the equipment in the future. Similarly, oil companies often hire drilling crews from abroad to help search for oil.

A special type of management contract involves a company that sets up a foreign factory, which it then turns over to the buyer. This arrangement is called a *turnkey project*. The construction company might design and build the facility and even train the local staff before "turning the key" over to the buyer.

FOREIGN PORTFOLIO INVESTMENT

Portfolio investment can involve either a marketable debt investment or a *noncontrolling* amount of marketable equity investment. Investors in portfolios of foreign investment, such as loans, Eurobonds, Eurocurrency deposits, foreign government debts, and noncontrolling shares of the stock of corporations, have a different type of international risk than do exporters or importers, for merchandise or for services. The lender must be able to analyze the credit-worthiness of the borrower. The investor must be able to determine the safety and investment appeal of various investment alternatives. Both investors and lenders must concern themselves with the problem of country risk—the likelihood that economic, governmental, or socio-cultural developments may adversely affect the lender's or investor's assets.

Investment and credit risks: Analysis of investment and credit risks tend to be much more difficult in most countries than they are in the United States, where public disclosure laws, such as those of the Securities Exchange Commission; generally accepted accounting principles; and the widespread prominence of security and industry analysts provide a significant amount of information to political lenders and investors. Even in most of Europe and in Japan the public availability of data about industrial companies is generally much poorer than in the United States. In developing countries the problem for the portfolio investor is much greater. As a result, most portfolio investors concentrate their investment efforts upon the more highly developed foreign economies. As the interest in such security markets grows, a greater availability of corporate data becomes available in many foreign countries. Also, special investment vehicles have been developed to aid the investor interested in such markets, but who lacks the expertise and the time to research foreign investment opportunities. For example, mutual funds that place a larger share, or all, of their investments in foreign markets have become increasingly popular.

Commercial banks are more venturesome than are most other types of portfolio investors. Their portfolios are comprised largely of the loans they make to other banks, corporations, and governments. For many large banks this type of portfolio provides a high degree of diversification among borrowers, countries, maturities, and so forth. Nevertheless, bankers must content themselves with the knowledge that even basic credit analysis can be much more difficult in many foreign countries than in their home countries, which are typically the United States, the United Kingdom, Continental Europe, or Japan. The rewards of foreign lending may often be very attractive. However, the lender, as well as the investor, must be prepared to do much extra research. Thus, credit or other investment analyses commonly absorb a greater share of an investor's time than in his or her traditional markets.

Country risk: This is another risk that is of greater concern to foreign investors than to exporters or importers. *Country risk* is the likelihood that political, legal, socio-cultural, economic, or even natural developments could occur within a nation's environment that could adversely affect the investment. Country risk differs from commercial (or credit) risk. The former involves developments in the environment. *Commercial risk* is more specific. It involves the likelihood that the borrower or issuer of a security will be unable to satisfy the terms of the investment or will function in such a way that the anticipated dividends, interest, or capital gains will not be forthcoming to the investor, even though nothing in the environment prevents such payments.

Country-risk analysis is a special type of task for the investor. It is discussed in detail in the next section.

Foreign-exchange risk: This is a problem for most foreign investors.[2] For short-term investments, the forward-exchange markets can often be used in the currencies of industrialized countries to eliminate the risk of currency-value alterations. However, forward markets are very weak for periods beyond one year, even for the major currencies. For the currencies of nonindustrialized nations and also for some industrialized nations, even the short-term forwards are virtually nonexistent. This should obviously be a major consideration in the making of a cross-currency investment.

---

[2]An exception would be a German company making a deposit in a Euro-DM account.

FOREIGN DIRECT INVESTMENT

FDI is an equity investment that is sufficient to give the investing company managerial control of a foreign company. This can be accomplished in a wide variety of ways. In many instances the foreign company is wholly owned by the investing company, that is, it is a *subsidiary*. In other cases the foreign affiliate may be jointly owned with others. These partners can be few in number such as is the case with a *joint venture*, or they may be widely distributed, such as occurs via a public sale of the stock in local capital markets abroad. The foreign partner might very well be a local government instead of a private-sector group. This is a *mixed venture*.

The foreign investment can be financed in a variety of ways. An infusion of equity capital is obviously one major source of funding a foreign investment. However, companies generally try to minimize their equity commitment as much as possible. Companies have proven to be very imaginative in putting together a financing package, a process commonly called *project financing:* sale of publicly traded debt, bank loans, supplier credits, loans or grants from the host government (often through a development bank), loans from international institutions (such as the World Bank), even loans from their home government or other companies (such as the lending of blocked funds). In some joint ventures an investor may not make any financial investment at all! Some investments are made in the form of other assets: patents, equipment, unused facilities, and so forth.

Regardless of the type of financial or ownership arrangement, a direct investment may either involve the construction of new (*de novo*) facilities or the purchase of existing facilities. In many instances the latter has very strong attraction to companies. The purchase of an ongoing operation is the quickest and often the least expensive way of making an effective investment. However, *from the perspective of the host country,* a takeover is commonly the *least* attractive approach, since it does not provide new construction and production jobs. One major exception occurs when the local company would otherwise collapse; in that instance, the host government frequently welcomes a reasonable takeover.

Corporate risk of direct investment: Typically, foreign direct investment is the type of international business activity that exposes the international company to the greatest degree of risk. The direct investor has committed his or her resources to the purchase of "bricks and mortar"—that is, investment in plant and equipment, warehouses, stores, agricultural land, mining development, and transportation equipment. By their very nature such investments are generally rather immobile, or they are mobile only with great difficulty.

Unlike exports, for which the company generally retains ownership until adequate compensation has been paid, or imports, where physical possession is taken outside the exporting country and where multiple sourcing can provide added protection, the foreign direct investor has committed his or her resources physically in a foreign country. And, unlike the foreign portfolio investor whose investment is in a form (1) that can easily be transferred across national borders, (2) that are commonly of short-term nature, (3) that generally have a convenient secondary market for resale, and (4) that can often be sold privately without attracting governmental attention, foreign direct investments cannot readily be transferred, are permanent in nature, do not usually have a strong secondary market, and usually cannot be readily sold without a government's knowledge and acceptance.

The ownership of tangible assets abroad exposes the company to the possibility of loss of the facilities as a result of events as diverse as bad weather (droughts, flooding), other natural calamities (earthquakes), civil rioting, war, and adverse governmental action (regulations, red tape, expropriation, capital controls). Thus, because of the long-term nature of direct investments, the foreign direct investor must take extreme care in investigating foreign investment opportunities. The importance of competent country-risk analysis cannot be exaggerated.

CAVEATS

Many observers and practitioners of international research have a misguided and exaggerated sense of the accuracy and indeed even of the "scientific nature" of such research. The reader should remain aware of such common tendencies to exaggerate the worth of international research. Although research is very important—indeed mandatory for a prudent company—it is necessarily subject to serious shortcomings as a result of both the very nature of the research and of the material upon which it is based. This is also true of most comparable research in the domestic context, but the limitations are greatly compounded in the international sphere.

The types of research with which we are most concerned here, such as market research, funding studies, country-risk analysis, and foreign exchange risk analysis, rely very heavily upon the evaluation of likely events that are dependent upon the decisions and actions of people—consumers, corporate managers, politicians, and so forth. In such instances the accuracy of quantatitve analysis is seriously limited. Even when the analysis is based upon readily quantifiable data (such as trade, investment, and debt information), the analyst of international conditions and outlooks is commonly confronted with data that are much less reliable than that of most comparable domestic research.

For example, market analysis that attempts to utilize data on population, income, spending patterns, and so forth has a serious problem of justifying the reliability of the data collected. In many foreign countries, especially (but not all) developing countries, even published governmental data are often questionable. Also, forecasting of events such as foreign exchange fluctuations relies very heavily on factors that are very difficult to quantify, for example, changes in governmental policies or in voting patterns of the electorate. As a result, it is not surprising that forecasting systems in areas that rely primarily on qualitative evaluation methods tend to do consistently better than econometric and other quantitative methods. There are indeed areas where quantitative analysis can be very appropriate, such as in international trade. However, the manager must choose with care the appropriate circumstances for the use of quantitative methods.

The type of international business activity contemplated obviously dictates the nature of the analyses that are necessary. The exporter or the direct investor who is primarily interested in serving the foreign market would naturally be very interested in the potential market demand in the various foreign markets under consideration. The prospective importer would focus heavily upon the nature of the alternative foreign sources of supply. The direct investor who is seeking access to foreign factors of production would need a careful study of the nature, cost, and availability of such labor, minerals, or other factors. The international lender would need to focus heavily upon the credit-worthiness of borrowers. The risks of foreign exchange-rate fluctuation and of foreign-exchange and capital controls would be of interest to several of these categories of international business operations. (These types of risks are discussed in Chapter 21.) So also would the question of country-risk analysis.

The rest of this chapter focuses on two of these managerial tasks: the assessment of the potential of foreign sources, with special attention to markets, plus country-risk analysis.

ASSESSING FOREIGN MARKET AND SOURCE POTENTIAL

After a firm recognizes a need to look overseas for profitable opportunities, it is immediately confronted with the task of selecting promising markets or sources from among more than 170 nations, estimating their potentials, developing marketing or purchasing programs, and assessing its ability to undertake the necessary activities by taking stock of its resources and capabilities and their current and planned rates of utilization.

This section briefly highlights some of the traditional methods and techniques used to assess and evaluate foreign market potentials. Also discussed are some of the key questions that need to be answered *before* an actual commitment of resources and capabilities takes place.

TRADITIONAL APPROACHES USED TO ASSESS FOREIGN POTENTIAL[3]

National markets are so varied that it is impossible to generalize easily. Some markets, especially oil exporters such as Saudi Arabia and Kuwait, are wealthy but not highly developed. Others, such as those of Western Europe and Japan, are not only relatively wealthy but also highly developed. Some, such as South Korea and Brazil, have been growing much more rapidly than others. These and many other historical differences mean that the demands and even the marketing systems of different countries can vary enormously.

The importance of the differences between the investor's home country and various foreign countries cannot be overemphasized. However, they also should not be exaggerated. The company that plunges in overseas without an adequate understanding of the differences between a foreign market and the company's home market (or even between a very different foreign market and a *group* of national markets with which an international company has had past experience) can fail badly, and needlessly. Likewise, the company that exaggerates the differences and difficulties of foreign markets can needlessly miss profitable opportunities.

The balanced approach requires careful analysis coupled with realistic evaluation. Many different techniques of market analysis are available. The corporate manager should know the techniques available as well as the strengths, weaknesses, and costs of each.

One approach found useful in reducing the number of potential national markets to a manageable few for further, more intensive scrutiny, is to classify markets according to their stages of economic development. However, since this approach greatly oversimplifies the real world, it should be used with extreme caution. First, different parts of the same country may be at different stages of development, as in the cases of Brazil and India. Second, stages of economic development are being skipped as the governments of developing countries attempt to

---

[3]The author is grateful for the assistance of Professor Brian Toyne of the University of South Carolina in the writing of this section.

bring their countries into the twentieth century in just a few years. Such is the case of some OPEC countries. Third, the influence of multinational corporations may also accelerate the rate of change as their presence is felt and the infrastructure of specific regions of countries advance more rapidly than others. Fourth, the person assigning countries to different stages of economic development may be misinformed or culturally biased. Because of these varying developments, pressures, and biases, the classification of countries and especially regions of the world by stage of economic development may result in lost, overlooked, or underestimated opportunities. The appraoch is useful, however, to the degree that it may help identify countries as having latent or incipient demand as well as actual demand.

Table 11.1 identifies six stages of economic development that countries may go through on their way from the agricultural, subsistence-type economies found in some regions of Africa, Asia and Latin America to the advanced and highly industrialized societies of the United States, Western Europe, and Japan. The table also lists some of the market characteristics and types of demand associated with each stage.

There are, of course, a large number of such classifications systems, each of which reflects the perspective of its author. It is only presented as an example of this particular approach. The classification system finally adopted by a firm for screening national markets should be based on the attributes of the products it intends to market internationally.

While manufacturers of textile machinery may find sufficient demand in fourth-stage markets, manufacturers of highly sophisticated and labor-saving consumer products may only be interested in sixth-stage markets. (See Table 11.1.) Manufacturers of mining and other extractive equipment could become interested in third- and even second-stage markets. Soft drink manufacturers, on the other hand, may find adequate demand in second-stage markets.

After a few potentially attractive markets have been identified, or more correctly, a larger number of markets eliminated on the basis of their economic development, it is then necessary to assess and evaluate the demand potentials of the remaining markets. Since potential demand is a function of size, recognized or emerging needs and wants, and the ability to satisfy these needs and wants through an exchange process, it should not be too surprising to learn that the traditional statistics used to measure foreign market potential include the market's population, gross national product (GNP), GNP per capita, and import statistics. An evaluation of these statistics must, of course, be coupled with a consideration of the market's language(s), culture, religion, political system, class structure, educational levels, and so on, in order to gain a broad overview of the country, its people, and its potential.

The use of these standard variables is not without problems. For example, population data for many countries are based on estimates rather than censuses. Some countries, especially developing countries, have found that taking periodic censuses, even at ten-year intervals, is too expensive and difficult. In many cases, the people are highly illiterate, ruling out the use of questionnaires. As a result, it would take an army of personnel to go around asking every family for information.

Even GNP may not be comparable for widely different cultures and economies and may underestimate consumer well-being because of what is and is not included in the statistic. Many developing countries have a very difficult job of estimating the scale of all economic activities, since many of these activities are based on barter. Problems may also be encountered when translating GNP estimates from one currency into another, since exchange rates do not necessarily reflect the true *domestic* purchasing powers of the two currencies.

The more relevant statistic for estimating consumer demand, GNP per capita, may be misleading for the same reasons. In addition, this statistic assumes that the income of a country is evenly distributed among all consumers—an assumption that is rarely realistic. For example, in 1980 GNP per capita for Kuwait, Sweden, and the United States were $24,384, $14,267, and $10,278, respectively.[4] In the case of Kuwait, the income is generated primarily through the sale of oil and is concentrated in the hands of a few families. As a result, most Kuwaitis do not share *pro rata* in this income. Even in the case of Sweden, which has a more uniform distribution of income than the United States, the GNP per capita figure may also be misleading. A GNP per capita income of $14,267 need not indicate that Sweden's per capita demand will necessarily be higher than for U.S. consumers with GNP per capita incomes of $10,278. Disposable income, purchasing power, and saving habits for the two types of consumers might very well be different because of cultural, social, and tax reasons.

Another problem with all statistics is that they are static, providing no information on trends, developments, and potential changes. Changes in GNP and GNP per capita, for example, might only reflect an attempt by a local government to describe more accurately economic activities within its boundaries, present a more glowing picture to international lending institutions, or, perhaps, result from domestic political expediency.

Also, increases in imports may not be a true measure of actual increases in a country's consumption. They may measure, instead, increases in such things as the presence of foreigners and export-related activities of local and foreign firms. Notwithstanding these problems,

---

[4]*International Financial Statistics,* August 1983; Vol. XXXVI, No. 8; pp. 207, 262, 400, 402 and 442.

TABLE 11.1 Stages of Economic Development and the Development of Markets

Stages	Description	Resources Employed	Marketing Functions	Marketing Institutions	Comments	Examples
1. Agricultural, self-supporting	Primary subsistence farming. Most people are not in a money economy.	Land Labor	Exchange	Periodic markets, fairs	Labor intensive High illiteracy No organized markets	Nomadic or hunting tribes
2. Preindustrial or commercial	Raw materials are extracted and exported. Sugar, rubber, and so forth grown and exported. Money economy developing alongside of barter economy.	Land Labor	Exchange	Traders, fairs, merchants Export-import	Labor intensive High illiteracy Local markets Import oriented, primarily mining, farm, and port facility equipment	Agricultural economy (products such as sugar and coffee)
3. Primary manufacturing	Processing of raw materials and agricultural products. Urbanization increasing as people enter manufacturing. Some local businesses developing as suppliers to primary manufactuers.	Land Labor Technology Transportation	Exchange Physical distribution	Merchants Middlemen Export-import	Labor intensive, some capital intensive activity (refining, and so forth) Import oriented, primarily basic plant and equipment Some consumer products	Cottage industry

	Description	Factors	Marketing functions	Distribution institutions	Characteristics	U.S. economy
4. Nondurable and semidurable consumer goods	Mass production of some consumer products start to replace imports. Middle class developed and part of the political scene.	Land Labor Technology Transportation Capital	Some demand creation Physical distribution	Merchants Middlemen Specialized institutions appearing	Capital intensive Product differentiation National, regional, and export markets develop Literacy increasing	U.S. economy—1885–1914
5. Capital goods and consumer durable goods	Commercial transition. Local manufacture of automobiles, refrigerators, and so on. Economy might still be heavily dependent on exports for capital generation.	Land Labor Technology Transportation Capital Communication	Demand creation Physical distribution Market information	Large retailers Increased specialization of intermediaries	High literacy High urbanization Capital intensive Development of distribution system	U.S. economy—1915–1929
6. Exporting of manufactured products	Export of manufactured goods begin to dominate. Country may have specialized in certain types of manufactured goods. Almost all consumers are in the money economy. Large middle-income class.	Land Labor Technology Transportation Capital Communication	Demand creation Physical distribution Market information Market and product planning and development	Integrated channels of distribution Increased specialization of intermediaries	Capital and land intensive Rapid product innovation National, regional, and export markets	U.S. economy—1950 to present

SOURCES: Adapted from E. Jerome McCarthy, *Basic Marketing*, 5th ed. (Homewood, Ill.: Richard D. Irwin, Inc., 1975), pp. 195–97; and Philip R. Cateora and John M. Hess, *International Marketing*, 4th ed. (Homewood, Ill.: Richard D. Irwin, Inc., 1979), p. 332.

GNP, GNP per capita, and imports are very useful indicators of a country's potential well-being and prospects.

ASSESSMENT TECHNIQUES
USING SECONDARY DATA

Notwithstanding the problems just described, if GNP and GNP per capita are used to indicate markets with potential demand, the international marketer is immediately confronted with additional problems not faced by domestic marketers. Instead of analyzing a single and massive national market, the international marketer is required to analyze a number of markets whose demand potentials are relatively small. For example, of the 148 countries included in the 1977 *World Bank Atlas,* only 24 had per capita incomes exceeding $4,000 in 1976.[5] However, some of these 24 countries have relatively low total income (for example, Luxembourg), whereas countries with much lower per capita income have relatively large total incomes (for example, India and Indonesia).

Because of the relatively small potentials of most foreign markets, international marketers cannot afford to use elaborate and expensive market assessment techniques requiring primary data bases and the development of economic models. They must rely, instead, on relatively inexpensive secondary data–based techniques that are in line with the profit potentials of the markets under investigation. The remainder of this section briefly describes three secondary data–based analytical techniques suggested by Moyer.[6] These techniques are as follows: (1) demand pattern analysis, (2) regional lead-lags, and (3) comparative analysis.

Empirical studies utilizing *demand pattern analysis* indicate that consumption of manufactured and agricultural goods change as a country's GNP per capita increases.[7] For example, the percent of total manufacturing production accounted for by the production of textiles, food, beverages, and tobacco declines as GNP increases, being replaced in importance by heavy industries producing metals, chemicals, and metal products. An analysis of these demand patterns for a particular country can provide the international marketing researcher with information on the country's stage of economic development and, more importantly, on what types of demand can be anticipated in the future.

Another useful technique, that of *regional lead-lag analysis,* extends the product life cycle concept to other countries. The technique assumes that generic product demand patterns in product-pioneering

---

[5] *World Bank Atlas,* World Bank, 1977.
[6] Reed Moyer, "International Market Analysis," *Journal of Marketing Research,* November 1968.
[7] Ibid.

countries will eventually be repeated in other countries with somewhat similar economic, social, and cultural conditions. The technique is useful in that it provides the international marketing researcher with information important for making strategic decisions concerning the timing of overseas introduction. For many industries, however, the lag period is shrinking, permitting some companies, such as IBM, to introduce new products in a large number of countries almost simultaneously. This enables such firms to reduce unit costs of new products as a result of large volume production and to quickly recover research and development expenditures.

The final technique described is that of *comparative analysis*. One of the unique advantages in international marketing is the ability to comparatively analyze market potentials and marketing performance. Three basic international comparison categories can be considered.[8] The first involves the *extension of intracompany and intercompany domestic marketing performance analysis* to other single-country situations. The second type of comparison involves *estimating marketing potential and marketing performance* in country Y on the basis of data for country X. This type of comparison assumes, however, that the economic, competitive, social, and cultural conditions of the two countries are sufficiently similar to justify a comparison. Assuming, for example, that income, stage of industrialization, and so forth are the same for countries X and Y, and yet the firms' sales per capita are different, the international marketing researcher might justifiably ask why such discrepancies in sales performance exist. Most probably there are conditions existing in the two countries that will explain the differences. However, comparisons such as this do increase the likelihood of disclosing problems in international marketing that would otherwise be overlooked. The third type of comparison involves *comparing subnational markets* and is really a special case of the second type. Because of the sweeping assumptions that must be made in order to compare national markets, a more accurate comparison may be possible if regional markets in countries X and Y are compared.

ANALYSIS OF COUNTRY RISK

As has been frequently noted, there are numerous variables that affect the operations of a specific company in different countries in different ways at different times. However, there are many other factors that have a more general impact upon the entire host country and therefore

---

[8]Warren J. Keegan, *Multinational Marketing Management*, 2nd ed. (Englewood Cliffs, New Jersey: Prentice-Hall, Inc., 1980), p. 195.

upon the companies, foreign as well as domestic, that are operating therein. The study of country risk requires a different type of analysis from most of the foregoing.

Each type of international analysis needs to be studied individually on its own merits rather than have the conclusions of that analysis clouded by the conclusions of other types of research. For instance, a bank's interest in making loans in a foreign country where there is a strong loan demand should not interfere with an independent effort to analyze the country risk in that country. Both types of analysis (that is, market potential and country risk) are important inputs to the final managerial decision. Therefore it is extremely important that the two elements of the decision should be reached separately, so that independent evaluations can be combined by managers who are responsible for making the final decision. Likewise, the results of other analyses, such as adverse results from foreign-exchange risk analysis, should not interfere with an analysis of marketing or sourcing opportunities. It may be very possible to avoid a foreign exchange risk by taking the appropriate defensive measures, thereby taking advantage of the opportunities.

THE COUNTRY ANALYSTS

Country-risk analysis (CRA) can be done either by corporate personnel or by outsiders. What is critical is that the analysts not only be competent but that their analysis accurately reflects the views and needs of the particular company.

Since there are many different types of international business activities; since the companies represent many different countries; and since the companies differ substantially between themselves in terms of corporate resources, philosophy, and goals; then it is essential that the CRA be one that is appropriate for that particular company. Thus, there will be a major difference in the CRA perspectives of commerical banks, extractive companies, retailers, manufacturers of consumer products, and construction companies.

If the company chooses to do the CRA in-house, then the system can be specifically designed for the company's needs. If outside specialists are hired, they must be properly indoctrinated to reflect the company's perspective, or someone within the company must make the necessary adjustments in the outsider's report.

Whatever the source of the report, it must be based upon competent analysis in several veins, not only economic but also political, legal, and even socio-cultural. Companies often choose junior managers for country-risk analysis. This is commonly a bad mistake. Just because an individual is a business school graduate does not necessarily qualify him or her to do economic analyses; much more training is necessary. Similarly (and often to an even greater extent), companies err in not choosing qualified political analysts. Most corporate employees are even poorer political analysts than they are economic analysts.

A growing number of research companies have been formed that specialize in country risk analysis. Although professional in-house analysis would be the optimal solution in most cases, many companies cannot afford such expenses or they simply opt for the less-expensive external service. Like so many external services, CRA can vary substantially in quality. Since the time horizon for many of the decisions that flow from country-risk analyses is very long term, the choice of analysts and the continuing evaluation of the quality of the analyses is critical. However, it is very difficult to gauge the quality of CRA services. The choice of either internal or external specialists warrants great care.

THE NATURE OF COUNTRY RISK

Country risk is the likelihood that events could occur that would extraordinarily disrupt the environment within which the company operates abroad. Risk can stem from economic, political, legal, or sociocultural sources. Analysts commonly refer to *risk analysis*. However, that procedure is *not* greatly different from *opportunity analysis*. For example, a marketing research program that spotlights markets with the greatest potential can also serve to spot those with the greatest market risk. Similarly, an effort by a bank to identify the relative risk of the various foreign countries identifies not only those of high risk but also those of low risk.

Country risk can arise either *directly* from events that have a direct impact upon the company itself, such as expropriation or confiscation of its foreign assets, or *indirectly* via the impact of environmental factors on another company, such as a customer or a supplier. This latter point is critically important but is very often overlooked by companies.

Such disruptions of the environment within which a company operates most commonly occur in the country in which the company is operating abroad. However, it could also stem from the home country of the international company or even from a third country. For example, in 1979 many American companies and banks with business in Iran were hurt more by the U.S. government's action of sequestering the assets of Iran than by the actions of the Iranian government. Likewise, many European and other foreign companies were hurt in the same process, not from the actions of the Iranian government or by their own government, but by a third government—that of the United States. All these types of country risk need to be examined.

Types of country risk: There are several aspects of country risk. The major components are as follows:

1. legal risk
2. foreign exchange risk
   a. FX fluctuation
   b. FX controls
3. money and capital-control risk
4. trade-control risk
5. sovereign risk
6. general country risk

Although all these are part and parcel of country risk, the analysis of country risk per se does not cover all these facets. Some of them are analyzed separately. For example, foreign exchange risk is commonly analyzed by a group of analysts that is separate from the economists and political scientists who perform CRA. The problem of FX risk is examined in the chapter on foreign-exchange exposure management. Similarly, legal risk is a very specific type of risk that requires the specialized services of legal experts.

The task of the country-risk specialist revolves around the last four of the categories listed above. In some companies, the problems of money, capital and even trade-control risk are assigned to the FX risk analysts as well. In these cases the CRA function concentrates totally on the problems of sovereign risk and general country risk. However, the risks of money, capital, trade, and exchange controls are all closely related to sovereign risk.

Sovereign risk: National governments are sovereign authorities in their own territories. Within their respective jurisdictions they are generally the supreme authorities. Sovereign risk is the threat that the government may take voluntary action to either renege upon its own obligations or interfere with the ability of private-sector companies to honor their obligations, such as using capital controls or confiscation. Note this refers to *voluntary* actions on the part of the government; sovereign risk does *not* involve the *financial inability* of the government to honor its own obligations, but its *willingness or unwillingness*. Financial inability would involve credit or commercial risk, not country risk.

Sovereign risk can thus be seen to be essentially a political risk.

General country risk: Any type of country risk that does not comfortably fit under any of the categories of risk above can be grouped under this catchall category. General risk includes economic, political, and socio-cultural components. Examples of general economic risk include *natural catastrophes*, such as the earthquakes in Algeria or

Greece, droughts in North Africa or Chile, floods in Bangladesh, and hurricanes in Central America; *man-made economic catastrophes,* such as the economies of Chile and Jamaica under the tutelage of Salvador Allende and Michael Manley, respectively; *depression,* collapse in the prices of critical exports, such as happens with very volatile commodities such as sugar, copper, phosphates, and coffee; and *soaring prices* for critical imports, such as petroleum and food. Examples of general political and socio-cultural risk are international war, domestic insurrection, and worker or student unrest.

These types of developments, even though they do not stem from deliberate governmental action to interfere with foreign companies, can either directly or indirectly have very negative impacts upon companies.

COUNTRY RISK VERSUS OTHER RISKS

Country risk obviously does not exist in a vacuum, totally separate from other types of international risk, such as market, credit, legal, and foreign exchange. For example, the actions of a government can potentially affect any of those types of risk. However, over and above the impact of governmental actions upon these specific risks, such actions can also have broader risks that would properly fall under the heading of *country risk.*

TECHNIQUES OF COUNTRY RISK ANALYSIS

Many efforts have been made to identify the "definitive" set of variables for a particular type of *international "risk and opportunity" analysis.* However, for each type of international analysis there is a particular set of variables that might be optimal for the analysis at hand. Yet, analysts are far more likely to err as a result of failure to consider enough variables than to have considered too many. Also, there are a large number of variables that are common to many different types of international analysis.

For a particular analytical task for a proposed direct investment, let's say foreign exchange-rate forecasting, a different combination of these variables might be necessary than for another purpose, for instance country-risk analysis. Also, even for the same variables different weights might well be advisable when the purpose of the analysis varies. Nevertheless, a very carefully structured set of variables is strongly recommended for whatever the purpose intended. This helps to lessen the chance that important elements have been overlooked and helps provide the mechanism for comparable analysis of different countries. (It should be obvious to the reader that different analytical techniques applied to different alternatives, whether they be currencies, markets, or investment prospects, make a valid comparison difficult if not impossible.)

There are essentially only three different approaches to country-risk analysis.

1. quantitative
2. free-form qualitative
3. structured qualitative

With the developments that have occurred in the past two decades in computers and statistical techniques, there has been a strong fascination with *quantitative efforts* to evaluate risk. Unfortunately, the results from the use of quantitative techniques have thus far *not* been too encouraging with respect to country risk.

The attractions of the use of quantitative techniques are many. If they prove to be feasible, massive amounts of information would be readily available to the decision maker. A wide variety of simulations could be applied. Also, the final output might be able to be used as a strong tool in making the final investment decisions.

Unfortunately, quantitative techniques of CRA are, of necessity, very complicated, very difficult to design, very difficult to implement, and very expensive. It is also often even more difficult to get the necessary personnel who can not only understand country-risk analysis but also know how to apply the necessary quantitative techniques. However, the greatest shortcoming of quantitative techniques is that CRA involves too many variables that are not readily quantifiable. If the number of qualitative variables was small, then the extent of possible error that might result from estimates of the likelihood of such events occurring might not introduce excessive amounts of potential distortion. Also, if it could be reasonably assumed that various errors of these estimates would tend to be offsetting, then quantifiable techniques might be plausible alternatives for country-risk analysis. However, the number of qualitative variables is very great (as will be seen in the following sections), and the errors are as likely to compound themselves as they are to offset one another.

As a result of these difficulties, quantitative techniques for country-risk analysis are much less common than are qualitative techniques. Not only are the qualitative techniques less complicated and less subject to the errors of attempting to make precise judgments about various variables, but these techniques are less expensive and can be readily understood by a wider range of managers.

A *free-form qualitative country-risk analysis* is unique every time. Each report is different. This makes it very difficult to compare different countries. This is often the initial type of CRA in which companies engage. However, because of the noncomparability of the results, most companies evolve to a more structured approach to CRA.

With a *structured* system of *qualitative* CRA, a company analyzes each country from essentially the same perspective and asks essentially the same questions. The qualitative analysis is generally supported by quantitative data and, where appropriate, testing and projections of the data, but not to the extent of quantitative techniques. In this way different countries, regardless of their location, stage of development, or type of government, can be compared. This is very important, since many decisions stemming from CRA are directed specifically at comparing the attractiveness of different countries.

FACTORS INFLUENCING COUNTRY RISK

For whatever the type of international operation intended, it is convenient, as noted above, to break the varieties of information necessary for CRA into three general groups, as follows:

1. politico-legal
2. socio-cultural
3. economic

Politico-legal and economic factors have the broadest impact upon international business operations. However, for some types of activities and in some situations the socio-cultural variables can be of critical importance.

The ranking listed above is not intended to indicate the order of priority. In many instances, such as the consideration of a direct investment in manufacturing facilities abroad for servicing the local market, all three types of analysis may well be done simultaneously. In other cases it may be clear to the management team that one particular category of analysis far outweighs the others in priority. In such instances a lot of time, effort, and cost might be saved by concentrating the first stage of the analytical process upon that one key area. For example, consideration of producing in foreign markets for export back to the home country requires a knowledge of the sophistication of the local workers in various countries. Likewise, a company that insists upon 100 percent ownership of its facilities might do well to initiate its international analysis with a look at the relevant laws and governmental attitudes in various countries.

There is a very wide range of variables that may be relevant in a particular analysis or for a particular country. Unfortunately, variables that might be very significant in one country (such as money and capital controls in Argentina), may be rather insignificant in another.

Political components of country risk: Many of the critical factors of country-risk analysis are political in nature. Table 11.2 lists many of the principal categories that any type of approach to country-risk analysis would, of necessity, need to consider. The list is certainly not exhaustive. It is intended to be very general. Depending upon the particular type of project for which the country-risk analysis is being performed, the analyst should consider more specific subcategories in some of these areas and some other important categories.

As with the other two major groups of components that need to be studied as part of country-risk analysis—economic and socio-cultural variables—the listing in Table 11.2 includes both domestic and international elements. Among the domestic political variables, the principal

TABLE 11.2   Political Factors Affecting Country Risk

I. DOMESTIC
    A. The political system
        1. Its basic strength
        2. Its resiliency—capacity for change without disruptive conflict
    B. The group in power
        1. Philosophy
        2. Policies
        3. Government officials
            a. Ability and number of qualified officials
            b. Willingness and capability for making tough decisions
        4. Strength, capability of implementing plans
    C. Opposition groups
        1. Strength of opposition groups
            a. Likelihood of system-disrupting conflict arising from within the country
        2. Philosophies of strong opposition groups
    D. The governmental system
        1. Efficiency
        2. Red tape
        3. Flexibility
        4. Responsiveness
II. INTERNATIONAL
    A. Likelihood of system-disrupting conflict arising from outside the country
        1. Due to country's own problems
        2. Due to treaty or other obligations
    B. Relations with major trading partners
    C. Relations of the company's home country with other countries

categories are the basic political system itself, the group presently in power, any major opposition groups, and the governmental bureaucracy.

The primary question regarding the overall political system is addressed to the strength and resiliency of the system. In the event of conflict within the system, does the country have the ability to absorb conflict without serious disruption to the political system? In many countries transfers of government take place regularly without any major disruption, for example, in the United Kingdom, Mexico, and Japan. In other cases, governmental change appears rather chaotic and disruptive, when in fact the country absorbs the uncertainty with a minimum of disruption, such as is the case with Italy. However, in many other countries the political system is not strong and has very little resiliency. This is especially true of many developing countries, for example, Iran, Argentina, and Greece. Dictatorships often rule or come to power as a result of unstable political conditions.

The type of governmental system, for example, democratic, Communist, military, and so forth, is not necessarily an issue of political risk. Any type of governmental system might prove to be risky from a foreign investment perspective. Correspondingly, each of the governments noted above also have examples of attractive investment environments.

Both the group in power and groups with strong aspirations for power also need to be carefully studied. What is the likelihood of the party in power remaining in power? What are its philosophy, policies, and degree of competences? If there are opposition groups that may be able to gain power (by whatever means appear to be their choice, whether it be by systematic means [an election] or by nonsystematic means [a revolution or *coup d'état*]), their strengths, philosophies, policies, and competency also need to be analyzed. Finally, how efficiently does the governmental bureaucracy function? (The Egyptian bureaucracy, for instance, has often proved so fraught with red tape that desired policies of the government are often frustrated. Foreign companies that have been interested in investing in Egypt have been known to give up simply out of exasperation.)

On the international scene, the critical question involves the likelihood of a politically destabilizing conflict arising from outside the country's borders. Conflict can arise either directly as a result of that government's own relations with other countries, or it can occur indirectly as a result of the government's close ties with another government, for instance, via a treaty.

Socio-cultural components of country risk: When a company operates in a foreign country, it must consider the possible effects of many socio-cultural variables. Table 11.3 lists many of the principal categories of socio-cultural variables that should be considered in a

TABLE 11.3   Socio-Cultural Factors Affecting Country Risk

I.   DOMESTIC
   A.   Social groups
      1.   Homogeneity of population
         a.   Ethnic
         b.   Religious
         c.   Linguistic
         d.   Class
      2.   Extent of cohesiveness or divisiveness
   B.   General psychology of population; work ethic
   C.   Unemployment
   D.   Political activism of population
   E.   Extent of social unrest
      1.   Strikes
      2.   Riots
      3.   Insurgency
II.   INTERNATIONAL
   A.   Cross-border ties
      1.   Ethnic
      2.   Religious
      3.   Linguistic
      4.   Historical
   B.   Cross-border antagonisms
      1.   Ethnic
      2.   Religious
      3.   Linguistic
      4.   Historical

proper CRA. As noted in the last section, this list is not intended to be comprehensive; it covers most of the major types of variables, but many more can be important, especially for specific types of investments.

Among the domestic socio-cultural factors, a very important element of any risk analysis is in the relative degree of homogeneity or heterogeneity of the population. Significant divisions can occur on the basis of ethnic groups (for example, there are three major tribal groups in Nigeria and three different racial groups in Malaysia [Malay, Chinese, and Indian]), religious groups (Hindus and Moslems in India and Protestants and Catholics in Northern Ireland), linguistic groups (the Flemish and the Walloons in Belgium), or class groups (the Brahmans and the "untouchables" in India).

Other socio-cultural factors of interest are the general psychology of the population (such as the work ethic, which is very prominent in some countries such as South Korea), the degree of political activism, and the extent of unemployment of the population. The final major category of domestic socio-cultural risk—the extent of domestic social unrest—can be projected from the previous variables.

In the international vein, important factors include cross-border ties (based on ethnic, linguistic, religious, or simply historical considerations), which can be either favorable or unfavorable from the perspective of socio-cultural risk analysis.

Economic components of country risk: Economic factors can obviously be of great importance in determining the degree of country risk confronting a foreign company. Table 11.4 outlines many of the most important of these variables. There is nothing really unique about these variables; they are the same basic variables that are involved in most analyses of a country (for example, the analysis of FX risk).

The principal domestic variables are factors such as the trends in economic growth, investment, and inflation. In addition, factors such as the diversity of the economy, its cyclicality, and the strength of the local infrastructure, especially the financial infrastructure, are of great interest to the country-risk analyst.

In the international arena the focus is typically on economic factors such as the overall balance of payments and the breakdown of the current and capital accounts into their components.

The economic analysis in the process of country-risk analysis, like the political and socio-cultural, is directed toward answering the question about the dangers from doing business in that particular country. Many other answers can be provided by the appropriate analysis of much of this same data, for example, the market potential of the country, but CRA is focused only on the question of country risk.

The ultimate decision of whether a company is going to export, license, or invest in a particular country or the decision concerning which of several countries to choose for any of these operations is ordinarily based on several different types of risk analysis. The corporate managers must be careful not to allow their judgment in any particular type of risk analysis to be clouded by the known results of other risk analyses or policy decisions of the company. This is not to say that policy decisions or the results from completed analyses should not affect the pattern of CRA analyses. Obviously they can. For example, if geologic analyses have already narrowed down the list of possible countries in which bauxite or some other natural resource can be found, then obviously the resource-seeking company should be guided by that information to concentrate its CRA on those countries. Similarly, if the company has already made a policy decision not to do business with a certain country due to philosophical or other reasons, then the country-risk analysts would probably be wasting a lot of time in researching that country.

TABLE 11.4 Economic Factors Affecting Country Risk

I. DOMESTIC
    A. Economic growth, investment trends
    B. Cyclicality of economy, economic diversification
    C. Inflation
        1. Monetary policy
        2. Fiscal policy, budget deficits
    D. Strength of local financial markets, portion of total
        investment financed locally
II. INTERNATIONAL
    A. Balance of payments
    B. International Trade
        1. Importance of trade in GNB
        2. Stability of trade earnings
            a. Diversity of exports
            b. Elasticity of export demand
            c. Elasticity of import demand
                (1) Capital equipment
                (2) Necessities
                    (a) Degree of self-reliance in food
                    (b) Reliance on imported energy
                (3) Luxuries
        3. International trade ties, proximity to major markets
        4. Extent of trade controls
    C. International capital
        1. Currency
            a. Strength
            b. Stability
            c. Quality of exchange markets
            d. Depth of exchange markets
            e. Extent of controls over exchange markets
        2. Debt
            a. Total
            b. Short-term as share of total
            c. Debt-service ratio
            d. Debt-service schedule
        3. International financial resources
            a. International reserves, gold valued at market
            b. International borrowing capacity
                (1) History of debt repayment
                (2) Credit rating
            c. Autonomous capital inflows
        4. Share of total investment financed from abroad

SUMMARY

The decision to internationalize has many long-term consequences for a company. Therefore, it is not something a company should undertake casually. Nevertheless, the initial steps are indeed often taken somewhat casually without much planning. Such steps can occur, for example, as the result of unsolicited demand from abroad or from an emotional impulse to "go international" without adequate preparation. However, if the company is to expand overseas in a rational fashion, then careful planning is necessary.

The appropriate research for international operations of a company is a function of the type of activity in which the company is engaged. The international research has many different components: market research, credit analysis, legal research, FX forecasting, and country-risk analysis, among others.

The evaluations of the potentials of a foreign country and specific suppliers or customers are obviously very serious matters for a company as it prepares to venture abroad. The nature of the analyses in these various fields that are needed by a particular company is a function of the nature of the business of the company, the desires of the company, and its resources and weaknesses. This is true whether the international activity is to be export or import, licensing or foreign investment, portfolio or direct investment.

Yet, whatever the parameters within which the company must operate, the task for international management of the evaluation of the potential of foreign countries is quite complicated and should not be undertaken casually. There is a very wide range of variables that might have potential bearing upon the choice of the country (or countries) to be chosen for the foreign operations.

Country-risk analysis (CRA) is another very complicated task involving economic, political, and socio-cultural components. It specifically focuses on sovereign risk plus the elements of general country risk that can arise from forces outside the government's control. Country-risk analysis is not a highly developed field. Quantitative techniques have not proven to be very effective. Qualitative techniques are widely available but until the late 1970s were not widely utilized. Especially in the area of political analysis—a critically important aspect of CRA—companies have been careless in obtaining competent assistance.

Once the company has done both the market and country-risk analyses, it is prepared to incorporate the recommendations that ensued from those analyses along with the company's own self-analysis. With these inputs the company is able to determine not only where to expand internationally but also in what form.

The next two chapters examine the impacts, unfavorable as well as favorable, that a company, as a result of its international operations, can have upon its home and host countries.

KEY TERMS

COMMERCIAL RISK	MANAGEMENT	SOVEREIGN RISK
COUNTRY RISK	CONTRACTS	SUBSIDIARY
INVESTMENT RISK	MIXED VENTURE	TURNKEY
JOINT VENTURE	PROJECT FINANCING	

REVIEW QUESTIONS

1. Identify and define the various types of international risks a firm encounters in its international operations.
2. What is licensing? In what way can it be more valuable internationally than domestically?
3. What are management contracts? What are turnkey projects?
4. Discuss the advantages of portfolio and direct investments relative to each other. When might a company choose to employ each?
5. Why might a host country try to place severe limits upon direct foreign investments from abroad?
6. What were the three market-assessment techniques that rely upon secondary data? How do they differ?
7. What are some of the major dangers of relying upon secondary data for market and country-risk assessment?
8. What are the various types of country risk? What type of specialist is likely to be responsible for each type? Could all these types of risk analysis be handled by specialists outside of the company?
9. How does sovereign risk differ from country risk?
10. Describe the basic types of country-risk analysis.
11. What are the three basic groups of factors that affect country risk? What are the major subcategories of each?

SUGGESTED REFERENCES

AGMON, TAMIR, AND CHARLES P. KINDLEBERGER, eds. *Multinationals from Small Countries.* Cambridge, Mass.: MIT Press, 1977.

AHARONI, YAIR   *The Foreign Direct Investment Decision Process.* Cambridge, Mass.: Division of Research, Graduate School of Business Administration, Harvard University, 1966.

AJAMI, RIAD A., AND DAVID A. RICKS "Motives of Non-American Firms Investing in the United States," *Journal of International Business Studies,* Winter 1981.

BEHRMAN, JACK N. *Decision Criteria for Foreign Direct Investment in Latin America.* Council of Americas, 1974.

————*National Interests and the Multinational Enterprise.* Englewood Cliffs, N.J.: Prentice-Hall, Inc., 1970.

BROOKE, MICHAEL Z., AND H. LEE REMMERS *International Management and Business Policy.* Boston: Houghton Mifflin Co., 1978.

CALVET, A.S. "A Synthesis of Foreign Direct Investment Theories and Theories of the Multinational Firm," *Journal of International Business Studies,* Spring–Summer 1981.

DUNNING, JOHN, ed. *Economic Analysis and the Multinational Enterprise.* New York: Praeger Publishers, 1974.

FARMER, RICHARD N., AND BARRY RICHMAN *Comparative Management and Economic Progress.* Homewood, Ill.: Richard D. Irwin, Inc., 1970.

FRANKO, LAWRENCE G. *European Multinationals.* New York: Harper & Row Publishers, Inc., 1976.

FRY, EARL H. *Financial Invasion of the U.S.A.* New York: McGraw-Hill Book Company, 1980.

GILPIN, ROBERT *U.S. Power and Multinational Corporation,* New York: Basic Books, Inc., Publishers, 1975.

GLADWIN, THOMAS N., AND INGO WALTER *Multinationals Under Fire.* New York: John Wiley & Sons, Inc., 1980.

GROSSE, ROBERT *Theory of Foreign Direct Investment.* College of Business, University of South Carolina: Essays in International Business, December 1981.

HYMER, STEPHEN H. *International Operations of National Firms: A Study of Direct Investment.* Cambridge, Mass.: MIT Press, 1976.

KINDLEBERGER, CHARLES P. *American Business Abroad.* New Haven, Conn.: Yale University Press, 1969.

KOBRIN, STEPHEN J. "The Environmental Determinants of Foreign Direct Investment: An Ex-Post Empirical Analysis," *Journal on International Business Studies,* Fall 1976.

KOLDE, ENDEL-JAKOB *Environment of International Business.* Boston, Mass.: Kent, 1982.

KORTH, CHRISTOPHER "Developing a Country-Risk Analysis System," *Journal of Commerical Bank Lending,* December 1979.

LAMONT, DOUGLAS F. *Foreign State Enterprises.* New York: Basic Books Inc., Publishers, 1979.

LITTLE, JANE SNEDDON "Locational Decisions of Foreign Direct Investors in the United States," *New England Economic Review,* July–August 1978.

MICHALET, CHARLES A., AND MICHEL DELAPIERRE (David Ashton, trans.), *The Multinationalization of French Firms.* Cleveland: World Trade Education Center—Academy of International Business, 1975.

MILLER, ROBERT, AND DALE WEIGEL "Motivation of Foreign Direct Investment," *Journal of International Business Studies,* Fall 1972.

RAGAZZI, GIORGIO "Theories of the Determinants of Direct Foreign Investment," *IMF Staff Papers,* July 1973.

RICKS, DAVID A., AND RIAD AJAMI "Motives of Non-American Firms Investing in the U.S.," *Journal of International Business Studies,* Winter 1981.

RUTENBERG, DAVID P. *Multinational Management.* Boston: Little, Brown & Company, 1982.

TERPSTRA, VERNON *Cultural Environment of International Business.* Cincinnati: Southwestern Publishing Co., 1978.

TUGENDHAT, CHRISTOPHER *The Multinationals.* New York: Random House, Inc., 1972.

VERNON, RAYMOND *Sovereignty at Bay.* New York: Basic Books, Inc., Publishers, 1971.

12

The Positive Impacts of Foreign Direct Investment

International business brings various types of advantages to all countries involved. In Chapter 2 many of the advantages of international trade were considered. In Chapter 3 the focus was on some of the impacts of international flows of factors of production. In this chapter the focus is upon the *positive effects* that foreign direct investment (FDI) might bring to either the host or the home country.

THE NATURE OF THE IMPACTS OF FOREIGN DIRECT INVESTMENT

INTERNATIONAL AND DOMESTIC INVESTMENT

Any FDI, whether by a multinational firm or not, can have either negative or positive effects. As noted in Chapter 1, most observers of FDI refer to companies making foreign direct investments as *multinationals,* although in fact they may be very domestically oriented, with only a marginal degree of involvement in international business. Therefore, the reader should bear in mind that observations made here about the favorable and unfavorable effects of multinationals also tend to apply to foreign direct investments made by nonmultinational firms as well.

Any investment has a wide variety of potential effects, some good and some bad. This is *true of domestic as well as foreign direct invest-ment.* Thus, if a French company opens a new factory in Normandy or an American company in Michigan, then, if that company is not local to the area, it can have many of the exact same types of impacts that are examined in these two chapters.

However, when the investing company is foreign, it tends to be much more visible, and local residents can be much more sensitive to its effects. As a result, it is worthwhile to focus upon as many of these impacts as possible: the positive effects are noted in this chapter and the negative effects in Chapter 13.

The consequences of FDI that are examined in these two chapters are *possible* consequences. No one investment or even no one company is ever likely to produce all these favorable or unfavorable results. Nor will even one country necessarily experience all the different effects. Howev-er, they are results that have occurred and can be expected to occur in conjunction with some foreign direct investments in some countries as seen from the perspective of some observers. The participant and observ-er of FDI need to be aware of the many possibilities of both favorable and unfavorable impacts in order to be able to intelligently evaluate such investment.

PERSPECTIVES OF THE OBSERVERS

There are many observers of, and direct participants in, direct investment: workers, suppliers, customers, competitors, political observ-ers (both those presently in power and those seeking power), tax authori-ties, labor unions, banks, and so forth. Each has a different perspective. Each sees different advantages and disadvantages from a given invest-ment.

The views of the different participants and observers of FDI not only do not necessarily agree, but they are often diametrically opposed. The following approach to analyzing FDI is designed to take into account perceived advantages or disadvantages from *all* possible perspectives. Therefore, the reader might not find some of the "advantages" advanta-geous from his or her perspective; in fact, some may be actually seen as disadvantages. This should not be too surprising. For example, the local company that loses business to a new local competitor from abroad is not likely to view the new company in the same light as the worker hired by the new company or the supplier who has just gotten the new contract.

This issue of different perspectives and philosophies is examined in detail in the next chapter. The last chapter of this section, Chapter 14, integrates the favorable and unfavorable impacts of FDI, which are discussed in this and the following chapters, with the strengths and weaknesses of both the investor and the company. From this discussion the reader can draw the basis for compromise and cooperation, with maximum benefits to both the company and the country and minimum disadvantages to each.

The impacts of FDI are examined using the following outline:

1. host-country perspective
   a. economic effects
   b. socio-cultural effects
   c. politico-legal effects
2. home-country perspective
   a. economic effects
   b. socio-cultural effects
   c. politico-legal effects

The greatest, most readily observable, and generally the most politically sensitive impacts of foreign direct investment are those seen from the host country's perspective. Therefore, most of the discussion will focus on the host country. This pattern is used in the next chapter as well.

FAVORABLE ECONOMIC IMPACTS OF FDI: HOST COUNTRY'S PERSPECTIVE

Table 12.1 outlines the major categories of favorable effects from the host country's perspective.

POSITIVE IMPACTS OF FDI ON BASIC FACTORS OF PRODUCTION

Table 12.2 outlines some of the major favorable impacts upon host countries involving the factors of production.

Capital: The favorable effects relating to *capital flows*, as with so many of the variables that are examined in this and the next chapter, have both primary and derivative effects, that is, both immediate and subsequent effects.

The primary capital effects result directly from the actual flow of capital itself, if indeed a capital inflow actually is involved in the investment, instead of locally generated earnings on existing investments or local borrowing. There is a net addition to the available capital stock in the country. This brings a greater variety of capital sources to the country. Such an inflow is especially important for countries with limited domestic savings and weak domestic capital markets, particularly if those countries have been having difficulty in directly tapping the capital markets abroad. This has been a very serious problem for many developing countries and Communist countries since the mid-1970s following the massive buildup of foreign debt following the oil crisis of 1973–1974.

This infusion of new capital from abroad sometimes also serves to indirectly augment local investment capital by *attracting local capital* that was not being productively employed locally or that was being held abroad. It can be invested in either the same project or a related investment. Related investment opportunities derive from either *linkages* (that is, direct ties with a particular project through suppliers, contractors, and so forth) or via the *multiplier* effect (that is, indirect ties with the investment through workers' earnings being spent and respent in the local company).

Another, and critically important, primary effect results from the *financial capacity* of the investor *to bear the financial risk* of the investment. If the investment is large or in any other way inordinately risky, it is often beyond the capacity or willingness of local companies to absorb the risk. Even the local government may not be able to afford the risk. This is especially true of large projects involving raw material extrac-

---

TABLE 12.1   Potential Favorable Impacts of Foreign Companies upon Host Countries: Major Groupings[a]

    I.   POSITIVE *ECONOMIC* EFFECTS
       A.   Basic factors of production
           1.   capital
           2.   labor
           3.   entrepreneurship
           4.   technology
           5.   raw materials
       B.   Effects resulting from basic factors of production
           1.   balance of payments
           2.   structure of economy
           3.   stability of economy
           4.   effects upon local companies
   II.   POSITIVE *SOCIO-CULTURAL* EFFECTS
       A.   General public
       B.   Workers
       C.   Customers
  III.   POSITIVE *GOVERNMENTAL* EFFECTS
       A.   General political system
       B.   Governmental finances
           1.   revenue
           2.   expenditures
       C.   International relations

[a]Table 12.1 corresponds to Table 13.1.

TABLE 12.2   Postive Impacts of FDI on the Basic Factors of Production[a]

   I. CAPITAL
    A. Initial inflow
    B. Access to additional capital abroad
    C. Capacity to attract local capital
    D. Financial capacity to bear risk
    E. Increased savings in local economy
    F. Retention of locally generated cash flow by the foreign
        investor
    G. Attraction of other foreign investors
  II. LABOR
    A. Unskilled (and semi-skilled)
    B. Technological skills
    C. Managerial skills
    D. Introduction of nontraditional mental attitudes
    E. Offset to brain drain
 III. ENTREPRENEURSHIP
    A. Search for new products, markets, methods, and so forth
    B. Willingness to bear risk
  IV. TECHNOLOGY
    A. Introduction of existing patents, and so forth
    B. Access to ongoing research and development programs
    C. Responsiveness to local needs and resources
    D. Appropriate technology
   V. RAW MATERIALS
    A. Bringing access to important sources of raw materials from
        abroad
    B. Providing materials at lower prices

---

[a]Table 12.2 corresponds to Tables 13.2 and 13.3.

tion. Recent examples of this type of project would include copper projects in Panama and Peru, iron ore in Brazil, oil in Indonesia, and bauxite in Cameroun.

Labor: A second factor of production that can flow into a country as part of a foreign investment is *labor*—both unskilled (or semi-skilled) and skilled (technological and managerial). (See Table 12.2, section II.) Foreign investors do not typically take their own unskilled or semi-skilled labor with them. However, such labor flows do occasionally occur when local workers are not available or are unwilling to do the heavy, dirty work. An example would be the South Korean workers who are brought to Saudi Arabia by Korean countractors.

Much more common, indeed almost the norm, is the infusion of highly trained technicians and managers. It is rather unusual for a company to make a new investment in a country without assigning some of its own personnel. Occasionally, if the investment involves a buy out of an existing and well-run operation, the foreign investor may choose to simply absorb the existing management and technological staff. However, in the vast majority of cases, the company brings in some of its own people—either from abroad or from other operations that the company already has in the same country. Such individuals can be natives of the home country, the host country, or a third country. For example if an American company hired a German to run its Malaysian operations.

Technicians, of course, bring with them the specialized skills that can be so critical to a company in the modern world; not only less-developed countries but also industrialized countries are often lacking individuals with such skills. Examples include not only productive techniques, but also financial techniques, marketing techniques, and so forth.

The other type of skilled labor involves managerial expertise. This is *perhaps the most valuable of the factors of production* that foreign investors bring to the host countries. This is especially true of investments in less-developed countries, but it is also very true even in industrialized countries. For example, the introduction of American managerial techniques into Europe after World War II helped to revolutionize European management techniques. Now there are numerous European business schools that not only have adapted these techniques but have built upon them as well. Also, the major influx of foreign banks into London substantially agitated the staid British clearinghouse banks; the infusion of new ideas and techniques caused the major British banks to become more imaginative and competitive.

The process of adapting and adopting managerial techniques continues even in the United States and Europe. Today there is much interest in studying Japanese managerial techniques to see how they might be adapted into Western enterprises.

The introduction of highly trained personnel not only brings the particular skills that the tasks require, but, often of very great importance also, it brings an infusion of *nontraditional mental attitudes*. In peasant societies especially there is often a strong attitude that problems are the "will of God" or the "will of Allah." Such attitudes are very obstructive to economic and social "progress." Such attitudes must be overcome if such societies are to be able to throw off the shackles of poverty. (Nevertheless, as will be seen in the next chapter, such change may also be highly disruptive to a society.)

The infusion of foreign talent in many countries can help to offset the effects of "brain drain." When many highly trained personnel leave a country, it can impose a high social cost. Countries such as India, Pakistan, and Egypt as well as many Communist countries such as Cuba,

East Germany, and Poland have suffered very heavy losses of skilled workers.

Inflows of technicians and managers in conjunction with foreign direct investment can be an important aid in offsetting some of these losses, especially in developing countries.

Entrepreneurship: Closely allied with the flow of trained managers is the very special asset known as *entrepreneurship*. (See Table 12.2, section III.) The entrepreneur is the risk taker, the searcher for new products, markets, and productive methods. The two roles of manager and entrepreneur are tightly interwoven. However, they are quite distinct. The leader with the imagination to seek out new paths and the ability to personally accept risks may or may not be a good manager. For example, Henry Ford, for all his entrepreneurial genius in building the Ford Motor Company, almost destroyed it by his inability to manage it well and by his inability to let others do it for him. In a similar vein, there are many "good" managers who have neither the personal ability to lead a company imaginatively into new ventures nor the courage to take entrepreneurial risks; they merely represent the status quo.

Some observers may feel that a good manager must also be an entrepreneur. However, the roles are quite distinct, and it is useful to keep the two concepts separate. Each has its own function in the developmental process of a business.

Technology: The fourth factor of production that is mobile is *technology*. (See Table 12.2, section IV.) It can involve the introduction of new patents, processes, and so forth. But equally important may be the ongoing access to continuing research and development programs. This may not be important for the investment in stable products such as Coca-Cola or canned foods. However, it is critically important in technologically dynamic fields such as pharmaceuticals, computers, and consumer electronics. In these instances the initial infusion of foreign investment is only sufficient to get a country in the door of the particular market involved. However, in order to remain competitive, access to continuing technological developments is mandatory.

Finally, in many instances products or productive techniques may need technological modification as a result of unique conditions in the local environment. Access to "appropriate" technology can be extremely valuable to a country in some circumstances. For example, farm equipment that is satisfactory in industrialized countries often proves inadequate in developing countries, where the grains and their plants can be much tougher and where the maintenance facilities and technicians for the equipment can be much less satisfactory than in industrialized countries. Also, food products often require special modification in different countries (or even regions); this sometimes requires technological flexibility as well as product flexibility.

Raw materials: *Raw materials,* especially minerals, are a critical resource in many industries. (See Table 12.2, section V.) Generally, this particular advantage of FDI is rather limited. Most raw materials can be readily purchased on world markets. Therefore, if the rest of the necessary package of productive factors can be put together by a domestic investor, then the raw material can usually be obtained.

However, when FDI gives a country access to some vital mineral from abroad, which it might have had difficulty obtaining directly, this can be a major gain for the country, especially if the mineral is available at favorable prices. For example, if an OPEC country chose to set up oil refineries or petrochemical plants in a foreign country and to provide the base feedstocks, the access to the raw material (especially if at favorable prices) would be a vital component of the investment.

The flow of these basic factors of production (capital, labor, entrepreneurship, technology, and raw materials) can be very valuable contributions to the development of a country. Lack of balance in the necessary factor proportions is a serious impediment to the development of many countries. However, there are also many other advantages (economic, socio-cultural, and politico-legal) for the host country. These derive from the influx of the basic factors and are examined in the rest of this chapter.

POSITIVE ECONOMIC EFFECTS RESULTING FROM THE BASIC FACTORS OF PRODUCTION

In addition to the direct impacts resulting from FDI, there are many positive *derivative effects.*

Balance of payments: The *balance of payments* can be favorably affected in both the trade and capital accounts.

In the trade account, the investment can be beneficial either by providing import-substituting production or by the creation of export-expanding production. (See Table 12.3.)

1. *Import substitution* (Table 12.3, section A-1) involves the initiation of a type of production that was not previously produced in the country or that was only produced in an inadequate quantity. The new venture enables the local production to supplant what had formerly been imported and thereby reduce the merchandise or service import drain on the balance of payments. The lack of local production can reflect any of several factors: unrealized opportunities, lack of willingness of local investors to make the investment, or the unavailability of the necessary complementary factors of production.

TABLE 12.3   Positive Effects of FDI Resulting from Basic Factors of Production (Section I)[a]

I. BALANCE OF PAYMENTS
  A. Trade
      1. import substitution
          a. unrealized opportunities
          b. lack of willingness of local investors
          c. unavailable complementary factors or components
      2. export expansion
          a. export orientation of company
          b. exporting expertise
              (1) knowledge of mechanics
              (2) knowledge of foreign markets
          c. captive foreign markets
          d. existing foreign distribution network of company
          e. attractiveness of reputation, brand names, and so
              forth in foreign markets
          f. greater ability and willingness to extend credit
              abroad
  B. Money and capital
      1. initial infusion of capital
      2. attraction of additional capital from abroad
      3. inducement for locally owned capital to be returned from
          abroad
      4. increase in local savings resulting from higher income
      5. incentive to keep locally owned capital from flowing
          abroad
      6. retention of local cash flow of FDI in the host country

[a]See Tables 12.4 and 12.5 for sections II, III and IV.

Import substitution has tremendous appeal for many promoters of economic development. Indeed, in many circumstances, imports which occurred because of inefficiencies in the local economy and which prevented profitable production from being initiated can economically be replaced by local production; countries should search out such opportunities.

However, *there has been a strong tendency for many governments to abuse the logic of important substitution* by promoting types of import displacement that can only be economical via trade protectionism. If quotas exist or if tariff levels are high enough or if subsidies are given, almost any production can be profitable if the demand is strong enough. Even greenhouse gardening in Sweden could produce bananas and coffee, but the cost would certainly be prohibitive, although a small but profitable market might survive. In a similar fashion, the *average* Chilean tariff in the early 1970s exceeded 100 percent. As a result, at one time there were more than fifteen automobile companies in Chile—a nation of only 8 million people. Such gross inefficiency and very high-cost production could never have survived under more competitive conditions.

There is little doubt that an almost obsessive interest in import subsitution has led to many inefficient and costly investments.

2. As the preceding discussion indicates, import substitution, while remaining basically valid, must be utilized with great restraint. As a result of this, there has been a shift toward more emphasis in recent years upon *export expansion* (Table 12.3, section A-2). A willingness to forego the easy temptation of artificially stimulating import substitution and instead allowing imports to remain high, while at the same time encouraging exports to grow even faster, is a more sophisticated political and economic decision, but it is not really much more complicated. Import substitution attempts to reduce the growth in the country's trade by allowing exports to grow under normal market conditions while trying to trim the growth in imports or to even reduce them via import substitution. Unless this reduction of imports is economically justifiable without trade protectionism, then, as was seen in the trade chapters, productive efficiency in the country and the world will decline.

Export expansion, on the other hand, encourages an increase in trade and a greater realization of the economic benefits of freer trade. Thus, the country's imports are allowed to grow under normal market conditions, while the exports are stimulated in such a way as to take advantage of competitive advantages that exist but have remained un-utilized. Examples of export-promoting efforts of a government include information programs (for example, the investment promotion offices of such states as South Carolina and Michigan in Brussels and Tokyo and similar offices of foreign countries in the United States), financing packages, and tax holidays.

Obviously, even in this instance there is a very thin line between helping foreign and local companies learn about the advantages of production in a particular country and artificially stimulating investment. (With so many countries struggling to attract textile and electronic investments, a small country may easily be overlooked unless it "toots its own horn".) If the governmental support becomes too extensive, it may be the only thing that makes a particular investment worthwhile. In that case, the governmental support program is as deleterious to economic efficiency as the negative trade barriers mentioned above with respect to import substitution. *"Positive" barriers are no more justifiable than are negative barriers.*[1]

If the governmental support program can attract economically

---

[1]Refer again to the related discussion in Chapter 4.

worthwhile investments in the absence of further inducements, then the program is justified and the investment desirable. But if the investment would not be sufficiently profitable on its own, then the government is encouraging another misallocation of resources.

Some of the benefits of an export-expanding type of investment from abroad can include something as simple as the *export orientation* of the company. For example, when the German company, Thyssen, purchased controlling interest in the Budd Company in the United States, it kept the American managers but gave them some new policies. These new policies included a major orientation toward exporting. This manufacturer of railroad cars had made less than 10 percent of its sales overseas, primarily because of a lack of effort. The new parent company was convinced that, without sacrificing the traditional domestic markets, the Budd Company could greatly expand its international sales.

Another export-expanding asset that the foreign investor can bring to a host country is *exporting expertise*—the knowledge of exporting mechanics and of foreign markets.[2]

If the investor has a *captive foreign market* or at least an existing *foreign distribution system,* this can be a critically important contribution to the host country. When a manufacturing company has parts shipped to its plant in Malaysia for assembling, the completed products are shipped back to the intracompany captive market. Similarly, the canned fruit company that opens a pineapple plantation in the Philippines has its own distribution network in the United States or Europe through which fruit can be sold, an advantage that a domestic Philippine company might not have.

If the foreign investor brings a valuable market *reputation or brand name,* this is another monopolistic asset that local companies might not be able to match. Thus, if Malaysia, for instance, is anxious to become a major producer of electronic goods, the effort would be greatly aided by investors with names such as Sony, Phillips, and General Electric.

Credit plays a very significant role in many areas of exports. Banks, of course, provide much of this. However, companies still provide a large amount of export credit in some industries. If local companies lack the financial strength or the willingness to provide financing services, then they may be valuable assets that the foreign investor can contribute.

Foreign investment also can favorably affect the capital account of the balance of payments (see Table 12.3, section B). The initial infusion of capital, the attraction of additional capital from abroad, the inducement for an inflow of locally-owned capital being held abroad, and an incentive for keeping more domestic savings from flowing abroad are all

---

[2]See Chapter 16 for a discussion of the mechanics of exporting.

ways that the BOP capital account can be favorably affected. These were discussed under the section on capital flow above. (See Table 12.2.)

Another result involves an increase in the local capacity to generate savings as a result of the increased income. An additional source of increased capital results from the retention of part or all of the locally generated cash flow by the foreign investor. Occasionally all the cash flow might be kept in the country for a period of years as the foreign investor expands the initial investment. (However, the country should not expect this from the normal investment; it is definitely the exception rather than the rule.)

As previously discussed, much investment also results as a response to the investment by other companies. This might be a defensive investment of the "follow-the-leader" type. Or it might result from international linkages. For example, American automotive parts companies and advertising agencies received strong incentive to invest in Europe following the wake of the investment there by American automobile manufacturers. Likewise, an *international multiplier effect* can lead to totally unrelated investments coming from abroad as a result of the rising incomes engendered by the initial investment.

Structure of the economy: Foreign direct investment can also have a strong impact upon the basic structure of the ecomony—the physical resources, the infrastructure, and the industrial structure. (See Table 12.4.)

Physical resources include such assets as land, raw material, climate, and plant and animal life. (See Table 12.4, section A.) Even in the most industrialized and intensively developed countries, there remain resources yet to be developed or even explored. For example, three out of every four oil wells that have *ever been drilled anywhere in the world* have been drilled in the continental United States! If any major raw material has been adequately explored and exploited, it would appear to be oil in the United States. Yet a massive search still continues under the impetus of high oil prices. And, despite the size of the American oil giants, foreign investors such as British Petroleum have joined in this search.

Potentially unique inputs of the foreign investor in the realm of physical resources include exploration, development of the productive system, and the actual exploitation of the resources (for example, mining the ores or growing the crops).

In countries where the *economic and social infrastructure* is inadequate for a company's purposes, the foreign investor may have to build the basic infrastructure itself. (See Table 12.4, section B.) In some instances the infrastructure is virtually nonexistent. A major mining

TABLE 12.4   Positive Effects of FDI Resulting from Basic Factors of Production (Section II)[a]

II. **STRUCTURE OF THE ECONOMY**
   A. Physical resources (raw materials, land, climate, plant and animal life)
      1. exploration
      2. development of the productive system
      3. exploitation
   B. Expansion or improvement of infrastructure
      1. basic economic infrastructure
         a. transportation
         b. communication
         c. power
      2. social infrastructure
         a. housing
         b. health
         c. education
      3. financial infrastructure
      4. marketing infrastructure
         a. market research
         b. distributional channels
         c. promotional channels
      5. integration with the rest of the country's infrastructure
   C. Industry
      1. new productive capacity
      2. enhanced efficiency (productivity)
      3. diversification of economy
         a. geographical
         b. type of production

---

[a]See Table 12.5 for sections III and IV. Table 12.3, section II, corresponds to Table 13.4.

venture in the heart of the Amazon jungle in Brazil is expected to cost in excess of $1 billion. A significant part of that developmental cost will go toward the creation of the following types of infrastructure:

1. *Basic economic infrastructure,* consisting of the elementary transportation, communication, and power systems. Without adequate systems in each of these categories, no modern investment is possible. In the Amazon mining venture, initial supplies had to be brought in by helicopter so that roads, railroads, communication, and power-generation systems could be built.

2. *Social infrastructure,* consisting of housing, health, and educational systems. Even when local facilities are available, they may be wholly inadequate for the needs of the foreign investor. For example, even if a mud hut suffices for the local populace (which, especially in remote areas, can be very primitive) and if there is a local doctor, their availability may be totally unacceptable to the workers who are brought to the investment site.

3. *Financial markets*—the foreign investor may help to strengthen these markets by the prestige which its use of the markets might bring, by the attraction of more funds through the basic channels and by the attraction of foreign banks to the country.

4. *Marketing system*—this is often one of the inefficiencies of a system that can be the most difficult to surmount. If there is an inadequate delivery system, storage system, or means for advertising, then the foreign company may have to provide them itself, or it may need to induce some other party to assume the task.

The investors' contribution to the country's infrastructure is especially beneficial if it is designed to tie in with the existing or planned infrastructure of the country and if it is made available to the general public. For example, railroads that were built by mining and plantation companies have often been key elements in the early development of infrastructural systems for many countries, such as the roads and railways built by the banana companies in Central America.

In some cases, however, new infrastructural systems do not tie in well with an integrated, rational, infrastructural system for the host country. For example, a large part of the railroad lines that exist in Latin America run from the interior to the coast, that is, from the mines to the loading docks. The lines do not tie together nationally and certainly not internationally between the various South American countries, and the gauges of track often vary.

In addition to the impact of the foreign investor upon the development of physical resources and infrastructure, the investors naturally can have a very significant impact upon the *industrial capacity* of the country (see Table 12.4, section C). That, after all, is one of the strongest motives for a large share of foreign investments, that is, the building of productive capacity. This can involve either totally new capacity or enhanced productivity of existing capacity. It can also be very valuable to the country qualitatively as well as quantitatively. For example, diversification of the industrial base (either geographically or in the type of production) can be a major gain by the country from the FDI.

Also, in many types of business ventures there is the need for a "critical mass" before industrial growth accelerates. For example, a single factory or even a small group of factories may not be sufficient to attract supporting industries such as banks, suppliers, and so forth. However, a major new investment might be all that is necessary to go beyond that "critical mass" to a point where there is enough industry and supportive companies in place that, when other investors look at that particular production site, it may have strong advantages relative to other investment alternatives.

Stability of the economy: If a foreign investment brings greater diversity to the productive base of a country or to the markets of a country's exports, this can help to provide a cushion against domestic business cycles or even against the business cycles in different foreign markets. (See Table 12.5, section III.) This benefit is especially true for small, undiversified economies. For instance, Chile is very heavily dependent upon its copper exports. Copper is by far the major industry in the country. The government was anxious to diversify the nation's industrial base and welcomed foreign investments that would contribute

---

TABLE 12.5   Positive Effects of FDI Resulting from Basic Factors of Production (Sections III and IV)[a]

III. STABILITY OF THE ECONOMY
    A. Greater diversity of production
    B. Foreign demand as cushion for domestic business cycles
IV. EFFECTS UPON LOCAL COMPANIES
    A. Commercial relations
        1. suppliers
            a. increased sales for local firms and wholly new
                market opportunities
                (1) directly via linkages (financing)
                (2) indirectly via income multipliers
            b. advice
        2. customers
            a. lower prices
            b. better quality
            c. greater variety
            d. better service
            e. advice
            f. financing
    B. Competitors
        1. demonstration effect of new products and techniques
        2. stimulus to work harder
    C. Capital effects
        1. gain from sale of facilities to foreign investor
            a. saving from bankruptcy
            b. shift of resources to more profitable investment
        2. money and capital
            a. stronger markets
            b. introduction of new financing methods
    D. Training of workers
    E. Training of technicians and managers
    F. Sharing of technology

---

[a]Sections III and IV of this table correspond to Tables 13.5 and 13.6, respectively.

to this process. One type of investment has involved large-scale foresta-tion for the purpose of paper making in the coming years.

This type of diversification is generally beneficial even to the com-panies that are part of the industry of greatest importance, such as copper in Chile; these companies can be excessively visible when so much of the health of the economy depends upon them. For instance, when world copper demand and prices slackened in the past, the Chilean economy suffered excessively, and the copper producers were very (and often uncomfortably) visible. The more the Chilean economy is able to diversify away from its past overwhelming reliance on the copper indus-try, the less subject it will be to the vicissitudes of the market and the less exposure that one industry will likely feel. This visibility, or high profile, can often be unhealthy for a company.

Positive effects of FDI on local business: Foreign investors can very often bring major benefits to local companies. Suppliers, customers, and even competitors can benefit from commercial relations with a foreign investor. *Suppliers* can benefit from new investment either di-rectly via linkages with the new investment or indirectly via the multi-plier effects upon the local economy resulting from the expenditures of the investor. (See Table 12.5, section IV, Part A-1.)

Linkages are *direct* ties with a particular investment. Thus for a supplier, the flow of new orders can bring either increased sales in traditional lines of production or lead to the introduction of entirely new goods or services. Suppliers also sometimes benefit from the direct assis-tance of the buyer in stimulating the quantity or quality of the supplier's output.

The income-multiplier effect works *indirectly* upon companies that do not have direct contact with the investor. They benefit indirectly because of increased economic activity of employees, whose income has risen, or from companies that are expanding operations because of the linkage effects. For example, local stores benefit from greater demand for food, clothing, furniture, housing, and so forth, and local sellers of industrial supplies enjoy increased demand for their products as their customers expand operations in response to the demands from the new investor.

Customers (see Table 12.5, section IV, part A-2) also benefit in a variety of ways. The new company may bring lower prices; if existing competition in the particular industry is low, local suppliers may be enjoying very high markups, which, of course, may have been one of the basic reasons that attracted the foreign investor in the first place. The new company may also bring a better quality product, after the sale, service or advice than local competitors. If product differentiation exists (that is, if the product is not a commodity), the customer can enjoy not only variety of supplier but some variety in products as well. Also, a foreign company might offer better credit terms than local companies.

Even *competitors* (see Table 12.5, section IV, part B) can sometimes benefit. Often all that the inherent potential of local companies requires is the stimulus of needing to work harder. Sometimes the foreign investors bring new ways of doing business.

The infusion of *capital* (see Table 12.5, section IV, part C) from abroad can affect local business in several ways. Many foreign investments involve the takeover of already existing facilities. In some instances these facilities would have (or already have) gone out of business. Finding a buyer for such facilities can be extremely important to the owner. Even if the facilities were not on the road to bankruptcy, the appearance of a buyer who is willing to pay an attractive price is very appealing to the owner, who might now be able to redivert his or her own investments into other assets.

The participation of the foreign company may help to strengthen the local money and capital markets. Such financial markets are very weak in most countries. It is often a very laborious process to raise weak markets to effective institutions. The local borrowing by attractive foreign borrowers can attract more local investors to the market, although there is always the risk of too much local money and capital flowing to prime foreign borrowers, but this can be regulated.

Many local companies look to the employees of foreign companies as a prime *source of trained manpower* (see Table 12.5, section IV, parts D and E). For example, Citibank with its hundreds of foreign offices in dozens of different countries is famous as a fertile training ground for local nationals who are often subsequently hired by local competing banks. In Ecuador several of the major local banks are heavily staffed with Citibank alumni. This can be an expensive part of the investment cost for a foreign investor, but it can be a very attractive contribution to the local companies that can take advantage of such trained personnel. IBM is another classic example of a company that has many well-trained alumni in many local companies.

Foreign investors often bring with them important *technology* that was not formerly available locally (see Table 12.5, section IV, part F). This technology can, of course, be valuable to the purchasers of the goods or services. Also, sometimes, as was mentioned above, foreign investors either on their own initiative or in response to requirements of the local government, stimulate the initial creation or subsequent expansion of local supplies. This may require the infusion of capital and also technology to the potential suppliers.

FAVORABLE SOCIO-CULTURAL IMPACTS OF FDI: HOST COUNTRY'S PERSPECTIVE

POSITIVE EFFECTS OF FDI ON THE GENERAL PUBLIC

Direct investment can have many effects that go well beyond those who are directly affected. Even the general population of the locale, region, and even the country can feel the favorable effects of foreign direct investment, even though they are often not aware of the source of the benefits (see Table 12.6). As noted in the discussion of trade barriers, those who benefit from free trade are often unaware of all the benefits that unfettered trade brings in the way of lower prices, better quality and service, and greater variety. In a very similar fashion, the general public is often unaware that many of the goods and services they consume are produced locally by foreign-owned firms. Also, conditions such as increasing living standards and greater stability of the local economy and government can stem in some cases from the prosperity the investment may have brought.

Higher living standards can accrue to the general public via linkages and income multipliers, as discussed above. Higher standards of living can also result from an improved infrastructure resulting from the investment and from additional expenditures by the government because of increased tax revenues (see Table 12.6, section I).

Increased employment and income, especially if coupled with job stability, the broadening of the economic base, the enlarging of the

TABLE 12.6   Positive Socio-Cultural Effects of FDI on the General Public[a]

I.   HIGHER LIVING STANDARDS
   A. Via multipliers
   B. Via infrastructure improvements
   C. Increased expenditures by government
II. GREATER STABILITY FOSTERED BY PROSPERITY
   A. Economic stability
      1. broadening of economic base
      2. enlarging middle class
   B. Socio-cultural stability
   C. Politico-legal stability
      1. diversification of political base
      2. reduction of socio-economic unrest
III. STIMULATING DESIRE FOR SOCIO-ECONOMIC GROWTH

[a]Table 12.6 corresponds to Table 13.7

middle class, and the diversification of the political base, can help foster greater economic, social, and political stability (see Table 12.6, section II).

Foreign investment can also help stimulate the desire for further socio-economic growth (see Table 12.6, section III). This is, of course, a mixed blessing, as are so many of the impacts from economic growth. Some groups do not find socio-economic growth, which tends to be identified with modernization, to be a blessing. For example, the Ayatollahs of Iran were rejecting just such a trend in their revolution against the Shah.

Nevertheless, socio-economic development is seen as a laudable goal by most observers. The example and impacts of FDI can help disrupt the traditional "shackles" of fatalism and provide some of the economic thrust that is necessary to begin the process of growth once the inertia is psychologically overcome.

POSITIVE EFFECTS OF FDI ON WORKERS

Workers are affected in three definite ways (see Table 12.7): *directly,* by being hired by the foreign investor, *indirectly,* by being hired by companies that are favorably affected via linkages with the new investment; and *even more indirectly,* by being hired by companies that have benefited by means of the income multiplier. Benefits include not only the salaries, which are commonly higher than local companies are paying, but also the special training and more highly skilled jobs that might

TABLE 12.7   Positive Effects of FDI on Workers[a]

      I. INCREASED EMPLOYMENT
          A. Direct
          B. Via linkages
          C. Via other income multipliers
     II. INCREASED WAGES
   III. NATURE OF EMPLOYMENT
          A. Steady work
          B. Special training
          C. Skilled jobs
          D. Higher compensation
              1. those working for the company
              2. those working for other companies
   IV. EFFECT ON ATTITUDES
          A. Decline of fatalism
          B. Expanded awareness

[a]Table 12.7 corresponds to Table 13.8.

be opened, hopefully offering steady employment. Some of these benefits can filter over to the employees of other firms as well, even to direct competitors, who may have to improve their treatment of workers and managers in order not to lose them (see Table 12.7, sections II and III). This trend can be inflationary, but, if it is coupled with greater productive efficiency as well, the effects can be balanced and the inflationary effect reduced or eliminated.

The exposure to nonlocal firms from abroad can also have an important *psychological impact* upon workers (see Table 12.7, section IV). It can help to overcome a fatalistic mentality and expand the workers' awareness of income, living-standard, training, and job opportunities. This impact of FDI and of the exposure to foreign influences has been termed a "revolution of rising expectations." It reflects the fact that, once traditional patterns of expectations have been broken, people's hopes remain at a permanently higher level. For many peoples of the world, the current generation is virtually the first generation in history to have a legitimate hope that improvements are possible for them and their children that were not available to their parents. This hope is crucial for the development of a modern society and the realization of higher incomes. However, this psychological impact is not a desirable goal for extreme traditionalists, who do not view development as progress, and for groups who will not benefit from a change in the existing socio-economic structure (such as the large land-owning families in many countries, who would be reluctant to lose farm workers to the cities). Again, it is a matter of perspective. These are benefits as seen by some but not when seen by others. The latter view is examined in the next chapter.

POSITIVE EFFECTS OF FDI ON CONSUMERS

For investment aimed at serving the local market, the local consumers are the major beneficiaries in the host country. (See Table 12.8.)

TABLE 12.8   Positive Effects of FDI on Consumers[a]

I.	**GREATER VARIETY OF GOODS**
	A. Satisfying unmet demands
	B. Education regarding new products and services
II.	**IMPROVED QUALITY**
III.	**BETTER SERVICES**
	A. Convenience
	B. Service after the sale
IV.	**LOWER PRICES**

[a]Table 12.8 corresponds to Table 13.9.

As previously indicated, these benefits include a greater variety of goods —both new goods to satisfy demands not being met (or those not even "recognized" by consumers) and different goods and services to compete with existing producers. Other advantages flow from improved quality of goods and services that are sold as well as service after the sale, which is so important in the markets for many sophisticated products. Finally, the greater competition and improved productive techniques may well result in lower prices for the consumer.

FAVORABLE IMPACTS OF FDI ON THE GOVERNMENT: HOST COUNTRY'S PERSPECTIVE

POSITIVE EFFECTS OF FDI ON THE GENERAL POLITICAL SYSTEM

Foreign direct investment that has a significant impact on the local economy can, under different circumstances, either increase the degree of concentration of political power (such as happened under the late dictator Anastasio Samoza in Nicaragua) or broaden the power structure (such as occurred in Ecuador, where the oil wealth helped to offset the old wealth of the banana oligarchy). (See Table 12.9.) Naturally, depending upon the viewer's perspective, either pattern may appear to be beneficial. Also, depending upon circumstances, *either* effect might enhance political stability.

POSITIVE EFFECTS OF FDI ON GOVERNMENTAL FINANCES

Revenues: Foreign investors can contribute to a government's revenues (see Table 12.10, section I) through both increased tax collection and the government's ability to obtain aid and loans from abroad.

TABLE 12.9   Positive Politico-Legal Impacts of FDI on the Host Government[a]

    I. EFFECT UPON POWER STRUCTURE
        A. Greater concentration
        B. Greater diversification
   II. EFFECT UPON GOVERNMENT'S POWER BASE
        A. Enhancement
        B. Reduction
  III. INCREASED STABILITY

---

[a]Table 12.9 corresponds to Table 13.10.

TABLE 12.10   Positive Impacts of FDI on the Host Government's Role in the Economy[a]

I. INCREASED REVENUE
    A. Increased tax base
        1. direct, via linkages and multipliers
        2. import and export tariffs
    B. Tax collection
        1. visibility of foreign firms
        2. sophistication of accounting systems of foreign firms
    C. Aid from company in attracting foreign grants and loans
    D. Increased base for earning foreign exchange
II. PRIVATE EXPENDITURES REDUCING NEED FOR GOVERNMENT EXPENDITURES
    A. Less poverty and welfare costs
    B. Infrastructure improvement and expansion with nongovernmental funds

[a]Table 12.10 corresponds to Table 13.10

The increasing industrial base enlarges the tax base of the government via the aforementioned direct, linkage, and multiplier effects. Also, governments can sometimes successfully impose export taxes. If the new company imports, then import duties increase too.

Not only can the tax base be improved by the presence of foreign companies, but so also can the tax-collection process be improved. Because of the visibility of foreign firms and their well-known financial sophistication, it is frequently much easier for a government to identify the tax liability of foreign companies and to collect it than might be true for comparable domestic companies. For example, tax evasion is extremely rampant in many countries, including some major industrial countries such as Italy. Under these circumstances, the government's tax revenues can often be enhanced disproportionately by the presence of foreign firms.

Foreign investors can sometimes be helpful in lobbying with their home governments or even with multinational organizations in attracting loans and grants. Also, if the FDI increases the nation's export capacity, it can make a major contribution to the country's ability to earn foreign exchange.

This, as has been amply demonstrated, can be very important in helping underpin the value of the country's currency and in helping the country to finance its imports.

Expenditures: In some circumstances, foreign investors can even help reduce the government's expenditure requirements, either existing or potential (see Table 12.10, section II). For example, welfare costs can be reduced as a result of the decline in unemployment. Also, in those instances in which the foreign investor expands or improves the nation's infrastructure, this can remove the need for the government to do so.

POSITIVE IMPACT OF FDI
ON INTERNATIONAL RELATIONS

Host countries are sometimes anxious to strengthen political as well as economic ties with another country. For example, a former colony may wish to diversify away from its excessive dependence (both economic and political) upon its former colonial landlord. Also, a country that is in the process of shifting political alliances may use its treatment of foreign investors as part of the evidence to other governments of its shift (for example, as did Egypt after the death of Gamal Abdul Nasser). This can also lead to an increase of foreign aid. Thus, the foreign investor can favorably contribute to, as well as benefit from, a changing political climate.

FAVORABLE IMPACTS OF FDI:
HOME COUNTRY'S PERSPECTIVE

The first part of this chapter looked at the positive impacts of FDI on the host country. The rest of the chapter concentrates upon the favorable impacts for the home country of the investor.

There are a variety of favorable effects on the home country—economic, socio-cultural, and politico-legal (see Table 12.11).

POSITIVE ECONOMIC EFFECTS OF FDI
ON THE HOME COUNTRY

Effects on basic factors of production: As discussed in Chapter 3, many foreign investments involve a search for increased productive efficiency. Two of the primary benefits involve natural resources and technology. Each of those factors of production can be beneficial to the home country. Obviously, natural resources (for example, chromium, petroleum, and lumber) that are not available at home can be brought from abroad by foreign investors. Likewise, technology obtained via the purchase of a foreign company can often be utilized by the company's affiliates in the home country. Even though natural resources and technology might also be available via imports, foreign direct investment is often the only way to obtain these types of assets, especially technology. Also, direct investment often results in lower prices or increased confidence in a regular supply (e.g., with raw materials).

TABLE 12.11   Positive Impacts of FDI: Home Country's Perspective[a]

I.   POSITIVE ECONOMIC EFFECTS
   A.   Basic factors of production
        1.   technology
        2.   raw materials
   B.   Effects resulting from basic factors of production
        1.   balance of payments
             a.   trade
             b.   money and capital
                  (1)   revenues from foreign operations
                  (2)   loans from foreign offices
        2.   effects on companies in home country
             a.   revenues
             b.   export demand
             c.   diversification
                  (1)   productive capacity
                  (2)   earnings
             d.   technology and product or service ideas
             e.   supply of components
             f.   access to new money and capital markets
II. POSITIVE SOCIO-CULTURAL EFFECTS
   A.   Increased employment for workers
   B.   Greater product availability to customers
III. POSITIVE EFFECTS ON THE GOVERNMENT
   A.   Government revenue
        1.   increased import taxes
        2.   increased taxes on repatriated earnings
   B.   International relations
        1.   FDI as a complement to foreign aid
        2.   Encouraging closer political ties between home and host
             governments

[a]Table 12.11 corresponds to Table 13.11

Effects on the balance of payments: The derivative economic benefits principally involve the balance of payments and the impact upon companies in the home country. (See Table 12.11, section I, part B-1.)

The BOP can be improved (if it is assumed that improvement is measured by a decrease in the balance on current account deficit) by either an *increase in exports or a repatriation of foreign revenues.*

Many foreign investments do rely upon critical exports of vital subassemblies or supplies from the home country. If these sales exceed any export decline that the investment caused, then the investment will benefit the trade account of the BOP. Also, in the short run during the construction phase, the demand for productive equipment from the home country can increase the exports of the capital goods industry in the home country. These goods could, of course, be purchased in a third country, but companies show a strong predilection to buy from companies in their home country if that is their normal source of equipment.

A second BOP advantage results from the *inflow of revenues from the foreign investment*. This includes not only dividends and interest but fees, royalties, commissions, capital gains, and so forth. These revenues can, of course, be retained abroad and reinvested there. Strictly speaking, it is only when these revenues are actually repatriated back to the home country that they benefit that country's BOP. However, the United States and some other countries list "earnings reinvested abroad" as a way of improving the appearance of the BOP statement.

Another favorable BOP impact is associated with the inflow, not of foreign earnings, but of *loans from the foreign operations*. International banks, for instance, frequently borrow from their foreign subsidiaries to help finance domestic needs.

Effects on companies in the home country: Obviously, the investing company stands to gain substantially from the FDI—otherwise there would be little incentive for investing. (See Table 12.11, section I, part B-2.) These rationales were discussed in Chapter 3. Among the benefits noted then were, of course, the export demand, the inflow of revenues, and the access to new technology and raw materials just mentioned above.

In addition, diversification of investments was seen in Chapter 3 as a way of self-insuring against disruptions of needed supplies or products and as a way of balancing the company's sales and profits in markets that experience different economic cycles. For example, companies such as Ford Motor Company and Citibank have had more profitable operations abroad than in the United States. In the case of Ford, in some years heavy losses in the United States were offset by large profits from its foreign operations. The foreign profits provided a very important cushion to the overall company, including stockholders, creditors, and even employees, since the company was better able to absorb its domestic losses.

Companies can also become very reliant upon the supply of goods and components from abroad, called *vertical integration*. Their exposure to other companies overseas can often provide valuable input into the technology, products, and servicing of the parent company. Many European companies are drawn to the United States in order to have a personal window into technological developments and marketing trends, since developments are often very difficult to perceive satisfactorily from overseas. In a similar fashion, some companies can gain greater access to foreign capital markets via subsidiaries in those countries. Indeed, foreign financing subsidiaries are very common across a wide spectrum of industries and countries.

POSITIVE SOCIO-CULTURAL EFFECTS OF FDI ON THE HOME COUNTRY

Effects upon workers and corporate customers: Socio-cultural benefits can accrue to the home country in only limited ways. (See Table 12.11, section II.) Two of these involve the increased availability of products from abroad and the increased employment resulting from greater exports. An example of the former would be an investment in a plantation or mines in a foreign country for the specific purpose of feeding the factories and markets of the home country. An example of the latter is Volkswagen, which, after developing a very successful export market to the United States with the "Beetle," saw its U.S. market disappear as a result of the soaring value of the deutschemark. In response, VW bought a factory from Chrysler in Pennsylvania in order to set up U.S. assembly operations. Many of the components are shipped from VW factories in Germany, thereby providing jobs in Germany that would have been lost otherwise.[3]

POSITIVE EFFECTS ON THE GOVERNMENT OF THE HOME COUNTRY

Effects upon government revenue: Government revenue (see Table 12.11, section III) can be enhanced in several ways. For instance, if imports from the foreign operation increase, tariff revenues will grow if there is a duty on the particular good that is imported. And, naturally, to the extent that the parent company's profits are affected by repatriated foreign revenues of the type noted above, the company's income tax liability may be increased to the advantage of the government's tax revenues. Such potential is, however, subject to an offset resulting from foreign tax payments on the same and related income. (See Chapter 22, "International Taxation.")

Effects on international relations: Governments often encourage foreign direct investment by their domestic companies in the foreign countries which the government is anxious to aid or with which it hopes to develop closer political ties. If a home government is interested in furnishing foreign aid to a certain country (or in furnishing investments in lieu of it), the government will often encourage its nationals to invest

---

[3]See Robert B. Stobaugh, "How Investment Abroad Creates Jobs at Home," *Harvard Business Review*, September–October 1972, pp. 118–26.

in that country, often by providing investment insurance and other assistance. The French government strongly encourages investments in some of its former colonies in order to aid them and to maintain tight economic ties between France and the former colony.

SUMMARY

As discussed in Chapters 2 and 3, uninhibited movement of goods, services, and factors of production increases the welfare of the world and generally of each country involved. Obstructions to these flows reduce gains, as discussed in Chapter 4.

Foreign direct investment is a special type of international flow that can involve movements of goods and equipment, services such as managerial advice and construction work, and factors of production such as capital, labor, and technology. FDI is much more personal and permanent than international economic movements such as exports or licensing. As a result, the range of the impacts of FDI is much greater than those of any other type of international flow.

This chapter's focus is on the favorable impacts of foreign direct investment. These favorable effects can be economic, socio-cultural, or governmental. They include the views of any pertinent observer: customers, suppliers, workers, competitors, government officials, the general public, social workers, and so forth. Obviously, these groups have different views of the impacts.

Not all the impacts discussed here will be judged favorable by all observers; indeed, some of them will also be listed in the next chapter as "unfavorable" impacts, because that is how other observers may view them. These observations are designed as a general overview of a very wide variety of potential effects of direct investment, especially FDI. The more the critical observer (whether supporting FDI, against it, or neutral to it) understands the economic, socio-cultural, and politico-legal impacts of FDI, the better the observer will be able to make a sophisticated evaluation of the investment.

Unfortunately, either investors or their supporters have unrealistically optimistic images of the favorable impacts of their operations upon both the host and home country. On the other hand, critics in both the host and home countries commonly underestimate the advantages of such flows. This chapter is designed to show the favorable side of foreign direct investment.

The reader may well observe that many of these positive impacts are not unique to *international* investments; they can result from domestic investment as well. This is very true. The observation is also true of the negative impacts that are discussed in the next chapter. However, many observers fail to be aware of such impacts even for domestic investments. This very wide array of possible impacts is discussed in order to provide the reader with a realistic perspective of a foreign company's impact. The manager from a company can thereby be prepared to maximize the favorable impacts of the investment and let such information be known by the appropriate people, such as governmental officials, workers, or the nearby population.

KEY TERMS

APPROPRIATE TECHNOLOGY	INFRASTRUCTURE	LINKAGE
IMPORT SUBSTITUTION	ECONOMIC	MULTIPLIER
	FINANCIAL	
	MARKETING	
	POLITICAL	
	SOCIAL	

REVIEW QUESTIONS

1. Which of the potential favorable impacts upon the basic factors of production do *you* think are most important to a host country?
2. How can the socio-cultural conditions in a country be favorably affected by investments from abroad?
3. Discuss the likely attitudes of the home and host governments to the types of favorable political impacts described in the chapter.
4. How are the balance of payments of both home and host countries *favorably* affected by direct foreign investment? How does the time horizon of these effects differ between the two countries?
5. To what extent can local investors provide the same types of favorable impacts as do foreign investors?
6. If these favorable impacts are available from local investors, should investment from abroad be restricted? Explain.

SUGGESTED REFERENCES*

JOHNSON, HARRY G.   "The Multinational Corporation as a Development Agent," *Columbia Journal of World Business,* May–June 1970.

STOBAUGH, ROBERT B.   "How Investment Abroad Creates Jobs at Home," *Harvard Business Review,* September–October 1972.

---

*See also the references at the end of Chapter 14.

13

The Negative Impacts of Foreign Direct Investment

That there are many possible gains for home and host countries from foreign direct investment, as was discussed in the last chapter, is acknowledged by all observers. Even Communist ideologues recognize this fact. As a result, it is not too surprising to note that Communist countries from Yugoslavia to the People's Republic of China are prepared to welcome "appropriate" foreign investment.

However, many observers, not only Communists but many non-Communists as well, are nevertheless very critical of some of the effects of foreign direct investment (FDI). While they may acknowledge some of the contributions mentioned in the previous chapter, they often are convinced that the benefits of foreign direct investments are not sufficient to offset the negative impacts. As a result, there is widespread criticism of foreign direct investors. Such investment is often considered to be at best a necessary evil. Not too surprisingly, when governmental permission for FDI is given, there is often very strong control imposed on the investors at the same time. As is discussed in the next chapter, appropriate controls are necessary for the country and, in some respects, even for the investors.

This chapter completes the picture begun in the last chapter, so that the reader will be familiar with both the positive and negative aspects of foreign direct investment. It is critical that all observers of the FDI process be able to analyze the possible impact of such investment in a realistic manner.

It is very important that the governments involved, especially the host government, have a clear understanding of the various possible negative consequences that can stem from foreign direct investment. In many instances the negative effects can be substantially reduced or even completely eliminated if they are anticipated and controlled. Even if the unfavorable effects cannot be significantly modified, the government is in a better position to confront the effects and possible political criticism if the disadvantages of the investment have been foreseen. The government is also in a better, more realistic position from which to negotiate with the company if the government has a clear impression of possible consequences, bad as well as good, from the FDI.

It is equally important for the business manager to be able to understand the basis for much of the opposition the company's investment might encounter in both the home and the host country. An understanding of the objective and subjective criticisms of the possible negative effects of the investment can enable the company to avoid many potential problems, prepare the company's representatives to intelligently negotiate with national governments, and prepare the company for some of the criticism that may well be forthcoming despite the company's best efforts.

In this chapter the major causes of the opposition to foreign direct investment are examined as follows:

A. Consideration of the nature of the opposition to the MNF
B. Examination of perceptions of unsavory impacts of the performance abroad of multinational corporations on
    1. the host country's perspective
        (a) economic effects
        (b) socio-cultural effects
        (c) politico-legal effects
    2. the home country's perspective
        (a) economic effects
        (b) socio-cultural effects
        (c) politico-legal effects

As was true in the last chapter with the positive effects of FDI, this compilation of the negative effects includes many impacts that could result from either foreign or domestic investment: Only some stem uniquely from FDI. However, the same negative results are commonly viewed much more critically when they stem from a foreign company rather than a domestic company. This double standard needs to be understood by both investing companies and local observers.

THE NATURE OF OPPOSITION
TO FOREIGN DIRECT INVESTMENT

PHILOSOPHIES CHALLENGED

The traditional business view: The typical manager tends to be a staunch defender of the private enterprise system. In a similar fashion, multinational managers are likely to be apologists for the notion that the MNC is one of the best, most efficient, and quickest means available to a country to aid its development. They tend to feel that the ability of their companies to efficiently combine factor inputs with market demand internationally, as well as in their domestic home environment, is an important, indeed perhaps the surest, path to development.

There have indeed been a few notable exceptions—for example, the briberies of the old United Fruit Co. in the "Banana Republics" and even ITT in Chile during the early 1970s—to what most multinational managers perceive as a favorable record of MNC performance abroad. However, on the whole most MNC personnel feel that the record they and their peers have carved attests to their claims. As evidence they can point out, as we have seen, that these companies have created numerous jobs, improving living standards and the balance of payments, have paid billions in taxes, and have produced numerous other effects that have benefited host countries throughout the world and their home countries as well.

Unfortunately, this evidence has left much of the public unconvinced. Included among this number are, of course, the absolute socialists for whom private capitalism has no role, but they are usually only a minority of the unconvinced in most countries. The majority are less dogmatic in their approach and, while willing to listen to a recital of the contributions made by the MNCs, they remain negatively disposed. It is important that the international business community understand the rationale of such people, because many of them are very influential in their countries and their ideas appear to be spreading. For instance, witness the apparently antiprivate enterprise positions that have been assumed in recent years by many countries in Latin America, the Middle East, Africa, Asia, Australia, and even Canada. The extensiveness of this action suggests that perhaps this attitude against private enterprise represents an idea whose time has come.

The private enterprise system: The private enterprise philosophy is not universally accepted. Indeed, even in the United States there is strong pressure from many labor leaders, consumer advocates, politicians, and other groups calling for much tighter governmental control over and even ownership of many basic industries such as oil, steel, railroads, airlines, power companies, communication companies, and so forth. Governmental ownership (at the state and municipal level as well as at the federal) of power systems (the Tennessee Valley Authority, Boulder Dam), transportation (Amtrak, Conrail), local services (water supply, garbage disposal), and many others is extensive. Also, strict governmental regulation of private enterprises is even more pervasive. Many of these are generally accepted even by business personnel—at least for someone else's company! (Consider these prominent examples: the Pure Food and Drug Act, the Securities Exchange Commission, and the Federal Reserve System.)

Many of these agencies and their enabling legislation have helped to strengthen the financial and economic systems of the United States. Of course, there are also many legislative acts and their agencies whose efficacy is questionable. Nevertheless, the point is that neither the American manager nor those of any other country are strangers to governmental enterprises or extensive governmental controls.

The nature of governmental controls varies substantially by country. Indeed, one of the many incentives for investing in some foreign countries has been greater freedom from governmental constraints. Countries that may tightly control some industries may be much more liberal in their treatment of other industries, which in turn might be tightly controlled elsewhere. For example, American banks generally have much greater freedom of action in London than they do in the United States, whereas oil companies have much greater freedom of action in the United States than in the United Kingdom.

Thus, an intellectual of a developing country does not need to be indoctrinated in a Communist country to be exposed to notions of governmental regulation and ownership. Education in Western Europe, the United States, and Canada provides ample opportunity to observe these trends. In addition, the intensive analysis of MNCs by private organizations, U.S. governmental agencies, foreign governments, and international organizations provides extensive food for thought for the inquisitive mind. Thus, the alert student who is studying political science, economics, or any other field will have plenty of opportunity to study criticism of foreign direct investors. Many of them will undoubtedly return home with negative attitudes relating to the real or allegedly enormous strength of MNCs and their abuses.

It should obviously follow that it is imperative for the interests of the multinational business executive that his or her side of the story should be clearly told. Also, however, it is mandatory that he or she understands the nature of criticism which confronts him.

Maximizing economic wealth: One of the basic doctrines of the private enterprise system is that the inherent efficiency of the system leads to the realization of greater overall economic wealth in a shorter time than by more socialistic means. The realization of this wealth maximization is inherently accepted by proponents of the system. However, many people in the world have conflicting goals that have a higher priority than wealth maximization.

Probably the most prominent of these conflicting goals is that of greater equalization of social welfare. In terms of economic growth this is generally a submaximization goal; but, in terms of social-welfare maximization, it has high priority in governmental planning, even in the wealthiest of industrialized countries.

Therefore, it is hardly surprising that countries whose stage of economic development is far below that of the developed countries and whose relative poverty is accordingly far greater, tend to be very conscious of social-welfare goals. Most of these social-welfare goals do not maximize economic gains. Therefore, it is often difficult for multinational business executives with an economic-efficiency orientation to adequately understand the rationale of the actions of governments or groups that are motivated and activated by other goals such as social welfare.

Nonphilosophical opposition: The problem of understanding and empathizing with the goals and aspirations of the host country would be difficult enough if they stemmed solely from the philosophical positions described above. Unfortunately, there are other, usually less rational, bases for opposition as well.

Political expediency and maneuvering are obvious examples in which the multinational corporation can be caught in the middle. This is true of any political system, but it can take on new dimensions when, for example, labor unions are wings of political movements (or vice versa). Labor unions in many countries are often more interested in, and more efficient at, instituting work stoppages for political rather than for economic reasons. Labor criticism of foreign investors can occur for the same reason.

Another source of opposition that does not stem from philosophical rejection of the free enterprise system is *nationalism*. This is a strong identification with one's own country, even if it leads to actions that may not be in the *economic* self-interest of the country. Economic losses are often accepted in order to obtain social gains in the form of an increase in national pride. Thus companies may be required to expand the local ownership or production of parts when they operate in a particular country.

All countries display nationalism to some extent: It is part of human nature. However, nationalism is an especially prevalent condition in newly independent countries. Since the end of World War II, dozens of countries have gained their independence. Political leaders in these countries often find it politically expedient to emphasize nationalism in the face of proposed foreign investments. That such actions may drive the investors away and cause the loss of potential jobs (economic losses) is often not as important as the demonstration of political independence (social gains).

THE VIEWPOINT OF THE HOST COUNTRY

Numerous groups in a host country can be affected by multinational investments. Even in the absence of significant philosophical differences, there is a great disparity between the attitudes of these disparate groups. As a consequence, there is seldom a singular "national viewpoint," but rather there are many viewpoints of different groups within the country. Just as in the firm's home country, many viewpoints of groups outside the firm weigh upon business decisions. However, groups that at home can safely be ignored or given little notice may be very significant abroad.

Unfortunately, this can often have the effect of "losing if you do and losing if you don't" for many of a firm's actions abroad, since there is no single viewpoint confronting the investor. If there is not a "national viewpoint," however, there are groups that carry the greatest weight. These are what must be identified. Correspondingly, the following types of criticisms must be considered according to their source. The relative weightings, moreover, vary from country to country and from time to time. As an example, the Shah and his followers were obviously for many years the most important group to satisfy in Iran. However, as opposition to the Shah grew, the attitudes of religious leaders became increasingly important.

NEGATIVE IMPACTS OF FDI:
THE HOST COUNTRY'S PERSPECTIVE

The following examination of unfavorable effects that may accrue to some sector of the host country from foreign investment attempts to cover a large number of possible criticisms. Some criticisms apply to a particular investment; some do not. Some can be avoided; some cannot. Some apply in an individual country; some do not. Some exist at a particular point in time; some do not. As with the favorable impacts of FDI that were seen in the last chapter, the individual reader has a particular, rather than a universal, perspective. As a result, he or she may disagree with the listing of a particular effect as unfavorable.

Table 13.1 outlines the major groupings of the unfavorable effects of FDI. (It is parallel to Table 12.1.) The lists that follow indicate many of the types of criticism leveled against foreign investors. Although some impacts occur sooner than others because of their nature, there is no chronology to the listing.

TABLE 13.1 Potential Unfavorable Impacts of Foreign Companies Upon Host Countries[a]

I. NEGATIVE ECONOMIC EFFECTS
    A. Basic factors of production
        1. capital
        2. skilled personnel
        3. technology
        4. entrepreneurship
        5. raw materials
    B. Economic effects resulting from basic factors of production on
        1. balance of payments
        2. structure of the economy
        3. stability of economy
        4. effects on local business personnel
II. NEGATIVE SOCIO-CULTURAL EFFECTS
    A. General public
    B. Workers
    C. Customers
III. NEGATIVE GOVERNMENTAL EFFECTS
    A. General impact
    B. Governmental finances
        1. revenue
        2. expenditures
    C. International relations

[a]Table 13.1 corresponds to Table 12.1.

NEGATIVE ECONOMIC EFFECTS OF DIRECT INVESTMENT BY FOREIGNERS ON HOST COUNTRY

Basic factors of production: The most immediate impacts of foreign direct investment upon a host country are commonly the inflow of some or all of the most mobile of the basic factors of production: capital, labor, technology, and so forth. Unfortunately, while the productive factors may be badly needed, their inflow is not an unalloyed blessing from the viewpoint of the host country. Each of these three most mobile factors of production bring distinct disadvantages.

Capital inflows (see Table 13.2), for example, give rise to future money and capital *outflows*. If the investment earns sufficient foreign exchange to cover future outflows (for example, an export-creating investment), the investment will have much more appeal to local authorities than if it will be a net drain on exchange earnings in the future (for example, via interest, dividends, and capital repatriation). Most investments fall into the latter category, however.

Countries are often reluctant to increase their reliance upon for-

TABLE 13.2　Negative Economic Effects of FDI Resulting from Capital Flows[a]

  I.　RELUCTANCE OF COUNTRY TO DEPEND HEAVILY ON FOREIGN SOURCES OF CAPITAL

 II.　POTENTIAL OUTFLOWS
    A.　Interest and principal payments
    B.　Dividend and capital payments
    C.　Royalty and fee payments and so forth

III.　INCREASING EXPOSURE TO SUDDEN, DISRUPTIVE INFLOWS AND OUTFLOWS

IV.　RELUCTANCE OF FIRM TO BRING IN ADDITIONAL CAPITAL

 V.　ABILITY TO EVADE MANY LOCAL MONEY AND CAPITAL CONTROLS BY RESORTING TO FOREIGN SOURCES

---

[a]Table 13.2 corresponds to Table 12.2, section A.

eign capital. This is especially critical in light of the massive increase in foreign debt that has resulted from the sky-rocketing price of oil. On the other hand, it may not be in the country's best interests if the foreign investor fails to bring in additional capital in order to finance future expansion. For example, if the company funds future operations primarily via local borrowings, this may pose a disruptive drain upon the local financial markets.

If the openness of the economy results furthermore in great exposure to sudden disruptive outflows (or inflows) by the foreign investor or by the attempt of those companies to avoid local monetary controls, the foreign investor may again be the focus of sharp criticism. Access to many sources of funds and a high level of financial sophistication do indeed make these actions possible. MNCs have shown themselves to be quite capable and often willing to act in this manner. As will be seen in Chapter 20, this method may well be viewed as sound business practices.

The inflow of *skilled personnel, managers,* and *technicians* can be even more important than the inflow of capital for many countries. (See Table 13.3.) However, these resources are commonly viewed by host governments as only a temporary need and a short-term solution until local nationals can be trained for the jobs. However, many companies fail to train and upgrade local workers as rapidly as is efficiently feasible. In many firms this is a deliberate foot-dragging policy, whereas in others it is largely a result of inertia.

Governments are growing increasingly sensitive to such failure to train local nationals. A corporate policy of rapid training and promotions of local nationals is not only good for public relations but also is frequently wise economically. The cost of employing a person from the

TABLE 13.3 Negative Economic Effects Resulting from Flows of Skilled Personnel and Technology[a]

I. SKILLED PERSONNEL
    A. Reluctance of government to rely heavily upon expatriates
    B. Reluctance of company to train local nationals
II. TECHNOLOGY
    A. High technology, which provides relatively fewer jobs
    B. Higher costs of modern technology
    C. Fear of becoming a technological satellite
        1. reluctance of firm to establish research and development facilities locally
    D. Reluctance of firm to bring modern technology
    E. Technology inappropriate to environment

---

[a]Table 13.3 corresponds to Table 12.2, sections B and D.

home country abroad is often two or three times the cost of employing a comparable local national.

Modern technology is mandatory for many productive processes and for many products. (See Table 13.3.) However, its infusion is expensive in terms of foreign exchange and brings fewer jobs than alternative, more labor-intensive, productive processes. On the other hand, criticism sometimes arises in host countries due to what is considered outdated technology or an inadequate inflow of modern technology. The more labor-intensive technology may be economically more justifiable and have a much more favorable impact upon the local economy, but local pride may cause it to be rejected. Thus, both too much and too little technology can be criticized, and there may not be a middle ground that satisfies all critics.

Effects resulting from basic factors of production: As noted when capital inflows were discussed above, the balance of payments can be very adversely affected by the MNC. In addition to those capital-account flows, many foreign investments can negatively affect the current account. Often such investments require a large amount of imports, both capital goods and components. The latter, of course, can be a constant drain on the BOP. Where local sourcing is feasible, it would tend to be much more favorably viewed than foreign sourcing.

Export-producing investment is almost universally attractive to host governments. But many companies that could export significant amounts are reluctant to do so. In many instances it can be argued that it is not economically feasible to do so. However, many other companies base their decisions upon corporate policies that even objective observers might dispute (for example, reluctance to compete with exports from the home country). Either type of company can have a large and continuing negative BOP impact.

The ability of a foreign investment to alleviate this problem of foreign exchange shortages on a continuing basis via import substitution or export expansion, for example, cannot only be one of the most welcome contributions that a company can make but often a strong argument against nationalization as well.

The basic *structure of the economy* can also be profoundly affected negatively by foreign investment. (See Table 13.4.) One of the principal reasons why investors are attracted to less-developed countries is to tap the *physical-resource potential* of a country (see Table 13.4, section I). This leads, however, to some of the most virulent criticisms of the multinational firms. Many nations have little economic potential other than their physical resources and often relatively little of that. They are

---

TABLE 13.4   Negative Impacts of FDI on the Structure of the Economy[a]

I.   PHYSICAL RESOURCES (RAW MATERIALS, LAND, CLIMATE, PLANT, AND ANIMAL LIFE)
     A.   Government dissatisfied with its share of benefits
     B.   Unsatisfactory development of concessions
         1.   too slow or not intensive enough
         2.   monopolization of resources
         3.   too fast or intensive
         4.   major fluctuations in output
         5.   improper balance of exploitation
             a.   high grading
             b.   low grading
         6.   failure to process locally
         7.   failure to adequately service local markets
     C.   Deterioration of resources
         1.   depletion
         2.   erosion
         3.   pollution
         4.   failure to replenish renewable resources
II.   INDUSTRY AND COMMERCE
     A.   Nonproductive, non–growth-oriented investment
     B.   Geographical concentration
     C.   Output restrictions
III.   INFRASTRUCTURAL EXPANSION OR IMPROVEMENT
     A.   Failure to improve local infrastructure
     B.   Lack of integration of basic infrastructural improvements with rest of economy
     C.   Failure to mesh infrastructural investments with government's developmental plans

---

[a]Table 13.4 corresponds to Table 12.4.

understandably very sensitive regarding its exploitation. The primary complaint revolves around the distribution of shares of benefits between the country and the company. The oil-producing countries have demonstrated how the government's share of the gains can be increased and redistributed for the countries' benefit. It is less clear whether producers of other primary products such as bauxite, coffee, and bananas will be similarly, though certainly less spectacularly, successful. Since no other product is so uniquely critical as is petroleum, it is very doubtful that other producer cartels will be able to pay such rich dividends. Where the monopolistic power of the country is less (or unrealized), the alleged inequity of the distribution of the gains from the exploitation of the resources can be one of the most sensitive and explosive issues dividing the firm and country.

Again, this is an area where the resourcefulness and flexibility of the company are paramount in importance. After all, the resources do ultimately belong to the country, which has the sovereign authority to expropriate the operations at any time. As a result, a variety of *modi operandi* have been conceived for the development of raw material deposits. One arrangement that is certain to gain in significance is one in which the country retains total ownership and ultimate control of all resources with private companies being hired to serve the state company. A myriad of alternative agreements is possible. The least imaginative multinational companies are going to be left behind, whereas some of their brethren who are capable of adaptation will profit handsomely.

Other complaints involving physical resource utilization revolve around unsatisfactory exploration or development of *concessions,* a monopoly granted to a company. Usually the complaint refers to inadequacy. The defensive investor who gains a resource concession but who is slow to develop it is demanding a high price from the host economy. This is especially true if the company has a monopoly on the control of the resources in that country. Once development commences, governments are anxious that the extent of local processing be maximized. For example, countries that are suppliers of primary products such as ores are generally anxious to also become processors. However, companies that have their own processing facilities elsewhere are often reluctant to shift production abroad. Nevertheless, pressure for local processing will become very strong in coming years. The willingness of companies to invest in local secondary processing operations may be a *sine qua non* for many raw material concessions in the future.

Development of concessions can be too fast or too imbalanced. Countries not only need their resources to be developed adequately, but the resources must be conserved as well. Some producers allow their concessions to deteriorate or they "high grade" their resources by stripping only the richest or high-grade ore and ignoring lower-quality but still economical ore. This is contrary to sound mining principles. Also, producers can be guilty of inadequate control of erosion, depletion, and pollution and of failure to replenish agricultural land. The time horizon of the country as well as that of the firm must be kept in mind in developing raw materials.

In a similar vein, governments are very sensitive to the nature of *industrial and commerical development* (see Table 13.4, section II). Nonproductive investment in unnecessary fields such as soft drinks and other "junk foods" are facing greater and greater criticism. Also, governments are very concerned about an excess of geographical concentration, which can greatly aggravate social and infrastructural difficulties for the country.

A company with operations in other countries may choose to reduce the output of local operations while maintaining full-scale production at home. This may be very rational from the company's viewpoint but very objectionable from the perspective of the country.

Infrastructure that accompanies an investment can be a major benefit for a country, if it is designed to meet other needs of the people. (See Table 13.4, section III.) Drilling and land-moving equipment that are brought into remote regions can be utilized at a relatively small marginal cost to the company to dig wells, build roads, and so forth.

For example, foreign companies drilling for oil in the Amazonian basin of Ecuador sometimes existed for months near villages whose primary source of water was contaminated river water. For a relatively small marginal cost the companies could have drilled wells for the villages. The marginal impact on the local population and the ensuing goodwill from providing assistance can be immense. Shortsightedness in failing to do so can be very counter-productive.

Investments in infrastructure should also be designed, as far as practical, to be integrated into the basic infrastructure of the rest of the economy and in accordance with the government's expansion plans. For example, railroad gauges, electrical voltage, and communications equipment should all be compatible with local standards. This type of accommodation mostly involves common sense and careful planning and rarely leads to much additional expense. Yet, incompatible investments in infrastructure by foreign investors have often occurred.

Foreign direct investment can add a degree of instability to an economy (see Table 13.5). This is especially true if the FDI is concentrated in one major export industry—copper in Chile and Zambia, sugar in the Dominican Republic, bauxite in Jamaica and Guyana, or tea in Sri Lanka. Major foreign investments sometimes reduce a host country's economic diversity; this can be an especially sensitive issue if agricultural diversity is reduced, for example, if local farmers divert production from traditional crops needed to feed the local populace and shift to

TABLE 13.5   Negative Impacts of FDI on the Stability of the Economy[a]

I.   REDUCTION IN DIVERSIFICATION OF ECONOMY
II. WEAKNESS IN FOREIGN DEMAND AS DAMPER ON
     DOMESTIC ECONOMY
III. HIGH IMPORT PRICES AGGRAVATING DOMESTIC
     INFLATION

[a]Table 13.5 corresponds to Table 12.5, section III.

export crops that will not feed the local people (coffee, tea, coconut oil, cocoa, sugar, and so forth). Critics claim that so much agricultural land in Brazil has been diverted to large export-oriented plantations that the country's ability to feed its own population has been sharply reduced.

Unless the overall benefits from the investment are very high, some countries might be better off without such a destablizing investment! This is an example of the importance of a government promoting some degree of balance in its program of economic growth.

Even if the foreign investment increases economic diversification, it does not necessarily improve economic stability in the host country. If export-oriented investment is in an industry of highly volatile demand, such as is the case with most minerals, the local economy is more strongly affected by international economic fluctuations than if it didn't have the investment. These effects can, of course, result from domestic investment as well as investment from abroad.

Another destabilizing impact of the economic expansion and modernization that either FDI or domestic investment can bring is the greater exposure to the inflationary impact of reliance upon imports. As noted in the last chapter, imports can reduce inflation by replacing more expensive goods and services. However, if the investment requires goods or services that are not available locally and that are subject to rapid price increases (for example, petroleum, vehicles, meat), then the imports can be inflationary, not by replacing existing consumption but by changing the consumption mix.

Local business personnel are adversely affected by multinational investments in three ways: as customers, suppliers, and competitors. *Customers* (see Table 13.6, section I) usually gain from a new investment in the ways discussed in the previous chapter. However, if the new company is able to use its strength to monopolize the market, then even the customers may stand to lose, at least in the long run. This can be a problem in any country of any size and at any stage of development. The antitrust laws in the United States, for example, are designed to protect customers and competitors against just such misuse of economic power.

Another risk to local companies arises if the dominant supplier should suddenly choose to divert its production to affiliates overseas; thus local customers would suffer.

Suppliers (see Table 13.6, section II) of local companies that lose market share to the new company are naturally also losers, unless they can become suppliers to the new company. However, even in the latter capacity suppliers can be losers if a dominating buyer uses its power to excessively depress prices or chooses to arbitrarily switch suppliers.

Undoubtedly, the principal impacts upon local businesses are usu-

TABLE 13.6   Negative Impacts of FDI on Local Companies[a]

    I.   NEGATIVE IMPACTS UPON CORPORATE CUSTOMERS
        A. Monopoly power of seller
        B. Diversion of production to foreign markets
   II.   NEGATIVE IMPACTS UPON SUPPLIERS
        A. Suppliers to local competitors
        B. Suppliers to foreign investor
  III.   NEGATIVE IMPACTS UPON COMPETITORS
        A. Capital-related effects
            1. domination of local money and capital markets
            2. ability to gain access to foreign money and capital markets
        B. Effects on labor force
            1. attracting away best workers from local firms
            2. driving up wages
        C. Effects from marketing strength
            1. inability to match the following of foreign firms:
               a. economies of scale
                  (1) buying large amounts of supplies
                  (2) large-scale production
               b. financial strength
                  (1) bearing risk
                  (2) extending credit
               c. quality
               d. service
               e. variety
               f. innovations
               g. reputation, trademarks, and so forth
               h. marketing sophistication
               i. foreign contracts
               j. distribution network
            2. monopolization of major industries by foreigners
               a. concentration of local firms into suppliers and subcontractors
               b. thwarting local business initiative

[a]Table 13.6 corresponds to Table 12.5, section IV.

ally a result of the competitive strength and actions of the foreign company (see Table 13.6, section III). Even suppliers and customers, which may otherwise benefit from the new investment, may suffer as *competitors* for resources such as capital and manpower.

The experience, size, and resources of the large multinational corporation can be overwhelming for the local competitor. The MNCs can dominate not only the local product markets but also the money, capital, and personnel markets. In addition, access to foreign markets and resources creates many monopolistic advantages.

Of course, many of the factors referred to here are the exact types of oligopolistic or monopolistic advantages that induce MNCs to invest abroad. By definition, these advantages are someone else's disadvantages. This is certainly not to imply that the firm should fail to utilize its advantages, but rather to suggest that by bearing this dichotomy in mind the investor can hope to understand some of the criticism of his or her role.

Local businesses can find themselves being squeezed out of their traditional domestic *financial markets* by foreign companies with stronger credit ratings (see Table 13.6, section III, part A). Also, those same foreign companies might have a strong financial advantage via the option of funding either locally or abroad as credit conditions fluctuate; this option is commonly not available to smaller, less sophisticated, less credit-worthy local companies.

Foreign companies are often very successful in attracting some of the best *local workers* (see Table 13.6, section III, part B). The foreign investor often promises better wages and training and job-promotion opportunities. This can hurt not only competitors, suppliers, and customers but also the government. At the very least, local wage costs can be driven up. Antagonism can easily result. Also, the foreign company can sometimes be a vehicle for adding to brain drain by deploying top local nationals abroad.

The most damaging competitive impact of an investment is upon those local companies that produce the same goods or services as the foreign investor (see Table 13.6, section III, part C). They may well lack the managerial and technological sophistication of their foreign competitor. They quite probably lack the economies of scale and financial strength. Competition from the MNC can completely overwhelm local companies, and the former can end up with a virtual monopoly or oligopoly. Also, the local company may be unable to match the *marketing* mix of price, quality, innovations, service, variety, trademarks, reputation, and promotion that the foreign company offers. If the companies are competing for foreign markets, the foreign investor commonly benefits from business contacts abroad and from an established distribution network.

This arrangement may indeed be more efficient from a strictly economic perspective. However, if the local government is anxious to stimulate local companies and is already wary of excessive dependence upon foreign companies, then this outlook may be very unsatisfactory. Also the local companies that are hurt are certainly likely to object. Even if the foreign investment stimulates some local suppliers, the government many not find that to be a satisfactory alternative—they may not want to be "drawers of water and hewers of wood."

Negative Socio-Cultural Effects of FDI on the Host Country

Foreign companies have social as well as economic impacts upon their host countries. Those in the host country that perceive negative socio-cultural impacts from the presence of foreign companies can be grouped into three categories: the general public, workers, and consumers. The government's view of negative socio-cultural effects basically reflects one or more of these perspectives.

The general public: The developmental process itself, of which the multinational firm is a major cause, can have a *revolutionary effect upon a society*. (See Table 13.7.) If the society is large, modern, dynamic, and familiar with outside influences, foreign investment will frequently not cause major changes. In small, traditional, static societies, however, the foreign investor may bring not only the revolutionary impacts of development but also exposure to foreign influences. This may cause much adverse reaction. An unfavorable response may also occur, of course, in developed countries, but it is likely to be most severe in less developed nations.

Economic development almost inevitably brings social change with it. Modernization disrupts traditional patterns (Table 13.7, section I). This cannot be avoided, but observers who criticize often fail to foresee or accept this fact.

There is not, however, only a single path to modernization of an economy and society. It is quite feasible for a country to adhere to major portions of its Asian, African, or Latin culture. Yet, modern development is largely American and European in origin. As a result, many aspects of the brand of modernization American and European investors bring with them reflect the socio-cultural background from which the process sprang.

This "Americanization" or "Westernization" is often opposed by many groups in the host country who are anxious to preserve as much of the traditional culture as possible. Such socio-cultural reaction is most

TABLE 13.7 Negative Socio-Cultural Effects of FDI on the General Public[a]

I. UNHAPPINESS WITH CULTURAL CHANGES OR RATE OF CHANGE
   A. Modernization
   B. Westernization
II. INCREASED SOCIAL INSTABILITY
   A. Accentuated population mobility
      1. breakdown of traditional family and community patterns
   B. Accentuated differences between the very rich and very poor of the "dual economy"
   C. Stimulation of insatiable consumer demands
   D. Creation of a new power elite
III. URBANIZATION PROBLEMS
   A. Inadequate infrastructure
   B. Increase in crime
IV. ECOLOGICAL PROBLEMS
   A. Pollution
   B. Destruction of natural resources
   C. Nonconservation of renewable resources
V. RELATIONS BETWEEN LOCAL NATIONALS AND FOREIGNERS
   A. Lack of empathy of nationals for foreigners
      1. xenophobia
      2. chauvinism
      3. thoughtlessness
   B. Lack of empathy of foreigners for nationals
      1. xenophobia
      2. chauvinism
      3. thoughtlessness

[a]Table 13.7 corresponds to Table 12.6.

prevalent in small, developing countries where the pace of change can be most disruptive. However, even the French government, which is very sophisticated in most respects, has reacted very chauvinistically to alleged threats to the French langauge from English words.

Table 13.7 (section II) lists several problems of *increased social instability* that can ensue from the increased investment. Investment, especially foreign investment, tends to concentrate in specific cities or regions, except for extracting raw materials and agriculture, which must locate where the resources are found. Investments are most commonly concentrated in the major economic centers, such as Mexico City, Seoul, Cairo, Lagos, and Barcelona. These centers attract large migrations from rural areas, which tends to break down the traditional extended family and community patterns; this breakdown can be very destabilizing for a society.[1]

Social instability can also be enhanced by an increase in the gap between the very rich and the very poor, which is so prevalent in many developing countries, even if the poor are made better off in absolute terms. It is often the *relative* degree of poverty rather than the absolute degree that causes the most unrest.

Under conditions of abject poverty, the poor are often fatalistically resigned to their fate and may be so sick and poor that social unrest is unlikely. Initial progress, which breaks the chains of poverty and fatalism, often awakens the desire for continued progress (the "revolution of rising expectations") and can cause dissatisfaction and unrest if such continuous progress is not forthcoming. It is important that the company, especially a foreign-owned company, be perceived as a continuous source of contribution to progress or at least not as an obstacle.

Another social problem stemming from FDI can be the stimulation of insatiable consumer demands. Even if advertising campaigns are directed only toward the wealthier strata of a country, the posters and advertisements in the news media can arouse the interest and unrest of those who cannot afford the merchandise.

Also, foreign investment often helps to create a new power elite among local nationals. This upsets traditional social balances and can lead to unrest and even violence, with many innocent people being caught in the middle.

The migration from the countryside to the city increases *urban problems* (see Table 13.7, section III). The urban infrastructure can be overwhelmed, leading to slums, inadequate schools, health problems, and crime.

Industrialization can lead to *ecological problems* as well (see Table 13.7, section IV)—pollution (for example, the air pollution in cities such as Mexico City and Sao Paulo is some of the worst in the world), destruction of depletable natural resources (strip mining), and failure to conserve and renew non-depletable resources (forests and farmlands).

These aforementioned social problems are, despite their seriousness, rather impersonal. Also, there are frequently ugly personal sociocultural problems (see Table 13.7, section V). These can involve the actions, reactions, or omissions of either the foreigners or the local nationals. Problems can result from xenophobia (the fear of things foreign), chauvinism, or mere thoughtlessness. These types of unfavorable personal contacts tend to worsen the attitudes of the individuals involved. Many executives have returned from foreign assignments with a very negative attitude toward the nationals. The same individuals

---

[1]See the Glossary at the end of the book for a definition of the *extended family*.

have quite probably left comparable attitudes among the local nationals abroad. Their companies might well suffer as a result, and other companies may also suffer.

These negative personal experiences can occur when dealing with superiors, peers, or subordinates at work, when dealing with representatives of other companies or the government, or during one's private life with neighbors, social acquaintances, servants, or businesses (the doctor or the local grocer).

In many areas of the world, foreign business personnel live in specifically identifiable high-income enclaves. Some governments require this (for example, Saudi Arabia, which requires it of most non-Moslems; also East European governments commonly require it of their personnel working abroad). In other cases, social and economic conditions, such as overwhelming poverty, force the creation of an enclave. In yet other cases, social pressures dictate the trend toward enclaves; note, for example, the Jewish, Black, Indian, or Chinese ghettos in numerous cities throughout the world. However, in many instances an enclave is created largely from personal preference, most commonly involving a single nationality. For instance, note the concentrations of Japanese families in many parts of the world where significant Japanese investment has occurred and the concentrations of German families in specific areas and in special clubs or restaurants of a city, such as in Charlotte, North Carolina.

Enclaves prevent their "inmates" from learning from and about the local culture, often allowing ignorant misunderstandings to develop. Enclaves also tend to encourage misconceptions by outsiders of those within the enclave.

Workers: Employees can be some of the principal beneficiaries of new foreign investment. However, companies can find themselves exposed to criticism on many fronts in regard to labor (see Table 13.8). Foreign companies are commonly accused of underpaying their workers ("exploitation of cheap labor"), even if they are paying at or above local wages. Actually, exploitation charges are more likely to come from overseas (from labor unions) than from local sources. On the other hand, MNCs are commonly charged locally with overpaying workers and causing dissatisfaction among workers for other companies. This is another example of a difficult tightrope: No matter what the company does, it might well be subject to criticism.

If expatriates are employed by a foreign company (as is generally the case), criticism greatly increases (see Table 13.8, sections II, III, and IV). There is common criticism of the *use of expatriates* under any circumstances. When expatriates are employed, charges of discrimination in hiring, firing, compensating, and promoting are frequent. Person-

TABLE 13.8   Negative Effects of FDI on Workers[a]

I.   WAGES
    A.   Underpaying: charges of exploitation of cheap labor
    B.   Overpaying: charges of inducing dissatisfaction
II.   OPPOSITION TO USE OF EXPATRIATES
III.   PREFERABLE TREATMENT OF EXPATRIATES BY COMPANY
    A.   Employment
    B.   Promotion
    C.   Compensation
    D.   Firing
    E.   General treatment
IV.   PERSONAL CONFLICTS BETWEEN LOCAL WORKERS AND EXPATRIATES
V.   JOBS LOST IN COMPETING COMPANIES
VI.   DEMANDS THAT CONFLICT WITH LOCAL CUSTOMS
VII.   ADVERSE CONSEQUENCES OF
    A.   Rationalization of worldwide operations
       1.   preferential treatment by firm to home country's operations
       2.   scaling down of host-country operations
    B.   Changing management strategy
    C.   Response to declining demand

[a]Table 13.8 corresponds to Table 12.7.

al conflicts between local workers and expatriates can also be a problem. Other difficult issues revolve around violations of local taboos and other customs. A company needs good advice on local conditions to avoid unforeseen pitfalls.

Economic readjustment resulting from foreign investment is always grist for the mill of criticism. If competitors are hurt by the new venture, workers from the local competitors are also hurt, even if there is a net gain in jobs for the country or region. However, often a modern investment, being more efficient, may lower net employment, for instance, because of large farm machinery replacing numerous workers utilizing primitive tools (see Table 13.8, section V).

A chronic problem surfaces as a result of the very common need for a company to view its local operations as only part of its worldwide operations (see Table 13.8, section VII). Decisions to *rationalize* worldwide organization of the company (that is, to reorganize for greater economic efficiency), to change management strategy, or simply to scale down local production in response to declining sales, all of which have a negative impact on the local employment scene, can easily be targets of criticism. It is quite normal for companies to prefer that these decisions be made from a local perspective rather than worldwide. Since there is frequent suspicion of preferential treatment of the home country's operations over the host country's, local sensitivities can be aggravated. For instance, will the French or American company facing strong union, public relations, and perhaps even governmental pressures at home be as likely to scale down those operations or other (perhaps even more efficient and economical) operations in the host country? It is a realistic concern.

Consumers: One of the most difficult social issues that arises from economic development is the stimulation of *unsatisfiable demands*. (See Table 13.9.) The promotion of its products by the MNC can be a prominent contributor to this trend. Just as in the ghettos of industrialized countries, in poor countries the exposure to attractive advertisements can cause substantial dissatisfaction and unrest among the poor. Related criticism can arise from inducements to buy *wasteful or very frivolous items*, where poverty and capital needs are great and where foreign exchange is limited. Conversely, the more important the product is deemed for local needs, the more welcome the company is likely to be.

Other consumer-related complaints involve destruction of local market patterns (see Table 13.9, section II). Supermarkets may be much more economical than small bakeries, butchers, fruit and vegetable merchants, and so forth. However, the supermarkets are often less conveniently located and very impersonal. These innovations disrupt not only economic but also social patterns.

Another criticism of foreign companies is that product promotion is often in poor taste by local standards or is misunderstood (see Table 13.9, section III). Also, brand names or slogans may often have a different

---

TABLE 13.9 Negative Effects of FDI on Consumers[a]

I. STIMULUS TO BUY GOODS THAT ARE
   A. Unaffordable
   B. Wasteful
   C. Unnecessary
II. DESTRUCTION OF TRADITIONAL MARKET PATTERNS
   A. Impersonal trade
   B. Displacement of local suppliers
III. PRODUCT PROMOTION
   A. Poor taste
   B. Misunderstandings and blunders

---

[a]Table 13.9 corresponds to Table 12.8.

connotation. Of course, the company may well be penalized in the market as a result. For example, "General Motors made an embarrassing mistake when its 'body by Fisher' came out as 'corpse by Fisher' in Flemish (Belgium). . . . Pepsi's familiar U.S. ad of 'Come Alive with Pepsi' had problems in Germany because the translation of 'come alive' in German meant 'come alive out of the grave.' "[2]

NEGATIVE POLITICO-LEGAL EFFECTS OF FDI ON THE HOST COUNTRY

The multinational firm is not merely an economic and social animal: It also has strong political characteristics and impacts. Most critically, the very political system of a country can also be strongly affected by multinational investments, both directly and indirectly.

General impact: Economic development, especially if it is associated with foreign companies and foreign living styles, can produce the "revolution of rising expectations" previously mentioned (see Table 13.10). Once the traditional fatalism or passivity of a culture is shaken by the introduction of new aspirations, *political instability* often tends to grow.

The most notable direct impact of the MNC upon a government is perhaps *interference with governmental affairs* (see Table 13.10, section II). Prime examples are bribery, political subsidies (à la ITT in Chile in the early 1970s), or even efforts to overthrow governments.

Also, foreign investors are often adept at playing off one country against another. This may be good business and develop a strong negotiating posture for the company, but it can offend local sensitivities, especially if the country is newly independent! (See Table 13.10, section III.)

The domination of an economy by one or several foreign firms (for example, the Firestone Rubber Company in Liberia, the old United Fruit Company [now United Brands] in Central America, and ARAMCO in Saudi Arbia) can easily be viewed as a threat to the sovereignty of almost any government. Governments (especially of poor or small countries) often feel frustrated by the control of the domestic economy by foreign companies (see Table 13.10, section IV). The aggregate size of such investment could thus hurt the company, even if its own particular investment is small.

The creation of *new economic elites* can strengthen or weaken a

---

[2]David Ricks, Marilyn Fu, and Jeffrey Arpan, *International Business Blunders* (Columbus, Ohio: Grid Publishing, Inc., 1974), p. 11.

TABLE 13.10   General Negative Politico-Legal Effects of FDI[a]

I. INCREASED POLITICAL INSTABILITY
II. POTENTIAL INTERFERENCE OF FOREIGN FIRMS IN
LOCAL GOVERNMENT
    A. Bribery
    B. Subversion
III. COMPANY PLAYING HOST COUNTRY OFF AGAINST
OTHERS FOR BEST ADVANTAGE
IV. PROPENSITY OF FEW LARGE FOREIGN FIRMS TO
DOMINATE THE FOLLOWING:
    A. Important industries
    B. Regions of the country
    C. Whole country
V. EFFECT ON POWER STRUCTURE
    A. Greater concentration
    B. Greater diversification
    C. Effect on government's power base
        1. enhancement
        2. reduction
VI. REVENUES AND EXPENDITURES
VII. INTERNATIONAL RELATIONS

[a]Table 13.10 corresponds to Tables 12.9 and 12.10.

government (see Table 13.10, section V). Depending upon circumstances it can lead to a concentration of greater power in the hands of a small group (such as the military in Libya), or it can diversify the concentration of power with the creation of new power elites. This happened in Ecuador, where in the early 1970s the old agricultural elite saw its power diluted in the face of the new oil revenues that were controlled by the central government. Either effect can be seen as favorable or unfavorable depending upon the observer's viewpoint.

Revenue and expenditure: Economic expansion caused by foreign investors, especially when coupled with population shifts, can greatly increase demand for *governmental services*. The government's efforts to increase its revenues to finance these and other programs are often thwarted by the MNC's actions. *Transfer pricing* is a prime example of this, but so also is the corporate *manipulation of fees, royalties,* and so forth as a means of avoiding taxation. Countries are becoming much more sophisticated in controlling alleged abuses in these areas; multinational agreements are being sought to greatly decrease the flexibility of companies to reduce or delay taxation by these means.[3]

---

[3]These managerial actions are discussed in Chapters 20–22.

International relations: The MNC is often viewed abroad as an arm of its home government. The home country's government further reinforces this notion when it intervenes with a host government in the event of an expropriation or—as with the U.S. government's directive to American banks to seize Iranian assets in their offices at home *and abroad*—when it imposes *extra-territorial controls* on its companies' operations abroad.

Intervention in relations between companies and the governments of their host countries can often involve the home country's government in undesirable disputes. An important source of these problems is the old mentality of "gun-boat diplomacy," where governments were accustomed to using political and military pressure to protect commercial and industrial interests. This misuse of power has no place in today's world. Governments would be better off if they did not insure foreign investments and if they allowed MNCs to assume all of their own risks. A move in this direction may well occur in coming years. Many foreign governments do not insure their investors abroad. Such a laissez-faire policy would undoubtedly discourage some investments. However, it would not only reduce the occasions for intergovernmental disputes but would remove some of the basis of criticism of the firms. Foreign investments should be based upon their economic merits, not their political clout! The right to earn profits abroad must be tempered by the prospect of losses, just as it is at home.

NEGATIVE IMPACTS OF FDI:
THE HOME COUNTRY'S PERSPECTIVE

The foregoing discourse concentrated on the most obvious country-company relationship in international investment: namely, the host country versus the investor. This section considers a second very important country-company relationship: the home country versus the investing firm.

Just as with the host country, the foreign investor can cause unfavorable economic, socio-cultural, and politico-legal effects in its home country.

NEGATIVE ECONOMIC EFFECTS OF FDI
ON THE HOME COUNTRY

Table 13.11 section I, outlines the negative economic effects that can be caused by foreign investors in their home country.

TABLE 13.11   Unfavorable Political Impacts of Foreign Investors on Their Home Countries[a]

   I. NEGATIVE ECONOMIC EFFECTS
      A. Basic factors of production
          1. capital
          2. skilled manpower
          3. technology
      B. Effects resulting from basic factors
          1. balance of payments
          2. structure of the economy
          3. local businesses
          4. local economy
  II. NEGATIVE SOCIO-CULTURAL EFFECTS
      A. Workers
      B. General public
 III. NEGATIVE POLITICO-LEGAL EFFECTS
      A. Governmental control of domestic economy
      B. International relations

---

[a]Table 13.11 corresponds to Table 12.10.

Factors of production: The flow of factors from the home country may be a drain on the available supply of the factors. (See Table 13.11, section I, part A.) The firm's efforts to optimize the utilization of its resources may be suboptimal from the home country's viewpoint and therefore subject to criticism.

Capital outflows can be viewed as detrimental even by wealthy industrialized countries, including the United States. The series of capital controls that were introduced in the mid-1960s to diminish the capital outflows from the United States and to strengthen its balance of payments included FDI controls—the Foreign Direct Investment regulations. If capital outflows can trouble the world's wealthiest nation (although they were rather ill-conceived policies), it should come as no surprise that they can also be a concern for smaller countries. Some FDI even flows out of developing countries. Some of this basically represents geographical diversification in the same industry, for example the FDI in Hong Kong and elsewhere of San Miguel beer of the Philippines. Other FDI represents political insurance, that is, an international diversification of investments in response to the threat of adverse political changes at home. Governments of capital-poor countries may well oppose such outflows.

Similarly, a country with limited *skilled manpower*, such as scientists, might be rather opposed to a company's decision to shift research and development facilities and their skilled workers abroad.

In a similar vein, a country whose companies have a monopoly upon a certain type of technology might like to maintain the monopoly. The selling or licensing of the technology abroad could hurt the country's competitive position. (This is analogous to the smuggling of rubber plants out of Brazil to Malaya to begin the Asian rubber industry.)

Effects resulting from the basic factors: The home country's *balance of payments* can be adversely affected by capital outflow and any decline in exports resulting from the foreign investment. (See Table 13.11, section I, part B.) The capital outflow can be expected to eventually be more than offset in the long run with capital, interest, dividend, and fee inflows. However, the temptation is to attack the short-term problem with controls, as the United States did for ten years (1964–1973).

The *structure of the economy* can also be affected; for example, consider the negative impacts upon industries such as television and textile manufacturing as U.S. producers shifted production abroad. Opponents to foreign direct investments can sometimes make a strong case against the "legitimacy" of FDIs. If the foreign investment represents a replacement for home country investment, there can be a strong surge of resentment. If the connection between the foreign direct investment and a close-down of domestic operations can be demonstrated, the opposition from displaced workers, displaced suppliers, local commerce, and the local government can be quite vehement. (As was seen in Chapter 5, the FDI might not be the cause of the loss at all; the facilities might have closed up in any event. However, the FDI often serves as a convenient scapegoat.)

NEGATIVE SOCIO-CULTURAL EFFECTS OF FDI ON THE HOME COUNTRY

Foreign direct investment can have deleterious socio-cultural effects upon the home country of the investor parallel to the negative economic effects (see Table 13.11, section II). In the event that domestic production seems to be producing adverse effects, then workers and the general public may indeed perceive themselves to be worse off as a result of the FDI. As noted above, workers can be displaced, even if other jobs are created elsewhere, such as sales positions in the after-market. The basic problem is that often (and indeed, generally) the workers who bear the initial brunt of the loss of jobs are not the same ones with the appropriate skills or in the right place to be the beneficiaries of the newly created jobs. Thus, even if the overall economy and workers in general are better off, some parts of the economy and some groups of workers will perceive themselves as being worse off. This situation is analogous to that in the host country.

NEGATIVE POLITICO-LEGAL EFFECTS OF FDI
ON THE HOME COUNTRY

Control of the domestic economy: There are two specific ways in which the home government is primarily affected (see Table 13.11, section III). The first involves the government's efforts to control conditions in the domestic economy. If the investor is able to identify investment options abroad, while the government is trying to encourage investment at home, the company's FDI would be contrary to the government's wishes. Also if the government is attempting to strengthen the domestic currency or to improve the balance of payments, the foreign investment would again be "against the grain" of governmental policy.

The movement by local companies into foreign production facilities can also affect the home government's revenues and expenditures. If the foreign investment replaces an existing or potential domestic investment, then it may well cause a loss of tax revenues to local governments as well as to the national government. At the same time, if a local company is closed, then the ensuing unemployment adds to the government's social costs. In many or most cases, the local facility might have been closed anyway. However, if it is replaced by investment in another country, then the attitude of the home country's government may well be more unfavorable to the company.

International relations: The second major way in which FDI can affect the home country's government involves relations between the government and other governments abroad. As has been discussed, foreign investors commonly call upon their home government for support in some of their disputes with host countries. However, in general, it is not in the best interests of a government to allow the private economic transactions of its citizens to drag it into tense international situations. Yet this frequently happens. There is still a strong tendency for governments to let the "tail wag the dog." For example, in 1968 the new military government of Peru expropriated the local subsidiary of Exxon. In response, the U.S. government suspended all economic and military aid to Peru. Yet the behavior of the local subsidiary—the International Petroleum Company (IPC)—had been so blatantly antagonistic to the government that most foreign business personnel with whom the author spoke to in Peru shortly after the expropriation felt that IPC had gotten what it deserved. Nevertheless, U.S.-Peruvian relations were badly affected by the situation.

Related to this type of situation in which companies can easily drag their home governments into undesirable foreign entanglements, are situations in which the government specifies foreign behavior which it expects its companies to avoid, for example, the trade and investment embargo that was imposed by the United Nations upon Rhodesia, the banning of trade with certain other countries (even from foreign plants owned by the home country's nationals) and the Foreign Corrupt Practices Act in the United States (which, among other things, forbids the payment of certain business fees abroad by U.S. companies—even if such payments are legal in the foreign country!) Prior to the rapproachement between the United States and the People's Republic of China, most exports to the PRC were banned for American companies, wherever they were located. Thus, when the French subsidiary of the Fruehauf Trailer Corporation received a large order from the PRC, the command of the U.S. government directing the company not to make the shipment was greeted with dismay within France (which was not embargoing such trade). U.S.-French relations were badly strained over the event. The French government seized the disputed trailers and made sure that they were shipped. This problem of extraterritoriality of one government inside the borders of another country is a very sensitive issue in international relations.

SUMMARY

Direct investment inevitably has a strong influence upon the locale in which it is made. Many different local groups find themselves affected. Many of the effects, as shown in the last chapter, are favorable. Yet many others are viewed unfavorably. Some are viewed ambiguously— seen as favorable by some and unfavorable by others or favorable at one point in time but unfavorable at a later point in time. The negative impacts of foreign direct investment cover the same range of variables as was examined in the last chapter. The perception of those who find fault with the effects of the foreign investment runs the gamut of all of the observers who are in any way affected by the foreign direct investment: workers, suppliers, competitors, the government, social workers, etc. No matter how favorable one may be toward the potential advantages of FDI, there are many at least potential consequences that may be disturbing to the observer. To the non-sympathetic observer, of course, the disadvantages are numerous. Such adverse consequences may be, as they were with the favorable consequences which were discussed in the last chapter, of an economic, socio-cultural or politico-legal nature. Also, the disadvantages can be seen from either the perspective of the host or the home country.

However, it is important for all observers to bear in mind that not all these impacts, favorable or unfavorable, are unique to investments from abroad. Local direct investment can also be highly disruptive to a local community. It is just that, when the effects of an investment are joined with the foreignness of the investor, the disadvantages commonly tend to be perceived as more onerous than if the same effects had been caused by local investors. The foreign investor must always realize that this foreignness will frequently be an extra burden. He or she often *cannot* do with impunity what the local investor can do.

These two chapters have examined a wide array of the impacts, both favorable and unfavorable, which the foreign investor can bring, either intentionally or unintentionally, to the host country in which the investment is made. From a study of such pluses and minuses it is hoped that the manager or prospective manager will gain a more realistic perspective of both the strengths and weaknesses of potential foreign investments. The relationships between the multinational company and the governments with which it must negotiate and cooperate in the company's international investments have changed substantially in recent decades—especially as governments have become more sophisticated about their relationships with foreign investors. Both parties, corporate and government, to the negotiations can expect that the negotiations will be more difficult and balanced than in the past. Both sides will be buttressed by professional advisors. As a result, hopefully in the future the negotiations will produce more balanced, equitable and less sensitive contracts than have been so common in the past. The basis for compromise will be examined in the next chapter.

KEY TERMS

CHAUVINISM	EXPATRIATE	NATIONALIZATION
CONCESSION	EXTRATERRITORIALITY	TRANSFER PRICE
DUAL ECONOMY	NATIONALISM	XENOPHOBIA
ENCLAVE		

REVIEW QUESTIONS

1. Certain groups have a philosophical opposition to the free enterprise system. Which groups tend to feel this way?

2. Certain other groups, which do not necessarily have a philosophical opposition to the free enterprise system, are nevertheless frequently very critical of foreign investment. Identify these groups and explain their positions.

3. Discuss the negative *economic* impacts of foreign direct investment. How serious an issue do you think that they are? To what extent are they uniquely the result of foreign direct investment rather than domestic investment?

4. Discuss the negative *socio-cultural* impacts of foreign direct investment. How serious an issue do you think that they are? To what extent are they uniquely the result of foreign direct investment rather than domestic direct investment?

5. Discuss the negative *politico-legal* impacts of foreign direct investment. How serious an issue do you think that they are? To what extent are they uniquely the result of foreign direct investment rather than domestic direct investment?

6. Should the host government take action to oppose negative impacts from FDI? What can it do?

7. Should the foreign investor take action to reduce the negative impacts? Why or why not? What would you suggest the company do?

8. Governments of young developing countries sometimes take actions that please the local populace but which chase foreign investors away and lose jobs. Is this rational behavior? Could it be avoided?

SUGGESTED REFERENCES*

GOLDFINGER, NAT "A Labor View of Foreign Investment and Trade Issues," *International Trade and Finance,* ed. Robert Baldwin. Homewood, Ill.: Richard D. Irwin, Inc., 1971.

LEVITT, KARI *Silent Surrender: The American Economic Empire in Canada.* Toronto: Liveright Publishing Co., 1970.

Maryknoll (special issue on the multinational corporation), Maryknoll, N.Y.: Maryknoll Press, September 1975.

RICKS, DAVID A., MARILYN FU, AND JEFFREY ARPAN *International Business Blunders.* Columbus, Ohio: Grid Publishing, Inc., 1974.

SOLOMON, LEWIS D. *Multinational Corporations and the Emerging World Order.* Port Washington, NY: Kennikat Press, 1978.

---

*See also the references at the end of Chapter 14.

14

The Mutual Dependency between the Multinational Firm and Its Host Country

The two previous chapters isolated a very wide range of the positive and negative impacts of foreign investments. As noted, these categorizations are subjective. They reflect the views of many observers: business executives, labor leaders, government officials (of both home and host governments), Marxists, competitors, social workers, and so forth.

It is vitally important that managers of foreign companies be aware of the wide range of economic, socio-cultural, and politico-legal impacts that their investments might bring or, perhaps even more important, that observers *think* they might bring. A realistic perception by managers can enable a company to avoid many potential pitfalls in its relations with the government of the host country.

In a similar vein, the host government has an obligation to familiarize itself with the various favorable and unfavorable impacts that can result from investments. Alertness to such possibilities, careful planning, tough bargaining, and conscientious enforcement of rules can greatly increase the potential net gain to the host country.

At the same time the government should be aware that *any* investment, domestic as well as foreign, can produce many of the impacts that were noted in the previous two chapters. The criticism that is frequently levied against foreign investors often fails to make this distinction.

It is important for the government to be able to distinguish between those impacts, both good and bad, that are unique to foreign investors and those that domestic investors could also produce. If the disadvantages are inevitable whether an investment is from foreign or domestic sources (for example, urbanization or ecological problems), then the governmental officials should recognize this fact.

Similarly, if domestic investors that can provide the desired advantages while avoiding some of the problems foreign investors might bring—profit outflows and extraterritorial interference by foreign governments—then the government should also be aware of that. The very foreignness of a company makes it more visible, which commonly makes both the company and local nationals more sensitive to criticisms, problems, misunderstandings, and so forth.

However, domestic direct investment is often inadequate, either because of inability or a lack of willingness. When only foreign investors can bring certain needed assets, then the identification of such assets is an important piece of information for the host government in its negotiations with the potential foreign investor.

Any investment, whether domestic or foreign and whether privately owned or government-owned, will produce many impacts, both favorable and unfavorable, upon the host country. The critical question to the government (as to the company when it makes its investment analysis) relates to the *net* balance between the costs and the benefits. It also relates to the comparison between the net benefits from a foreign investment and, if it is available, a comparable domestic investment. Unfortunately, because of the qualitative nature of many of the feasible impacts, both the advantages and disadvantages are difficult to quantify.

A POSITIVE-SUM RELATIONSHIP

An investment generally brings advantages to both the investor and its host country: The relationship is a positive-sum opportunity. However, as a result, the basic relationship between a foreign investor and the host government is one of mutual dependency. The relative strengths of the two sides depict a pattern of *bilateral monopolies or oligopolies.*

If it is not clear to each side that it stands to potentially gain from the proposed investment, then obviously the entire basis for negotiation would disappear. The investor is interested in the country only if the opportunity presented is not only profitable but more profitable than other alternatives in both its home country and alternative host countries. Conversely, countries, even Communist countries in Eastern Europe and China, recognize the advantages of the assets that foreign investors can provide.

The relationship between the investor and the host country is somewhat analogous to that described between different countries earlier in the book when the benefits of free trade were discussed. The gains from investment, as is true of the gains from trade, can be distributed in different proportions. However, the relationship is complicated by the fact that the possible negative impacts upon a host country can be far more complicated than those noted as a result of a freer trade, such as, for instance, displacement of workers.

BARGAINING STRENGTH

The distribution of the potential benefits is going to depend to a significant extent upon the relative assets, weaknesses, and negotiating skills of the two parties. Some countries have such strong monopolistic or quasi-monopolistic assets that they are able to attract significant amounts of foreign investment quite readily. For example, countries that are rich in raw materials, for example, Peru and Malaysia, have a strong appeal for companies seeking minerals. Likewise, countries with large domestic markets (for example, Germany, Japan, and Brazil) have strong, natural appeal to companies seeking foreign markets. Other countries must overcome natural disadvantages or disadvantages based upon their past reputation in order to attract the attention of foreign investors. Some countries can deliberately create conditions to attract foreign investors (for example, favorable banking laws in Singapore and the Bahamas and the provision of investment incentives such as tax holidays in many countries such as Taiwan and Argentina).

In a similar vein, some companies have such strong inherent advantages that they not only are extremely attractive to most host countries but are often able to obtain unusually attractive concessions; IBM is a classic example. Most other companies are less favorably endowed and must market their proposals more aggressively; they know that, if they do not make a proposal that is attractive enough to the host country, there are other companies that might be quite willing to do so.

NEGOTIATIONS

The negotiating process between the company and the host country can thus be seen to be a function not only of the relative strengths and weaknesses and goals of the two parties but also of the perception by each of the relative strengths and weaknesses and goals of the other, together with the appropriate negotiating skills of each.

Given the conditions that each party brings to the bargaining table, an acceptable agreement *may* be possible. However, it is also possible that alternatives available to either party may be more attractive, so that the negotiations may fall through. It is also very possible that irreconcilable differences will develop. Both the company and the country need to be realistic about their minimum conditions.

Sometimes the terms demanded by the two parties are completely irreconcilable. However, in other negotiations potentially attractive agreements fall through because of unrealistic demands and failure to give adequate consideration to cultural differences; either the investor or the host country or both could be responsible. For example, Citibank, which had been well established in Nigeria by the mid-1970s, refused to accept a demand that it sell 60 percent of its Nigerian operations to local interests. The bank was fearful that, if it capitulated to the government's demands in Nigeria, it would also have to do the same in Colombia and Saudi Arabia (two countries in which Citibank was even more deeply entrenched than in Nigeria). As a result of its refusal, Citibank was forced to withdraw from Nigeria (much to the satisfaction of the other foreign banks there, which were able to pick up the Citibank business). However, Citibank later capitulated to the governmental demands in both Colombia and Saudi Arabia anyway. It belatedly regretted its Nigerian decision and was subsequently anxious to return to Nigeria but was unable to do so: The Nigerian government was not very favorably inclined toward a bank that had earlier withdrawn from the country rather than accept the government's demands.

THE HOST COUNTRY

WHY DOES THE HOST COUNTRY ACCEPT FOREIGN INVESTMENT?

It is not only the developing countries that are aided by foreign direct investment. All countries can benefit from such foreign influences. Indeed, the countries with the most foreign investment are Canada and the United States. The greatest concentration of American investment is in Canada and Western Europe. Thus, not only have companies found these nations to be attractive, but the countries have been willing to accept large amounts of such investment. Developing countries receive a minor share of the foreign direct investment from the industrialized countries, but, as the impacts noted in the previous two chapters suggested, that investment is nevertheless relatively very significant in those countries. An investment that is relatively small by the standards of the industrialized countries can be relatively quite large by local standards when the local industrial and commercial base is small.

Open economy: The simplest explanation why much of the capital flows occur, especially into the more highly developed countries, is simply that the economies are relatively open to these flows: A minimum of barriers is imposed to obstruct the factor movements. Countries such as the United States, the United Kingdom, and Germany fall into this category. However, many countries, including not only most developing countries but also such developed countries as Canada and Australia, have imposed various types of serious impediments to flows of direct investments. Such obstacles can be against outflow of capital funds as well as against the inflow. Since we are interested in the flows that can actually occur, we are most interested here in the barriers to the inflow of capital that is capable of emigrating from its home country.

Access to needed factors: Many countries actively court foreign investors. Their rationales are often compatible with the investment rationale of the companies, but in some respects they are very different. Obviously, if the foreign investor has a unique factor to bring that is largely lacking in the local economy, such as technology or sophisticated management, this is often a very attractive contribution from the perspective of the host country. In a similar vein, other monopolistic assets such as captive foreign markets, which would be virtually impossible for companies in the host country to establish abroad, would be another incentive for accepting foreign investment. These and related advantages were discussed in detail in Chapter 12.

Even when many of the necessary resources are available locally in adequate supply, it may be necessary for foreign producers to complete the combination of complementary resources that are necessary for production. Indeed, the very fact that there are attractive local resources not being adequately employed by local companies is often a very strong argument on behalf of attracting foreign investors. For example, the existence of an empty automobile factory in Pennsylvania was a strong incentive for the government of that state to make an attractive bid to Volkswagen to begin their first American manufacturing operation in Pennsylvania. Similarly, when Ford made known its intention of building a large new assembly operation, the government of the Canadian province of Ontario offered an attractive package if Ford would make the investment in that province, outbidding an aggressive bid from the state of Ohio.

Peter Drucker observed that what developing countries (or even developed countries or regions) lack "is the full ability to mobilize their resources. . . .What they need are 'triggers,' stimuli from abroad . . . which will energize the resources of the country and will have a 'multiplier impact.' " Drucker goes on to note that, in and of themselves, the foreign investor cannot *cause* development of a host country, but they can be an important aid. ". . . They can only turn the crank but not push the car."[1]

---

[1] Peter F. Drucker, "Multinationals and Developing Countries: Myths and Realities," *Foreign Affairs*, October 1974, pp. 124, 127.

Development of local markets: Many foreign investors are primarily interested in the development of the local market. Often this involves imported products. Nevertheless, in many instances it is still attractive to the host country for such investments to occur as a means of stimulating the local economy by satisfying existing demand, improving the efficiency of the local economy, and stimulating demand-pull pressures. For example, the foreign investment by commercial banks not only improves the local financial infrastructure but also provides local jobs; these two factors together also serve to stimulate further growth in the economy as a result of the increased infrastructural efficiency and via the multiplier effect.

Balance of payments: A very prominent potential impact of foreign direct investment is upon the balance of payments. The oil crisis coupled with rampant world inflation, widespread world economic slowdown, volatile foreign exchange rates and commodity prices, and ambitious local developmental programs have all combined to cause unprecedented balance-of-payments deficits for the majority of developing countries and many of the developed countries as well. Commerical banks have been called upon to finance a very major share of such deficits, but their capacity to continue doing this on the scale of the past decade are very limited. Furthermore, debt financing entails heavy interest charges and the periodic need to refinance the debt.

Equity investments, together with private-sector loans, despite the negative factors that were seen to be sometimes associated with the former in Chapter 15, are less onerous politically. "As a rule (they) constitute a smaller (and, above all, a clearly delimited) burden than grants and other political subsidies from abroad. The latter always create heavy obligations, both in terms of foreign and domestic policy, no matter where they come from."[2]

THE DEVELOPMENTAL PROCESS

Complexity: The majority of countries in the world are at a level of development they themselves would describe as unsatisfactory, whether the term they use to describe their stage is *developing, less developed,* or *underdeveloped.* Development is a very complicated process that is still inadequately understood even by developmental specialists. Often in the past, development has been equated with economic development. Too little attention has been placed upon politico-legal and especially socio-cultural development. As a result of the unbalanced nature of developmental programs, the efforts were very often unbalanced and inadequate and were fraught with unanticipated and unsatisfactory side effects.

---

[2]Ibid., p. 125.

The previous two chapters very carefully considered politico-legal and socio-cultural implications of foreign direct investment. They can often be as significant as the economic ramifications and can enhance or thwart the anticipated economic gains from the investments.

The need for outside assistance: No country has been able to attain development completely on its own. Japan has borrowed heavily from the United States and Europe in order to foster its development. The Soviet Union, despite its socialist rhetoric, has also had to draw heavily upon non-Marxist countries. The United States drew very heavily upon Europe. Even the United Kingdom, the first industrialized country, had the benefit of financial resources from continental European countries.

The resources that these countries have drawn upon from other countries have included not only financial resources but all the various factor and nonfactor assets that we have noted as being valuable contributions made by foreign investors.

Of course, foreign direct investors are not the only source of such assets. Debt financing and the licensing of technology, for example, are two prominent alternatives through which the needed resources can be rented. Also, the source of the resources from abroad can be from foreign governments rather than from the foreign private sector. However, as was noted earlier in this chapter, the availability of the necessary resources from foreign governments is often inadequate and typically comes with strings attached.

Many countries, if they were single-minded enough, could develop largely on their own—autarkically, without the assistance of foreign capital and resources other than what they could acquire through imports. However, this process would be extremely slow and horribly wasteful and would occur as the developmental gap with the rest of the world increased steadily. For example, even the Soviet Union with all of its resources and single-minded confidence in the Communist system realizes the folly of limiting itself to the resources (mineral, technological, and so forth) of itself and its Communist allies. Thus, the USSR buys massive amounts of sophisticated equipment and difficult-to-make products such as computers, large-diameter pipes (for natural gas pipelines), machine tools, and so forth.

Fortunately, autarky is not necessary. The gains that are possible via trade and factor flows can foster much higher rates of development than could any country on its own.

The developmental process of countries such as the United Kingdom and the United States was long and slow. However, since there was no higher level of development with which the British and the Americans of that earlier era could compare themselves, the pace was deemed to be very satisfactory. They were not catching up to the level of development of anyone else. They were themselves creating much of the initial means of development, and they were setting the standard for development.

Today, developing nations do not need to devise their own means to development. The way has already been pioneered by the "developed" countries. As a result, the pace of development can be greatly accelerated over any pace that was ever attainable by the pioneering countries. For example, countries such as Japan, South Korea, and Brazil were able to increase their real per capita incomes from 8 to 12 percent per year during the 1960s and 1970s, rates of growth that were only possible because they could tap into technology, capital, and foreign markets that already existed. In a similar vein many other developing countries will be able to advance rapidly in the future by building upon the resources and experiences of other countries. As a result, those countries will be able to grow at a far faster pace than was possible for the United States and the United Kingdom.

As we have already seen, the multinational firm is an important vehicle for the transmission of the various assets needed by a country for development. As a result, if the conditions are right, foreign investment can be very attractive to the host country as a vehicle of fostering economic, socio-cultural, and politico-legal development.

POWER OF THE COUNTRY

Sovereignty: The core of the power of the host country is that it is a sovereign nation with very extensive control over matters within its own borders. This includes control over corporations, domestic or foreign.

This sovereign right extends to the ability to selectively expropriate an individual company, to nationalize an entire industry (such as was done to the Venezuelan oil industry), or even to socialize an entire private sector of an economy, such as occurred in Cuba. This sovereign right is acknowledged by virtually all governments in the world and in virtually all the courts of the world, including those of the major investing countries. Seizure of private enterprises is permissible as long as adequate compensation is paid. On the other hand, confiscation (seizure without compensation) is legally unacceptable to most governments in most neutral courts, unless justifiable cause can be shown. For example, the position of the U.S. government was stated in a speech by Cecil Hunt, Acting General Counsel of the Overseas Private Investment Corporation (the U.S. government agency that insures foreign investments by U.S. companies against expropriation): "We recognize the right of any country to expropriate the property of a U.S. investor . . . so long as the undertaking is nondiscriminatory, for a public purpose and accompanied by prompt, adequate and effective compensation." In actual fact, even if the expropriation was discriminatory and even if it was not for a public purpose, expropriation would generally be accepted as long as adequate compensation was paid.

Barriers: The earlier discussion of barriers to the free movement of factors of production and the subsequent effective control of such exported factors detailed the extensive array of tools available to the host government with which to control or punish a foreign (or domestic) investor. In addition to the outright barriers that were discussed, governments also have an array of tools available to control the activities of the foreign investor subsequent to the investment. Included in this collection are controls such as local content requirements*, local hiring demands, and export requirements.

Monopolistic or oligopolistic assets of the host country: The sovereign authority of the host government and the power of its various potential controls are, of course, negative factors in most corporate analyses of a potential host country. Offsetting these disadvantages are a number of prominent assets. These were discussed in Chapter 3, "The Basis for International Factor Movements."

A country's basic assets are its endowments of natural resources: minerals, water, climate, labor force, agricultural land, and so forth. Countries are extremely diverse in the allocation of these resources, which are, of course, strong incentives for companies seeking these factors of production.

Other countries have large populations, a critical location, a highly developed infrastructure, favorable laws, or attractive investment incentives. These assets appeal to other groups of investors.

Governments have little control over the availability of many of these assets. Other assets such as favorable laws and investment incentives are very much within a country's control.

DEGREE OF RISK FOR THE HOST COUNTRY

The risks for the host country are threefold, as follows:

1. the risk of inadequate protection against the type of negative impacts that can ensue from investment (as seen in the last chapter)
2. the risk of inadequate realization of the type of advantages that can ensue from investment (including difficulty in attracting investment) (as seen in Chapter 12)

---

*A government demand that a certain proportion of the value of components must be locally produced.

3. the negotiating risk of overplaying the country's bargaining position to such an extent that an attractive investor is driven away (This risk is discussed later in this chapter.)

THE FOREIGN INVESTOR

COUNTERVAILING POWER OF THE INVESTOR

As was noted, the foreign investment holds many of the keys that can enable a country to unlock its resources. For the host country to insist upon autarky—"going it alone"—would be very expensive, very wasteful, and very slow. Common sense dictates that host countries avail themselves of the resources that are available in the private sector of foreign countries. This collection of resources is, of course, the basis for the monopolistic or oligopolistic strength of the foreign investors (their "countervailing power") in their dealings with host governments.

Corporate management has a responsibility to the shareholders and employees of its company to drive the most profitable bargain possible for the company in negotiations with a host government. This requires a thorough knowledge of both their own company's strengths and weaknesses. It also requires an ample knowledge of the corresponding strengths and weaknesses of the host country. The countervailing powers of the company stem from its own strengths and from the weaknesses of the country.

WEAKNESSES OF THE INVESTOR

The company must thoroughly analyze its own weaknesses before initiating an investment venture. Does it, for example, have the necessary financial resources to fund the venture and to bear the risks? If the financial resources are available or can be obtained from outside sources, does the company have the necessary managerial capability to plan and implement the investment, or would the venture overwork the existing or potential management? Also, does the company have the necessary resources, the necessary ongoing research and development, to be able to make a continuing contribution to the host country in order to increase the likelihood of the company's continued welcome in the host country?

How badly does the company need the particular host country? If the country plays too dominant a role in the overall operations of the company, that exposure to unfavorable developments greatly increases the relative strength of the host country. For example, when the Libyan government sought to increase its power over the foreign oil companies in the 1970s, it concentrated initially on those companies that were very heavily reliant upon Libya for their major source of oil, such as Occidental Petroleum. Having first wrung concessions from those companies, the Libyan government was then able to focus pressure for concessions upon the more balanced companies, which were relatively much less dependent upon Libyan oil.

THE DEGREE OF RISK
FOR THE FOREIGN INVESTOR

The risk to the investor is a function of many factors, as follows:

1. the absolute amount of the investment
2. the relative reliance of the company upon that particular investment
3. the essentiality of the investment to the host country
4. the industry in which the investment is made
5. the political nature of the host country
6. the means of financing the investment
7. the organizational format of the investment
8. the outside support available to the investor

The absolute amount of the investment: The larger the investment, the greater the risk to the company. Obviously, this is true of any investment whether foreign or domestic. The size of an investment is relative to the size of the company. A $100 million investment would be a major commitment to any company. However, for a company with only $1 million in assets, even an investment of $100,000 would be large.

In some industries the average size of an investment can be quite huge. In the mining industry, investments of $500 million or more are not uncommon. In addition such investments must often rely heavily upon equity rather than debt financing, a factor that can greatly increase the risk to the investor.

Some other industries typically make relatively small average investments. Banking is a prime example; the cost of the average banking facility abroad is a mere shadow of that required for a major mining or industrial investment. Furthermore, bank investments are invariably highly leveraged, that is, they are largely financed from debt.

The relative reliance of a company upon a particular investment: As noted in the Libyan example above, if a company is highly exposed in a particular country, then its risk to adverse actions by the host government is obviously greatly increased. Exposure is not solely a matter of total monetary investment. It is also a matter of the strategic importance of the particular facility to the company. If the facility produces a component that is critical to the overall operations of the company and that cannot satisfactorily be replaced by alternative sources, then the investing company would be highly exposed to risk in that country, even if the relative size of the investment is small for the company. For example, if a critical raw material is produced in a particular facility, or if the company shifted its entire production of a critical manufactured component to that facility, then the company would be very highly exposed to disruption of that source. Such disruption could come from many sources—action of the local host government, action of the home government, labor unrest (either direct, such as labor strikes at the facility abroad; or indirect, such as labor strikes or rioting, which severely disrupt the transportation system), weather, and so forth.

The essentiality of the investment to the host country: Corresponding to the signficance of the investment to the investing company is the importance of the investment to the host country. Investments that bring great benefits to the country may be well insulated from harsh discriminatory action. For example, major industrial or mining investments are commonly of great importance to the host country. However, they are also highly visible and may be convenient targets for criticism.

On the other hand, investments in nonessential products, such as soft drinks or cigarettes, are of much less urgency. Also, the latter type of investment is seldom unique to foreign investors: Local investors can typically acquire the necessary equipment, technology, and skills to produce such standardized products. These industries are therefore more susceptible to various forms of discriminatory action. After all, Coca-Cola and Marlboros are not essential products!

Time horizons can play an important role in the question of essentiality. Many investors, that might be deemed critical when the investment was originally made, may no longer be so essential once the investment is completed. An investor, therefore, needs to try to ensure that its investment continues to provide a uniquely favorable input long after the investment is initiated. Companies, such as those in high-technology and consumer goods industries in which styles or technology are in constant flux (for example, fashionable clothing and consumer electronics) and those that offer a long-term promise of extensive exports to foreign captive markets are much less vulnerable to unfavorable actions of the host government.

The above are examples of *vertical integration,* which can either weaken or strengthen the bargaining position of the company.[3] For example, if critical inputs would be unavailable to the foreign facility in the event of a governmental seizure of that facility or if the market for

---

[3]See the Glossary at the end of the book for a definition of *vertical integration.*

the output of the facility would be cut off, then the investor's hand is greatly strengthened. On the other hand, if the company's production and/or sales would be severely affected by the seizure, then the company is highly exposed as a result of its vertical integration.

The industry in which the investment is made: Industries vary significantly in the likelihood that a host government will seize them. Investments in industries such as mining, petroleum, infrastructure (transportation, communication, and power), banking, insurance, and land have a particularly bad record of foreign seizures. These types of investments are not simply the target for takeover by socialist governments, but they are often seized even by governments that favor a strong private enterprise system.

The political nature of the host government: As the reader may well assume, governments with a strong socialistic bent are much more likely to seize private property than those with a strong democratic bent. Any type of government, from democracy to dictatorship, may opt to seize certain foreign-owned companies. However, a socialistically minded government is much more likely to do so.

Socialistically minded governments can come in many guises— from democratically elected governments in countries like the United Kingdom, France, and Venezuela to political dictatorships in countries like those of Eastern Europe to military dictatorships as in countries such as Libya. Therefore, the investor must apply political labels with great care. No particular type of government is a guarantee against discriminatory action against foreign investors. However, careful analysis of political risk can greatly reduce a company's ignorance of this prospect. The threat is too great for a company *not* to take special efforts to try to anticipate such dangers and to either avoid them or to take steps (as discussed below) to minimize those risks.

The means of financing the investment: An investment that is financed substantially by the infusion of equity into a foreign operation represents a major commitment of the investor. If such a facility is seized or destroyed, the cost to the investor as a proportion of the total investment is very great. However, if the equity investment is shared, for instance, through a joint venture, or if the investment is highly leveraged through the use of debt, then much of the potential risk can be shifted to others. This is especially true if much of the borrowing or infusion of equity is from local sources in the host country. However, even if the foreign operation is financed from sources in the home country or even a third country, then the risk *may* be able to be shifted to the lenders. Also, such a diversification of financial interest in an investment can provide some powerful allies in the event of difficulties with the host government. These allies may be banks, other companies, or even the governments of those banks or companies.

Whether or not debt financing can be effectively used to shift the risk to the lender depends upon whether the foreign facility or the parent (or even a separate financing subsidiary) is the ultimate obligor. If the foreign subsidiary is financed on its own merits with no recourse to the parent, then the effective incidence of risk is likely to be shifted away from the parent. However, if the parent extends a loan or guarantees a loan that is extended to its foreign affiliate by an outside source, then the parent is not generally avoiding that share of the risk of the investment.

A company may be reluctant to reveal to a government that it has guaranteed loans to a subsidiary; the knowledge of guarantees could encourage a government that is considering confiscation. For similar reasons, companies sometimes use a bank as a "front" to make a loan to the company's subsidiary: The company places a deposit with the bank, which then extends a loan to the foreign subsidiary of the company; in this way the true source of the loan is hidden.

The organizational format of the investment: The most common forms of organization of foreign investments are the branch and the subsidiary. A *branch* is essentially an extension of the headquarters. It is not a separate legal entity for either legal or tax purposes. A branch must be registered with local authorities, and it must conform to local laws. It is only permitted to do what those laws permit. It pays local taxes. This organizational format leaves the investor with a significant degree of exposure. The headquarters is legally responsible for the obligations of the branch. It is also liable for taxes at home on the profits earned abroad by the branch, whether the earnings are repatriated or not.

A common alternative to the branch is the subsidiary. A *subsidiary* is separately incorporated under the laws of the host country. As such, the subsidiary provides a wide variety of insulation between the parent and its foreign affiliates in the area of taxes as well as in legal matters. The headquarters is not usually liable for taxes on the earnings of a subsidiary unless they are repatriated. Also, in the absence of guarantees by the parent, it is not generally legally responsible for the obligations of the subsidiary.

If a foreign government should take discriminatory action against a subsidiary of a foreign company, the company loses not only the assets of that affiliate but also the legal responsibility for the liabilities of the seized subsidiary, unless the parent company guaranteed the liabilities of its subsidiary. On the other hand, if a government seizes the branch of a foreign company, the company may well find itself the unhappy owner of branch liabilities without the offsetting assets.

The outside support available to the investor: If an investment is made independently by a single company without any financial, commerical, or political backing, then the investor must bear the entire risk, at least the equity portion. However, many foreign investments are made with outside backing. This can involve either private-sector or public-sector support.

A common type of private-sector support comes in the form of a *joint venture*. This occurs when a subsidiary is owned jointly by two or more companies. The joint-venture partners may be either from the private sector of the investing company's home country, a third country, the host country or from the public sector of the host country.

Joint-venture partners from the investor's own country can make valuable contributions to the investment—capital, technology, markets, and so forth. However, they may provide little extra protection against adverse action against the subsidiary that might result from conflict between the host and home country.

Similar contributions can be obtained from investors from a third country. However, in addition, these investors may be able to bring additional pressure on a host country's government from the third country, especially if governmental pressure might be brought to bear.

A partner from the host country can bring unique assistance in the form of knowledge of local conditions and perhaps valuable contacts in the host country's government. If the local partner is from the private sector, the investing company needs to explore what the implications would be if there was a change of government. If the local partner is tied to a political group, then a change of government could have strong implications for the joint venture, for better or for worse.

The partner from the host country is very often the local government. In many instances, this is mandated by local law. In other instances, the local law merely requiries a local partner. However, in many instances private-sector investors cannot be found, either because of the size of the investment, the nature of the investment, or the risk of the investment. In these instances, the government may be the only local partner available.

Having the host country's government as a local partner has often proved to be a very risky propositon. Governments tend to get into investments of the highest priority to them. However, once involved, that often tends to be only a first step to an eventual total takeover. The record of joint ventures with governments is among the worse of the various types of joint ventures in terms of governmental seizure of facilities. Nevertheless, it may be the only way for a company to get involved. Also, many of these investments have indeed worked well.

COMPROMISE

NEED FOR UNDERSTANDING

Self-analysis: The first step in successful bargaining requires a thorough understanding by each party of not only its own strengths but also its own weaknesses. In the past, foreign investors have tended to be much better prepared for this than the host countries. The companies knew what they had to offer the country and knew what they wanted to avoid. However, very frequently in the past, the representatives of the host government were ill-prepared for the task before them. Often they lacked the sense of responsibility for safeguarding the welfare of their people. They certainly failed in a very significant portion of the negotiating sessions to be as expertly prepared as their counterparts in the investing company in understanding the major issues with which they were confronted. As a result, many contracts and concessions were signed that did not do justice to the host country.

Imbalances of this nature have been substantially reduced. There has been a vast increase in the cadre of trained specialists from various host countries, in the support of advisory services available from international organizations such as the IMF, World Bank, and U.N. and in the accessibility of independent specialists—a variety of different experts on whom the host country is now able to call in order to obtain the best possible advisors in its negotiations.

Another part of the self-analysis that each party to the negotiations needs to consider is what its own options are. If negotiations should fail, what is its fallback position? How many concessions is it willing to make in order for those negotiations to succeed? What is the cost of failure? What are the benefits of the possible alternatives?

Analysis of the other party: The second recommended step in the negotiation process is to analyze the position of the anticipated partner in the negotiation. What is the other party (whether it be the government or a company) likely going to seek? What are its strengths and weaknesses? What are the advantages that will be sought, and what are the disadvantages that it will try to avoid? This analysis also includes determining the other party's alternative options. If one party is unwilling to accede to the other's demands, how readily can the latter find an attractive alternative?

This is an area where investing companies have traditionally done their homework better than have host countries. Host countries have frequently been woefully unprepared. This will, however, be much less the case in the future. The proliferation of experts has greatly strengthened the position of host countries in their negotiations with investing companies.

Realistic goals: The third logical step by which both the prospective investor and the prospective host country can prepare themselves is the setting of reasonable goals. The company must certainly identify what it wants to get out of an investment. However, it should also decide what the least acceptable conditions would be. Similarly, the country should evaluate the proposed relationship from the same perspective—specifically, what would be the least acceptable conditions under which the country would be interested in the investment.

The setting of goals must be realistic. It must take into account the goals that the other party is likely to have set for itself. Otherwise, a lot of time can easily be wasted in fruitless discussions. Also, potentially attractive partnerships may be lost.

Codes of conduct: Because of serious concern about all the criticism that has often been levied against multinational companies in the past, a number of different efforts have been directed toward drawing up *codes of conduct* to guide foreign investors in their operations in host countries. Two of many codes of conduct were designed by the United Nations (basically reflecting the host country's perspective) and by the International Chamber of Commerce in Paris (reflecting the corporate viewpoint). These codes can be useful guidelines for helping foreign investors avoid "inappropriate" behavior. They can also guide host governments in terms of what to expect from foreign investors. However, even sincere efforts to observe all the recommendations of the codes will not insure an investor against troubles with the host country. Also, the codes themselves may not be completely applicable in many investment situations. The codes of conduct can be very useful guidelines, but they must be used with discretion. Also it must not be assumed that their implementation is the end of the investor's or the country's need to act with further discretion.

BARGAINING AND COMPROMISE

Bargaining is a function of all the foregoing preparation and the goals that each party to the negotiations has set. It also is a function of the personalities involved.

Neither party will get everything it wants. No bargaining opportunity is going to offer each party its maximum goals. Therefore, compromise is going to be necessary. In any positive-sum relationship there is likely to be a wide variety of combinations of the distribution of both the gains and disadvantages resulting from the relationship. This was seen in the discussion of the gains from trade. It is also very true in the relationship between an investor and the country in which it invests.

If the expectations of each party have been realistic and if the bargaining has been carried on with careful awareness of the advantages and disadvantages that the other party might be expected to anticipate, then a successful conclusion to the negotiations will often be possible.

Even under these circumstances, however, many negotiations will fail. This is to be expected. Therefore neither party should make the mistake, if it has any options, of relying excessively upon a successful outcome of this one particular set of negotiations. By the same token, each party should weigh the cost to itself of an excessive prolongation of the negotiations, which, in the final analysis, might fail anyway.

The relative bargaining position of the two parties changes over time. Generally, the foreign investor's bargaining strength is greatest before the investment is actually made—at the time of preinvestment negotiations with the host government. Once the investment has been made, the bargaining strength generally shifts to the advantage of the host country, since, once the facilities have already been constructed, it may well be within the abilities of the host country's nationals to manage without the help of the investor. (Figure 14.1 is a rough sketch of the changing position of the investor and the host country.) After the facilities have been completed, there may be a strong temptation for the host government to utilize its relatively stronger position to demand renegotiation of the investment contract to the government's advantage.

Since the host government has sovereign authority and since the government's relative strength increases once the investing company has committed its resources, the company needs to demonstrate that it continues to bring net advantages to the country. A continuing infusion

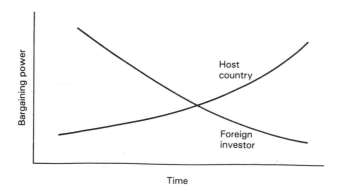

FIGURE 14.1   Relative Bargaining Power: A

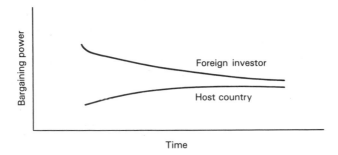

FIGURE 14.2   Relative Bargaining Power: B

of capital or technology and purchases from or sales to affiliated organizations abroad (that is, vertical integration) are excellent means to this end. This is especially effective if there are no other sources or customers for the subsidiary. Thus, the bargaining power of the company may remain above that of the country for extended periods. (See Figure 14.2.)

RENEGOTIATION

Under "normal" commercial relations, a contract between two parties is a legally binding agreement that will last until the end of the contract period. This is certainly the norm within the domestic experience of most companies. However, even under normal circumstances, it is not at all unusual for contracts to be retroactively renegotiated. This is sometimes done when the market conditions have shifted substantially against one of the parties to the contract. A buyer for example may be able to negotiate for extended delivery terms. Or a borrower may be able to renegotiate a fixed-term loan when interest rates have fallen. These situations are especially likely when the party in the more favorable position (i.e., the seller and the lender, respectively, in the examples above) is anxious to do more business with the other party in the future.

Investment contracts with a host government have the same binding relationship. However, the sovereign authority of the government, coupled with the tendency for governmental awareness and goals and even the groups in power to change over time, have produced a long history of governmental demands for retroactive changes in contracts. An *expropriation* is, of course, the ultimate in "renegotiation." However, there are many less extreme forms as well.

One of the most common causes of demands for renegotiations results from governmental perception that the foreign investment is no longer making significant marginal contributions to the host country; that is, the majority of the unique contributions of the foreign investor were made with the initial investment. What the government would like to see is an investment that continues to make marginal contributions over what a domestically owned company could do. In the absence of new oligopolistic advantages flowing to the country, many governments decide that the advantages are exceeded by the disadvantages the investment continues to impose upon the country, for example, a continuing drain upon the balance of payments in the form of outflows of profits, fees, and even capital. Companies in this situation are tempting expropriation targets.

Companies that tend to be able to maintain their welcome in a wide variety of host countries are those that continue to provide a unique contribution via continuing inflows of new technology such as in electronics or computers, via expanded local investments, or via providing continuing access to captive foreign markets.

ANTICIPATING PROBLEMS

Many companies can see "the handwriting on the wall" and plan for anticipated future difficulties with host governments. Some companies opt to avoid the issue by utilizing licensing rather than investment as their vehicle for penetrating the local market or for tapping the local resources. Another means involves purchase agreements whereby the local government or local company produces to the specification of the buyer. In Eastern Europe, for example, many arrangements have been made between Western companies and the governments of East European countries that involve the Western companies helping the governments to build a productive facility, often with the company's technology, equipment, and even capital. The Western company is subsequently compensated in the form of a share of the shipments of the goods that the factory manufactures. (This is called *buy-back,* a type of barter).

Divestment: In other instances, direct investment may still be the most attractive solution, despite the anticipation by the company of future difficulties with the host government. One approach a company can take (although it may be at the insistence of the host government) is to phase out all or part of its ownership either over a period of years or in one fell swoop. This is called *disinvestment* or simply *divestment.*

Many governments have introduced or can be expected to introduce "indigenization" programs: *Peru*vianization, *Nigeria*nization, *Malaysian*ization, and so forth.[4] These programs are designed to maximize the local control of the national economy and to maximize the perceived local benefits from the investment. Unfortunately, a shift to local control often results in a sharp decline in the overall benefits, although that

---

[4]See Glossary at the end of the book for a definition of *indigenization.*

may be acceptable from the local perspective because of psychological or political advantages. (For example, an agrarian reform program might require that a foreign-owned plantation be sold to local farmers. Very commonly, production will decline sharply under the new arrangement. Nevertheless, the distribution of the land might relieve local political pressures by peasants and might satisfy the nationalistic philosophy of government officials.)

Divestment does not need to be total nor does it need to involve sacrifice of control by the foreign investor. Many governments are primarily interested in an increase of the advantages to local groups but are aware of advantages that continued managerial control by the foreign investor can entail. As a result, these governments are not adverse to continued foreign control in some cases, even though local ownership may be mandated at 51 percent, 60 percent, or even more. Foreign control is, of course, easiest to maintain if the local share of the ownership is dispersed among many individuals.

One of the problems with divestment is that in many developing countries there may not be enough local capital in the private sector to buy the divested equity. As a result, the local government may be the only feasible partner, which may be exactly what the government was intending, even though the local divestment law may not mandate sale to the government. With the government as a partner, local ownership is, of course, very concentrated.

Divestment has often been forced upon foreign investors after the investment has been made. For example, Nigeria in the mid-1970s demanded that 60 percent of the ownership of all banks be sold to Nigerian nationals. Most of the foreign banks acquiesced.

More and more commonly, however, indigenization programs are already in force, including divestment requirements, *before* foreign investments are made. In these instances, although the investor may initially be able to hold 100 percent control, plans must be made *a priori* to divest some share or all of the ownership over a period of years.

Many foreign investors have strongly opposed any form of joint venture. This opposition is against either the formation of the joint venture at the time of the original investment or subsequently via divestment. However, shared ownership is becoming more and more common in international investments. Even developing countries that might have little to offer to the investment other than access to an attractive local market are increasingly inclined to demand some form of sharing.

Investment insurance: Because of the risks inherent in many foreign investments, investors are often anxious to find protection in the form of insurance or guarantees. This protection can come from either the private sector or from governmental agencies.

Governments typically limit their insurance and guarantee programs to the coverage of *new* investments *in developing countries;* thus, an American company could not obtain protection for an investment in France or even for uninsured outstanding investments in developing countries. The governments of most major industrialized countries, including the United States, the United Kingdom, France, Germany, and Japan have investment insurance agencies.

The American program is handled by the *Overseas Private Investment Corporation* (*OPIC*). OPIC provides the following two major types of assistance:

1.   insurance for the investor against three types of country risk
     a.   inconvertibility
     b.   expropriation
     c.   war, revolution, and insurrection
2.   loan guarantees for the lender

Insurance coverage is provided directly to the investor. The investor may choose to insure against any one or all three of the risks outlined above. The cost of the insurance varies for the type of coverage sought and sometimes also for the type of investment. Nevertheless, the insurance cost is relatively quite low; the vast majority of foreign investments by American companies that have been eligible for such protection are actually covered (at the option of the investor).

The loan guarantee program offers protection to the lender (a commercial bank or insurance company) that is interested in financing the project.

Arbitration of disputes: Despite all the various efforts that the investor and the host country might make in an effort to ensure a smooth relationship, irreconcilable differences sometimes arise. These differences can occur either when the two parties wish to continue working together (although relations often deteriorate to such an extent that this is not feasible) or in the event of an expropriation.

Contracts between an investor and a country typically specify exactly what the legal alternatives are in the event of a dispute. The local courts may be accepted by the company as having the appropriate jurisdiction. However, since the government is the sovereign authority in the country in which the investment is made, the local legal system is often considered by the investing company as not being sufficiently independent from governmental influences or as being philosophically biased against the company. Accordingly the investing company does not view it as the appropriate avenue for settling its disputes with the country. The country may accept the legal system of the investor's home country. However, a neutral jurisdiction noted for its efficiency and experience in disputes of this nature is commonly chosen. The British and the American courts are the most commonly chosen.

Because of the sovereign status of the country and the option of declaring *sovereign immunity* against prosecution for actions within its own borders, most contracts between an investor and country include a *waiver of sovereign immunity* by the government.

In addition to the use of private-sector legal channels, there are two multinational channels that might also be of assistance. In 1966 the World Bank created the *International Center for the Settlement of Investment Disputes* (ICSID) to provide a channel for binding arbitration between an investor and a host country. The host country must be a member of ICSID (only governments can belong). The International Center can be used only if both parties consent to the *binding* conclusions of the Center.

One final legal avenue is the *International Court of Justice* in the Hague in the Netherlands. Only governments can present cases to the International Court. Therefore, a company could only utilize this channel if its host government were willing to present its case.

Support from the home country's government: In extreme cases, such as the refusal of a host government to negotiate or in the case of outright confiscation, the government of the investing company's home country may take direct action against the host country. This is a very unfortunate situation. Private business problems thus become the basis for international diplomatic troubles.

Any investment is risky. A company will typically only make an investment that it thinks will be profitable. Many investments eventually turn out to be unprofitable, whether they are made domestically or abroad. Governments are wise to avoid involvement in such problems. Governments generally avoid the temptation to bail out individual domestic investments.

Governments do not, however, act as intelligently in international affairs when they allow the conflicts between their domestic companies and foreign governments to aggravate the home government's international diplomatic relations. A government has responsibilities that are far greater and more important than protecting individual (or even overall) international operations of its companies.

Fortunately the days of gunboat diplomacy seem to be behind us. However, international power politics are still very much with us. Only the weapons have been up-dated—they are now generally economic or political.

If a company has the right to earn an attractive profit in its foreign investments, it also has the "right" to absorb any losses from making the wrong investments. It would be ideal for governments to remain aloof from the international activities of their companies. However, in reality governments are willing to be involved especially if the investments are made in developing countries in support of governmental policy. Also, since other countries are doing the same thing to encourage and protect their own companies, competitive pressures between governments encourage them to offer comparable protection to their companies. It is not the ideal from the perspective of international diplomatic relations, but it is an excellent opportunity for companies, who should certainly consider the use of such protection.

SUMMARY

When companies expand overseas in coming years, they will hopefully do so with greater empathy and flexibility than in the past. Countries are changing, becoming more sophisticated, and demanding more from foreign investors. The countries are receiving better advice and will increasingly have the appropriately trained counselors to aid them when negotiating with foreign firms.

Foreign investment remains a positive-sum game, and both parties can share the gains. Furthermore, the oil crisis has illustrated that in some instances the size of the gains can be changed by these negotiations. However, distribution of the gains will be significantly affected by the bargaining power and skill of the two sides.

The relationship between the MNC and the host country takes many forms. In some instances countries insist upon total ownership while sharing the development and financing with the firm; payment is often a share of production. Other governments are only willing to hire companies via a performance contract. But most commonly perhaps, many investments are made that must be divested (partially or completely) over a span of years. Investors are going to need to accustom themselves to substantially less control than in the past.

In many respects, although each side should gain, the relationship between the country and the multinational firm is like a bridge or poker game. There will be bidding, betting, finessing, and bluffing. The successful player needs to be able to objectively evaluate not only its own strengths and weaknesses but also those of the opponent. The more monopolistic or oligopolistic assets the firm has that are needed by the country, the more likely the company will be able to make a profitable investment and avoid expropriation. Conversely, the more assets the country has that are needed by the investor, the stronger that party's bargaining position and the more likely it will be for the country to attract foreign investments on terms favorable to the country.

In the extreme, the country can always nationalize the firm's investment, hopefully with compensation. However, the forward-looking company is the one that will be most able to live and profit in the coming decades. The MNC can avoid or minimize many potential complaints by understanding the position of the host country.

KEY TERMS

ARBITRATION

AUTARKY

CLOSED ECONOMY

CODE OF CONDUCT

DIVESTMENT

EXPROPRIATION

INDIGINIZATION

INTERNATIONAL CENTER
   FOR THE SETTLEMENT
   OF INVESTMENT
   DISPUTES (ICSID)

INTERNATIONAL COURT
   OF JUSTICE

LOCAL-CONTENT
   REQUIREMENT

JOINT VENTURE

OPEN ECONOMY

OVERSEAS PRIVATE
   INVESTMENT
   CORPORATION (OPIC)

SOVEREIGN IMMUNITY

SOVEREIGNTY

VERTICAL INTEGRATION

REVIEW QUESTIONS

1. What is an open economy? Is it wise for a developing country to have an open economy?

2. What would be the results of a developing country's decision to develop internally without outside assistance?

3. What would be the impact, if any, upon the United States if it attempted to cut off its international trade and capital flows? Does it need outside assistance?

4. What is sovereignty? What is sovereign immunity?

5. What are three major categories of risk for a host country in accepting FDI?

6. Discuss how the following affect the investor's degree of risk:
   a. extent of the vertical integration of the investment with the rest of the company
   b. essentiality of the investment to the host country
   c. industry of the investment
   d. means by which the project is financed

7. What are codes of conduct? How do they affect foreign investors?

8. What is expropriation?

9. What is divestment? Do you think that divestment is a wise part of a company's FDI policy?

SUGGESTED REFERENCES

BALL, GEORGE   *Global Companies.* Englewood Cliffs, N.J.: Prentice-Hall, Inc., 1975.

BARANSON, JACK   *Technology and the Multinationals: Corporate Strategies in a Changing World Economy.* Lexington, Mass.: Lexington Books, 1978.

BARNET, RICHARD, AND RONALD MULLER   *Global Reach, the Power of Multinational Corporations.* New York: Simon & Schuster, Inc., 1974.

BASSIRY, R.   *Power vs. Profit: Multinational Corporation–Nation State Interaction.* New York: Arno, 1980.

BEHRMAN, JACK   *National Interests and the Multinational Enterprise.* Englewood Cliffs, N.J.: Prentice-Hall, Inc., 1970.

————*U.S. International Business and Governments.* New York: McGraw-Hill Book Company, 1971.

BERGSTEN, C. FRED ET AL.   *American Multinationals and American Interests.* Washington, D.C.: The Brookings Institution, 1978.

BLAKE, DAVID, ed.   "Multinational Corporation," *The Annuals,* September 1972.

BUSINESS INTERNATIONAL CORPORATION   *Effects of U.S. Corporate Investment Abroad.* 1974.

DRUCKER, PETER F.   "Multinationals and Developing Countries: Myths and Realities," *Foreign Affairs,* October 1974, pp. 121–34.

FATEMI, NASROLLAH, GAIL WILLIAMS, AND THIBAUT DE SAINTE-PHALLE   *Multinational Corporations* (2nd ed.), San Diego: A.S. Barnes & Co., 1976.

GUISINGER, STEPHEN   *Private Enterprise and the New Global Economic Challenge.* Indianapolis: The Bobbs-Merrill Co., Inc., 1979.

HAWKINS, ROBERT, ed.   *Economic Effects of Multinational Corporations.* Greenwich, Conn.: Jai Press, 1979.

HOOD, NEIL, AND STEPHEN YOUNG   *The Economics of Multinational Enterprise.* London: Longman, 1979.

JACKSON, RICHARD A., ed.   *The Multinational Corporation and Social Policy: Special Reference to General Motors in South Africa.* New York: Praeger Publishers, 1974.

LOWENFELD, ANDREAS, ed.   *Expropriation in the Americas: A Comparative Law Study.* New York: Dunellen Company, 1971.

MORGAN, ALAN, AND ROGER BLANPAIN   *Industrial Relations and the Employment Impacts of Multinational Enterprises.* Paris: Organization of Economic Cooperation and Development.

ORGANIZATION OF ECONOMIC COOPERATION AND DEVELOPMENT   *Investing in Developing Countries.* Paris, France.

RAVEED, SION   *Joint Ventures Between U.S. Multinational Firms and Host Governments in Selected Developing Countries.* New York: Arno, 1980.

ROBINSON, RICHARD *National Control of Foreign Business Entry.* New York: Praeger Publishers, 1976.

SAUVANT, KARL, AND FARID LAVIPOUR *Controlling Multinational Enterprises.* Boulder, Colo.: Westview, 1976.

TAVIS, LEE, ed. *Multinational Managers and Poverty in the Third World.* South Bend, Ind.: University of Notre Dame Press, 1982.

TRUITT, J. FREDERICK *Expropriation of Private Foreign Investment.* Ann Arbor, Mich.: University Microfilms, 1969.

UNITED NATIONS *Transnational Corporations in World Development: A Re-examination,* New York, 1978.

U.S. DEPARTMENT OF COMMERCE *Foreign Direct Investment in United States,* 1976.

U.S. DEPARTMENT OF COMMERCE *Multinational Corporation,* 1972.

U.S. TARIFF COMMISSION *Implications of Multinational Firms for World Trade and Investment and for U.S. Trade and Labor,* 1973.

VERNON, RAYMOND *Storm Over the Multinationals,* Cambridge, Mass.: Harvard University Press, 1977.

15

Organization of International Operations

The international activities of a company expose it to many new opportunities but also simultaneously to new difficulties and potential troubles. Careful planning together with appropriate systems of organization and control can help the company to best take advantage of the opportunities, to minimize the difficulties, and to head off or to respond to the problems.

The optimal approach for attaining these ends is a function of the nature, extent, and location of the company's international activities. It also depends upon the stage of internationalization in which a company finds itself. Companies seldom spring into well-organized international companies all at once. The vast majority move through a series of evolutionary stages. This chapter examines the various types of international business activities in which a company may be involved internationally, the evolutionary process of internationalization of companies, and the organizational structures by which the companies attempt to control those international activities.

VARIETIES OF INTERNATIONAL ACTIVITIES

There are a wide variety of different types of international activities in which companies engage. The more complicated companies can be engaged in an extensive variety of these different business activities simultaneously. Three categories of international activity are foreign trade, foreign managerial or technical assistance, and foreign production.

FOREIGN TRADE

The simplest form of international business activity involves the myriad forms of exporting or importing. Whether it is merchandise or a service that the company is trading, the essence of this form of international business is that the good or service is sold in a different country from that in which it was produced. Thus, domestic production is exported and foreign production is imported. The most common type of transaction involves *merchandise,* for example, U.S. grain, computers, or aircraft; Japanese automobiles and electronic goods; German machine tools and chemicals; Brazilian coffee, soy beans, and iron ore.

The international trade of *services* is also vitally important, for example, banking and insurance services, licensing of technology, franchising, and so forth. As was seen in Chapter 7, commercial banks export many services to companies, governments, or banks in other countries. (In Chapter 16 those banking services that help to facilitate international trade are examined in further detail.) Also, a company such as Coca-Cola franchises the production of its beverages in foreign markets and licenses its trademarks, such as Coke.

FOREIGN MANAGERIAL AND TECHNICAL ASSISTANCE

International trade in goods and services is the oldest and probably best known of the major categories of international corporate activities. A less well-known, but nevertheless very important and rapidly growing international business activity is the provision of *advisory services* in foreign countries. Unlike international trade, which involves the international sale of domestically produced goods or services, international managerial and technical assistance is a service that is produced in a foreign country in offices, factories, or mines.

This field of international business is becoming much more prominent as countries seek to control more and more of their own economic destiny (as was seen in the previous chapter). Since most developing countries do not have sufficient expertise in many technological and managerial areas, in mineral exploration and development, in negotiation with foreign companies, and so forth, they are increasingly attracted to the availability of a growing cadre of specialists who are available to assist them.

This renting of expertise is analogous to the domestic situation where many companies hire outside specialists on contracts to come into the company to help to run computers, to do productivity studies, to negotiate for the company, or to clean the company's buildings. In each of these cases, the providers of the specialist services take their services to wherever the work is needed by the client rather than delivering a finished product to the buyer.

Some examples of managerial and/or technical contracts that are commonly purchased internationally are engineering studies, oil well drilling, turnkey construction contracts, and negotiations with foreign companies. When the degree of expertise needed, the immediacy of the task, or the short duration of the project dictate the need to hire individuals from outside the company (or government), then the use of temporary outside assistance can be very attractive, if not mandatory. For example, as was seen in the last chapter, when the governments of host countries are in the process of negotiating with potential foreign investors, it is highly desirable that they have available on their behalf very highly qualified specialists to advise them in areas such as the technical aspects of the proposed project and the proposed relationship between the government and the investing company.

FOREIGN PRODUCTION

The third basic type of international business activity is the production of goods and/or services in a company's own facilities in a foreign country. Such production is often virtually the same as the company's domestic production, except that it is carried out in a foreign country, is subject to the laws of that country, and utilizes locally available resources.

Among services that are produced and sold abroad are banking, stock brokerage, and accounting. A special category of service is that which is provided by retailers (for example, Sears Roebuck). Manufacturers can produce almost any type of product in foreign countries; indeed, they sometimes produce products that they might find it difficult to produce back home, for legal reasons such as environmental regulations or for economic reasons such as restrictive labor practices. Another category of foreign producers are the natural resource producers. These include such activities as mining, pumping, farming, lumbering, fishing, and so forth.

The market served: The production of goods and services overseas can be to satisfy the needs of any customer. It may be for a foreign local market (for instance, Michelin, the French tire giant, produces tires in the United States to sell in the U.S. market), for a market in the home country (for example, a television producer that exports from its production facilities in Taiwan back to its domestic market), or for a market in a third country (for example, U.S. oil companies that ship crude oil from their Middle Eastern concessions to their European operations). As seen in the last chapter, the export of some or all of such production may be mandated by the host country's government.

THE INTERNATIONAL CORPORATE EVOLUTION

For most companies, the expansion and increase in sophistication of their international activities are evolutionary processes. There are, of course, unique cases of companies that aggressively plunge into foreign manufacturing without a gradual buildup in their international expertise; this can most readily be accomplished if a company enters into a joint venture with an experienced partner. For most companies, however, the internationalization process is one of steps.

In a very large, diversified economy, such as that of the United States, a company may become very large domestically before becoming extensively involved in international operations. In smaller countries, a company is much more likely to become involved internationally at a much earlier stage of corporate expansion. In either case, however, the internationalization process normally evolves through several steps.

THE PATTERN OF CORPORATE EVOLUTION

Corporations follow a variety of paths in their growth processes. To a large extent the pattern is a function of the nature of the company's business. Some companies immediately aim for national (and sometimes even international) markets. Thus, Apple Computer never viewed only California as its basic market. Instead, its founders realized that they had to aim for a much broader market from the very beginning. However, such companies are a distinct minority.

Most companies begin as local companies before they ever expand to wider markets. This is true of strictly domestic companies as well as multinational companies. For example, even the Ford Motor Company originally developed as a local company in Detroit. Only later did its sales spread to wide areas of the state. It was even later that the company began to "export" heavily to other states such as Ohio and eventually to the entire nation. Initially this production was almost entirely based in the Detroit area. It was only later that output expanded to other states ("foreign investment"). Thus, slowly, the rapidly growing company expanded from a local to a regional to a national company.

Some companies are, of course, created for the primary purpose of serving an international market. For example, the author once was co-owner of a small import firm; the entire orientation of the firm from its very inception was toward the international business sphere. Also, U.S.

commercial banks often create special subsidiaries in the United States, whose operations are limited by law to certain types of international banking. Similarly, many companies in the United States set up Domestic International Sales Corporations (DISCs) as export vehicles for their products. However, most companies evolve into the international arena in a pattern similar to that in which the Ford Motor Company expanded domestically. Indeed, Ford continued to evolve from a local to a regional to a national and then to an international company in a rather continuous progression.

Initially, just as with its penetration of markets outside the Detroit area, Ford first entered foreign markets via export and then via foreign production. Although the American automobile industry has not fared very well in the international-trade field in recent generations, it has not always been thus. For example, in the 1920s the American automobile industry enjoyed a healthy export surplus in its trade with the rest of the world. This success was followed by foreign production. Ford had assembly plants in the United Kingdom, Germany, Brazil, and Argentina even before World War I.

ORGANIZATIONAL STRUCTURE

There are a variety of different ways in which companies can organize themselves for greatest efficiency. The specific format chosen is a function of many things: the industry of the company; the philosophy, experience, and personal preferences of senior management; legal constraints; the stage of the company's evolution; and so forth. This section examines the major varieties of organizational formats.[1]

International organizational structure is essentially patterned after its domestic cousin. There are basically four formats depending upon the organizational focus chosen by the company. These basic formats are (1) *product orientation,* (2) *functional orientation,* (3) *geographical orientation,* and (4) *customer orientation.* The opportunity to choose between these various alternatives allows the company to utilize to the company's advantage the differences in focus and strengths of the four alternatives. However, it also exposes the company to inherent weaknesses in each particular structure. A fifth format, which is a hybrid combination of at least two of these basic formats, also exists. This *matrix structure* or grid, however, is also no panacea and has its own shortcomings. Thus, the choice of organizational structure is something that companies, domestic or international, should not take casually.

---

[1] If the reader is interested in pursuing this topic of international organizational structure in greater detail, an excellent discussion can be found in Richard D. Robinson, *International Business Management,* 2nd ed. (Hinsdale, IL: Dryden Press, 1978), pp. 643–84.

The following sections examine each of these formats briefly together with a discussion of essential international adaptations. However, first we examine the very simplest forms of international organizational structure—*appendages* that are attached to the domestic product, functional, geographical, customer, or matrix structure.

INTERNATIONAL APPENDAGES TO THE BASIC ORGANIZATIONAL STRUCTURE

The simplest type of international organizational structure makes no formal adjustment for the international activities of the firm. Companies that choose this approach are typically in the first or second degree of internationalization.[2] In this instance, the international business of the firm is handled by each division or group of the company independently of all the other international efforts of the company. The organizational structure of this firm could take the form of any of the basic formats mentioned above—with each product, functional, geographical, customer, or matrix group handling responsibility for the international needs of its own divisions.

The obvious disadvantages of this approach are that the international activities of the company are likely to be disjointed and probably will not grow as rapidly or with as high a profit potential as would be possible with a more coordinated effort. Under this approach some divisions are likely to ignore the international opportunities altogether. As seen in earlier chapters, the many aspects of international business that are very different from domestic business often serve to deter corporate managers who are unfamiliar with and overwhelmed by the unknown elements of international business. The existence of such "managerial barriers" makes a concerted effort to tap these markets very unlikely in such units.

The international department, division, or subsidiary: In order to overcome the disadvantages of the noncoordinated approach discussed above, a very common option is for a company to set up a separate unit to develop and coordinate the company's international efforts. Initially such a unit may be only a department. Later it may tend to evolve into a division or subsidiary. Figure 15.1 shows an international division attached to a product structure; it can just as readily be attached to a functional, customer, or geographical structure.

Companies in the second and third degrees of internationalization are common users of this form of organization. It provides for a concentration of international expertise on the task of optimizing the company's international opportunities and problems. As such, it is a distinct

---

[2]Refer back to chapter 1.

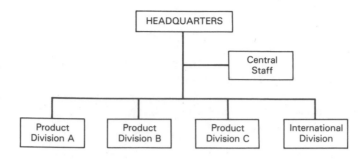

FIGURE 15.1   International Division Structure

improvement over organizational formats that make no specific allowance for concentrating international business efforts. However, the company utilizing this form of structure is still basically a domestically
oriented company in most cases. The international division must compete with the other divisions of the company for the resources that it
needs. Since the managers of these other divisions are typically very
familiar with the domestic markets and may be required to make product modifications to serve the international markets, they are sometimes
reluctant to provide adequate service to the international division. The
latter suffers from having to rely upon units of the company that are
basically domestically oriented. In short, it commonly lacks a sufficiently
strong power base.

     An international division or subsidiary has a number of distinctive
advantages over a structure that involves dispersed international efforts
in different parts of the same company or simply an international
department. By concentrating all international activities under a single
group, economies of scale can be realized. By grouping the company's
international skills, knowledge, and interests in one area, the international activities and personnel of the company may produce the most
efficient efforts. In the absence of such concentration, independent efforts in disparate units may well have a minimal effect. However, with a
unified group headed by a senior officer, the company is likely to pay
more attention to its international activities. When the senior management of the company has not yet developed a strong commitment to the
internationalization of the company, this unified effort is especially
important as a means of helping to educate the company's management
and in producing noticeable and favorable initial international performance.

     The international division, or even the international subsidiary, is
not always the optimal solution to a company's international structural
problems. In many cases, this form of organization has distinctive draw-

backs. Foremost among these is the fact that the international division often relies heavily upon domestically oriented divisions, especially production but also different portions of the corporate staff. If these ties are not maintained efficiently, the international operation may find itself shortchanged and therefore rendered less efficient. Thus, the international division may be treated as a poor cousin. This tends to be the greatest problem in those early stages of second-degree internationalization when most corporate managers are not strong supporters (and perhaps are even active opponents) of the company's international operations.

GLOBAL ORGANIZATIONAL STRUCTURES

As companies expand or plan to expand further, the international department, division, or subsidiary structure may prove to be unsatisfactory. Any of four basic corporate organizational structures plus the combination of two or more of them in a matrix can be utilized. The following five sections discuss these global structures. These structures, without the international orientation, are the basic structures of domestic companies as well.

When a company's international activities attain a status within the company that the corporate management views to be at least as important as domestic activities, then the company should seek an organizational format that better serves the need of the company than does the international division. This stage of evolution of the company does not require that the international sales, production, or purchases of the company actually need to be greater than or equal to the company's domestic sales. What is required is that the corporate management *perceives* that the international side of its operations is or will likely become as important as the domestic. Thus, it can be a response to either the existing facts of corporate activity or the corporate plans for the future. Managerial perspective is the measure—not percentages of sales, profits, or assets.

Corporate reorganization is always a complicated and traumatic step for any company. Therefore, it should not be undertaken casually. The costs, both financial and for the personnel of the company, should be carefully considered. However, if properly planned and executed, a reorganization can bring a significant improvement in efficiency to the company once the transition period is past.

Among the primary advantages to the company from reorganization into a global organizational structure are the reduction or avoidance of the diseconomies that often occur with the international division from the failure of domestically oriented divisions to adequately support the international activities of the company. Global structures can also enable the company to be better prepared to take advantage of international opportunities when they arise. This results from the ability of the company to concentrate any and all of its specialized resources on a particular opportunity or problem. The global structure is also a good mechanism for training managers who will later rise to senior positions at headquarters. More and more companies are not only ensuring that such experience is gained by promising executives but are also arranging that part of such executives' training should be overseas.

Product orientation: The organizational format that is based upon major product groups is illustrated in Figure 15.2. For example, such groups could be cars, trucks, buses, and farm equipment for a major motor vehicle manufacturer. Although there is a corporate central staff needed to provide companywide expertise and to provide some degree of assistance to each product group, each group also has its own functional staff (for example, marketing, finance, and so forth). This structure focuses upon and optimizes the company's production strengths. However, the decentralization of nonproduction functions such as marketing and finance tends to result in duplication and inefficiency in those fields.

The international activities of the company with this product-oriented structure are distributed between the various product divisions. The significance of the international activities can still vary substantially between divisions: Some of the company's products may be more amenable to export or import markets than others, or the management of some divisions may simply have more international experience than do managers in other divisions.

The product structure is best suited for companies with very diverse product lines; with this form of organizational format the company is placing principal emphasis upon coordination within groups rather than among groups. This diversity is accentuated for companies whose diverse products are marketed to very different end-users and through

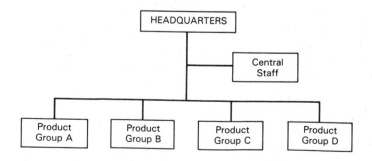

FIGURE 15.2   The Product-Oriented Organizational Structure

very different distributional channels (divergences that are magnified internationally). The more varied the company's products, end-users, and distribution channels, the more attractive this type of structure becomes. However, for companies with compatible product lines, end-users, and channels, other organizational structures are more appropriate.

The product-oriented structure typically tends to require a fairly high degree of managerial decentralization. Product-group managers need to be able to function autonomously, and central management must be willing to permit this. One of the most promising aspects of this autonomy involves the planning of new products for different markets. Thus, managers in this type of structure are truly product specialists on a worldwide basis.

A major drawback to the product structure stems from the failure of the various product divisions to coordinate their efforts even when they are operating in the same country. Such a failure can lead to excessive duplication of staff in foreign markets and often confusion among customers. Within a particular country it could well be feasible to coordinate some of its efforts across divisional lines, especially in the creation of specialized staff such as legal, accounting, financial, and so forth. However, the effective implementation of such coordination is commonly elusive under the product-oriented structure.

Other potential problems from the product structure include a tendency toward excessive independence by product-group managers with the accompanying problems of control and communication for corporate management. Also, there is a common tendency toward provincial thinking by product-group managers who are excessively oriented toward the welfare of their own division rather than that of the company as a whole.

Examples of companies that utilize the global product structure include Pan American World Airways and Westinghouse.

Functional orientation: Figure 15.3 illustrates the organizational format that emphasizes the various corporate functions rather than simply product as in Figure 15.2. For example, the functions could be manufacturing, marketing, finance, and research and development. This structure does indeed allow for the development of highly specialized cadres of experts. However, coordination among the different functions can be a serious problem. Corporate central staff is oriented more toward helping to integrate the various functions than to providing additional expertise, since there is already a concentration of such strengths in these various functional areas.

The manufacturing function is sometimes subdivided into major

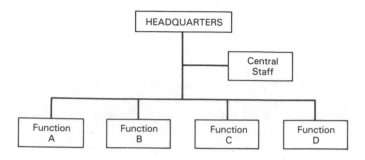

FIGURE 15.3   The Function-Oriented Organizational Structure

manufacturing processes.[3] This structure is called a *process-oriented structure*. However, it is really a special case of the functional-oriented organizational format.

Within the functional framework, all the company's functional operations (such as finance, production, marketing, personnel, and research and development) throughout the world would be concentrated in one sector of the company. An example of a company with this type of organizational structure is the Ford Motor Company. It is also very common among large European companies.

This form of organization can work well for companies with a relatively narrow range of products. Economies of scale are gained within each functional area. Duplication of specialties is kept to a minimum with the consequent savings in manpower.

The disadvantages of this type of global structure include the need to duplicate the regional specialists, the failure of such specialists to coordinate their efforts, the separation of the manufacturing and marketing operations, and the natural tendency for managers to have too narrow a perspective in emphasizing their own functions rather than the overall welfare of the company.

Geographical orientation: The third basic organizational format is based upon a geographical orientation, either the geographical location of customers or of the company's productive facilities. As shown in Figure 15.4, the company is organized around regions rather than products or functions. In the domestic U.S. corporation, such a format might be divided into groups for the Northeast, the South, the Midwest, and the West. In the United Kingdom, such a format might provide different groups for Southern and Northern England, Wales, Scotland, and Northern Ireland.

---

[3]For example, see Robinson, *International Business.*

With the geographical form of organization of the multinational company, the domestic operations of the firm are just one (or only a part of one) of a group of geographically distinctive subsidiaries. Under this scenario, the United States could be either a separate geographical subsidiary or part of a North American, North American/Caribbean, or even Western Hemisphere subsidiary. For multinational companies whose home market is small relative to its international markets (for example, Dutch and Belgian companies), treating the domestic home market as only part of a larger regional market is fairly common. When the domestic home market is very large, such as for U.S. and Japanese companies, it is more common to separate the home market as a separate unit.

The geographical-oriented corporate structure places greatest emphasis upon coordinating regional productive or marketing efforts. However, it has a major difficulty of trying to coordinate different geographical areas, and the dispersion of product and functional efforts may be less than optimal in many companies. Corporate central staff serves a coordinating function, but this task is often difficult to accomplish successfully.

Under this form of organization, most or all of the corporation's activities relating to any good or service that is bought, sold, or produced within a region, are under the control of the regional group head. Each of the geographical regions is a separate profit center.

Such an organizational format works well for companies with a narrow range of products, markets, and distribution channels. It is also attractive if the particular product requires localization in order to be attractive in the local markets in which it is sold. Oil companies and major money-center banks are examples of industries in which this form of corporate organizational structure is popular.

Advantages of the geographical-oriented format center around the

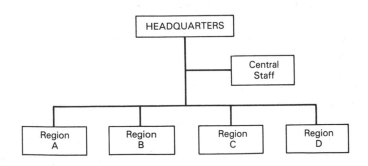

FIGURE 15.4 The Geographical-Oriented Organizational Structure

fact that a concentration of all a company's regional assets into one group offers an economy of scale and concentrated efficiency that permits a coordinated effort to develop in that particular market. All of the various functional specialists can gain synergistic advantages from working with others who specialize in the same geographical area.

This particular form of organization does not generally work well for companies with diverse products, markets, and marketing channels. For such companies, the effort to gain efficiency geographically is generally offset by significant diseconomies in functional and production terms. Such factors as production, development, and marketing on a worldwide basis are disturbed by the artificial geographical organization.

There are special personnel problems with this type of organization. There is the need to duplicate specialists in the different divisions, since such services are not centralized in the geographically structured company. In addition there is the need for a large cadre of internationally experienced executives capable of living and operating comfortably in a variety of foreign cultures and political and economic systems. Another disadvantage of this system is that the geographical orientation tends to give the managers in such groups a geographical rather than a company-wide perspective.

Customer orientation: One of the bases for designing a corporate organization along geographical lines is the location of customers. This serves as a useful criteria when a particular group of customers can be clearly identified with a specific geographical area, such as the consumer market in a particular country. However, when the customer base involves companies with many operations in many parts of the world, then this format is not satisfactory. Therefore some companies organize according to the types of customers they wish to serve rather than the locations of customers (see Figure 15.5). For example, commercial banks

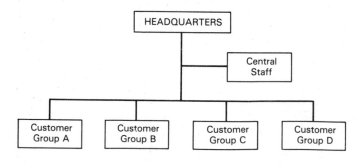

FIGURE 15.5   The Customer-Oriented Organizational Structure

are commonly organized into groups such as the personal, corporate, mortgage, and trust departments. Alternatively, corporations might be divided into industrial, commercial, and governmental divisions according to the nature of the major customers of that group.

This fourth type of basic global structure is commonly overlooked in discussions of international (and even domestic) corporate structure. Under this format the company is divided to provide service for various groups of customers wherever their business activities may take them. Like the geographical structure, each group may have the capacity to produce and market a full range of the company's goods or services; but like the functional or product structures, the groups are organized on a worldwide basis.

Major advantages of this approach are the avoidance of duplication of efforts and consequent confusion and inefficiency both within the company and with the customer. For example, a major international bank such as Continental National Bank of Illinois has certain domestic customers who are not engaged in business anywhere except in the United States (although this could include exporting or importing to the extent described above as first-degree internationalization). These customers would be serviced by the Domestic Group.

Since Continental is a major international bank with many foreign offices, the bank also services local companies overseas (that is, the foreign domestic market). These customers are serviced by the Foreign Group.

There are additional very important customers of the bank that it services both at home in the United States and in many of its overseas facilities as well. This creates the possibility of duplication and conflicting and wasteful efforts. In order to avoid this, the Multinational Group exists. Within this group all the company's relations with the customers are controlled on a worldwide basis.

This form of structure obviously places greatest stress upon the customer and can indeed provide the most specialized and perhaps personalized service. However, it also tends to require duplication of skills in each group and a separation between such specialists in the different groups, which prevents them from developing as strongly as they might otherwise do. Again, corporate central staff can reduce some of these disadvantages but can never totally overcome them.

A structural hybrid—the matrix or grid: There are advantages to each of the organizational formats described above. However, none of them is ideal for all companies. That is, of course, why so many different formats have been developed by different companies to serve their different needs. Indeed, it is probably safe to say that all these formats have drawbacks for most or even all the companies that have adopted them. Nevertheless, most companies settle upon one basic format as the most satisfactory structure overall for that company's needs at a given point in its evolutionary growth—or create a combination of two types.

Since each of these structural forms has its own drawbacks, it is not surprising that efforts have been made to integrate two or more of these into a structure that attempts to combine the best characteristics of each while avoiding the major disadvantages of each. The result, commonly called either a *matrix* or a *grid,* is structurally much more complicated than the relatively simple formats that were examined above. Furthermore, these efforts toward integration are still somewhat rudimentary; few companies have implemented such structures yet. Figure 15.6 is an example in which the company attempts to integrate both product and

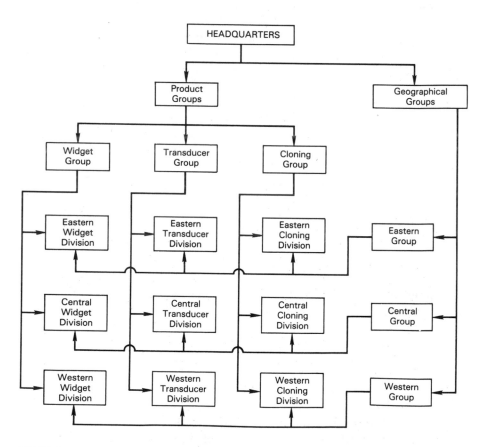

FIGURE 15.6   A Geographical-Product Matrix

geographical dimensions into one matrix structure. Several additional combinations of the four basic structures are also obviously possible.

In theory the matrix structure seeks to create collegiality among managers stemming from a combination of a power balance and a sharing of responsibility. This experience, relationship, and interdependence should ideally lead to broader, less parochial points of view—a companywide perspective that tends to measure recommendations and decisions by their impact upon the entire company and not just upon one particular division or group.

A major hurdle to widespread adoption of the matrix structure is that it is such a radical departure from the traditional formats discussed above. Each of the above, whether based upon product, function, geography, or customer, is structurally simple. One of the principal appeals of the structures noted above is that they clearly delineate lines of authority and communication. Each individual in the structure has only one boss. However, in a matrix structure many managers might have at least two different supervisors. This can be very confusing and disruptive. For example, in Figure 15.6, the different geographical-product groups (for instance, the Eastern Cloning Division) are responsible to both a regional group head (that is, the Eastern Group) and a product-group head (the Cloning Group). This duality poses many potential problems for the effective management of a company.

For many individual companies there is no optimal structure. However, some structures are more appropriate and efficient than others. Therefore, the search for a structure that is best for a particular company at a particular stage of its history, with the current management and under existing laws, is not only desirable but vital.

As noted above, the company with international operations may need to modify its organizational structure from that of the solely domestic company. These modifications are described in the next section. They are based upon the domestic formats but with the addition of some new wrinkles.

FACTORS AFFECTING THE CHOICE OF ORGANIZATIONAL STRUCTURE

With a variety of basic organizational arrangements from which to choose, what determines the format a company might choose? There are many factors that can affect this choice—factors stemming from within the company and from its environment. Also, it should be remembered that the appropriate organizational structure is not permanent: What is most appropriate today may not be the ideal in ten or even five years. Some companies change their organizational structure with bewildering (and one is tempted to say, inefficient, and costly) frequency.

CORPORATE FACTORS AFFECTING
INTERNATIONAL ORGANIZATIONAL STRUCTURE

There are many factors within the company and the markets that it chooses to serve that help guide it in choosing the appropriate structure. Thse guidelines stem from both constraining factors and opportunity factors, including considerations such as the company's strategies, size, international expertise, the risk involved, the importance of the foreign venture(s), and the overall cost-benefit analysis of the foreign operations.

Corporate strategies: A company needs to have very carefully delineated goals for its worldwide operations. However, not all companies have such clearly identified goals. The failure of a company to set these goals can be a very costly oversight, since in the absence of such guidelines the company may well stumble into ventures that it will later regret and that might prove to be very expensive.

A company's strategies dictate the manner in which a company approaches its foreign (as well as domestic) investments. Perhaps the company is satisfied to simply "follow the flag" by chasing its existing customers as they move abroad. For example, the suppliers of auto parts and major service companies, such as banks, advertising agencies, and accounting firms, followed the major U.S. auto companies abroad. Obviously, this strategy would dictate where and how the former might expand.

Perhaps the company wishes to do all its production from its home base, with foreign operations being limited to marketing. Does the company insist upon tight central controls for all its foreign operations? If production quality and patents or unpatented technological processes are involved, then the company will tend to seek an organizational structure that provides tight controls on its foreign operations. IBM is a classic example of a company demanding such tight controls.

Time horizon of the venture: If the company envisions that its international ventures represent a permanent commitment on the part of the company, then the organizational structure should rightly reflect this perspective. However, if the company is primarily envisioning temporary or other short-term ventures (such as turnkey construction contracts or limited-horizon management or technological assistance contracts), then a permanent organizational structure should not be designed.

Size of the company's international versus domestic operations: As noted, when a company is initially getting involved internationally, it typically evolves through a series of steps. As a result, the early organizational structure of companies is commonly of the international department or division format. When the scale of the international activities has grown relatively important, a more global organizational structure becomes attractive. There are, however, companies that have growth goals that are clear from the beginning; these companies may choose an internationally flexible structure (for example, a functional structure) at an early stage of its evolution.

Risk: Risk is always associated with any investment. International investments may expose companies to a greater variety or at least a very different variety of risk than that to which the company is accustomed. Risk can often be either insured, guaranteed, or shared. However, the existence of extra risk may well dictate, at least from the perspective of the investing company's management, a high degree of control of the foreign operations.

An added factor is the attitude toward risk taking of the management. Risk-taking managers are less disturbed with the scale of risk than managers who are chronic risk avoiders. On the other hand, risk-averse companies usually seek an organizational format that will reduce undue risk.

The company's resources: The company's weaknesses and strengths are critical in determining not only what investments to make and where to make them but also how to make them. If a company already has extensive international business experience, it may be prepared to plunge ahead into a new venture. The company requires other resources such as capital and managerial expertise to be able to unilaterally make the investment. For companies without the required capital, expertise, or confidence, a logical alternative may be a *joint venture.* Finding a partner (or partners) to complement the company's strengths and offset its weaknesses can be an excellent approach to entering into foreign ventures. Many companies begin this way and, after "learning the ropes," are later prepared to venture abroad on their own. In some cases one partner will buy out the other partner, so that the joint venture reverts to a wholly owned operation.

In the past, many companies have been very reluctant to enter into joint ventures. There can be many disadvantages, primarily stemming from conflicts over control and goals. However, a joint venture can be very successful. It can be critical in sharing risk and great investment expense, such as are typical of large mining projects. Also, in a growing number of countries joint ventures with local investors, either private-sector or government, are mandated by the government in order for the investment to be permitted.

Joint ventures are becoming increasingly common in the arena of international investments. Companies that would not have even considered them at one time are accepting them as normal and even desirable in some instances.

Importance of the investment: Many investment projects are optional for a company: If the investment does not occur, the company would still prosper, although perhaps not to the extent or in the fashion desired. It may then be necessary for the company to retrench, reinvest, or set off in new (or old) directions.

Many other investment projects may be critical for a company. In these instances the company is much more exposed. It will also probably be much less flexible. It certainly is likely to be more susceptible to the application of pressure, either imposed by markets or governments. When a project is critical to a company—for example, as it is in the case of a company that needs to integrate vertically into raw material resource production, such as a copper company, or into a vitally important manufacturing component, such as semiconductors—then this urgency is likely to be reflected in an organizational structure in which the venture is pivotal.

Nature of the product and foreign operations: Relatively simple products and foreign operations can be readily managed with several different organizational forms. However, if the productive process, the product itself, the end-use market, and/or the distribution channels are complicated, then the company needs to seek an organizational format to alleviate potential problems in these areas. For example, a complicated production process might suggest the desirability of a product-oriented structure. Similarly, wide variance in distribution channels and end-users might benefit most from a customer-oriented format.

Location of the foreign operation: Proximity can be measured in several ways. Obviously, geographical proximity is very important: If the foreign operations and markets are close to the company's home market, then great latitude in organizational format is possible. For example, the Canadian or Mexican markets are near to American firms and French, Belgian, and German markets are close to Dutch firms.

Cultural and linguistic proximity is also important. Thus exporting companies marketing British products in Canada or Australia, and Chinese or Mexican products among the Chinese and Mexican ethnic communities in the United States can probably readily adapt to the end-user without need for major structural reorganizations.

ENVIRONMENTAL FACTORS AFFECTING INTERNATIONAL ORGANIZATIONAL STRUCTURE

It is not only the company and its markets that help direct a company in its efforts to choose an appropriate organizational structure. There are also factors in the company's environment that affect the appropriate choice of structure.

Laws and other governmental influence: The demands of a host government or even of the home government can sometimes impose severe constraints upon or open up attractive options affecting the organizational flexibility of a company. For example, a host government's insistence upon the use of a joint venture would likely preclude the inclusion of such a facility in a functional-oriented company. On the other hand, regional integration, such as in the European Economic Community, acts as a very strong inducement for a company to adopt a geographical orientation.

The nature of the competiton: The activities of other companies can also affect the organizational structure of a company. If a major competitor is vertically integrating its worldwide operations and thereby gaining a competitive edge, there is a strong inducement for other companies to copy the successful structure. For example, Ford Motor Company's success with worldwide integration of its production has accelerated efforts by General Motors and European companies to do likewise. Similarly, if one company has been able to gain an edge by functional specialization, then there will be a stong incentive for other companies to try to succeed in areas such as marketing, financial innovations, and efficiency.

SUMMARY

Small companies can often succeed with a very informal, often amorphous organizational structure. However, when a firm grows and becomes increasingly complex, it becomes imperative that a formal organizational structure be designed for the company as a means of controlling its growing resources, of better preparing the company to take advantage of emerging opportunities, and of helping it avoid potentially serious problems. When the growing firm becomes extensively engaged in international business, then the need for an appropriate organizational structure becomes even more critical: Complexity, and numerous opportunities, and potential problems make this vital.

The form of structure chosen by a company and the nature of the control patterns which its worldwide operations will demand are a function of the nature of the company's international operations. A company's international activities fall into three categories: foreign trade, foreign managerial and technological assistance, and foreign production. The combination of these activities in which a company is engaged is an important factor in its choice of organizational format.

Few companies jump suddenly into international production with special organizational needs. Instead, most companies evolve through a series of degrees or phases of internationalization. As internationalization increases in complexity, so does the need for an explicit modification of the organizational structure to account for the international activities of the firm.

The company has several design options available to it. The simplest of these involves the addition of an international department or division to the domestic structure. When the firm is prepared to move beyond this point, it can adapt one of various international organizational structures, which are analogous to their domestic counterparts: product, functional, geographical, or customer orientation, plus the hybrid form known as a matrix.

Given this variation among companies and the various organizational structures they can choose, the company's decision concerning the best format reflects several factors: the stage of its development, its current management and ownership, and the existing environmental constraints.

The choice for any individual company is not necessarily an easy one. However, it is of great importance. Furthermore, it should be kept in mind that any significant change in organizational structure is expensive for the company and imposes heavy strains upon its personnel. However, if the choice is carefully made and if the changeover is carefully managed, the results can be very rewarding to the company.

KEY TERMS

GRID

INTERNATIONAL
   DEPARTMENT

INTERNATIONAL
   DIVISION

INTERNATIONAL
   SUBSIDIARY

MATRIX

ORGANIZATIONAL
   ORIENTATION:
   CUSTOMER
   FUNCTION
   GEOGRAPHY
   PRODUCT

REVIEW QUESTIONS

1. How important do you think international managerial and technical assistance is? Why?
2. How do the departmental, divisional, and subsidiary structures differ?
3. What are the advantages and disadvantages of the five types of global organizational structure?
4. How would you select a structure for your company's international operations?
5. How would a company's resources affect its choice of organizational structure?

SUGGESTED REFERENCES

BERKMAN, HAROLD W., AND IVAN R. VERNON *Contemporary Perspectives in International Business.* Skokie, Ill.: Rand McNally & Company, 1979.

BROOKE, MICHAEL Z., AND H. LEE REMMERS *The Strategy of Multinational Enterprise.* New York: American Elsevier Publishing Co., 1970.

BUSINESS INTERNATIONAL "Reorganizating the Corporation," *100 Checklists: Decision-Making in International Operations.* New York: Business International, 1970.

CLEE, GILBERT H., AND WILBUR M. SACHTJEN "Organizing a Worldwide Business," *Harvard Business Review* (November–December 1964).

CULLMAN, W. ARTHUR, AND HARRY R. KNUDSON *Management Problems in International Environments.* Englewood Cliffs, N.J.: Prentice-Hall, Inc., 1972.

DAVIS, STANLEY *Managing and Organizing Multinational Corporations.* Elmsford, N.Y.: Pergamon Press, Inc., 1979.

DYMSZA, WILLIAM A. *Multinational Business Strategy.* New York: McGraw-Hill Book Company, 1972.

FARMER, RICHARD *Multinational Strategies.* Bloomington: University of Indiana Press, 1975.

FAYERWEATHER, JOHN *International Business Strategy and Administration.* Cambridge, Mass.: Ballinger Publishing Co., 1978.

———, and ASHOK KAPOOR *Strategy and Negotiation for the International Corporation.* Cambridge, Mass.: Ballinger Publishing Co., 1976.

KAPOOR, ASHOK, AND PHILIP GRUB, eds. *Multinational Enterprise in Transition.* Hinsdale, Ill.: Darwin Press, 1972.

KOLDE, ENDEL-JAKOB *Multinational Company: Behavioral and Managerial Analysis.* Lexington, Mass.: D.C. Heath & Co., 1974.

KUHNE, ROBERT   *Co-Determination in Business: Workers' Representatives in the Boardrooms.* New York: Praeger Publishers, 1980.

PHATAK, ARVIND V.   *Managing Multinational Corporations,* pp. 172–88. New York: Praeger Publishers, 1974.

PRASAD, S. BENJAMIN, AND V. KRISHNA SHETTY   *Introduction to Multinational Management.* Englewood Cliffs, N.J.: Prentice-Hall, Inc., 1976.

RINGBAKK, KJELL-ARNE   "Strategic Planning in a Turbulent International Environment," *Long-Range Planning,* 1976.

ROBINSON, RICHARD D.   *International Business Management,* 2d ed. Hinsdale, Ill.: Dryden Press, 1978.

STOPFORD, JOHN M., AND LOUIS T. WELLS   *Managing the Multinational Enterprise.* New York: Basic Books, Inc., Publishers, 1972.

TOYNE, BRIAN   *Host Country Managers of Multinational Firms: An Evaluation of Variables Affecting Their Managerial Thinking Patterns.* New York: Arno, 1980.

TSURUMI, YOSHI   *Multinational Management: Business Strategy and Government Policy.* Cambridge, Mass.: Ballinger Publishing Co., 1977.

YOSHINO, MICHAEL   *Japan's Multinational Enterprises.* Cambridge, Mass.: Harvard University Press, 1976.

16

Export and Import Procedures and Financing

International trade is the most pervasive form of international operations. Most international firms are engaged in international trade. Indeed, that is the only significant international activity for many firms. However, many other companies with much more complicated forms of international business operations (such as foreign direct investments) are also involved in importing and/or exporting. Therefore, familiarity with the basic procedures and means of financing international trade is very important for any international manager.

DOMESTIC VERSUS INTERNATIONAL TRADE

Domestic trade is generally much simpler to conduct than international trade. This is true for many reasons, several of which have already been noted in this book as unique characteristics of international business: distances, languages, laws, foreign exchange, country risk, lack of familiarity with customers, and so forth. As a result, over the centuries a wide range of specific procedures for facilitating and financing international trade have evolved.

Most domestic trade is not as structured as foreign trade: In domestic trade, contracts tend to be informal (often verbal), and financing is generally on open account—that is, direct supplier financing (accounts payable for the buyer, accounts receivable for the seller).

International trade is not generally so trusting, so informal. Although companies can communicate easily throughout the world today, although merchandise can be moved to most parts of the world almost as quickly as it can domestically when the urgency for speed is great, and although there have been substantial improvements in the area of international credit analysis, traditional methods of international trade continue to prevail. These methods prevail not simply as a result of inertia, but because they have proven themselves to be effective and convenient. Indeed, as is noted later, some of these techniques are now being adapted for domestic use.

THE PROBLEM OF FOREIGN EXCHANGE

Most international trade involves foreign exchange exposure for either the exporter or the importer or both (that is if the billing is in a third currency). This special problem of international trade is discussed in detail in Chapter 21.

FINANCIAL PROBLEMS OF INTERNATIONAL TRADE

PROBLEMS FOR THE EXPORTERS

The exporting firm has the dual problem of obtaining financing for its export ventures and of being offered a satisfactory means of payment by the foreign purchaser. It is often possible to tie the two needs into one neat package. If the exporter can obtain some guaranteed commitment by the foreign importer or some intermediary working on its behalf, this guarantee could serve as security for a domestic export-financing loan.

PROBLEMS FOR THE IMPORTERS

The importer is confronted with the task of offering the exporter some form of assurance that the bill will indeed be paid. Cash in advance is one option (indeed, the ideal from the perspective of the exporter), but not a very favorable option for the importer. Billing on open account is generally the ideal situation for the importer. However, unless the exporter is very familiar with the importer or has received a guarantee by a third party—a government agency or an insurance company—this will not likely be acceptable. A very large amount of international trade does occur on open account, but it is primarily between different units of the same company, between companies that have had a long association, or on purchases by large companies with a very strong international credit rating.

Since a very large volume of international trade does not fall under any of these categories, it was necessary for some other form of guaranteed payment to be devised. What is generally used is a type of bank guarantee—the letter of credit.

THE LETTER OF CREDIT

The basic international financial tool that is used in international trade is the *letter of credit* or simply L/C. A letter of credit is issued at the request of the importer. It is issued by a commercial bank (typically the importer's bank) as a guarantee of payment to a beneficiary (usually either the exporter or its bank). (See Figure 16.1.)

The bank's promise to pay has thus been substituted for that of the importer. For this service, the importing company pays a fee. Also, if the importer's credit rating is not satisfactory for the bank, then a deposit or some other type of collateral may be required by the bank from the importer.

From the exporter's perspective, its claim is now on the bank. The bank in turn now has a claim upon the importer. Thus, the L/C is a special type of credit line that is issued to the importer.

REVOCABLE VERSUS IRREVOCABLE

Since the exporter now has the promise of payment of the importer's bank instead of that of the importer itself, the exporter should now be willing to ship the merchandise, as long as it is confident in the creditworthiness of the bank. Letters of credit are usually *irrevocable*— that is, once the L/C is issued, the exporter knows that it cannot be cancelled. Some L/Cs, however, are *revocable*—a fact that greatly reduces their attractiveness; they are not guarantees but can help to facilitate payments.

If the exporter is unfamiliar with the foreign bank that issued the letter of credit, it can check the quality of that bank by talking to its own bank. If the exporter is unwilling to ship the merchandise simply based upon the L/C of a foreign bank with which it is not familiar, it can request that its own bank add its guarantee to that of the foreign bank. This the local bank will be very willing to do if it is familiar with and

4

The First National Bank of Chicago   ORIGINAL   7
INTERNATIONAL BANKING DEPARTMENT
One First National Plaza/Chicago, Illinois 60670

Cable address: NATIONAL CHICAGO   Telex number: 2-53801   Date of issue: JAN. 1, 19--

| Irrevocable Documentary Letter of Credit | ISSUING BANK'S NUMBER | ADVISING BANK'S NUMBER |
| Advising Bank | cc. 123456 | Applicant |

BANCO ESPANOL DE CREDITO   LEATHER GOODS INC.
BARCELONA, SPAIN   CHICAGO, ILLINOIS

Beneficiary   Amount

FABRICAS MAJORCA S.A.   US$100,000.00 (ONE HUNDRED THOUSAND
(COMPLETE ADDRESS)   U.S. DOLLARS)
                                          Expiry

Draft must be presented for negotiation or presented
to the drawee on or before: JUNE 30, 19--

Dear Sir(s),

We hereby issue in your favor this documentary letter of credit which is available by negotiation of your draft(s)
at -----180 DAYS SIGHT----- on THE FIRST NATIONAL BANK OF CHICAGO, CHICAGO, ILLINOIS, U.S.A.,
accompanied by the following documents:

DISCOUNT CHARGES ARE FOR ACCOUNT OF THE APPLICANT.
1. COMMERCIAL INVOICE IN TRIPLICATE,
2. U.S. CUSTOMS INVOICE IN TRIPLICATE,
3. FULL SET OCEAN CARRIERS CLEAN BILLS OF LADING, DATED ON BOARD, ISSUED IN
    AT LEAST TWO ORIGINALS PLUS ONE NON-NEGOTIABLE COPY TO ORDER OF SHIPPER,
    BLANK ENDORSED, MARKED FREIGHT COLLECT NOTIFY ABC FORWARDING CO., 38 S.
    DEARBORN ST., CHICAGO, ILLINOIS 60670.

NOTE: ALL BANK CHARGES OTHER THAN THOSE OF THE FIRST NATIONAL BANK OF
         CHICAGO, CHICAGO, ILLINOIS ARE FOR BENEFICIARY'S ACCOUNT.

Covering:

2,000 LEATHER COATS AT $50.00 EACH. 1,000 EACH OF STYLE NUMBER 95 AND 96.
TERMS: F.O.B. VESSEL, SPAIN.

Dispatch/shipment from	Partial shipments	Transhipments
SPAIN (ANY PORT)	PROHIBITED	PROHIBITED
To		
CHICAGO, ILLINOIS VIA THE GREAT LAKES	INSURED BY [X] Buyer [ ] Seller	

Special conditions: NEGOTIATING BANK MUST AIRMAIL ONE ORIGINAL COMMERCIAL INVOICE,
CUSTOMS INVOICE AND BILL OF LADING TO ABC FORWARDING CO., 38 S. DEARBORN
STREET, CHICAGO, ILLINOIS 60670, FOR OUR ACCOUNT, AND A CERTIFICATE TO
THIS EFFECT MUST BE SUBMITTED WITH THE REMAINING DOCUMENTS.

DRAFT MUST BEAR THE CLAUSE "DRAWN UNDER DOCUMENTARY CREDIT NO. 123456   OF THE FIRST NATIONAL BANK OF CHICAGO"

We hereby engage with drawers and/or bonafide holders that drafts drawn   Advising bank's notification
and negotiated in conformity with the terms of this credit will be duly
honored on presentation and that drafts accepted within the terms of this
credit will be duly honored at maturity.

The amount of each draft must be endorsed on the reverse of this credit
by the negotiating bank.   SPECIMEN

        Yours faithfully,
     THE FIRST NATIONAL BANK OF CHICAGO

JOHN DOE John Doe   DAVID DOE David Doe
Authorized Signature   Authorized Signature   Signature of Official of Advising Bank

Except so far as otherwise expressly stated this credit is subject to the "Uniform Customs and Practice for Documentary Credits (1974 Revision), International Chamber of Commerce, Publication No. 290

Reprinted by permission of First Chicago Bank.

FIGURE 16.1   Letter of Credit

confident in the issuing bank; such a guarantee is called a *confirmed
letter of credit.* With a confirmed L/C, the exporter now has a claim upon
its own bank, which has a claim upon the importer's bank, which has a
claim upon the importer. Under either confirmed or unconfirmed L/Cs,
the exporter is no longer concerned with the importer's credit rating.

CONDITIONALITY

The letter of credit is typically issued only subject to certain (often very restrictive) conditions. The conditions usually involve the presentation of a series of specific documents before payment is made against the L/C. Thus, the standard commercial L/C is called a *documentary letter of credit*.

The L/C specifies exactly what conditions must be satisfied in order for the issuing bank to honor the document. Figure 16.1 is a sample of a typical letter of credit. It names the beneficiary (Fabricas Majorca, S.A.—the exporter), the company on whom the L/C is drawn (Leather Goods, Inc.—the importer), the amount of the L/C, and the conditions under which it will be honored. If the exporter satisfies all the conditions listed, then the bank *must* pay as promised—even if the importer is dissatisfied for some reason. Therefore, it is crucial to the importer that the document specifically list the conditions that must be met in order for that company (on which the L/C was drawn) to be satisfied.

ADVANTAGES OF THE L/C

With the L/C, the importer has the advantage of being able to establish the credit indirectly via its own bank, which is necessary for the company to import. The importer is thus able to buy without having to pay in advance.

The exporter is able to sell with a high degree of confidence, since, even though it may not be very familiar with the buyer, its credit will be paid. Also, with an irrevocable L/C, the exporter will find it much easier to obtain export-production financing. Obviously, if the exporter's bank has confirmed the L/C, then that bank will be willing to help finance the merchandise on a credit the bank itself has guaranteed. Even if the L/C has not been confirmed by the exporter's bank, that bank, if it is confident in the quality of the bank which issued the L/C, will then also be willing to provide export financing.

THE BANK DRAFT

THE NATURE OF A DRAFT

The letter of credit offers assurance to the exporter that, if the conditions listed on the L/C are satisfied, the issuing bank will pay the amount specified on the L/C. The exporter's claim for payment against an L/C is in the form of a *bank draft* (or *bill of exchange*). As the sample letter of credit illustrates (Figure 16.1), the promised payment under the

L/C is made when a draft is submitted with all documentation specified in the L/C. As a result, these drafts are often called *documentary drafts*.

A draft is similar to a personal check written on a checking account at a local bank. (See Figure 16.2.) A personal check, like any other type of draft, is a written request by one party that a second party make payment to a third party. It need not even involve a bank, but most commonly does.

With a personal check the owner of the checking account (the first party) directs the bank in which he or she has deposited the funds (the second party) to pay the third party. The third party may even be the same as the first or second party. For example, the check may be written out to cash (for payment to the first party), or it may be written in favor of the bank (for example, as a payment on an automobile or mortgage loan). Personal checks seldom require documents in order to be valid: They are generally written unconditionally.

Documentary draft: A documentary draft is somewhat different. It, of course, does require documents. It is also issued in a different fashion. It is not the payor (the one doing the paying) who draws up the draft as was true with the personal check. Instead, it is the payee (the one who is being paid, for example, the exporter) who draws up the draft. Thus, the exporter (the first party) directs the bank of the importer (the second party) to pay a third party (either the exporter or its bank).

A letter of credit is *not* a means of payment. It is a very strong promise to pay but is not itself the means of payment. Thus, the L/C is not a marketable financial instrument. However, the draft that is drawn against the L/C may become highly marketable.

A bank's credit rating is typically better than that of most of its

F B D 368		Form No. 16-0368

U.S.A. ___MAY 1,___ 19—

Exchange for _$100,000.00_

At _- - - - - 180 DAYS - - - - -_ Sight of this _FIRST_ of Exchange (Second being unpaid)

Pay to the order of __FABRICAS MAJORCA S.A.__

the sum of __ONE HUNDRED THOUSAND AND NO/100 UNITED STATES DOLLARS__

Drawn under Letter of Credit No. ___G.C. 123456___ Dated _____

Issued by __THE FIRST NATIONAL BANK OF CHICAGO, CHICAGO, ILLINOIS__

Value received and charge to the account of _____

To _THE FIRST NATIONAL BANK OF CHICAGO_   FABRICAS MAJORCA S.A.

CHICAGO, ILLINOIS   *John D. Brown*

SPECIMEN

Reprinted by permission of First Chicago Bank.

FIGURE 16.2 Time Draft

customers. That is, of course, the very reason that banks are asked to issue letters of credit—by substituting their credit rating in place of that of the company on whose behalf the L/C is issued.

When a draft is written that directs the bank to honor the terms of the L/C, the bank will review the L/C and the documents that have been submitted together with the draft. If the conditions stipulated in the letter of credit have been satisfied, then the bank *must* honor the draft. *It is a legally binding obligation.*

Drafts can be payable either upon presentation (that is, a sight draft—payable on sight) or at some specified period after presentation (that is, a time draft—for example, payable thirty or ninety days after presentation).

OTHER USES OF LETTERS OF CREDIT

The L/C has proved to be such a useful tool of international trade that its use has spread to other commercial areas. The domestic use of L/Cs has grown substantially. Most of the advantages which were noted for their international use hold true for domestic use. Thus it is a natural development for L/Cs to extend into domestic trade financing between companies that are not familiar with one another or where the buyer's credit rating is low.

In addition, L/Cs have also been widely used as a type of guarantee for other types of financial, commercial, or industrial contracts. For example, letters of credit have been widely used as guarantees of contractor's performance on international construction contracts. In this capacity they are also called *letters of performance.*

The user of *performance L/Cs* must proceed with great caution. This is a financial area that is fraught with grave risks. Remember that the bank *must* honor the L/C as long as the specified conditions have been satisfied. However, unlike trade financing (1) where it is relatively easy to identify satisfactory performance, (2) where there is a long history of experience with their use and in the adjudication of disputes, (3) where the size of the contracts is not usually large enough that errors could lead to serious economic consequences for the issuing bank, and (4) where the contract is essentially self-liquidating within the relatively near term, performance L/Cs can be more easily challenged as to satisfactory performance, have little history of adjudication, can be very substantial in size, and are not as readily self-liquidating. Thus, both the contractor for whom the L/C was drawn and the bank may find such L/Cs to be much less satisfactory than standard trade L/Cs.

With such words of warning, it should be added that performance L/Cs are likely to continue to grow in importance. So long as the financial manager approaches the use of performance L/Cs with appropriate caution, they can be attractive tools.

Sight draft: The *sight draft* is the type of documentary draft that is most like a personal check. It is immediately payable when the bank receives the draft—if all the documents are in order. As a result, the issuing bank must pay the exporter or the confirming bank and the importer must in turn make payment to the issuing bank immediately upon presentation of the sight draft. Since the importer presumably will not be able to sell the merchandise until some time in the future, it will either need to draw down existing funds or obtain a loan from the bank. This is frequently an uncomfortable strain upon the importer. Thus, bank drafts are commonly time drafts rather than sight drafts. By that means the issuing bank does not need to make payment to the exporter or the confirming bank until sometime in the future, and the importer does not need to pay its bank until then.

Time drafts: The essence of the *time draft* is that, although the bank that issued the L/C must pay according to its promise, the letter of credit clearly specifies that payment is not to be made until some time after the documentary draft is submitted to the issuing or confirming bank. (Figure 16.2 is a time draft.) Thus, the exporter has, in effect, extended credit beyond the point of presentation of the draft.

For the importer this provides time to sell the merchandise and thus obtain the necessary funds in order to pay its obligation to the bank that issued the L/C. (Note that the importer does not ordinarily need to pay its bank until it is time for the bank to honor the draft drawn against its L/C, whether it be a sight or a time draft.)

The exporter now has a draft that the bank which confirmed or issued the letter of credit promises to pay at a specific date—with no conditions. The documents will no longer be attached. (The time draft is similar to a postdated check.)

When the bank receives the documentary draft and has been satisfied that the draft accurately fulfills all the conditions specified in the letter of credit, then the bank stamps the word "accepted" on the draft. The draft has become a *bankers' acceptance.*

BANKERS' ACCEPTANCE

A *bankers' acceptance* (see Figure 16.3) is an *unconditional* guarantee by the bank to pay at a specific date, whereas the L/C is a *conditional* guarantee. The bankers' acceptance is very similar to a large certificate of deposit (CD). Both types of bank obligations are negotiable or marketable. Thus, although the exporting company has not yet received payment, it can sell the bankers' acceptance in the money markets. It has virtually the same credit rating as the CD of the same bank. They are

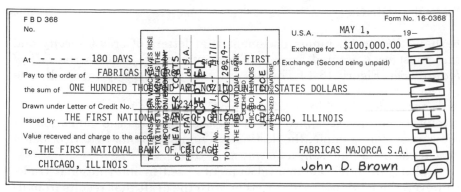

Reprinted by permission of First Chicago Bank.

FIGURE 16.3   Bankers' Acceptance

both sold in the market in competition with commercial paper and U.S. Treasury bills. The following four types of negotiable financial instruments are the major types of marketable securities that comprise the money markets: (1) T-bills, issued by the U.S. federal government, (2) commercial paper, issued primarily by nonbanking corporations, (3) certificates of deposit, issued by commercial banks, and (4) bankers' acceptances, also issued by commercial banks.

A bankers' acceptance thus provides indirect financing for the importer (that is, from the exporter for the duration of the time draft) and provides the exporter with a means of obtaining immediate payment for the goods upon receiving the accepted draft back from the bank. Of course, the disadvantage to the exporter is that, unlike a sight draft, which the bank pays in full upon sight, a time draft is paid in full only at some future date. The exporter may choose to keep the acceptance until maturity. However, if the exporter chooses to sell the acceptance, it must be sold at a discount (as are T-bills, CDs, and commercial paper). The issuing or the confirming bank will very often buy its own acceptances— at a discount, of course, and thereby earn interest on an investment in itself!

The importer pays a fee for the issuance of the original letter of credit and also for the bankers' acceptance. However, in exchange, it has been given not only the use of the good name of the bank for the company's imports but also the use of credit. The bank may even offer credit to the importer at the maturity of the acceptance.

Hundreds of billions of bankers' acceptances are issued annually. They are even becoming quite common domestically, because they provide a marketable form of trade and inventory financing.

BILL OF LADING

Perhaps the most common document that letters of credit specify and that must be presented as part of a documentary draft is the *bill of lading*. (See Figure 16.4.) The bill of lading is a receipt given by the carrier (for example, the steamship line, the airline, and so forth) to the exporter (called the shipper). It commonly serves as more than a simple receipt. Generally, it is also a *contract* that specifies the obligations of the carrier (for example, the destination and approximate date of delivery). It can even represent a *document of title*.

There are other common documents used in international trade. However, the letter of credit (together with the draft that results from it) and the bill of lading are the most ubiquitous.

GOVERNMENTAL SUPPORT FOR EXPORTS

Most governments view the encouragement of exporting from their countries as an important public policy. As a result, many governments have created agencies for promoting, facilitating, and even subsidizing exports. International agencies also encourage international trade via their financial support.

THE U.S. EXPORT–IMPORT BANK

The U.S. Export–Import Bank (Eximbank) is the major U.S. agency for providing financial support for exports. It is analogous to those of many other countries. The *Eximbank* is a U.S. governmental agency that was set up in 1934 to finance both exports and imports. It was specifically intended to promote trade with the Soviet Union. However, no trade with the USSR has ever been financed by Eximbank, since an act of the U.S. Congress forbids the extension of government credit to any country that is not satisfactorily paying the U.S. government for past loans. Since the Soviet Union is in default on a significant amount of such credits, it has been ineligible for new trade credits.

The title—Export–Import Bank—implies that imports as well as exports are financed. Indeed, this was the original intention. However, no imports have ever been financed. The agency should more appropriately be entitled the U.S. Export Bank! It supports the purchases abroad of American-made products, whether the purchasers are foreign companies, foreign governments, or U.S. companies abroad.

SEA-LAND SERVICE, INC.

INTERNATIONAL BILL OF LADING
NOT NEGOTIABLE UNLESS CONSIGNED "TO ORDER"
(SPACES IMMEDIATELY BELOW FOR SHIPPERS' MEMORANDA)

(2) SHIPPER/EXPORTER (COMPLETE NAME AND ADDRESS)	(5) BOOKING NO. / (5A) BILL OF LADING NO.
	(6) EXPORT REFERENCES
(3) CONSIGNEE (COMPLETE NAME AND ADDRESS)	(7) FORWARDING AGENT, F.M.C. NO.
	(8) POINT AND COUNTRY OF ORIGIN
(4) NOTIFY PARTY (COMPLETE NAME AND ADDRESS)	(9) ALSO NOTIFY-ROUTING & INSTRUCTIONS

(12) INITIAL CARRIAGE BY (MODE) *	(13) PLACE OF INITIAL RECEIPT *	
(14) VESSEL VOY. FLAG	(15) PORT OF LOADING	(10) LOADING PIER/TERMINAL	(10A) ORIGINAL(S) TO BE RELEASED AT
(16) PORT OF DISCHARGE	(17) PLACE OF DELIVERY BY ON-CARRIER *	(11) TYPE OF MOVE (IF MIXED, USE BLOCK 20 AS APPROPRIATE)

PARTICULARS FURNISHED BY SHIPPER   SEA-LAND-U.S. CUSTOMS CONTAINER BOND IIT 145

MKS. & NOS./CONTAINER NOS.	NO. OF PKGS.	HM **	DESCRIPTION OF PACKAGES AND GOODS	GROSS WEIGHT	MEASUREMENT
(18)	(19)		(20)	(21)	(22)

(23) Declared Value $_____ If shipper enters a value, carriers "package" limitation of liability does not apply and the ad valorem rate will be charged.

RATE OF EXCHANGE | (24) FREIGHT PAYABLE AT/BY

ITEM NO.	RATED AS	PER	RATE	PREPAID	COLLECT	LOCAL CURRENCY	
							If this box is checked, goods have been loaded, stowed and counted by Shipper. Carrier has NOT done so and is not responsible for accuracy of count, condition or nature of goods described in PARTICULARS FURNISHED BY SHIPPER.
							THE RECEIPT, CUSTODY, CARRIAGE AND DELIVERY OF THE GOODS ARE SUBJECT TO THE TERMS APPEARING ON THE FACE AND BACK HEREOF AND TO CARRIER'S APPLICABLE TARIFF.
							In witness whereof three (3) original bills of lading all the same tenor and date one of which being accomplished the others to stand void have been issued by Sea-Land Service, Inc. or its designated agent on behalf of itself, other participating carriers, the vessel, her master and owners or charterers.
TOTAL CHARGES							

* APPLICABLE ONLY WHEN USED FOR MULTIMODAL OR THROUGH TRANSPORTATION.
** INDICATE WHETHER ANY OF THE CARGO IS HAZARDOUS MATERIAL UNDER DOT, IMCO OR OTHER REGULATIONS AND INDICATE CORRECT COMMODITY NUMBER IN BOX 20.

AT . . . .

BY . . . .

SL 2265 5/82	BILL OF LADING NO.	DATE	FOR SEA-LAND SERVICE, INC.

Reprinted by permission of Sea-Land Service, Inc.

FIGURE 16.4   International Bill of Lading

The Eximbank has a wide range of authority in order to foster U.S. exports. (1) It can extend *loans* with its own funds. These loans can be extended either directly to the importers abroad or to foreign banks or other foreign financial institutions that combine the funds with their resources to finance U.S. exports. It also sometimes buys bankers' acceptances that were used to finance U.S. exports. (2) It can issue *guarantees* on the loans made by commercial banks. (3) It can issue *insurance* on the trade credits extended by exporters.

The Export–Import Bank wishes to encourage as much export financing as possible. Therefore, it is careful to avoid disrupting the private sources of trade financing. Indeed, the Emibank works very closely with such institutions. When it extends loans directly, it is only on condition that part of the funds must also come from the private sector. The Eximbank's share is always less than 90 percent. These direct Eximbank loans are generally for the financing of long-term credits—longer maturities than commercial banks will generally issue.

The bank is a strong proponent of *cofinancing* with commercial banks. Under this arrangement, a joint loan is extended by both the Eximbank and the commercial bank. The commercial bank lends the short- and medium-term funds (for example, the first five years), and the Eximbank funds the long-term portion. Thus, the commercial banks will be paid back much sooner; therefore, they are more interested in participating in the financing of these long commercial credits. In addition, the Eximbank may well extend a guarantee for the commercial bank's share of the loan. The commercial bank's share of the loan is at standard commercial loan rates, whereas the Eximbank's loan is at a subsidized rate.

THE COMMODITY CREDIT CORPORATION (CCC)

Another U.S. agency that finances American exports is the *Commodity Credit Corporation* of the U.S. Department of Agriculture. As the name and parentage of the CCC suggest, this agency promotes the exportation of American agricultural commodities.

The Commodity Credit Corporation extends its credit to export firms in the United States. The credits are provided through the purchase of the exporter's accounts receivable. The financing cannot exceed three years, and the total amount of the discounting is limited to the export value of the commodities without any allowance for shipping, insurance, and financial charges. An irrevocable standby letter of credit must back up all discounted trade credits.

In conjunction with the Eximbank, the CCC also helps finance the export of agricultural storage and processing facilities. It is felt that the increase of these facilities abroad will encourage the export of U.S. agricultural products.

AGENCIES OF OTHER GOVERNMENTS

All major exporting nations and also many smaller countries have governmental agencies that act in a similar fashion to the Export–Import Bank of the United States in subsidizing their exports. Some of the major agencies are the Export Credits Guarantee Department (ECGD) in the United Kingdom, COFACE in France, and the Export–Import Bank of Japan. Unfortunately, these agencies tend to periodically escalate their competitive subsidy programs into a pricing war as a means of giving their exporters an edge over foreign exporters. This is another form of interference with free trade. It is very likely that most of the export trade would occur even without these subsidies. If such programs successfully divert some purchase orders from abroad, it may very well mean that such trade could not be supported upon its own merits.

However, this is conjecture. So also is the speculation of trade without agencies. The agencies will continue to play a major role in international trade, and prospective importers and exporters should be familiar with them. Commercial banks are the prime source of information on the facilities offered by these agencies.

NONFINANCIAL INVOLVEMENT BY GOVERNMENTS

The efforts by governments to encourage the exports by their companies extend beyond the provision of loans, guarantees, and insurance. For example, agencies such as the U.S. Department of Commerce publish helpful materials, offer training seminars, suggest trade leads, and even arrange trade contracts.

Sometimes domestic laws, policies, and taxes discourage exports. Since these parameters are designed to protect domestic companies and consumers and to finance governmental deficits, they are counterproductive if they obstruct exports. As a result, governments commonly exempt exports and exporters from the burdens of some of these constraints.

In Chapter 22 international taxation is discussed. Among the issues examined then are the laws that exempt exports from the value-added tax, a type of indirect tax that is the major form of corporate taxation in Europe. Also, the Domestic International Sales Company (DISC), a special export company that permits U.S. exporters to defer most profit taxes for extensive periods of time, is discussed.

American antitrust laws are among the most constraining antitrust laws in the world. They are intended to discourage anticompetitive practices domestically—practices that are in many instances normal and legal in Europe, Japan, and elsewhere. One of the results of domestic antitrust laws in the United States has been the discouragement of the creation of joint ventures for promoting exports.

Special laws have been created in the past to surmount some of these obstacles. However, what is potentially the most fruitful law of all was passed in 1982: the *Export Trading Company Act.* This Act encourages the creation of *export trading companies* (ETCs). ETCs will hopefully offer special encouragement to small- and medium-sized companies that were not active exporters in the past. Companies, including commercial banks, will be permitted to form consortia to promote exports jointly. Some of the major advantages will be as follows:

1. significant exemption from antitrust laws
2. the chance to employ export specialists—something the individual companies may not be able to afford
3. easier access to export financing, since commercial banks are likely to be involved in many of the ETCs and because the export specialists are very familiar with the extensive array of financing that is available

Hopefully, once ETCs become well known, many companies that have done little or no exporting in the past will recognize their untapped opportunities in foreign markets.

Any country could benefit from the development of export trading companies. The Japanese have been by far the most successful; their trading companies handle not only the majority of exports but also a very large share of Japanese imports. Developing countries should also explore the potential of ETCs; access to exporting expertise would be perhaps the greatest advantage for them.

INTERNATIONAL AGENCIES

There are a number of international agencies that have been created to encourage development of developing countries. These were discussed in an earlier chapter. By far the largest of these agencies is the International Bank for Reconstruction and Development (the World Bank). Other important agencies are the Inter-American Development Bank (which, next to the World Bank, is the largest and most significant), the Asian Development Bank, and the European Investment Bank. These agencies were all jointly created by a number of different governments. Both developed and developing countries are members of each group, but only developing countries can borrow. Most loans can only go to governments, although some of their special lending facilities permit funds to be extended to private-sector companies as well.

PRIVATE-SECTOR SUPPORT
OF INTERNATIONAL TRADE

The aggressive efforts of the governmental agencies such as those mentioned above provide a significant amount of export financing. However, the vast majority of exports are financed by private sources—primarily through direct supplier credits and commercial bank credits. Some of these, especially long-term credits, are insured or guaranteed by government agencies. Nevertheless, the greatest share of trade financing is provided by private forces without governmental encouragement.

SUPPLIER CREDITS

Between affiliates: Supplier credits between different affiliates of the same companies are the norm for the financing of such trade. Indeed, since the affiliates have a common owner, letters of credit are not necessary. Drafts that ensue from such arrangements are called *clean drafts,* since they do not require documents.

Between nonaffiliated companies: Although international trade between nonaffiliated companies is not generally financed on open account, that is, through supplier credits, it does frequently occur between companies that have had a long trading relationship. For example, the two companies may have a strong relationship in their domestic trade (for example, Bendix is a major supplier of automotive parts to Ford both in the United States and abroad).

Direct supplier credits are also provided when the buyer is believed to be a very strong company. For example, Ford would generally be able to buy on open account even from suppliers outside the United States. Trade credits are also used if the exporter has received insurance on the payment from, for example, the Eximbank.

BANK CREDITS

The most important single source of international trade financing is the commercial banking sector. This includes borrowing at home, in a foreign country, or in Euromarkets.

Commercial banks facilitate international trade in a variety of ways. This includes not only the extension of importer loans and export-production loans, but also a variety of services: for example, L/Cs and bankers' acceptances. These services earn fees for banks.

Lending limits: In some countries, such as the United States, commercial banks are restricted by governmentally imposed *legal lending limits* (LLL). Such limits typically apply to a bank's lending to an individual borrower (for example, Toyota) throughout the world. LLLs are generally tied to the net worth of the bank—not to the size or strength of the borrower.

Banks that are subject to legal lending limits must consider all of their loans and financial commitments to a company. For example, if a bankers' acceptance has been issued that will likely involve the need for the bank to extend a loan to the company to cover the acceptance at maturity, this contingent liability must be kept in mind by the bank when any new credits are considered.

Since the LLL is a function of the bank's capital rather than the size of the borrower, the legal lending limit is primarily a constraint on large companies (since the same LLL applies to all customers of the bank). However, banks generally also have self-imposed internal lending limits for individual companies. This is simply a prudent precaution. These lending limits can limit the access that companies of *any* size have to an individual bank.

Although some bank regulatory authorities do impose legal lending limits, none impose *country lending limits* (CLLs). Thus, although an American bank has an absolute limit to the credits that it can extend to even a large and prime-quality company like IBM, there is no corresponding limit on its loans in a country, such as in Peru.

Nevertheless, most major banks have prudently adopted their own self-imposed country lending limits. These CLLs can be flexible, but in some cases they will lead banks to ration their credit in certain countries.

Lines of credit: A major type of bank credit facility is the promise to extend a loan at some time in the future. This arrangement is called a *line of credit.* There are many times when companies anticipate that they will either need or may need funds at some point or during some period in the future. Sometimes the company knows exactly when the funds are needed, for example, when a large international account payable comes due. At other times the company may not know when or even if the line of credit is needed. (For example, in early 1979 IBM arranged for $1.3 billion of credit lines.) On the average, 30 to 40 percent of all credit lines are never drawn down. Nevertheless, they are a very important asset for a company to have available.

Sometimes, especially when credit is readily available, banks will issue lines of credit without charging a service fee. However, this credit is not generally binding on the bank: *If* funds are readily available, the funds are provided to the company. The major advantage of this type of arrangement is that all the paperwork for a loan is done in advance, and the money is available at very short notice.

If a company wants the line of credit to be guaranteed, then it will need to pay a fee for the extension of the line. This fee is a proportion of the total line and is charged on the unused portion as long as the line is outstanding. When part or all of the line of credit is drawn down, the fee no longer applies against the portion that has been drawn down. However, that portion now becomes a loan, and, of course, interest is charged against it. The interest rate is determined by the interest rates prevailing at the time when the funds are borrowed, not prevailing when the credit line was arranged.

Private Export Funding Corporation: Governmental agencies are generally anxious to promote the financing of exports by private-sector commercial banks. One such corporation is the Private Export Funding Corporation (PEFCO) in the United States. PEFCO was established in 1970 under the initiative of the Bankers' Association for Foreign Trade and with the encouragement of the Eximbank. It is owned by a large group of banks and some major exporters.

PEFCO's principal focus is upon the extension of medium- and long-term credit to foreign purchasers of U.S. capital goods such as aircraft, power plants, railroad equipment, and mining and industrial installations. PEFCO, although a private-sector company, is designed to supplement other private-sector sources of financing, including, but not limited to, loans from the banks and companies that own it. If alternative funding sources are available, then PEFCO will not ordinarily lend. However, when credit conditions are tight or when the project is large and the financing is lengthy, then PEFCO can play a very major role.

PEFCO never extends loans without significant participation from commercial banks. Very often, the Eximbank is also a lender. If the Eximbank is lending, then it will take the long-term maturity share of the loan, PEFCO will take the middle range, and the commercial banks will take the shorter-term range of the loan. If Eximbank is not a lender, the PEFCO will take the long-term portion, and the banks will take the shorter-term share.

All of PEFCO's loans (principal and interest) are unconditionally guaranteed by the Eximbank. This is true whether or not the Eximbank is sharing in the project as a lender.

The majority of the funds of the Private Export Funding Corporation come from borrowings in the private money and capital markets. With the Eximbank guarantee of all of its lending, the company's credit rating is very strong.

INSURANCE AND GUARANTEES

There are also private-sector agencies that insure and guarantee international credits. In the United States the primary agency is the Foreign Credit Insurance Association (FCIA), an association of private insurance companies. Its primary goal is to insure the trade credits of exporters. Not only political risk but also commercial risk can be insured. (However, potential losses from a devaluation cannot be insured.)

Under commercial risk coverage the exporter is insured against the inability of the importer to pay resulting, for example, from such factors as a decline in sales of the buyer, fraud, or a natural calamity such as a fire and so forth. Political risk also covers a wide variety of factors: for example, currency inconvertibility (that is, exchange and capital controls), confiscation by the government of either the importer or the goods shipped, war, insurrection, and so forth.

If the exporter that is going to finance its own customers is able to obtain FCIA coverage, this arrangement makes it much easier for the company to secure bank financing for its export-production needs.

SPECIALISTS WHO HELP TO FACILITATE TRADE

All private-sector and public-sector institutions mentioned above provide a variety of ancillary services to help the exporter and importer. In addition, there are a variety of other international trade services that are commonly provided by other companies that specialize in such services.

These specialist companies are of three varieties. The first group is comprised of *agents*—institutions that act on the exporter's behalf in selling its goods but who do not take title. The second group is the *merchants*—companies that not only sell the goods of the exporter but who also buy and take title to the goods. The third group involves what might be called the *facilitators*—institutions that are not directly involved in the sale but that help to facilitate the sale for the company that is not capable of handling all export or import duties or that simply does not want to assume those responsibilitites.

Most of these groups of trade specialists are located domestically relative to the exporter or importer who hires them. However, some are located abroad.

INTERNATIONAL TRADE AGENTS

As noted, agents act solely on behalf of whoever hires them. They do not buy or take title to the merchandise.

Agents who represent the exporter: There are a variety of export agents. This first group of agents reside in the exporter's country and represent the exporter.

The *export broker* is typically a specialist in a limited variety of bulk commodities (especially food and raw materials) or sometimes in a geographical area such as Eastern Europe. The ties between the exporter and the broker are not ordinarily very close. It is not a long-term relationship, but rather it may be limited to individual contracts. The exporter may work with the same broker many times but not on the basis of a long-term contract. The broker earns a commission on the total amount of the goods sold.

The *combination export manager* (CEM) or the *export management company* has a much more intimate type of relationship with the seller. The CEM serves as the exclusive agent of the company and, in effect, acts as the export department of the exporting company. The combination export manager not only has a specialized domestic staff but in many instances has a marketing organization set up abroad as well. Thus, if a company that has export opportunities but either no experience or little interest in devoting corporate resources to serving the export markets, the CEM is available to fulfill the needs. The CEM often handles a wide variety of goods for the exporter. It also commonly handles closely related products of other exporters. The contract is typically for at least several years. The CEM's services are entirely in the name of the exporter. Indeed, customers often have no idea that they are not dealing directly with the exporter. The services include at least the contacting of the customer and the negotiating of a contract. Other services can include handling promotion, credit, shipping, and so forth. For these services the CEM is paid a commission and also sometimes a retainer.

Sometimes other exporting companies offer to handle some or all of the products the exporter wishes to sell in other countries. They already have their own distribution network and may be able to fill in their product line and realize greater economies of scale by thus offering to *piggyback* the products of another company.[1] For this service the company that does the piggybacking is paid a commission.

The exporter can economize in its export efforts and also learn much about exporting by combining with other companies in a *selling group*. The selling group might involve companies with complementary products, or it might even involve competitive companies that find an advantage in combining their export efforts. In the United States, the Webb-Pomerene Act permits such joint exporting associations to be set up without violating the antitrust laws, as long as they do not act in such a way as to reduce domestic competition in that industry.

There are also agents who represent the exporter abroad. The *import broker* is analogous to the export broker, except that the former resides in a foreign country. Naturally such a broker specializes in a particular country or group of countries. The import broker is also to be found primarily in the bulk commodity field. Like any broker, the import broker is paid a commission.

---

[1]See Vernon Terpstra, *International Marketing*, 2nd ed. (Hinsdale, IL: Dryden Press), pp. 316–18.

A *manufacturer's representative* works abroad under contract to the exporter. Representatives can exist in almost any industry. They generally represent several exporters, usually in complementary product lines. However, they work very closely with each exporter and, if they are competent, can very effectively cover a market for each exporter. Their basic function is to contact customers, take the orders, and see that the customers are satisfied. The exporter is responsible for shipping, providing credit, collections, and so forth. The manufacturer's representative is paid a commission.

Agents who represent the importer: In addition to the agents which the exporter may employ, many exports result from contacts from the agents for the buyers. Agents such as these could, of course, also be very useful to the domestic company that wishes to import.

Most of these purchasing agents operate on commission but some may be paid a retainer. Some, such as the *resident buyer,* specialize in a narrow range of products and have close ties to the buyer. Others, such as the *export commission house,* are more generalized and may have only erratic contact with the buyer.

INTERNATIONAL TRADE MERCHANTS

Merchants, unlike agents, buy for their own accounts. Therefore, they are principals in the international trade: They take title; they offer credit; they often handle the shipping; they bear the risk. Their net income results from the margin between their buying and selling prices. From the exporter's perspective, such specialists, as with agents, may be located either domestically or internationally.

Domestic merchants: These merchants reside in the home country of the exporter. As a result, since these companies actually buy the merchandise, the "exporter," in effect, only makes domestic sales. The actual export work is handled by the merchant. Obviously, the seller is generally isolated from the final customer. In the extreme case, the manufacturer may not even be aware that the sales are for export.

Export merchants operate in a wide variety of consumer or industrial fields. Their ties with the manufacturer are tenuous, with little loyalty; they may even be handling competitive lines. Sometimes they relabel the merchandise before exporting it. They do not represent a channel for exposing a company's products to foreign markets, but they do represent additional sales, and the export merchants do all the actual export work.

Foreign merchants: This group of intermediaries buy for their own accounts while residing abroad. *Distributors* have exclusive territories. The territories may be part of a country, the entire country, or even a group of countries. The distributor and manufacturer rely heavily on each other and work closely together.

Import jobbers are wholesale merchants who do not get exclusive territorial rights. Accordingly, their loyalty to the manufacturer is likely less than that of distributors.

INTERNATIONAL TRADING COMPANIES

A very unique breed of trade specialist is the *international trading company*. The ITCs do not fit neatly into any of the categories above. Indeed, they may fit into any one or all of them.

Trading companies may be oriented around either exporting or importing, but, because of the obvious profit potential and economies of scale, many engage in both exporting and importing.

The most famous of the trading companies are the Japanese trading companies, the *sogo shoshas,* such as Mitsui, Mitsubishi, and Sumitomo. These and similar companies handle the bulk of Japanese exports and imports, although not the trade of the major auto companies (such as Toyota and Nissan) or the major electronics companies (such as Panasonic and Sony). Some of the individual trading companies handle billions of dollars of exports and imports annually. An individual trading company can handle hundreds or thousands of different products. Although they can act as agents, in most respects they act as merchants.

Trading companies can obviously be very effective ways of increasing a country's exports. As a result, some governments actively encourage them. In the United States, antitrust laws have been effective enough barriers that trading companies have never become prominent. However, as the discussion of the Export Trading Company Act indicated, this is likely to change in the 1980s.

The brief descriptions of agents and merchants above cover only some of the many different varieties of international trade intermediaries that are available to aid the exporter or importer.[2] Unfortunately, there is much confusion over titles of many of these specialists; also, different authors choose different terms. However, the description of the function is what is most important.

FACILITATORS OF INTERNATIONAL TRADE

Some of the agents and many of the merchants mentioned above assume most or all of the actual export or import activity for a company. In such cases the company's selling or buying may be little different

---

[2]For a more detailed list, see Philip R. Cateora and John M. Hess, *International Marketing,* 4th ed. (Homewood, Ill.: Richard D. Irwin, 1979), pp. 556–75.

than domestic business (what might be called *domestic exporting* and *domestic importing*).

However, many companies must handle many of the export and import procedures themselves. It has already been shown how commercial banks can be critically important in trade financing, collections, foreign exchange, and so forth. Commercial banks also provide invaluable service in identifying trade leads (either exports or imports), arranging credit checks of potential customers, suggesting agents and merchants, suggesting governmental financial assistance, and so forth. There are a couple of additional trade facilitators who can greatly simplify the domestic company's exporting and importing.

Foreign freight forwarder: Most exporters utilize the services of freight forwarders. They are specialists in arranging for the shipping of exports (although not usually the packing) and preparing the necessary paperwork such as the bill of lading and any necessary export and foreign import documentation. Many large exporters handle such responsibilities directly, but the majority of companies find it to be more appealing to hire the services of outside specialists. In the United States the foreign freight forwarder must be licensed and bonded under the rules of the Federal Maritime Commission.

Customhouse broker: The task of getting merchandise through customs (or the "customhouse") where tariff duties and other trade rules are imposed can be both complicated and time consuming for the importer. The customhouse broker is a specialist in the laws, policies, and procedures of this task.

The broker checks the arrival of goods, prepares customs documentation, pays the duty on behalf of the importer, and delivers the goods to wherever the importer specifies. The importing firm generally finds these services to be to its benefit. The same firm can often be a foreign freight forwarder and a customhouse broker.

SUMMARY

Exporting and importing can be a very bewildering and complex undertaking for the company with little or no previous experience. However, there is a wide variety of advisory and financial services available to assist the international trader. These services are available from both private-sector and public-sector sources.

The services range from foreign exchange advisory services, customhouse brokers, and freight forwarders to the credit facilities of commercial banks and governmental agencies.

Some international trade is financed directly by supplier credits.

Transactions such as trade between affiliates of the same company, purchases by major, prime-quality international corporations, and trade between companies that have a long history of trading together (either internationally or domestically) are commonly shipped on open account. Also, if the exporter has received a guarantee of the payment of its international receivable by either a governmental or private-sector agency, it is likely willing to provide trade credits.

Governmental agencies (such as the U.S. Export–Import Bank and the Export Credits Guarantee Department of the United Kingdom), international agencies (such as the World Bank and the Inter-American Development Bank), and private companies (primarily commercial banks) are all important sources of financing international trade.

Down through the years a variety of tools have been devised to overcome the major diseconomies of international trade (such as the distances, lack of familiarity of seller with the buyer, differences in currencies, and so forth). The most critical instruments for facilitating international trade are the letter of credit, bank draft, bankers' acceptance, and the bill of lading. Several other valuable tools, such as foreign exchange advisory services and cable transfers, are discussed in the chapters on international financial management.

KEY TERMS

BANK DRAFT
BANKERS' ACCEPTANCE
BILL OF EXCHANGE
BILL OF LADING
COFINANCING
COMBINATION EXPORT
  MANAGER
COMMODITY CREDIT
  CORPORATION (CCC)
CONFIRMED LETTER OF
  CREDIT

CUSTOMS-HOUSE
  BROKER
DOCUMENTARY DRAFT
EXPORT BROKER
EXPORT–IMPORT BANK
  (EXIMBANK)
FOREIGN CREDIT
  INSURANCE
  ASSOCIATION (FCIA)
FOREIGN FREIGHT
  FORWARDER

INTERNATIONAL
  TRADING COMPANY
  (ITC)
LETTER OF CREDIT (L/C)
LINE OF CREDIT
PERFORMANCE LETTER
  OF CREDIT
SIGHT DRAFT
TIME DRAFT
TRADE AGENT
TRADE MERCHANT

REVIEW QUESTIONS

1. Why are special documents and different techniques needed for international trade in comparison to domestic trade?
2. What is an L/C? Who initiates it? Who issues it?
3. What are irrevocable, documentary, and confirmed L/Cs?
4. Why is an L/C important?

5. What is a bank draft? What are the two major varieties? How do they differ?
6. What is the relationship between an L/C and a draft?
7. What is a bankers' acceptance? Why is it so important?
8. What is a bill of lading?
9. Explain the roles of the Eximbank and the CCC.
10. Explain legal lending limits and country lending limits. How is each set?
11. What are lines of credit? How important do you think they are for companies?
12. What is the FCIA? What are its primary functions?
13. Explain the functions of
    a. export and import broker
    b. combination export manager
    c. international trading company
    d. foreign freight forwarder
    e. customhouse broker

SUGGESTED REFERENCES

ALEXANDRIDES, C.G., AND GEORGE MOSCHIS　*Export Marketing Strategy.* New York: Praeger Publishers, 1977.

BANAITIS, SY J.　*International Letters of Credit.* Chicago: First National Bank of Chicago, 1977.

DOWD, LAURENCE P.　*Introduction to Export Management.* Eljay Press, 1977.

HALL, R. DUANE　*International Trade Operations.* Jersey City: Unz & Co., 1984.

HARRIS BANK　*International Trade Guide,* 1978.

KORTH, CHRISTOPHER M.　"International and U.S. Lending Agencies," in *International Banking: Principles and Practices,* ed. Emmanual N. Roussakis, New York: Praeger Publishers, 1983.

MORGAN GUARANTY　*Export and Import Procedures* (latest edition).

RICKS, DAVID A., AND MICHAEL CZINKOTA　"Export Assistance: Are We Supporting the Best Programs?" *Columbia Journal of World Business,* Summer 1981.

SCHNEIDER, GERHARD W.　*Export-Import Financing.* Willowdale, Ontario: Ronald Press, 1974.

SMALL BUSINESS ADMINISTRATION　*Export Marketing for Smaller Firms,* 1971.

U.S. DEPARTMENT OF COMMERCE　*Basic Guide to to Exporting,* 1978.

17

Marketing Management in International Operations*

Marketing is the process by which a company chooses a target market and develops and implements a marketing program to successfully serve that market. The *target market* has several different parameters: for example, it has a geographical dimension (that is, local, regional, national, foreign, or worldwide) as well as other dimensions (level of product sophistication and price range). The choice of the market to be targeted also involves the identification of the company's needs and wants.

The *marketing program* is the plan of action the company chooses to employ in order to reach the target market: developing, implementing, and controlling the necessary strategies and tactics to satisfy the needs and wants of the target market. The marketing program incorporates the choices of the *product* to be provided, the *price* to be charged, the method of *communication* (promotion), and the method of *distribution* (delivery).

The international firm serves both its domestic market and foreign markets. The same marketing activities are required in either location, but *foreign marketing* is generally more complicated, since it is undertaken in different national environments than that with which the company's executives are most familiar.

---

*THIS CHAPTER IS PRIMARILY THE WORK OF PROFESSOR BRIAN TOYNE OF THE UNIVERSITY OF SOUTH CAROLINA.

Two related but distinct concepts with which the reader should also be familiar are international marketing and international trade. *International or multinational marketing* involves the multinational coordination and integration of the firm's many national marketing programs into an effective global marketing program. *International trade* refers to all shipment of goods between nations—not just those that are marketed (for example, between affiliates of the same company).

INTERNATIONAL MARKETING MANAGEMENT TASKS

As discussed above, the primary task of a firm's marketing function is to identify a target market and to implement a program for reaching that target. In addition, these tasks are to be performed within the constraints imposed by the external environment and the firm's limited resources, capabilities, and goals. These tasks are schematically shown in Table 17.1. Part A is the environmental analysis that is necessary to identify the target market. Part B is the building of the marketing program itself; it involves strategic and tactical planning, the necessary corporate organization, and the control procedures for the program.

With this framework as a reference, the rest of this section looks at many of the problems faced by marketing management when the performance of these tasks cross national boundaries. The added dimension of coordinating and integrating national marketing programs into an effective international marketing program is also included. The program to be discussed can be classified into three broad categories, which, while distinct, are interrelated and strongly influence one another.

1. those problems encounterd when making adjustments for the differences between and among the firm's domestic and foreign *environments*
2. those problems concerned with the development of *marketing programs* that must meet the conditions within specific markets
3. those problems that are concerned with the development of an overall coordinated and integrated international marketing program

It should be immediately obvious, however, that these categories merge in the real world.

ENVIRONMENTAL ADJUSTMENTS

When developing, implementing, and administering foreign marketing programs, the international marketing manager must effectively adjust and adapt to the environmental context of the foreign market.

TABLE 17.1 Global Marketing Management Process

The Multinational Marketing Management Process	Key Questions for Analysis, Planning, and Control of Global Marketing
	A. Identification of Target Market
Environmental Analysis 1 . . . . nth National Markets (see Table 17.2 for detail of Environmental Dimensions)	1. What are the unique characteristics of each national market? What characteristics does each market have in common with other national markets? 2. Should we cluster national markets for operating and/or planning purposes? If we do cluster, should we use proximity, market characteristics, or both?
	B. Building of Marketing Program
Strategic Planning	3. Who should make marketing decisions? 4. What are our major assumptions about target markets? Are they valid? 5. What is the need satisfied by our product in target markets? 6. What is the customer benefit provided by our product in target markets? 7. What are the conditions under which our product is used in the target markets? 8. How large is the ability to buy our product in target markets? 9. What are our major strengths and weaknesses relative to our existing and potential competition in target markets? 10. Should we extend, adapt, or invent our products, prices, advertising, and promotion programs? 11. What are our objectives given the alternatives open to us and assessment of opportunity, risk, and company capability? 12. What is the balance of payments and currency situation in target markets? Will we be able to remit earnings?
Structure	13. How do we structure our organization to optimally achieve our objectives, given our skills and resources? What is the responsibility of each organizational level?
Tactical or Operational Planning— Plan Implementation	14. Given our objectives, structure, and our assessment of the market environment, how do we develop effective operational marketing plans? Specifically, what products, at what prices, through what channels, with what communications, and for which markets and market clusters?
Controlling the Marketing Program	15. How do we measure and monitor plan performance? What steps should be taken to bring actual and desired results together?

SOURCE: Adapted from Warren J. Keegan, *Multinational Marketing Management,* 2nd ed. (Englewood Cliffs, New Jersey: Prentice-Hall, Inc., 1980), p. 25.

The influence and impact that each uncontrollable element of the foreign environment has on the foreign marketing program and its administration must be correctly interpreted.

The initial step involves the identification of the appropriate target market(s) (part A in Table 17.1). This is accomplished via the process of an analysis of foreign marketing environment (see items 1 and 2); this, essentially, is a study of the nature of the potential customer.

Once the target market has been determined, the company can proceed to the second step: the building of a marketing program (part B). This involves strategic planning (items 3 through 12), structural reorganization (item 13), tactical (or operational) planning (item 14), and the creation of a control system (item 15).

Once these determinations have been made and the appropriate structure created, the company is prepared to proceed with the implementation of the entire program. A summary of many of these uncontrollables is presented in Table 17.2. In effect, the unique blending of these uncontrollables and the framework they have established for doing business constitute (1) the culture of each market, impacting as they do on the customer's values, beliefs, and behavior and (2) the economic and political framework within which the customer and company operate. As a result, the foreign or international marketing executive must gain, through exposure and experience with "alien" cultures, the ability to correctly interpret the influence that these uncontrollables, singularly and combined, have on national marketing programs. Some of the more obvious differences encountered and their influence on marketing programs are also described in Table 17.2.

When marketing domestically, reaction and adjustment to the uncontrollable changes and developments taking place in the environment in which the firm operates can frequently be automatic—almost subconscious—since there is a reasonably high level of consistency in many of these variables over time and since the manager is very familiar with them. For example, we make automatic assumptions about the political and legal systems, the form that competition will take, and the degree and level of technology each potential customer is familiar with. We also make automatic assumptions about our economic system, adjusting only to changes in economic conditions. In effect, we only see what we are culturally trained to see and find solutions to problems that are in keeping with and accepted by our culture. We would be surprised and, perhaps angry, if we had made a business appointment for 2:00 p.m. and the other person did not arrive or was not ready to see us until 2:30 p.m. Yet this would be quite acceptable behavior in many parts of the world. Also, Westerners automatically assume that black is worn for mourning and that green connotes safety and health. In some parts of the world, white is worn for mourning and green connotes danger and disease.

Cultural bias: A very real danger when marketing overseas is to interpret the foreign environment and its market using one's own *cultural frames of reference*. In addition, it needs to be stressed that the dangers of misinterpretation actually increase when two cultures, such as those of the United States and Canada, appear to be similar. For example, Philip Morris, a large U.S. tobacco company, discovered that

TABLE 17.2 Environmental Variables Affecting International Marketing Strategies

Factors Limiting Standardization	Elements of Marketing Program				
	Product Design	Pricing	Distribution	Sales Force	Advertising and Promotion, Branding and Packaging
Market characteristics					
Physical environment	Climate Product use conditions		Customer mobility	Dispersion of customers	Access to media Climate
Stage of economic and industrial development	Income levels Labor costs in relation to capital costs	Income levels	Consumer shopping patterns	Wage levels, availability of manpower	Needs for convenience rather than economy Purchase quantities
Cultural factors	"Custom and tradition" Attitudes toward foreign goods	Attitudes toward bargaining	Consumer shopping patterns	Attitudes toward selling	Language, literacy Symbolism
Industry conditions					
Stage of product life cycle in each market	Extent of product differentiation	Elasticity of demand	Availability of outlets Desirability of private brands	Need for missionary sales effort	Awareness, experience with products
Competition	Quality levels	Local costs Prices of substitutes	Competitors' control of outlets	Competitors' sales forces	Competitive expenditures, messages
Marketing institutions					
Distributive system	Availability of outlets	Prevailing margins	Number and variety of outlets available	Number, size, dispersion of outlets	Extent of self-service
Advertising media and agencies			Ability to "force" distribution	Effectiveness of advertising, need for substitutes	Media availability, costs, overlaps
Legal restrictions	Product standards Patent laws Tariffs and taxes	Tariffs and taxes Antitrust laws Resale price maintenance	Restrictions on product lines Resale price maintenance	General employment restrictions Specific restrictions on selling	Specific restrictions on messages, costs Trademark laws

SOURCE: Robert D. Buzzell, "Can You Standardize Multinational Marketing?" Harvard Business Review (November–December 1968), pp. 108–109.

411

market proximity and a common heritage and language are not sufficiently strong factors to guarantee success. When developing their Canadian marketing strategy, they assumed that the Canadian smoker was
basically the same as the U.S. smoker and would respond in similar
fashion to promotional appeals developed for the U.S. market. Much to
its chagrin, the firm found that Canadians preferred a different type of
tobacco and preferred their cigarettes packaged in a slide-and-shell box
rather than the U.S. "soft" package. These differences were partly
responsible for the company's failure to strongly penetrate the Canadian
market.

One author identified this "unconscious reference to one's own
cultural values" as a natural "self-reference criterion" (SRC) and proposed the following four-step approach to be used to isolate it, so that its
effect on marketing decisons could be minimized if not eliminated:

Step 1:   Define the business problem or goal in terms of the Amer-
          ican cultural traits, habits, or norms.
Step 2:   Define the business problem or goal in terms of the for-
          eign cultural traits, habits, or norms. Make no value
          judgments.
Step 3:   Isolate the SRC influence in the problem and examine it
          carefully to see how it complicates the problem.
Step 4:   Redefine the problem without the SRC influence and
          solve for the optimum business goal situation.[1]

It should be obvious, however, that the success of this approach
demands a thorough understanding and knowledge of the two cultures—
a requirement that is not easily met, since most of us are unaware or
unconscious of the influence that culture has on our way of life and
decision-making processes. Even after living in an "alien" society for
many years, expatriated business personnel may still be surprised by
facets of the "alien" culture—and even some of their own culture.

DEVELOPMENT OF FOREIGN MARKETING PROGRAMS

The development of marketing strategies for foreign markets follows more or less the same sequence of steps involved when developing a
domestic marketing strategy. Basically, the process includes those decisions and actions involved in selecting potentially attractive target markets and establishing suitable product policy (for example, product de-

---

[1]James A. Lee, "Cultural Analysis in Overseas Operations," *Harvard Business Review* (March–April 1966), pp. 106–14.

sign, product characteristics, and servicing levels), pricing policy and sales price–related services (credits and discounts), promotion policy (blend of advertising and sales activities, media selection, and advertising content), and distribution policy (channels, means of transportation, and territory covered).

Decision making and activities in each of these areas should follow a basic format. Activity objectives and goals that are congruent with the firm's overall objectives and the market's environment have to be decided upon, defined, and quantitatively established. Relevant information has to be gathered and analyzed in terms of the various possible alternatives and their consequences, and evaluated according to internally accepted standards of the firm. The alternative that is closest to the standards is then selected, implemented, and controlled. It should be noted that each of the five elements that constitute a marketing strategy (that is, identification of the target market coupled with the choices of product, promotion, distribution, and price) is only one part of the total process. A successful marketing strategy is one that blends these five elements in such a manner as to simultaneously and successfully meet the needs and wants of the target market and the objectives of the firm.

The remainder of this section discusses some of the problems encountered when developing a company marketing program. Specifically, the discussion centers on marketing research and the four controllable factors of product, promotion, distribution, and price. Although a detailed discussion of the target market is omitted, it will quickly become clear that the four controllable factor decisions are dependent upon the characteristics of the target market. Production, promotion, distribution, and price decisions are, for example, interrelated and dependent upon the market's size, income, location, and so forth.

The more general problems of coordinating and integrating many foreign marketing programs into one comprehensive international marketing program are discussed in the next section.

International marketing research: International and domestic marketing research involves the systematic collecting, recording, and analyzing of data to provide information required to make decision about the target market and the choices of product, promotion, distribution, and price. However, international marketing research is broader in scope and involves problems not generally encountered domestically.

International marketing research is broader in scope in three ways. The first way is the potential magnitude of the research effort. There are more than 170 countries, each of which may represent a potential marketing opportunity. Yet, since each is unique to some degree, it might be desirable to research and rank them according to their potentials. However, from a practical point of view, this is not generally feasible, so many preliminary but effective screening and ranking methods have been developed.[2] For example, an analysis of the basic needs served by a product may indicate that the product may have worldwide, regional, or only single-country potential. The nature of the product is the critical consideration; thus, although a manufacturer of soft beverages may eventually want to research the marketing potential of a large number of countries, a manufacturer of sophisticated, capital-intensive coal-mining equipment may only have a limited number of countries to research.

A second aspect of the broader scope of international marketing research is the number of activities undertaken by this function. Domestic marketing research is generally responsible only for specific information required for decisions regarding marketing strategy. International research, on the other hand, can involve all types of information essential for conducting business overseas. As such, it may be responsible for general information about the country and the forecasting of social, economic, and political trends.[3]

The third aspect, which flows from the activities required of the international marketing research function, is the number of variables on which data must be gathered and analyzed. In other words, all the variables implicit in Table 17.1 are subjects for research. They include, as a minimum, the following:

1. competition (U.S., local, third country)
2. transportation
3. electrical characteristics
4. trade barriers
5. economic environment
6. business philosophies
7. legal systems
8. social customs
9. languages
10. political climate
11. consumption patterns
12. relevant cultural patterns
13. religions and moral backgrounds
14. philosophies of major political parties[4]

---

[2]See Vern Terpstra, *International Marketing,* 2nd ed. (Hinsdale, Ill.: Dryden Press, 1978), pp. 188–95, for a detailed discussion of several useful methods for screening and ranking countries according to their market potentials.

[3]Philip Cateora and John Hess, *International Marketing,* 4th Ed. (Homewood, Ill.: Richard D. Irwin, 1979), p. 254.

[4]Ibid., p. 255.

The problems somewhat unique to international marketing research are of three kinds: (1) problems associated with the number and size of foreign markets; (2) problems associated with secondary data; and (3) problems associated with primary data.[5]

Even when a preliminary screening and ranking method has been employed, many firms may still need to research several countries to determine their potential and collect information helpful in developing marketing strategies. The challenge is to find economical ways that are cost effective in terms of the country's market potential. Part of the problem arises because research costs money, the firm cannot spend more money for the research than the resulting information is worth, and the value of the information is directly related to the market's potential. Another part of the problem arises because many foreign markets are small in terms of population and income. The information collected is of less value in smaller markets and therefore less research can be profitably undertaken.

Secondary data are data available from all published sources, such as governments, trade associations, banks, international organizations, and company records. The international problems arising from secondary data are of the same types as encountered domestically: *scarcity, reliability, comparability,* and *timeliness.* However, the problems are more acute in other countries. First, in general, the availability of secondary data corresponds to the level of economic development of a country; thus, the United States is unparalleled for the wealth of economic and demographic data systematically made available to the public. Second, governments are the major data gatherers and are concerned about their images and the political implications that the data may convey. As a result, they may overstate or understate items such as industrial production, illiteracy, and so on. In addition, the reliability of the data varies according to the country's skills and sophistication in data gathering and analyzing. Third, to be of value to the international researcher, data must be compared between countries. However, items necessary for ranking countries are often defined or classified differently from country to country. Finally, the data frequently made available have been collected at different times in different countries, which creates problems when attempting to establish base years for comparison purposes. The data are also very often out of date before they are even released.

Since secondary data, by definition, are not specific to a particular marketing problem, the gathering of *primary data* is often necessary.

---

[5]Vern Terpstra, *International Dimensions of Marketing* (Boston, Mass.: Kent Publishing Company, 1982), p. 70.

However, as previously noted, the firm may not be willing to undertake primary research because of the trade-off between the cost of the research and the market's potential. Even when primary research is economically feasible, other kinds of problems are encountered: response problems, language-translation problems, literacy and education problems, and problems of inadequate infrastructure.[6]

First, since people's response behavior is culturally conditioned, response problems vary from country to country. For example, the Japanese always attempt to give answers that please the interviewer, even if they are misleading, because of a strong tradition of courtesy. Muslim women often cannot be interviewed because of religious reasons. Even business personnel in many countries are reluctant to be interviewed because of a desire for competitive secrecy.

Second, most international research necessitates the translation of questionnaires and other research materials into other languages. If attitudes, beliefs, and motivations are to be measured, the ideas and concepts must be translated, not just the words. Third, low levels of literacy and education also pose problems. Written questionnaires are of no value if the interviewee cannot read or comprehend the questions. Misunderstanding of the true meaning of the questions and the intent of the research results in erroneous information. Finally, inadequate infrastructure, such as telephones, unreliable postal service, and the lack of marketing research organizations in many countries, is a very serious problem.

Thus, it can be seen that the task of international marketing research is not easy. It is challenging and requires familiarity with the cultures and marketing environment of other countries. It is also critically important: a poor marketing research job can be very costly.[7]

Product: It was stressed earlier that the choice of the appropriate product for a foreign consumer should be made in fundamentally the same way as decisions for domestic consumers. Yet it is necessary to beware of the easy assumptions that any well-developed product, successful in the domestic market, will repeat that success overseas. The similarities in market performance end where the similarities in needs, resources, and the perceptions held by the consumer end. So long as the foreign consumer has the same needs as an American counterpart, and perceives these needs in a similar way, he or she will be receptive to the same product, be it a razor blade, an automobile, or a woodcarving. As long as the resources of the U.S. and foreign consumer are similar and perceived as expendable in a similar fashion, the customer is also likely

---

[6]Ibid., pp. 73–75.

[7]See David A. Ricks, *Big Business Blunders: Mistakes in Multinational Marketing* (Homewood, Ill.: Richard D. Irwin, 1983).

to be receptive to purchasing or using the same degree of quantity and special features of a product. In most cases, however, a foreign or international marketer would be hard pressed to find any consumers in foreign market who meet these criteria, except for U.S. tourists and expatriates.

The vast majority of foreign consumers do not share the resources or perceptions of needs and resources with the typical American consumer. A marketer can find a large number of a particular type of consumer—with matching characteristics such as age, sex, education, occupation, income, and family background—in Iowa, New York, California, and Georgia. As a result, reasonably good-sized market segments exist for almost any product in the United States. Even more important, these potential market segments can be expected to have sufficient income to purchase products, if not outright, at least on an extended payment basis.

This degree of similarity does not necessarily occur overseas. Special-purpose products, disposable products, and sophisticated products that require a great deal of technical skill to operate are not going to find large markets in most foreign countries. The second car for the family, the summer cottage, and the camping trailer are purchased by Americans even when a summary inquiry into the relative cost of alternatives such as cabs, resorts, motels, and trailer rentals would suggest that a better economic choice is available. This happens in the United States because the economic criteria for the decision are now less important than the psychological or social ones. In many markets around the world, product characteristics have to be matched primarily to the economic resources of the market segment in which they are sold.

Some of the more basic and critical questions related to product are listed in Table 17.3, part A. A review of these questions should indicate how product decisions can be influenced by considerations other than income, such as culture, psychology, laws, case of servicing, and so forth.

Beyond the specific economic constraints, the international marketing executive has to be concerned with sophistication of the intermediaries who handle or service the product, legal constraints such as safety and labeling, as well as the sophistication of the end user.

Fayerweather has suggested five important product characteristics that are relevant to making decisions about products for overseas markets. These are: primary functional purpose, secondary purpose, durability and quality, method of operation, and maintenance.[8] For example, in the United States, the bicycle is primarily used for leisure and health purposes. In Holland, however, it is a primary means of transportation

---

[8]John Fayerweather, *International Marketing*, 2nd ed. (Englewood Cliffs, N.J.: Prentice-Hall, Inc., 1970), p. 51.

TABLE 17.3 Key Marketing Mix Questions to Answer in Each Market or Country

Marketing Mix Elements	Questions
A. Product policies	1. What products and product lines should the company sell, for example, how broad and deep should the product line be for this market?
	2. To what extent should the company adapt and modify products to cultural, sociological, and national characteristics for this market?
	3. What improvements of existing products should be undertaken, and should the firm introduce a new product or products in this market?
	4. How should products be packaged and labeled in this market? (Includes a review of existing packaging and labeling laws.)
	5. How much emphasis is there on brand names and trademarks? Does the firm wish to use the same brand names and trademarks used in the United States and/or elsewhere in this market?
	6. What warranties and guarantees, if any, are desirable or must be offered and what other postsale service(s), such as repair service, is required in this market?
B. Advertising policies	1. To what extent should advertising themes and campaigns be differentiated from other markets to accommodate cultural, sociological, and national characteristics in this market? (Is standardized advertising a recommended and appropriate alternative in this market?)
	2. Should a local advertising agency, a branch, or subsidiary of the firm's international advertising agency be used in this market?
	3. What media are available, and what are their costs and unusual requirements? How reliable are media circulation or audience data?
	4. What is the availability and quality of media research organizations?
	5. What are the regulations on media advertising that would affect the firm's strategy in this market? What are the regulations on point-of-purchase and in-store materials?
	6. What roles do channel members play, and what advertising assistance, such as cooperative advertising, in-store promotion, and point-of-purchase materials, do channel members expect?
C. Distribution policies	1. What is the typical retail and wholesale structure for comparable products in this market?
	2. Should the firm use existing channels of distribution or attempt to alter the established distribution patterns in this market?
	3. Does the firm wish to sell directly to the retailer or through intermediaries in this market?
	4. Should the firm attempt to obtain wide distribution at the retail level or rely on exclusive dealerships or outlets in this market?
	5. How much channel control does the firm want in this market?
	6. What discount structure and credit terms are competitive and appropriate for this market?
	7. What is the quality of the available transportation, warehousing, and the firm's other physical distribution needs in this market?
	8. How much channel advertising support is necessary and appropriate for this market?
D. Pricing policies	1. What tariff and dumping laws are applicable in this market?
	2. Should the firm establish (or attempt to establish) uniform base prices?

TABLE 17.3 (Continued)

Marketing Mix Elements	Questions
	3. What specific pricing approach should be used in the market? (Examples are cost-oriented, competitor-oriented, and customer-oriented.)
	4. What are the price regulations (that is, price fixing and cartel arrangements) in this market?
	5. As an overall strategy, is penetration or skimming pricing preferable for new products in this market?
	6. What pricing approach do competitors use in this market?

SOURCE: Adapted from Richard T. Hise, Peter L. Gillet, and John K. Ryans, Jr., *Basic Marketing* (Cambridge, Mass.: Winthrop Publishers, Inc., 1979), pp. 546–50.

to and from work. In an African tribal community, the same bicycle may have an important secondary purpose of status. In fact, it may actually never be used yet displayed in a prominent place, so that other members of the community are aware of the owner's possession.

Durability and quality are also factors that must be appropriate for the proposed market. The heavy use to which bicycles are put in Holland more or less mandates a product that is highly reliable and durable. The same may not be the case for the African owner. Another factor that enters into the picture that affects durability and quality characteristics is the cost of repair. Because repair costs are generally significantly higher in the United States than in Europe, an emphasis has been placed on disposable products. In Europe, the emphasis is on repairability.

Other important characteristics are mechanical standards (for example, electrical voltage), conditions of use, method of operation, level of maintenance, and the availability of replacement parts. For example, driving conditions vary considerably from country to country and need to be accounted for in the product's design. Thus, the engines and radiators that are standard in the United States, Europe, or Japan may be very inadequate for use in the Bolivian Andes or Saudi Arabian desert. Also, the electrical current used varies; although 120 volts is the U.S. standard, 220 volts is a very widely used standard.

Promotion: The three basic elements of promotion are (1) identification of feasible promotional media, (2) analysis of the potential customer, and (3) the choice of the appropriate promotional program.

Consider the inputs needed to reach a decision on promotion strategy for a mass-produced consumer item such as toothpaste. The initial inputs will be related to the availability of *promotional media*. In the United States one would quickly conclude that television, radio, daily papers, magazines, billboards, direct mail, and sales personnel are feasible means of moving promotional messages to potential consumers.

Next, information is required on these potential consumers. Who are they? What do they look like from a marketer's viewpoint? How many are there? Where are they located? What do they read, listen to, view? How often? How much do they earn? How much do they spend? What do they spend their income on? Where do they shop? What is their educational level? Do they brush their teeth? How often? Do they use toothpaste? If so, which brand? A list of questions involving promotion was presented in Table 17.3, part B; included were considerations such as customer characteristics, media alternatives available, and governmental regulations.

These are just some of the question that need explicit or implicit answers before a rational promotion strategy can be developed. Once the correct questions have been identified and listed, the next question is where the marketer can get answers.

In the United States, there are many sources of information. Probably most information about the U.S. population comes from secondary sources such as the federal government. The U.S. Bureau of Census gathers extensive data on the population every ten years (the most recent census was in 1980) and carries out frequent sample surveys in between. Thus demographic information is available about Americans in terms of numbers, sex, age, family status, education, income, living conditions, and location. The Bureau also uses sophisticated techniques to forecast characteristics of the population for five, ten, and even twenty years into the future.

The Department of Commerce also publishes a vast amount of economic data, including the income and expenditure patterns of U.S. citizens, broken down to cover almost any macroeconomic information need of the U.S. business manager.

Besides the official sources mentioned above, there are many commercial and private sources of information. Industry and trade groups gather, analyze, and publish information pertaining to their particular fields of endeavor. Private organizations carry on research into consumer characteristics on a continuing basis and sell the results for profit. Perhaps the best known of these are the Gallup and Nielsen organizations.

As a final alternative, a company can always conduct its own primary research. In the United States, there is a ready supply of social scientists, mathematicians, and other trained personnel, as well as computers and the communications and transportation systems that make consumer research possible at reasonable cost. Most large American companies such as General Motors, Procter & Gamble, and DuPont, as well as many of the smaller companies, conduct continuing research concerning their customers, both actual and potential.

The point being made here is that there is a huge amount of useful information available, at a relatively low cost, on which promotion decisions can be based. Once sufficient information has been gathered about the size, composition, location, and responsiveness of the target market, the intricate national communication network can be used in a way that minimizes wasted effort. A media mix can be developed using local or national broadcasting, local and national newspapers and magazines, and the mails in such combinations that most of the selected target market will be reached by the promotional message. Furthermore, the costs of this type of activity can be accurately predicted, since these media publish reliable indices of the costs of their services.

A firm wishing to promote its product *in a foreign market* has the same basic promotion decisions to make. It must decide about its target market, its media mix, and its promotional message. In principle, the firm is doing nothing more or less than it was doing in its domestic efforts. Decisions have to be made about the same elements of the promotion mix. The inputs into the decision process, however, are different. Very few countries have any source of reliable information comparable to the U.S. Census Bureau or other Department of Commerce bureaus. Whereas a U.S. manager has access to many library shelves of research output concerning the American consumer, very little research has been done on most foreign consumers. Most of the world, and in particular the less-developed areas, has not subjected itself to academic introspection to any great extent. Thus, although a large number of books describing American motivations or the "American way of life" can be found, it is, for example, extremely difficult, if not impossible, to find any information that describes the "typical" Ethiopian or Indonesian, his or her motivations, and lifestyle.

Thus, the first promotional question—What is our target market?—is often hard to answer accurately. Reliable estimates usually originate with a United Nations agency or other international body rather than local sources. For example, the United Nations publishes a large volume of books, pamphlets, and reports on economic developments in various regions of the world (for example, *Economic Survey of Latin America),* and GATT makes available such publications as *Compilation of Basic Information on Export Markets* and *Market Surveys by Product and Countries.*

The second question—Which media should we select?—is often answered by default. In the United States, the difficult choice between national or local television may have to be made; however, no such choice is possible in most other countries. There may be only one television station (or none) operating only a few hours per day or even per week. Also even where TV and radio are readily available, commercials may be totally banned (such as in Belgium) or sharply curtailed (such as in the Netherlands). Moreover, a large portion of the population may have no access to a television set. Similarly, where illiteracy rates run in the 80 to 90 percent range, the press becomes a mass communication device for only a limited market. The development of media to carry a promotional message for a firm becomes dependent on the inventiveness of the marketing manager.

Despite the problems associated with the first two elements of promotion (that is, the identification of the availability of promotional media and of the demographic characteristics of consumers), the last element is probably the most difficult with which to deal—and certainly the most controversial. Even when a target market has been selected and a means of reaching it has been adequately developed, the question—What message should I use?—or, more accurately—Which message will elicit a purchase response?—still needs to be answered.

It has been said that the epitome of the ability to sell is the sale of a refrigerator to an Eskimo. The germ of truth in this is the relative importance of the sales message that translates the product into a means of satisfying some need or want. It should be readily apparent that modern advertising in the United States does not just provide product information (often not much product information is even given). Toothpaste is rarely advertised as merely a toothcleaning agent. Regular use of certain brands will lead anywhere from an interesting date, through marriage and success in business, to a happy retirement with contented grandchildren. Toothpaste is not the only product that will do this for a person. Advertising suggests that deodorants, shampoos, automobiles, razor blades, shoes, socks, underwear, even breakfast cereals will perform similar miracles. Such campaigns are, of course, generally most prominent in the United States and other developed countries but are frequently found in the major urban centers of most developing countries as well.

The success of such promotional messages is not accidental. Many years of study and research have led to the format of these advertisements. They are specifically engineered to influence certain target markets within the U.S. population. They are tailor-made for Americans and based on knowledge of their motivations and life styles.

What reasons are there for believing that these messages will have similar success with English, French, Latin American, Asian, and African consumers? Clearly, human beings everywhere have similar physical needs. They get cold, hungry, thirsty, and tired. Thus, they have needs that shelter, food, drink, and appliances will satisfy. However, as pointed out above, the content of modern promotional messages is not merely informational. It has appeals to the psychological and cultural makeup of potential consumers. Thus soft drink advertisements go beyond informing the public that the product will quench a thirst. They include some degree of social interaction as part of their appeal. Furthermore, they ignore (unless required to do so) any unsavory information such as the amount of sugar or lack of nutritional value—facets of information that may be very relevant to the consumer's needs and goals but that will likely have a negative or, at best, a neutral impact upon the consumer's image of the soft drink.

Careful research into the target market's cultural and attitudinal stance is needed, so that the promotional message can be used effectively. Furthermore, the degree of cultural sensitivity to promotional themes depends on the product that is being sold. Some firms have been very successful with a single promotional strategy that is used in almost all its markets. In general, though, one can safely assume that the nature of the product dictates the actual form of the strategy to a great extent. This point will be made clearer.

> In most of the dialogue regarding the common advertising approach, two key considerations are generally either ignored or only briefly noted. These considerations are the product to be marketed and its place in the market.
>
> The nature of the product may be the single most important factor in determining whether or not it is feasible for a firm to employ a common or universal approach in its multinational advertising. Certainly, there are low-priced, nondurable goods fulfilling basic needs that have broad potential markets. Firms selling such products may not be too concerned about many of the differences among global areas. Coca-Cola, for example, has successfully appealed to a broad market and become a by-word among consumers around the world. However, Coca-Cola is so low priced and appeals to such a basic biological need—thirst—that its potential market includes a large number of consumers wherever it is introduced.
>
> Virtually all durable goods producers, and most nondurable goods producers, are not blessed with such a broad potential market for their products. Questions relating to the product and its market need to be considered to determine whether or not the common approach is desirable.[9]

Distribution: Decisions on channel strategy are subject to similar environmental influences and informational constraints. Table 17.3, part C, presents a list of the types of questions that need answers before distribution decisions can be rationally made: for example, type and quality of distribution channels available, credit terms, and choice of corporate distribution policies in general.

In the United States, the corporate decision maker is very familiar with the capabilities of each of the distributional channels available (for example, mail order, wholesaler, and retailer) and the transportation channels available (for example, mail, truck, airplane, rail, and so forth). Accumulated information and experience enable the marketing executive to select those institutions that are best suited for the firm's products.

---

[9]John K. Ryans, Jr., "Is It Too Soon to Put a Tiger in Every Tank?" *Columbia Journal of World Business* (March–April 1969), p. 72.

In many foreign countries some of these distribution channels may be unavailable. Also, the executive's domestic experience with the channels that do exist in a particular foreign country may prove to be invalid. Thus attempts to transfer a successful domestic distribution pattern overseas will run into problems. The first problem is that there may not be a foreign institution equivalent to the company's traditional retail outlets (for example, a supermarket or a drugstore). Also, the patronage motives for using a particular type of outlet may differ from country to country. Time saving, packaging, breadth of product line, and pretty surroundings may not be as important to an Indian housewife as the money savings that would result from visiting many smaller, poorly built and maintained outlets, each with only a limited choice. The British housewife may not have a car to drive to a suburban supermarket. She may not have the consumption pattern or the refrigeration and storage capacity that would make large-scale, once-a-week shopping attractive to her; she may find it more economical to patronize the corner grocery store. The Peruvian housewife may prefer the daily personal contact with the baker, butcher, and so forth. All relevant environmental variables must be considered before a decision on outlets can be made.

It is also important to realize that differences in outlet characteristics do not arise at random. Entrepreneurs have experimented to develop channels that fit the requirements of their customers and the environmental conditions of the market. A firm that is new to a foreign environment might do well to analyze existing patterns of distribution to see why they work and how well they work before attempting to use American methods simply because they worked well in the United States. For example, the Japanese system of wholesale distribution is complicated (even cumbersome and inefficient), but foreign companies have generally found it very difficult to circumvent this expensive network.

Once the environment has been analyzed to determine how much of each type of service must be offered to derive full benefit from the environmental mix of a given country, the channel can be structured to provide these services to the degree required. If price is the crucial consideration for the Indian housewife, then inexpensive stores with a minimum of amenities may be the appropriate distribution channel. If a British housewife does not have a car, then a great deal of decentralization is required; the product must be placed where she can conveniently obtain it. If she does not have refrigeration and other storage facilities, then she requires small lot sizes or package sizes. Insofar as she has to feed her family daily and does not have adequate storage facilities, she needs a short delivery time for her food needs. All these requirements for the various services indicate that a small retail outlet may be appropriate for the British market. As it happens, the retail stores in Britain do tend to be smaller than those in the United States. Even the supermarkets that have been so successful in Britain in recent years are, on the average, much smaller than those in the United States.

In addition to the need to develop a distribution system designed to meet the environmental and target market characteristics of the foreign market, the firm must also develop a system of institutions that will enable it to reach the foreign market. Figure 17.1 shows a generalized form of the institutions involved in international marketing. The major *operating institutions* (line 1 in Figure 17.1) are the ones that produce and handle the product from the production line to the customer. They perform all the functions that are necessary in the operations of a marketing channel just as they would for domestic marketing. Ownership of the institutions by the producer can extend all the way from general intermediaries in Country A to the consumer in Country B, or it can stop anywhere in between. The extent of ownership depends in general on the economics of the situation. If the flow of goods is large enough, the producer might find it economically worthwhile to own, or to financially or otherwise control, its own intermediary institutions (that is, the intermediaries). Thus the producer may own distributing, wholesaling, and even retailing facilities. The volume of trade would have to be very great to make this type of ownership worthwhile. In the United States, only the oil companies have a structure that is close to full ownership of the marketing channel, and even the oil companies generally own retail outlets by default rather than by choice. Usually, therefore, the channel functions in domestic or international marketing are performed by specialists who have only a trading relationship with others in the channel. In a foreign area where specialists are not available, the producer may need to finance the intermediary institutions by itself or in collaboration with nationals of the area.

It should be noted that ownership is not the crucial factor here. The crucial factor is the extent to which the behavior of the intervening institutions in the channel can be relied upon to make the firm's marketing programs most effective and, in the longer run, most profitable.

Table 17.4 illustrates some of the many domestic and foreign marketing intermediaries to which reference was made in Figure 17.1. Export merchants, trading companies, and distributors fall under the heading of "general intermediaries." All others usually qualify as "special intermediaries." Description of these types of firms can be found in the Glossary at the end of the book.

The *controlling institutions* (line 2 in Figure 17.1) represent national policy at the borders. National policy involving the economic well-being of the nation is reflected in restrictions on the flows of certain types of goods. These restrictions, generally available from governmental agencies, are very detailed and specific. In order to assure compliance, several kinds of documents must be prepared and presented to the authorities, who in turn allow or block a flow of goods across the border.

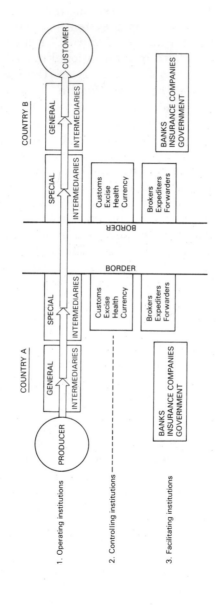

FIGURE 17.1 Institutions Involved in International Marketing Flows

TABLE 17.4 Characteristics of Intermediaries Involved in the International Flow of Goods

Type of Intermediaries	a Take Title?	b Take Possession?	c Control Price?	d Continuing Relationship?	e Representing Buyer or Seller?	f Arrange Shipping?	g Handle Competitive Lines?	h Type Goods?
Domestic:								
• Combination export manager	no	yes	advisory	yes	seller	yes	no	manufactured goods and commodities
• Manufacturer's export agent	no	yes	advisory	yes	seller	yes	no	staples and commodities
• Export broker	no	no	yes	no	either	not usually	yes	staples and commodities
• Export merchant	yes	yes	yes	no	self	yes	yes	manufactured goods
• Export jobber	yes	no	yes	yes	self	yes	yes	bulky and raw materials
• Trading companies	yes	yes	no	yes	self	yes	yes	manufactured goods
Foreign:								
• Import broker	no	no	nil	no	either	no	yes	commodity, food
• Factor	no	no	nil	sometimes	either	no	yes	commodity, food
• Manufacturer's representative	no	seldom	nil	often	seller	no	no	manufactured goods
• Import commission agent	no	seldom	nil	with buyer	buyer	no	yes	manufactured goods
• Distributor	yes	yes	partial	yes	seller	no	no	manufactured goods
• Dealer	yes	yes	partial	yes	seller	no	no	manufactured goods
• Import jobber	yes	yes	yes	no	self	no	yes	manufactured goods

SOURCE: Adapted from Philip R. Cateora and John M. Hess, *International Marketing*, 4th ed. (Homewood, Ill.: Richard D. Irwin, 1979), Exhibits 18–2 and 18–3, pp. 560–69. Chapter 18 of this book is entirely devoted to an excellent treatment of the international distribution system.

National policy on the physical well-being of the nation is also reflected in restrictions at the borders. Goods, particularly perishable and edible ones, must conform to specific standards concerning production, packaging, and sources. Thus meat shipments from areas suffering cattle diseases will be blocked, as will certain drugs, plants, and animals.

Almost all countries also have specific regulations concerning the flow of currencies across boundaries. These regulations may only insist on the reporting of amounts for information purposes, so that a country can know its position in an international monetary sense. More often, the regulations are for control purposes and are aimed at hindering some kinds of currency flows and fostering others (see Chapter 4).

The *facilitating institutions* (line 3 in Figure 17.1) are of three types. The first type is concerned with easier movement and reduced risk of financial flows across countries. The services of banks and insurance companies provide security against certain types of losses that can easily occur when buyer and seller are separated by distance, languages, laws, and culture. The second type of institution is more directly concerned with the product itself. Customs expediters, for example, specialize in and gain a thorough knowledge of a particular country's customs regulations and procedures. Then, for a commission, they ensure that a shipment passes a customs examination with minimum delay and at lowest cost. Freight forwarders accept responsibility for the movement of a shipment from point A to point B; they handle all the documentation and transshipments required for a client and charge a fee for their services, which the client merely adds to his or her costs of doing business. The client does not have to train someone or have someone available to perform this type of function when the volume of foreign business is large enough to warrant such fixed expenditure. The third type is the shipper, for example, the airline, shipping line, railroad, and trucking line.

Price: A list of key questions that need to be answered before a foreign pricing policy can be formulated and adopted is also presented in Table 17.3, part D: for example, regulations, competition, and pricing policies. Essentially, the firm can select from among three pricing alternatives: (1) a standardized worldwide base price; (2) a domestic price and a standard export price; and (3) a market-differentiated price. For each of these alternatives, the firm can choose a cost-oriented or market-oriented pricing policy.[10]

Cost considerations are fairly straightforward. The initial production costs for foreign-made products are often higher than for comparable domestic products, since the volume of production is generally smaller for foreign market segments. This smaller volume arises both from

[10]Richard D. Robinson, *International Business Management,* 2nd ed. (Hinsdale, Ill.: Dryden Press, 1978), pp. 94–99.

the relatively smaller total size of the effective market and from specific differences in batch requirements to fit differences in electric current or to accommodate other supporting services. The decision whether to produce in a foreign country (and probably incur higher production costs) or to produce at a home plant and export the product into the foreign market (and incur tariff and transportation costs) can also have a strong influence on the ultimate price of a product in a foreign market. If the product can actually be manufactured more cheaply abroad, the producer might have little choice other than to manufacture overseas; otherwise it might be impossible to meet foreign competition.

Transportation and handling costs are likely to differ also. The cost per hour of a transportation crew may be lower overseas, but it might take much longer to accomplish a job, so one should not rely solely on the savings from the lower wage rates that are quoted in this respect. The lack of adequate facilities for handling and storage of goods in most places may lead to extra costs for stronger packaging, smaller units, or greater spoilage. Finally, account has to be taken of the mandatory additions to final price that will arise from tax agencies in the market countries.

The market considerations affecting price are, of course, equally important. Cost data only determine a price floor below which the product would be unprofitable. The most immediate market consideration is the economic characteristics of the target market. This has already been discussed at some length. The other considerations define the firm and its policies in relation to the market. A firm that is established in a market behaves differently from a firm just entering a new market. Also, if it is decided to skim the market rather than to penetrate it for a long-term stay, change in pricing policy is necessary.

The competition the firm faces is different from that faced at home. Although competition may be lacking for products that are fairly new to a market, it is likely to be strong for items that have a traditional place in the consumer's shopping list. In such cases, changes in price are likely to be ineffective in changing the buying habits of consumers, since foreign-made (for example, American) items, with their greater sophistication, generally have higher purchase prices than their traditional counterparts, even though the cost to the consumer of the foreign-made product may be lower over time.

PROBLEMS UNIQUE TO INTERNATIONAL MARKETING MANAGEMENT

As emphasized, a critical question that must be answered when developing a coordinated and integrated international marketing program is the degree to which national marketing programs can be standardized across national boundaries. That is, what elements of the marketing mix can be universally applied and still permit each national marketing program to be effective? Can the same product be used for all markets? Can one price be charged the final consumer regardless of his or her nationality? Can the same appeal be used in all markets? And so on.

A basic motivating force behind the desire to standardize the international marketing program is the ability of the firm to exploit six potential advantages that accrue to firms operating internationally. These advantages are

1. *Program transfer.* International marketing management can draw upon the strategies, products, advertising appeals, sales management practices, promotional ideas, and so on that have been developed and tested in one or more markets and apply them in other comparable markets.

2. *Systems transfer.* International marketing management can introduce planning, budgeting, product development, personnel, and other systems developed and tested in the company into new markets.

3. *People transfer.* International marketing management can assign people across national boundaries, thus developing a cadre of personnel experienced in several national markets and using particular skills and talents more effectively on a global scale.

4. *Economies of centralization of functional activities.* International marketing management can eliminate, or at least reduce, duplication and dispersal of the marketing staff by concentrating at single locations particular activities and thereby developing greater competence and, at the same time, reducing costs.

5. *Resource utilization.* While all firms are constrained in their business activities by their resources and capabilities, an international marketing perspective enables the international marketing management to scan the entire world to identify sources of manpower, money, and materials that will enable it to most effectively compete in world markets.

6. *Global strategy.* Because of the five advantages listed above, international marketing management is also in a better position to scan the world for marketing opportunities and to apply its skills, resources, and marketing programs where and when necessary to more effectively exploit these opportunities. The ability of the firm to maximize the benefits derived from these advantages is directly, if not fully, dependent upon the international marketing executive's ability to standardize his or her national marketing programs.[11]

For example, profitability depends ultimately on both sales and costs, and there are significant opportunities for cost reductions via standardization. The most obvious, and usually the most important, area for cost savings is product design. By offering the same basic product in

---

[11]Adapted from Warren J. Keegan, *Multinational Marketing Management,* 2nd ed. (Englewood Cliffs, N.J.: Prentice-Hall, Inc., 1980), p. 26.

several national markets with some possible variations in functional and/or design features, a firm can frequently achieve longer production runs, spread research and development and administrative costs over a greater volume, and thus reduce total unit costs.

Standardization also permits international firms to achieve consistency in their dealings with customers and ultimate consumers (who may or may not be the same). Many international marketing executives believe that consistency in product design, post-sale servicing, brand name, and packages has a direct and positive influence on sales. International travel by tourists and business personnel and the development of international communication add credence to this belief. If a British tourist in Spain, for example, sees his or her favorite brands in a store, he or she may well buy them during a visit and, importantly, reinforce his or her brand loyalty in this international product. Also, as is the case in Europe and Canada, radio and television messages extend across national boundaries, thus heightening the possibility of confusion if different brand names and promotional appeals are used. Nestle, Unilever, and Exxon are examples of firms that have successfully adopted a standardized approach in promotional appeals.

> Many companies have found real benefits in a multinational approach to marketing strategy. The gains have included greater effectiveness in marketing, reduced costs, and improved planning and control. Moreover, especially in Western Europe but also in some other parts of the world, social and economic trends are working in favor of more, rather than less, standardization in marketing policies. Tourism, international communication, increased numbers of multinational customers, and other forces are all tending toward greater unification of multinational markets.[12]

The standardization approach is well established in some industries. For example, as shown in Table 17.5, a recent survey of 100 executives from 27 multinational firms in the food, soft-drink, soap-detergent-toiletries, and cosmetics industries indicated that 63 percent believe their international marketing programs were highly standardized (line 1). Further, 71 percent felt that their basic advertising message was standardized (line 6); 76 percent used standardized packaging (line 4); 81 percent had standardized product characteristics (line 2), and an overwhelming 93 percent employed standardized brand names (line 3). However, on the other hand, only 43 percent employed standardized media allocation (line 9)—a fact that reflects the different media laws and infrastructure in various countries.

---

[12]Robert D. Buzzell, "Can You Standardize Multinational Marketing?" *Harvard Business Review* (November–December 1968), p. 107.

TABLE 17.5   Standardization of Marketing Decisions among European Subsidiaries of Selected
Multinational Enterprises

Elements of the Marketing Program	Distribution of Executive Ratings of the Degree of Standardization of Their Marketing Programs as a Percent of All Ratings		
	Low Standardization	Moderate Standardization	High Standardization
1. Total marketing program	27	11	63
2. Product characteristics	15	4	81
3. Brand name	7	0	93
4. Packaging	20	7	76
5. Retail price	30	14	56
6. Basic advertising message	20	6	71
7. Creative expression	34	4	62
8. Sales promotion	33	11	56
9. Media allocation	47	10	43
10. Role of sales force	15	10	74
11. Management of sales force	17	10	72
12. Role of Intermediaries	13	7	80
13. Type of Retail Outlet	34	7	59

SOURCE: Adapted from Ralph Z. Sorenson and Ulrich E. Wiechmann, "How Multinationals
View Marketing Standardization," *Harvard Business Review* (May–June 1975), p. 39.

If, as has already been suggested, standardization offers many potential benefits to the international firm, why don't all international marketing executives standardize their international marketing programs? The answer to this question depends on several factors, some of which have already been discussed. Variations in market characteristics are possibly the most important. However, the executive's attitude toward foreign markets and the marketing function also play significant roles. The remainder of this section presents three types of attitudes that have been found to be prevalent among international executives and show how these attitudinal categories affect the international marketing approach adopted. The section concludes with a discussion of one approach that can be used to determine whether selected marketing mix elements can be standardized across national markets.

MANAGEMENT ATTITUDE AND EXPERIENCE

Management attitude has a pervasive and enduring influence on a firm's operations and functions. International marketing management is no exception. How international marketing management views its foreign markets and the tasks to be performed has a direct influence on the organizational structure adopted and even on the national and international marketing programs developed. As noted in an earlier chapter, executives can be classified by their ethnocentric, polycentric, or geocentric perspectives. In the real world of business, the lines between these three types of attitudes are often not distinct. People, in general, have a mixture of attitudes that may fall within two or all of the categories. They also may change with time as they grow older and gain experience in international activities.

The *ethnocentric approach* to international marketing assumes that all markets are basically the same. This approach assumes that people throughout the world have basically the same needs and wants to be satisfied and will react to specific products and appeals in the same fashion. A U.S. marketing executive who has been successful in the United States, if ethnocentric in his or her attitudes, will naturally believe that what has been successful domestically will also be successful elsewhere. He or she will, therefore, be prone to introduce the same product in other countries and will use the same promotional appeals, distribution systems and oulets, and so on. Some companies, such as Coca-Cola, Pepsi-Cola, and Exxon have been quite successful using this approach. The majority of companies, however, will not find this to be a successful approach. Campbell Soups, for example, lost $30 million dollars over a five-year period when it first attempted to penetrate the European markets by assuming that European tastes were the same as those of U.S. customers and that Europeans would therefore respond to promotional appeals designed for U.S. customers.[13]

An ethnocentric approach also implies that all marketing activities can be centralized at the firm's domestic headquarters, and that new products and new promotional appeals can be tested in that domestic market and then later extended into other national markets without change.

The *polycentric approach* to international marketing is at the opposite extreme; it assumes that all markets are irreconcilably different. As a result, the marketing programs including product and promotion must be tailored to each market, necessitating a totally decentralized approach. The polycentric marketer would feel that local marketing executives must have complete charge of all marketing activities, since it is only the local executive who can know and be sensitive to the particular needs and wants of his or her market and how these needs and wants are to be appealed to and satisfied. Generally, this approach is adopted by many firms when first entering international activities or by those that have experienced calamities as a result of using an unsuccessful ethnocentric approach.

The *geocentric approach* to international marketing is a more balanced view; it assumes that there are some marketing activities that can be centralized and some that need to be decentralized. Such an approach is reflected in the survey results shown in Table 17.5. A geocentric

---

[13]"The $30 Million Lesson," *Sales Management*, March 1, 1967, p. 31.

marketing perspective is the result of experience and the accumulation of trade-offs between the need to tailor the various elements of the marketing program to the individual needs and wants of each national market, the need for international coordination and control of these national marketing programs, and the resulting costs versus the sales generated. For example, most large multinational firms show a tendency to eventually centralize their product design activities while decentralizing their promotional activities.

PRODUCT AND PROMOTION PLANNING

Product: One approach that can be used to determine whether national marketing programs can be standard is to analyze the firm's product in terms of the needs or wants to be satisfied.[14] There are, of course, many ways to classify products. They can be classified as durable and nondurable, industrial and consumer, and so on. Each classification system is developed to meet certain requirements. When classifying products for sale internationally, the classification system used should give some clue as to the degree that cultural, social, and other factors influence buying behavior.

The durable and nondurable classification system does not provide information such as this, and consequently it does not assist the international marketing executive to develop his or her marketing programs, either national or international. A better approach is to divide products into consumer and industrial categories. For example, consumer products are usually much more sensitive to cultural and sociological forces than are industrial products. The reason for this is that most industrial products are purchased to help solve problems that are production or product related; industrial products are generally not heavily affected by the ego needs of the buyer or user. As such, and since the technologies and production processes are very similar the world over, the problems these products help to solve are also similar. Although such motives as prestige can play a role even in some industrial purchasing decisions, the buyer is acting more like the rational economic buyer who is generally envisioned by economic analysts. Delivery, reliability, durability, and price play significantly more important roles in industrial purchasing. Thus, permitting a high degree of worldwide standardization of all marketing program elements is possible.

Promotion: It should not be too surprising to learn, therefore, that international marketers of industrial products are not faced with the same promotional problems as are international marketers of consumer products. The marketers of consumer goods must understand the

---

[14]This section is based largely on Warren J. Keegan, "Multinational Product Planning: Strategic Alternatives," *Journal of Marketing* (January 1969), pp. 58–62.

psychological and social forces that motivate purchases and the types of appeals that are effective, necessitating more worldwide diversification of the marketing program elements.

These points can be clarified by discussing the various planning alternatives identified in Table 17.6. There are five possible product-communication alternatives available, as follows:

1. The *same product* is sold worldwide, and it is promoted with the *same message* (that is, "extension" of both product and marketing strategy into foreign markets).
2. The *same product* is sold worldwide, but the approach to the *promotion* of the product is *adapted* to each market (that is, extended product, adapted promotion program).
3. The *product* is *adapted* to local market conditions but is promoted with essentially the *same message* (that is, adapted product but extended marketing strategy).
4. Both the *product and promotional message* are *adapted* to local market conditions.
5. *New products* and *new promotional* strategies are devised for foreign markets.

The selection of any particular strategy from among these five alternatives is dependent upon three factors: the function or need to be satisfied by the product (column d in Table 17.6), the conditions under which the product will be used (column e), and the cost incurred in adapting the product to local conditions (column c).

The first strategy involves the use of *the same product and message worldwide*. It is the least costly, since the product and communication techniques are extensions of what is used in the country of product origin.[15] Most soft drink and cosmetics firms sell the same basic product worldwide and use essentially the same advertising and promotional appeals developed and tested in their domestic markets. Very little variation exists from country to country in target consumer groups in terms of the function or need to be satisfied and the conditions of product use. As noted above, many industrial product firms have also found that they can use this particular strategy successfully, since most business-related problems are the same the world over. Even in less-developed countries, product specifications for equipment and plant, computers, and the like, generally follow those developed in the industrial countries. This is often true, even if that is not the optimal economic approach for a poor country. For example, many governments of developing countries insist that foreign investors or government agencies buy only the most up-to-date equipment, despite the fact that such equipment is capital-intensive, requires highly trained operators, is expensive to repair, and

---

[15]The country of product origin is commonly, but not necessarily, the home country of the company.

TABLE 17.6 Strategic Product-Communication Alternatives

| | Marketing Strategy | | | Foreign Country's Use of Product Versus Home Country's Use | | |
| | a | b | c | d | e | f |
	Product	Promotional Message	Relative Cost of Adjustment	Product Function or Need Satisfied	Conditions of Product Use	Product Examples
Strategy 1	Same product	Same message	1	Same	Same	Soft drinks, cosmetics, most industrial equipment and supplies
Strategy 2	Same product	Adapted message	2	Different	Same	Bicycles, motor scooters
Strategy 3	Adapted product	Same message	3	Same	Different	Gasoline, detergent
Strategy 4	Adapted product	Adapted message	4	Different	Different	Clothing, greeting cards
Strategy 5	New product	New message	5	Same	—	Cars, trucks, food products

SOURCE: Adapted from Warren J. Keegan, "Multinational Product Planning: Strategic Alternatives," *Journal of Marketing,* January 1969, p. 59.

may also be very energy intensive. In countries that are capital poor, suffer from high unemployment, have a shortage of highly skilled labor, and have extremely high energy costs, such purchasing mandates are very shortsighted.

This particular marketing strategy has great appeal to companies because of its associated cost savings and because of the opportunity for the firm to take advantage of its international economies of scale. Unfortunately, and as already noted, this strategy does not work for all products.

The second basic promotional strategy utilizes the *same product* worldwide but with *different messages*. When a product fills a different need or serves a different function but is used under conditions similar to those in the market of origin, the only adjustment required is the message. As previously noted, bicycles satisfy basically different needs in the U.S., Dutch, and African markets. The condition of use, however, is basically the same. [Thus, the appeal of selling the same product but with a communication adaptation strategy stems from the savings resulting from *product* standardization.] The only additional costs are those incurred in identifying the different needs or functions to be satisfied and the development or promotional appeals around the newly identified functions or needs.

Strategy three employs a *modified product* but promotion with the *same message* worldwide. This approach assumes the product will satisfy the same needs or function, but under different use conditions. Exxon used this approach when it modified its gasoline to meet different climatic and user conditions, yet it used its "Put a Tiger in Your Tank" theme worldwide. In general, soap and detergent companies also use such a strategy, adjusting the product to meet local water and washing machine characteristics and yet using universal appeals.

The fourth strategy utilizes both a *modified product and message*. It is introduced when the function of the product is different from the traditional market for the product. This strategy is basically a combination of strategies two and three. For example, U.S. greeting card companies have had to change their product and message in Europe. In contrast to U.S. greeting cards, European greeting cards are designed to provide space for the sender to write his or her own message. Also, European greeting cards are used for both personal and business purposes. Clothing must also usually be adapted, since there can be considerable variation in tastes in clothing fashions between countries and in climatic conditions.

Strategy five employs *product invention* and development of *new messages*. This approach is used when existing products are unsatisfactory for the new market and cannot be adopted. The problem could be of either function or price. For example, when potential customers cannot afford one of the firm's products, an opportunity exists to invent or design an entirely new product that satisfies a particular need or function at a price the customer can afford. This strategy may be quite rewarding for the mass markets of developing countries—provided, of course, that the research, development and production costs are not excessive. For example, some multinational companies have developed or brought licenses for entirely new products designed specifically for the low-income markets of developing countries. Quaker Oats sells a high-protein, low-cost food product for some South American markets which was developed by a Guatemalan research group. Ford and General Motors designed vehicles that are small, relatively inexpensive, and easily assembled with an emphasis on utility, durability, and ease of repair.

SUMMARY

The basic functions of marketing and the elements of the marketing program and marketing activities are the same for domestic, foreign, and international marketing. However, the implementation and control of foreign and international marketing can be quite different from domestic marketing because of environmental differences and the evolving need for the coordination and integration of foreign marketing programs into comprehensive international marketing programs. Thus, the international marketer is not only faced with finding some optimum combination of price, product, promotion, and distribution policies and practices, but he or she has to be aware of the way environmental factors abroad affect each segment of the mix and the total marketing effort.

These environmental and organizational differences, and the implications that flow from them for international marketing management, result in many special and unique problems. Throughout the many dimensions of the international marketing function, conflicts arise over the need to standardize marketing activities and marketing programs to reduce costs and improve the coordination and integration of the firm's marketing efforts. The conflict basically revolves about product, price, promotional strategy decisions, and the way in which the marketing activity is organized and viewed by the international marketing executive. Unfortunately, there are no general or fixed rules for resolving these conflicts, subject as they are to the environmental constraints imposed by foreign markets, the firm's resources and capabilities, and the firm's objectives.

KEY TERMS

COMPARATIVE MARKETING	INTERNATIONAL MARKETING	MARKETING PROGRAM STANDARDIZATION
FOREIGN MARKETING	INTERNATIONAL TRADE	TARGET MARKET

REVIEW QUESTIONS

1. Why are the terms *international trade* and *international marketing* not interchangeable?
2. What is international marketing?
3. What are some of the internal pressures that encourage firms to seek overseas opportunities? What are some of the external pressures?
4. When and why is it necessary to limit the analysis of market potential to secondary data for some foreign markets?
5. Why do some firms have highly standardized international marketing programs and others do not?
6. Which elements of the marketing program are likely to be standardized? Which are not? Why?
7. Identify the five product-communication strategies available to the international firm, and explain the reasons why one strategy may be preferred over another.

SUGGESTED REFERENCES

BAKER, JAMES C., AND JOHN K. RYANS, JR. *Multinational Marketing Dimensions in Strategy.* Columbus, Ohio: Grid Publishing, Inc., 1975.

BARTELS, ROBERT, ed. *Comparative Marketing: Wholesaling in Fifteen Countries.* Homewood, Ill.: Richard D. Irwin, 1963.

BODDEWYN, JEAN *Comparative Management and Marketing.* Glenview, Ill.: Scott, Foresman & Company, 1969.

CARSON, DAVID *International Marketing—A Comparative Systems Approach.* New York: John Wiley & Sons, Inc., 1967.

CATEORA, PHILIP R., AND JOHN M. HESS *International Marketing* (4th ed.). Homewood, Ill.: Richard D. Irwin, 1979.

FAYERWEATHER, JOHN *International Marketing.* Englewood Cliffs, N.J.: Prentice-Hall, Inc., 1970.

KEEGAN, WARREN J. *Multinational Marketing Management* (2nd ed.). Englewood Cliffs, N.J.: Prentice-Hall, Inc. 1980.

KORTH, CHRISTOPHER M. "Barter—An Old Practice Yields New Profits," *Business,* September–October 1981.

TERPSTRA, VERN *International Marketing* (2nd ed.). Hinsdale, Ill.: Dryden Press, 1978.

18

Personnel Management in International Operations

One of the most important differences between business operations in one country and business operations encompassing more than one country is the nature of the human resource problems and opportunities of the firms. The success of a company abroad is very much a function of the quality of the managers and other key employees—both those at headquarters who control or maintain liaison with the foreign operations and the managers of the foreign operations. The domestic problems of motivation, leadership, and productivity remain when a firm becomes multinational in its operations, but a whole new group of behavioral issues becomes as important as the old ones. How can the best people be selected to go abroad to work in a foreign environment? How should they be trained? Once selected, how can a cultural transition be made? If the firm has a force of workers distributed over the world, how can consistent personnel policies be administered to so many different kinds of people in so many different environments? What do the nationals of one country working in another country need in order to be effective, productive workers in the new environment? These questions and many others are added to the domestic behavioral questions when a firm emerges from operating in a single national environment.

The international personnel function is examined in the following three parts:

1. the *selection and training* of the appropriate personnel for the company's international operations

2. the *management of personnel* worldwide
3. the *adjustment problem* for employees who are sent to work in a foreign country or who must at least travel there

The selection and training of those employees who will play sensitive roles in the company's international operations (item 1 above) includes not only those who will be working abroad but also the personnel from the home country who interact with the foreign staff and who must travel abroad often. Likewise, the adjustment problems (item 3) affect traveling officers as well as those who reside abroad. The worldwide management of personnel (item 2) can affect all of the company's employees, both international and domestic.

THE STATUS OF FOREIGN ASSIGNMENTS

Some companies find it much easier to induce employees to accept foreign assignments than do other companies. The difference may stem from the image that foreign assignments have within a particular company.

Some firms treat foreign assignments as second-rate positions. They might send individuals with relatively little growth potential at home. For those companies it obviously is going to be much more difficult to attract top-level managers abroad, even if the company's priorities change to favor foreign operations. The company's performance in its foreign operations is likely to reflect the quality of the managers who were sent. Fortunately, this attitude toward foreign jobs is much less common than it was in the 1950s and 1960s.

At other companies, foreign assignments are virtually prerequisites for promotion to senior management. In those companies, many of the best managers are likely to be anxious to accept challenging (and appropriately rewarded) foreign assignments. The relative cost of inducing such transfers is likely to be less in such a company. Also, the performance of the company's foreign operations is likely to reflect the quality of the managers and technicians assigned to those operations.

THE SELECTION OF PERSONNEL
FOR INTERNATIONAL OPERATIONS

THE NUMBER OF EMPLOYEES SENT ABROAD

Contrary to popular misconception, most international business jobs are in the country of the company's headquarters. Most employees, including managers, who are actively involved in the international operations of the company seldom, if ever, even travel abroad.

There are probably also more employees who travel abroad for their company from its domestic operations than there are employees who are sent by their companies to actually live abroad. Many managers spend several months a year outside of their home office visiting various corporate facilities in foreign countries.

Finally, most of the employees who work abroad are typically going to be nationals rather than *expatriates* (that is, people from foreign countries). In past years companies were commonly much more inclined to send their nationals to live abroad. However, the high costs and the availability of rapid worldwide transportation, coupled with the host country's demands for the hiring and training of local nationals in important corporate positions and the much greater availability of competent nationals in the host country make the use of expatriates much less attractive (and even impossible in some cases). Even high-income countries such as Switzerland have tight controls over the use of foreign nationals by foreign companies or even by Swiss companies.

THE TYPES OF EMPLOYEES SENT ABROAD

The most prominent type of expatriate employee is a manager. However, as was seen in Chapter 3, there are also very large numbers of technicians and other skilled workers who work abroad. For example, oil exploration throughout the world is heavily populated by oil drillers from Oklahoma and Texas.

In some cases companies even bring semiskilled and even unskilled workers to work on foreign construction projects. For example, South Korean construction projects in the Middle East use tens of thousands of Korean workers. However, this latter is a very special and limited case. Our discussion only focuses upon the choice of managers and technically-skilled employees.

THE TYPES OF SKILLS NECESSARY IN THE EXPATRIATE EMPLOYEE

Both expatriate employees and the domestic counterparts must be highly skilled in their function whether it be accounting, production, drilling, or so on. Yet, as in any endeavor, the more varied and complicated are demands that are placed upon a job, the fewer the individuals who can competently fulfill the job. A first-class accountant or engineer is not necessarily a first-rate manager. Similarly, the top-rated domestic accountant–manager or engineer-manager is not always going to make the best foreign manager even in a comparable job. The selection process for foreign assignments is extremely important but very difficult and, unfortunately, not very scientific.

A strong argument can be made for many foreign assignments that the individual chosen must be even better than the domestic counterpart. In domestic operations managers or technical workers often encounter a situation for which they must seek the assistance of a specialist. However, distances, time differentials, staffing limitations, and communication problems often make it much more difficult for the expatriate to obtain assistance. Therefore, the expatriate must often be much more self-reliant than in a corresponding domestic job.

Another requirement of an assignment abroad is the ability to adjust to local conditions. *Cultural shock* is a major part of this, but so also is *political shock* and *economic shock*. Operating in an Asian or Arabic culture, under a dictatorship, or in a primitive or socialist economy can be a major change for a manager. Adaptability to differing conditions is an important managerial skill for expatriate managers.

Many individuals cannot make the adjustment. Unfortunately, before making an assignment abroad, it is not easy to identify individuals who will be able to make a successful adjustment. Tests and other screening techniques have been developed to attempt to differentiate between those likely to adjust successfully and those likely to fail. However, test results have not generally been satisfactory.

Successful adjustment to foreign conditions is also a challenge for the manager's family. Many foreign assignments have failed, at a very high cost to the company, not because the manager was unsuccessful, but because his or her family failed to adapt. Therefore, before sending a manager on a foreign assignment, companies commonly interview the spouse as well as the manager. However, the same shortcomings of screening techniques exist that were mentioned above concerning the choice of the manager.

THE LEVEL OF RESPONSIBILITY IN THE FOREIGN ASSIGNMENTS

Foreign assignments commonly expose expatriates to levels of responsibility far beyond what would be true in a corresponding domestic assignment. Indeed, this opportunity to assume greater responsibility is a strong attraction for many people in their choice of a foreign assignment. However, for the company it means that the individual chosen must not only be at least as competent as the domestic counterpart, but commonly must also be more mature, able to operate more independently, and capable of making responsible decisions.

In some foreign assignments expatriates find themselves faced with the need to negotiate with government officials and senior managers of other local companies; these people are commonly older and more experienced. Not all domestically successful employees can fill such requirements.

Thus, the choice of the employee for foreign assignment focuses upon the following three primary factors:

1. *job competence* (relative to a corresponding domestic job—with allowance for any additional difficulties in the foreign job slot)
2. *maturity* to accept increased responsibility
3. *adaptability* of both the manager and his or her family to a foreign culture

The three criteria could be termed the three "abilities": *capability, responsibility,* and *adaptability.*

THE NATIONALITY OF OVERSEAS EMPLOYEES

Except in relatively isolated cases, unskilled and semiskilled workers for a company's foreign operations are hired in the local market abroad. However, a company has a greater variety of options when it is in the process of choosing managerial and technical personnel. It may be able to find the optimal personnel locally in the foreign country. The company may also choose to hire nationals from the home country of the parent company. A third choice is the hiring of *third-country nationals* (TCNs). For example, at one time the First National Bank of Chicago had a Syrian running its Lebanese operations, a Lebanese national managing its Jamaican operations, a German running its Venezuelan operations, and an American managing its German facilities.

Experienced managers generally agree that the single most important requirement for appointment to a foreign operation is managerial or technical competence. If the individual is not highly competent, he or she will likely not only do a poor job for the company but may also find it difficult to earn the respect of the other employees in the foreign affiliate. On the other hand, if the manager is competent, then a manager of any nationality could be appropriate. The idea is to find the best manager or technician for each particular job, regardless of nationality. However, in some cases a manager's nationality itself could be a serious barrier, for example, an Israeli would not be welcome in most Arab countries, and a South African would be unwelcome in most of Africa.

The host-country national: In many respects, the ideal candidate for most overseas jobs with a company would be a host-country national with extensive experience in the parent company's headquarters or elsewhere where he or she could absorb a wealth of knowledge about the company's policies, practices, and technological skills. There are tens of thousands of foreign nationals at colleges in the United States and European countries such as the United Kingdom, France, and Germany. This group is a prime source of employees for a company's foreign operations. Not only do such individuals have the benefit of training in modern techniques and the opportunity to be trained at the corporate headquarters, but they also know the language and customs of their home countries. The most adaptable of these may even become *bicultural*—the ability to live comfortably in either of two cultures.

Other advantages for hiring a local national can include lower salary and hiring costs, often substantially less than a foreign counterpart. That individual may also have valuable local contacts.

If the company has a very long time horizon for its operations in that particular country, then it may be especially important if local nationals play a prominent role in the company from the very beginning. Even if these individuals may have other shortcomings relative to a foreign national, the company may opt to hire and train local nationals for future needs in that country. This choice is especially likely if a local image is important for the company in that country. Finally, local nationals are often chosen because the government insists upon locals being hired!

There are also certain potential disadvantages from choosing local nationals. The most common of these is probably that of communication problems with the parent or other affiliates of the same company. Although the local national has an advantage over foreign nationals when dealing with local workers, suppliers, customers, and so forth, they can be at a linguistic or cultural disadvantage when trying to communicate with nonlocal nationals at foreign affiliates of the same company or with important suppliers or customers from another country. Some of these difficulties can, of course, be reduced by choosing an appropriate mix of local and foreign nationals for various managerial and technical roles within the foreign facility. However, the potential troubles need to be considered.

Other possible disadvantages from hiring local nationals stem from some of the political advantages mentioned above. The local national may be more likely to be drawn into local social or political conflicts, may find it difficult to view developments from the corporate perspective when there is a potential conflict with some local interests, and may be subject to local political or social pressure to a much greater extent than would a foreign national. Also, sometimes host-country nationals may not be the best choice for managing local employees. For example, where there is a definite religious or caste division among the workers, a foreign manager may be the best compromise, since any local choice might antagonize one group or the other.

Some foreign companies experience a high rate of turnover among local nationals. This is analogous to domestic conditions in the United States, where companies such as IBM, Litton Industries, Citibank, Ford, and General Motors have long been viewed as excellent training grounds by young employees before they move on to other companies. To a certain extent, such mobility is inevitable. It may very well provide a company with a cadre of excellent contacts in other companies. However, in a foreign country where training may be especially difficult, a high rate of turnover may be a real problem. Of course, the company that may be confronted with such a situation should carefully analyze the difficulty. Perhaps the problem is remedial (for example, perhaps the pay scales or benefits may be inadequate). Another related problem may be that the company simply does not offer sufficient promotion opportunities. If the foreign operation is small, aggressive employees may feel frustrated. Furthermore, they may be unwilling to move to other slots in the company that are outside their home country. Conversely, the company may not make such transfers available. In such instances, the company may find that foreign nationals may pose fewer problems than local nationals.

The parent-country national: There are also a strong set of arguments for a company to choose a home-country national for foreign operations. Often these are the very factors which make the host-country nationals less desirable. Foremost among the competitive edges that the parent-country national has to offer over the host-country national is the cultural and linguistic affinity to the managers of the parent and with customers and suppliers from the home country. The home-country manager is familiar with the parent company; its practices, policies, personnel, and so forth.

Home-country nationals are more likely to identify with the worldwide goals of the company. Similarly, they are less susceptible to local political and social pressures than are local nationals.

Other motivation for deliberately utilizing parent-country nationals includes the need for a start-up manager for a new operation, when the time horizon of the venture is too short to justify the training of a host-country national or to provide on-the-job training in foreign operations for the parent-company national.

The company may also choose this approach by default instead of deliberately. Even if the company would like to utilize local nationals, there may not be enough available to satisfy the company's needs. Sometimes, as seen above, there may be political or cultural reasons for introducing a foreign national. For example, because of political, religious, or cultural divisions in the local workforce, no local national may be able to avoid serious problems when dealing with the local peers, subordinates, or superiors; a foreign national may be the only expedient compromise—someone whom all local groups would accept as the best of available alternatives—even if viewed merely as the least unattractive option.

It was noted above that a host-country national can be an advantage by conveying the local image of the company. However, in other instances a foreign image may be a company's strongest asset. In that event the use of expatriate managers may be the most successful approach to a company's staffing needs abroad.

Finally, although it would be hoped that whatever decision the company finally made would be rationally based upon a careful analysis of the various relevant variables, many foreign staffing decisions are unfortunately made through a process of what could best (and perhaps most charitably) be described as *corporate inertia*. This often occurs simply because the company is most comfortable with hiring parent-country nationals, whether it is optimal or not. Such companies simply take what appears to be the most expedient path of hiring expatriates, whether that is likely to be in the company's long-term interest or not.

There are, of course, a number of disadvantages with the use of expatriates. Many of these are the same factors that make the choice of a local national optimal in many instances. There is the natural diseconomy of the foreign national resulting from his or her lack of familiarity with such factors as the local language, culture, and political system and the corresponding difficulty of adjusting that may (and often does) result.

There can also be serious local impediments. For example, local workers may be very reluctant to work for or even with foreign nationals. Also, the local laws may require the hiring of local nationals. In such instances, of course, the foreign company has little choice.

Finally, there are managerial difficulties as well. Not the least of these is the cost. As noted above, expatriate managers and technicians generally cost much more than local-country nationals. This is frequently true even when the investment is made into a relatively expensive country such as the United States. Local employees generally cost less than bringing their counterparts from abroad.

Other managerial problems include the difficulty of evaluating, rewarding, promoting, and reintegrating the expatriate when the time for reassignment arrives. The use of a local manager who does not need to be compensated on the same scale as comparable managers in operations of the company in other countries, who does not need to be evaluated on the same basis as those managers, and who will not be moved abroad in the future can minimize many of these difficulties. More will be said of this later in the chapter.

THE TRAINING OF PERSONNEL FOR FOREIGN ASSIGNMENTS

All companies find it necessary and desirable to educate new employees about the company as well as the job. Old employees must also be educated when they assume new positons. This is true of domestic jobs as well as international jobs.

The multinational company is faced with the task of training all its employees wherever the company operates. With far-flung operations in many different countries and with employees of many different cultures who speak a wide variety of languages, this task is much more difficult, encompasses many more areas, and is much more important than for domestic jobs.

THE TRAINING OF HOST-COUNTRY NATIONALS

Local employees of foreign facilities can generally be trained in the host country. It involves both technical training and indoctrination in the company's way of operating: its history, products, philosophies, policies, and so forth. This preparation not only improves communication and efficiency, but also reduces misunderstanding and increases esprit de corps. Sometimes local nationals are brought to the headquarters or another facility of the company for further training. However, for non-managers, this additional training would be unusual. It is indeed expensive.

THE TRAINING OF EXPATRIATES

Foreign nationals who are sent to work in a host country (whether they are home-country nationals or third-country nationals) pose an especially difficult training problem for the MNC. For most companies this is undoubtedly the most difficult training task. Unfortunately, in the past and even today, companies often assign a manager or technician abroad with little or no predeparture training and preparation. The results can be disastrous for both the individual and the company.

There are relatively few educational programs that deliberately prepare a manager for foreign assignments. Many schools offer graduate and undergraduate courses in the field of international business.[1] However, very few offer training specifically oriented toward jobs in international business. One school that does offer just a program is the University of South Carolina through its Master in International Business Studies (MIBS) program. The MIBS program not only offers an internationalized MBA curriculum but also incorporates training in a foreign language and eight months spent in a foreign country; six of those months are spent working in that country. Another well-known program is that of the American Graduate School of International Management in Arizona. However, such programs train only *junior* managers.

Most employees who are sent to foreign assignments do not have the advantage of such internationalized training as part of their formal

---

[1] For example, Robert Grosse and Gerald W. Perritt, eds. *International Business Curricula: A Global Survey* (Cleveland: World Trade Education Center—Academy of International Business, 1980).

education. However, even these individuals typically need some additional predeparture training, unless they have acquired specific training in the country to which they will be assigned and unless they are already very well versed in the job, philosophies, procedures, and so forth of the company. Thus, every company has an important task of educating its employees prior to departure.

Since most of the employees who are likely to be assigned abroad have families, the problem also arises of the training of the family, especially the employee's spouse. Many foreign assignments have been ruined for even highly qualified and well-prepared employees, because their families could not make the adjustment. Therefore, it is very important that the predeparture preparation, and even the choice of which manager or technician to send, should include the spouse.

Unfortunately, many companies give very inadequate consideration to the employee's family when making assignments and providing training. Unfortunately also, employees themselves often give inadequate consideration to the difficulties of family adjustment in their decision regarding a foreign assignment and in the predeparture training.

The remainder of this discussion focuses upon optimum types of training programs for the employee and, where appropriate, for the family as well. As noted above, job competence is the most critical asset that a person can take to a foreign country. If the individual chosen does not yet have those skills, then it is very important that these skills be acquired, typically prior to departure.

A second type of job preparation involves familiarizing the manager or technician with the specific job, the foreign office, lines of communication, plans for that office, policies, competitive conditions, business and legal environment, relations with the local and parent-country government, and so forth. Indeed, many of these issues can be important in the individual's decision concerning the position. For example, if the company's plans for the foreign operation (for example reducing its scale of operations) are unattractive to the individual, then it should be known to the employee before he or she accepts the position.

Often a prospective transferee may not ask all the relevant questions regarding a proposed new assignment. The company should raise the sensitive issues from the start, so that they are carefully considered by the individual before the acceptance decision is made. The costs, both financially and from disrupted plans resulting from failure of a manager to adjust to a foreign position, are too great for the company to fail to take all reasonable precautions to ensure that the best person is chosen.

Another very important part of the training process involves the preparation of the transferee and his or her family for adjustment to the foreign environment. This problem of adjusting to the foreign environment is often called *cultural shock,* since the disruption caused by living in a foreign culture can be such a major part of the adjustment problem of the manager or technician and his or her family. However, as noted above, adjusting to cultural differences is only part of the adjustment problem. There can also be *economic shock* and *politico-legal shock.* Indeed, there is a very wide range of the types of adjustment difficulties that expatriates can encounter. Training programs can help to prepare the transferees to anticipate the painful shocks. In general, the more that is known in advance about potential adjustment difficulties, the easier the adjustment is likely to be. For example, a course in the history, religion, and culture of India would make the strangeness of the country more acceptable—and interesting—to the Westerner.

Preparation for these types of personal adjustment problems obviously should not only include the job transferee but also his or her family. Unfortunately, many companies are very negligent in failing to provide adequate preparation for the family as well. In such instances the company may later find that it has been penny wise and dollar foolish if the transfer fails because of the failure of the employee's family to make a successful adjustment.

The provision of language training is a major part of the preparation process. Such training should begin for at least the transferee and spouse before departure. It will need to continue after the couple reaches their foreign assignment.

Preparation is also necessary regarding living conditions, including basics such as how and where to shop, medical and educational facilities, and housing areas. Discussion should also involve foods, climate, customs, the local currency, and attitudes toward foreigners. Similarly, transferees should be primed to anticipate cultural attitudes regarding races, castes, nationalities, sexes, religions, tribal groups, linguistic groups, and political parties.

Another area of preparation, indeed of selling the executive on the transfer, is a thorough understanding of the support services and special perquisites the foreign assignment entails. Included in this area are such factors as salary, bonuses for hardship, housing, and education, tax offsets, shipping allowances, assistance in selling or renting the transferee's home. Finally, the manager or technician who is being transferred should receive a clear picture of the type of support services that are provided when the family returns to its home country, whether or not their transfer was successful and lasted full term. Included in this repatriation adjustment plan should be a program telling how the individual will be reintegrated into the corporate hierarchy upon his or her return to the home country. More will be said about this in the last section of this chapter.

COMPENSATION OF EXPATRIATE MANAGERS

One of the most difficult international personnel problems is the task of designing an equitable and effective compensation package for its internationally mobile employees. This is a very complicated and dynamic issue with which even companies with long international experience continue to struggle. Unfortunately, there is no simple answer; nor is there any consistent approach.

The basic goal of a compensation program for foreign assignments must be to provide adequate incentive to induce managers or technicians to accept, even seek, overseas assignments without causing dissatisfaction among their peers. This is a delicate balance.

The incentive problem with respect to the prospective expatriate involves the threefold task of, first, making the move attractive, second, maintaining his or her satisfaction while abroad, and third, not making the foreign compensation package so attractive that the individual will be reluctant to return home or transfer elsewhere in the company. Each of these three components of the compensation task has its own difficulties.

Because of the various approaches to the compensation question, the varying conditions between different companies, and the dynamic nature of the task, it is impossible to generalize about ideal approaches. There is none. However, there are general prevailing patterns that can be outlined. Most compensation packages have various combinations of the following four components:

1. base salary
2. a special bonus or premium to induce the manager to accept an international transfer
3. special cost-of-living allowances
4. special additional fringe benefits

Within this framework, however, different companies have developed widely differing packages. Furthermore, these packages continue to evolve. Nevertheless, there is widespread dissatisfaction on the part of companies because of a perception by a company that its program is not "ideal."

BASE SALARY

The prospective expatriate is not likely to accept a loss of income or living standard from a foreign move. The individual is accustomed to a certain level of income and will likely be returning to the home country to a position with at least the same salary that he or she received before departure. Thus, a starting point for the overseas compensation package is generally the home-country base salary.

In many instances a foreign assignment is not merely a lateral move but involves a promotion. In such instances, even the base salary is increased. This base salary is also important for the rest of the expatriate compensation package, since some of the components of the premium, the cost-of-living adjustments, and the special fringe benefits are all functions of the size of the base salary.

THE EXPATRIATE PREMIUM

There are some foreign assignments that do not seem to require a special inducement to attract managers and technicians. For example, London, Paris, and most major Canadian cities are sufficiently attractive to most Americans that special compensations to accept "hardships" are not necessary. However, for most locations abroad this is not true. For hundreds of other locations the inducement of a special hardship and/or adjustment premium is given. The inducement may be required simply because of the inevitable adjustment problems from living in a foreign culture, even if the standard of living in that location is high and the hardship is minimal, for example, most of Northern Europe for Americans and the United States for Europeans. However, in many other cases the climate or the living conditions are sufficiently difficult that a hardship bonus is necessary in addition to the adjustment allowance. For example, most locations in Latin America, Asia, Africa, and the Middle East generally warrant such allowances for most American and European managers.

These two allowances—one for adjustment and one for hardship—comprise the *expatriate premium*. The hardship component of the allowance is generally an annual bonus that does not change much during most foreign assignments. However, the transferee's adjustment problem can be expected to decline with the length of the foreign assignment. Therefore, that portion of the premium may be either only a first-year payment, may be phased out over several years, or may be permanent. The pattern is, of course, a function of both the company and the degree of foreignness of the overseas assignment.

COST-OF-LIVING ALLOWANCE

The expenses of living in different parts of the world can vary significantly. Indeed, there can be substantial differences even within the same country. For example, many companies find that they must pay adjustments even in the United States when they reassign employees to such high-cost locations as New York City or Washington, D.C. Overseas cities such as London, Caracas, and Tokyo are relatively high-cost locations. Some companies make their own cost-of-living calculations. Most appear to use special indices such as those of the U.S. Department of State, which are published annually. (See Table 18.1.) Using published indices has the advantages of convenience and objectivity. It has the disadvantage that the indices do not cover hundreds of smaller cities and remote locations where the cost of living bears little resemblance to costs in the cities on the index. In such instances the company is forced to make its own calculation or to hire an outside specialist to make the calculation for it.

In addition to a general cost of living allowance, there are often additional allowances. For example, special subsidies for local housing (and perhaps also for housing maintenance back home), education of grade- and high-school children, and tax equilization are very widespread.

Tax equalization has often been an especially difficult burden for companies, especially for American companies because of the nature of U.S. tax laws. The United States is virtually the only country that taxes the income of its citizens that is earned abroad. Throughout most of the 1970s U.S. expatriates had an exemption from U.S. taxes on as little as $15,000 of their foreign earned income. This was too low to provide much relief. It acted as an expensive hurdle to sending employees abroad and placed U.S. companies at a competitive disadvantage. Fortunately, the Economic Recovery Tax Act of 1981 increased this exemption to $75,000 for 1982 with annual raises until it reaches $95,000.[2]

OTHER FRINGE BENEFITS

In addition to the expatriate premiums and the various cost-of-living adjustments, expatriates are often also given other perquisites such as special insurance (for example, on political hazards such as kidnapping), compensation to offset the need that the transferees may have to contribute to local social security programs (from which they may never be able to benefit), and continuing language and area training for both themselves and their families.

Since the employee will be working in a foreign country, part or all of the compensation will generally need to be in the local currency. However, since the employee may have financial obligations back home or may simply desire to invest the money outside the local country, both fluctuations in the exchange rate and exchange or capital controls can be a problem. (On the other hand, variations in the exchange rate

---

[2]Commerce Clearing House, *Explanation of Economic Recovery Tax Act 1981.*

TABLE 18.1 U.S. Department of State Indices of Living Costs Abroad

Country and City	Index
Argentina: Buenos Aires	112[a]
Australia: Canberra	126
Belgium: Brussels	113
Brazil: Sao Paulo	101
Canada: Ottawa	105
Chile: Santiago	156
China: Beijing	96
Colombia: Bogota	102
Dominican Republic: Santo Domingo	106
Egypt: Cairo	111
France: Paris	153
Germany: Frankfurt	138
Greece: Athens	107
Hong Kong: Hong Kong	114
India: New Delhi	93
Indonesia: Jakarta	121
Italy: Rome	108
Ivory Coast: Abidjan	141
Jamaica: Kingston	124
Japan: Tokyo	142
Korea: Seoul	125
Kuwait: Kuwait	136
Malaysia: Kuala Lumpur	123
Mexico: Mexico City	110
Netherlands: The Hague	125
Nigeria: Lagos	164
Pakistan: Karachi	106
Peru: Lima	100
Philippines: Manila	104
Poland: Warsaw	77
Saudi Arabia: Riyadh	137
Singapore: Singapore	119
South Africa: Johannesburg	103
Spain: Madrid	114
Switzerland: Geneva	134
Taiwan: Taipei	115
Turkey: Istanbul	92
United Kingdom: London	124
USSR: Moscow	142
Venezuela: Caracas	140

[a]Indices do not include housing and education allowances.

SOURCE: *Indexes of Living Costs Abroad, Quarters Allowances, and Hardship Differentials,* U.S. Department of State, October 1982, pp.2–4.

sometimes work to the expatriate's advantage.) It is very common for part of the payments to a worker to be made in the home-currency or in a third-country currency. These payments are usually outside of the country in which the job is located.

PERSONNEL POLICIES OF HOST GOVERNMENTS

CONTROLS ON MIGRATION

All governments carefully regulate international migration. Regulations can be extensive for temporary as well as permanent movement of people. This can often be an important constraint upon the international staffing decisions of a company. For example, even the United States has laws that tend to make it very difficult for companies to hire foreign citizens unless a very strong case can be made for the unique qualities of the individual. Foreign students with American educations are often hired with a temporary (twelve- or eighteen-month) "training" visa. However, after that time the company may be forced to reassign the individual overseas or to release him or her. Switzerland is especially notorious for the difficulties that companies often encounter in trying to get their employees admitted for even several years.

In most countries, including virtually all developing countries, there is the recognition that a foreign company needs to utilize some of its own home-country nationals. However, even this acceptance of reality is commonly coupled with an extensive array of controls.

Understandably, host governments are very concerned about insuring that its citizens receive extensive employment benefits from the foreign companies which are permitted to invest in that country. In many respects this is not very inconsistent with the long-term well-being of most foreign companies. However, the managerial and ethnocentric inertia discussed elsewhere in this book has aggravated this issue as an especially sensitive one between foreign investors and their host countries.

In general, it makes economic and managerial sense for a company to hire, train, and promote local nationals to the greatest feasible extent. Except in special instances, such as those mentioned earlier in this chapter—the intitial need during start-up of a new facility, when corporate secrets are involved, or when corporate communications are critical (for example, either with the corporation, its suppliers, or its customers) extensive managerial, financial, and public relations dividends are likely from hiring local nationals.

However, many companies have traditionally been very lax about utilizing as many local nationals as possible. Therefore, governments have often felt that they need to be very explicit about the personnel demands made upon the company. Unfortunately, much of this attitude is traceable to past intransigence and shortsightedness on the part of foreign companies.

CONTROLS ON PERSONNEL MANAGEMENT

Among the specific categories of controls that governments impose upon foreign investors are those involving local hiring, training, promotion, layoffs, and firing. Most foreign companies hire local nationals for production work. However, managerial jobs are sometimes disproportionately weighed with foreign nationals. Governments therefore sometimes place a limit upon the number of foreign nationals who can work in the country; this limit may either be an absolute limit in numbers or relative to the total employment of the company. The limit is often reduced over time.

Since regulations on the hiring of expatriates are obviously designed to encourage not only local hiring but also the training and promotion of local nationals into managerial and technical positions, such pressures may often push a company beyond what efficiency and economy would dictate. But, unless the government can be convinced to grant an exception, the company may have little choice.

Even more widespread than hiring, training, and promotion regulations are very restrictive rules involving the laying off and firing of employees. Even in many industrialized Western European countries, there are labor laws that place very severe severance burdens upon a company; both Italy and France are examples of countries where such rules are far more burdensome than in the United States and Canada.

RELATIONS WITH LABOR UNIONS

The nature of labor unions varies substantially between different countries. Therefore, managers who are familiar with unions in their home countries may not be properly prepared to deal with a different breed of unions in another country. In countries such as the United States, Canada, Germany, and Japan, labor unions are principally concerned with economic issues. They do not generally mix politics into their negotiations with companies. Furthermore, when labor disruptions occur they are either directed against one company or one industry. If, as with the annual Japanese spring labor offensive, there are multi-industry strikes, the interruptions are relatively short and not greatly disruptive.

POLITICIZED LABOR UNIONS

In many other countries labor unions are deeply involved in politics. Such politicized labor unions are found in Europe in organizations such as the British Trade Unions Council. They are also found elsewhere in Europe in countries such as France and Italy. In many Latin American countries there is a very widespread tradition of political disruption.

When a firm operates in countries where union politicization and militancy are strong, the company may find its operations disrupted even if the unions have nothing specific against the company, but rather because the workers are striking against some governmental policy. In many of these countries, labor disruptions can also be very violent (against either property or persons).

INTERNATIONAL LABOR UNIONS

Labor union leaders often feel frustrated by the ability of some multinational companies to absorb strikes in one country by increasing output in their facilities in another country. As a result, labor unions have been discussing multinational action against companies. Such unity has been discussed for many years, but with little success. Nevertheless, even this limited success is likely to encourage further joint efforts in the future.

PERSONAL ADJUSTMENT TO LIVING ABROAD

Learning to live in a foreign culture requires many personal adjustments, large and small. These adjustments can be of many different types: adjusting to different languages, foods, manner of living, schools, health facilities, recreation, social customs, political structure, ease of travel, and so forth.

Expatriates, both the transferred employee and his or her family, differ significantly in their ability to learn to adjust to the foreign country. As noted earlier, some transferees never do make the adjustment. Some foreign assignments collapse very quickly or are never totally satisfactory because of this.

ENCLAVE LIVING

Some expatriates avoid exposing themselves to the foreign country in which they live as much as possible. For example, some of the foreign enclaves for oil families in Saudi Arabi are so complete (schools, churches, theaters, social clubs, stores, hospitals, and so forth), that many of the wives and children of the expatriate employees have very little contact with the country in which they are living. It is as though they were on a tiny American or British island.

No one nationality has a monopoly on enclave mentalities. Russians are notorious for trying to isolate their citizens when the government sends them abroad; this is, of course, done for political reasons. The Japanese also have a very strong tendency to concentrate in enclaves, but for social reasons.

The expatriate employee is generally forced to confront the country. However, some of the wives and children return after the assignment abroad with little or no knowledge of the language, customs, history, or politics of the country.

The penalties of enclave living: Failure to try to adapt to a country in which one is residing, to learn as much as possible about the country, and to try to learn to appreciate the culture and history of the area is a most unfortunate waste. The individual, of course, loses from failing to have grown and to have learned from the opportunity of living abroad. (And, having failed once, the probability of failing to adjust in a future foreign assignment where there is no enclave is much greater.) The company loses if the employee is affected by his or her family's attitudes or if local contacts react negatively to the attitudes of his or her family.

LIVING SUCCESSFULLY ABROAD

The individuals who reside in enclaves, whether such enclaves are physical or only psychological, succeed in surviving abroad but not in truly living there. If an expatriate seeks to merely survive in a foreign country without truly living within that country, it is a shame that the foreign assignment was ever made.

It is possible for most people to make at least a reasonably successful adjustment to a foreign job assignment. Careful screening of employee and spouse prior to assignment can greatly improve the probability of success. So also will predeparture and postarrival training in the language, history, and customs of the country. However, the strongest single attribute for success is personal attitude. The next two sections examine two important attitudinal factors in making a successful adjustment: *empathy* and *avoiding stereotypes*.

Empathy: *Empathy* is the generalized ability to see the world through the eyes of other people. This personality trait enables one to see why the other person feels the way he or she does about specific issues or to see how someone else views the world. If this trait is expanded to include the ability to see the world as the members of another culture see it, then it becomes *cultural empathy*. Without cultural empathy, the views and actions of members of another culture may well seem odd or perhaps even immoral or ridiculous. However, when actions are examined from the viewpoint of the persons making the actions, the reasons and assumptions behind the action become much clearer.

For example, in the past American health workers sometimes had little success in some parts of the world in introducing birth control techniques in order to stem the rapid rate of population growth. However, after an initial analysis of the failures, it was concluded that the problem could be solved if a technically better method of birth control could be devised. Nevertheless, success did not come even as better methods were developed.

Later observations indicated that the initial analysis of the problem was misleading because it was from an American perspective. It seemed very logical from this point of view that better products were the solution. However, it was soon realized that the failure of the program was not caused by the technical product; rather, it was because of the beliefs prevalent in many foreign parts of the world about having children. In some countries, a man's virility is measured by the number of offspring he has. The degree of attractiveness and sexual desirability of a woman in certain tribal societies is indicated to her friends by the number of children she has borne. In many countries, children often act as "old age insurance," since they will care for their parents in later years. And, in a society which through its high fatality rate has had a low probability of any single child reaching maturity, parents need to have many children in order to be assured that some of them will survive. Thus, there was not a strong desire among many of these groups to reduce the number of their children.

The initial American solution—to simply improve and promote the technical products—could never be successful alone, because it only looked at the problem from an American viewpoint. These other social factors were considered seriously once this early lack of cultural empathy was recognized, and the programs became more successful.

When individuals enter a foreign environment they use a *self-reference criterion* (SRC) to evaluate and interpret events and behavioral actions in the new environment. They unconsciously refer to their own cultural values in judging situations in the new culture. As an individual matures and gains experience in the world, a system of personal standards of judgments and points of reference is built that helps the individual to make decisions and to take appropriate actions.

These standards or reference points are, quite naturally, intimately intertwined with the specific culture in which the individual learned to deal with life. This causes no difficulty until one travels to another culture, where a different set of standards or points of reference is required for effective performance in that culture. A foreigner in a new environment often makes decisions and judgments by referring to the standards that were relevant to his or her home culture (thus using an SRC for judgment) without sufficiently considering the differences between the criteria he or she naturally tends to use and those used by local nationals.

Only rarely is an individual from one culture able to develop a relatively complete sensitivity to the nuances of another, significantly different, culture. Therefore one must usually train oneself to examine the basic assumptions and reference points that are used in determining his or her own actions and behavior in order to identify "culturally rooted" criteria. Since one can probably never totally suspend his or her self-reference criterion, bases for action must constantly be monitored in foreign countries in order to be sensitive to important differences that might require a modification of behavior.

Whether considering introduction of a new product, hiring new employees, dealing with present employees, or negotiating with a local government, management of a multinational firm must be aware of the assumptions and viewpoints of members of the local culture if it is going to be effective.

Stereotyping: The world is much too complex for an individual to catalog in his or her mind each trait and quality of every individual he or she meets or hears about. Since the human brain does have a limited capacity, one must resort to mental shortcuts, such as stereotyping. A *stereotype* is a mental picture used to identify and think about certain groups of people. A stereotype usually contains a mental list of traits that are associated with members of the group. When the label is applied to some national group, the stereotype is a *national stereotype*. This is the most significant kind of stereotype in international business, since it is important to know what kinds of qualities (mental list of traits) an individual associates with a particular country. This is important from the viewpoints of both the manager going abroad and of the foreigners with whom he or she will deal—employees, customers, officials, and so on. In additional to national sterotypes there are, of course, racial stereotypes, sexual stereotypes, regional stereotypes, educational stereotypes, job stereotypes, and so forth.

Table 18.2 gives two very different sets of stereotypes about Americans. (Will the "real" Americans please identify themselves?) Obviously, the self-reference criteria of Mexicans and Taiwanese strongly influence their perceptions of other cultures. Such stereotypes are likely to affect their attitudes toward, and perhaps their working relationships with,

TABLE 18.2 Foreign Perceptions of Americans

Mexican Perceptions	Taiwanese Perceptions
Americans are:	Americans are:
Reserved	Friendly/Outgoing
Rushed/Time conscious	Relaxed/Easygoing
Realistic/Hardheaded	Optimistic
Team worker	Independent
Quality-conscious	Output-oriented
Unemotional	Emotional
Serious/Businesslike	Fun-loving/Joking
Self-controlled	Self-indulgent

SOURCE: *Newsletter,* National Council for International Visitors, 1981.

Americans. All nationalities and regional groups are subject to such stereotypes—and often other conflicting stereotypes. Knowledge of our own stereotyping tendencies and the stereotypical attitudes of others toward us can be important in our efforts to work with people of other nationalities (or even other groups within our own country).

An American traveling to a country where the label "American" calls forth a fairly negative picture in the minds of the local population, will probably act in a certain way. But the American would act very differently if he or she had gone to a country where Americans were the object of a more favorable stereotype. Obviously, effectiveness in business matters could be seriously impaired if one made erroneous assumptions about the stereotype evoked in the minds of foreign associates. Likewise, each individual should be aware of his or her own stereotypes used in classifying and thinking about other people.

Sensitivity to various national stereotypes will enable the internationally oriented manager to understand the actions of behavior of certain individuals and groups. The stereotypes used by non-Americans to envision Americans vary greatly from area to area. If Americans are thought to be arrogant, overbearing, and rude, one can expect very different treatment than if the dominant local stereotype of Americans is composed of traits such as industriousness, friendliness, and efficiency. The difference is simply related to the point of view taken by the observer. A sensitivity to this point of view in the local population can provide a much improved and more accurate basis for effective behavior.

CULTURAL SHOCK

When members of one culture are displaced and begin living in a new and different culture, they are often subject to a phenomenon known as *cultural shock*. This term is descriptive of the general disorientation and discomfort experienced by an individual placed in a new society.

An individual often seems to go through an initial phase of enchantment with the new culture, but this is usually followed by a period of disillusionment and negative feelings about the culture. In some instances there is no initial enchantment, only disillusionment.

The intensity and duration of cultural shock vary from person to person, but the phenomenon is present in most instances of cultural migration. The sudden absence of the familiar indicators and behavioral guideposts normally used to regulate one's life causes some discomfort. The customs and often the language are different, and different outlooks and attitudes may be required for effective functioning in the new environment. If an American has great difficulty in adjusting to these new requirements, he or she may retreat to the security of an American circle of friends, because he or she understands them and knows what they expect. With these people, the American can retain his or her old guideposts for behavior and can use the subtle cues of social intercourse. This is the safe route, but, of course, this may not result in furthering his or her effectiveness in the foreign environment.

Overcoming cultural shock is often a matter of time. It is a function of the type of reaction provoked by the shock. As an individual begins to learn the more subtle aspects of the new culture, the country begins to lose its strangeness and, consequently, much of its threat. Simply living in the culture and gaining experience in it often promote a reduction in cultural shock and disorientation. However, the reaction of various individuals to cultural shock usually exhibits one of two patterns. The shock may be viewed as a temporary obstacle, and the effort necessary to overcome it may be considered well spent. A person responding to cultural shock in this pattern will probably be able to recover quite satisfactorily and learn to be effective in the environment.

The second pattern of reaction, however, is quite different. The early severity of the shock may be sufficient to force the person back into more familiar surroundings. This may mean increasing social and business contacts with individuals of his or her own nationality in the foreign environment or, in extreme cases, it may mean physical retreat to one's home country. Even a retreat to the community of one's own nationals can seriously threaten any chances of gaining real insight into the host culture, since others, probably also suffering from cultural shock, will be quick to commiserate. This position exhibits a minimum of cultural empathy and a maximum usage of a self-reference criterion; it does, however, serve as an emotional salve to the troubled expatriate and/or his or her family.

A firm might decide to try to overcome cultural shock in its expatriate employees, it might decide to try to minimize the severity of the shock, or it might decide simply to live with it or to totally ignore it. But no matter what strategy is selected, a knowledge of the causes and symptoms of this "occupational disease" of expatriates is important in carrying out that strategy more effectively.

RETURNING HOME

Most companies intend to reassign their managers or technicians with the same company after several years at a particular foreign post. It is relatively unusual today for companies to make permanent foreign assignments for expatriates. Some expatriates may receive a series of foreign assignments (often interspersed with at least one home assignment). For example, one of the author's colleagues at the First National Bank of Chicago successively headed the Indonesian office, the branch in Rome, and then all Latin American operations—an unusually diverse series of foreign assignments. However, the day of permanent overseas assignments to one foreign location appears to be past. It was not such an unusual situation in past generations when transportation and communication was slow. British companies as well as the British government were often very inclined to do this. Such permanent assignees are still to be found today, but as their generation retires, the practice is declining.

REASSIGNMENT AND READJUSTMENT PROBLEMS OF THE EMPLOYEE

Since the expatriate has been away from the domestic mainstream of jobs, obtaining an attractive reassignment must be carefully planned by both the company and the employee. Obviously, the longer the expatriate has been away, the more difficult the task of finding an appropriate reassignment.

It is axiomatic that the company should keep its overseas employees in mind when new job opportunities arise. A continuous flow of information to its executives abroad about developments elsewhere in the company is an indispensable way of maintaining worldwide corporate morale; information about job opportunities is a critical part of this process.

Presumably, a company should be seeking the best employee for each job. The special skills and experiences of expatriates can be very important contributions to the company, even in its domestic operations.

The new assignment is not always an easy task even when the company has kept the expatriate aware of the opportunities. Expatriates have worked under very different conditions within the corporation than are likely to exist back at headquarters and many other operations of the company in the home country. For example, the expatriate likely played a much bigger role and carried much more independent responsibility in the overseas assignment because of staff limitations (the expatriate was a big fish in a little pond). This chance to develop a variety of managerial skills is a very definite attraction of many foreign assignments.

Also, the expatriate often has much greater visibility in the overseas assignment. For example, when the corporation's senior management tours the foreign operations, all or most of the foreign managers and technicians may well be involved in hosting the visit. As a result, the *repatriate* (the returned expatriate) may not feel as close to the decision-making center at headquarters and perhaps not as important as he or she did "in the field."

Thus, the task of finding a comparable reassignment is not an easy one. Even when the jobs appear comparable on the surface, the different nature of the responsibilities and corporate exposure may be perceived very differently by the employee. Readjustment back home is not always easy. Some companies find a reassignment into a very different type of job helpful rather than to try to match the jobs. This may not, however, be feasible, and it may lose the advantages of the employee's experiences abroad.

READJUSTMENT PROBLEMS OF THE EMPLOYEE'S FAMILY

Reassignment home is sometimes also not easy for the repatriate's family. As with the employee, the family has enjoyed a rather unique position abroad. Even with all the difficulties of adjustment mentioned above, once the adjustment is made expatriate families often find the perquisites of the foreign assignment to be very attractive. Such factors as luxury housing, servants, private clubs and schools, company-financed travel, and their relative wealth in the host country are just a few of the many perceived advantages.

If the family is able to return to their former home upon reassignment back to their home country, then there is a strong element of stability and insulation from psychological and financial shock. This is one reason, along with the rental income and capital gains potential, that many expatriates choose to keep their homes when they are assigned overseas.

If the reassignment involves the need to relocate (even in the same general area), there can be a cultural and economic shock of re-entry. The longer that the family has been abroad the more difficult this process is likely to be.

The children need to adjust to a new neighborhood and to new schools (although hopefully their foreign schooling, whether private or public, has kept them at least abreast with their peers at home). The entire family may need to find new friends and activities.

If the family failed to keep their former home or to at least keep their money invested, they may be unpleasantly shocked at the cost of new housing.

Many expatriates are able to accumulate a comfortable "nest egg" while abroad, so that their overall wealth has risen. However, many families find that they are not as relatively prosperous as they were abroad. They will have lost their foreign bonuses and allowances. Even if on a "real income" or purchasing power basis the family is better off, they may perceive themselves to be worse off without servants, private clubs, participation in the diplomatic set, and so forth. Thus, this problem can have a strong psychological base.

Ordinarily the readjustment process can be relatively smooth. The resettlement traumas are usually temporary. However, the expatriate family needs to remain aware of the potential difficulties before they actually return home.

SUMMARY

The personnel task is an important one for any company, domestic or multinational. However, when the personnel roster of the company includes individuals from many different countries and expatriates in many foreign assignments, then the basic personnel tasks of selection, training, compensating, and so forth become much more complicated.

Many companies have had difficulty integrating their foreign personnel operations into the rest of the company. Who should be assigned to foreign operations, our best people or only those who can be conveniently spared from domestic operations? Should foreign managers be home-country nationals, third-country nationals, or foreign local nationals? What training should be received, and how much autonomy should be provided?

Compensation is an especially difficult problem. It must be sufficient to attract the appropriate personnel to the foreign assignment and to keep them satisfied while they are there, but it must not be so extensive that the individual may be unwilling to accept reassignment.

Re-entering the corporate and personal mainstream of the home country may be a problem for many expatriates and their families. Both the company and the employee's family need to anticipate re-entry problems and plan for them. The company needs to be systematic and cautious about providing an attractive re-entry job for the "repatriate." The family needs to have retained a financial base in the home country (for instance, by keeping their own home). Keeping their home can also make the return to home-country living easier for the entire family.

KEY TERMS

BICULTURAL	FRINGE BENEFIT	STEREOTYPE
CULTURAL SHOCK	REPATRIATE	THIRD-COUNTRY
EMPATHY	SELF REFERENCE	NATIONAL
ENCLAVE	CRITERION	
EXPATRIATE		

REVIEW QUESTIONS

1. How is a company's attitude toward the status of foreign assignments likely to affect its ability to attract qualified personnel to accept those assignment?

2. How do the responsibilities of foreign assignments tend to differ from comparable domestic assignments?

3. Compare the advantages and disadvantages of hiring host-country versus parent-country nationals.

4. a. How would you feel about working for a foreign company in your home country? Outside of your country?

   b. How would working for a foreign company differ from working for a company from your home country at home and abroad?

5. What kind of preparation would you like to receive from your company before accepting a foreign assignment.?

6. a. Should a company have the right to consider not only your appropriateness for a foreign assignment but also that of your spouse and children?

   b. If you were making the personnel recommendations, would you include the spouse and children of your employees in your decision?

7. Design a compensation package for yourself for an overseas assignment to (a) London and (b) Jakarta, Indonesia. Consider each of the various allowances and fringes that were discussed.

8. How can dealing with labor unions in other countries differ significantly from dealing with those in the United States?

9. a. What do you perceive to be the advantages and disadvantages of enclave living?

   b. Would you prefer an enclave in a foreign culture that is very
       different from your own?
10. a. What is cultural empathy?
    b. How will it affect your success in working abroad?
11. a. What is cultural shock?
    b. How would you expect it to affect you on a one-month and on a
       two-year overseas assignment?
    c. Do you think that it will be a serious problem for you?
12. What are your stereotypes about the British, French, Haitians,
    Americans, Mexicans, and Japanese? Consider (a) work ethic,
    (b) pace of living, (c) degree of emotionalism, (d) attitude toward
    foreigners, and (e) whether they are fun-loving or serious.
13. What type of resettlement problems can occur upon returning
    home?

SUGGESTED REFERENCES

GLADWIN, THOMAS, AND INGO WALTER *Multinationals Under Fire.* New York:
    John Wiley & Sons, Inc., 1980.

GROSSE, ROBERT, AND GERALD W. PERRITT, eds. *International Curricula: A Glob-
    al Survey.* Cleveland: World Trade Education Center—Academy of Interna-
    tional Business, 1980.

HELLINGER, STEPHEN H., AND DOUGLAS A. *Unemployment and the Multination-
    als.* Port Washington, NY: Kennikat, 1976.

KRUGG, NEIL B. "A Unique Approach to Tax Equalization for Foreign Employ-
    ees," *Compensation Review, 12,* no. 4, 1980, pp. 34–43.

KUHNE, ROBERT J. *Co-Determination in Business.* New York: Praeger Publish-
    ers, 1980.

KUHNE, ROBERT J., AND ROBERT F. SMITH, "The Terrorist Threat to Corporate
    Executives," *Business Horizons,* December 1979.

KUJAWA, DUANE, ed. *International Labor and Multinational Enterprise.* New
    York: Praeger Publishers, 1975.

SEHAM, MARTIN C. "Transnational Labor Relations: The First Steps Are Being
    Taken," *Law and Policy in International Business,* Spring 1974.

19

Accounting for International Operations*

The accounting system of any business firm is designed to record the transactions of that firm and report their impact on the firm's assets, liabilities, and owner's equity. When the firm in question is multinational in its operations, accounting techniques and procedures must be provided to handle the international transactions and activities.

The accounting process is governed by a set of accounting principles, and these can be complicated even in a domestic setting. When coupled with the complexities of international business, the resulting accounting principles for international activities are among the most difficult of all. In this chapter the fundamental concepts and basic procedures for accounting for international operations are examined. The emphasis is on the topics contained in the two major U.S. accounting rules that apply to this area. These rules were issued by the Financial Accounting Standards Board (FASB): FASB 8, "Accounting for the Translation of Foreign-Currency Transactions and Foreign-Currency Fi-

---

*THIS CHAPTER IS PRIMARILY THE WORK OF PROFESSOR THOMAS EVANS OF THE UNIVERSITY OF SOUTH CAROLINA.

nancial Statements," which was issued in 1975, and FASB 52, "Foreign-Currency Translation," which was issued in 1981. The specifics of accounting practice vary for other countries, but the essential difficulties are similar.

This chapter examines the accounting principles for two major areas of international operations—the translation into U.S. dollars according to American accounting principles of

1. borrowing, investing international trade (for example, imports and exports), and
2. foreign financial statements

The chapter concludes with a discussion of recent efforts toward establishing worldwide accounting standards. Chapter 22 presents a brief introduction to a complicated but vitally important subject: the taxation of multinational operations.

TRANSLATION OF INTERNATIONAL TRANSACTIONS

A significant share of international transactions of U.S. firms is denominated in U.S. dollars. This includes almost all exports, many imports, and many capital flows. For such transactions there are no special accounting problems; indeed, most of the transactions are recorded exactly as they are in a domestic firm. Difficulties arise when such transactions are denominated in foreign currencies. In examining the difficulties this creates and the accounting standards employed, the discussion in this section focuses on importing and exporting activities. However, the principles are also applicable to other types of international transactions, such as lending, borrowing, and so forth.

The only currency allowed for recording transactions is the domestic currency (although the United Kingdom and Singapore allow the use of any currency). There are major problems associated with trying to add up the impact of many transactions that are denominated in different currencies. Thus, if a firm should purchase something from a seller in a foreign country and agree to pay for it in a foreign currency, some way must be found to translate and to record the transaction into the local currency.

When exchange rates were fixed, this did not pose a significant problem. However, floating exchange rates can create serious problems in accounting for transactions denominated in foreign currencies. If the exchange rate changes between the date of the transaction and the settlement date, an accounting adjustment is necessary. *Generally accepted accounting principles* (commonly called *GAAP*) in the U.S. require that no change be made in the dollar value of the transaction, but that instead recognition be made of the foreign exchange gain or loss on the subsequent settlement of the foreign currency account. The following illustration shows these problems and principles more clearly.

ACCOUNTING FOR IMPORTS AND EXPORTS

The Seymore Prophets Importing Company purchased and received DM 10,000 worth of merchandise from a West German supplier on May 1 with payment due on August 1. On May 1, the exchange rate was DM = $0.60. Seymore made the following entry to record this import on May 1:

	Debit	Credit
May 1:		
Merchandise	$6000	
Accounts Payable in DM		$6000

Since Seymore Prophets is an American firm, it cannot record in DM in its U.S. financial statements. The exchange rate on May 1 is used to translate the DM obligation into dollars. The resulting dollar amount is used to record the asset acquired and the resulting obligation to pay.

If no change in the exchange rate occurs between the time the transaction is initiated and the time it is settled on August 1, Seymore would acquire DM 10,000 (at the exchange rate of DM = $0.60) and send that to the German supplier. The company would record the following entry:

	Debit	Credit
August 1:		
Accounts Payable in DM	$6000	
Cash		$6000

Thus, the original $6000 entry will be matched by the eventual $6000 payment.

However, what is more likely in today's exchange markets is that the exchange rate for DM on August 1 will be different from the rate on May 1. If the rate on August 1 is DM = $0.62, then Seymore will have to pay $0.02 more for each of the DM 10,000 that it needs to send to its supplier. Accounting rules require that Seymore consider this $0.02 per DM as a foreign exchange loss. The entry needed to record payment at a rate of $0.62 is as follows:

	Debit	Credit
August 1:		
Accounts Payable in DM	$6000	
Foreign Exchange Loss	$ 200	
Cash		$6200

On August 1, a total of $6200 would be needed to acquire DM 10,000 to send to the creditor. If the exchange rate fell to below $0.60, say $0.58, then Seymore would have had a foreign exchange gain on the settlement. Of course, if the German company had billed Seymore in American dollars, there would be no foreign exchange gain or loss to Seymore, because no foreign currency would be involved. The Germany company would then have to bear the foreign exchange risk.

This, "splitting" of an import or export transaction into two parts is called the "*two-transaction view*," and it has been GAAP since FASB 8 was issued. Notice that, in our illustration for Seymore Prophets, no matter what happens to the exchange rate subsequent to the purchase, the merchandise that was acquired abroad stays at $6000 and any change in the rate from that point on is recorded as a separate item—a foreign exchange gain or loss. These basic principles (the *two-transaction view*) also generally apply to export sales; payment and receipt of interest, dividends, and royalties; foreign lending activities; foreign borrowing; and foreign direct investment.

An additional complication is introduced if the end of an accounting period occurs between the transaction date and payment date. Below are the proper entities to record a French franc–denominated export sale by Seymore to a customer in France. Seymore exported some American goods on December 1, 1982, for 50,000 francs with payment to be made on January 31, 1983. On December 1, the FF – $0.25; on December 31, 1982 (the end of Seymore's accounting year), the FF = $0.26; and on the payment date, January 31, 1983, the FF = $0.24. All figures have been translated into U.S. dollars at the prevailing exchange rate on each date.

	Debit	Credit
December 1:		
Accounts Receivable in FF	$12,500	
Export Sales		$12,500
December 31:		
Accounts Receivable in FF	$ 500	
Foreign Exchange Gain		$ 500
January 31:		
Foreign Exchange Loss	$ 1,000	
Accounts Receivable in FF		$ 1,000
Cash	$12,000	
Accounts Receivable in FF		$12,000

The original sale is recorded in dollars using the rate on December 1. But at the end of the year, the outstanding receivable in francs would have to be updated using the most recent rate and recognizing an exchange gain. At the time of payment, the most recent rate is used to again update the receivable and recognize an exchange loss from the reversal in the rate. Finally, receipt of the francs and their conversion into dollars are recorded. Notice that in this case, an overall foreign exchange loss is shown, but it is broken down into two components—one part as a gain in 1982 and the second a loss in 1983.

The next section explores the problems and appropriate techniques for translating foreign currency–denominated financial statements.

TRANSLATION OF FOREIGN FINANCIAL STATEMENTS

A second accounting area of importance to the multinational corporation is accounting for foreign investment activities. When a firm invests in the stock and bonds of another firm, the resulting investment must be classified as either short-term or long-term, depending upon how long the firm intends to keep the investment. If the firm is only temporarily investing excess cash in the securities of another firm, this is considered short-term and is classified as a current asset on the balance sheet. It is valued at the original cost of the investment or at the current market price, whichever is lower.

If the investment is long-term, however, a different accounting treatment is necessary. In the United States, because many American firms are actively involved in the acquisition of other firms, some special accounting methods have been developed to account for this activity. The key element is how much of the voting stock is owned.

COST METHOD VERSUS EQUITY METHOD

If one firm owns insufficient voting stock is another firm to enable the former to significantly influence the policies of the latter firm, the former is considered as having only a "minor influence" on the latter and must use the *cost method* to account for its investment.[1] Essentially, the cost method requires that the investment be recorded at the total amount paid to acquire the stock. Thereafter, any dividends

---

[1]For balance-of-payments purposes, the definition of *control* is somewhat different. The U.S. Department of Commerce defines a *direct investment* as one in which a company owns 10 percent or more of the voting stock.

declared and paid on the stock would be considered revenue when received.

When one firm owns sufficient voting stock in another firm to significantly influence the latter's policies, the investor firm is said to have a "substantial interest" in the other firm and must use the *equity method* to account for the investment. The equity method requires that the investment be periodically adjusted to recognize the investor's share of increases or decreases (from profits or losses) in the net worth of the investee company. Any dividends received from the investee reduce the value of the investment account.

CONSOLIDATION

A special situation exists when one firm owns over 50 percent of the voting stock of another firm; this is called *control*. The investor firm in this case must prepare *consolidated financial statements*.

Consolidated financial statements present the financial affairs of a single economic entity that is made up of a number of separate legal entities (that is, the parent company and each of its subsidiaries). The typical nonconsolidated financial statements are prepared for just one entity—the firm in question. But if one firm owns or has controlling interest in (as opposed to merely "substantial interest" in) another firm, then an investor in the parent company should know that his or her investment really represents a share in more than one firm. If you look at the financial statements of most large American firms, you will see that they are consolidated. This procedure is required in the United States for controlled companies.

To prepare consolidated statements, the basic procedure is to obtain the individual financial statements of each of the firms and then to simply add them up, line by line, to get the consolidated total (of their assets, liabilities, owners equity, revenues, expenses, and profits). Double-counting of the same financial total must be avoided, and certain other adjustments must be made, especially when one firm does not own 100 percent of another. The basic idea is simple.

ACCOUNTING FOR FOREIGN INVESTMENTS

Special accounting procedures are necessary when an American firm makes investments in foreign subsidiaries. To be consolidated, the financial statements of *all subsidiaries* (the name for firms owned by other firms) are added together to form one consolidated balance sheet, one consolidated income statement, and so forth to represent the group as a whole. When foreign firms are subsidiaries, there are two major barriers to consolidation.

1. The accounting principles used to prepare the foreign financial statements may not be GAAP in the United States.
2. The monetary figures in the foreign statements are in foreign currencies.

U.S. generally accepted accounting principles require that both these barriers be overcome before consolidation can occur.

FOREIGN ACCOUNTING PRINCIPLES

The accounting principles that exist in a given nation at a point in time are related to that nation's type of economic system, legal framework, business environment, social system, national tradition, strength of its accounting profession, and patterns of historical development. Thus, as these factors differ among nations in the world, it is quite natural to expect that each nation's accounting principles differ as well. And in varying degrees, this is true.

When a firm is owned by another firm in a different country, the subsidiary continues to be a legal entity in its home country and must comply with the national laws, business customs, and accounting principles where it is located. Thus, even though a French firm may be wholly owned by an American firm, the French subsidiary must comply with French law, business customs, and accounting rules. It will issue French financial statements and pay French taxes. It will follow French accounting rules and principles in its books, and the monetary unit of account will be the French franc.

The French accounting statements are the starting point for consolidation. Generally accepted accounting principles in the United States must guide the consolidation. The first step is to determine whether or not the French accounting principles embodied in the subsidiary's financial statements are in conformity with U.S. GAAP. If not and if the difference is material (that is, by causing a major distortion), then the French subsidiary's financial statements must be adjusted to comply with U.S. GAAP.

Obviously, if the differences between the national accounting principles among the nations of the world were great, this would greatly complicate the preparation of consolidated financial statements. Fortunately, *the differences in accounting principles are generally not substantial.* Furthermore, as we shall describe more fully in a later section, there is a movement today among the nations of the world to reduce the diversity in their national accounting principles to aid in comparisons and consolidations.

Table 19.1 lists some typical areas where foreign accounting principles and practices can differ significantly from U.S. GAAP. A multinational corporation's accounting system and accounting personnel must

TABLE 19.1   Common Areas Where Foreign GAAP Differ from U.S. GAAP

In some nations, accounting for the impact of inflation (general price-level increases or specific price-level increases) is either required or at least permitted by national law.

In some nations, firms can smooth year-to-year net income by creating *expense reserves* within discretionary limits specified by their GAAP. This can also permit overconservative reporting of lower-than-actual net income.

Some nations' GAAP do not require the preparation of consolidated financial statements, or they may utilize a consolidation policy that is different from that which is used in the United States, such as requiring the consolidation of only controlled *domestic* subsidiaries.

Some national acounting principles permit or require excessive depreciation or the immediate write-off of fixed assets.

Some other specific areas where major differences in national accounting principles can be found are inventory methods, currency translation methods, goodwill amortization, treatment of stock dividends, accounting for the cost of pension plans, and accounting for leases.

---

be familiar with the accounting practices that are followed by their foreign subsidiaries. They must develop methods to adjust, where necessary, foreign financial statements that do not conform to U.S. GAAP. Not infrequently, two sets of books may be kept for foreign subsidiaries: one according to the local accounting principles and one according to U.S. GAAP.

FOREIGN CURRENCIES

In addition to overcoming the problem of foreign accounting principles, the parent company that desires to consolidate the financial statements of its foreign subsidiaries must also deal with the foreign currencies in which these statements are expressed. Until these currencies are transformed into the common monetary denominator of the home currency, consolidation is impossible.

The major problem that arises in the translation of financial statements expressed in a foreign currency is the choice of which exchange rate to use. This is especially important in a period of volatile changes in exchange rates.

Given the importance of translation and the difficulties presented by volatile currencies, it would be convenient if all financial accounts on the balance sheet, income statement, and other financial reports could all be translated at a single exchange rate. Unfortunately, this is not always possible, as will be explained in the following section.

TRANSLATING FOREIGN CURRENCIES

Since World War II, there have been three major translation models that have been used by accountants in various countries to translate foreign currency amounts of foreign affiliates into a domestic currency: the *current-noncurrent,* the *monetary-nonmonetary,* and the *current-rate* methods. These models indicate which of three exchange rates should be used for each amount of foreign currency on the balance sheet and income statement of a foreign affiliate in order to translate these amounts into the particular domestic currency. The three different exchange rates are (1) the *historical rate,* which is the rate in effect when a transaction takes place; (2) the *current rate,* which is the rate at the end of the accounting period (the quarter or year) when the consolidation is being done; and (3) the *average rate,* which is some average rate over a particular period of time.

The three translation models have different rules regarding when these three rates are to be used. The major differences among these models deal mainly with items on the balance sheet and two items on the income statement (described below).

Income statement: In general, all three models require that sales, other revenues, and most operating expenses on the income statement be translated into the domestic currency by using the *average rate* for the period covered by the revenue or the expenses. The major exceptions to this rule concern the translation of costs of goods sold and depreciation expenses on the income statement. Each model has a different approach to these two elements on the income statement. Thus, in the following comparison of the models, items on the income statement other than cost of goods sold and depreciation expense are all translated at the *average exchange rate* for the period covered by the income statement, unless otherwise stated.

Balance sheet: current-noncurrent: The *current-noncurrent model* adopts the traditional accounting classification scheme for the balance sheet and applies it to translation methodology. Under this method, those balance sheet items classified as current (expected to be used up, converted into cash, or paid within one year) are translated into the domestic currency at the current rate. Those elements that are classified on the balance sheet as noncurrent are translated at their historical rate. Thus, current assets and current liabilities are translated at the current rate; fixed assets, noncurrent liabilities, and shareholders' equity (except for retained earnings) are translated at the historical rate. Retained earnings are not translated but are the residual needed to make the balance sheet actually balance after the other accounts have been translated. On the income statement, cost of goods sold is translated at the current rate as the flow of inventory occurs through the income statement, and depreciation expense is translated at the appropriate historical rate.

The current-noncurrent classification scheme is designed primarily for the benefit of creditors to assess the short-term solvency of the firm. It is convenient and well established and thus is "available" for adoption as a basic translation scheme. However, there is no conceptual support for the relating of exchange rates and accounting classification.

Balance sheet: monetary-nonmonetary: The *monetary-non-monetary model* focuses on the financial character of the foreign element in the financial statement to determine the rate to translate into the domestic currency. Foreign currency assets and liabilities that are expressed in a fixed number of currency units are defined as *monetary;* those that do not fit this description are *nonmonetary.* The monetary items are translated at the current rate, and the nonmonetary items at historical rates.

Monetary items are assets such as cash, claims to cash, and almost all liabilities. The main nonmonetary items are assets such as inventory, prepaid items, and fixed assets. Stockholders' equity (except for retained earnings) is translated at the historical rate. Again, retained earnings are not translated but are the residual necessary to provide balance. The main differences between the current-noncurrent and monetary-non-monetary methods involve the translation rates used for noncurrent receivables, payables, inventory, and prepaid items. Under the current-noncurrent method, all noncurrent items are translated at their historical rate, whereas all current items are translated at the current rate. However, under the monetary-nonmonetary method, current and non-current receivables and payables, which are monetary, are translated at the current rate; current assets, such as inventory and prepaid items, which are nonmonetary items, are translated at their historical rate. Under the monetary-nonmonetary method, cost of goods sold is translated at the historical rate as the flow of inventory through the income statement proceeds, and depreciation expense is translated at the appropriate historical rate.

A variant of the monetary-nonmonetary approach was generally used in the United States under FASB 8 from 1976 to 1981. FASB 8 referred to this approach as the *temporal model.*

Balance sheet: the current rate: The *current-rate* (or *closing-rate) model* is the simplest of all the translation methods. It calls for the use of the current rate for translation of all items on the balance sheet, except for capital stock and retained earnings (which are, as with the other two translation methods, a residual). All assets (whether current or noncurrent, monetary or nonmonetary) and all liabilities (whether current or noncurrent) are translated at the current rate. All elements on the income statement, even the cost of goods sold and depreciation expense, are translated at an average rate.

Table 19.2 lists the main differences among the three translation models for items on the balance sheet and income statement. Note that all three systems employ the current rate for cash, receivables, and payables. Each method utilizes the historical rate for paid-in capital and surplus. Retained earnings are not translated but are the residual under each system, although a special translation adjustment account may be introduced in some systems (such as FASB 52). Revenues and most expenses on the income statement are generally translated at the average rate. However, there is considerable variation between the three systems in the translations of the other accounts on the balance sheet and income statement.

The current-rate model is the most prevalent method used throughout the world. With the introduction of FASB 52 in 1981, FASB 8 was superseded. The current-rate model became the basic U.S. approach, replacing the monetary-nonmonetary system.

U.S. TRANSLATION PRACTICES

The first translation model adopted in the U.S. was the current-noncurrent. It became generally accepted in the late 1930s and was used

TABLE 19.2 Comparison of Translation Models for Items on the Balance Sheet and Income Statement

	Translation Rate Used[a]		
	Current-Noncurrent	Monetary-Nonmonetary	Current-Rate
Balance Sheet Item			
Cash	C	C	C
Current receivables	C	C	C
Inventories (cost)	C	H	C
Prepaid items	C	H	C
Plant, property and equipment	H	H	C
Long-term intangible assets	H	H	C
Current payables	C	C	C
Long-term debt	H	C	C
Paid-in capital and surplus (capital stock)	H	H	H
Retained earnings	X	X	X
Income Statement Item			
Cost of good sold	C	H	A
Depreciation expense	H	H	A
Revenues	A	A	A
Operating expenses	A	A	A

[a]C = current rate; H = historical rate; A = average rate; and X = not translated, a residual.

until 1975. During the mid-1950s, the monetary-nonmonetary model became popular, and it too was used by American firms until 1975. The year 1975 is very important, because it represented an abrupt change in U.S. GAAP for translation. Prior to that year, many translation methods (the current-noncurrent, monetary-nonmonetary, and variations of them) were employed by American firms to translate their international operations. In 1975, the FASB issued FASB 8, which narrowed the diversity in this area by allowing the use of only one translation model—the *temporal model*. Although this model was quite close to the monetary-nonmonetary model, most American firms had to make at least some change in their translation practices to conform to FASB 8.

In addition to requiring the use of one translation method, FASB 8 required that translation gains and losses be included in the determination of net income. Prior to this, many firms used a variety of treatments for translation gains and losses. But under FASB 8, these were required to be included in current net income. For these and other reasons, FASB 8 became a very controversial pronouncement of the FASB and was the subject of a number of studies.

In March of 1979, the FASB created a Task Force on Foreign Currency Translation to recommend changes to FASB 8; these changes came forth as FASB 52, which was issued in December of 1981. This new translation pronouncement, while adopting much of the content of FASB 8, required most American multinationals to adopt the current-rate model. However, under certain circumstances FASB 52 still requires the use of the translation model of FASB 8, the temporal method. Perhaps of greatest significance, FASB 52 requires that translation gains and losses that arise in applying the current-rate method, instead of being included in net income, be moved from the income statement to a special component of stockholders' equity on the balance sheet.

TRANSLATING FOREIGN OPERATIONS

The following illustration demonstrates the principles of FASB 52 in detail. Assume that the Seymore Prophets Company created a subsidiary and built a factory in the country of Examplandia. On December 1, 1983, when one FC (the currency of Examplandia) equaled one U.S. dollar), the subsidiary had the following balance sheet:

	FC	$		FC	$
Cash	1500	1500	Accounts payable	1800	1800
Merchandise inventory	1800	1800	Long-term debt	1000	1000
Fixed assets	1500	1500	Capital stock	2000	2000
	FC 4800	$4800	Retained earnings	0	0
				FC 4800	$4800

Seymore's investment in the new subsidiary was $2000 (that is, the capital stock in the balance sheet). Operations were to begin on January 2, 1984. However, by the close of business on December 31, 1983, the exchange rate for the FC dropped to a new rate of FC/1 = $0.90. If GAAP are the same in Examplandia as in the United States, then the consolidated financial statements can now be prepared for Seymore.

In applying FASB 52 to this subsidiary, the current-rate method will be used, assuming that this subsidiary is to be operated as a separate firm that primarily services the local market in Examplandia. Under this method, all the assets and liabilities on the balance sheet are translated into dollars at the year-end rate. Since there have been no operations (no revenues or expenses) for this subsidiary, its year-end balance sheet in the local currency is exactly the same as it was on December 1, 1983. However, the exchange rate has changed from $1.00 to $0.90 per FC.

From an accounting standpoint, since the FC declined in value, the *dollar* value of every asset in this subsidiary has dropped and the dollar value of every liability has dropped as well. Since the assets exceed the liabilities (a *net asset position*), the result is a *translation loss*. (If the FC had increased in value, there would have been a *translation gain*.) Under the old FASB 8, any loss or gain would have appeared in the consolidated income statement of the parent and thus would have affected the net income. However, under the FASB 52, a loss or gain appears only on the balance sheet as a separate component of stockholders' equity. This translation is shown for the Examplandia subsidiary in Table 19.3.

Under FASB 8, although the total asset value remained unchanged in terms of the *local* currencies at FC 4800, the *dollar* value of the monetary assets (FC 1500 of cash) declined from $1500 to $1350 because

TABLE 19.3 Translation Schedule of Examplandia Subsidiary (December 31, 1983)

Financial Statement Element	Predevaluation		Exchange Rate	Postdevaluation	
	FC	$		FC	$
Cash	1500	1500	current ($0.90)	1500	1350
Merchandise inventory	1800	1800	current ($0.90)	1800	1620
Fixed assets	1500	1500	current ($0.90)	1500	1350
	FC 4800	$4800		FC 4800	$4320
Accounts payable	1800	1800	current ($0.90)	1800	1620
Long-term debt	1000	1000	current ($0.90)	1000	900
Capital stock	2000	2000	historical ($1.00)	2000	2000
Retained earnings	0	0		0	
Translation adjustment					(200)
	FC 4800	$4800		FC 4800	$4320

of the exchange-rate decline from \$1.00/FC to \$0.90/FC. Since *all* liabilities are monetary liabilities, the total liability exposure was FC 2800; it declined in value from \$2800 to \$2520. Thus, the asset decline of \$160 was more than offset by a liability decline of \$280 for a net translation *gain* of \$120.

Under FASB 8, the \$120 net translation gain would have been used to calculate the consolidated net income on the 1983 income statement for the parent firm. This impact upon net income (whether a loss or gain) was very controversial since most managers and many accountants viewed them as unrealized and thus as "paper losses." However, these paper losses were a determinant of net income under the old translation rules.

However, under FASB 52, the result would be quite different. As Table 19.3 shows, although the total assets of this subsidiary still remain constant in terms of the local currency at FC 4800, their dollar value after translation dropped from \$4800 to \$4320. In a similar way the dollar value of the total liabilities declined from \$2800 to \$2520 (\$1620 plus \$900). Thus, the assets declined by \$480 (\$4800 minus \$4320), and the liabilities declined by \$280 (\$2800 minus \$2520), for a net translation loss of \$200 (\$480 − \$280).

Thus, it can readily be seen that the type of translation method used can have a significant effect upon the reported results—and whether the net loss or gain is reported in the income statement.

Under FASB 52, as can be seen in Table 19.3, the \$200 net decline appears on the balance sheet in an account in the stockholders' equity section which is called *translation adjustment.* Note that the adjustment occurs *only on the balance sheet,* and that *it does not affect the net income* for 1983.

Translation of the financial accounts of the Seymore Prophets subsidiary in Examplandia is necessary on a quarterly basis as long as Seymore controls the subsidiary. Business commences on January 2, 1984, and the firm begins to buy and sell and to incur expenses. Table 19.4 shows the financial statements for the subsidiary on March 31, 1984, the end of the first quarter.

Assume that the exchange rate at the end of January was FC = \$0.89; at the end of February, FC = \$0.93; and at the end of March, FC = \$0.94. For translation purposes, as of March 31, 1984, the current rate would be \$0.94, and the average rate of the end-of-month rates for the first quarter would be \$0.92. Table 19.5 illustrates the translation schedule for these statements into dollars. Study it carefully.

The top half of Table 19.5 represents the income statement for the first quarter in 1984 for the Examplandia subsidiary. It shows that in the local currency, FC, this subsidiary operated profitably. The first quar-

TABLE 19.4   Financial Statements for Examplandia Subsidiary (Quarter ending March 31, 1984)

Income Statement (in FC)			Balance Sheet (in FC)		
Sales		FC 3600	Cash	FC 2540	
Cost of goods sold	FC 1800		Merchandise inventory	1800	
Salary expense	360		Fixed assets (net)	1360	
Depreciation expense	140		Total assets		FC 5700
Advertising expense	300		Accounts payable	1800	
Miscellaneous expenses	100		Long-term debt	1000	
Total expenses		2700	Stockholders' equity	2900	
Net profit		FC 900	Total claims on assets		FC 5700

ter's profit of FC 900 is shown as the balance in retained earnings on the balance sheet as of the end of the first quarter.

Under the provisons of FASB 52, all revenues and expenses on the income statement are translated into dollars using the average rate for the period, which in this example is $0.92. This procedure is simple to implement and does preserve the relationships in the income statement that are of concern to management—the gross profit rate and the ratio of operating profit to sales. These ratios are the same in FC and in dollars. For example, in FC, the sales minus the cost of goods sold equals the gross profit: FC 3600 − FC 1800 = FC 1800. In terms of a percentage, gross profit divided by sales produces the gross profit percentage. In FC, FC 1800 ÷ FC 3600 = 50 percent. Notice that this ratio has been preserved by the translation procedure in dollars: $3312 − $1656 = $1656; $1656 ÷ $3312 = 50 percent.

On the balance sheet, all the assets and liabilities are translated at the current rate of $0.94, except for the amount of capital stock, which is shown at its historical rate; the amount of retained earnings, which is taken from the income statement; and the translation adjustment account. Please note that the translation adjustment account exists only in dollars: It does *not* appear on the *FC* balance sheet.

It is important to recognize that ($102) is the ending balance in this account. Recall that the beginning balance in the translation adjustment account as of January 2, 1984, is ($200) (see Table 19.3). Thus, for the first quarter of 1984, this subsidiary must have produced a positive translation adjustment of $98, which, when added to the balance as of the beginning of the year, resulted in the ($102) that appears on the translated balance sheet of the first quarter of 1984. It is important to distinguish between the overall balance in the translation adjustment account and the current period's translation adjustment amount (that is, the difference between the beginning and ending amounts). FASB 52

TABLE 19.5 Translation Schedule

Financial Statement		FC	Exchange Rate	$
		Income Statement[a]		
Sales		FC 3600	$0.92 average	$3312
Cost of goods sold	FC 1800		0.92 average	$1656
Salaries expense	360		0.92 average	331
Depreciation expense	140		0.92 average	129
Advertising expense	300		0.92 average	276
Miscellaneous expenses	100		0.92 average	92
Total expenses		FC 2700	Not translated	$2484
Net profit		FC 900	Not translated	$ 828
		Balance Sheet		
Cash	FC 2540		0.94 current	$2388
Merchandise inventory	1800		0.94 current	1692
Fixed assets (net)	1360		0.94 current	1278
Total assets		FC 5700		$5358
Accounts payable	1800		0.94 current	1692
Long-term debt	1000		0.94 current	940
Capital stock	2000		1.00 historical	2000
Retained earnings	900		From income statement	828
			Translation adjustment	(102)
Total claims on assets		FC 5700	Total claims on assets	$5358

[a]Assumptions: Sales were made, and wages, advertising, and miscellaneous expenses were incurred uniformly throughout the first quarter.

requires the disclosure of the details in the translation adjustment account.

TRANSLATING FOREIGN BUDGETS

Our focus thus far has been on currency translation for external reporting. It should be noted that exchange rates can cause problems in the budgeting and planning operations in the multinational firm as well. A special problem in this area concerns the translation of the budgets for foreign operations into dollars. If the management of the multinational emphasizes the preparation of comprehensive business plans, then each part of the firm will prepare its budget in terms of its own local currency. The management must then decide whether these budgets that are in the variety of currencies should be assembled into one master budget in dollars and, if so, which budget should be used to evaluate the performance of the foreign operations.

The following example demonstrates the special problems inherent in this area. Suppose that Seymore Prophets Corporation requires that each of its foreign subsidiaries prepare operating budgets for future quarters. Suppose further that the Examplandia subsidiary submits the following budget at the end of 1983 for the first quarter of 1984:

Operating Budget (First Quarter, 1984)

Sales	FC 3600
Cost of goods sold	(1800)
Salaries expense	(360)
Depreciation expense	(140)
Advertising expense	(200)
Miscellaneous expense	(200)
Operating net profit	FC 900

Although this may be a perfectly valid operating plan for this subsidiary, the management of the multinational may want to translate it into dollars, so that all the operating plans can be combined into meaningful totals. But this requires the use of an exchange rate. Thus, management faces a decision concerning what rate to use to translate this budget into dollars for the coming quarter. It could use the spot rate at the end of 1983 of $0.90, or it could have some estimate made for the average rate for the first quarter of 1984 and use that rate. But whatever management decides to do, it may run into problems later on if it tries to compare the actual results for this subsidiary (in dollars) with the translation of the budget. Differences may exist between the plan and the actual dollar results simply due to changes in the exchange rate, and this may cause personnel problems in the evaluation system. Table 19.6 shows the difference caused for the Examplandia subsidiary's operating results if the FC budget is translated into dollars at an estimated rate of $0.93 and then compared with the results translated into dollars at the average rate of $0.92, as used for external reporting purposes.

If we assume that the subsidiary actually achieves the budget figures in FC, then, depending upon which exchange rate is used to translate the budget into dollars, the actual results in dollars may not agree. For example, if the management of the firm translates the original FC budget into dollars at a rate of $0.93 and then in the following quarter the actual results were in agreement in FC but the exchange rate averaged only $0.92, there would be a difference between the expected profit in dollars and the actual dollar results. The management would have to take this into account and adjust for it.

WORLDWIDE ACCOUNTING STANDARDS

As shown earlier in this chapter, the accounting principles of the nations of the world are not the same, for a variety of reasons. Each nation has carefully guarded its own right to set the accounting principles to be followed within its national boundaries. The resulting diversity in national accounting principles makes the preparation of consolidated financial statements more difficult and has a second negative effect: It acts as an obstacle to the flow of international investment capital. From an international viewpont, this second detrimental impact is the more important one.

For example, assume an investor is seeking to invest some funds in an automotive firm. If the investor takes an international viewpoint, the funds could be invested in any of a number of firms, located in the

TABLE 19.6 Subsidiary Evaluation Report (First Quarter, 1984)

	FC		FC = $0.93	FC = $0.92
Sales		3600	3348	3312
Expenses		2700	2511	2484
Cost of goods sold	1800		1674	1656
Salaries expense	360		335	331
Depreciation expense	140		130	129
Advertising expense	200		186	184
Miscellaneous expense	200		186	184
Net profit		900	837	828

United States or abroad. To make the decision as a prudent investor, the published annual report (which contains the financial statements) for each of the firms could be obtained, examined, and compared. However, if the accounting principles underlying the financial statements in the annual reports are not similar, then the comparison cannot easily be made, and the investor will not benefit from such a comparison. Thus, the efficiency of the final investment decision can be questioned. If national accounting principles were less diverse, such comparisons could be more easily made, and the flow of investment capital across national boundaries would be facilitated.

Throughout the years, some accountants have been aware of the international dimensions and implications of their profession. The seriousness of the two problems caused by national diversity in accounting principles has not escaped the attention of the accounting profession either. In recent years, there is growing support for efforts to reduce this diversity and solve the problems.

Some real progress has been made since the mid-1970s to deal with the problems created by national diversity in accounting principles. The European Economic Community is engaged in a program that is intended to harmonize the accounting principles of member nations. Also, the United Nations has sought to influence the quality, quantity, and consistency of published financial data from multinationals. Another organization—the International Accounting Standards Commitee (IASC)—has committed itself to the establishment of worldwide accounting standards. It is likely that such efforts will continue in the near future.

Keep in mind, however, that the goal of this movement is not to establish one set of accounting principles to be used in all nations. Given the differences in nations, that is an impossible dream. But what is needed and possible is the reduction of national diversity in GAAP to facilitate international investment. Progress will continue to be made toward this goal.

SUMMARY

The accounting dimension is an important aspect of multinational operations. Improper understanding of the accounting implications of such international business factors such as changing currency values and different accounting systems can hamper efficient operations. The accounting implications are explained in the national accounting rules; in the United States these are FASB 8 and FASB 52. These two pronouncements of the FASB cover such important topics as accounting for international transactions and translating foreign financial statements for consolidation. When coupled with volatility in exchange rates, these accounting rules can result in the reporting of translation gains and losses that are difficult to understand.

The differences in national accounting principles tend to inhibit efficient international investment and make the preparation of consolidated financial statements more difficult. The recent change in the United States from one currency translation method to a method more in harmony with other countries' translation methods shows that some progress is being made to reduce the international diversity.

KEY TERMS

AVERAGE EXCHANGE RATE

CONSOLIDATED FINANCIAL STATEMENTS

COST METHOD

CURRENT EXCHANGE RATE

CURRENT-NONCURRENT METHOD

CURRENT-RATE METHOD

EQUITY METHOD

FASB 8

FASB 52

GENERALLY ACCEPTED ACCOUNTING PRINCIPLES (GAAP)

HISTORICAL EXCHANGE RATE

MONETARY-NONMONETARY METHOD

NET ASSET

NET LIABILITY

PAPER GAIN

PAPER LOSS

TEMPORAL METHOD

TRANSACTION

TRANSLATION

TRANSLATION ADJUSTMENT ACCOUNT

TWO-TRANSACTION VIEW

REVIEW QUESTIONS

1. The Dewey Cheatum Company exported some merchandise to a customer in the United Kingdom on September 1, 1983. The goods were shipped on that day and invoiced at £1000 (the exchange rate on that day was $2.22/£). Payment was due on January 31, 1984. Record the sale of September 1, 1983, in dollars, for Dewey Cheatum. Make any adjusting entry necessary on December 31, 1983, when Dewey closes its books (assume that the rate was $2.25/£, and then record the collection of this account on January 31, 1984, when the rate was $2.23/£.

2. Below is the year-end balance sheet of a foreign subsidiary of the Odom International Corporation. This subsidiary was acquired by Odom on December 30, 1983, when the exchange rate between that nation's currency, the LC, and the dollar was LC1 = $1.00. However, on December 31, 1983, the rate declined to LC1 = $0.95. Translate the balance sheet according to FASB 52 as of the end of 1983, and determine the balance of the translation adjustment

account. Assume no operations had taken place and that this subsidiary had operated at break-even prior to its acquisition by Odom and therefore has no retained earnings balance.

Odom International Corporation
LC Subsidiary (12/31/83)

Cash	LC 1400	Accounts payable	LC 1600
Inventory	1600	Long-term debt	2000
Fixed assets	1200	Stockholders' equity	600
	LC 4200		LC 4200

3. Below is the income statement for 1984 for a foreign subsidiary of the Ingram International Corporation.

Ingram International Corporation
Subsidiary (Income Statement for 1984)

Sales		FM 7200
Expenses		5300
Cost of goods sold	3600	
Wage expense	720	
Depreciation expense	280	
Advertising expense	400	
Auto expense	300	
Net Profit		FM 1900

The exchange rates for the year were as follows: January 1, 1984, FM1 = $0.80; July 1, 1984, FM1 = $0.82; and December 31, 1984, FM1 = $0.84. Translate the income statement into dollars using FASB 52.

SUGGESTED REFERENCES

ALHASHIM, D., AND J. ROBERTSON *Accounting for the Multinational Enterprise.* Indianapolis: The Bobbs-Merrill Company, 1978.

ARPAN, JEFFREY S. *International Intracorporate Pricing: Non-American Systems and Views.* New York: Praeger Publishers, 1972.

————, AND LEE H. RADEBAUGH *International Accounting and Multinational Enterprises.* Boston: Warren, Gorham & Lamont, 1981.

CHOI, F.D.S., AND G.G. MUELLER *An Introduction to Multinational Accounting,* Englewood Cliffs, N.J.: Prentice-Hall, Inc., 1978.

Evans, Thomas G., William R. Folks, Jr., and Michael Jilling   *The Impact of Statement of Financial Accounting Standards No. 8 on the Foreign-Exchange Risk Management Practices of American Multinationals.* Financial Accounting Standards Board, 1978.

Fantl, Irvin L.   "Control and the Internal Audit in the Multinational Firm," *Journal of Accounting,* Fall 1975.

Financial Accounting Standards Board   *Statement of Financial Accounting Standards No. 8,* "Accounting for the Translation of Foreign Currency Transactions and Foreign Currency Financial Statements," 1975.

————*Statement of Financial Accounting Standards No. 52,* "Foreign Currency Translation," 1981.

Fitzgerald, R.D., A.D. Stickler, and T.R. Watts, eds.   *International Survey of Accounting Principles and Reporting Practices.* New York: Price Waterhouse International, 1979.

Granick, David   "National Differences in the Use of International Transfer Prices," *Management Accounting,* Summer 1975.

Greene, James, and Michael G. Duerr   *Inter-Company Transactions in the Multinational Firm.* New York: National Industrial Conference Board, 1970.

Stamp, E., and M. Moonitz   *International Auditing Standards.* Englewood Cliffs, N.J.: Prentice-Hall, Inc., 1979.

Stanley, Marjorie, and Stanley Block   "Response by U.S. Financial Managers to Financial Accounting Standards #8," *Journal of International Business Studies,* Fall 1978.

Watt, George C. et al.   *Accounting for the Multinational Corporation.* Financial Executives Research Foundation, 1977.

20

Financial Management in International Operations

THE INTERNATIONAL FINANCIAL MANAGER

International financial operations are one of the managerial functions in which the international operations differ most significantly from the domestic and is also one of the functions that is potentially the most lucrative to the astute manager. It is true that some of the most unique and potentially perilous differences between the domestic and international occur in the financial vein (for example, foreign exchange markets). However, it is also the vein in which such opportunities as diversified financial markets can lead to attractive funding profits.

Earlier chapters examined many of the major aspects of the international financial environment in great detail: foreign exchange markets, international capital and money markets, international controls, accounting practices and so forth. In this and the following chapter we examine how the multinational corporate manager reacts to these constraints. Some of these environmental conditions are simply obstacles to be overcome. However, others provide opportunities to be exploited.

Several different aspects of international financial management are examined. After first considering the basic question of the financial structure of the firm, the focus shifts to international cash-flow management, international capital budgeting, and, finally, what can be done with blocked funds. The next chapter examines the special problems in managing foreign exchange exposure.

WHOSE PERSPECTIVE: PARENT OR SUBSIDIARY?

We are examining the international financial management function of the firm as a whole—as an entire system. When the role of the manager of a foreign subsidiary of the company is discussed, it is assumed that that manager is seeking to optimize the performance of the entire firm. This is not, of course, universally true. Some managers of subsidiaries are able to concentrate upon optimizing the performance of the subsidiary, even if such performance is not optimizing the overall performance of the entire company. If this is possible, it is because of a breakdown in the normal pattern of controls that should tie subsidiaries to the parent; either the controls were never instituted or, if instituted, are not being employed. As indicated in an earlier chapter, the lack of such prudent and normal controls can greatly reduce the attractiveness of a company's international operations. Of course, these controls are typically more difficult to implement than they are in corresponding domestic relationships. However, that is no excuse for failing to properly implement them. With the wide range of financial risks to which a company is exposed in its international operations, the company simply cannot afford such laxity. Therefore, the discussion assumes that the company is acting accordingly.

LOCUS OF FINANCIAL CONTROL

As seen in the discussion about control of international operations, the locus of control of financial operations can be quite varied between different companies. With highly centralized controls, financial decisions and operations are controlled by central headquarters. Many companies, however, choose to decentralize control either to regional or even local managers of their foreign operations. Other companies utilize centralized control for some functions, such as capital budgeting and controlling cash reserves, but use decentralized control for other needs, such as local working-capital requirements. The rapid development of modern communication and computerized information technology has greatly increased the options for financial managers for choosing between centralized or decentralized control.

The major hurdles confronting the international financial manager help to dictate for each company exactly what type of control system to implement. In the rest of this chapter problems such as time lags, inflation, governmental controls, and taxation are addressed.

CORPORATE FINANCIAL STRUCTURE

The analysis of corporate financial structure is highly developed in the study of financial management. For instance, one of the basic concepts in capital budgeting is "optimal capital structure." Each industry, indeed each mature company, has its own optimal capital structure. However, the aspiring international manager should be aware that the patterns with which he or she may be familiar are not necessarily the norms in other countries. For example, a study in the mid-1970s indicated that in the United States the average debt ratio among a wide range of manufacturing companies was 42 percent. In contrast, the corresponding figure was approximately 57 percent in France and the Netherlands, 67 percent in Japan, and 79 percent in Norway.[1] These discrepancies may have narrowed somewhat since then, but the differences remain very significant. Thus, the financial manager must realize that the providers of funds may be using very different analytical criteria in foreign countries from what is the norm at home.

EQUITY CAPITAL

A company with an international perspective can expand its own equity funding opportunities to foreign domestic markets. There are already many foreign companies listed on stock exchanges in the United States, Europe, and Japan. Of course, as has been seen, there is no international or Euro-equity market.

The sources of equity financing for the foreign subsidiary are, of course, somewhat more extensive for the foreign subsidiary than for the parent, since the subsidiary can draw upon the resources of the parent as well as outside resources. Indeed, the most obvious source of equity funding for the fledgling subsidiary abroad is the parent corporation. It matters little to the subsidiary what the source of such funds is for the parent: it could derive from retained earnings, a new sale of stock in the domestic markets, or even debt financing.

A second source of equity financing for a foreign subsidiary is from one or more other companies: a joint venture or consortium. A third alternative is for the subsidiary to sell its own stock, typically in the country in which the investment is being made. It could involve either public or private sale of stock. (If it is a private stock sale, the arrangement might be a joint venture unless the stock is widely dispersed.)

---

[1]Arthur Stonehill et al., "Financial Goals and Debt-Ratio Determinants: A Survey of Practices in Five Countries," *Financial Management,* Autumn 1975, p. 40.

Private sales of stock by the subsidiary have the advantage of generally not being subject to governmental regulation. If the sale is to be a public one, then typically local regulations need to be satisfied regarding the initial or primary sale and subsequent resale on the secondary market.

DEBT CAPITAL

Debt financing is even more varied than equity financing. First, it can come from a much broader geographical base. Either the parent or the foreign subsidiary may have access to debt markets in the home country, host country, third-country markets, or the Euromarkets. (It should be remembered that organizational formats such as a branch, agency, or representative office are not separate corporate entities from the parent. Any external funding to which they may have access are a direct obligation of the parent.)

Second, debt can also derive from a wide variety of sources: public markets, commercial banks, development banks, or private placements. Third, debt financing is also more variable than equity financing, since it can be for the long or short term.

FUNDING DIVERSITY

This wide range of funding options is, of course, an attractive opportunity to many international firms. A company does not have to have foreign subsidiaries in order to tap foreign and international money and capital markets. More and more companies are coming to realize that opportunities for both funding and investing are available if the company is willing to search for them.

At one time the Euromarkets and the foreign capital markets were the private preserve of only the largest and most credit-worthy companies. As the markets developed, however, and as the competition grew between bankers and merchant bankers, a wider and wider range of companies have been partaking of these markets. This, of course, adds a greater element of risk to the provider of funds to or through these markets. However, greater diversification was inevitable and is a welcome development.

This is especially true of the Euromarkets. The greater *depth* (that is, placing power—the ability of the market to provide large sums of money) and greater *breadth* (that is, the ability for the markets to serve a wide variety of needs for a wide range of borrowers) have made it possible for the Euromarkets to become the dominant financial markets of the world by the late 1970s.

INTERNATIONAL CASH-FLOW MANAGEMENT

The management of international current assets and liabilities is one of the most dynamic responsibilities of the international financial manager. This task, which is called *international cash management* or, more accurately, *international cash-flow management,* is essentially the control of short-term–liquid and near-liquid accounts that are on the company's balance sheet, such as cash, marketable securities, receivable, and payable accounts.

International cash-flow management is directed toward an optimal utilization of the firm's current resources and financing sources (that is, its current assets and liabilities) on a systemwide basis. Therefore, a few words about the basic mechanisms for moving funds internationally would be useful.

AVAILABLE MEANS OF INTERNATIONAL CASH TRANSFER

Mail transfer: The traditional means of moving funds internationally is the *mail transfer* (or *mail payment order*) via a commercial bank. It is similar to a cashier's check wherein the bank withdraws the funds from the remitter's bank when the payment order is sent. As the name suggests, the payment is sent by mail. At one time this was the only means available, and it was very slow. Today the mail payment mechanism is much faster; airmail is the standard method of transmitting. Nevertheless, the clearance of claims by mail can take weeks, even between the United States and Europe. Since every day of delay of receipt of the payment represents the loss of use of funds to the company to which the funds are sent, delays can be very costly. For example, when interest rates are 15 percent, the *daily* cost of delay of a $100,000 receipt (not an especially large transfer by international standards) is more than $41; at 20 percent it is more than $55.

This daily cost can be viewed in either of two ways. The first is the *opportunity cost* of not having the excess funds to invest. The second is the *realized cost* when funds are short from needing to borrow the equivalent amount of funds (which would not be necessary if the payment had been received). Such problems not only trouble intercompany payments but even payments between different affiliates of the same company.

Obviously, if a quicker means of payment is available, then the company receiving the payment could either invest the money profitably or reduce its borrowing costs by eliminating the "float" of the payment. The company would logically even be willing to pay for the faster service in order to speed up the payment.

Cable transfer: The basic mechanism that has traditionally been used for facilitating international financial payments is the cable transfer. The *cable transfer* involves a direct transfer of funds electronically (by "cable") from a bank in one country to one in another country. The two banks would ideally be correspondent banks with either deposit accounts with each other or credit lines that could be drawn upon. In this way the funds can be transferred almost anywhere in the world very quickly, usually with next-day delivery.

The cost of such service is relatively cheap, perhaps $25 to $50, depending on the amount. Thus, it does not pay for a company or individual to transfer small amounts of money. However, as seen in the example above, gaining the use of large amounts of funds for even one additional day could pay for the cost of the mail transfer, and the time saved could be one or two weeks or more. Thus the receiving company should indeed be willing to be billed for such charges. If the amounts of the transfer are really large, the savings can be very substantial. At a 12 percent cost of borrowing or investment rate, a $2 million cable transfer would represent a savings of more than $650 per day! At 20 percent the savings would exceed $1000 daily!

In addition to the time factor, the use of cables reduces the likelihood of loss or theft of payments. Also, mistakes (or fraud) can be much more quickly identified.

MANAGEMENT OF INTERNATIONAL FLOWS BETWEEN COMPANIES

Before examining the special problems relating to intracompany accounts, the management of international cash flows with *outside companies* or other organizations are considered.

Receivables: Cable transfers should generally be insisted upon for large international movements of funds such as the receipt of payment on receivables. For small amounts it is usually best to accept the delay. The cost of cabling simply does not justify the time saved for small payments. However, if there are a large number of small payments emanating from the same region (for example, payments from numerous credit-card customers or insurance policyholders), it may be desirable to arrange for regional collection points. This can be accomplished by such means as the use of lockboxes (primarily in the United States), or regional collection points.[2]

These steps have addressed the question of how to move the funds once payment is being made. The other problem of the utilization of

---

[2]For a definition of lockboxes, see the Glossary at the end of the book.

receivables is that of prompt, or even accelerated, payment by the debtor. This problem in international finance is essentially the same as in domestic finance. If the company wishes to accelerate future payments on receivables, then it needs to tighten credit terms or, conversely, sweeten the appeal for prepayments. For example, if normal international terms for a given industry are 2/10, net 50, it may be desirable to change the terms to 3/10, net 40).

In the late 1970s an alternative system to cable transfers was developed which speeded up the transfers even more and reduced both costs and mistakes. Traditional cable transfers relied upon outside communication systems such as telegrams or telex. The new system, however, is mutually owned and controlled by a group of banks.

The new system is cleverly called *SWIFT*, the acronym for the *Society of Worldwide Interbank Financial Telecommunications.* SWIFT employs one transfer center in the United States and one in Europe. A bank that is on the system notifies the center and receives confirmation within minutes. The process is inexpensive, fast, and safe (since SWIFT confirms the transfers).

Banks that participate in the SWIFT system utilize it whenever possible. However, they must revert to cable when transferring funds to countries or banks that are not members of SWIFT.

The greater speed and safety of SWIFT are, of course, also of great importance to bank customers. As the system becomes more prevalent, competition may also force down the fees.

The problem of past-due payments on existing accounts in international sales is complicated by the distances involved, the problem of currency-value changes, the threat of capital controls, and so forth. These and other threats simply mean that the risks to a company of not keeping its receivables current can be much greater than for domestic accounts where such problems are not an issue. Pursuing past-due accounts promptly is, therefore, critically important.

Payables: When the company is in the position of debtor, its perspective is, of course, the reverse of its role as creditor. For example, if a company's creditor is not too sophisticated and permits payments by means of a check instead of a cable transfer, then the debtor might have use of the funds for an extra week or two. As seen in the previous section, this could be quite profitable. It is generally in the debtor's interest to delay payment as long as possible.

Many aspects of the disbursement-management function are essentially the same as they are in domestic operations. The alert manager will pay no sooner than necessary. (Remember that the debtor's payments have to be financed in some way, and that it can be expensive.) If the creditor is slow in pressing for payment on overdue accounts (for example, on trade credits or even tax bills), there can be a strong temptation for the debtor to delay payment beyond the payment date. This is, of course, unpopular with the creditor and may lead later to more restrictive credit terms. However, such excessive delays, even by companies that are not short of funds, is very common, especially in periods of high interest rates.

MANAGEMENT OF INTERNATIONAL INTRACOMPANY ACCOUNTS

When receivables or payables are between different affiliates of the same company, the company has much more control than in the examples above. Also, the motives of the company as creditor do not conflict with those of the company as debtor.

Float is generally undesirable with intracompany accounts. If payments were to be made via a mail transfer, the float would benefit the debtor unit's bank, and both the paying and the receiving units would lose the use of the funds during the period of the float. With the added risks of loss, theft, error, and fraud, it is all the more clear why cable transfers are most attractive for intracompany transfers.

Netting: Since both the paying and the receiving units are within the same company, it very often occurs that payments are flowing back and forth between the same two or same group of affiliates. If this is true, the company is exposing itself to unnecessarily high transaction costs (such as transfer and foreign exchange charges) and may also be exposing itself unnecessarily to risks in the currency exchange rate and bank errors in the transfer. For example, even if cable transfers are utilized, mistakes do occur that at the very least can be irritating and time consuming. Also, since international payments commonly involve foreign exchange transactions for at least one of the parties, service fees that are buried in the spread between the buy and sell quotes, as well as transaction expenses result. If the number of these transactions is large, the cost can be high. Furthermore, the processing within the company of these transactions is also expensive.

To resolve this inefficiency, many companies utilize a type of in-house clearing system known as *netting*. Under this arrangement, the company tries to determine what the inflows and outflows are among various affiliates. In this way it identifies the *net* inflows or outflows for each affiliate. That affiliate then pays only its net debt or receives its net credit.

Table 20.1 illustrates a simple example involving only two affiliates that are located in two different countries. Subsidiary A is scheduled to make three payments to subsidiary B during the week of February 9.

TABLE 20.1 Bilateral Netting[a]

| | Due To | | |
Due From	Subsidiary A	Subsidiary B	Gross Payables
Subsidiary A			
Feb. 9		$2,500	
Feb. 10		4,900	
Feb. 13		1,800	$9,200 (for A)
Subsidiary B			
Feb. 10	$5,200		
Feb. 11	9,400		14,600 (for B)
Gross receivables	$14,600	$ 9,200	$23,800
— Gross payables (column 3)	− 9,200	−14,600	
Net receivables	$ 5,400	($5,400)	

[a]All figures are in thousands of U.S. dollars.

During the same period, subsidiary B is scheduled to make two payments in the other direction. At least one of the subsidiaries must utilize the foreign exchange market. (Note that if the company utilized a policy of transferring all intracompany accounts in the currency of the parent, a policy that is not really unusual, then *both* affiliates may need to use the foreign exchange markets. For example the French affiliate may be required by corporate policy to buy dollars—the currency of the parent—in order to pay the German affiliate, which then exchanges the dollars for deutschemarks.) In the absence of a netting system, transfers would total $23.8 million, payable in five transactions. On the other hand, if the company is employing a netting system, the company could reduce the flow to only $5.4 million, which would be paid in a single payment from B to A. This represents a considerable savings in foreign exchange and transaction costs.

If the netting system includes more than two affiliates,the arrangement is very similar. The only difference is that the individual who controls the netting arrangement needs to specify exactly how the net payments are to be made and by and to whom they are to be made. Table 20.2 illustrates an extension of the example above. For simplicity, all payments are to be made on the same date. This is indeed one of the adjustments that the implementation of a netting system commonly involves. The company would use the same payment dates throughout the system.

As Table 20.2 shows, this company has a variety of different intracompany payments. Some of the subsidiaries have mutual interchange. Others have only a one-way pattern of trade. In the absence of the

TABLE 20.2 Multilateral Netting[a]
(February 13, 198X)

Due From	Due To Subsidiary A	Subsidiary B	Subsidiary C	Subsidiary D	Gross Payables
Subsidiary A		$ 9,200	0	$ 4,100	$13,300
Subsidiary B	$14,600	—	$1,800	3,800	20,200
Subsidiary C	3,100	0	—	1,500	4,600
Subsidiary D	0	12,800	7,900	—	20,700
Gross receivables	$17,700	$22,000	$9,700	$ 9,400	$58,800
Gross payables	−13,300	−20,200	−4,600	−20,700	
Net receivables	$ 4,400	$ 1,800	$5,100	($11,300)	

[a]All figures are in thousands of U.S. dollars.

netting system, total payments from the entire system would be $58.8 million. With a netting system, the total amount of net payments has been reduced to $11.3 million. As the net receivables line shows, subsidiaries A, B, and C are all net creditors. They have no net payments to make at all on these intracompany accounts. Subsidiary D is a net debtor to each of its three affiliates. Of course, two or even three of the affiliates could be net debtors instead of creditors. Regardless of the net relationships, netting can be a very valuable tool.

The companies for which netting offers the greatest potential are those that are vertically integrated, with different subsidiaries specializing in the production of different components that are shipped among the various facilities. The electronics and automobile industries are just two industries that find netting attractive.

Netting can be an especially important aid to a company if exchange or capital controls exist. It can also be useful under credit controls. However, in many countries (even in Europe) multilateral netting requires specific governmental permission. In many other countries it is banned completely.

A company that is considering netting needs to weigh the savings with the cost of implementing the system; many companies will not find it to be justified.

Pooling: Another very common tool of international cash-flow management within a company is the use of accumulation, or pooling, accounts. *Pooling* involves the consolidation of the control of excess cash and near-cash assets into one centralized unit within the company. The goal of pooling is the increase in efficiency in the use of such assets. This efficiency is primarily attained by providing the means for internal financing within the company and by taking advantage of economies of scale in the investment of excess funds outside of the company. However, pooling can also provide the additional advantage of increasing the extent of corporate control over its foreign operations.

Pooling can be very useful within a single country as well as internationally. A company with many subsidiaries can increase the efficiency of the use of its systemwide resources by viewing all of its affiliates' cash and securities as part of the corporate pool. Such a system is relatively simple, since such factors as the currency, laws, and taxes are the same, and since there are no problems of capital controls.

Internationally the situation is more complicated than it is within a single country, since there is a difference in currencies, laws, and so forth. Nevertheless, the potential of pooling for improved efficiency is substantial. Not only might there be savings from intracompany financing and greater profit from the pooled investment of excess funds outside company, but the company may more easily avoid the risks of capital and exchange controls and the threat of devaluation. Pooling may also give certain affiliates from countries with very weak money markets investment opportunities that they could not otherwise tap, especially if capital or exchange controls exist.

The pool does not necessarily have to be collected. In fact, to do so may be unnecessarily expensive. The key to a successful pool is having one office control the resources, wherever they may be located.

The pool does not consist of all liquid funds of the company. Instead it is comprised of the *excess* funds of the various affiliates. Therefore cash-poor affiliates are not in a position to contribute to the pool but are instead drawers from the pool.

The individual who controls the fund needs to draw together not only the information on the excess funds but also on the cash needs of the various affiliates that might be funded by the pool. The pool can be profitable not only to the company as a whole but also to each of the participants. For example, if subsidiary D needs to borrow $1 million for which its banks will charge 20 percent, whereas at the same time subsidiary B can invest $1 million at 16 percent, then an intracompany loan at 17, 18, or 19 percent would make both the borrowing unit and the lending unit better off.

Since the funds that are pooled in the form of cash and marketable securities can be in many different currencies, the manager of the pool must make currency decisions when making investments outside or even within the company. When an intracompany loan is made, then a foreign exchange risk is being taken by either the lender or the borrower. This is not necessarily bad. As is seen in the next chapter, companies, or their affiliates as in this case, can sometimes reduce their exposure to fluctuations in the exchange rate by acquiring foreign currency assets (if the local currency is expected to decline in value) or liabilities (if the local currency is expected to rise in value). This reduction of exposure may result from either intracompany or intercompany transactions.

If an investment is made outside the company, it can be made by the pool manager either in the same currency (for instance, French francs invested by the pool in either France or in the Euro–French franc market) or in another currency (for instance, French francs invested either in pound sterling in London or Eurosterling). In the latter case, the pool manager would usually "cover" the investment against possible fluctuations in currency value between the franc and sterling. (This and other procedures of foreign-exchange exposure management will be discussed in Chapter 21.)

FINANCING AND INVESTING

The international orientation and international expertise of the multinational business firm provide it with a unique opportunity to escape the confines of its own domestic money and capital markets. At their own discretion these managers have the option of utilizing either local or international financial markets. These options are available whether the company is seeking to borrow funds or to invest funds.

At various times, most companies have excess funds available that are either not needed immediately or are precautionary funds that must be readily available as a cushion against unexpected charges. Prior to the late 1960s when inflation rates were much lower than they are now, interest rates were also relatively low. Therefore, the opportunity cost of not having such funds invested aggressively was not very high.

However, with the high rates of inflation and the corresponding high interest rates of the 1970s and 1980s, corporate treasurers have been under pressure to use such funds in order to generate nonoperating earnings. This has caused many corporate treasurers to look to the Euromarkets and foreign domestic markets for more attractive investment opportunities. These investments are almost always made in the home-country currency (for example, a U.S. company depositing funds in the Eurodollar market) or, if in a foreign currency, with forward cover. These are funds the corporate treasurer must handle conservatively. Such investment mechanisms are sufficiently safe (indeed, often as safe as domestic investments).

In a parallel vein, a company's financing needs can be met from much wider markets than in the past. In the chapter on international money and capital markets, it was shown how extensively markets such as the Euromarkets are used as funding sources by international companies. Indeed, at one time, corporations were the major nonbank customer for these markets.

CAPITAL BUDGETING

Investment of a firm's capital for long-term periods should be handled in as sophisticated a manner as possible. The anticipated receipts including terminal or salvage value should be compared with all the various costs and the various incumbent risks of the project. Inflation needs to be taken into account. So also should the cost of capital and the possible return on alternative projects. The process of comparing the costs of a project with the returns from that project is called *capital budgeting.* (See the discussion entitled "The Tools of Capital Budgeting.")

THE TOOLS OF CAPITAL BUDGETING

Two basic tools of capital budgeting are the *internal rate of return* and the *net present value.* The latter, NPV, is the most prevalent tool; if the two tools were to give conflicting recommendations between alternative projects, most anlaysts would recommend that the decision suggested by the NPV method should be followed. Therefore, this discussion focuses upon that method.

Both these basic capital-budgeting tools are based upon *discounted cash flows.* Future cash flows are reduced in value (that is, discounted) at a particular interest rate (the *discount rate*) for every year between the time of that cash flow and the present time. The result is the *present value* (that is, the value at the beginning period of a cash flow that is expected to be received or paid at some date(s) in the future).

If an amount equal to the present value is invested to earn interest at the same interest rate as that used for the discount rate and if the interest earned is reinvested each period, then the *future value* of the total earnings plus principal would exactly equal the *future cash flow(s).* This process is called *compounding.*

Thus, another way of defining the present value is that amount which, if invested at the beginning of a period of time and with the earnings reinvested each period, would equal the future cash flow: discounting, or seeking the present value, is the opposite of compounding, or seeking the future value.

Within the field of capital budgeting the question of how to incorporate the problem of variable risks between alternative investments is very important. Risk differentials can either be incorporated into the discount rate (the greater the risk, the higher the discount rate) or into the anticipated cash flows (the greater the risk, the lower the cash flows, all else being equal). Most analysts of both domestic and international capital budgeting prefer the adjustment of cash flows so that the same discount rate is applied to each alternative investment. A major advantage to the use of the adjustment of cash flows is that it allows a finer degree of tuning of cash flows. If a higher discount rate is used, then the total present value of the cash flows in the more distant years would be very sharply reduced.

Capital budgeting is basically the same for either a domestic or an international investment project. However, the task of calculating the various inputs into the international decision is much more involved than for the corresponding domestic decision.

Eiteman and Stonehill list some of the complications that can make the international capital budgeting analysis more difficult.

1. differing tax systems
2. constraints on capital flows
3. differences in financial markets and institutions
4. different rates of inflation
5. fluctuations in foreign exchange rates
6. political risks
7. greater difficulties in estimating terminal value[3]

Because of the factors listed above, the international financial manager is generally confronted with serious difficulties in estimating the two critical elements of calculating net present value: future cash inflows and the appropriate discount rate. Both may be much more difficult to obtain for international investments than for domestic investments. It is difficult enough in domestic capital budgeting to estimate future cash flows, especially with the wide variability in inflation, interest, and economic growth rates. When the same criteria have to be evaluated for foreign countries with which the evaluator is not as familiar as with his or her home country and where a wide variety of additional risks exist as mentioned above, the greater difficulties of the task should be apparent.

Some assumptions and some arbitrary definitions are commonly utilized in order to make the task more manageable. For example, the NPV is usually calculated on total cash flows but sometimes only on those that are considered to be freely remittable. This latter option is a conservative policy which may, in fact, undervalue the investment. Also, in order to alleviate the problem of fluctuating exchange rates, it is commonly assumed that purchasing power parity is effective; that is, that the differential in inflation rates is exactly offset by the adjustments in the exchange rates. As already discussed in an earlier chapter, although purchasing power parity is generally not valid in the short term, there is ample evidence to indicate that it does function in the medium to long term—the very period with which the capital budgeter is concerned.

Foreign investment is not always fraught with greater risk than at home. For instance, investors from oil-exporting countries or other devel-

[3]David K. Eiteman and Arthur I. Stonehill, *Multinational Business Finance*, 3rd ed. (Reading, Mass.: Addison-Wesley Publishing Co., 1982), pp. 340–41.

oping countries are often seeking a reduction of risk. Similarly, when Francois Mitterand won the 1981 election in France, companies and individuals who feared his socialist policies sought protection in foreign investments. Also, American companies, such as General Motors, that are fearful of antitrust action if they expanded at home, are thereby encouraged to expand abroad. Such investors should appropriately reduce their estimates of future cash flows at home to reflect the greater risk there.

As a final note, it should be emphasized that not everything is more difficult in international capital budgeting relative to domestic budgeting. As we have seen, there are often very attractive alternatives to domestic investments; otherwise, there would not be so much interest in foreign investments. Also, the access to a wider variety of capital markets when foreign investments are made can sometimes help companies to diversify their funding base and, perhaps, even reduce their cost of funding.

BLOCKED FUNDS

Despite the best analytical effort of capital budgeters, conditions sometimes develop within a country that lead a government to impose severe exchange and capital controls to the extent that funds are temporarily or permanently *blocked;* that is, they cannot be *repatriated.* Thus, as far as that company is concerned, the currency is inconvertible to some extent.

Blockage of funds may be either absolute or relative. For example, countries that are actively blocking funds need to leave some loopholes in order to allow the international sector of their economy to continue to function. Also, some countries allow some repatriation of funds, but only up to a certain percentage of capital. For example, dividend payments from 10 to 15 percent of capital may be permissible but no more than that.

The avoidance of these controls is an important job for financial managers. (*Avoidance* refers to actions that are legal under the local laws of the country imposing the controls. *Evasion* refers to actions that the local government considers improper.) Unfortunately, actions that a firm might use quite legally in some countries can be very illegal in others. Obviously, it is important to know the difference in each country of operation.

Transfer pricing: A *transfer price* is simply the price charged between different affiliates of the same company. If all such pricing were done on an "arm's-length" basis (that is, as though the buyer and the seller were independent entities), then transfer pricing would have little unique significance. However, since companies do indeed have extensive control over many of their pricing decisions, the concept of transfer pricing has great significance. This is compounded by the fact that it is very difficult for an outsider (such as a host-country government) to have a very accurate idea of what the realistic "arm's-length price" should actually be, for example, for subassemblies for which there is no market outside the company.

Governments have become much more sophisticated in understanding and controlling transfer pricing, which can be a very powerful tool for shifting funds from one country to another.

Transfer prices can be used to avoid (or evade) various controls and taxes. For example, if the desire is to avoid paying high import duties in a particular country, then an artificially low import price may be feasible. This approach also tends to have the effect of shifting the locus of the profit to that country. If the local tax rates are low, the attraction of this use of transfer pricing is enhanced. Of course, if it is a country with a high tax rate, the appeal of low import transfer prices is reduced.

With the use of transfer pricing a company can adjust intracompany accounts in such a way that even though dividend repatriation is blocked the profits are shifted "upstream" (that is, to an earlier stage of the company's operations such as a supplier—outside the blocking country).

Unbundling: Capital controls often place strict limits upon the ability of the local affiliates of foreign companies to repatriate their earnings. Many countries limit dividend repatriation to some proportion of equity capital, for example, 12 or 15 percent. This might be wholly inadequate for many companies based on their own worldwide norms, relative to the perceived risk and headquarter costs of a particular investment. Many governments, while severely limiting the amount of dividend repatriation, have been amenable to additional payments in lieu of dividends.

In the past, for simplicity many companies often lumped all their charges against a foreign affiliate under the heading of dividends. Since this is often no longer feasible, many companies now *unbundle* the charges for parent-company services to the subsidiary. Some unbundled charges, which at one time may have simply been absorbed in the overall heading of dividends, are royalties for the use of patents, allocations against corporate overhead and research and development, specific charges for the use of trademarks, and direct expenses incurred by the headquarters for expenses such as travel and communication related to that affiliate.

Swaps: Countries tend to allow repayment of international debts by companies located within their borders, especially if the loan is from a bank. Therefore, it is very common for companies to channel loans to foreign affiliates in risky countries via banks. The funds may come directly from the bank (usually with a parent-company guarantee) or the arrangement may be merely a pass-through of the company's own funds.

Swaps are commonly made, for instance, via what are known as *credit swaps*. Under a credit swap, a company arranges with a bank to make a deposit in a safe country (e.g., in London). In exchange, the bank makes a loan to the subsidiary in the risky currency (e.g., Brazilian cruzeiros). When the loan is repaid to the bank, the parent company regains its deposited funds. If the loan is not repaid, either because of financial inability of the subsidiary or because of the extensive degree of the capital controls, the bank generally has the "right of offset"—that is, the right to seize the deposit, since it is, in effect, being provided as a type of collateral.

Another type of swap occurs between two business firms in different countries. The two companies swap currencies or, in effect, extend loans to each other. Thus, this arrangement is often called a *parallel loan* or *back-to-back loan*. For example, two British firms with operations in Argentina may arrange for the subsidiary of one company to lend Argentine pesos to the subsidiary of the second company. At the same time, the second company would lend pounds sterling to the first company in the United Kingdom. Part of the arrangement is that the currencies will be swapped back at a later date. Thus, the loan is a covered contract for each company.

Other antiblockage techniques: When governments impose capital contols, they are very suspicious of any unusual applications for outflows by a company. On the other hand, if a company has a long record of certain types of payments (for example, 20 percent dividend payments paid in regular quarterly installments), the government might be much more lenient about allowing most or all of these flows to continue. Thus, some companies are careful to establish a pattern of dividend repatriation—a reflow of some or all of dividends—even if, in order to maintain the working capital of the firm, it is necessary for the subsidiary to borrow funds or, in some cases, even to get new capital infusions from the parent.

When, after all these various avenues have been tapped to whatever extent is feasible, the company still has blocked funds, then other decisions must be made. In some cases companies can use blocked funds to make local purchases for exporting to other affiliates. Or the company might pay for as many expenses in that country as possible (for example, buy airline tickets for much or all of the travel that must be done in the entire region, not just in that country).

Finally, the company may opt to invest in local real estate or some other local asset that may be valuable if, in the future, the controls are loosened. For example, in the early 1970s Argentina had extensive controls over the repatriation of the earnings of foreign companies. Some of the companies used the funds to buy offices or factories to increase their productive base. In Peru at about the same time the government seized many foreign companies. Part of the compensation was in the form of rather unattractive Peruvian bonds, which paid relatively low interest and matured over many years. One option to holding these bonds was to reinvest them in Peru in permitted types of ventures (for example, hotels) together with an additional infusion of an equal amount of foreign funds, whether from the blocked company or not.

SUMMARY

International financial management is one of the managerial functions most strongly affected by the international environment. Although the financial risks of international finance are much greater than domestic finance, the financial opportunities are also greater.

International financial management involves responding to the special risks and hurdles that are encountered in international operations and to the opportunities of the special alternatives offered.

The first of these areas is that of managing international cash flows. This includes, of course, the financing and investing in Euromarkets and foreign domestic markets. It also includes the international control of cash, marketable securities, receivables, inventories, payables, and so forth.

The analysis of long-term investments falls under the heading of capital budgeting. This is a very unique and challenging topic in the international arena.

The final responsibility of the international manager discussed in this chapter was the problem of blocked funds. Antiblockage techniques include transfer pricing, unbundling, swaps, establishing a dividend repatriation pattern, and local investments and purchasing.

KEY TERMS

BACK-TO-BACK LOAN	NETTING	SWAP
BLOCKED FUNDS	PARALLEL LOAN	TRANSFER PRICE
CABLE TRANSFER	POOLING	UNBUNDLING
CAPITAL BUDGETING	REPATRIATION	
CASH-FLOW MANAGEMENT	SOCIETY OF WORLDWIDE INTERBANK FINANCIAL TELECOMMUNICATIONS (SWIFT)	
MAIL TRANSFER		

REVIEW QUESTIONS

1. **a.** Compare the corporate debt ratios which Arthur Stonehill gives the United States, Germany, France, the Netherlands, Norway, and Japan.
   b. How would their debt ratios tend to affect their capital budgeting decisions?
   c. How would they affect their costs?
   d. How would they affect their production decisions?
2. **a.** Compare mail transfers, cable transfers, and SWIFT transfers. Compare their speed, cost, and safety.
   b. When does the company lose the transferred funds? Under what circumstances should a company use the various methods?
3. How does netting work? How is it beneficial to the company?
4. Describe pooling. How is it beneficial to a company?
5. How are international cash-flow projections and the calculations of discount rates different from their domestic counterparts?
6. What are blocked funds? How can companies avoid this problem.

SUGGESTED REFERENCES

EITEMAN, DAVID K., AND ARTHUR I. STONEHILL *Multinational Business Finance* (3rd ed.). Reading, Mass.: Addison-Wesley Publishing Co., Inc., 1982.

FEIGER, GEORGE, AND BERTRAND JACQUILLAT *International Finance*. London: Allyn and Bacon, 1982.

FOLKS, WILLIAM R., JR. "The Analysis of Short-Term Cross Border Financing Decisions," *Financial Mangement*, Autumn 1976.

GIDDY, IAN "Exchange Risk: Whose View?" *Financial Management*, Summer 1977.

HENNING, CHARLES N., WILLIAM PIGOTT, AND ROBERT H. SCOTT *International Financial Management*. New York: McGraw-Hill Book Company, 1978.

LESSARD, DONALD R. *International Financial Management*. Boston: Warren, Gorham and Lemont, 1979.

RICKS, DAVID *International Dimensions of Corporate Finance*. Englewood Cliffs, N.J.: Prentice-Hall, Inc., 1978.

ROBBINS, SIDNEY M., AND ROBERT STOBAUGH *Money in the Multinational Enterprise*. New York: Basic Books, Inc., Publishers, 1973.

RODRIQUEZ, RITA M., AND E. EUGENE CARTER *International Financial Management* (3rd ed.). Englewood Cliffs, N.J.: Prentice-Hall, Inc., 1984.

SHAPIRO, ALAN C. *Multinational Financial Management*. London: Allyn and Bacon, 1982.

———— "Payments Netting in International Cash Management," *Journal of International Business Studies,* Fall 1978.

STONEHILL, ARTHUR, THEO BEEKHUISEN ET AL.   "Financial Goals and Debt-Ratio Determinants: A Survey of Practices in Five Countries," *Financial Management,* Autumn 1975.

21

Management
of Foreign
Exchange Exposure

The previous chapter examined most major aspects of the field of international financial management. However, the discussion of one special, very critical part of international money management was deferred to this chapter. This is the corporate treasurer's task of confronting the potential impact upon the company that results from the threat of fluctuation of exchange rates.

FOREIGN EXCHANGE EXPOSURE

THE THREAT OF EXPOSURE

Any time a company is forced to operate in a foreign currency it runs the risk of suffering financial losses by the change in the value of that country's currency.[1] Even if the company is not operating in a country whose currency's value is changing, the firm can sometimes be hurt if it is doing business with that country; for example, if may export

---

[1]Except in those relatively rare cases where the foreign country uses a currency that is inflexibly tied to the company's home currency (for example, the Guatemalan quetzal, which has not changed value relative to the U.S. dollar since the 1920s, or the Irish pound in the period to the late 1970s, when its value had been immutably the same as that of the pound sterling).

and denominate its receivables in the currency of the importer, such as Saudi Arabian oil exports to the United States, which are priced and paid in dollars. This can affect both intracompany and intercompany financial accounts. The company can be adversely affected even if it has no *direct* financial exchange exposure. It can also be hurt *indirectly* if the foreign customer is badly affected by a change in currency value.

A two-edged sword: It should be remembered that changes in currency values can affect a firm either unfavorably or favorably. For example, in the second quarter of 1981 Exxon reported extraordinary income resulting from foreign exchange movements of more than $550 million. A year earlier the company had reported a corresponding $300 million loss. Of course, such losses are often primarily the result of the need to adhere to a somewhat arbitrary accounting convention (in that case, FASB 8).

THE TYPE OF EXPOSURE TO HEDGE

Transaction versus translation versus economic exposure: There are several different ways in which a company can be exposed to the movement in the value of a currency. If specific outstanding contracts are affected (for example, a receivable, a payable, or even off–balance sheet contracts such as purchase orders), the company has *transaction exposure*—that is, the transaction would be affected when payment is made or received, if a change in the currency's value occurs.

If the balance sheet of the parent company is affected when the financial statements of foreign affiliates of the company are consolidated into the home-country currency of the parent company, then the company has *translation exposure*. This was the crux of the international accounting chapter. Translation exposure for an American company is, of course, a function of the rules of FASB 52.

The accounting convention (that is, monetary-nonmonetary, current-noncurrent, or current-rate method), which is required by law or accounting practices or which is chosen by the company, determines what types of adjustments to make in order to reduce the net *unfavorable* translation exposure (or increase the net favorable exposure). As seen in the discussion of FASB 52 and other systems of foreign exchange accounting, each system defines translation exposure differently.

Table 21.1 summarizes the translation exposure of different balance sheet accounts for both anticipated devaluations and revaluations. The various accounts are identified as *exposed, unexposed,* and *hedged* as they relate to the anticipated foreign exchange change.

Beyond any transaction or translation exposure, if the future prof-

TABLE 21.1 Translation Exposure of Parent Company

	Anticipated Devaluation			Anticipated Revaluation		
	Monetary-Nonmonetary Method[a]	Current-Noncurrent Method	Current-Rate Method	Monetary-Nonmonetary Method[a]	Current-Noncurrent Method	Current-Rate Method
Cash: foreign currency[b]	E[d]	E	E	H[d]	H	H
Cash: parent currency[c]	U[d]	U	U	U	U	U
Securities: foreign currency	E	E	E	H	H	H
Securities: parent currency	U	U	U	U	U	U
Receivables: foreign currency	E	E	E	H	H	H
Receivables: parent currency	U	U	U	U	U	U
Inventories	U	E	E	U	H	H
Fixed assets	U	U	E	U	U	H
Payables: foreign currency	H	H	H	E	E	E
Payables: parent currency	U	U	U	U	U	U
Long-term debt: foreign currency	H	U	H	E	U	E
Long-term debt: parent currency	U	U	U	U	U	U
Paid-in capital and surplus	U	U	U	U	U	U
Retained earnings	Residual	Residual	Residual	Residual	Residual	Residual

[a] The temporal method is very similar to the monetary-nonmonetary accounting method.

[b] Any currency other than that used by the parent company for accounting purposes.

[c] The reporting currency used by the parent company for accounting purposes.

[d] E means exposure; U, unexposed; and H, hedge.

itability of a company may be affected, the company has *economic exposure. Any* company engaged in *any* international business operations is subject to economic exposure.

Translation exposure, transaction exposure, and economic exposure each measure a different type of impact upon a company engaged in some form of international operations. The defensive strategies a firm can employ in the face of these threats depend upon which type of exposure is of the greatest concern to the company.

The traditional assumption that is made about corporate management is that the basic financial goal that motivates a firm is the maximization of long-term shareholder wealth. This is the basic premise for most textbooks and theorizing in the area of financial management. Surveys strongly support the legitimacy of this belief, especially within the United States. In addition, there is evidence that it is also valid in many foreign cultures. (See box entitled "Financial Goals of Firms in Five Countries." This goal stresses economic exposure.

However, there are other, more immediate considerations that lead a company to focus upon transaction and translation exposure. These two approaches are discussed below in turn.

Net asset exposure versus net liability exposure: When the company's exposure is calculated, it has either (1) a balanced (or zero) exposure (that is, exposed assets equal exposed liabilities), (2) a net asset exposure, or (3) a net liability exposure. With zero exposure the company, of course, is not threatened by either a devaluation or a revaluation, since its exposed assets and exposed liabilities are affected in such a way that the effects offset each other. However, if there is a net asset or net liability position, then this amount is affected by the change in currency value.

Such an effect may be either beneficial or harmful to the company. For instance, a net asset exposure is detrimental to the company in the event of a devaluation but beneficial in the event of a revaluation. The converse is true for a net liability exposure. Table 21.2 summarizes these effects.

TABLE 21.2 The Impact from Changes in Currency Value

	Change Expected in the Foreign Currency	
	Depreciation or Devaluation	Appreciation or Revaluation
Net Asset Exposure	Loss	Gain
Net Liability Exposure	Gain	Loss

FINANCIAL GOALS OF FIRMS IN FIVE COUNTRIES

In the last chapter, reference was made to a survey which was taken in the mid-1970s of financial executives in manufacturing companies in five different countries: France, Japan, the Netherlands, Norway, and the United States. In all of the countries except Norway the survey results indicated that maximizing the growth of earnings (a long-term perspective) was the primary goal.

Other major factors that received strong emphasis in most countries were the guaranteed availability of funds and the maximization of return on equity. Again, these are goals that emphasize long-term priorities.

SOURCE: Arthur Stonehill, Theo Beekhuisen, Richard Wright, Lee Remmers, Norman Toy, Antonio Pares, Alan Shapiro, Douglas Egan and Thomas Bates, "Financial Goals and Debt-Ratio Determinants: "A Survey of Practices in Five Countries," *Financial Management,* Autumn 1975, pp, 27–41.

Headquarters versus subsidiary perspective: The problem of exposure is complicated enough on its own merits. However, as noted at the beginning of this chapter, for the international financial manager there is the added difficulty that the problem of exposure does not appear the same from all viewpoints within the company. Foreign subsidiaries, for example, have different amounts of exposure than does the parent. In Table 21.3 assets and liabilities of the subsidiary that are denominated in the local currency are considered to be exposed from the parent's viewpoint, that is, since the current-rate method of translation is being used. However, the same assets and liabilities would be viewed as unexposed by the subsidiary. On the other hand, assets and liabilities denominated in the currency of the parent company are considered exposed from the subsidiary's point of view but not from the parent's perspective. Thus, from the parent's perspective the subsidiary has a $1220 *net asset exposure* (translation exposure)—$2050 of asset exposure less $830 liability exposure—while from the subsidiary's point of view it has a $620 *net liability position* (transaction exposure)—$80 of asset exposure less $700 liability exposure.

This is, of course, another example of the numerous types of control and coordination problems that can confront a firm in its international operations. If each unit is in control of its own exposure position, then in the example above the parent would be interested in hedging its *net asset translation exposure* in the anticipation of a devaluation of the host-country currency. At the same time, the subsidiary would be attempting to hedge its *net liability transaction exposure.*

Fortunately, in this case both the parent and the subsidiary are

TABLE 21.3 Subsidiary, Inc., Balance Sheet (August 1, 198X)

	Dollar-Denominated	Local-currency Denominated (Dollar Value)[a]	Total (Dollar Value)
Cash	$ 10[b]	$ 200	$ 210
Marketable securities	50	100	150
Accounts receivable	20	1000	1020
Inventory	0	250	250
Fixed assets	0	500	500
Total assets	$ 80	$2050	$2130
Accounts payable	$300	$ 130	$ 430
Long-term loans	400	700	1100
Equity	0	600	600
Total claims on assets	$700	$1430	$2130

[a]If local-currency devaluation is expected, then translation exposure (current-rate method) from Headquarter's perspective is $200 + $100 + $1000 + $250 + $500 − $130 − $700 = $1220 (net asset exposure). The transaction exposure from the Subsidiary's perspective is $10 + $50 + $20 − $300 − $400 = −$620 (net liability exposure).

[b]All figures are in thousands of U.S. dollars.

attempting to attain the same goal. However, who should hedge? How much should be hedged? ($1220 or $620?) Would the same hedging effort have an equal effect upon both parent and subsidiary?

In general, most companies choose to view the exposure from the perspective of the headquarters. The manager of the foreign subsidiary should be evaluated upon the impact of the subsidiary's operations upon the parent after translation. This places an added responsibility upon the corporate headquarters. If the manager is going to be evaluated upon the subsidiary's translated performance after changes in currency value, then an effort must be made by the company to distinguish between nominal and real performance. For example, the manager of the Mexican subsidiary might have appeared to have done extremely well in the 1973–1975 period at a time when Mexican inflation was artificially stimulating profits. Then in 1976 and 1977 the subsidiary's profits would likely have suffered significantly, even if the manager was doing just as well, when measured in pesos after the peso's 40 percent devaluation.

The reader should try to bear in mind throughout the following discussion the different perspectives that might affect different parts of the corporation, the problem of apparent and real performance on the part of subsidiaries, and the need to fairly evaluate managers apart from the nominal effects resulting from changes in currency value. This latter would include the sophistication to depreciate artificially inflated earnings prior to a devaluation and to appreciate subsequent earnings after a devaluation (and do the converse for a revaluation). Consider the case of the manager whose performance looked so exceptional prior to the Mexican devaluation that he or she was promoted back to headquarters or to another subsidiary outside of Mexico. Then the unfortunate successor had to report a substantial decline in the subsidiary's performance—not the result of poor managerial performance of that manager but because of the devaluation.

CORPORATE RESPONSE TO FOREIGN EXCHANGE EXPOSURE

HEDGING, COVERING, AND SPECULATING

If the company's net exposure is such that it will benefit from the anticipated change in currency value, then there is no need for the company to take further action in the face of the potential change. However, if the company's net asset or net liability exposure is detrimental to the company, then the managers must consider what actions are available to the company. They must decide whether the cost of those measures justifies their use by doing a cost versus benefit analysis. If the remedy is more expensive and damaging than the disease, the remedy should be rejected. Thus, companies often decide that the best course of action is to do nothing, although this is not always easy to do and may be impossible in the face of corporate and market pressures.

THE RISK PSYCHOLOGY OF THE MANAGER,
THE COMPANY, AND THE MARKET

Corporate decision making is never made in a psychological vacuum. Corporate managers, creditors, and investors are not "economic men and women." Among other influences, they are affected by their own attitude toward risk and the time horizons of their decisions. These factors can have an important bearing upon the responses that the company makes to foreign exchange exposure.

For example, the final decision about whether to hedge or not to hedge net foreign exchange exposure may suggest that hedging would be too expensive relative to the risk. In this case the company should not hedge. Nevertheless, in many instances managers will hedge anyway, either because of their own reluctance to accept avoidable risk or because of the reluctance of senior management or the board of directors to accept such risk. (Many managers would rather accept the outright cost of hedging rather than the probability of a smaller but indefinite cost of not being hedged.)

Also, the market does not necessarily perceive foreign exchange losses with a long-term perspective. Accounting principles can distort short-term results in such a way that the market's perceptions of that company are affected. As a result, if a company would have to report a foreign exchange loss at the end of the accounting period, even if the loss is unrealized, many managers would choose to hedge the exposure, even if there are existing hedges that do not appear on the balance sheet, such as forward foreign exchange contracts.

Hedging and covering: Companies often choose to hedge or to cover their exposure. The terms *hedging* and *covering* are very closely related. As a result, they are very often confused and misunderstood. Essentially, *hedging* refers to action taken to offset existing exposure, for instance, net exposed assets or liabilities on the balance sheet. *Covering*, on the other hand, refers to actions taken to offset *anticipated* exposure, for instance, from a purchase order that requires payment in a foreign currency. The exposed contract is offset by a covering contract, whereas there was no specific exposed contract to offset with the hedge.

The same type of actions can sometimes be used for either hedging or covering motives. However, a much greater variety of alternatives is available for hedging.

Speculating: Note also that it is very possible for a company with no net foreign exchange exposure to take the exact same type of steps that are discussed below. For example, there is no reason why a company with favorable exposure would not want to cover new contracts or to even take some of the balance sheet adjustments to be discussed in order to increase its favorable condition. It could also take some of the extraordinary steps to be discussed (that is, in effect, to hedge nonexisting exposure). This is *speculation*—actions that are taken merely to generate profit as a result of currency fluctuation. There would not be an offsetting contract; it is a deliberately exposed position. Speculation is strongly criticized by governmental officials and others. It is not considered a "nice" thing to do, and very seldom will any corporate executive admit to speculating. Nevertheless, it is a very common practice.[2] The author has seen some extremely favorable exposures to impending devaluations or revaluations—the results, managers tell me, of very fortuitous conditions in that industry for that country, but certainly not speculation! Of course, this is often very true, but in many other instances suspicion is amply justified.

---

[2]Thomas G. Evans, William R. Folks, Jr., and Michael Jilling, *The Impact of Statement of Financial Accounting Standards No. 8 on the Foreign-Exchange Risk Mangement Practices of American Multinationals* (Financial Accounting Standards Board), 1978, p. 122 (items 6 and 7).

The approach that a company takes with regard to its perceived exposure depends upon the following factors:

1. type of exposure being measured
   (a) transaction
   (b) translation
   (c) economic
2. direction of the exposure
   (a) favorable
   (b) unfavorable
3. options available for defending the company
4. cost of possible defensive measures
5. extent and probability of expected change in the currency value
6. corporate philosophy regarding defensive actions

Some companies have a simple, indeed simplistic, strategy of hedging, or offsetting, *any* translation or transaction exposure. This approach is encouraged by such accounting rules as FASB 8, which subjects financial managers to quarterly "exposure" of any translation losses to the view of unsophisticated shareholders and financial analysts. Thus, there is a strong incentive to offset exposure, even though the cost may be high and even if the movement in the currency's value is expected to reverse itself in the next quarter and produce a translation gain.

Other companies take an equally simplistic view that purchasing power parity (PPP) will equalize the inflationary differences between countries. Therefore, those companies choose to do nothing. This, of course, eliminates the explicit costs of hedging. Also, as was seen during the 1970s, the attainment of PPP may not only require the passage of many years but in the process may produce extensive overvaluation and then undervaluation of a currency. Figure 21.1 illustrates the swings in the value of the deutschemark–U.S. dollar exchange rate. Between 1979 and 1980, the deutschemark rose more than 125 percent in dollar terms. In the following two years, the dollar rose 40 percent against the deutschemark.

Companies with dynamic management programs for foreign exchange exposure weigh the costs of hedging carefully. For them and for those companies that cover all exposure, the following sections review many of the major hedging alternatives.

RESPONSE TO ECONOMIC EXPOSURE

If a company's actions are truly guided by long-term financial goals, then the logical emphasis should be on economic exposure. All firms with continuing international operations have economic exposure. This is even true of the company that heavily exports but bills its customers entirely in its own currency. It may not have translation or transaction

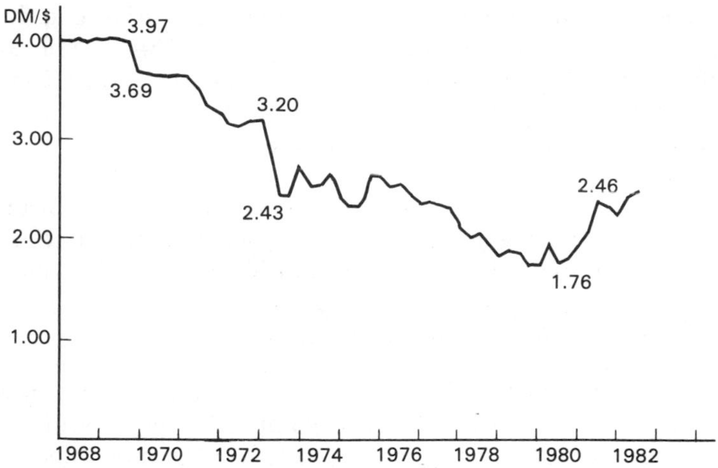

[a]When the line is descending, the dollar is losing value and the deutschemark is gaining value, and vice versa.

SOURCE: International Monetary Fund, *International Financial Statistics,* various issues.

FIGURE 21.1 Exchange Rate Variability (Deutschemarks/U.S. Dollars)[a]

exposure, but the mere fact that it is involved internationally on an ongoing basis necessarily results in economic exposure. Economic exposure is likely to be an even more critical problem for the company with foreign direct investments.

The first step in avoiding unnecessary economic exposure is the training of managers to recognize the nature of this exposure, how it is created, and how it can be avoided. Stress needs to be placed upon the word *unnecessary.* Not all economic exposure can be successfully avoided, at least not at an acceptable cost. However, if financial, marketing, and purchasing managers are alert to the problem of economic risk, the problem can be kept to a minimum.

Response to economic exposure involves the application of long-term strategy. Management training and policies should guide the company until conditions warrant a change.

Marketing response: From a marketing perspective, consciousness of the problem of economic exposure can be reflected first in the choice of market target. For example, if the foreign manufacturing subsidiary of a company is faced with the choice of expanding either in a foreign domestic market, where the economic exposure risk would be increased (i.e., because of a growth in local currency sales), or in an export effort, where the economic risk would be less, the consideration of economic exposure should be a logical factor in the final decision.

The choice of the pricing and credit policies are other decisions that affect economic risk. For example, if a company wishes to minimize the receivables in a subsidiary in order to reduce asset exposure, then credit policies should be designed to encourage early payment. Also, sometimes pricing can be changed to a foreign currency from the local currency. Or, when faced with devaluation, if pricing is in the local currency, the company can strive to keep price increases at least abreast of inflation. Thus, many potential negative economic impacts of a devaluation will be avoided. The sourcing of inputs into the production process should also take this element of risk into consideration! Would domestic or foreign sourcing expose the company to less risk?

Financial response: Financial decisions in the past have most commonly reflected sensitivity to the potential problems of economic risk. However, many companies continue to err. As noted above, corporate treasurers today have a wide variety of financing channels open to them, not only in terms of different financial instruments and geographical markets but also of different currencies. This fact suggests another area in which the financial manager should be alert to the risk of economic exposure: The choice of borrowing and investing alternatives should be compared not only on the basis of nominal cost or return but also on the basis of expected real cost or return, that is, after the impact of a change in currency value is assessed.

RESPONSE TO TRANSACTION AND TRANSLATION EXPOSURES

Transaction and translation exposures are closely related. The same protective actions that reduce transaction exposure can also reduce translation exposure. However, there are additional responses that can reduce translation exposure that do not offset transaction exposure.

As already seen, certain assets or liabilities are favorably affected by the anticipated change in the value of a foreign currency, although assets *and* liabilities would not be favorably affected *simultaneously: Either* assets *or* liabilities would be favorably affected, and, of course, either assets or liabilities, not both, would be unfavorably affected. Those assets or liabilities which are affected favorably by changes in currency values are, in effect, *implicit* or *natural hedges;* through these hedges the company gains some measure of protection without taking any explicit action.

Thus, all assets (in the event of an expected revaluation) or liabilities (for an expected devaluation) that are *favorably* affected by changes in the currency values are types of hedges. The fact that some of these hedges came about unintentionally is irrelevant. Their function as a hedge is implicit in their nature relative to the type of change in the value of the currency. (Remember that the asset or liability that serves as a hedge by being favorably exposed under one change would be negatively exposed if the opposite change in currency value occurred.

Balance sheet hedges: Since some assets or liabilities are favorably affected by a change in the value of a foreign currency, it stands to reason that the company could *deliberately manipulate* these same accounts on its existing balance sheet, so that the exposure is reduced and/or the hedges increased. This is the first example of an *explicit,* as opposed to an implicit, *hedge.* These balance sheet hedges result in one of two ways: either by shifting *exposed* assets or liabilities to unexposed accounts (for example, by replacing exposed liabilities with unexposed liabilities) or by replacing *unexposed* assets or liabilities with those that provide a hedge.

If a company is expecting a depreciation in the value of a foreign currency and has a net asset exposure in that currency, protection can be obtained by reducing the exposed assets in exchange for other assets that are unexposed. This can be done for a translation exposure, by the liquidation of cash and securities in a local currency in order to buy assets in a foreign currency that would not be hurt by the change in that currency's value, or by using those unfavorably exposed monetary assets to pay off an unexposed liability in a foreign currency. The other alternative is to replace an unexposed liability with an unexposed liability by, for example, substituting a debt in a local currency with one in a foreign currency.

A logical extension of this method of the balance sheet hedge to protect against exposure is to go beyond the mere shifting of existing balance sheet accounts to the augmentation of the existing accounts. A common step is for the subsidiary to borrow the local currency, which the company thinks is going to decrease in value, and invest it in some unexposed asset, such as a marketable security in a foreign currency. Also, swaps and transfer pricing, as discussed in the previous chapter, could also provide protection.

There are many other ways in which a company can attack the problem of its exposed balance sheet, that is, its translation exposure. For example, an accelerated dividend payment could be used to reduce the subsidiary's holdings of excessive cash in a local currency. Another very common tool is the use of leading and lagging. *Leading* refers to the prepayment of unfavorably exposed liabilities (that is, those in strengthening currencies). The concept of leading also includes the encouragement of the prepayment of receivables that are unfavorably exposed by the offering of special discounts on the outstanding receivables. *Lagging* refers to delayed payment of favorably exposed liabilities (that is, those in weakening currencies). The method of determining translation exposure (selecting the monetary-nonmonetary, current-noncurrent, or current-rate method) determines exactly which balance sheet accounts are exposed or unexposed. Table 21.4 outlines the appropriate balance sheet adjustments to anticipated devaluation or revaluation.

The forward hedge:　Another prominent method of hedging, one that can be used to hedge either translation or transaction exposures, is the *foreign exchange market forward hedge,* or simply the *forward hedge.* This method involves the use of the forward contract to cover an existing exposure (a covered hedge) or to hedge the part of the existing translation exposure that is not subject to specific maturing contracts, such as demand deposits or inventories. The latter are uncovered hedges, since there is no explicit existing contract against which the hedge can be applied. The forward hedge is a legal contract. Therefore, the hedging company is guaranteed that its exposure is protected.

An alternative hedge involves the use of an Fx futures market contract or even a futures option. However, they are primarily available only in the U.S. and only for a small number of currencies. Nevertheless, they can broaden a firm's hedging choices.

TABLE 21.4　Balance Sheet Hedges by Parent Company
(Translation Exposure)

	Anticipated Devaluation of Currency in Subsidiary's Country	Anticipated Revaluation of Currency in Subsidiary's Country
1. Cash		
Foreign currency[a]	Exposed: reduce	Natural hedge: increase
Parent currency	Unexposed: no change	Unexposed: no change
2. Securities		
Foreign currency	Exposed: reduce	Natural hedge: increase
Parent currency	Unexposed: no change	Unexposed: no change
3. Receivables		
Foreign currency	Exposed: reduce	Natural hedge: increase
Parent currency	Unexposed: no change	Unexposed: no change
4. Inventories[b]	If exposed, reduce	If a hedge, increase
5. Fixed assets[b]	If exposed, reduce	If a hedge, increase
6. Payables		
Foreign currency	Natural hedge: increase	Exposed: prepay
Parent currency	Unexposed: no change	Unexposed: no change
7. Long-term debt		
Foreign currency[b]	If a hedge: increase	If exposed: prepay
Parent currency	Unexposed: no change	Unexposed: no change
8. Paid-in capital and surplus	Unexposed: no change	Unexposed: no change
9. Retained earnings	Unexposed: residual account (which absorbs any foreign exchange loss or gain)	Unexposed: residual account (which absorbs any foreign exchange loss or gain)

[a]Local currency of the subsidiary or currency of a third country.

[b]Only if exposed: Exposure is determined by translation method used. Under the current-rate method these accounts would be considered exposed.

Money-market hedge: The money-market hedge is probably the most sophisticated of the standard tools for reducing exposure. It is certainly the one that tends to cause students the greatest amount of difficulty. Like the forward hedge, the money-market hedge can be used to hedge either transaction or translation exposure. Also, like the forward hedge, it is a contractual arrangement that provides the company with protection that is as safe as a large corporate deposit at the bank where the money-market hedge is made.

The essence of a *money-market hedge* is (1) to borrow funds in the currency of a net asset exposure or in the other currency if a net liability exposure exists, (2) to translate such funds at the *spot* exchange rate, and (3) to invest the proceeds in that currency. A forward contract is *not* used, since that would eliminate the hedge.

Returning to the example of the company with a foreign subsidiary in a country whose currency is expected to devalue, the translation exposure results from an excess of assets in the local currency. A money-market hedge can be made by borrowing local currency (this would result in an increase in liability exposure) and investing the proceeds in a foreign currency at the spot exchange rate (this would result in an increase in an unexposed asset). This is an *uncovered money-market hedge*. If the exposure being hedged is a transaction exposure, then the money-market hedge is designed to cover the existing commitment (that is, the transaction), and it is a *covered money-market hedge*. The local borrowing would be an unexpected liability, whereas the investment in a foreign currency provides a hedge.

If, on the other hand, the subsidiary's currency is expected to increase in value, then the money-market hedge would work in the opposite direction. Foreign currency is borrowed, converted into the local currency, and invested in that country. Again, this would be favorable to either transaction or translation exposure. Also, this type of money-market hedge can be either covered or uncovered.

CAVEATS OF RESPONDING TO EXPOSURE

The discussion above examined many different types of responses to the problem of economic, transaction, and translation exposure. The reader should bear in mind several important caveats about the use of these tools.

1. Governmental controls are often designed to prevent some of these steps. For example, money-market hedges that accelerate the outflow of funds from a country that is already experiencing weakness in the value of a currency are often obstructed by capital or exchange controls.

2. The feasibility of using any of these tools, even if they are legal and available, needs to be weighed against the impact of the step upon the future strength of the company. Obviously, even a good thing can be carried too far. If, for instance, the conversion of cash into foreign securities or into unexposed local assets dangerously impaired the liquidity of the company, it should be rejected.

3. The tax implications, for example, the forward and money-market hedges against translation exposure must be considered. The profits of successful forward and money-market hedges are taxable income. However, the translation losses they are used to hedge are not tax deductible. Thus, some of the gains are lost to taxes. The hedge needs to exceed the exposure: hedge (FX) $(1 - T)$ = exposure (FX), where T is the marginal tax rate. Since FX is included in both sides of the equation, the formula reduces to: hedge $(1 - T)$ = exposure. This converts to: hedge = exposure $\div (1 - T)$. Thus, at a marginal tax rate of 50 percent (that is, $T = 0.5$), $1,000,000 of exposure would require $2,000,000 of hedges. A 40 percent marginal tax rate would require a total hedge of $1,666,667.

4. The financial manager must never forget that most hedging efforts, and even defensive changes in policies for items such as receivables and inventories have a cost. Therefore, a cost-benefit analysis needs to be made between the various alternatives available, including the choice of doing nothing at all, which may prove to be the optimal decision.

5. Finally, it must be remembered that the actions described above are a type of insurance for the company. If the anticipated change in currency value does not actually occur, the expenses involved in hedging and other responses to the exposure were *not* therefore *unnecessary*. Just as a husband who buys life insurance for himself to protect his family has not wasted the money simply because he happens to survive, neither has the company wasted money when the anticipated devaluation or revaluation does not occur. If the decision to hedge was prudently made, then the hedging costs are merely necessary costs of doing business.

SUMMARY

The management of foreign exchange exposure confronts any company that is involved in international operations. Economic exposure affects every company. In addition, transaction exposure affects a company with foreign currency contracts that are either assets or liabilities. Translation exposure affects a company that has a subsidiary or branch abroad.

Exposure can have either favorable or unfavorable consequences for a company. Some companies benefit from a devaluation or depreciation of a currency whereas some are hurt. Similarly, some companies benefit from a revaluation or appreciation whereas other companies are hurt.

Corporate managers have many options for confronting the threat imposed by foreign exchange exposure. Most of these tools, such as balance sheet modifications plus forward and money-market hedges, are the responsibility of financial managers. Some of the tools for responding to economic exposure also involve marketing and purchasing managers as well. However, all managers need to remain alert to the constant threats from foreign exchange exposure.

KEY TERMS

BALANCE SHEET HEDGE	FORWARD HEDGE	NET LIABILITY EXPOSURE
COVERING	MONEY-MARKET HEDGE	SPECULATION
DEFENSIVE ACTION	NATURAL HEDGE	TRANSACTION EXPOSURE
ECONOMIC EXPOSURE	NET ASSET EXPOSURE	TRANSLATION EXPOSURE

REVIEW QUESTIONS

1. Define transaction, translation, and economic exposure. Which is likely to have the greatest impact upon the long-term profitability of a firm?

2. What is the impact of devaluation upon a net asset exposure? of revaluation?

3. How do hedging and covering differ?

4. Distinguish between speculative and defensive actions in the FX markets.

5. How would you implement a balance sheet hedge?

6. How would you implement a forward hedge?

7. How would you implement a money-market hedge?

8. Is it ever impossible to use any of the hedges listed in questions 5 through 7?

9. Would you ever opt *not* to hedge, even if you expected to lose from an anticipated change in a currency's value and if hedging was possible?

SUGGESTED REFERENCES

AGGARWAL, RAJ *Financial Policies for the Multinational Company: the Management of Financial Exchange.* New York: Praeger Publishers, 1976.

ALIBER, ROBERT *Exchange Risk and Corporate International Finance,* New York: Macmillan, Inc., 1978.

CORNELL, BRADFORD, AND J. KIMBALL DIETRICH   "The Efficiency of the Foreign
    Exchange Market Under Floating Exchange Rates," *Review of Economics
    and Statistics,* February 1978.

ENSOR, RICHARD, AND BORIS ANTL, eds.   *Management of Foreign Exchange Risk.*
    London: Euromoney, 1978.

FOLKS, WILLIAM R., JR.   "Decision Analysis for Exchange Risk Management,"
    Financial Management, Winter 1972.

GEORGE, ABRAHAM   "Cash Flow vs. Accounting Exposure to Currency Risk,"
    California Management Review, Summer 1978.

JACQUE, LAURENT   *Management of Foreign Exchange Risk.* Lexington, 1978.

KOHLHAGEN, STEVEN W.   "A Model of Optimal Foreign Exchange Hedging
    Without Exchange Rate Projections," *Journal of International Business
    Studies,* Fall 1978.

KORTH, CHRISTOPHER M.   "A Devaluation Dichotomy: Headquarters vs. Subsid-
    iary," *MSU Business Topics,* Autumn 1972.

————   "Future of a Currency," *Business Horizons,* June 1972.

LIETAER, BERNARD A.   *Financial Management of Foreign Exchange Risk.* Cam-
    bridge, Mass.: MIT Press, 1971.

MURENBEELD, MARTIN   "Economic Factors for Forecasting Foreign Exchange
    Rate Changes," *Columbia Journal of World Business,* Summer 1975.

New Techniques in International Exposure and Cash Management, New York:
    Business International, 1977.

PRINDL, ANDREAS   *Foreign Exchange Risk.* New York: John Wiley & Sons, Inc.,
    1976.

RADEBAUGH, LEE   "Accounting for Price-Level and Exchange-Rate Changes for
    U.S. International Firms: An Empirical Study," *Journal of International
    Business Studies,* Fall 1976.

RIEHL, HEINZ, AND RITA M. RODRIGUEZ   *Foreign Exchange Markets.* New York:
    McGraw-Hill Book Company, 1977.

SHAPIRO, ALAN, AND BRUNO SOLNIK   "A Pure Foreign Exchange Asset Pricing
    Model," *Journal of International Economics,* May 1977.

22

International Taxation *

International taxation is another very complicated aspect of international operations. If a firm has foreign earnings it will likely be subject to foreign tax jurisdictions. It may also have to pay domestic taxes on foreign earnings in its home country. In some instances the company pays taxes to more than one country on the same income. Fortunately, international agreements exist that can greatly reduce the risk of *double taxation.* Also, home-country tax rules often provide relief or deferral of domestic taxation on foreign earnings. However, the international manager needs to be well aware of the nature of tax laws and the company's potential liability.

A special type of tax, known as the *value-added tax* (VAT), is becoming very prevalent abroad, especially in Western Europe. VAT is introduced in this chapter, not only to familiarize the manager of foreign operations, but also because it is being considered by the U.S. Congress for use in the United States.

If an international manager is stationed abroad, he or she is also threatened by double taxation on his or her earnings. This is especially true for American managers, since the U.S. government taxes U.S.

---

*THIS CHAPTER IS PRIMARILY THE WORK OF PROFESSOR RONALD TAYLOR OF THE UNIVERSITY OF SOUTH CAROLINA.

citizens who are living abroad. The last section of this chapter examines this taxation of persons living overseas.

TAXATION BY THE UNITED STATES OF FOREIGN CORPORATE INCOME

BASIS FOR INTERNATIONAL TAXATION

The United States asserts its power to tax on the basis of jurisdiction over (1) individuals and (2) transactions or property. As a result, citizens or residents of the United States, including domestic corporations, are subject to United States income taxation on their worldwide income. In addition to this, foreign individuals and corporations are subject to U.S. income taxation to the extent that the United States has jurisdiction over the transactions or property involved (e.g., U.S.-earned income).

Double taxation occurs when two countries claim jurisdiction and tax the same income. This may occur, for example, if a U.S. corporation earns income in a foreign country and is forced to pay income taxes to the foreign government as well as to the U.S. government. The resulting tax burden could place the U.S. corporation at a competitive disadvantage, which is generally undesirable. Therefore, the tax statutes of the United States allow taxes paid on foreign income to be either deducted from taxable income or credited to tax liability.

TAX DEDUCTIONS VERSUS TAX CREDITS

A very basic feature of tax law is that certain costs of a taxpayer can be subtracted from taxable income before tax liability is calculated. These costs are *tax deductions*. They directly reduce taxable income.

Other costs directly offset part of the tax liability; they do not reduce taxable income or the overall tax liability but rather are considered an acceptable means of settlement of part or all of the tax liability. These offsets are called *tax credits*. However, not all foreign taxes are creditable. In order to be creditable, the tax must be a tax on income or a tax in lieu of an income tax. Property, value-added, and excise taxes are not creditable.

BRANCHES VERSUS SUBSIDIARIES

The organizational form of the foreign operations of a company doing business abroad has a major impact on the tax consequences of its operations. If the foreign sales, service, consulting, and so forth are handled by personnel operating "out of a suitcase" away from the home office, from a tax perspective the operations are little different than are domestic operations. In this case there is likely to be little foreign tax liability of any sort. Likewise, if a representative office is set up abroad from which sales representatives operate to promote sales from outside the country, there may well be no foreign tax liability.

However, there are two major organizational arrangements that have important implications in the matter of foreign taxation.

Branch: This is a type of foreign operation that is essentially an extension of the parent; it is not a separate legal entity. The branch can buy, sell, earn profits, or suffer losses. It is also subject to foreign local taxes.

Since the branch is actually an integral part of the parent company, all expenses, income, profits, and losses are actually part of the financial performance of the parent company during a given accounting period. Note that this unification of financial accounts plus any tax liability or tax credit is true even if no money is repatriated from the branch to the parent.

The branch can be particularly attractive to corporations that anticipate losses in the initial phase of foreign operations. However, the additional exposure to liability by the headquarters and legal requirements of the host country may make this alternative undesirable or impossible.

Subsidiary: The second major type of organizational format with important tax implications is the subsidiary. A *subsidiary* is a separately incorporated legal entity in the country within which it operates. Two major advantages are realized. First, the U.S. parent corporation is generally shielded legally from the liabilities of the foreign subsidiary; this "shield" is not absolute, however; either the issuance of parent-company guarantees or local laws can establish liability. Second, the earnings of the foreign subsidiary are generally not taxable to the U.S. parent corporation until they are actually repatriated as dividends. However, except in rare circumstances, a foreign subsidiary cannot file a consolidated tax return with its domestic parent. As a result, losses from the foreign subsidiary's operations cannot be used to reduce the taxable income of the U.S. parent corporation.

TAXATION OF FOREIGN EARNINGS

Taxation of earnings of branches: The total income or loss from the operation of a foreign branch of a U.S. corporation is combined with the U.S. corporation's other income from domestic operations in the calculation of taxable income. When the foreign branch has paid foreign taxes on its income, the U.S. corporation may, when it files its U.S. tax statements, elect to claim either a deduction or a credit for the foreign taxes paid.

The election to claim a deduction reduces the impact of double taxation, but it does not eliminate double taxation entirely. Assume, for example, that the effective tax rate in the United States is 46 percent and in the foreign country is 40 percent, and that the net income before taxes of the foreign branch is $100,000. This suggests a nominal tax rate of 86 percent (46 percent + 40 percent) and a tax bill of $86,000. Fortunately, the results are not quite that bad. Treatment of the foreign tax as a *deduction* by the U.S. corporation results in the following:

Foreign taxable income	
Income earned by the branch	$100,000
Foreign tax at 40 percent (deducted)	$ 40,000
U.S. taxable income	$ 60,000
U.S. tax at 46 percent (deducted)	$ 27,600
Income after all taxes (foreign and U.S.)	$ 32,400

As a result, a total of $67,600 ($40,000 + $27,600) was paid in taxes on the foreign income. This is equivalent to an *effective tax rate* of over 67 percent, which is higher than either country imposed alone. This occurs because only 46 percent of the foreign taxes paid (46 percent of $40,000 = $18,400) resulted in an offset of U.S. tax ($46,000 − $18,400 = $27,600) (by reducing the taxable income of the company). If the U.S. tax rate was higher or lower, the offset of U.S. tax would also be accordingly higher or lower.

An election to claim the *foreign tax credit,* on the other hand, results in a dollar-for-dollar offset of U.S. taxes for foreign taxes paid. Therefore, using the example above, a credit would result in the following:

Income earned by foreign branch		$100,000
Foreign tax at 40 percent (deducted)		$ 40,000
U.S. tax at 46 percent (on total income)	$46,000	
Less foreign tax paid (credit)	$40,000	
U.S. tax paid (deducted)		$ 6,000
Net income after tax		$ 54,000

Note the impact upon tax liability and after-tax earnings of the three alternatives:

	Total Tax Liability	After-Tax Earnings	Effective Tax Rate
Double taxation	$86,000	$14,000	86.0%
Deduction for taxes paid abroad	$67,600	$32,400	67.6%
Credit for taxes paid abroad	$46,000	$54,000	46.0%

Quite obviously, double taxation can be a huge penalty if both countries are high-tax countries. It is also apparent that the taxpayer will almost always be better off if foreign tax payments (or any other costs) qualify as tax credits rather than tax deductions.

Taxation of earnings of subsidiaries: A foreign subsidiary is a separate entity from the U.S. parent corporation. The income and losses of the foreign subsidiary are not combined with the taxable income of the U.S. parent corporation. The foreign subsidiary pays its own taxes, and the parent receives no credit for them. In order to equalize the tax treatment of these two forms of business operation, the tax code provides for a *tax credit,* but only when a foreign subsidiary distributes a dividend to its U.S. parent corporation. A pro-rata share of the foreign taxes paid by the subsidiary on the profits that produced the dividend are "deemed to have been paid" by the U.S. shareholder if the shareholder owns at least 10 percent of the foreign corporation voting stock.

All dividends received from foreign subsidiaries must be "grossed up" or increased by the amount of the foreign taxes deemed to have been paid by the U.S. corporation. The tax deemed to be paid by the U.S. corporation is the proportion of the foreign tax that the amount of the dividend received bears to the accumulated after-tax foreign profits. This may be expressed by the following formula:

$$\text{Foreign tax deemed paid} = \text{Foreign corporation's income tax} \times \frac{\text{Dividend received (before gross up) from foreign corporation's earnings}}{\text{Accumulated profits (after taxes) for the foreign corporation}}$$

For example, if a wholly owned foreign subsidiary earned $100,000, which was subject to tax at the rate of 40 percent, the net profit after tax would be $60,000. If the foreign corporation paid a taxable dividend of $50,000 to its U.S. parent corporation, the deemed-paid tax credit would be

$$\text{credit} = \$40,000 \times \frac{\$50,000}{\$60,000} = \$33,333$$

As a result of the "gross-up" requirement, the U.S. corporation would report a dividend of $83,333 ($50,000 + $33,333). If the U.S. corporation was subject to 46 percent tax rate, its U.S. tax would be $38,333 ($83,333 × 46 percent) less a credit for $33,333 in foreign taxes, for a net tax of $5,000.

The treatment of foreign taxes as a credit instead of a deduction is an election that must be made annually on the tax return of the taxpayer. As a general rule, the taxpayer may take a credit for taxes paid or accrued, depending on the pertinent method of accounting. However, a cash-basis taxpayer may make an additional election to credit foreign taxes as though they were on an accrual basis. This enables the cash-basis taxpayer to match his or her tax paid with the income that gave rise to it, even though the tax is paid in a subsequent year.

LIMITATIONS ON THE FOREIGN TAX CREDIT

The basic purpose of the foreign tax credit is to prevent double taxation. However, it would not be reasonable to subtract taxes paid abroad from taxable income from operations in the U.S. when calculating domestic U.S. tax liability. Therefore, the U.S. tax law imposes a *limitation* on the amount of foreign income that may be taken as a credit. The taxation of a U.S. citizen's worldwide income coupled with the limitation has the effect of taxing him or her at the higher of the U.S. or the foreign tax rate. As a result, taxes are not avoided by conducting business in a "low-tax" country, and U.S. income is not reduced by foreign taxes that exceed U.S. rates. However, as long as the earnings of a foreign subsidiary are not paid to the parent as dividends, the U.S. tax liability on such earnings is deferred. Furthermore, there is generally no limit on the amount or the duration of the deferral. (The major exception to this generalization is covered by Subpart F of the U.S. tax code, which is examined below.) The allowable tax credit on foreign income taxes is based on the total amount of taxes paid to *all* foreign countries. This is known as the *overall credit limitation*. The maximum allowable credit is limited to a percentage of U.S. tax before credits. The percentage is determined by the ratio of foreign-source taxable income to worldwide taxable income. This may be expressed by the following formula:

$$\text{Limitation} = \frac{\text{Total foreign-source taxable income}}{\text{Worldwide taxable income}} \times \text{U.S. tax before credits}$$

The operation of the overall limitations may be illustrated by the following example. Usco, a U.S. corporation, has taxable income in the United States of $275,000, of which $200,000 is from foreign sources (country Y and country Z). If the U.S. tax rate is 46 percent, the U.S. tax, before credits, is $126,500. During the taxable year, Usco pays $45,000 in income tax to country Y and $50,000 in income tax to country Z. The maximum allowable credit which Usco may claim for foreign taxes paid is $91,965, which is calculated as follows:

(1) $\dfrac{\text{Total foreign-source taxable income}}{\text{Worldwide taxable income}} = \dfrac{\$200,000}{\$275,000} = \begin{array}{l} 0.727 \text{ (or 72.7 percent of} \\ \text{earnings and income taxes} \end{array}$

(2) U.S. tax before credits = income × tax rate
    = $275,000 × .46 = $126,500

Limitation = (0.727) ($126,500) = $91,965

When, as in the example above, more foreign tax is paid than may be claimed as a credit, the "excess foreign tax credit" ($3035 in the example above) may be treated as a *carry-back* and a *carry-forward* to other tax years. As a general rule, the excess tax credit is first carried back to the second preceding year from the excess credit year. Any unused portion is carried back to the first preceding year. Any further excess is carried forward to future tax liabilities up to a maximum of five future years. Any portion remaining after five years expires. An excess foreign tax credit can only be claimed in a carry-back or carry-forward year in which the overall limitation has not been reached (that is, when an "excess limitation" exists).

TAX MINIMIZATION THROUGH INCOME AND EXPENSE ALLOCATION

It is clear from analyzing the limitation formula that the identification of the total foreign-source income is critical in determining the allowable foreign tax credit. In addition to this, the more foreign-source income that exists in proportion to worldwide income, the greater the U.S. tax savings. Therefore, when the foreign tax rate is lower than the U.S. tax rate, it may be desirable for management, via transfer pricing, to maximize foreign-source *income* while maximizing U.S.-source *expenses* whenever possible. Almost any intracompany transaction provides management with these opportunities.

The U.S. tax code attempts to prevent the arbitrary shifting of profits between and among related businesses that are seeking a tax advantage. It gives the Internal Revenue Service power to *reallocate* items of income, deductions, and credits between and among businesses that are "owned or controlled directly or indirectly by the same interests." The reallocation is made whenever it appears that the U.S. corporation is absorbing expenses that result in increased income to a foreign affiliate, or it is charging unrealistically low sales prices to it. The purpose of reallocation is to place a controlled taxpayer on a "tax parity" with an uncontrolled taxpayer. The basic concept is that a U.S. taxpayer should deal with affiliates on "arm's-length" terms. As a result, any U.S. corporation engaged in foreign operations should be prepared to justify its pricing policies and changes made between domestic and foreign affiliates, and should keep adequate records to support its position. Nevertheless, within these constraints proper allocation of income and expenses by management can lead to signficiant tax savings.

TAX MINIMIZATION VIA TAX HAVENS

As a general rule, the income of a foreign subsidiary is not taxed to the domestic parent until the income is repatriated as a result of dividends, liquidations, and so forth. This can lead to the temptation for a company to try to avoid a significant share of its foreign taxes by the use of *tax havens*. These are countries such as the Netherlands Antilles, which are noted for very low tax rates. Special nonoperating subsidiaries that are located in these tax havens are used to "book" financial transactions of operating subsidiaries of the same parent but located in different foreign countries in such a way as to concentrate as much taxable income as possible in these low-tax countries. For example, a U.S. corporation may sell its goods near cost to its tax haven subsidiary, which would then resell the goods at normal markups. Actual shipments of the goods would be from the U.S. corporation to the customers of the tax haven corporation. As a result, the tax haven subsidiary would not actually ship or receive any goods, but it would "earn" the profit on the foreign sales of the U.S. parent. With the use of such a tax dodge, taxation on foreign earnings could be avoided indefinitely. Such a subsidiary could even loan its funds to the parent!

In order to prevent the foreign subsidiaries of U.S. corporations from operation in "tax haven" countries and thereby avoiding U.S. taxation, *Subpart F* of the Internal Revenue Code taxes certain types of income whether or not the income is repatriated. The determination of Subpart F income is very complex. It includes foreign-based company sales and service income, foreign personal holding company income, and the sum of all illegal bribes, kickbacks, or other "sensitive payments." These sources of income are added to the earnings of the parent and taxed *as if* they were paid as a dividend; foreign tax credits can be taken if these are available. Any undistributed income which has already been taxed under Subpart F can be distributed without incurring an additional tax.

Actually, very little tax is collected under Subpart F, since its threat alone is sufficient to cause companies to avoid creating foreign subsidiaries that might be subject to it.

SPECIAL TYPES OF DOMESTIC CORPORATIONS WITH INTERNATIONAL OPERATIONS

Congress has created special taxation status for certain types of domestic corporations to stimulate export activities and/or to encourage investments in certain areas of the world. The following is a brief discussion of these provisions, which may be elected by management to minimize the total tax liability.

Domestic international sales corporation (DISC): DISC was created to provide special incentives for U.S. corporations to increase their exports. The provision was also designed to decrease the tax inequalities between U.S. companies that export their products and either foreign or U.S. companies that manufacture abroad through the use of foreign subsidiaries. The qualifying profits of a DISC enjoy preferential tax treatment. A portion of the profits of the DISC from export activities is taxed directly to the shareholders. The untaxed portion becomes subject to taxation only when it is distributed, the parent company sells the DISC's stock, or when the subsidiary no longer qualifies as a DISC.

The major requirements necessary to elect DISC status are: (1) 95 percent or more of gross receipts must be from export activities, and (2) 95 percent or more of its assets must be export assets. Only incremental export sales of a company can take advantage of the special DISC tax benefits. The typical DISC is a subsidiary of its parent manufacturing corporation, which does the actual manufacturing. A DISC is a marketing company, not a manufacturing company. DISCs have been strongly criticized by GATT; the U.S. Congress may soon eliminate or modify them.

Possessions corporation: The Tax Reform Act of 1976 provided a more beneficial system of allowing for qualifying corporations with operations in U.S. possessions (especially Puerto Rico). Corporations making the election receive a foreign tax credit equal to their full U.S. tax liability on their business and qualified investment income from U.S. possessions, even if the tax is not paid to the government of the possession. The companies, in effect, pay no U.S. taxes on these earnings.

INTERNATIONAL TAX TREATIES

Tax treaties are agreements between the governments of two countries. They may be considered to be the "supreme law" of taxation in the United States, since the provisions of a tax treaty supercede the provisions of the Internal Revenue Code.

The purpose of a tax treaty is generally to facilitate commerce between the two participating countries. As a result, the presence of a tax treaty may benefit the taxpayer or, at worse, leave his or her position unchanged. It does not usually work to his or her disadvantage.

One of the primary needs for tax treaties arises from the desire to reduce the impact of *double taxation.* The United States treats taxes that have been paid to another country on foreign-source income as a direct offset (credit) to the taxes it imposes. However, a number of factors may cause the problem of double taxation to persist. For example, if the definition of source income in the U.S. differs from that of the other country involved, the tax credit will not be adequate to deal with the problem. Tax treaties deal with the particular problems involved by reaching mutually acceptable definitions for terms that apply to the residents of both countries.

Tax treaties generally benefit residents of the participating countries by reducing the rate of tax paid by the residents of one country on income subject to taxation in the other country. Tax treaties may also exempt certain types of activity from taxation. For example, if a foreign manufacturer in a nontreaty country regularly sells its product in the United States through a general agent, it would be subject to tax. However, if the foreign manufacturer is the resident of a treaty country, it would probably be exempt from tax if it did not have a permanent establishment in the United States.

THE VALUE-ADDED TAX

The *value-added tax* (VAT) system is currently being used by many European countries as the primary revenue-raising tax. In recent years, the VAT has also been considered in the United States as an additional source of tax revenue.

How It Works

The basic concept of the VAT is to impose a tax on the value that a producer of goods or services adds to its output. As a result, the VAT is assessed and collected at various output stages in the manufacturing process. The amount of tax is based on the total price at which the goods or services are sold. To avoid double taxation, a credit is allowed for the tax that has already been paid for value added to the product by other entities. In other words, *value added* is equal to the selling price of outputs, less the cost of qualified inputs.

This process may be illustrated by the following example. Assume that Supplier Inc. uses its own raw materials to make parts that are purchased by Assemble Company, which makes widgets that are sold to Big Store, a retail outlet. The transactions may be summarized as follows:

Entity	Cost of Input	Selling Price of Output	Value Added	VAT (at 10 percent)	
				Marginal	Cumulative
Supplier, Inc.	0	$ 2	$2	$0.20	$0.20
Assemble Company	$2	$ 6	$4	$0.40	$0.60
Big Store	$6	$15	$9	$0.90	$1.50

In the example above, the VAT imposed on each entity is the value added multiplied by the imposed tax rate. If the rate is 10 percent, the VAT imposed on Assemble Company is $0.40. Another method of calculating the tax relies on information taken directly from purchase and invoices. If the VAT is separately stated on the invoices, then the VAT becomes the tax on sales (output tax) less the tax on purchases (input tax).

As can be seen from the example, the VAT is very similar to a national sales tax, except that collection of the VAT is made in stages.

The direct taxpayer under the VAT system is the producer; however, this cost is usually passed on to the consumer, subject to pricing constraints that may be imposed by the marketplace. It is important to note that both profitable and unprofitable businesses incur a tax liability under the VAT system, whereas only profitable businesses incur an income tax liability.

The European VAT favors export activity. This is accomplished by subjecting imports not only to import duties but also to VAT while allowing the exporter a credit for the VAT element in its purchases. Thus, exports are free of VAT.

U.S. TAXATION OF U.S. CITIZENS LIVING ABROAD

As a result of the 1981 Economic Recovery Tax Act, new rules have been introduced that are intended to restore the competitiveness of U.S. companies sending U.S. citizens and resident aliens to work overseas. Prior laws subjected these persons to taxation of their compensation as well as any allowance they might receive to meet the higher cost of living abroad. Very few other countries tax their citizens while they are living and working abroad.

EXCLUSION OF FOREIGN INCOME

The new law establishes an election to exclude foreign earned income of $80,000 for 1983. Further increases are a matter of intense debate in Congress. Earned income includes wages, salaries, professional fees, or other compensation for personal services. However, income that is received outside of the foreign country in which it was earned to avoid paying income tax in that country does not qualify for the exclusion.

U.S. citizens are eligible for the exclusion if their tax home is in a foreign country and they have been a bonafide resident of that country or countries for an uninterrupted period, which includes an entire taxable year. A U.S. citizen or resident who is present in a foreign country for at least 330 full days during a period of twelve consecutive months also qualifies. A husband and wife are each eligible for an exclusion of their own earnings.

In addition to the election to exclude foreign earned income, a new provision in the law allows an election to exclude a portion of the reasonable housing expenses paid during the taxable year by an individual, and his or her family if they also reside in the foreign country. For

1983, the excluded amount is equal to housing costs in excess of approximately $6600. Housing expenses do not include interest and taxes that would normally be deductible.

TAX PLANNING

Under the old law, there was little incentive to minimize foreign taxes, since U.S. taxes were usually larger, and the foreign tax would simply result in a credit against the U.S. tax. As a result of the new law, overall taxes may be reduced as a result of minimization of foreign taxes.

Nevertheless, persons living in high-tax countries may benefit from not electing the exclusion, because their U.S. income tax liability is offset by foreign taxes paid. In addition to this, the election may have an adverse effect on certain retirement-plan deductions, such as individual retirement accounts, which are based on taxable income. As a result, careful planning is necessary to achieve the best possible combination of benefits.

SUMMARY

It is said that death and taxes are two certainties that we can never escape. However, just as good living habits can delay the former, good planning can reduce or delay the latter. In general, tax planning is a question of timing. For example, a decision to repatriate income from a foreign subsidiary next year instead of this year may temporarily defer taxes. The election by an individual to exclude the allowable portion of foreign earned income from taxable income permanently avoids taxes. Only by understanding the "rules of the game" can the international manager effectively and legally minimize the impact of taxes.

Taxation is one of the most complicated aspects of international management. Some of the opportunities and pitfalls of international taxation were discussed in this chapter. Implementation of a corporate tax plan should always involve the use of tax specialists who stay abreast of the never-ending changes occurring in this challenging field.

KEY TERMS

ARM'S-LENGTH PRICING	DOUBLE TAXATION	TAX HAVEN
DOMESTIC	EFFECTIVE TAX RATE	TAX TREATY
INTERNATIONAL SALES	POSSESSIONS	TRANSFER PRICING
CORPORATION (DISC)	CORPORATION	VALUE-ADDED TAX (VAT)

REVIEW QUESTIONS

1. Define double taxation. How can it be avoided?
2. Distinguish between a tax deduction and a tax credit. Which will produce the lower worldwide effective tax rate for the corporation?
3. Distinguish between a branch and a subsidiary. What are the major advantages of each?
4. Do both foreign branches and subsidiaries pay taxes abroad?
5. Why is the pricing of products sold between affiliates of the same company of prime importance to governmental tax officials?
6. Can taxes paid by a company in a high-tax foreign country be used to shelter income in a low-tax foreign country from U.S. taxes?
7. XYZ Inc., a U.S. domestic manufacturing corporation, opened a branch in Germany during the year. XYZ Inc. also has an office in Spain. Taxable income derived from the branch in Germany was $30,000, and taxable income derived from the office in Spain was $20,000. A total of $350,000 taxable income was derived from U.S. operations. Germany imposed a tax on income in that country totaling $15,000. Spain imposed a tax on income in that country totaling $6000. Assuming that the U.S. income tax is $164,750, compute the total foreign tax credit that may be used by XYZ Inc. this year.
8. ABC Inc., a U.S. domestic manufacturing corporation began operating a wholly owned subsidiary in Canada this year, which earned $350,000 before income taxes. The subsidiary paid income taxes to Canada of $150,000, and it paid a dividend to its U.S. parent totaling $50,000. Assuming a marginal tax rate of 46 percent, what is the net tax liability (if any) after credits to ABC Inc. as a result of receiving the dividend?
9. Explain why you would or would not expect the limitation on the foreign tax credit to take effect in questions 7 and 8 above.

SUGGESTED REFERENCES

ARPAN, JEFFREY S. *International Intracorporate Pricing: Non-American Systems and Views.* New York: Praeger Publishers, 1972.

ARTHUR ANDERSEN AND COMPANY *Tax and Trade Guides* (periodically updated).

AUDERIETH, STEPHEN, AND ELMER M. PERGAMENT *Tax Guide to International Operations.* Greenvale, NY: Panel Publishers, 1975.

CHOWN, JOHN   *Taxation and Multinational Enterprises.* London: Longman, 1974.

COOPERS AND LYBRAND   *Expatriate Tax Planning,* Washington, D.C., 1982.

ERNST AND WHINNEY   *Foreign and U.S. Corporate Income and Withholding Tax Rates* (periodically updated).

——— *E&W International Series,* New York, various booklets.

PAULES, EDWARD P.   "A Guide Through the Tax Maze," *Euromoney,* October and November 1980.

PRICE WATERHOUSE   *Corporate Tax Rates in 80 Countries* (periodically updated).

SPILLER, STEPHEN R.   "Two Types of Credit for Foreign Taxes Help Offset Double Tax on International Income," *Taxation for Accountants,* January 1980.

Glossary

Absolute advantage: the ability of one country (or company) to produce a product at a lower cost than another.

Accounting exposure: translation or transaction exposure to foreign exchange-rate fluctuations.

Ad valorem duty: a duty or tariff which is charged as a percentage of the value of goods. (See *duty, specific duty, compound duty.*)

African Development Bank (AFDB): a multinational financial institution which lends funds to African countries for purposes of economic and social development (similar to the *Inter-American Development Bank or Asian Development Bank*).

Agency: a wholly-owned foreign office of a bank which can make loans but cannot accept deposits. (See *branch, representative office, subsidiary.*)

Agency for International Development: an agency of the U.S. State Department which is responsible for most U.S. foreign aid.

Agreement corporation: a state-chartered subsidiary of a commercial bank which is permitted to engage in international banking and finance more readily than can the bank's domestic offices (similar to *Edge Act* subsidiaries).

AID: *Agency for International Development*

Appreciation: an increase in the value of a currency in foreign exchange markets which is caused by market forces rather than a formal *revaluation* by the government. (See also *depreciation.*)

Arbitrage: simultaneous purchase and sale of assets in different markets at different prices (or simultaneous borrowing and investing in different markets). The contracts offset each other (and are therefore riskless) with the investor profiting from the different terms. The arbitrageur's actions help to keep the prices in the different markets in relative balance. (See *interest arbitrage* and *foreign exchange arbitrage.*)

Asian Development Bank (AsDB): a multinational lending institution which lends only to developing countries in Asia. It lends for economic and social development projects. (See *African Development Bank, International Bank for Reconstruction and Development,* and *Inter-American Development Bank.*)

Asian dollar: the Asian portion of the Eurodollar market. Although geographically separated, the markets are closely tied.

Asking quote: the price at which an FX dealer is willing to sell. The opposite is the *bid quote.* (See also *offer price, selling rate.*)

Asset exposure: the total of assets which will be adversely affected by a depreciation or devaluation of a currency. (See *liability* and *net exposure.*)

Autarky: an effort by a country or region to be as economically self-sufficient as possible with little reliance upon other countries or regions.

Average rate: the average FX rate over a period of time (e.g., the annual or quarterly average). (See *current rate, historical rate.*)

Back-to-back loan: (1) an intra-corporate loan which uses a bank as a "front" so that the transfer appears to be a bank loan; the funding unit of the company deposits the funds with a bank which then lends the money to a second unit of the company; also called a *fronting loan.* (2) offsetting loans between two different companies in different countries, thus, in the U.S., Company A lends to Company B while in a foreign country Company B lends an equivalent amount to Company A; also called a *parallel loan.*

Balance of payments: a statistical tabulation of all of the economic transactions (i.e., goods and services, transfers and funds) between the residents of one country or region with the rest of the world (or simply another region or another country) during a period of time (usually a calendar year).

Balance of trade: the net difference between a nation's or region's exports and imports of merchandise or goods during a particular period of time; a subset of the *balance of payments.*

Bank draft: an unconditional order directing the bank to which it is addressed to pay a designated third party at the time when presented or at a specific period after presentation. Also called a *bill of exchange.* (See also *sight draft* and *time draft.*)

Banker's acceptance: a bank *time draft* which the bank has formally agreed to pay (i.e., it has "accepted") at the future time specified on the draft. The word "Accepted" will be stamped or written on the draft. It then becomes a negotiable *money-market instrument* which can be sold and resold at a discount up to maturity.

Bank for International Settlements (BIS): an international organization which helps major central banks to exchange information and to coordinate some of their joint international monetary arrangements; located in Basel, Switzerland.

Barter: the direct exchange of goods or services for other goods or services. Money is not used. Also called *countertrade*.

Benelux: a customs union of *Be*lgium, *N*etherlands and *Lux*embourg.

Bid quote: the price at which the bank is willing to purchase a currency. Also called the *buy quote*. The opposite is the *offer price* or *asking quote*.

Bill of exchange: see *bank draft*.

Bill of lading (B/L): a receipt given by a carrier (e.g., shipping line) to an exporter. The B/L is also the contract which details the carrier's responsibilities. It may also serve as a document of title for the merchandise.

BIS: *Bank for International Settlements*

Blocked funds: financial assets owned by non-residents which cannot be freely transferred out of a country or into another currency because of governmental controls.

Bond: a type of negotiable debt instrument whose original maturity was long term—usually at least five years.

Branch: a department of a company which is located away from headquarters. It is not a separate legal entity. Therefore, the obligations of the branch are the legal obligations of the headquarters and the full resources of the latter are available to protect the branch. A bank's branch can take deposits as well as make loans. (See *agency, subsidiary*.)

Bretton Woods: the location of a major international meeting of treasury and bank officials of the Allied countries in 1944. The meetings designed the IMF, the IBRD and indirectly led to the creation of GATT.

Broker: an intermediary who brings buyer and seller or borrower and lender together in the foreign exchange or Eurocurrency markets.

Buy quote: the foreign-exchange rate at which a foreign-exchange dealer is willing to purchase a currency (and therefore the price at which a vendor can sell FX to that dealer). The opposite is the *sell quote*. (See also *bid quote*.)

Cable or telegraphic transfer: movement of funds via the use of cable or telegraph. (See also *mail transfer, SWIFT.*)

Capital account: the section in the balance of payments that records changes in most financial assets and liabilities.

Capital control: restriction on the movement of money or capital across national borders.

Capital intensive: production techniques which require high concentrations of capital per unit of output relative to labor or land input. (See *labor intensive*.)

Capital markets: long-term financial markets (as opposed to *money markets*).

Cartel: an organization of sellers or buyers which is capable of manipulating price and/or supply.

CD: *Certificate of Deposit*

Central bank: an agency (usually of a country's central government) which exercises monetary policy: issuing currency, managing money supply, managing interest rates and credit availability.

Central rate: an exchange rate to which a government agrees with other governments to tie its currency; central rates are similar to the *par values* that existed under the IMF system of fixed exchange rates.

Certificate of deposit (CD): a short-term promissory note issued by commercial banks. Large CDs are negotiable *money-market instruments.*

CIF: *Cost, insurance and freight*

Clean float: an exchange-rate system which permits supply and demand pressures to dictate exchange rates with no governmental intervention. Clean floats are very rare in the real world. (See *dirty float, managed float.*)

Clearing account: an arrangement between two or more countries or their central banks to channel trade and capital flows among themselves through special accounts. Convertible foreign currencies will only be used to settle *net* balances at settlement dates—not on a daily basis. Clearing accounts are intended to expand trade between the countries and to conserve scarce FX.

Closing a position: covering an open forward contract prior to maturity by means of a second but offsetting, forward contract with the same maturity.

Closing-rate method: see *Current-rate method.*

CMEA (also COMECON): *Council for Mutual Economic Assistance*

Co-determination: an agreement between management and labor which permits labor to participate in controlling the company.

Collateral: security which is offered to a creditor as added protection against the possibility that the debtor will fail to pay an obligation. (If the debtor defaults, the creditor may seize or sell the collateral. If the debt is paid off, the collateral is released to the debtor).

Combination export manager: an export company which handles the products of other companies. The CEM does not own the goods, but is typically paid a retainer plus commissions. Typically, all of the transactions are handled in the exporter's name by the CEM—even utilizing their letterheads.

COMECON: *Council for Mutual Economic Assistance* (CMEA)

Commercial paper: a short-term, unsecured, negotiable, promissory note issued by a corporation with high credit ratings. Commercial paper can be either placed directly with investors or sold through investment bankers.

Commercial risk: see *credit risk.*

Commission: special fees charged by financial institutions, such as commercial banks or brokers, for handling financial transactions. Commissions are usually a percentage of the value of the transaction but can also be a fixed price.

Commitment fee: a charge imposed by lenders for the guarantee that funds will be loaned at a future date (e.g., for a *line of credit*).

Commodity agreement: an agreement between buyers and sellers of commodities to regulate price and output; the agreement can regulate supply and demand and provide for buffer stocks as well as control price.

Commodity Credit Corporation (CCC): an agency of the Department of Agriculture of the U.S. Government. One of its many responsibilities is to help finance U.S. agricultural and agricultural-equipment exports.

Common market: a form of economic integration between countries which provides not only for no internal trade barriers and common external trade barriers (as does a *customs union*) but also free factor mobility.

Comparative advantage: the theory that the true basis for trade is not *absolute advantage* in production (and distribution) but relative (or comparative) advantage. This is obtained when the producer focuses upon producing what it can produce more efficiently (i.e., sacrificing less of alternative products) than another country. All countries have comparative advantages: comparative advantage can be either the efficient country's greatest absolute advantages or the inefficient country's least absolute disadvantages.

Compensatory duty: an extra duty imposed upon imports to offset some artificial trade advantage of those products (e.g., export subsidies in the producing country). Also called *countervailing duty*.

Compound duty: a combination of both *ad valorem* and *specific duties*.

Confirmed letters of credit: a *letter of credit* which is guaranteed by a second bank as well as the issuing bank. For example, an exporter may not be satisfied with the safety of the issuing bank and request that its own bank also add its own guarantee (or "confirmation").

Confiscation: seizure of private property by a government without fair compensation. (See also *expropriation*.)

Consolidated financial statement: combines balance sheet, income statement, etc. of parent and all subsidiaries as though they were a single unit.

Consortium: a *joint venture* of banks which will provide joint financing to customers.

Conversion: the exchange of one currency for another.

Convertible currency: currency which can be freely converted to another currency (or gold) without governmental permission. (See *inconvertible currency* and *blocked funds*.)

Convertible Eurobond: Eurobond which can be exchanged for equity in the issuing company.

Correspondent bank: a bank which provides banking services for a client bank which is located in a different geographic area (either foreign or domestic). Often the two banks serve as correspondents for each other and keep reciprocal deposits with each other so that each can receive and make payments on behalf of the other. The two banks are generally independent of one another with no equity ties.

Cost, insurance and freight (CIF): a shipping term under which the selling price includes not only the basic price of the merchandise (i.e., the cost) but also insurance and transportation (i.e., freight) charges.

Council for Mutual Economic Assistance (CMEA or *COMECON*): an economic organization of Communist countries which attempts to coordinate some of their economic programs and gain some of the advantages of economic integration. The members are Bulgaria, Cuba, Czechoslovakia, East Germany, Hungary, Mongolia, Poland, Rumania, and the U.S.S.R.

Countertrade: see *barter*.

Countervailing duties: see *compensatory duty*.

Country exposure: total of assets (net of appropriate offsetting liabilities) which would be affected by *country risk*.

Country lending limit: the most that a bank will lend to all borrowers (or guarantors) in a particular country.

Country risk: the threat that adverse governmental action (*sovereign risk*) or other adverse development in a particular country will threaten a company's investments in that country. (See also *credit risk*.)

Coverage: an indication that a particular item in a corporation's balance sheet or income statement would be favorably affected by a change in the value of the currency or denomination.

Covered interest arbitrage: the process of borrowing one currency, buying a second currency spot, investing the second currency and simultaneously selling it forward. The procedure is designed to profit from either favorable interest-rate or forward-rate differentials between two countries. Because of the forward hedge there is no exchange risk to the investor. (See *arbitrage*.)

Covering: buying or selling a foreign currency (either spot or forward) in order to offset a future payable or receivable contract which is denominated in a foreign currency. Covering eliminates the foreign-exchange risk. (See *hedging*.)

Crawling-peg system: an exchange-rate system where the exchange rate is fixed but changes frequently by relatively small amounts.

Credit (in the balance of payments): a decrease in foreign assets owned by local residents or increase in liabilities to foreigners. A credit represents a source of funds or international purchasing power. (See *debit*.)

Credit risk: likelihood that a debtor will be financially unable to repay principal and/or interest (called *commercial risk*). (See also *country risk*.)

Credit tranche: one of the four conditional IMF lines of credit against which a country can borrow after it has drawn its *reserve tranche*. The terms become more stringent with each credit tranche.

Cross-border exposure: risk which arises from an asset or liability which is located in a foreign country. The term is most frequently used with financial assets or liabilities. Cross-border exposure occurs whether or not a foreign currency is involved. (See also *cross-currency exposure.*)

Cross-currency exposure: risk which arises from a financial asset or liability which is denominated in a foreign currency—even if a national border is not crossed. (See also *cross-border exposure.*)

Cross rate: a foreign-exchange rate between two currencies which is calculated from the ratio of the value of each currency in terms of a third.

Currency band: range within which monetary authorities allow a currency to fluctuate around a par or central rate (e.g., $\pm 2\frac{1}{4}\%$).

Current account: the portion of the balance of payments which records trade in goods and services plus unilateral transfers.

Current/non-current method: translation method for foreign-currency-denominated financial statements which translates current assets and liabilities at the *current* (or *closing*) *exchange rate;* non-current items are translated at *historical rates.*

Current-rate method: the translation of foreign-currency-denominated financial statements at the exchange rate which was in effect on the closing date of the financial statements. Also called *closing-rate method.* (See *historical rate, average rate.*)

Customs-house broker: a firm which contracts to bring other companies' imported goods through local customs.

Customs invoice: an export document which declares the value of the goods covered.

Customs union: an agreement between countries in which import tariffs and other barriers are eliminated between the members (as does a *free trade area*) but also common barriers imposed upon imports from all other countries.

Dealer: specialist in a bank's foreign-exchange department who executes transactions on the bank's account (also called *trader*).

Defensive hedge: action taken to protect a company against exposure to an FX change (i.e., to offset anticipated loss); *speculation* would involve similar actions but without any exposure—simply seeking profit rather than offsetting losses. (See also *hedging.*)

Depreciation: a decline in a currency's value caused by market forces. By contrast, *devaluation* is a decline caused by official government action. (See *appreciation.*)

Depth: a measure of the capacity of an FX or capital market to accept a large trade without significant movement in price. A strong market has depth and can absorb large trades. A thin or shallow market cannot absorb such trades without significant movement in price or interest rate.

Devaluation: a decline in a currency's *par* or *central* value caused by official government action rather than market forces (which is called *depreciation*). (See *revaluation*.)

Development bank: an investment and/or loan fund which aids economic and social development of developing countries (e.g., IBRD, IDB, or national development banks such as Mexican financieras).

Direct investment: purchase of enough of the equity shares of a company to offer some degree of managerial control. Governmental statistics often set the minimum level at 10%. (See also *portfolio investment*.)

Direct quotation: the currency which is being used to value another currency (e.g., DM/$ is DM direct and $ *indirect*). In most markets the local currency is quoted directly.

Dirty float: a floating currency whose value is controlled by the government to a level higher or lower than the market would produce. (See *clean float* and *managed float*.)

DISC: *Domestic International Sales Corporation*

Discount: forward exchange rate which is less than the spot rate. (See *premium*.) Also, selling of a financial contract below its face value (e.g., a banker's acceptance).

Domestic International Sales Corporation (DISC): a special domestic subsidiary of a U.S. company which received special tax advantages if 95% of its revenues were qualified export sales and 95% of its assets export-related. DISCs were eliminated in 1984.

Draft: a written word by one party (the drawer) to a second party (the drawee) to pay a third party. (A personal check is a draft.) An exporter will issue a draft to an importer directing payment to the exporter's bank (also called a *bill of exchange*). Drafts may be payable on presentation (*sight draft*) or if a draft is payable at a specified future time after sight (e.g., 30 or 90 days) it is a *time draft*.

Dual economy: a country in which there are great extremes between the rich and the poor.

Dumping: the selling of goods more cheaply in a foreign country than in the country of production.

Duty: a tax imposed upon goods when they are imported, exported or in transit. (See *ad valorem duty, specific duty, compound duty, tariff*.)

Economic exposure: the *exchange-rate risk* that *future operations* of a company or one of its foreign offices will be adversely affected by the change in value of a currency.

Economy of scale: a decrease in average production costs resulting from large-scale production.

Edge Act Corporation: a domestic subsidiary of a U.S. commercial bank that engages in international banking and investment. It may not engage in domestic banking in the U.S. An Edge Act subsidiary can engage in some foreign activities which are forbidden to the bank domestically in the U.S. but are permitted to it by the host country (e.g., equity investment and underwriting of corporate bond issues). (See also *agreement corporation.*)

EEC: *European Economic Community*

Effective interest rate: the true interest rate which is paid or received. It reflects not only the *nominal interest rate* but also the premium or discount on the purchase price and in the forward foreign-exchange market.

EFTA: *European Free Trade Association*

Embargo: prohibition of the trade of goods or services with a particular foreign country. (See also *quota.*)

EMS: *European Monetary System*

Entrepot: a trade or financial center *through which* goods or services flow but from which they do not originate (e.g., Switzerland is an entrepot for funds; Hong Kong is a trade entrepot for merchandise to and from China).

Ethnocentric: an attitude which is home oriented and ignores differences of foreign people or environments—assumes all of the world is the same. (See also *geocentric, polycentric.*)

Eurobond: a long-term negotiable debt instrument (i.e., a bond) which is underwritten by an international *syndicate* and sold principally or entirely in countries other than the country of the currency in which the issue is denominated. (See also *Euromarket, international bond, foreign bond.*)

Eurocurrency: a currency deposited in a commercial bank outside the country of origin. Principal and interest will be paid in that currency. (See *Euromarket.*)

Eurodollar: the major form of *Eurocurrency.*

Euromarket: the international or external financial markets which usually exist only outside of the country whose currency is utilized. (See *Eurocurrency, Eurobond.*)

European Common Market: see *European Economic Community.*

European currency unit (ECU): a unit of account established by the *European Monetary System.* Its value is determined by the weighted value of member currencies. The EMS eventually hopes to make the ECU a common currency for the bloc.

European Economic Community (EEC): a regional economic grouping of European countries (originally Germany, France, Italy, Belgium, Netherlands and Luxembourg with the later additions of the United Kingdom, Ireland, Denmark and Greece). Often called the European Common Market, it is actually more like a *customs union.*

European Free Trade Association (EFTA): a *free-trade area* in Western Europe. It was originally comprised of Austria, Denmark, Norway, Portugal, Sweden, Switzerland, and the United Kingdom. However, Denmark and the United Kingdom later joined the EEC.

European Monetary System (EMS):   an effort by most of the EEC countries to keep their currencies within established limits to one another. Each currency has a *central rate*. The value of the bloc's currencies *float* relative to the U.S. dollar and most other currencies.

Exchange control: restriction on free dealings in foreign exchange. Controls include multiple exchange rates, *inconvertibility*, and *quotas* on the amount which can be bought or sold.

Exchange rate: the price of one currency in terms of another. (See *spot* and *forward markets; buy, bid, sell, ask* and *offer*.)

Exchange rate risk: the possibility of a loss resulting from the rise or fall in the value of a foreign currency. (See *economic exposure, transaction exposure, translation exposure*.)

Expatriate: (1) (verb) to take funds out of a country; (2) (noun) someone living outside his or her country of nationality.

Export: a good, service or capital that is sent abroad.

Export-Import Bank (Eximbank):   a U.S. Government agency which promotes exports from the U.S. by intermediate and long-term financing. The Eximbank provides loans to foreign importers and guarantees to exporters and banks in the U.S.

Export management company: acts as export dept. for other companies; it provides all export services needed.

Export merchant: a distributor who buys stocks and distributes goods made abroad.

Expropriation: governmental seizure of the assets of a foreign entity—either with or without compensation. (See also *confiscation, nationalization*.)

Extraterritoriality: attempt by a government to apply its laws outside of its territorial borders.

Factor of production: one of the fundamental economic inputs into any productive effort—land, labor, capital, entrepreneurship and technology.

FCIA: *Foreign Credit Insurance Association*

Fixed exchange rate: a system of relatively stable exchange rates with a *par* or *central value* (e.g., tied to another currency, gold, or SDRs); frequently limited fluctuations above and below the fixed rate are permitted. (See also *floating exchange rate*.)

Floating exchange rate: an FX system which lacks both par and central values; the exchange rate moves according to the forces of supply and demand. (See also *clean, dirty,* and *managed float*.)

Floating rate loan: a loan which is priced at a fixed differential (or *spread*) above a base rate (e.g., prime, LIBOR, CDs, etc.).

FOB: *Free on board*

Foreign bond: a bond sold in a domestic market by a foreign borrower. (See also *international bond, Eurobond*.)

Foreign Corrupt Practices Act: an American law against bribery by U.S. companies operating abroad.

Foreign Credit Insurance Association (FCIA): an association of private insurance companies in the U.S. which, in cooperation with the Export-Import Bank, provides credit-risk insurance for exports of goods from the U.S.

Foreign Credit Restraint Program: U.S. capital controls (1964 to 1973) which limited the ability of U.S. financial institutions to lend abroad. (See also *Foreign Direct Investment Regulation* and *Interest Equalization Tax*.)

Foreign Direct Investment: see *direct* investment.

Foreign Direct Investment Regulation (FDIR): U.S. capital controls (1968 to 1973) which limited the ability of U.S. companies to make direct investments abroad. (See also *Foreign Credit Restraint Program* and *Interest Equalization Tax*.)

Foreign exchange: foreign money (including currency, bills of exchange and bank deposits); also, the process of exchanging one currency for another.

Foreign exchange arbitrage: the simultaneous purchase and sale of FX; the arbitrageur profits from price discrepancies. (See also *arbitrage*.)

Foreign freight forwarder: a company which assists exporters by handling the export of goods; the freight forwarder will perform many services (including booking freight space, delivering the goods to the carrier, preparing documents and advancing shipping expenses).

Foreign portfolio investment: see *portfolio investment*.

Foreign tax credit: a credit against home-country taxes because of taxes already paid abroad.

Forward contract: an agreement between two parties to exchange currencies at a future date at a set price. (See also *spot market*.)

Forward exchange rate: the price for a foreign currency for delivery at some future time; also called simply the *forward rate*.

Forward hedge: protecting a foreign-exchange exposure (e.g., a payable or receivable) by use of a forward contract. (See also *money-market hedge*.)

Forward market: FX market for the purchase or sale of FX in the future. (See also *spot market*.)

Free on board (FOB): export price quotation which includes the cost of delivery (at the seller's expense) and the cargo is loaded on board a carrier at a specified location.

Free trade area: an agreement between a group of countries to eliminate trade barriers among themselves while maintaining their own individual barriers toward non-member nations. (See also *customs union* and *common market*.)

Free trade zone: an area where goods may be imported free of duties for packaging, assembling, or manufacturing and then exported; only if the goods are transferred into the domestic market will *duty* need to be paid.

Front-end fee: in syndicated loans, all fees which are paid when a loan agreement is signed or when the draw-downs begin; includes both the *management* and *participation fees*.

Fronting loan: see back-to-back loan.

GAB: *General Arrangements to Borrow*

Gains from trade: the increase in production and consumption realized from the greater economic efficiency which results from international trade.

GATT: *General Agreement on Tariffs and Trade*

General Agreement on Tariffs and Trade (GATT):   an international agency, headquartered in Geneva, Switzerland, which encourages countries to reduce tariffs and other barriers to international trade.

General Arrangements to Borrow (GAB):   a special agreement between the IMF and a group of 10 major industrialized countries whereby the IMF can borrow from the group to make a special loan to any member of the group.

Geocentric: an attitude which is essentially world-oriented—viewing the entire world as subject to relatively similar approaches and solutions. (See also *ethnocentric* and *polycentric.*)

Gold tranche: the part of an IMF member country's subscription quota which was paid in gold; gold is no longer used for this purpose. (See *reserve tranche, credit tranche.*)

Grace period: a period of time during which the payment of principal (and sometimes the interest) on a loan is deferred to a later date.

Group of Ten (G-10):   a group of major industrialized countries which have agreed to support the IMF's *General Arrangements to Borrow* by lending their currencies to the IMF. The members are Belgium, Canada, France, Germany, Italy, Japan, Netherlands, Sweden, the United Kingdom and the United States—with Switzerland as an associated member.

Hard currency: a strong, freely-convertible currency; one which is expected to maintain its value or to appreciate. (See also *soft currency.*)

Hedge: an action which will offset the exposure to a change in exchange rates, interest rates or other prices. (See *forward hedge* and *money-market hedge.*)

Historical rate: the exchange rate which was in effect on the date when assets were acquired or the liabilities were incurred. (See *current rate, average rate.*)

Host country: the country in which a foreign investment is made.

Hot money: investible funds which move very quickly in response to changes in interest rates or to avoid impending regulations.

Hyperinflation: very high rates of inflation.

IBRD: *International Bank for Reconstruction and Development*

ICSID: *International Centre for Settlement of Investment Disputes*

IDA: *International Development Association*

IDB: *Inter-American Development Bank*

IFC: *International Finance Corporation*

IMF: *International Monetary Fund*

Import: a good, service or capital which is brought into a country from abroad.

Inconvertible currency: currency which cannot be exchanged for another currency either because of the absence of demand or because of regulations. (See also *blocked funds, convertible currency.*)

Indirect quotation: the value of one currency (usually the domestic currency) in terms of a foreign currency (e.g., DM 2.3/$ is $ indirect & DM direct). (See *direct quotation.*)

Infant industry: a young industry which, it is argued, needs tariffs or other protective barriers until it matures to a point where it is efficient enough to compete successfully with imports.

Infrastructure: the basic networks which help economic activities to operate—communication, transportation, energy, water supply, sewer, schools, hospitals, financial institutions, marketing institutions, etc.

Inter-American Development Bank (IDB): a regional development which extends loans for economic and/or social development to developing countries in Latin America and the Caribbean. (See *African* and *Asian Development Banks.*)

Interest arbitrage: simultaneously borrowing in one market and investing in another to profit from favorable interest differentials. (See *arbitrage.*)

Interest Equalization Tax (IET): special tax imposed on U.S. residents from 1963-1973 when they bought securities issued by foreign borrowers.

Interest-rate parity: the tendency for the differential between the spot and forward exchange rates to equal the annual interest-rate differential between the two countries.

International Bank for Reconstruction and Development (IBRD): a multinational development bank which makes loans to developing countries throughout the world at commercial rates of interest; also called the *World Bank.* (See *World Bank Group.*)

International bond: a bond sold outside the country of the borrower. (See *Eurobond* and *foreign bond.*)

International Centre for Settlement of Investment Disputes (ICSID): an organization designed to provide a voluntary channel for conciliation or arbitration between a contracting ICSID government and foreign investors from other countries.

International Development Association (IDA): an adjunct to the IBRD which provides loans with generous interest and repayment terms to poorer developing countries. (See *World Bank Group.*)

International Finance Corporation (IFC): an adjunct to the IBRD which provides either loans or equity investments to private-sector companies in developing countries. (See *World Bank Group.*)

International Monetary Fund (IMF): an international agency which attempts to encourage cooperation between the FX policies and actions of countries and which provides loans to help maintain FX stability during periods of temporary FX-market instability.

International reserves: the international liquid assets of a government which are readily available to meet its international obligations or to buy its currency in FX markets; the principal reserve assets are convertible currencies, gold, SDRs and reserve position in the IMF (also called official reserves).

Intervention: actions of a central bank to influence the FX rate of its currency either by buying it with *international reserves* or selling it for foreign currencies.

Investment bank: see *merchant bank.*

Joint venture: an enterprise which is undertaken by two or more parties (e.g., a jointly owned subsidiary, a *consortium,* or a *syndicate.*)

Labor intensive: productive process which requires a relatively high amount of labor and relatively low amounts of other factors of production, such as capital or land. (See capital intensive.)

L/C: *letter of credit*

LDC: *Less Developed Country*

Lead and lag: process of accelerating (leading) or delaying (lagging) international payments in anticipation of the rise or fall in the value of a currency.

Less developed country (LDC): a country with a low level of per capita income.

Letter of credit (L/C): a written agreement issued by a bank promising to pay a specified amount (or up to a specified amount) at some future time when the conditions specified in the L/C have been satisfied.

Liability exposure: the total liabilities which will be adversely affected by a revaluation or appreciation of a currency. (See *asset* and *net exposures.*)

LIBOR: *London Interbank Offer Rate*

Licensing: the rental of patents, trademarks or technology in exchange for royalty payments.

Line of credit: an agreement by which a lender promises to make a loan at some future time of the borrower's choice.

Liquidity: ability of an asset to be able to be quickly converted to cash with a minimum risk of significant loss of value.

Lock box: an arrangement whereby a commercial bank controls a post-office mailbox on behalf of a corporate customer; the bank collects the mail, opens letters and deposits the checks on behalf of the customers.

London interbank offer rate (LIBO or LIBOR): the interest rate at which one Eurobank in London offers to make a deposit in another Eurobank; LIBOR is commony used as the base rate for loans to corporations and government's (e.g., LIBOR + 1%).

Long position: when a party (either bank, corporation or governmental agency) has purchased more of something for future delivery than it has sold (e.g., buying more of a currency than is sold, having more receivables than payables in a currency or investing funds for a shorter period than that for which they were borrowed). (See *short position, square position.*)

Mail transfers: movement of funds via mail. (See *SWIFT* and *cable transfers.*)

Make a market: to be willing to both buy and sell at almost any time (e.g., an FX trading desk).

Managed float: when a government intervenes in the FX market to avoid currency volatility. (See *clean float* and *dirty float.*)

Management fee: commission received by the lead commercial or merchant banks for organizing and managing a *syndicate*. (See also *participation fee, front-end fee.*)

Manager: in a loan or *underwriting syndicate,* the bank which receives the *mandate* from the borrower and solicits other lenders or underwriters to participate.

Mandate: the directive by the borrower to a bank or underwriter to *syndicate* the offering on the agreed terms.

Merchant bank: specialist in underwriting and distributing new debt and equity issues. (Also called *investment bank.*)

MFN: *Most-Favored Nation*

Mixed venture: a *joint venture* in which one of the partners is an agency of a government.

MNC: *multinational corporation.*

Monetary/non-monetary method: all monetary assets and liabilities are translated at the current exchange rate; non-monetary items are translated at historical rates.

Money-market hedge: in order to hedge a future payable or receivable or other exposure, the currency at risk is borrowed, converted spot to the desired currency and invested. Used as an alternative to forward hedge. (See *forward hedge.*)

Money-market instruments: short-term, negotiable promissory notes—including treasury bills, *commercial paper, certificates of deposit* and *banker's acceptances.*

Most-favored nation (MFN):   a policy of treating all, or a group of countries, equally in international commercial policy—extending to each of these countries the *tariff* and *NTB* treatment that is given to the most favorably-treated nation.

Multinational corporation (MNC):   a firm which considers its international activities to be at least as important as its domestic activities; the term is also used to identify a company with extensive production abroad coupled with significant overseas markets. (Also called *multinational firm* or *enterprise* or *transnational corporation.*)

Nationalization: government takeover of an entire industry; however, may also refer to any government take-over. (See also *expropriation.*)

Negotiable: marketable; describes a security for which there is an active secondary market.

Net exposure: a *net* asset or liability position in a currency; applies to any type of FX exposure (e.g., translation, transaction, etc.). (See *asset* and *liability exposures.*)

Netting: an intra-company process of subtracting the receivables from the payables between different affiliates of the same company; only the net amount will be paid or received.

Nominal interest rate: the interest rate which is stated on a debt contract; it may differ from the *effective interest rate* as a result of a discount or premium on the purchase price or on forward FX cover.

Non-tariff barrier (NTB): obstacles to trade other than tariffs.

NTB: *Non-tariff barrier*

Numeraire: the unit of accounting; may be an existing currency or a basket of currencies such as the *SDR* or *ECU.*

OECD: *Organization for Economic Cooperation and Development*

Offer price: either the price at which an FX trader will sell a currency (asked or asking price) or the rate at which the lender will lend money.

Official reserves: see *international* reserves.

Offshore market: a financial market which is exempt from ("offshore" from) the *Euromarket's* regulations on the domestic market of the country where the transactions occur.

OPEC: *Organization of Petroleum Exporting Countries*

Open position: being either *long* or *short* in holdings of a foreign currency. (See also *square position.*)

OPIC: *Overseas Private Investment Corporation*

Organization for Economic Cooperation and Development: an agency of 24 of the industrialized countries that studies and attempts to encourage cooperation of economic policies of its member countries.

Organization of Petroleum Exporting Countries (OPEC): the international cartel of oil-producing countries.

Outright quotation: an FX quote which is stated fully as the amount of one currency required to buy a specific amount of another; spot quotes are always outright, while forward FX quotes may be (1) outright; (2) stated as a percent of premium or discount; or (3) stated as a *swap quote.*

Overseas Private Investment Corporation (OPIC): A U.S. Government agency which insures foreign direct investments by U.S. companies abroad against risks of expropriation, war or currency inconvertability.

Overvaluation: an exchange rate which is above its realistic value either because of market pressures or governmental action; an overvalued currency will be expected to weaken in the future.

Parallel loan: *see back-to-back loan.*

Participation: the sharing in a large loan or merchant-bank *syndication.*

Participation fee: commission which is paid to participants in a syndication. (See also *management fee, front-end fee.*)

Par value: the official value which a government sets for its currency in international markets; parity can be relative to gold, the dollar, another currency or a basket of currencies (e.g., the SDR). (See also *central rate.*)

Performance letter of credit: an L/C which is issued as a guarantee of performance in accordance with the terms of a contract; unlike an import L/C which promises payment if an export contract is fulfilled, a performance L/C pays if a contract (commonly for construction contracts) is not fulfilled. (See *letter of credit.*)

Petrodollars: FX earnings from the export of petroleum.

Point: the last decimal in a foreign-exchange quote (e.g., for a quote of FC 2.5972, a point is 1/10,000 of the FC).

Polycentric attitude: the view that each foreign country or market is unique with little in common with others; host-country oriented. (See also *ethnocentric* and *geocentric.*)

Pooling: the cash-management process of transfering excess funds of affiliates into a common account (or pool)—often in a low-tax country.

Portfolio investment: purchase of debt or equity without gaining any managerial control. (See also *direct investment.*)

Premium: the amount by which a forward quote exceeds a spot quote or the amount by which the price of a debt security exceeds its face value. (See also *discount.*)

Private placement: the sale of non-negotiable debt or equity directly to the investor.

Product life cycle: the evolution of a product from a condition of being new, expensive, difficult to produce and unique to a condition of being standardized in production, relatively inexpensive and readily available.

Protectionism: an effort to protect domestic producers by means of controls on imports.

Purchasing-power parity: the tendency for the percentage change in the exchange rate between two currencies to be equal but opposite in direction to the relative percentage change in inflation between the two countries; as a result, the purchasing power of the two currencies relative to one another should remain unchanged (i.e., remain at parity).

Quota: a quantitative limitation on imports (e.g., quantity, weight, etc.); also, the amount of each country's subscription in the IMF.

Quotation (or quote): rate at which an FX dealer is prepared to buy or sell foreign currencies.

Repatriation: the transfer home of assets held abroad.

Representative office: an office of a foreign bank which can neither accept deposits nor extend loans but which can solicit business for other affiliates of the bank. (See *agency, branch, subsidiary.*)

Reserve account: That portion of the balance of payments which reflects changes in the government's international reserves.

Reserve currency: Any convertible currency which central banks hold in their *international reserves.*

Reserve tranche: the portion of an IMF member country's subscription quota which was not paid with its own currency; the amount of the reserve tranche can be borrowed automatically by the member.

Revaluation: an increase in the *par* or *central value* of a currency caused by official government action rather than by market forces (which is called *appreciation*). (See also *devaluation.*)

Rollover: the negotiated or contractural extension of a loan at maturity or at regular periods—usually with changes of interest rates; (e.g., a two-year Eurodollar term loan with a six month rollover is available to the borrower for the full two years, but the interest rate will fluctuate every six months with changes in LIBOR).

SDR: *Special Drawing Right.*

Selling rate: the price which an FX trader is *offering* or *asking* for a currency.

Services: balance of payment accounts such as travel, transportation, insurance and banking. Also called *invisibles.*

Short position: an excess of liabilities over assets in a particular currency.

Sight draft: a bill of exchange which is payable upon presentation; a bank check is a sight draft. (See also *time draft, bank draft.*)

Smithsonian Agreement: an IMF agreement (December 1981) which realigned FX par values and the price of gold; the agreement was necessitated by the U.S. decision to end the convertibility of the dollar into gold.

Snake: an arrangement in the mid-1970s whereby several European countries established central values for their currencies and permitted fluctuation only within central limits.

Society of Worldwide Interbank Financial Telecommunications (SWIFT): an international electronic network for transferring funds between member banks.

Soft currency: a weak currency, one likely to decline in value and/or threatened by the imposition of exchange controls. (See also *hard currency.*)

Soft loans: loans issued with very lenient repayment terms (e.g., low interest, long *grace period*, repayable in soft currencies, etc.). (See *International Development Association.*)

Sovereign immunity: a government is immune from lawsuits either in its own courts or abroad—unless it submits voluntarily.

Sovereign risk: the threat that a government will either default upon its own obligations of its own volition (rather than because of credit problems) or will prevent private sector borrowers from repaying their obligations. Also, risk that a government will seize a company's assets.

Sovereignty: power of a government over the people, organizations and assets within its borders.

Space arbitrage: the simultaneous purchase and sale of identical or similar assets in geographically-separated markets. (See *arbitrage*.)

Special drawing right (SDR):   international reserve asset created by IMF; created simply by agreement of its members. The SDR's value is the weighted average of a basket of currencies. SDR's are issued only to governments.

Specialization: concentrating production upon a limited range of goods or services (ideally those upon which a country has a comparative advantage).

Specific duty: calculating duties based upon some quantitative measure (e.g., number, weight) rather than value. (See also *ad valorem* duty and *compound duty*.)

Speculation: taking or maintaining (long or short) positions in the hope that a favorable price change will occur. (See also *defensive hedge*.)

Spot market: FX market for delivery within one or two business days. (See also *forward market*.)

Spread: the difference between buying and selling FX quotes; also the difference between a lender's funding cost and the rate at which it lends.

Square position: when the cash inflows of a given currency equal the cash outflows (i.e., are covered) for all maturity dates. (See also *long* and *short positions*.)

Subpart F income: a special category of foreign-source income which will be taxed in the U.S. whether or not it is remitted back to the U.S.

Subsidy: export encouragement by a government in the form of lower taxes, tax rebates, low-interest loans, etc.

Swap: (1) the exchange of currencies between two companies or governments (e.g., the swap lines between major central banks); the swap will later be reversed. (2) the simultaneous buying and selling of a currency for two different maturities.

Swap rate: the difference between spot and forward rates expressed in points.

SWIFT: *Society of Worldwide Interbank Financial Telecommunications*

Switch trading: the exchange of barter contracts. (See also *barter, countertrade*.)

Syndicate: a group of commercial or investment banks that cooperate for a short time to float a loan or a security issue.

Target market: a group of potential customers with a fairly homogeneous set of wants which the seller hopes to satisfy with a single product or service.

Tariff: a schedule of duties. (See *duty*.)

Tax credit: a reduction of the actual tax liability. (See also *tax deduction*.)

Tax deduction: a reduction of taxable income. (See also *tax credit.*)

Tax-haven country: a country with low or no taxes on foreign-source income and/or capital gains.

Tax incentives: tax holiday (i.e., tax-free period) or reduction in taxes offered by a government in order to attract investment.

Tax treaty: an agreement between countries to lower taxes on residents of the other country, to agree to offer credits on taxes paid by its residents in the other country and/or to cooperate in the enforcement of tax matters.

Telegraphic transfer: the transfer of funds via cable, wire, telex, SWIFT, etc.

Temporal method: translating financial statements of a foreign affiliate of a U.S. company by the regulations of FASB 8, similar to monetary/nonmonetary.

Term loan: a medium to long-term bank loan.

Terms of trade: relative price levels of exports relative to imports for a country.

Thin market: when there is little activity in a market—even small orders can affect prices.

Third world: all developing countries; the first world is comprised of the industrialized countries of the West and the second world is the Communist countries.

Time arbitrage: the use of forward exchange to take advantage of the price differentials between various forward maturity dates. (See *arbitrage.*)

Time deposit: placement of funds with a bank for a fixed period of time.

Time draft: *a bill of exchange* drawn to mature at a fixed period of time after sight. (See also *sight draft, bank draft.*)

Tranche: a portion or a slice of a line of credit (e.g., the *reserve tranche* and *credit tranches* of the IMF or the several tranches of a bank loan with several draw-downs).

Transaction currency: a currency which is commonly used to pay for international goods and services or financial contracts; also called *vehicle currency.*

Transaction exposure: the net total of existing contracts (e.g., receivables and payables) which will be affected by a currency-value change. (See also *translation* and *economic exposure.*)

Transfer price: an intra-company price charged by one unit of the company to another unit of the same company for goods or services.

Translation exposure: a measure of the net asset or liability exposure on the balance sheet of a company's foreign subsidiary; it is the amount which would be changed in value by a currency-value exchange. (See also *transaction exposure* and *economic exposure.*)

Turn-key: a construction project in which the contractor not only plans and builds the project but trains the buyer's personnel and initiates operation of the project—only then is the key turned over to the buyer.

UNCTAD: see United Nations Conference on Trade and Development.

Undervaluation: an exchange rate which is below its realistic value either because of market pressures or governmental action; an undervalued currency will tend to strengthen in the future.

Underwriting: the guarantee by the lenders or merchant bankers to provide the funds specified, regardless of the issue's acceptance in the market.

Unilateral transfer: in the balance of payments the account which measures money which is paid unilaterally rather than in exchange for goods, services or financial assets (e.g., foreign aid, gifts, worker remittances, pensions). (See also *current account*.)

United Nations Conference on Trade and Development (UNCTAD): a U.N. organization with little statutory authority comprised of most developing nations but which serves as a forum for discussion, study and publication of common problems of its members.

Unit of account: see *numeraire*.

Value-added tax (VAT): a tax which is levied on the value added at each stage of production; VAT is a type of national sales tax.

VAT: *value-added tax*

Vehicle currency: see *transaction currency*.

Withholding tax: a tax collected from the payment before it is distributed to the recipient (e.g., a borrower will withhold the tax portion of its interest payment and remit the funds to the local government—not the government of the lender).

World Bank: International Bank for Reconstruction and Development.

World Bank Group: the *International Bank for Reconstruction and Development* plus its two associated agencies, the *International Finance Corporation* and the *International Development Association*.

Xenophobia: fear of foreigners.

Index